The Life of St. Katharine of Alexandria.

BY

JOHN CAPGRAVE, D.D.,

PRIOR OF THE AUSTIN FRIARY AT LYNN, NORFOLK,
AND PROVINCIAL OF HIS ORDER.

EDITED BY

CARL HORSTMANN,

WITH FOREWORDS BY

F. J. FURNIVALL,

AND NOTES ON THE SOUNDING OF *gh* IN CHAUCER'S DAY,
AND OF LONG *i* IN SHAKSPERE'S.

LONDON:
PUBLISHED FOR THE EARLY ENGLISH TEXT SOCIETY
BY KEGAN PAUL, TRENCH, TRÜBNER & CO.,
PATERNOSTER HOUSE, CHARING-CROSS ROAD.
1893.

Unaltered reprint 2000
ISBN 0 85991 855 6
Distributed for the Early English Text Society by
Boydell & Brewer Ltd, PO Box 9, Woodbridge, Suffolk IP12 3DF
and Boydell & Brewer Inc, PO Box 41026, Rochester, NY 14604-4126
Printed and bound in Great Britain by Antony Rowe Ltd, Chippenham, Wiltshire

The Life of St. Katharine.

Early English Text Society.
Original Series, No. 100.
1893.

BERLIN: ASHER & CO., 5, UNTER DEN LINDEN.
NEW YORK: C. SCRIBNER & CO.; LEYPOLDT & HOLDT.
PHILADELPHIA: J. B. LIPPINCOTT & CO.

FOREWORDS.

§ 1. *Capgrave's Life*, p. v.
§ 2. *Capgrave's Works*, p. xiii.
§ 3. *Capgrave's Character*, p. xv.
§ 4. *St. Katharine*, p. xxii.
§ 5. *Apology for the Text*, p. xxiv.
§ 6. *Miscellaneous*, p. xxxi.

§ 1. *Capgrave's Life.*—In his *Chronicle of England*, John Capgrave tells us under the 17th year of King Richard II (22 June 1393 to 21 June 1394), "In þis ȝere, in þe xxj day of aprile [in Easter week, 1394], was þat frere bore whech mad þese annotaciones";[1] and in the present text he tells us, p. 16, l. 240, "Myn cuntre is Northfolke, of the town of Lynne." Of his parentage we know nothing, though if we construe his word "faderes," p. 17, l. 243 below, strictly, we shall have to hold him one priest's bastard son and another's grandson:

"God yeue me grace neuere for to blynne
To folwe the steppes of *my faderis* before,
Wiche to the reule of Austyn were swore."

But he doubtless meant only by "faderis before" the spiritual fathers or Austin Friars who had gone before him. In 1400 the boy, with his playfellows and townsmen, must have felt proud of the Lynn fishermen:

"In that same ȝere, the schippis of Lennes, which fischid at Aberden, took certeyn schippis of Scotlond, with her amyrel, Sir Robert Logan, knyte, and broute hem to Lennes."—*Chronicle*, p. 266-7. (Note the absence of *gh* in *knyte* and *broute*.)

And in 1401 he must have wonderd at the comet:

"In this same ȝere . . . appered a sterre, whech thei clepe cometa, betwix the west and the north, in the monthe of March, with a lie bem, whech ben bowed into the North. It betokened, as men seid, the blod that schuld be spilt at Schrouisbury."—*Chronicle*, p. 278. [The battle of Shrewsbury was on July 22, 1403.]

[1] Facsimile of leaf 175 of the Cambridge University MS Gg. 4. 12 in Hingeston's edition of the *Chronicle* in the Rolls Series; also p. 259 of the print.

vi   *Forewords.*   § 1. *Life of Capgrave,* 1406—16.

In 1406 he was still in his birth-town, for he tells us in his Latin *Book of the Illustrious Henries,* as englisht by Mr. Hingeston in the Rolls Series, 1858, p. 117 :

"I saw [Princess Philippa] the only daughter of this most excellent king [Henry IV] in the town of Lynn, where she went on board the ship in which she left England, and went to be married to [Eric XIII] the king of Norway ... She indeed is the offspring of this king [Henry IV], and I saw her with my own eyes."[1]

And it was no doubt in Lynn that he experienst the hard winter of 1407 :

"In the IX ȝere of this Kyng was a gret wyntir, that dured both Decembir, Januari, Februari, and March, that the most part of smale birdis were ded."—*Chronicle,* p. 295 :

and the floods of 1413—*Henries,* p. 125 :

Now he [Hen. V] was crowned at Westminster on the ninth day of the month of April, in the year of our Lord 1413. In the winter of the same year there were great floods of snow and rain, and in the summer several fires,[2] from which signs some men foretold that he would be a warlike king, and would experience many dangers in war. —*Chronicle,* p. 303 :

as well as heard of the stealing of three Lynn children in 1416, and the later recovery of them :

"In the same ȝere [A.D. 1416] III. beggeres stole III. childyr at Lenne ; and of on, thei put oute his eyne ; the othir, thei broke his bak ; and the thirde, thei cut of his handis and his feet, that men schuld of pite gyve hem food. Long aftir, the fadir of on of hem, whech was a marchaund, cam to London, and the child knew him, and cryed loude, 'This is my fadir.' The fadir tok his child fro the

[1] No doubt Capgrave saw the rest of the Court too, for he says in his *Chronicle,* p. 292 (but under 1404), "In this ȝere were sent embassiatouris fro the Kyng of Denmark for to have the Kyngis doutir Philip to be joyned in wedlok to her Kyng. The Kyng broute hir to Lenne, for to take schip there. And in that towne he lay nyne daies, the too qwenes, thre sones of the Kyng—Herri, Thomas, and Umfrey—and many othir lordes and ladies." Capgrave also notes on p. 291 before the visit of the King to Lynn, that after Henry IV's forbiddal of pilgrimages to the place where the Archbp. of York and the Earl of Nottingham were beheaded, "The Kyng ... lost the beute of his face. For, as the comoune opinion went, fro that tyme onto his deth he was a lepir, and evyr fowlere and fowlere. For in his deth, as thei recorded that sey him, he was so contracte, that his body was scarse a cubite of length."

[2] As one of these, Mr. Hingeston (*Henries,* p. 125 *n.*) reckons the Norwich fire of 1414.

Forewords. § 1. *Life of Capgrave,* 1416.

beggeris, and mad hem to be arested. The childirn told alle the processe, and the beggaris were hangen, ful wel worthy."—*Chronicle,* p. 316.

In this year, 1416, Capgrave also notes the tremendous thunderstorms on June 14 :—*Chronicle,* p. 314 :

"In the XVIII. kalend of Julij were the moost horribil thunderes and litynnyngis that evyr ony man herd." (No *gh* again.)

When and where Capgrave went to school he does not tell us, but as the Augustine Friars settled at Lynn in the beginning of Edward I's reign, A.D. 1293, and had their Monastery in the northern part of the town, in Hogman's Lane, alias Hopman's way,[1] and as they had a Professor of Sacred Theology, one John de Beston, in 1382 (p. xi, note 1), Capgrave may have gone to their school, assuming that they had one.[2] If not, there were in Lynn, a Benedictine Priory, a House of Black Friars or Preachers, and Convents of Franciscan or Grey Friars, and Carmelite or White Friars, at the school of such of which as had one, Capgrave could have got his education. Leland says that he went to Cambridge,[3] but Pamphilus, Bale, and others assign him to Oxford. He tells us himself that he knew William Millington, the first Provost of King's College, Cambridge.[4] The probability is that he went first to Cambridge, the University nearest to him, and then took his degree of D.D.[5] at Oxford[6]; but nothing is known about this for certain.

[1] Dugdale's *Monasticon,* vi. 1594, col. 2, quoting the Continuator of Blomefield's *Hist. of Norfolk.*

[2] If they'd had a school in 1446, Capgrave 'ud surely have put the fact into his *Illustrious Henries,* p. xi below. I doubt whether his "youthful offshoots" mean a general school.

[3] "Granta, fœcunda eruditorum parens, quæ illum, ut ego conjectura colligo, juvenem docuit, idem testabitur."—*Com. de Script. Brit.* (1709), p. 453.

[4] "Over these colleges [Eton, and King's Coll. Camb.] he set two influential men as provosts; one of them—Master William Millington [of Clare Hall]—I know personally. He presides over the college at Cambridge, and in the questionings of the schools, as well as in profound literature and in the perfection of his morals, surpasses many who had gone before him."—*Book of the Illustrious Henries,* p. 154.

[5] In his Dedication of his "Book of the Illustrious Henries" to K. Henry VI, he calls himself "Brother John Capgrave, the laast of Doctors, and the meanest of the pore Brethren of Saint Augustin," p. 1 and 226.

[6] Pamphilus (Works, 1581, Rome, fol. 139) says: "Joannes Capgrave,

viii   *Forewords.*   § 1. *Life of Capgrave,* 1416—38.

In 1416 or 1417, when 23 or 24, that is, four or five years before the birth of Henry VI on Dec. 6, 1421, Capgrave tells us that he was ordaind Priest, and that in Dec. 1421 he was studying in London :—*Book of the Illustrious Henries,* p. 146 :—

"I heard the voice of the churches, and the ringing of the bells, when the birth of our king [Henry VI] was made known in London, for I was then studying there, in the fourth or fifth year after I was raised to the priesthood; and the rejoicing of the people has not yet faded from my memory. For I deem that that praise and that rejoicing were omens of the peace which a great company of wise men expect to come in your days, my king . . .   I deem that those voices and rejoicings will in time be fulfilled, that, as the people wishes and the devout pray, there may come to be one heart in the two kingdoms [England and France], as they have both of them already one God, one Faith, one Baptism [*Ephesians* iv. 5]."

In 1422 he preacht at least 7 Sermons at Cambridge, p. xiv below.

I suppose that after this, and before he settled down to write his Annals, his Legends of Saints, and his Commentaries on the books of the Bible, Capgrave went to Rome, was taken ill there, was helpt by Bp. Grey, and had to stay some time in that city. In the Dedicatory Letter to William Grey, Bishop of Ely, set before his Commentary on the Acts of the Apostles, Capgrave says :

" Reminiscor, sancte Antistes, quanta pia visitatione vestra in me, miserum peregrinum atque Romae infirmum, dilectionis exenia tribuistis ; et nunc, a sollicitudine officii mei penitus absolutus, licet tarde veniens, munus possibilitatis meae vobis decrevi mittendum."
—*Liber de illustribus Henricis* (1858), p. 221.

On coming home, Capgrave may well have settled down at the Austin Friary at Lynn to write his Biblical Commentaries, &c. That on the Book of Genesis he tells us he began on 6 Sept. (or Oct.) 1437, and finisht on 21 Sept. 1438, while Humfrey, Duke of Gloster, says it was in the same year presented to him at Penshurst. The MS is now at Oriel, is in Capgrave's writing, and has the Duke's inscription on its fly-leaf :—

" Feliciter per Capgrave.   Incipit Frater Johannes Capgrave hoc

---

Anglus, Oxonii publice Divinas Litteras docuit, et Vetus et Novum Testamentum interpretatus est ; " and in his "Chronicon Ordinis Fratrum Eremitarum Sancti Augustini," he includes Capgrave in his List of " Viri qui in publicis Scholis functi sunt docendi munere."—*Chronicle,* p. x.

Forewords. § 1. *Life of Capgrave,* 1438—44.

opus in Translatione Sancti Augustini Doctoris, quae occurrit mense Octobris [*really Sept.* 6], anno Domini M. CCCCXXXVII; et fecit finem ejusdem in festo Mathei, Apostoli et Evangelistae, anno Domini M. CCCCXXXVIII."[1]

"Cest liure est a moy, Humfrey duc de Gloucestre, du don de Frere Johan Capgrave, quy le me fist presenter a mon manoyr de Pensherst, le jour de l'an M. CCCCXXXVIII." [This must mean Jan. 1, 1439.]

Before this time, Capgrave had either written part of his *Chronicle or Annals of England,* or had got together some materials for it. In the Dedicatory Epistle to the Duke, Capgrave says, that while

"turning over *my Annals* . . I found written in them that A.D. M. CCXLVIII the Order of Hermits of St. Augustine in England was founded by Richard of Clare, the son of Gilbert of Clare, and Earl of Gloster."[2]

As Capgrave's Commentaries on Exodus, and the first and third Books of his Commentaries on the Books of Kings (I *Samuel* and I *Kings*) were given to Oxford early in 1444—see last note —we may legitimately suppose that Capgrave had by that date workt consecutively through the books of the Bible, and finisht his Commentaries on Leviticus, Numbers, Deuteronomy, Joshua, Judges, and Ruth. And as he would give the Duke only those MSS which he dedicated to him, Capgrave may well have written by Feb. 1444 several more Commentaries, as well as other books; but the dates of his other Biblical Commentaries and his Latin Lives of Saints—

[1] The vellum MS is a large folio of 181 leaves in double columns. In its first fine initial is a figure of the Duke seated and hatted, while Capgrave, in his friar's dress, kneels before him and offers his MS. The first initial of the Prolog contains a figure of the author seated at a desk, with four books bound in red before him, and several in the cupboard beneath.—*Lib. de illustr. Henricis,* p. 225. The Duke gave the MS to the University of Oxford by Indenture dated 25 Feb. 1444, with three other of Capgrave's Commentaries, no doubt also presents from him to the Duke, as witness this extract from the Schedule to the Deed—*Chronicle,* p. xv:

"Item, Capgrave super Regum Primum ... 2º fo. sint viv.
Item, Capgrave super Regum 3 ... ... 2º fo. fulgorem.
Item, *Capgrave super Genesin* ... ... 2º fo. arduum.
Item, Capgrave super Exodum ... ... 2º fo. et beatitudinem."

[2] "Sed et *Annualia mea* revolvens, aliud inveni quod me monet. Scriptum enim in iis reperi, quod anno Domini M. CCXXVIII. fundatus fuerat Ordo Heremitarum Sancti Augustini in Anglia per Ricardum de Clara, filium Gilberti de Clara, comitemque Gloverniae."—*Lib. de illust. Henricis,* p. 230-1.

x   *Forewords.* § 1. *Life of Capgrave*, 1446.

printed by Wynkyn de Worde in 1516 as *Nova Legenda Anglie*—are not yet known, and his English Life of St. Katharine in the present volume is undated. So is the fragment of his Guide to the Antiquities of Rome, while the MS of his English Life of St. Gilbert of Sempringham was burnt in the Cotton fire.

On August 1, 1446, Henry VI visited Lynn, and Capgrave gave him information about the first founding of the Austin Friars[1] there. Capgrave was no doubt then Prior of his monastery, if not also Provincial or Controller of all the Friaries in the Eastern province, or whatever the limits of his jurisdiction were. In his *Book of the Illustrious Henries*, as englisht by Hingeston, p. 158—160, Capgrave says, under the year 1446 :

" In the twenty-fourth year of his reign,[2] this most devout king [Henry VI], in the course of the solemn pilgrimage which he made to the Holy Places, received into his favour the place of the Hermit Friars of S. Augustin in the town of Lynn, promising to his priests who dwelt there, by his (p. 159) own mouth, that from thenceforth that place should be regarded as closely connected with himself, and also with his successors lawfully begotten of his body. That he himself, also, and his successors, as before, should be regarded as its founder, or founders, not in name only, but in deed and in truth. These events occurred in the feast of S. Peter ad Vincula [Aug. 1], in the year of our Lord 1446, and in the twenty-fourth year of the reign of our illustrious lord king, as we said above.

" And forasmuch as many lying and double-tongued men have, as I have heard, taken occasion to say, after the departure of our king,[3] that the place had had a founder from its very earliest days,—whose name, however, they know not how to insinuate,—on that account *the writer of the present work, who also gave his lord information*

[1] It seems that when Henry VII visited Lynn with a large retinue on Aug. 25, 1498 (14 Hen. VII), he too stayd at the Austin Friary, for, says the entry in Hall Book 3, p. 17 : "which King was met at the Green At [this] half Witton [or Wootton] Gapp, with the foresaid Mayor and the Commons of Lynn, which King was presented *at the Friars Augustines* with ten great pikes, ten tenches, three couple of breams, twelve swans, two oxen, twenty sheep, a ton of wine, thirty dozen bread, two tons of ale, two tons of beer, two loads of wood ; and a pipe of wine was given to the Mayor for his guests." The next Monday the King hunted with the Mayor, and went off on Tuesday.—Harrod's *Report on King's Lynn Records*, p. 112. I saw the folio entries at Lynn last August.

[2] In the autograph MS the words "Data compilatoris" are written in the margin opposite this passage.—Hingeston.

[3] The Privy Seals of the 24 Henry VI show that on the 6th of August the King was at Colchester.—Hingeston.

concerning this matter, seeing that his character has been partially injured by the imputation that *the information which he gave his lord the king* was false, here clearly sets forth the whole truth of this matter, as collected from ancient charters and sealed instruments :—

"Be it known then that the said Hermit Friars of S. Augustin[1] first entered the town of Lynn, with the intention of making their abode there, in the twenty-second year of the reign of the second [that is, first] king Edward [A.D. 1293], counting from the Conquest. This is found to be capable of proof from the licence of the king (who wrote that he was the son of king Henry, and marks this as the number of the years of his reign) in his charter to a certain widow of good conversation, whose name was Margaret Southmere. Now the land which was granted first by this lady to the Friars measured a hundred feet in length, and twenty-four in breadth. Our place thus begun in a narrow spot, increased by the presentation of many parcels of land, as is set forth in divers royal charters. For we have another charter granted to Humphrey de Wykyn [3 Edw. III, A.D. 1329], concerning his land; and another to Robert de Wykyn [12 Edw. III, A.D. 1338] for his messuage[2]; also yet another to Thomas de Lexham [? 33 Edw. I, A.D. 1304-5] for his messuage. Also another,[3] of a larger benefaction to certain inhabitants of Lynn [38 Edw. III, A.D. 1364], for five messuages.

"See, then, most dear lord, thy little plot, composed of many small parcels of ground, and united into one; and impress on thy heart that there are there *thirty priests*, besides deacons, subdeacons, and youthful offshoots[4] of the inferior order, to the number of sixteen; and consider that these hold thee in special remembrance.

---

[1] For a full account of this Friary, see Capgrave's *Chronicle*, ed. Hingeston, Appendix V, p. 368.

[2] In the Appendix to the 11th Report of the Historical MSS. Commission, 1887, Mr. J. C. Jeafferson notes (p. 231) that "On the eleventh of the kalends of May, 1352, Margaret Frenghe, widow, left vis. viiid. to the Friars of the order of St. Augustine tarrying in Lenn," and (p. 232) "all that tenement with its edifices and appurtenances in the town of Lenn, *opposite to the Friars of the order of St. Augustine of Lenn*," to be sold for the payment of her debts and the fulfilment of her will. On p. 245 is the entry :—

"26 August 1382. Acknowledgment and Bond of the Prior and convent of the Friars of St. Augustine of Lenn, for fifty marks of gold received by them for the said convent's use, of John de Beston, Professor of sacred Theology of the same order and convent, under conditions set forth in the instrument."

On p. 246 is this further entry :—

"20 October, 5 Henry VI and 1426 A.D. Bond of the Prior and Convent of the Friars of the Order of St. Augustine of Norwich for payment of twenty marks to the Convent of Augustine Friars of Lenne."

[3] There were still more, see *Chronicle*, p. 368-9, notes.

[4] Namely, acolytes, and others of the inferior orders.—H.

"If, however, thou dost desire any more minute information, let thy Majesty command, and thy servants will obey.

"May thy royal Majesty live long to the honour of God, the support of the Church, and the settlement of the realm!"[1]

In this same year 1446, Capgrave no doubt finisht Part II of his *Liber de Illustribus Henricis;* and before Oct. 13, 1453, when Henry VI's only son Edward—kild at Tewkesbury, May 4, 1471—was born, Capgrave must have finisht his Third Part and ended his book. For, in his last paragraph he says, p. 218 of the englishing—

"So also may my lord ever preserve the Faith inviolate, may he nourish up *his children, when any shall be born to him,* faithfully for God; that so his enemies may be frightened by his sword, and he may depart this life pure both in body and in soul," &c.

In 1456 we find Capgrave with the titles of Prior, and Provincial of his order of Friars Hermit of St. Augustine, and with jurisdiction extending at least as far as the city of Oxford. Kennet's *Parochial Antiquities* (ed. Bandinel, ii. 399-401; reprinted in *Chronicle,* p. 328-333) contains two deeds dated 1456, of which the first witnesses that the Prior and Brethren of the Convent of Augustin Friars at Oxford, which stood near the present site of Wadham College, accept as their Founder and Patron, Edmund Rede of Borstall. And their venerable Master John Capgrave, Prior Provincial, approves this, and testifies it by his letters.[2] By the second Deed, on the same day, the said Oxford Austin Prior and Brethren grant to the said Edmund Rede, and William his eldest son, some chambers within their house, and some part of their garden, for lodging and other accommodation whenever they shall visit the said Convent, or reside in Oxford. And they do this "licentiâ Fratris Magistri Johannis Capgrave, nostri Provincialis."

[1] Capgrave evidently intended to have added something more . . . and left a whole leaf of the vellum bare for the purpose in his autograph copy. He altered his mind, however, and wrote at the bottom of the page (for the direction of his scribe)—" Make no space, but writh forth—INVOCATO," *i. e.* the first word of the Third Part.—H.

[2] Et ad preces eorum [the Oxford Prior and Convent], venerabilis Magister Johannes Capgrave, Prior Provincialis, summo studio incitatus est, ut huic receptioni et recognitioni dicti Fundatoris nostri præsens esset, ut ad perpetuam rei memoriam suis literis testificaret, ne filii sine patris consensu aliquid novum conderent, nec labor filiorum sine patris consensu frustraretur.

In an Indenture of June 12, 1461, between the Prior of the Austin Friars of Lynn and the Executors of Richard Cosyn, printed in Blomefield's *History of Norfolk*, iv. 616, and in Capgrave's *Chronicle*, p. 370, note, the seal of the Venerable Prior Provincial is appended; and we may fairly assume that he was Capgrave.

Bale tells us in his *Scriptores Illustres*, 1548, that Capgrave died at Lynn on the 12th of August, 1464, and was buried there among the Austins in the reign of Edward IV.

§ 2. *Capgrave's works.* The only English works of Capgrave which have survived are, 1. his *Life of St. Katherine* here printed, and which exists in three Arundel MSS, nos. 20, 168, 396 in the Brit. Mus., and in the Rawlinson MS. 116 in the Bodleian. The Prolog is printed in *Chronicle*, p. 335.

2. *Chronicle of England*, autograph MS in the University Library, Cambridge, Gg iv. 12; a copy, MS CLXVII in Corpus Christi Coll., Cambridge, edited by Hingeston for the Rolls Series, 1858. It runs from the Creation to A.D. 1417; contains at first, short notices from the Bible, Isidore, St. Jerome, Eusebius, and of events all over the world; gets its early history of England from the Brute, Higden, &c., and, as it nears the writer's own time, confines itself almost to England, and gives accounts of Wat Tyler's rebellion, Oldcastle, the resignation of Richard II and the accession of Henry IV, &c.

3. *Guide to the Antiquities of Rome:* fragments of this were found in the fly-leaves of the two MSS of Capgrave's Latin treatise on the Creeds—? autograph MS, All Souls' Coll. Oxford, no. 17 (wherein he latinises his name as "Johannes de Monumento Pileato"[1]), and Balliol Coll. Oxford, no. 190. Mr. Hingeston claims that these Fragments (which he prints *Chron.*, p. 357-66) are in Capgrave's own handwriting; but I do not believe they are,[2] because they have the gutturals which Capgrave avoided in his *Chronicle:* *hight* was cald, *Chron.* p. 359, 361, promist 362 (*hite*, Chron. p. 5, 264, 316); *might* p. 362, *myght* p. 365 (*myte*, Chron. p. 188, 190, 191, 222, 225, 226, &c.); *monslaught* p. 362 (Chron. *manslawth* p. 185, 218); *mydnyght* p. 365 (Chron. *midnyte* 276); *knyghtes* p. 366

---

[1] *Monumentum*, a grave; *pileatum, a pileo*, a cap, *i. e.* Capgrave. Note in margin of All Souls' MS.—*Bk. Ill. Henrics*, p. 226 n.   [2] See p. xxxiv below.

(*knyte*, Chron. p. 186, 187, 217, 227, 230, 232, 234, 235, 237, 239, 249, 258, &c.); *knyghode* p. 357; but Capgrave's form *knyt* is kept on p. 357, and *heyth* (height) on p. 359. Moreover, Capgrave's 𝒥 monogram, ⚭, is not on these MS Rome-Guide leaves, and Mr. Hingeston was such a freshman at his work when he started, that I decline to accept his opinion on the fragments being written in Capgrave's hand.

4. *Life of St. Gilbert of Sempringham*: this existed in the Cotton MS Vitellius D xv, but was burnt in the fire of 1731, and only a few fragments remain. A note by Thomas Gybbons of the contents of the MS is in Harl. MS 980, p. 231 (*Chron.*, p. xviii). And the same MS gives an extract naming the twelve Orders of Augustinians, taken from "Joh. Capgrave in vii sermon at Cambridg. ann. 1422" (*Chron.*, p. 324 *n.*), when, or after, he was studying in London (p. viii above). Osbern Bokenham alludes to this 'Life' in his 'Lyvys of Seyntys,' Roxb. Club, 1835, p. 183, re-edited by Horstmann, "My fadrys book, Mastyr Joon Capgrave," Arundel MS, Brit. Mus., 327, lf. 118. (See p. xxxiii below.)

Capgrave's Latin works now known in MS are:—

1. His autograph MS of his *Commentary on Genesis* (A.D. 1437-8), Oriel Coll. Oxford, no. 32: see p. viii above.

2. His autograph MS of his *Commentary on the Acts*, Balliol Coll. MS, 189, given to the College by Bp. Grey of Ely (1454-78), to whom it was dedicated. (See p. viii above, and *De Ill. Hen.* 219—224.)

3. His *Commentary on the Creeds:* autograph MS, All Souls' Coll. Oxford, no. 17 (*De Ill. Hen.* 211—17); a copy, Balliol Coll., Oxford, 190.

4. *Nova Legenda Angliae* (Legendary Lives of Saints); MS in the York Minster Library; another in the Bodleian, Tanner MS 15; and a third, much damaged by fire, in the Cotton MS, Tiberius E 1. Printed by Wynkyn de Worde in 1516, when Pynson also printed a shortend englishing of it. It was compiled from the *Hist. Aurea* of John of Tinmouth (*De Ill. Hen.* xlix *n*). The Prolog is printed in *De Illustr. Henricis*, p. 195—209. Dr. Horstmann is now re-editing the book, with very large additions, for the Clarendon Press. It is to be some 2000 pages long.

5. His autograph MS of *De Ill. Hen.*, ed. Hingeston in Rolls Series.

§ 2. *Capgrave's lost Latin Works.* § 3. *His Character.* xv

Capgrave's lost Latin works—or those not now known to exist—are 14 theological, and one historical:

1. His Commentaries on Exodus, Leviticus, Numbers, Deuteronomy, Joshua, Judges, Ruth, Samuel, Kings, Psalms, Ecclesiastes, Isaiah, Daniel, the twelve Minor Prophets (Hosea, Joel, Amos, Obadiah, Jonah, Micah, Nahum, Habakkuk, Zephaniah, Haggai, Zachariah, Malachi), the 21 Pauline and Canonical Epistles, and on the Apocalypse (dedicated to Wm. Grey, Bp. of Ely, 1454-78). 2. 'Manipulus Doctrinæ Christianæ.' 3. 'De Fidei Symbolis.' 4. 'Super Sententias Petri Lombardi.' 5. 'Determinationes Theologicæ.' 6. 'Ad Positiones erroneas.' 7. 'Orationes ad Clerum.' 8. 'Sermones per Annum.' 9. 'Lecturæ Scholasticæ.' 10. 'Ordinariæ Disputationes.' 11. 'Epistolæ ad diversos.' 12. 'Vita S. Augustini.' 13. 'De sequacibus S. Augustini'; and (the same work or a continuation) 14. 'De illustribus viris Ordinis S. Augustini.' The lost historical work was 'Vita Humfredi Ducis Glocestriæ.'

§ 3. *Capgrave's character.* Capgrave, being an Englishman, was of course by race and nature a flunkey, and had an inordinate reverence for kings and rank. This vice or quality is ingrain*d* in the nation. While Henry VI was alive, Capgrave was his profound admirer, and " wholly devoted to his service" (*Henries*, p. 144); and his grandfather Henry IV, " gained the crown *by the providence*, as we believe, *of God*, who is mighty to put down the mighty from their seat, and to exalt the humble" (*Henries*, p. 115, quoting Luke i. 52). But as soon as York has turnd-out Lancaster, and Edward IV is on the throne, Capgrave dedicates his *Chronicle* to him, and then—

" He that entered be intrusion was Herry the Fourte. He that entered *by Goddis provision* is Edward the Fourt . . . We trew loveres of this lond desire this of oure Lord God, that al the erroure whech was browte in be Herry the Fourte may be redressed be Edward the Fourte. This is the desire of many good men here in erde, and, as I suppose, it is the desire of the everlasting hillis that dwelle above."—p. 40. (No *gh* in *broute*.)

And this " erroure" must be deduced from the facts stated by Capgrave (*Henries*, p. 116), that

" the said king Henry [IV] observed the ways of justice, honoured with all his power the servants of God, and, drinking from the

xvi *Forewords. § 3. Capgrave's Character and Flunkeyism.*

fountains of the Scriptures went not thirsting away . . . . he was mindful of that prayer of the most glorious Solomon, in which he asked, not for riches and honour, but for the assisting wisdom of God;"

that his son Henry V, the hero of Agincourt (Capgrave's *Henries,* p. 143),

"was felicitous in all things; felicitous in endowing the church, felicitous in ordering more clearly the divine offices, felicitous in the administration of justice, and in fine, felicitous in all his life. And as the blessed Felix laid low the statues by the breath of his most strong faith, so did this king shatter the statues of the heretics with the hammer of his justice, and burn them to ashes, lest the crop of the church should be spotted with their doctrines, and the company of the faithful be destroyed by the false-hearted.

"May the Lord grant unto him for the unbroken faith he kept with Him a ring of everlasting blessedness; for his defence of the church militant, the glory of the church triumphant; and in exchange for his earthly kingdom, whose laws he kept inviolate, an eternal kingdom with God the Father, God the Son, and God the Holy Ghost, for ever and ever. Amen;"

and that his grandson, Henry VI, was Capgrave's "desirable lord, the king," "to whose service I have wholly devoted myself" (*Henries,* p. 144). But as the Vicar of Bray had afterwards "still to be Vicar of Bray, Sir," so Capgrave had still to be Prior of Lynn, and Provincial of his province. He felt but as almost all Englishmen felt in his day; as almost all Englishmen would feel under like circumstances now. In the matter of kings, dukes &c., we are a poor lot.

And as Capgrave shared the social weakness of his nation, so he shared the hates and prejudices of his Papal Church and Order. This is how he spoke of the noble Reformer Wyclif, who lasht the abuses of the Romish hierarchy, and double-thongd the hypocrisy, the vice and corruptions of the Friars[1]:—

"In the IX. ȝere of this kyng [Richard II, A.D. 1384], John Wiclef—the organ of the devel, the enmy of the Cherch, the confusion of men, the ydol of heresie, the meroure of ypocrisie, the norischer of scisme—be the rithful dome of God, was smet with a horibil paralsie thorw-oute his body. And this veniauns fell upon

[1] See his English Works, ed. Matthew, E. E. Text Soc., and his Latin Works issued by the Wyclif Society.

§ 3. *Capgrave's Character. Hatred of Oldcastle.* xvii

him on Seynt Thomas [a Beket's] day in Cristmasse [Dec. 29]; but he deyed not til Seynt Silvestir day [Dec. 31]. And worthily was he smet on Seynt Thomas Day, ageyn whom he had gretely offendid, letting men of that pilgrimage [to his Shrine at Canterbury]; and conveniently deied he in Silvestir fest, ageyn whom he had venemously berkid for dotacion of the Church."—*Chronicle*, p. 240-1.[1]

Here is Capgrave's wind-up of Oldcastle,—*Henries*, p. 141-2, A.D. 1417. (Compare Hoccleve's Poem on him : *Minor Poems*, p. 8—24.)

"It was in the fifth year of the glorious king Henry [V] that *Oldcastle, that satellite of the devil,* was taken by the servants of Lord Powis, and adjudged to death.

"For their sakes into whose hands these writings may come, I will declare some of his errors to posterity, that they may not think he was put to so shameful a death except for a just cause.

"First, he declared that none ought to worship the Mother of Christ, or the other Saints.

"Also, that confession ought to be made to God alone, and not to man.

"Also, that in the Sacrament of the Altar, after consecration, the bread remains unchanged.

"He condemned civil property; and hated [Papal] priests and churches as abominations.

"He also was for destroying marriage, as far as in him lay.

"He is said to have inflicted severe injuries on his captors when they took him, for he was very strong. But a certain woman struck him on the shin with a footstool, and he presently fell to the ground. He was brought to London, hung, and burnt. He had pretended that he was Elias, sent for the conversion of the whole world; and

---

[1] See also p. 231 : "In this tyme [1376], on, Jon Wiclef, Maystir of Oxenforth, held many straunge opiniones :—That the Cherch of Rome is not hed of alle Cherchis. That Petir had no more auctorite thanne the othir Apostelcs ; ne the Pope no more power than anothir prest. And that temporal lordes may take awey the godes fro the Cherch, whan the persones trespasin. And that no reules mad be Augustin, Benet, and Frauncys, adde no more perfeccion over the Gospel than doth lym-whiting onto a wal. And that bischoppis schuld have no prisones ; and many othir thingis."—*Chronicle*, p. 231.

Again, at p. 236 : "In the V. ʒere of Richard [1381], Jon Wiclef resumed the eld dampned opinion of Berengari, that seide,—Aftir the consecracion of Cristis body, bred remayned as it was before. Mani foul errouris multipled Wiclef more than Berengari :—That Crist was there, as he is in othir places, but sumwhat more specialy ; That this bred was no bettir than othir bred, save only for the prestis blessing ; and, if Cristis body was there, it was possible to a man for [to] breke Cristis nek. He said eke it was lasse synne to worchip a tode than the Sacrament ; for the tode hath lyf, and the Sacrament non." (See also the references to 'Lollards' in the *Chronicle* Index.)

his prophecy was fulfilled, as some say, while he was being taken to the fire sitting in the cart, since the one was borne off in a chariot to Heaven, the other to hell. The duke of Bedford and those who were present at his death, urged him to make faithful and lowly confession of his sins, offering him time, and his choice from among many priests. But he said that though Peter and Paul were present he would not confess to them; and so, as a blasphemer, and abandoned abetter of heretics, he suffered the disgrace of death as he deserved. He was first dragged to the place of execution and hung; then he was dismembered and disemboweiled, and lastly his body was burned to ashes in the flame.

"These are the acts of this illustrious, noble, and most Christian king, Henry the Fifth, in the first lustrum of his reign."

Capgrave evidently approved of the burning of heretics: see *Chronicle*, p. 277, 297, 316, &c.

"In the third ʒere of this Herry [IV. A.D. 1401] was a Parlement at London, wher was mad a statute ageyn Lollardis,[1] that where evyr thei were founde preching her evel doctrine, thei schuld be take, and presentid to the bischop; and if they maynten here opiniones, thei schuld be committed to seculere hand, and thei schuld brenne hem and her bokes. This statute was practized in a prest [William Sautre], that sone aftir was brent at Smythfeld."—p. 277.

A.D. 1409. "In this ʒere was a Parlement at London in tyme of Lenton, where a smyth was appechid for heresie.[2] He held this conclusion, that the Sacrament of the Auter is not Cristes Body, but a thing without soule, wers than a tode, or a ereyne, whech have lyf. And whan he wold not renouns his opinion, he was take to the seculere hand, for to be spered in a tunne in Smythfeld, and to be brent. The Prince Herry had pite on the man, and counseled him to forsake this fals opinion; but he wold not. Wherfor he was put in the tunne; and when the fer brent, he cried horribly. The Prince comaunded to withdrawe the fire, came to him, and behite him grete;[3] but it wold not be. Wherfor he suffered him to be brent into asches."—*Chron.* p. 297.

A.D. 1416. "In this tyme, on Benedict Wolleman, a citeceyn of London, a gret Lollard, which had set up billes of grete errouris, was takyn, hanged, and drawe, on Myhilmesse day."—*Chron.* p. 316.

---

[1] A.D. 1400. Cicetir. "The erl of Salesbury was ded [beheaded?]; and worthi, for he was a gret favorere of the Lollardis, a despiser of sacramentis, for he wold not be confessid when he schuld deie."

[2] "This was John Badby, who was burnt in Smithfield in March 1410. See Foxe's *Actes and Monuments*, iii. 235, ed. S. R. Cuttley, 8vo. 1844."—T. Wright. Also see Hoccleve's long verses about him in *De Regimine*, p. 11—12, Roxb. Club, 1860. [3] *him grete*] grete thyngs to him. Corpus MS.

But—subject always to the Pope—Capgrave loved England, and desired its weal. In the Prolog to his Lives of Saints—*Nova Legenda Angliæ*—reprinted in *Lib. de illust. Henricis*, p. 195—209, he praises his country,—in the bit englisht by Hingeston, *Henries*, p. 223-4:—

"For England (*Anglia*), according to the definition of some, is (so) called from *En*, which is 'In,' and *Cleos*, which is 'glory,' as though (she were) 'all-glorious within,' nor indeed undeservedly. For although outwardly she rejoices in many and great prerogatives, as may be easily seen, for instance, in her fertile fields and abundant crops; in the vast weight of her wood-produce; in the loveliness of her meadows, streams and fountains; in the endless variety and beauty of her cities and towns, her castles and public buildings; and, finally, in the wonderful and angelic splendour and loveliness of the nation, both in countenance and in costume, in courage and vigour of mind, as well as in other countless worldly goods, in all of which, exclusive of that which lies concealed within, her beauty and her glory are resplendent.

"But, still more nobly and gloriously does her excellence and majesty of spirit shine forth from the virtues and examples of the Saints who have flourished in her, who all, like glowing constellations, lighted up the darkening world with their rays, while all men, in their clear light, could see that 'God is no respecter of persons, but that in every nation he that feareth God and worketh righteousness is accepted of Him' (*Acts* x. 35)."

He hoped to see England happy. He writes thus of the wise foreseers of evils to come under the weak child, Henry VI, who succeeded the hero of Agincourt (*Henries*, p. 148, 149-50):—

"Many persons of a malignant disposition, interpreting amiss this coronation of our king [A.D. 1431], continue to sow among the people such murmuring words as these,—'Alas for thee, O land, whose king is a boy, and whose princes eat in the morning'[1] (*Ecclesiastes* x. 16). . . . . .

"May the Lord take away from our realm these pestilent murmurers, who delight to prophesy evil things; for I trust in the Lord that I shall see our borders in peace and prosperity, and our days happy, before the day of my death!"

And as a mean to this end, Capgrave, like Chaucer's Merchant,

---

[1] And fyrste I remembred an olde prouerbe worthy of memorye, that "often ruithe the realme, where chyldren rule, and women gouerne." Halle's *Chronicle*, 1809, p. 386: the Duke of Buckingham is explaining to Morton Bishop of Ely, why he took Richard III's side.

xx *Forewords.* § 3. *Capgrave's Character. His Impartiality.*

wisht to see our then-scornd Navy strong, that England might keep the sea (*Henries*, p. 155-6) :—

"it is the opinion of many that, if the sea were kept by our navy,[1] many good results would follow : it would give a safe conduct to merchants, secure access to fishers, the quiet of peace to the inhabitants of the kingdom, to our king himself a large measure of glory. Our enemies laugh at us, and say—

"'Take the *ship* off from your precious money, and stamp a *sheep* upon it, showing thereby your own cowardice,'—since we who used to be the conquerors of all nations, are now being conquered by all nations. The men of old used to call the sea 'the wall of England'; and what think you that our enemies, now that they are upon the wall, will do to the inhabitants who are unprepared to receive them? Forasmuch as this matter has already for the space of many years been neglected, on that account it has happened that already our ships are scanty, our sailors few in number, and those unskilled in seamanship, from want of practice. May the Lord take away this our reproach, and raise up the spirit of bravery in our nation ! May He strip off the false and feigned friendships of nations, lest on a sudden, when we dread them not, they come upon us !"

Capgrave was not much moved by Agincourt (*Chron.* p. 312, *Ill. Hen.* p. 132—4), but he notes in his *Chronicle*, p. 313, the characteristic English answer of the Earl of Dorset in 1416 to the Comte d'Armagnac's summons to surrender :—

"Then sent to the erl of Dorcet this message, the erl Armenak,— 'Now art thou so streytid, that the se is on thin o side, and we on the othir. Therefor, be my councelle, ȝeld thee; for ellis schalt thou deye.' The erl of Dorcet sent this answer ageyn,—'It was nevyr the maner of Englischmen to ȝelde hem, whan thei myte fite.' And thouȝ the Englisch host had no mo men but XV. hundred, yet had thei bettir of XV. thousand, God and good prayeris hem helpyng." (No *gh* in *myte fite*.)

He evidently tried to be impartial where no church-doctrinal question was concernd. At p. 107 of his englisht *Henries* he says :

"Now forasmuch as different writers have given different accounts of the deposition of king Richard [II] and the elevation of king Henry [IV] to the throne,—and no wonder, since in so great a struggle one took one side, and one the other,—I, who stand as it were in the middle between the two parties, consider that I hold a

---

[1] A.D. 1522. Halle's *Chronicle* (1809), p. 634 : "and still the kynges great nauie kepte the narrowe seas, for then was neither peace betwene Englonde and Fraunce, nor open warre, as you have hard."

§ 3. *Capgrave's Character. Mr. Hingeston's praises of him.* xxi

better and a safer path, since, having investigated both sides of the question, I set myself diligently to elucidate the truth alone, not indeed to the prejudice of any one who may write of these things after me, if he shall undertake to discuss this matter with more accuracy and clearness."

Capgrave's biographers, says Dr. Thompson, in *Dict. Nat. Biogr.*, " eulogise his character in the highest terms. The most learned of English Augustinians whom the soil of Britain ever produced, he was distinguished as a philosopher and theologian, practically rejecting in his writings the dreams of sophists, which lead only to strife and useless discussions. Fulfilling the mission of his order, ' it was his wont to thunder against the wanton and arbitrary acts of prelates, who enlarge the borders of their garments beyond measure, catching at the favour of the ignorant herd; not shepherds, but hirelings, who leave the sheep to the wolves, caring only for the milk and fleece; robbers of their country, and evil workers, to whom truth is a burden, justice a thing of scorn, and cruelty a delight.'—BALE."

If Bale saw Capgrave's MSS in which this "thunder" was containd, I regret that they have been lost. To me the thunder sounds like the volleys of abuse which Wyclif and his followers fired against the Papal officials in religious England, and specially against the Friars, among whom Capgrave was a chief. Can Bale have mistaken a Lollard treatise for one of Capgrave's? But however this may be, our Friar made a very (a too) favourable impression on his Rolls-editor, Mr. Hingeston, who says—*Chron.* p. xxiv :—

" it is impossible not to be struck with the singular honesty and straight-forwardness of character which must have belonged to the writer . . . The appeal of Robert Grosteste, Bishop of Lincoln . . . from the authority of the Pope ' to the High King of Heaven ' is mentioned without a syllable of disapprobation[1] . . . He also men-

[1] *Chron.* p. 156, A.D. 1251 : "In the XXXVI 3ere of hir [his] regne deied Robert Grostede, born in Suffolk, and bischop of Lincolne. He beqwathe al his bokes to the Frere Menouris of Oxenforth. He had be at Rome, and pleted for the rite of the Cherch of Ynglond undir the Pope Innocent. For that same Pope reised many new thingis of this lond, and gaf the benefices without consent of the Kyng, or patrones, or any othir. And this same bischop Robert wrot and seid ageyn the Pope; and at Rome, in his presens, appeled fro him to the hy Kinge of Hevene. So came he hom, and deied. And in his deth he appered to the Pope, and smet him on the side with the pike of his crosse staf, and seid thus : ' Rise, wrech, and com to the dom.' This wordis herd the cubiculeris, and the strok was seyn in his side, for he deyed anon aftir that." (No *gh* in *nite.*)

Capgrave's entry as to Thomas a Becket is on p. 140 : " Aftir that fel gret strif

xxii *Forewords.* § 4. *Mr. T. A. Trollope on St. Katharine.*

tions the several instances of attempted aggression by the Pope on the prerogative of the King, and the liberties of English subjects, in the true spirit of an Englishman, and it is impossible to doubt that he heartily approved of the false claims of the See of Rome being disputed, although he does not venture to say so in as many words. The general impression left on the mind, after a careful review of the contents of the Chronicle, is favourable alike to the head and heart of the writer, and calculated to inspire us with the greatest confidence in his accuracy and credibility."[1] [Not, I hope, when he tells the absurd religious stories of miracles, &c., that he sometimes does.]

§ 4. *St. Katharine.* Of the heroine of the present volume, "St. Catherine, Virgin and Martyr, whose day of commemoration recurs on the 25th of November, and who is the person intended when the Roman Church speaks of St. Catherine without any additional designation," Mr. T. A. Trollope gives the following account in the 9th edition of the *Encyclopædia Britannica*, V. 229/2 (1876):—

"History has exceedingly little to tell of this saint; history, more properly so called, indeed has nothing at all. She is said to have been of royal parentage, and her life is referred to the early part of the 4th century. She was martyred at Alexandria. She was especially celebrated for her learning and philosophical culture, and has always been considered the especial patron of philosophical schools. But in proportion to the scantiness of authenticated fact, legendary fable has been abundant in furnishing forth lives of the saint. And it is to one of these legends that the well-known presentiment of the saint—which alone is likely to cause modern readers to feel any interest in her name—is due. It is said that in revenge for the discomfiture of a company of heathen philosophers, with whom she had been compelled to dispute, the holy and learned lady was bound to a wheel armed with spikes, in such sort that every turn of the machine would cause the spikes to pierce her body. But the cords were miraculously broken, and the malice of her enemies foiled. Hence St. Catherine, virgin and martyr, is always repre-

---

betwix him and the Kyng, for liberty of the Cherch; for whech first was the bischop exiled, and many wrongis do to him and to his kyn. Thanne cam he hom ageyn, and was killid." Not much in this Becket bit, and the Saint's holy-oil story at p. 273, to bear out Mr. Hingeston's statement.

[1] A.D. 1402. In this tyme cam oute a bulle fro the Court, whech revokid alle the graces that had be grauntted many ȝeres before; of whech ros mech slaundir and obliqui ageyn the Cherch; for thei seide pleynly that it was no more trost to the Pope writing than to a dogge tail; for as ofte as he wold gader mony, so oftyn wold he anullen eld graces, and graunt newe.—*Chronicle*, p. 281.

Forewords. § 4. *Capgrave's Life of St. Katharine.* xxiii

sented with a wheel [see Raphael's picture in the National Gallery[1]], and the extreme popularity of this saint, and consequent commonness of the pictures of her, is indicated by the fact that a wheel of a certain construction and appearance is to the present day called a Catherine wheel.

"The lover of mediæval painting may be warned against mistaking the pictures which he so constantly meets with, of St. Catherine with her wheel, for representations of St. Catherine of Siena, or of any of the other saints Catherine, who all of them lived a thousand years or more later than the first and original saint of the name."[2]

Capgrave says that he englisht the present *Life of St. Katharine* from a Latin translation of St. Athanasius's Greek 'Life' of her, made by Arrek, who died in Lynn many years before, and who had been "parson of Seynt Pancras in the Cyte of London a ful grete while," p. 14, 15. This St. Pancras must have been that in Soperslane, Cheapside, which was burnt in the Great Fire of London in 1666, and was never rebuilt, the parish being joind to that of St. Mary-le-Bow. The name Arrek does not occur in Newcourt's *Repertorium;*[3] and I don't know where else to look for him. The

---

[1] It is in Room VI, No. 168. Ruskin says that it was printed about 1507, in Raphael's second or Florentine period.—P. F.

[2] The other 5 Saint Catherines are given by Mr. Trollope, in col. 1, as—"2. *St. Catherine of Sweden,* who died abbess of Watzen, on the 24th March, 1381, and is commemorated on the 21st of that month; 3. *St. Catherine of Siena,* born in 1347, whose festal day is observed on the 30th of April; 4. *St. Catherine of Bologna,* whose family name was Vigri, and who died abbess of the Convent of St. Clairs in that city on the 9th of March, 1463; 5. *St. Catherine of Genoa,* who belonged to the noble family of Fieschi, was born about 1448, spent her life and her means in succouring and attending on the sick, especially in the time of the plague which ravaged Genoa in 1497 and 1501, died in that city in 1510, was canonized by Clement XII in 1737, and had her name placed in the calendar on the 22nd of July by Benedict XIV; and 6. *St. Catherine de' Ricci,* of Florence, born of that noble family in 1522, who became a nun in the convent of the Dominicans at Prato, died in 1589, and was canonized by Benedict XIV in 1746, who fixed her festal day on the 13th February."

[3] An Ecclesiastical Parochial History of the Diocese of London, A.D. 1708. *St. Pancras Soperlane,* Rectory :—This Church of S. Pancras Soperlane (so called, because near a Street formerly known by that name, but now, since the Fire [1666] call'd *Queen-street*) was a small Church, and stood in Needlers-lane, in Cheap-Ward. It is a Rectory, and one of the 13 Peculiars in this City, subject to the Jurisdiction of the Archbishop of Canterbury. vol. i. p. 517. . . . vol. i. p. 518. But being burnt down in the late dreadful Fire, it is since annext to the Church of S. Mary-le-Bow (as is also that of Allhallows, Honey-

xxiv   *Forewords. § 5. Apology for the Text.*

story of St. Katharine's Life being told in the side-notes, I will not trouble the reader with a sketch of it here. The author's appeal to the Holy Ghost for help, in the Prolog to Bk. III, p. 171, should be noted.

§ 5. *Apology for the text.* The Author and his subject having been dealt with, I turn now to his text in the present volume, and must start with an apology to our Members for the waste of some of their money in it, money that would have printed 130 pages of another MS. The material before Dr. Horstmann to enable him to

---

lane), which Church of S. Mary-le-Bow is made the Parochial-Church for all these Three Parishes. And the Site of this remains only as a Burying-place for the Inhabitants of this Parish. . . .

Reg. Cant.	Rectores.	Patroni.
Reynolds	25 Rob. de Sandwico, 2 Kal. Jul. 1319	
	26 Joh. de Hertford, prid. Id. Oct. 1320 per res[ignationem] Roberti	
	263 Ric. fil. Basil de Sudbury, 4 Id. Sept. 1326. Adam de Branketre	Prior & Capitulum Eccles. Christi Cant.
Islep.	287 Tho. Forster, cl. 6 Jul. 1361 per mort. Branketre	
	307 Will. de Drayton, 4 Kal. Mar. 1363 per res. Forster	
	Will. Gysors.	
Sudbury.	133 Rob. Martin, pr. 5 Oct. 1380. per res. Gysors	
	135 David Michell, 19 Maii 1381. per res. Martin	
Courtney ◁	277 Joh. Parker, cap. 12 Junii 1390 Joh. Wykyngston	
Arundel 2. P. ◁	67 Joh. Prata, 26 Maii 1413, per res. Wykyngston	
	69 Joh. Hody, 20 Dec. 1415. per res. Prata	Archiep. Can.
	77 Ric. Lofthouse, cl. 18 Oct. 1416, per res. Hody.	
	82 Ric. Grange, 31 Dec. 1416, per res. Lofthouse.	
Stafford. ◁	106 Joh. Kirkby, A.M. 12 Nov. 1450. per mort. Grange	
Bourchier ◁	74 Will. King, al. Holben, cap. 1 Maii 1459. per res. Bromh. Tho. Marks	

(A Robert Pratta was Vicar of East Winch in Norfolk in 1349.—Blomefield ix. 154, ed. 1808. I don't think *Prata* above can be a latining of *Akker*, acre, field. In the list of Prebendaries of St. Pancras, Kentish Town, Middx. in Newcourt i. 193-5, there is no name like Arrek.)

Forewords. § 5. *Capgrave's avoidance of Gutturals.* xxv

pick the best MS for his text, was, the autograph *Chronicle* printed in 1858, and its Appendix III, p. 335-354, containing the Prolog of the *St. Katharine* from the Arundel MS 396, collated with the Rawlinson MS Poet. 116, and Arundel 168; and the Editor's business was to see which of these MSS had spellings and forms most like those of the autograph *Chronicle*. Now even an eye so careless of peculiarities as mine was caught at once by one most prominent characteristic of Capgrave's spelling, his avoidance of the guttural *gh*. It is shown in the first page of his *Chronicle* (after the Dedication), "the man *hite* Cayn"; it is in the last page but one (316), "he *hite* the emperoure that he schuld withdrawe his obediens fro that same Petir"; and it occurs all through the work. See the *myte fite*, might fight, on p. xx, and other instances above. Take a few more samples:

aute (aughte, owed) 167, 171
boute (bought) 186, 257, 314, 315
broute (brought), 126, 127, 130, 131, 134, 135, 186, 219, 226, 271, 280
caute (caught) 189
dowtir (daughter) 126, 133, 134, 219, 221, 314
faut (fought) 136, 221, 260
fite (fight) 136, 184, 185, 189, 216, 230, 239, 256, 281, 313
fytyng (fighting) men 270
hey (high) 44; heyer (higher) 220
hite (1. was cald, 2. promist) 5, 133, 158, 264, 265, 316; be-hite 297
knites-mete (providing for knights) 293
knyte, knite (knight) 133, 134, 135, 186, 187, 217, 227, 230, 233, 234, 235, 237, 239, 249, 258, 276, 307, 313 &c

knythod 287
litynningis (lightnings) 314
midnyte 276
myte (might), 126, 188, 190, 191, 222, 225, 226, 236, 248
myty (mighty) 223, 238, 283
not (naught) 268
nowt (naught) 104
nyte 132, 284
ny (nigh) 159, 229
rite, ryte (right) 128, 129, 131, 153, 156, 225, 226, 228, 276
say (saw) 191
sey (saw), 89, 191, 363
sowte (sought) 147
streite, streith (straightway) 202
thorow, thorw (through) 78
thorow oute (throughout) 186, 271
thoute (thought) 245, 266

The only exception I have notist in turning over some of the pages is *wright*, p. 240, and the footnote to it says that it is "written in a later hand" upon an erasure.[1] The other way of avoiding the

[1] Cherborgh, p. 257, for Cherbourg in France, has justifiably the final *gh*, though the Corpus MS reads 'Cherborow.'

xxvi *Forewords.* § 5. *Dr. Horstmann chose the wrong MS.*

guttural *gh*, which Capgrave occasionally has recourse to, is by using *th: brithnesse* 58, *manslawth* manslaughter, 185, 218 ; *rith* right 81, 131, *rithful* 132, 312, *rithfuly* 40, *onrithfuly* 209.

Having thus Capgrave's autograph forms, Dr. Horstmann would turn to Mr. Hingeston's print of the Prolog to *St. Katherine* from Arundel 396 ; and what would he find in it? For Capgrave's *rite* (once *rith*), 'ryght' 337, 339 (twice), 340 (twice), 345, 351 ; for Capgrave's *knite* or *knyte*, 'knyght, knyghtes,' 345 ; for Capgrave's *hey* high, 'heygh' 338 (though 'hey' 349/1) ; for Capgrave's *brith*, 'bryght' 341 ; for Capgrave's *say* or *sey* saw, 'saugh' 343, 347, 348 ; for Capgrave's *thorow*, 'thurgh' 347, 354 ; for Capgrave's *not*, 'nought' 350 ; for Capgrave's *broute* and *sowte* p. t., 'isought' and 'brought' pp. 351. And that, to emphasize his love of *gh*, the Arundel man spelt *how* 'hough' 347.

On turning to Mr. Hingeston's foot-note collations, Dr. Horstmann would find, for the non-Capgrave forms *ryght*[1] 337, 339, 'rith Ar. 168, ryth Rawl.'; 340, 'ryth' Rawl. (righte Ar.) ; for the non-Capgrave *bryght* 341, 'brith' Ar. bryght Rawl. (bad); for the non-C. *saugh* 343, 348, the Capgrave 'sey' or 'saw' (347, 348) Ar. Rawl.; for the non-C. *knyghtes* 345, 'knythis' Ar., 'knyte' Rawl.; for the non-C. *thurgh* 347, 354, the Capgrave 'thorow' (through 354), Ar. 'thorw' (thorow 354) Rawl.; for the non-C. *hough* the Capgrave 'how' Rawl. ('who' Ar., both 'who' in 349) ; for the non-C. *nought* (350), the Capgrave 'not' Rawl. (noght Ar.) ; for the non-C. *Isought* 351, the Capgrave 'soute' Rawl. (sought Ar.). And the conclusion, before turning to the MSS themselves, would be, that of the three dealt with by Hingeston, the Rawlinson MS had most of Capgrave's forms, Arundel 168 rather fewer, and Arundel 396 least of all. This conclusion would be strongly confirmd by the rest of Arundel 396, for tho in 53/597-600 its *hyght, ryght, myght* are the same in Rawl.[2], yet in 61/737-40 its *whyght, nyght, dyght*

---

[1] Ar. 168 and Rawl. have the bad 'ryght' or 'righte' in 351 ; and in 345 Rawl. has the bad 'rygth.'

[2] In 65/814-17 Ar. has *spyryt, nyght, lyght*, and Rawl. badly *spryght, nyght, lyght* ; in 185/225-7 Ar. has *fyghte, lyghte*, and Rawl. *fyght, lyght* ; in 211/664-5 both have wrongly *plyght, nyght*, as they have *syght, bryght* in 225/888-9, and 229/953-5, and *bryght, lyght* in 251/1345-7.

Forewords. § 5. *Dr. Horstmann chose the wrong MS.* xxvii

are *wyte, nyth, dyth* in Rawl. ; in 73/939-41, its *fyte, hyghte* are *fyte, hyte* in Rawl. ; in 79/1-3 its *brygltt, ryght* are *bryth, ryth* in Rawl. ; in 91/191 its *vovgh* is *vow* in Rawl. ; in 93/237-8 its *thought, abovght* are þ*outh, abowth* in Rawl. ; in 117/615-16 its *nought, Ibought* are *nowth, Iboute* in Rawl. ; in 123/722-4, 205/568-70 its *nought, thought* are *nowte, thowte* in Rawl. ; in 127/783-4 its *whygt, disspyght* are *wyght, dispyte* in Rawl. ; in 141/1024-7, and 227/919-22 its *thought, nought, brought* are *thowte, nowte, browte* in Rawl. ; in 163/1373-5 its *whyt, endyght* are *wyght, endyth* in Rawl. ; in 177/106-8 its *myght, sight* are *myght, syte* in Rawl.; in 179/149-52 its *whight, ryght, bryght* are *whyte, ryght, bryte* in Rawl. ; in 217/751-4 its *nought, thought, bought* are *nouth, thowth, bouth* in Rawl. ; in 247/1266-7 its *nought, bought* are *noght, bowte* in Rawl. Moreover, these non-Capgrave forms continue in Arundel 396, as *hight* 264/81 ; *right, fight, might* 264/93-6 ; *myght, nyght, right* 266/135-8, &c. &c. *rightes* (= rites), *knyghtes, ryghtes* 271/324-7 ; *nought, bought, sought* 286/786-9, though in 267/163-5 the correct *wryte, knyte* occur, as doubtless elsewhere. And besides the wrong form in the rymes, Arundel 396 has them in the body of the lines : *sovght, novght* 13/193-5 (*soute, not*, Rawl.), *thorgh-ovte,* þ*urgh-ovte* 47/495, 508 (*thorow-oute,* þ*orw-out*, Rawl.), *movght* 53/588 (mouth, Rawl.), *thought* 195/400 (þouth, Rawl.), &c. &c.

In the face of this large number of gutturals in the Arundel MS 396, it is clear that any moderately careful editor would not have adopted it as the basis of his text before he had examind the Rawlinson MS, of which Hingeston's collation had—or ought to have—warnd him that it was nearer Capgrave's forms.[1] Nevertheless, Dr. Horstmann copied the Arundel 396, sent it to press, authorised the setting of the whole of it—tho' he knew of the existence of the Rawlinson MS ;—and not until the whole of the Arundel MS had been in type for several months did Dr. H. go to Oxford and collate the Rawlinson MS (of which he had not told me), and then found of course that it was a better MS than the Arundel one, independently

---

[1] Of course other forms in the Arundel MS differ from Capgrave's in the *Chronicle;* for *dreynt* drownd, *Kath.* 206/592, the *Chron.* has *dronch* 133, *dronchin* 74, and so on.

xxviii *Forewords.* § 5. *Dr. Horstmann chose the wrong MS.*

of the *gh*, which I knew nothing of till I took up the *Chronicle* some three weeks ago. I was savage about it,—as a testing collation could have been made at any time by Miss Parker at slight expense—but would not authorise the cost of setting the whole of the Rawlinson MS, as the text is poor, both in language and subject, and of little worth beside Capgrave's autograph Chronicle. I could not help telling Dr. Horstmann that his edition was a 'mess;' and I think his feeling that it is so, must have been one of the reasons that made him throw it up. I don't pretend to set myself over him as a person who hasn't made as bad or worse messes; no doubt I've made plenty more. The only thing is to confess the blunder, and beg our members to excuse it. All our workers can't be of the first class; we must often put up with some of the third and fifth; they show their good will, and we take the will for the deed. No very great harm has been done. (Some day we ought to have an edition of the *Chronicle* and this *St. Katharine* by a real language Editor.)

As to the gutturals, I feel sure that they had gone or were going in many parts of England much earlier than is generally supposed,[1] and I think that an occasional miswritten ryme like *white* (for *wight* active), *liȝte, myȝte*, in my *Parliament of Devils* volume, E. E. T. S. 1867, no. 24, p. 72/450-4—besides the like ones in the Text below—shows how the gutturals were pronounst even when they were written ȝ or *gh*. And as, according to my friend Mr. Walter Rye, all the good things and men in England come from Norfolk—or if they don't, ought to—I conclude that our standard English owes to Norfolk its exemption from harsh gutturals.

Thus far had I written (and printed) when a comment from our good friend Prof. Skeat came in, which makes me hope that fonetic folk will some day allow that Chaucer didn't guggle his *gh* as most, if not all, of the teachers of pronunciation have hitherto made him do. If any one in his England was subject to French influence, and was 'educated,' he was that man.

"I entirely deny your point about the loss of guttural coming from Norfolk! For it certainly came from France. It was the

---

[1] Compare the later 'slitingly,' 1654, *Nicholas Papers*, ii. 51 (1892); 'slitly,' *ibid.* 136; 'slited,' *ibid.* 212 (A.D. 1655).

Forewords. § 5. *The dropping of* gh. *Arundel MS* 396.

natural result of Frenchmen learning English; and of Englishmen (peasants) copying their superiors. The guttural *gh* became 'vulgar,' and was purposely got rid of. More's the pity. *ght* becomes *st* in *Domesday Book!* Such a change began first in the South, in Sussex and Kent,[1] &c., where French words most abounded. Then it attacked Mercian, and lastly Northumbrian; and to this day the guttural lingers in Scotland. That's the geography, and the facts. For all you know, Capgrave may have had a French-speaking father or grandfather. Or even being in the church would have helped. The educated classes sided, in *this* respect, with the nobles.

As for *th*, as *rith* for *right*, it would occur anywhere where the scribe was well up in Anglo-French. Why, it occurs in Havelok (and in Domesday Book, I believe) over and over again: all it proves is that the scribe was better up in writing out Anglo-French than in writing English: a *very* common thing. So much so that our modern spelling is wholly Anglo-French. See my *Principles of Etymology*, Series I, p. 304.

The Arundel MS 396 is a vellum one of about 1440, with red initials. At the end of its last treatise, one on the Mass, leaf 130 back, is:—

"Iste liber est ex dono *domine* Kateryne Babyngton, quondam subpriorisse de Campseye[2]; & si quis illu*m* alienauerit sine licencia

[1] I don't recollect any MS that avoids *gh* like Capgrave's *Chronicle* does.—F.

[2] The nunnery of "Campes, Campess, or Campsey Priory, in Suffolk,"— Dugdale's *Monasticon*, ed. Caley, Ellis and Bandinel, 1830, vol. vi, Part I, p. 583—7. "An Austin nunnery for the Nuns of the Order of Fontevrault" (Taylor, *Index Monasticus*, p. 99). "The Nunnery was six miles from Woodbridge, lying on the right of the high road." Its "ruins are now inconsiderable." "Previous to the dissolution there were nineteen Nuns of this house, besides the Prioress." "Before Ric. I, Theobald de Valoines gave all his estate in this place to his two sisters, Joan and Agnes, with design that they should build a Monastery to the honour of the blessed Virgin Mary, wherein they and other religious women might live to the service of God. Accordingly they founded here a Nunnery of the Order of St. Austin, of which the foresaid Joan was the first Prioress." K. John confirmd the founder's design by Charter; John de Framlingham, clerk, gave the nuns the manor and advowson of the Church of Karleton, and their third charter "relates to the foundation of a chantry at" Campsey Ashe "by Maud de Lancaster, Countess of Ulster, which in 1354 was removed to Rokehall in Brusyard." As to this, see also Dugdale, vol. vi, Part III, p. 1468.

"*Campsey-Ash*, a parish in the hundred of Loes in the county of Suffolk, 2½ miles to the E. of Wickham Market, its post town, which is a station on the Framlingham Junction of the East Suffolk railway. The par. lies on the E. side of the river Deben, and was the site of a nunnery of the order of St. Clare, founded in the latter part of the 12th century by Theobald de Valoines, and to

xxx *Forewords.* § 5. *The Arundel MSS* 168 *and* 20.

vna cum consensu dictarum [sanctimonialium?] conuentus, malediccionem dei omnipotentis incurrat, & anathema sit!"

The Arundel MS 168 is of paper, with a vellum wrapper to each sheet, and is a thin folio written in double columns, about 1440—50 A.D. Forty-six pages of collations of it are on p. 405—450 below. The Arundel MS 20 is a paper MS in double columns, ab. 1450—60, and has the *gh*. It has also the *xal, xulde* of the Lynn Gilds in the Society's *Gilds*, ed. Toulmin Smith, and other East-Midland texts. I copy, as a sample of Arundel 20, four stanzas that have *gh* rymes :—

lf. 23, bk., col. 1. (Bk. IV, Prol., p. 264 below.)
¶ But theis same ij For very werynes   92
left their honour & resynyd their ry3t.
Futt grete excusse had thei in) sykkernes ;
Thei seyd theyr grete labur & their sy3t
A-vaylle them ry3t nou3t nor yt my3t ;   96
for y{e} more thei dyd, y{e} more thei had to do :
wherfor in sykkernes thus thei twoo   98
¶ Resynyd theyr ry3t vnto this same man ....

lf. 23, bk., col. 2. (Bk. IV, Ch. 2, p. 267 below.)
Than) y{e} romayns with a cummyn assent   162
letters prevyly off grete sentence wry3t,
And in-to brytan) to constantyne them sent,
In whyche thei preyd hym), os he was kny3t,
That he cum helpe them ageyns this tyrant to fy3t ;[1]   166
Thei wolde be-tray hym), thei seyd, he xulde not spede ;
Thys was theyr ende : "cum helpe vs at oure nede."   168

lf. 26, bk., col. 1. (Bk. IV, Ch. 12, p. 286 below.)
Ry3t thus yt semys by oure creatore,   785
god off hevyn), that att made off nou3t,—
3e take a-wey From) hym that dew honore
That he xulde hathe, that he Futt dere bou3t,
when that in erthe byselye oure helthe he sou3te :   789
This same honor gyue 3e to dewls ymagys
Whyche 3e haue set here solemly off stagys.   791

---

which a chantry was attached by Maud de Lancaster. The nunnery, of which there are some remains, had a revenue at the Dissolution of £182 9*s.*, and was given to Sir William Willoughby." Hamilton's *National Gazetteer*, 1868, vol. i, p. 470, col. 1. *Campsie* in Stirlingshire is out of the question.

[1] Note that Dr. Horstmann prints in brackets the wrongly-spelt '*fyght*,' when he supplies the ryme-word to Capgrave's '*wryte . . knyte*,' which the Arundel scribe has, in this instance, rightly kept.

Forewords. § 6. *Index and Forewords. P. S. De Ill. Hen.* xxxi

Arundel MS 20, lf. 28, bk., col. 1, at foot. (Bk. IV, Ch. 18, p. 301 below.)

¶ Thus was she *con*fortyd, & lefte aft that nyght   1247
In *p*resone styft, in suche oryson) alone ;
The savowre abode, & sum-what of y*e* lyght,
After y*e* tyme the Aungeft was gone :
He hathe made hyr hardy & stable as y*e* stone :   1251
Ther xaft no peyn) hyr now remeue
Fro y*e* Feythe nor From) hyr be-leue.   1253

Gh rymes occur again, like *nouʒt, wrouʒt*, lf. 26, col. 1 ; *nouʒte, thouʒt*, lf. 27, col. 1 ; *nouʒt, brought*, lf. 27, bk., col. 2 ; *thouʒt, nouʒt*, col. 1, &c. &c.

§ 6. *Miscellaneous.* Mr. Thomas Austin has made the Index of Names and Glossary to the Text ; I put the side-notes and headlines ; and as our subscribers expect forewords of some kind to their volumes, I have knockt the present ones together, almost wholly from Mr. Hingeston's editions[1] of the *Chronicle* and *Illustrious Henries* in the Rolls Series. It has been a bore to do this, as other pressing work had to be set aside for it ; but no one else could be got. I cannot give time to hunt out the sources of the fictionary Life or write notes on the text. Dr. Schick's faithful work on his equally worthless *Temple of Glas* by Lydgate, shames me and makes me admire his thoroughness and zeal. He could not have workt more diligently and ably, had his author been Cynewulf, Chaucer, or Shakspere. I salute and honour him, and those of his nation and of mine[2] who edit in his spirit. At 67, and with five years' work in arrear, I am content to shirk ; and now I am off to bed.—F. J. F.

3, *St. George's Square, London, N. W., Feb.* 9, 1892, 1 *a.m.*

P. S.—Capgrave's *De Illustribus Henricis*, says its author, " prides itself on its brevity in its humble panegyrics on the men

---

[1] There is much research and good honest work in the volumes, for which I feel grateful to their Editor, whom I have so plunderd.—He is now the Rev. F. C. Hingeston-Randolph of Ringmore Rectory, near Kingsbridge, Devon, and has, since his *Capgrave*, edited several old texts, Exeter Bishops' Registers.

[2] In 'mine' I include Dr. Mary N. Colvin and her fellow-countrymen. Many of the Old French Text Society's men are of the right sort too ; above all, its Founders, Prof. Paul Meyer and Prof. Gaston Paris, who are an honour to their country.

who bear this name" (p. 100-1: Hen. IV of England). It is divided into three Parts. Part I contains the Lives of the 6 Emperors, Henry I—Henry VI,[1] A.D. 918—1198; Part II, the Lives of the 6 Kings, Henry I—VI of England,[2] A.D. 1100—1446; Part III, shorter Lives of twelve other Henries, A.D. 1031—1406: 1. Henry, King of the Dacians, that is, Eric VI of Denmark (A.D. 1241—1250); 2. Henry I, King of France (1031—59); 3. Henry, son of Richard, King of the Romans (1216—71); 4. Henry, Count of Champagne, made King of Jerusalem in 1192; 5. Henry, Archbishop of Sens (1122); 6. Henry, Duke of Lancaster, grandfather of Hen. IV, died March 13, 1361; 7. Henry Bohun, Earl of Hereford in 1199, died 1220; 8. Henry de Beaumont, died 1340; 9. Henry le Despenser, Bishop of Norwich, the suppressor of Litster's Norfolk rebellion 1381, died Aug. 23, 1406; 10. Henry of Huntingdon, the Chronicler, 1108—1135; 11. Henry, Archdeacon of Ghent, A.D. 1279; 12. Henry de Urimaria, of the Order of the Hermits of St. Augustine, A.D. 1340, D.D. of Paris, a writer of several theological works.

On Henry de Beaumont (1309—33), of the family who had large estates in Norfolk (Dugdale, *Baronage*, ii. 54), Capgrave says, *Ill. Henries*, p. 196:

"I have undertaken to commemorate the memory of the Illustrious Henries; and chief among these it delights me to leave a

[1] A compilation chiefly from the Chronicles of Martinus Polonus and Godfrey of Viterbo, less from Vincent of Beauvais, Matthew of Westminster and Henry of Huntingdon, with an anecdote of St. Jerome.—Hingeston, *De Ill. Hen.*, xx.

[2] From Henry of Huntingdon, Walsingham, Higden's *Polychronicon*, and Giraldus Cambrensis.

As to the dates of Part II, Mr. Hingeston says, *De Ill. Hen.* xxv:—"The fourth and two following Chapters were certainly composed not later than the year 1446, in which Humphrey, Duke of Gloucester, died, as the Author speaks of him in the first of them as still surviving. The 4th and 5th Chapters were probably written not long after the accession of Henry VI in 1421, as there are evident marks in the autograph MS. at the end of the latter of them, that the work was broken off there abruptly, and afterwards resumed with the sixth Chapter; and it is likely that this Chapter was finished between the date last mentioned in it, August 1, 1446, and February 1447, when the Duke of Gloucester died, or Capgrave would certainly have alluded to the death of his great friend and patron."

(On the household of Duke Humphrey, see his major-domo John Russell's *Boke of Norture* in my edition of *The Babees Book*, or *Early English Manners and Meals*, E. E. T. Soc.)

P. S. Early Decay of the Guttural gh in England.

record of those of the name of Beaumont, since I am their servant, and bound to this race by special affection."

Capgrave's Chronicle, tho begun before 1438, p. ix. above, was, I suppose, wound up and sent off, with its Dedication, to Edward IV, directly after his accession to the throne on 4 March, 1461. Like Chaucer's humorous appeal for money to Henry IV—his "*Purse*,"—the work would go to the new King at once; for fresh Sovereigns who bundle old ones out, are soothd by writers' assurances that God and the Right are on the winner's side. They generally do work with the big battalions.

With regard to the silence of *gh*, Mr. Gollancz instances the fact that in stanza 26 of the 13th-century *Pearl*—edited by him in his Series of early Texts, 1891, and by Dr. R. Morris in E. E. T. Soc., 1864—the scribe writes the disyllabic -*ie* as *yghe*: *yghe* eye, *lyghe* lie, to *dyghe* die, *syghe* saw, to *tryghe* try. In stanza 38 he rymes the adverb *hyghe* (meaning *hye*) high, with *cortaysye*; in 85 the past participle *tyght* with *crysolyt*, *quyt*, and *plyt* (n. plight, which rymes with *lyght*, *nyght*, *myghte* n., in st. 90, and, spelt *plyt*, with *delyt* in st. 93). Prof. Napier also reminds me that Chaucer rymes *plit* plight, with *appetit* in the Merchant's Tale, 473/2335-6 Six-Text;[1] but this is the O. Fr. *plite* condition, not the A. Sax. *pliht* peril. The author of the *Pearl* uses the two indifferently:—Gollancz, *Pearl*, 128. I wait for more MS evidence as to Prof. Skeat's theory.

In 1547, Salesbury says that *gh* is not guttural, and that Englishmen do not like the sound:

"*Gh* has the same sound as our [Welsh] *ch*, except that they sound *gh* softly, not in the neck, and we sound *ch* from the depth of our throats, and more harshly (p. 210); and as it is disagreeable to the English to hear the grating sound of this letter, so Welshmen in the South of Wales avoid it as much as possible."—Ellis, *E. E. Pron.* 779.

[1] Though the Minor-Poems Ryme-Index by Miss Marshall and Miss Porter shows other like rymes, they arise only from scribes' bad spelling. Robert of Brunne, Lincolnshire, in 1338 rymes a *lite* little, with to *fyghte*, Chron. 113/3180, and *sight*, with *desconfit*, ib. 36/1018.

If then, both West and East, the neglect of the guttural had spread far north in the Midlands before Chaucer's time, and was not used by Capgrave in Lynn some thirty years after Chaucer's death, we may fairly assume that "the Father of English Poetry" either didn't sound his *gh* at all,—or if he did, yet so slightly as to avoid all tone of harshness.

xxxiv *P. S. Capgrave's 'Guide to Rome' not Autograph.*

In 1569 John Hart writes 'higher' *heiër*, tho' he has *riht, rihtli, liht*. In 1599, Minsheu evidently hears no guttural in *gh*:
"Gue, Gui, Ghe, Ghi." "But if, after *u*, follow *e* or *i*, pronounce as the French like *Guerre, Guide:* as in English Guest, guide: so in Spanish *Guérra* war, *Guía* a guide: sound *Gherra, Ghia*,—except these wordes following " . . .—*Spanish Grammar*, p. 6.

" The Compendious Schoolmaster," 1687, says, p. 14 :

" *Gh* in the middle of a Syllable are but softly pronounced, as in *light, bright, might, night, right*, as also in *thought, straight, strength, slaughter;* and in *high, thigh, nigh, gh* are not sounded at all."

(As Capgrave was a Norfolk man,[1] we may note this book's "Essex stiles, Kentish miles, Norfolk wiles, many Men beguiles," p. 80. Misyn of Lincoln, in his *Fire of Love*, 1435, has *hily* for 'highly.')

The entry on p. xiv from Gibbons's MS, Harl. 980, p. 231, lf. 120, gives " Houeden fo 649 " as its authority for its account of St. Gilbert, and says also " Vid Joh Capgraue in Vit S^{tl} Gilberti manusc[r]ipt ex Museo Rob Kemp milit d Gissing "; and then, after a list of 11 of the 12 orders of Augustines, adds—

" The 12 An order onely in Norff which had 4 house[s], one of them is faln into the Kings hand, and he gaue it to Walsingham, hite Peterston [in Norfolk, see Dugdale. N. B. the *gh* is left out of *hight* cald].

" per Joh Capgraue in vii sermon at Cambridg Ann. 1422, et ex museo supradicto."

The doubt exprest on p. xiii as to the MS " Guide to the Antiquities of Rome" being in Capgrave's hand, is settled by the following letter from Prof. Napier :

" *Southfield, Cowley, Oxford.*
" *Wednesday, March 16, 1892.*
" MY DEAR FURNIVALL,
" I was in All Souls' Library this afternoon, and looked carefully at MS 17. The result of my examination confirms your supposition. The handwriting of the flyleaves is *entirely different* from that of the body of the MS, and can*not* be by the same scribe.

" Then I looked at the facsimile of the Cambridge MS of the Chronicle (given in *Hingeston's* ed. of the Chronicle), and I found

---

[1] The book contains, says the Author to the Reader (A 6 back), "some Raptures of Poetry on the Commandments, and on the Dolorous Ruins, and Glorious Resurrection [May 29, 1683] of the most Renowned City of *London*, from the devouring Flames [Sept. 4, 1666]," p. 104-6.

P. S. Arrek who wrote the Latin Life of St. Katharine.

that that is again in a different hand, *i. e.* that neither the flyleaves in MS 17 (All Souls'), nor the body of the MS No. 17, are in the same handwriting as the Camb. Univ. MS of the Chronicle. All three are different. Thence follows, that if the Cambr. Univ. Lib. MS of the Chronicle is really Capgrave's Autograph, that MS 17 (All Souls' = the Latin treatise on the Creeds) was not written by him. It is true that the sign ⚭ occurs twice in MS 17 (on p. 44, and on the last page), but that might have been copied from the MS from which MS 17 was copied.

"After examining the MS myself, I got Macray to come over with me to the All Souls' Library, and he looked at it, and came to precisely the same conclusion that I had formed.

"Yours ever, A. S. NAPIER."

18 March, 1892. Prebendary Hingeston-Randolph kindly sends me

"A word about Friend Arrek and Newcourt's List of the Rectors of St. Pancras', City (p. xxiii-iv). Some of the Canterbury Registers having been lost, the record of his Institution is no doubt lost with one of them. I suspect he came in between Rich. de Sudbury, instituted in 1326, and Adam de Branketre (who survived till Islip's time, but was instituted by a Bishop whose Register has perished). The Registers of Simon de Mepham, John de Stratford, John de Ufford, and Thomas de Bradewardin (1328—1349) have perished. As Islip became Archbishop late in 1349, and Branketre was, therefore, instituted before the end of that year, I think it very likely that Arrek was instituted, and either died or resigned, between the years 1327 and 1350. He died, it seems, at Lynn, probably of the 'Black Death,' which desolated England in 1349, and was especially destructive in Norfolk."

CORRIGENDA.

p. 14, v. 224, read rewarde instead of rewar
p. 40, v. 388, ,, y^t ,, ,, pat
p. 40, v. 394, ,, knew ,, ,, know
p. 78, v. 1043, ,, a rest ,, ,, a-rest
p. 81, v. 28, ,, wedded nedys, ,, ,, wedded, nedys
p. 148, v. 1156, ,, neybour ,, ,, neybour[s]
p. 172, v. 54, ,, baptym ,, ,, baytym
p. 230, v. 1003, ,, to ,, ,, te
p. 263, note v. 68, ,, trost ,, ,, trust
p. 276, v. 467, ,, am ful ,, ,, amful
p. 287, note, add 804 Wherfor
p. 316, add note : 1685 Rawl. hym instead of hem
p. 354, v. 507, read No[n] instead of N[o]n
p. 372, v. 1036, add to brent : [1]   [1] *al.* rent; and so in the notes : Rawl. rent

xxxvi *P. S. The Sound of long 'i' in Shakspere's Time.*

As there's an empty page, and I've long been exercised about the pronunciation of *i* in Shakspere's time, I note that when some fonetic friends told me that Shakspere pronounst *i* like our *ee* in *meet*, I quoted his Quartos in which *ay, aye*, yes, is, as a rule printed *I*,[1] and I took this as proof that Shakspere's long *i* was the same, or nearly the same, as ours. But seeing that Shakspere didn't correct his Quartos himself, my fonetic folk at first poohpoohd this *I* as a compo's vulgarism. Now, however, one repeats the late A. J. Ellis, and says that both *aye* and *I* were sounded as our *ai, ei, a*, in *vain, vein, vane*. I cannot away with this, further than to admit that the flat and dull long *a* may have existed alongside of our strong and sharp *i*. Scotchmen, I believe, still call *my* 'ma' (*a* in *father*), but then a Scotchman is capable of anything. As Andrew Borde says, "Trust yow no Skot" 59, 326 (E. E. T. Soc.).

In 1586, Baret's *Alvearie* clearly gives the diphthongal sound to *Ride, Hide* :—

"I Which standeth in the place of the third vowell, and hath bene taken for a single sound, is now so much doubted upon, that it is called in question both of his place and also of his name. It should be sounded (they say) like *ee*, as R*i*d, *Legere*, H*i*de, *Cauere*, to be pronounced as we corruptlie spell, *Reed, Heed*. And Ride, *Equitare*, Hide, *Abdere* (which commonly is written with I), as they say, should be written R*ee*d, H*ee*d, sounding I like the Greekes ει *diphthongus impropria*. But of this matter I said before, I would not here determine, leauing it to higher iudges .... Wherein you may be better resolued, if ye will consult with Maister H. Chesters booke, which he hath diligentlie written of Orthographie, after long and painfull trauell (as it well appeareth) in sundrie languages."

As Mr. Ellis has not (so far as I can see) quoted Minsheu's *Spanish Grammar*, 1599, on the point, I extract the passage here, for I think it makes for my side:

Definition of Orthopœia. "*Orthographie* . . Heereto belongeth *Orthopœia*, which is a right rule of true speaking, of ὀρθός right, and ἔπος word, that in speaking men pronounce not more grosse or smal, then the nature of language will allow, or otherwise then the accustomed

---

[1] As the derivation of *ay, aye* is unknown, Mr. Hy. Bradley, the President of our Philological Society, suggests that it is I itself. In Plato's Dialogs ἔγωγε is often used for Yes; and in some English dialects *Nich* ('Not I,' as we say) is used for No.

P. S. The Sound of long 'i' in Shakspere's Time. xxxvii

maner of pronunciation vsually permitted therein, as *Vino*, wine, not to pronounce it as Englishmen doe, *Veino*, but smaller, as they pronounce the double *ee*, *Veeno;* *Dios*, God, not *Deios*, but *Dheeos*. But of this hereafter in the letters more at large."—p. 5.

I three kindes. "I There be three kindes of I in the Spanish, that is, small *i*, Greeke *y*, and *j Jota*, or consonant. These two, *i, y* with a very small slender sounde, as the French and Italians doe, which is as the double *ee* in English, 'wee, shee, fee, decree': so in Spanish, *Tiráno*, a tirant, *Teerano:* *Vida*, life, *Veeda*, and not *A note for* as Englishmen pronounce *Teyrano, veida,* which all other *Englishmen.* nations mislike in hearing them speaking Latine; saying *Propino tibi,* they pronounce *Propeino tibi,*[1] which I would wish they woulde but marke, and take notice thereof: for the French, Italian, and Spaniard, do learne and are taught by their Schoolemaisters to pronounce the Latine different from their owne toong, otherwise one nation shoulde not vnderstand another speaking the Latine. But in this toong as in the Italian and French, they must obserue except they will fal into the vice of *Iotacismus* and be laughed at, and not be vnderstood by strangers when they speake or reade."

I think Minsheu meant that the Elizabethans pronounst long *i* as we do, as Mulcaster did in 1582, and not as long *a* in *wane*, tho' I admit that his words are consistent with his *ey* being our *ei, a,* in *vein, vane.* And he gives the Spanish diphthong " *ei* and *ey,* where *e* is more sounded than *i,* as *Réy* a king, *Léy* a law."

But Baret's acceptance of " Maister H. Chester" as the leading authority of his time, set me to find out who "H. Chester" was. His name, as given by Baret, was not in any Catalog in the British Museum; but a reference to the Bodleian Librarian, Mr. E. B. Nicholson, brought from one of his Assistants, Mr. W. H. Allnutt (an oarsman, and a fellow-member of mine in the National Amateur Rowing Association), the explanation that " Maister H. Chester" was no other than the well-known John Hart, the author of the English *Orthographie,* in MS 17 Reg. C. 7, Brit. Mus., A.D. 1551; in print, revised and with a fonetic appendix, 1569. The mistake as to his

---

[1] This confirms what the Dutchman, Justus Lipsius, said in 1586: "Pronunciant etiam nunc (ita accepi) recte soli pœne omnium Europæorum Britanni: quorum est *Regeina, Ameicus, Veita*. Recte, dico, quia non aliud insonuit hæc longa quam EI diphthongum."—*De recte Pron. Lat. Ling.,* p. 23. (Weymouth, *E. E. Pron.,* 1874, p. 18.) So too, Salesbury in 1550—67 blames those who "with their Iotacisme corrupting the pronunciation, make a diphthong of it (I), saying: *veidei, teibei,* for *vidi, tibi.*"

xxxviii *P. S. Long 'i' in Shakspere's time. Jn. Ha t 1551.*

name arose from his title-page saying his book was by "*I. H. Chester Heralt,*" and was made by more folk than John Baret; at least by Bullokar in 1580, and Gill in 1619.—*Ellis,* i. 35.

Well, I lookt thro' Hart's MS, and workt thro' his book, and I do not hesitate to say that every honest man not blinded by a theory *must* admit that Hart and his followers sounded his long *i* (or *ei*) much as we do, or at any rate made a markt difference between the sounds of our '*vein, vane,*' and '*vine.*' The evidence from his lists below is incontestable. I quote first from his autograph MS.[1]

MS Reg. 17 C 7, p. 101 or lf. 53, foot, by Jn. Hart, 1551.

"the same *e* lengthned (p. 102 or leaf 53 bk.) will serve for the commune abused diphthongs *ea, ai* or *ay,* & *ei* or *ey,* the powers of which voels we now myx together confuzibli, making the sound of the same long *e,* and not of any parfait
ea. diphthong; as in theis examples of the *ea* in *feare,* which we pronunce, sounding no part of the *a.*
ai, or And for the *ai* or *ay,* as in this word *faire,* pronuncinge nether the *a,*
ay. or *i,* or *y*: also in *saieth,* where we abuse a thriphthong.
ei, or Also *ei* or *ey* we pronunce not in theis wordes *cheine* and *theym,* and
ey. such lyke; where we sound the *e* long, as in all the others.
ee. Now for the *ee* we abuse in the sound of (p. 103, lf. 54), the *i* long; as in this sentence, "Take *heed* the birdes doo not *feed* on our *seed*"; also
ie. for the *ie* in *chief* and *pri·st*; in likewise for the *eo,* as in *people,* we onli
eo. sound the *i* long. We also abuse the *eo* in the sound of the *u* voel, as in *ieoperdi,* which we pronunce *iuperdie.*
oo. The *oo* we have abused as afore is said.

Thus now knowing the power of the voels, and considering the nature and office of diphthongs, we see how theis foresaid doo us not onli no pleasure, but great displeasure. Now lett us understand how part of theis foresaid, and others, shall serve us, and doo (p. 104) us great pleasure: even as coulo*u*rs necessari for us lyvely to contrefait the image of our pronunc!ation.
au. First the *au,* is rightly used as in *paul* and *lau,* but not *law.*
ua. Then the *ua,* is wel used in *uarre,* for *warre,* and in *huat,* for *what.*
ei. Further the *ei,* is wel and properli used in *bei,* for *by*; in *leif,* for *lyfe*; and in *seid,* for *syde.*
eu. Also *eu,* we use properli in *feu,* for *few*; in *deu,* for *dew,* and such lyke.
ue. The *ue* as in *question*; in *huen,* for *when*; in *uel* for *well.*
iu. Also the *iu* as in *triuth,* for *trueth*; in *rebiuk,* for *rebuke*; and in *riule* for *rule.*

---

[1] Both the MS and book are in course of copying, and will be edited for the Early English Text Society. Will any open-minded fonetic man volunteer for the work?

P. S. Long 'i' in Shakspere's time. Jn. Hart, 1569. xxxix

ui. And the *ui* alone for our (p. 105, lf. 55) false sounding of *we;* and as in *huich,* for *which; uitnes,* for *wittnesse,* and such like . . . ."

That Hart in 1551 pronounced *by, life, side,* much as we do, is clear. Let us take next his revised and printed book of 1569:—

Hart's *Orthographie,* 1569, fol. 43, p. 2.

"Now wil I shew you examples of the Diphthongs made of two short vowels, and of others of one short and of another long. And then of *ua, ue, ui,* triphthongs. With short vowels, as thus (*ui uil reid bei ionder ei, ie, iu, ou. uél, hu̱e̱r ðe uat uas uelne̱r ta̱kn bei ðe iung hound*) which is written for (we wyll ride by yonder well where the Wat [hare] was wel neare taken by the yong hound) which doe come very often in our speach. Of diphthongs whereof one vowell is short, and the other long as (*iu̱ u̱a, ue̱, u̱e̱r ua̱king in ðe fourt' tou̱r, hu̱e̱r az ðe bue*[1] *did pou̱r ua̱ter upón ðe hu̱e̱t iu̱, ou̱. flou̱r.*) which I write for (you were waking in the fowerth tower, when as the boye did poure water vppon the wheate flower) which also doe *uei.* come verie often. And for triphthongs as (*bi uciz ov ðe huciz buei*) for *ieu.* 'be wise of the hoyes bowy.' And (*hark ðe kat du̱t' mieu hucilz iu̱ milk ðe ieu*), for 'hark the Cat doth mewe, whiles you milke the yowe.' And *eau.* a Basin and *eaur,* for 'eawer,' and certaine others as will be seene hereafter. And for three vowels comming togither, and making (lf. 44, pa. 1) *iuë.* two sillables, as in example (*ðe viuèr se̱t', siuér it is puér*) for (the vewer sayth, sure it is pure) & as in these wordes (*ðis beier iz hciër ov pouér ðen ðe deiér bei hiz fciër*), For (this bier [buyer] is higher of power, than the dier by his fire)."

Hart's book, then, is consistent with his MS. He pronounced *ride, by, wise, whiles, buyer, higher, dyer, fire,* much as we do.

Now look thro' the lists of words that I have taken from the italic fonetic part of Hart's book. Let us start with the flat *ā* sound of "vane, vein, vain, wain, wane, may," &c., which one of my fonetic friends says that all the English, American and German authorities agree in holding to have been the pronunciation of long *i* in Shakspere's time, when John Hart livd and wrote.

Hart's *e̱* = *ay* or *ā,* in *may, wane.*

aku̱e̱ntans (acquaintance)	bre̱ðing
alue̱z (always)	bre̱ðs (breaths)
a-ue̱ (away)	[2]che̱r (chair)
be̱r (bear vb.)	de̱l (deal)
bre̱k	de̱z (days)
bre̱ðd (breath'd)	ech[2] (each)

---

[1] Hart's *e* has a curl or tail under it.
[2] As the printers havnt Hart's symbol for *ch,* they print *ch.*

xl *P. S. Long 'i' in Shakspere's time.* Jn. Hart 1569.

ęr (ear), Fr. *est le regne,* ęt le ręnah
ęðer (either)
extręm
ęzili (easily)
fęr (fear)   fęr (fair)
gręt (great)
hębriu (Hebrew)
huęr (where)
konstręn (constrain)
lęing (laying)
lęrn (learn)
lęv (leave)   lęving (leaving)
maintęner (maintainer)
mę (may)
męning (meaning)
nęr (near)
obę (obey)
pęr (pair)
persęv (perceive)
pęrz (pairs)

pęnted (painted)
plęnli (plainly)
Fr. *pain* (bread) pęn
L. *quæ,* Fr. kę
rędi (ready)
resęving (receiving)
ręzonable (reasonable)
sę (say)   sęd (said)
sęing (saying)
serten (certain)
sęt¹ (saith)
sęven (seven)
sęz (says)
spęk (speak)   spęking (speaking)
stęd and stęid (stayed)
¹tęching (teaching)
ðę (they)
ðę węr (they were)
ðęr (their)
ðęrin (therein)   ðęz (these)

Hart's *ei,* our long *i* in *life, thine,* &c.

bei (by)
boldlei
defeind (defined)
deivers (divers *adj.*), deiverslei
deveided
deueizd
dezeir, dezeiring
diskreibd   ei (I)
enterpreiz
especiãlei (especiaulei, 56 bk.)
feind (find)   feindet¹ (findeth)
feiv (five, 5)
fitlei (and by error ? fitli)
Florenteins
hięrbei (hereby)
huei (why)
huolei (wholly)
indifrentlei
komodiuzlei
komonlei
krusefeiing (crucifying)
leif (life)   leik (like)
leivli vois (living voice)
mei (my)   mein (mine)

meind
partlei   pasteim
peip (pipe)
perfetlei
perseited (? meaning, 57 bk.)
prezentlei (now)
satisfei   satisfeid
seifring (cyphering)
sertenlei
signifeing
signifeiet¹ (signifieth)
singulerlei
sufisientlei
teid (tied)
teim (time)
ðerbei (thereby)
treitlz (trifles)
triulei
uniformlei
ureit (write)
ureiter   ureiting
verelei
weiz or uaiz (-wise :) kontrari-, such-,
ðis-, uðer-

---

¹ *ch* is printed because we havn't Hart's single letter for it.

P. S. Long 'i' in Shakspere's time. Hart, Mulcaster, &c. xli

Hart's i̯, our *ee* in *teeth*, &c.

api̯r (appear)	mi̯ter (metre)
aspi̯r (aspirate)	ni̯dful
aspi̯rd (aspirated)	ni̯ds (needs)
bi̯ (be)	prosi̯deth (proceedeth)
bi̯ing (being)	L. *qui*, Fr. ki̯
bili̯v (believe)	ri̯d (read)
bli̯s (bless)	ri̯ding (reading)
bri̯fli (briefly)	si̯ (see)
[1] chi̯fest (chiefest)	si̯k (seek)
[1] chi̯z (cheese)	si̯md (seemd)
deri̯vd (derived)	spi̯ch[1] (speech)
exerci̯z	spi̯di (speedy)
exerci̯sing	stri̯k (the French have) ' litl stri̯ks under ðer konsonants.'
gi̯v (give)	
gri̯k (Greek)	ti̯th (teeth)[2]
gri̯ks (Greeks)	ti̯tl (title)
hi̯ (he) ' ui ma̯ si̯, hi ' (we may see, he)	tˈri̯ (three)
in sti̯d (instead)	to wi̯t (to wit)
i̯vn (even)	undiskri̯t
ki̯p (keep)	(*hih, liht, resitetˈ* (reciteth) *riht, rihtli*,
li̯kt of (liked of)	Hart sounded with short *i*.)
mi̯t (meet)	

Hart's a̯ was our *a* in father. He has a̯ges, bla̯m, dekla̯r, fra̯m, fra̯ming, ga̯v (gave), gra̯s (grace), ha̯v, ha̯ving, imita̯t, la̯burs, la̯di, ma̯d (made), ma̯ketˈ, na̯ms (names), pla̯sed, pla̯ces, sa̯m (same), tu separa̯t, [3] sha̯mfast (shamefast), [3] sha̯ps (shapes), spa̯k, ta̯bl, ta̯k (take), tha̯ms (Thames), wra̯t az ðe̯ spa̯k. Hart gives fonetic transcriptions of French, &c. On leaf 57, he says—

"iu me̯ si̯ bei ðiz litl treatiz, ei ha̯v bin a traveler bi-iond ðe seas, emong vulgar tungs, ov huich, ðat smaul kno̯leȝ ei ha̯v, hatˈ bin ðe kauz of ðís mein enterpreiz."

From the above lists and extracts it is abundantly clear that Hart and his followers did *not* sound the *i* in *mine*, &c., like the *ei, a* in our *vein, vane.* What other folk didn't? At least Mulcaster, I think; also Bullokar[4] (next page).

In his *Elementaire*, 1582, Mulcaster says (Ellis, *E. E. Pron.*, 912)—

"I . . . soundeth now sharp, as g*iue* [gyve], thr*iue, aliue, vviue, title, bible ;* now quik, as *glue, liue, slue, title, bible,* which sounds ar to be distinguished by accent, if acquaintance will not serue in much reading."

Ben Jonson in 1640 (*Ellis* 116), and when our long *i* was well establisht, shows us how to interpret Mulcaster's 'sharp' above. He says—

---

[1] *ch* is printed because we havn't Hart's single letter for it.
[2] ðe i̯ in ti̯th, huich ðe kómon man, and mani lernd, du̯ sound in ðe diphthongs *ei* and *iu*. leaf 47, p. 2.
[3] *sh* is printed because we haven't Hart's single symbol for it.
[4] See his fonetic writing in *Ellis* 838—45, and make your own lists from it.

xlii   *P. S. Long 'i' in Shakspere's time. Bullokar* 1580.

"I . . . is a Letter of a double power. As a Vowell in the former or single Syllables, it hath sometimes the sharpe accent ; as in *bínding. mínding. píning. whíning. wíving. thríving. míne. thíne.* Or, all words of one Syllable qualified by *e*. But, the flat in more, as in these—*bĭll. bĭtter. gĭddy, lĭttle.* incident. and the like . . . In Syllables, and words compos'd of the same Elements, it varieth the sound, now sharpe, now flat ; as in *gíve, gĭve. alíve, lĭve. dríve, drĭven. títle, tĭtle.*"

And Gil in 1621 says of our long *i* :

"retinebimus antiquum illum et masculinum sonum, atque unâ etiam laudem quam Justissimus Lips[i]us nobis detulit in Reginâ, in amicâ, vitâ," &c.— Weymouth, p. 18.

How ancient this long *i* (as we sound it) is, I must leave others to find out. That it existed in Shakspere's time is certain ; and we need not believe that he said 'ā want mā wān' when he needed a cup of sack, or cald a girl 'mā lāſ' when he meant 'my life.' Our late and lamented friend, A. J. Ellis, tho' he inclined far too much to the *i* = *a* theory, thus sumd up his views (*E. E. Pron.* i. 116) :—

"If the hypothesis here adopted for the pronunciation of long *i* by Palsgrave and Bullokar ; Salesbury, Smith and Hart ; and Gill, namely (*ii*, ei, ɵi) be correct, we have the phenomenon of the co-existence of two extreme sounds (*ii*, ɵi) with their link (ei), during the greater part of the xvith century, bringing the pronunciation of the xivth and xviith centuries almost together upon one point."

Bullokar, in "Bullokar's Booke at large, for the Amendment of Orthographie for English speech," 1580, tho' he gives only one vowel and one consonant sound to *i* and to *y* (p. 5), yet practically distinguishes between the short and long sounds of the vowel, and writes with his accented *ý* for long *i*.[1] His short sound is *i* or *y*: *thing, lyk = lick ;* he contrasts 'too *win,* or get,' with *wýn, wýnd,* and 'too *pýn, thýn*' and *wýnd* with *thin.* Here are some of his long *i* words :

besýd	lýf	rýnd	wrýt
být (bite)	lýk	rýp	wrýten (long)
declýnatiuz	lýuz	rýping	wrýting
declýning	merchandýz	strýf	wrýtor
derýuatiuz	mislýk	strýk	wýld
despýzed[1]	mýnd	suffýciently[2]	wýli
deuýd	paradýc' (-ise)	sýn (sign)	wýn
exercýz[2]	prouýded	thýn	wýnd
fýl (file)	prýc' (price)	tým	wýndi
fýnd	pýl (pile)	výl	wýuz (wives)
gýd	pýn (pine)	whýt	wýz
kýnd			

[1] Compare "a mauz nám (name) ; a he'l of the foot, an elm-tre', a heern (Heron) ; onesti, stónen, stóni, stón-lýk,"—p. 26.

[2] These are short *i* in B's *Æsopz Fabl'z*, 1585.

Pynson's shortening of Capgrave's 'Legenda Angliæ.' xliii

To the list above, Bullokar's *Æsopz Fabl'z* of 1585 adds, among other words :

abýdden	descrýbeth	mýcez	strýuingz
abýdeth	despýzed	mýn	strýkn
aduýzedly	despýzory	outsýdz	sýdz
alýu' (alive)	dezýr	prýc' (price)	sýnz (signs)
a-sýd	dezýred	prýd	týlz
behýnd	dezýring	pýn-tre'	výcez
bird-lým	dezýrous	reconc'ýl	whýl
blýnd	drýueth	reqýreth	whýlst
brýdl	empýr	reqýt	whýten
brýn	enqýreth	rýndz	wýld
býld (build)	fýnnes	rýp	wýldnes
býlded	grýnd	rýzn	wýzdom
býlding	hýdd	shýning	wýzly
býttn	hýding	smýling	ýdl'
chýding	hýred	strýf	ýdl'nes
chýld	knýf	strýpz	ýl'-land
chýlddern	lýknes	strýu' (strive)	ýrn (iron)
chýn (chine)	lým-twigz	strýuorz	

Bullokar's *ei* or *ay* sound was flat, as shown by his 'leizur, their, rein (reign), eight, plain, paier (pair), they, disdain, vain,' &c. 'Fire, desire,' he spells 'fyer, desyer' in 1580, but in *Æsopz Fabl'z*, 1585, they are 'fier, dezýr.'

Every one acknowledges that in 1621 Alexander Gil, Headmaster of St. Paul's School, sounded our long *i* ; see his table in his *Logonomia Anglica*, p. 12, contrasting "*kin*, kinne ; *k͞in*, keene ; *kjn*, kyne," &c. &c.

Pynson's englisht abridgment (1516) of Capgrave's *Nova Legenda Angliae* starts with " Here begynneth the Kalendre of the newe Legende of Englande," above a woodblock of the Crucifixion, and then begins

¶ The Prologe.

He firste treatyce of this present boke is taken out of the newe Legende of the sayntys of Englande / Irelande / Scotlande / and Wales, for theym that vnderstande not the Laten tonge / that they atte theyr pleasure may be occupyed therwith / and be therby y[e] more apte to lerne the resydue when they shall here the whole Legende / And it is to vnderstande, *that* not oonly those sayntes wer borne in theyse Countreys be in the sayde Legende and *in* this lytell treatyse / But also dyuerse other blessyd sayntes that were borne beyonde the see / and that came into any of theyse countreys, Englande / Irelande /

xliv *P. S. Capgrave's MS 'Life of St. Norbert.'* A. D. 1440.

Scotlande / and Wales, doyng there ony notable thynge to the honour of god / and to the profyte of the people—as to preche to theym the Faythe of oure Lorde / and to sette the people in good ordre / Or that haue lyued a blessyd lyfe i*n* any of theyse Countreys, to gyue the people example of good lyuynge /— Be also in the sayde Legende and in this present treatyse, & be accompted to be of that countrey that they so came into / As seynt Augustyne, the appostell of Englande, whom blessyd seynt Gregorye, then beynge pope, sent fro Rome with seynt Paulyn / seynt Laurence the confessoure, and dyuerse other in his company, to preche the faythe of our Lorde to the people of this Realme, then beynge Idolatroures and clerely alyenatyd fro trueth " . . . .

(The Life of St. Katharine of Alexandria is naturally not in Capgrave's or Pynson's book.)

Capgrave's metrical Life of St. Norbert, A.D. 1440.

Owing to my not having lookt before to my notes in the copy of Ritson's Bibliography which Henry Bradshaw gave me, I mist till now (28 April, 1892) an autograph (?) English poem of Capgrave's in 7-line stanzas (*ababb, cc*). At Sotheby's Sale of the Savile and other MSS on Feb. 6, 1861, was sold for £150 to " Powis " :

' 80. CAPGRAVE (John). The Life, Miracles, and Visions of Saint Norbert, with the Rules of Saint Austin, written in English Verse.

' The original Autograph Manuscript of an hitherto unmentioned English Poem, on 59 Leaves of vellum, in the old oak covers, folio.

' That this is the original Manuscript there can be little doubt, as its writer, on the reverse of the last leaf informs us of it, stating also the very interesting facts of the date of its composition and for whom composed, viz. :

"Go, litil book, to hem þat wil þe rede ;
Say you were made to þe Abbot of Derham ;[1]
Fast be Stoke it stant witȝ-outen drede.

---

[1] West Dereham in Norfolk, 1 mile S.E. of Downham, and 3½ miles N.W. of Stoke Ferry. It was the birthplace of Hubert, Dean of York, afterwards Archbishop of Canterbury, who founded an abbey here about 1188 for Premonstratensian canons from Welbeck. The site was granted to the Dereham family, and the ruins of the abbey were removed in the beginning of the (19th) century.—Hamilton, *Gazetteer*.

P. S. Capgrave's MS 'Life of St. Norbert.' A. D. 1440.

> It is to Lords and Gentilys alle in sam,
> And eke to pore men a very piliance (? pittance) ham.
> The Abbotes name was called at þatt tyde,
> The good Jon Wygnale,[1] þat never wold him hide
> For no gestis, but rather he wold them seke.
> The Freris namë þat translate þis story
> Thei called Jon Capgraue,[2] which, in assumpcion weke,
> Made a[n] ende of alle his rymyng cry,
> The ȝer of Crist our lord, witȝ-outen ly,
> A thousand four hundred & fourty evene.
> Aftyr þis lyfe, I pray god send us hevene."
>
>   ✥ ffelicit[er.][3]

'The first leaf of the volume has an Illuminated Capital Letter, in which the author is represented as delivering his work to his patron, whom in the proheme he addresses as follows:—

> "Joye, grace & pees, love, faith & charite,
> Evyr rest up-on ȝour goodly religious breest,
> To whom þat I, with moost humylite,
> Evyr recomende[4] lowly as ȝour preest;
> And þouȝ I be of rymeris now þe leest,
> Yet wil I now, obeying ȝour comandment,
> Put me in danger in þis Werk present." '—Catalog, p. 22.

Now "Powis" who bought the Norbert MS spells "Sir Thos. Phillipps," says Mr. F. S. Ellis; and Sir F. Madden signs "T. P." to "Powis" too. The MS proves to be in the Phillipps Collection at Cheltenham, tho I can't see it in Sir Thomas's Catalog of his MSS, in or near his "Sotheby MSS 1861," p. 301. I have askt Mr. Fenwick's leave to have the MS copied and edited for the E. E. Text Society; but he says it " is one of the MSS that we are not intending at present to allow being copied,"—more's the pity! Let us hope that it has no *gh*, and that its other forms match those of the Gg *Chronicle* (once Moore 40) at Cambridge.

In 1524 Thomas Messingham, in his *Florilegium*, or Lives and Deeds of the Saints of Ireland, reprinted from Capgrave's *Legenda*

---

[1] John Sadresson, *alias* Wygenhale, occurs 1429.—Dugdale vi. 899.

[2] ? 'Was J. C.' The line has now six feet instead of five.

[3] 'Feliciter per Capgrave' reads the Corpus MS of his *Liber de Illustr. Henricis*, ed. Hingeston, p. 186 *n*.

[4] ? comende me. I've put, above, þ for y, and ȝ for z, and have expanded the contractions.

Angliæ the Lives of St. Brigit (Brigida), virgin (p. 202-6), St. Fiacre (p. 390-2), and St. Fursey (p. 393-6). In 1625 at St. Omer was publisht "The Life of St. Patricke [abridgd from the Latin of Jocelinus, Monk of Furness] . . . Together with the lives of . . St. Bridgit (translated . . partly out of Cogitosus . . . and partly out of Capgrave) and of Saint Columba." The translator's dedication is signed "Fr. B. B., one of the Irish Franciscan Friars at Louvain."— Brit. Mus. Catalog.

In 1874 Bp. Stubbs reprinted Capgrave's Life and Miracles of St. Dunstan, from the Bodley Tanner MS 15, collated with the Rawlinson MS A. 294, & Wynkyn de Worde's edition of 1516: *Memorials of St. Dunstan*, Rolls Series, p. 325-353. In 1886 Canon Raine printed Capgrave's Life of St. Oswald, attributed to John of Tynmouth, from the Tanner MS 15, collated with MS A 16 C 1 of the Dean and Chapter of York, in *The Historians of the Church of York and its Archbishops*, Rolls Series, vol. ii. p. 502-512.

The Life of St. Katharine.

By JOHN CAPGRAVE.

THE LIFE OF ST. KATHARINE.

By JOHN CAPGRAVE.

[*MS. Rawlinson Poetry* 118.]

[fol. 1]
[1st hand]
PROLOGUS.

Iesu cryst,¹ crowne of¹ maydenys alle,   ¹ MS. crþst   1
A mayde bar' þe, a mayde ȝaue þe soke;
A-mong¹ þe lilies that may not fade ne falle
Thou ledyst þese¹ folk, ryth so seyth our' boke,   ¹ MS. yese
Wyth all her' hert euer on þe thei loke;   5
here loue, her plesauns so sore is on þe sette,
To sewe þe, lord, & folow þei can nott lette.   7

Ryth þus be ordyr we wene þou ledyst þe daunce: 8
Thi moder folowyth þe next, as reson is,
And after othir, þei goo rith as her chaunce
Is schap to hem of¹ ioye that may not mys;
But next that lady a-boue alle othir in blys   12
ffolowyth þis mayde weche we clepe kateryne.
Thus wene we, lord, be-cause þat þou and thyne   14

haue ȝoue to hir' of¹ grace so grete plente,   15
þat alle þe priuileges weche be in othir found
Ar sett in hyr as in souereyne hye degre,
ffor in alle þese rychely doth she habound—
loke alle þese seyntis þat on þis world¹ so round   19
leuyd her' sumtyme, & in sum spyce or kynde   ¹ MS. werd world, werd crossed out.
here uertues shal we in þis same mayde fynde.   21

THE LIFE OF ST. KATHARINE.

BY JOHN CAPGRAVE.

[*MS. Arundel* 396.]

PROLOGUS.

A ihesu criste, crovne of maydenes alle,   1   Christ, the Crown of Maidens,
A mayde bare the, a mayde ʒave þe sook;
A-mongis the lylyes that may not fade ne falle
Thov ledest these folk, ryght so scythe the book,
With al her hert cuere on the thei look;   5
her love, her plesavns so sore is on the sette,
To sewe the, lord, and folwe thei can not lette.   7

Right thus be ordre we wene thov ledest the davnce: 8   comes first;
Thy moder folweth the nexte, as resoun is,   next, His Mother;
And after other, thei go ryght as her chavnce
Is shape to hem of ioye that may not mys;
But next that lady a-bove alle other in blys   12
ffolweth this mayde whiche we clepe kataryne.   third, St. Katharine,
Thus wene we, lord, be-cavse that thov and thyne   14

have ʒove to hir of grace so greet plente,   15
That alle thy pryuileges whiche been in other fovnde
Arn sette in hir as in souereyn of (!) heygh de-gree
ffor in alle these rychely dooth she abounde—
Looke alle these seyntis that in this world so rounde   19   who had the virtues of all the Saints.
Leved here sumtyme, and in som spyce or kynde
here vertues shal we in this same mayde fynde.   21

Prolog.

Thou ȝaue to ion, lord, þe grete euangelyste,   22
Thin owne *presens* whan he hens shuld wende:
That same *presens* rithe euene, as þou lyste,
Thou ȝaue þis mayde at hyr' lyuys ende.
A welle of[1] oyle eke þou wold hyr' sende   26
Out of[1] hyr' graue, as had seynt nycholas;   [1] orig. her'
And for her' clennesse þou grauntede hyr'[1] þat gr*a*ce   28
Wheche seynt Paule had: mylke ryth at his throte   29
Ran owt w*yth* bloode, men sey in tokeny*n*g*'*[1]   [1] MS. tokenyngis
Þ*a*t martyrdam & maydenhode ryth i*n* o cote
Wer' medelede to-gydyr. þou douter on-to þe kynge,[1]   32
So had þou fully as these holy þingis.[2]   [1] corr. to king*is*   [2] r. þing

[fol. 1, b.]
[2nd hand]

To a-raye þi graue hese au*n*gellys eke godd sent
Ryth as he dyd su*m*tyme for seynt clement.   35
And as seynt margarete had her' petycyon)   36
At her' last ende graunted of godd allmyth:
What-maner man or woma*n* þ*a*t w*yth* deuocyon)
Askyth a bone of here, he hath it ryth
As he wyl haue, if he ask but ryth—   40
ffor ellys fayleth he, it is not to hys be-houe;
The same gr*a*ce hast þow of godd, þi loue,   42
Purchasyd, lady, on-to þi loueris alle.   43
Therfor wyl I þe serue so as I can,
And make þi lyffe, þat mor' openly it schalle
Be know a-bowte of woma*n* & of man.
Ther was a *p*r*e*ste, of flesch he was ful wan   47
ffor grete labour' he had i*n* hys lyue
To seke þi liffe ȝerys thyrtene & fyue.   49
Ȝet at þe last he fond it to hys gret ioye   50
ffer up i*n* grece I-beryed i*n* þe grownde;
Was neuyr no knyth i*n* rome ne eke i*n* troye
Mor glad of swerde or basnett bryght & rownde
Tha*n* was þis preeste wha*n* he had it fownde!   54
he blyssed þe ofte, & seyd all hys laboure
Was turned to solace, to ioye & socowr'.   56

Thov yave to Iohñ, lord, the greet evangelist,	22	_Prolog._
þin owyn presens whan he hens shuld weende:		
That same presens ryght evene, as þov lyst,		Christ was with St. Katharine at her death;
þov yave this mayde at hir lyves eende.		
A welle of oyle eke þov wulde hir sende	26	
Ovte of hir grave, as had seynt Nicholas;		
And for hir clennesse þou gravnted hir þat graas	28	
Whiche seynt pavle had: mylk ryght at his throte	29	
Ran ovte wyth blood, men seyne in tookenyng		
That martirdam and maydenhod ryght in on cote		
Were medeled to-gedyr. þou dovter on-to the kyng,		
So had þou fully alle these hooly thyng.	33	
To araye thi _grave_ his aungell_is_[1] eke god sent	[1] MS. aungell	and His Angels made her grave.
Ryght as he dede for seynt Clement.	35	
And as seynt Margarete had hir petycyon	36	
At hir laste eende gravnted of god almyght:		
What-maner man or woman that wyth devocyon		
Asketh a bone of hir, he hath it ryght		
As he wyl have, if he aske but ryght—	40	
ffor ellys fayleth he, it is not to his be-hove;		
The same _grace_ hast þou of god, thi love,	42	
Purchased, lady, on-to thi lovers alle.	43	
Therefore wil I the serve so as I kan,		
And make thi lyef, that more openly it shalle		I will make known her life.
Be knowe a-bovte of woman and of man.		
Ther was a preest, of flessh he was ful wan,	47	A Priest
ffor grete labovr he had in his lyve		
To seke thi lyef yeerys threttene and fyve.	49	
Yet at þe laste he foonde it to his grete ioye	50	found that Life in the ground, in Grece.
ffer vp in grece beryed in the grovnd;		
Was neuer knyght in rome ne eke in Troye		
More glad of swerd or basenet bryght and rovnd		
Than was this preest whan he had it fovnd!	54	
he blysshed it ofte, and seyde al hys labour		
Was turned to solace, ioye and sokour.	56	

| Prolog. | he mad þi lyff in englysch tunge ful well. | 57 |

But ȝet he deyed or he had fully doo:
Thy passyon, lady, & aH þat scharp whele
he left be-hynd, it is ȝet for to doo;
And þat he mad it is ful hard þer-too, 61
Ryth for straungenesse of hys derk langage.
he is now ded, þou hast ȝoue hym hys wage. 63

Now wyl I, lady, mor openly mak þi lyffe 64
Owt of hys werk, if þou wylt help þer-too;
It schall be know of man, mayde & of wyffe
What þou hast suffrede & eke qwat þou hast doo.
Pray godd, our lorde, he wyll þe dor on-doo, 68
Enspire our wyttys wyth hys priuy grace,
To preyse hyme & þe þat we may haue space! 70

Thys preeste of qwome I spake not longe ere, 71
In hys prologe telleth all hys desyre,
Who[1] þat he trauayled many a londe, to lere   [1] = how
[fol. 2] The byrth, þe cuntre, þe langage of þis martere,[1] [1] MS. martira?
Who was her moder & eke who was hyr syre; 75
A-boute þis mater he laboured ȝerys eytene,
Wyth prayer, fastyng, cold & mekyll tene. 77

So at þe last had he a reuelacyoun, 78
All mysty & derk, hyd all undyr clowde:
he thowte he sey þoo in hys avysyon
A persone honest, clothed in precyous schrowde,
Whech euer cryed vp-on þe preest ful lowde: 82
"Be-holde," he seyth, "þou man qwat þat I am,
What thyng I schew & eke qwhy I cam"— 84

ffor in hys hand he held a boke ful elde 85
Wyth bredys rotyn, leuys dusty & rent;
And euyr he cryed vp-on þe preest, "be-helde,
here is þi labour, her is all þin entente!
I wote ful welle what þou hast sowte & ment; 89
Ope þi mouth, þis book muste þou ete;
But if þou doo, þi wyll schall þou not gete." 91

he made this¹ lyf en englyssh tunge ful weel.   ¹ r. thi   57   *Prolog.*
But yet he deyed er he had fully doo :   This Priest who found St.
Thi passyon, lady, and al that sharpe wheel   Katharine's Life, englisht
he lefte be-hynde, it is yet not doo too (!) ;   it.
and that he made it is ful hard alsoo,   61   fol. 2.
Right for straungenesse of his dyrke langage.
he is now ded, þou hast youe hym his wage.¹   ¹ last words on erasure.   63

Now wil I, lady, more opynly make thi lyf   64   I will re-tell it from his
Oute of his werke, if þou wilt help ther-too ;   work.
It shal be knowe of man, of mayde, of wyf
What þou hast suffred and eke what þou hast doo.
Prey god, ovre lord, he wyl it may be soo,²   ² it m. b. soo on erasure.   68
Enspyre ovre wyttis wyth his prevy *grace*,
To preyse hym and the that we may have space !   70

This preest of whom I spak not longe ere,   71   This Priest
In his *p*rolog telleth al his desyre,
hov that he travayled many lond, to lere
The berthe, the contre, the langage of þis martire,   works for 18 years to find
ho was hir moder and eke hoo was hir syre ;   75   out the facts of St. Katha-
A-bovte this mater he labovred yerys eightene,   rine's life,
Wyth preyerys, fastynge, coold and mekel teene.   77

So at þe laste hadde he a revelacyon,   78   and then he has a revela-
Al mysti and deerk, hyd vnder clovde :   tion.
he thovte he saugh tho in a vysyon
A *p*ersone honest, clothed in a precyovs shrovde,
Wiche eue*r*e cryed on þe preest ful lovde :   82
"Be-hold," he seyth, " þov man, what þat I am,   In a Vision
What þing I shewe and eke why I cam "—   84

ffor in his hand he held a book ful eelde   85
With bredys rotyn, leues dusty and rent ;
And eue*r*e he cryed vp-on þe preest, " be-helde,
here is thin labo*ur*, here is¹ al thin entent !   ¹ overlined.
I wot ful weel what þou hast sovght and ment ;   89
Ope thi movth, this book muste þou ete ;   he is bidden to eat an old
but if þou doo, thi wil shalt þou not gete."   91   book.

Prolog.

"A, mercy, lorde," seyd þis preeste to hyme, 92
"Spare me now! who schulde I þis book ete?
The roten bredys, þese leuys derk & dyme
I may in noo wyse in to my mouth hem gete.
My mouth is small, & eke þei be so grete, 96
Thei wyll brek my chaules & my throte;
þis mete to me is lykly to do noo note." 98

"ȝys," seyd he, "þou mote nede ete þis book, 99
þou schalt ellys repente. ope þi mowth wyde,
Receyue it boldly, it hath no clospe ne hook,
let it goo down & in þi wombe it hyde,
It schal not greue þe neyther' in bake ne syde; 103
In þi mowth bytter', in þi wombe it wyll be swete—
So was it sume-tyme to eȝechyell þe prophete." 105

The preeste þo toke it in to hys mowth a-non, 106
It semed swete, ryth as it hony wer'.
þe other' man is passed & I-gon),
þe preest is stoyned as thow he turned wer'.
New ioye, new thowte had he than þere! 110
he a-woke & was ful glad & blythe,

[fol. 2, b.] Off þis dreme he blyssyd god ofte-sythe. 112
[3rd hand]
Aftyr þis not long depe in a felde 113
I-clad wyth flowris & herbys grete & smale,
He dalf', & fond þis boke whych he be-helde
Be-fore in slepe, rygth as I told my tale.
þere had he salue to all his byttyr bale! 117
It was leyd þere be a knyte þat men calle
Amylion fytȝ amarak', of cristen knytis alle 119

Most deuoute as on-to þis mayde. 120
He fond it a-mong old tresour in cipire-londe.
In kyng petris tyme, as þe cronycle sayde
Of þat same cipre where he þis boke fond,
And in pope[1] vrban tyme, as I vndyrstond [1] crossed out. 124
þe fyfte of rome, fell all þis matere   [2] MS. hane
wheche ȝe haue[2] herd and ȝet ȝe schall more clere. 126

[MS. Arundel.] *Vision of the Author of St. Katharine's Life.* 9

"A, mercy, lord," seyde this preest to hym, 92   *Prolog.*
"Spare me¹ nov! hov shuld I this book ete?   ¹ overlined.
The rotyn bredes, the leves derke and dym
I may in no wyse in to my movth hem gete.   He protests that he can't.
My movth is smal, and eke thei be so grete, 96
Thei wil breke my chaueles and my throte;
This mete to me is lykly to doo no note." 98

"Yes," seyde he, "þou muste nedes ete this book, 99   But, being orderd to,
Thou shalt ellis repente. ope thi movth wyde,
Receyve it boldely, it hath no clospe ne hook,
Lete it go dovn and in thi woombe it hyde,
It shal not greve the neyther in bak ne syde; 103
In thi movthe bytter, in thi woombe it wil be sweet—
So was it somtyme to Eȝechiel the prophet." 105

The preest tho took it in his movth a-noon, 106   he eats the book,
It semed sweet, ryght as it hony were.
The other man is passed and I-goon,
The preest is stoyned, as thou he turned were.
Newe ioye, newe thovght had he thanne there! 110
he a-wook and was ful glad and blythe,   awakes rejoicing,
Of his dreem he blyssed god ofte-sythe. 112

After this not longe depe in a feeld 113
I-clad wyth flovres and heerbes grete and smale,
he dalf, and fond þis book wiche he be-held   and finds the book (see l. 50—1)
Be-fore in slep, ryght as I told my tale.
There had he salve to all his bytter bale! 117
It was leyd there be a knyght þat men calle
Amylyon fitȝ amarak, of crysten knyghtis alle 119

Most devoute as on-to this mayde. 120
he fonde it a-mong old tresovr in Cypre lond.   in Cyprus (far up in Grece, l. 51),
In kyng petrys tyme, as the cronycle sayde
Of þat same Cypre where he his¹ book foond,   ¹ r. þis
And in pope Vrban tyme, I vndirstond 124   in the time of Urban V (A.D. 1362-70).
The fyfte of rome, fel al this matere   ¹ MS. haue
Wiche ye haue¹ herd and yet ye shal more clere. 126

10 *St. Athanasius's Life of St. Katharine.* [MS. Rawlinson.

Prolog.
Þere was a clerk wyth þis same kateryne, 127
whos name we clepe in latyne athanas;
He tawte here þe reules as he cowde dyuyne
Off god of hevyn, of Ioye & of grace,
And sche'hym also, for be here he was 131
I-turnyd on-to crist & to oure feythe;
He was here leder, as þe story seythe. 133
He wrote þe lyfe eke of þis same mayde; 134
He was with here at here last ende,
He say here martyryd, as hym-selue sayde,
He mote nede haue here lyfe in mynde!
He was a seruaunt on-to here, ryth kynde— 138
What schuld I lenger in his preysyng tary?
He was here chauncelere & here secretary. 140
He gate here maisterys thorw-owt þe partes 141
Off all grete grece, her' fadyrs empyre,
To lerne here be rowe all þe seuene artes;
Þis same man payd hem all here hyre.
He was as in þat courte fully lord & syre, 145
He knew here kynne & here counsell also,
Her' fadyr, here modyr, & all þe line þerto; 147
Here holy life he knew, here conuersacioun, 148
All here holy customys qwyll sche levyd here,
[fol. 3] He stode be here in here[1] grete passioun, [1] overlined.
He say þe awngelis how þei here body bere
ffer vp in to synay and leyde it down þere, 152
He saw þe weniaunce eke how it was take
On many a thousand eke for here deth[1] sake; [1] MS. ded deth; ded crossed out.
[2nd hand] he sey eke maxense who he was slayn, 155
Dropped from a bregge downn in a reuer',
Deyd so ful sodeynly in ful byttyr payn,
fforthe was he draw in to hell-feer';
Aungellys bar' her', þe deuelys bar' hys beer'— 159
Be-hold þe sundry reward of vertu & of syne!
On is in heuene, þe other' is hell wyth-inne. 161

St. Athanasius's Life of St. Katharine.

There was a clerke with þis same kataryne, 127 *Prolog.*
Whos name we clepe in latyn Athanas;   St. Athanasius (when a heathen) taught St. Katharine,
he tavghte hir the revles, as he covde dyuyne,
Of god of heuene, of ioye and of gras,
And she hym also, for be hir he was 131   was then converted by her,
I-turned on-to cryst and on-to oure feyth;
he was hir ledere, as the story seyth. 133

he wrote the lyf eke of this same mayde; 134   wrote her Life,
he was with hir at hir last ende,
he sav hir martird, as hym-self sayde,
he must nede hir lyf haue in meende![1]   [1] h. l. m. on erasure.
he was a servant on-to hir, ryght keende— 138
What shuld I lengere in this preysyng tary?
he was hir chavnceler and hir secretary. 140   and was her Secretary.

he gate hir maystrys thurgh-ovte the partes 141
Of alle gret grece, hir faderys empyre,
To leerne hir be rowe alle the .vij. artes;
This same man payed hem alle her hyre.
he was as in þat covrt fully lord and syre, 145
he knewe hir kyn and hir covnsel also,
hir fadir, hir moder, and all the lyne ther-to; 147

hir holy lyf he knew, hir conuersacyon, 148
Alle hir holy customes whil she leved here,
he stood by hir in hir grete passyon,
he savgh the avngellis hovgh thei hir body bere   St. Athanasius saw St. Katharine's body borne to Sinai.
ffer vp on-to synay and leyde it down there, 152
he savgh þe vengavnce eke hovgh it was take
On many a thovsende for hir dethes sake; 154

he saugh eke maxcence hovgh he was slayn, 155
Dropped fro a brygge down in a rever,
Deyed so ful sodeynly in a bitter payn,
fforth was he drawe in to helle-feer;
Avngellis bar hir, the deuellis bar his beer— 159
Be-hold þe sondry reward of vertu and of synne!
On is in heuene, þe tother is helle-with-Inne. 161

long aftyr þe deth of þis maxencyus 162
Byschop in alysaunder', caterynes cete,
Was þis sam mane, þis athanasius;
In whech he suffred ful mech aduersyte.
I wot not veryly ȝef it wer' he 166
þat made þe psalme qwech we clepe þe crede,
Wech we at pryme oft-tyme syng & rede. 168
he deyd euyn ther' &[1] holy confessour'. [1] r. an 169
And aftyr hys deth myth vnneth be knowe
þe lyuyng, þe lernyng of þis swete flowr'
And martyr kateryne, of hy ne of lowe;
Tyl on Arrek dyd it new I-sowe: 173
ffor owt of grew he hath it fyrst runge,
þis holy lyff, in to latyne tunge. 175

Thys clerk herd speke oft-tyme of þis mayde, 176
Bothe of her' lyffe & also of her' heende,
Who sche for lofe her' lyffe hath þus layde
Off our' lorde cryste, our' gostly spouse kende:
þis made hym seker' in to þat londe to wende, 180
To know of þis bothe þe spryng & þe welle,
If any man coude it any pleyner' telle. 182

Twelue ȝer' in þat londe he dwelt & mor', 183
To know her' langage qwat it myght mene,
Tyl he of her' vsages had fully þe lore,
Wyth ful mech stody, tary & tene.
fful longe it was or he myght it sene, 187
þe lyff þat Athanas made of þis mayde;
But at þe last he cam, as it is sayde, 189

Ther as he fonde it from mynde all I-ded. 190
ffor heretykys þat wer' thoo in þat londe
had brent þe bokys, boþe þe lesse & þe brede,
As many as þei soute & þat tyme ffonde;
But, blyssyd be godd of hys hye sonde, 194
þis boke founde þei not in no-maner' wyse—
Godd wolde not þat þe nobyll seruyse 196

Longe after the deth of this Maxcencius 162 *Prolog.*
Bysshop in alysavndre, katarynes Cyte,   St. Athanasius was afterwards Bishop in Alexandria.
Was þis same man, þis Athanasius;
In whiche he suffred ful meche aduersyte.
I wot not verely yet if it were he 166
Þat made þe salme wiche we clepe þe crede,
Wiche we at prime often-tyme synge and rede. 168

he deyed euene there an holy confessovr. 169
And after his deth myght vnnethe be knowe
The lyf, the lernyng of this swete flovr   His Greek Life of St. Katharine was turnd into Latin by Arrek,
And martyr kataryne, of hey ne of lowe;
Til oon arrek dede it newe I-sowe: 173
ffor ovte of grev he hath it first runge,
This holy lyf, in to latyn tunge. 175

This clerk herd spekyn ofte-tymes of þis mayde, 176
Bothe of hir lyf and of hir eende,
hovgh she for love hir lyf had thus layde
Of oure lord cryst, hir goostily spovse keende:
This made hym seker in to þat lond to weende, 180
To knowe of þis bothe þe sprynge and þe welle,
If ony man kovde it ony pleynere telle. 182

Twelue yeer in þat lond he dwelled and more, 183   who dwelt in Alexandria 12 years to learn Greek.
To knowe her langage what it myght mene,
Til he of her vsage had fully þe lore,
Wyth ful moche stodye, tary and tene.
fful longe it was er he myghte it sene, 187
The lyf þat athanas made of þis mayde;
But at the laste he cam, as it is sayde, 189

There as he fonde it from mynde al I-deed. 190   (See l. 121 & 50.)
ffor heretykes þat were tho in þat londe
hadden brent the bookys, bothe þe leef and þe breed,
As many as þei sovght and þat tyme fonde;
But, blyssed be god of that hey sonde, 194
This book fovnde thei novght in no-maner wyse—
God wolde not þat the noble scruyse 196

Prolog.

Off hys own mayde schulde be þus for-ȝete.   197
A hundred ȝer' aftyr' it was & mor',
þat þis arrek þis new werk had gete,
ffro þe tyme of Athanas—for so mech be-for'
Was he hens pased, I-ded & for-lore   201
As from euery tunge, bothe hys boke & he,
Off euery man & woman in þat cuntre.   203

And be þis preste was it on-to englischmen   204
I-soute & founde, & broute vn-to londe.
hyd in all counseyll a-mong nyne or ten,
It cam but seldom on-to any mannes honde;
Eke qwan it cam, it was noght vndyrstonde,   208
Be-cause, as i seyd, ryght for þe derk langage.
þus was þi lyffe, lady, kept all in cage.   210

Neuyrthelasse he dyd mych thyng þer-too,   211
þis noble preste, þis very good man:
he hath led vs þe wey & þe door' on-doo,
þat mech þe bettyr we may & we can
ffolow hys steppes.   for thowte he sor' rane,   215
We may hym ouyr-take, wyth help & wyth grace
Qwech þat þis lady schall vs purchasse.   217

he is now ded, þis goodeman, þis preste;   218
he deyid at lynne many ȝer' a-goo;
he is ny from mynde wyth mor' & wyth leeste.
ȝet in hys deying & in hys grett woo
þis lady, as þei sey, appered hym vn-to,   222
Sche bad hym be gladde in most goodely wyse,
Sche wold rewar hyme, sche sayd, hys seruyce.   224

[fol. 4]   Of þe west cuntre it semeth þat he was,   225
Be hys maner spech & be hys style;
he was sumtyme parsone of sent pancras
In þe cete of london a full grete qwyle.
he is now a-boue vs ful many a myle;   229
he be a mene to kateryne for vs,
And sche for vs alle on-to our' lorde ihesus.   231

Of his ovne mayde shuld be thus for-yete. 197 *Prolog.*
An hundyr yeer after it was and more,   *Arrek found St.*
þat this arrek this newe werk had gete,   *Athanasius's Life of St.*
ffro þe tyme of athanas—for so moche be-fore   *Katharine (A.D.1362-70),*
Was he hens passed, I-ded and for-lore 201
As fro euery tunge, bothe his book and he,
Of euery man and woman in þat cuntre. 203

And be þis preest was it on-to english men 204 *brought it to England, and*
I-sovght and fovnde, and brovght on-to londe.   *translated it (see l. 50, 57),*
hid al in covnseyll a-mong nyne or ten,
It cam but seeldom on-to ony mannes honde;
Eke whan it kam, it was not vndirstonde, 208
Be-cavse, as I seyde, ryght for þe derk lang[ag]e.   *tho' in hard words,*
Thus was thy lyf, lady, kepte in cage. 210

Neuerethelasse he did moche þing ther-too, 211
This noble preest, this very good man:
he hath led vs the weye and the dore on-doo,
That meche the beter we may and we can
ffolwe the steppys, for thov he sore ran, 215
We may hym ouer-take, wyth help and grace
Whiche þat þis lady shal vs purchace. 217

he is novgh ded, þis good man, this preest; 218
he deyed at lynne many yeer a-goo;   *and died at Lynn, long*
he is ny fro meende wyth more and wyth leest.   *ago.*
Yet in his deying and in his grete woo
This lady, as þei seye, appered hym on-too, 222
She bad hym be glad in most goodly wyse,
She wolde reward hym, she seyde, his seruyse. 224

Of the west cuntre it semeth þat he was, 225 *He was a west-country*
Be his maner of[1] speche and be his style;   [1] *overlined.*   *man,*
he was somtyme parson of seynt pancras   *and also Rector of*
In the Cyte of london a ful grete while.   *St. Pancras, in London.*
he is nov a-bove vs ful many myle; 229
he be a mene to kataryne for vs,
And she for vs on-to ovre lord ihesus. 231

Prolog.

Aftyr hyme nexte I take vp-on me 232
To translate þis story & set it mor' pleyn),
Trostyng on other' men þat her' charyte
Schall help me in þis caas to wryght & to seyn)
Godd send me part of þat heuynly reyne 236
þat apollo bar' a-bowte, & eke sent poule;
It maketh vertu to growe in mannes soule. 238

If ȝe wyll wete qwat þat I am : 239
My cuntre is northfolke, of þe town of lynne;
Owt of þe world to my profyte I cam
On-to þe brotherhode qwech I am Inne—
Godd ȝeue me grace neuyr for to blynne 243
To folow þe steppes of my faders be-for',
Whech to þe rewle of Austen wer' swore. 245

þus endyth þe prologe of þis holy mayde, 246
Ȝe þat rede it, pray for hem alle
þat to þis werk eyther' trauayled or payde,
þat from her' synnes wyth grace þei may falle,
To be redy to godd whan he wyll calle, 250
Wyth hym in heuyn to drynke & to dyne,
Thorow þe prayer' of þis mayde kateryne. 252

Bk. I. Ch. 1.

Ca^{m.} 1^{m.}

Svmetyme þer was a grete kyng in grees 1
Of surre & cypre boþe lord & syre,
As clerkes tel vs in elde storyes;
All thyng was rewlyd at hys desyr',
he gouerned full sadly þat ilk empire, 5
Costus men called þis kyng þoo be name;
A losyd lorde was he & of ful grete fame, 7

A lombe to þe meke, a leoun to þe prowde, 8
þus was he noted, if ȝe lyst to lere.
he was so wel I-know boþe styll & lowde,
All dede hym homage bothe fer & ner';
kyng, duke, erle, baron, & bachilere 12

After hym next I take vp-on me 232
To translate this story and set it more pleyn,
Trostyng on other men þat her charyte
Shal helpe me in this cas to wryte and to seyn.
God sende me part of þat Heuenly reyn 236
That apollo bar a-bovte, and eke seynt poule;
It maket vertu to growe in mannys sovle. 238

If ye wil wete what þat I am: 239
Myn cuntre is Northfolk, of þe tovn of lynne;
Ovte of the world to my profite I cam
On-to þe brotherhod wiche I am Inne—
God yeve me grace neuere for to blynne 243
To folwe þe steppes of my faderis be-fore,
Wiche to the revle of Austyn were swore. 245

Thus endeth þe prolog of þis holy mayde. 246
Ye that reed it, pray for hem alle
That to this werk either travayled or payde,
þat from her synnes wyth grace thei may falle,
To be redy to god whan þat he wil calle, 250
With hem[1] in heuene to drynke and to dyne,   [1] r. him
Thurgh þe preyer of þis mayde kataryne. 252

Marginal notes: Bk. I. Ch. 1. I english his Life of St. Katharine. I, Capgrave, am of Lynn in Norfolk, an Austin friar. Pray for me and all concerned in this Life!

Liber primus. Ca^m. primum.

Somtyme ther was a grete kyng in Grece, 1
Of surre and Cypre bothe lord and syre,
As clerkys telle vs in olde storyce;
Alle þing was revled at his desyre,
he gouerned ful sadly þat ilke empyre, 5
Costus men called þat kyng tho be name;
A losed lord was he, and of ful grete fame, 7

A lomb to þe meke, a leon to þe provde, 8
þus was he noted, if ye liste to lere.
he was so weel I-knowe bothe stille and lovde,
Alle dede hym homage bothe fer and nere;
Kyng, Duke, Erl, Baron, and Bachelere 12

Marginal notes: Bk. I. Ch. 1. King Costus of Greece. bore wide rule.

18 K. Costus of Greece, St. Katharine's father. [MS. Rawlinson.

[fol. 4, b.]
[1st hand]

ffor her be-houe to his presens soute,
And to his help eke whan hem nedyd oute. 14
Many yldes longed þoo on-to his grete lande, 15
And alle wer' þai¹ buxum at his request'; ¹ orig. þan?
þe grete see holy had he in his hande,
And all þe hauenes both est & west',
He welded hem alle ryth as hym lest; 19
Wer' þei marchauntis, wer' þei marineris,
Alle wer' þei than to hym as omageris. 21

þis kyng' in pees regned many ȝeres. 22
And be-cause he was fayr' & strong' of' bones,
he was wele be-loued of' all his omageres;
A noble man, þei sayde, he was for þe nones,
Gracious in feld, peisible in wones, 26
ffre of' his speche, large of' his expens,
fful gladly wyth peynes wold he dispens. 28

Was no lorde be-syde þat hym wold do wrake, 29
ffor whath man þat dede he shuld it sone wayle,
Whan þat he gan veniaunce to take—
Preyer as þan wold not a-vayle;
To many a kyngdom made he a-sayle, 33
And many a castell beet he ryth down
Whan þai to his lawes wold not be bown. 35

A goode man was he, þis is þe grounde: 36
Meke as a mayde, manful at nede,
Stable & stedfast euyr-mor' I-fownde,
strong' man of' hand, douty man of' dede,
helper of' hem þat to hym hade nede; 40
Wrong' þinges þo wroute he neuer',
Petous of' spiryt & mercyful was he euer'. 42

Pees wold he put debate euer a-boue— 43
þat uertew cleymyd he only to hym-selue;
Alle hys noble werkys on-to pees & loue

[fol. 5]
[2nd hand]

Wer' mad as mete as ex on-to helue.
A-mong all þe lordes þat men dyd þoo delue 47

ffor her be-hove to his presens lovte,[1]　　　[1] r. sovte
And to helpe eke whan̄ hem neded ovte.　　　14

Many Ildes[1] longed tho on-to his[2] grete londe,　[1] orig. yldes　Many isles belongd to
And alle were thei buxum at his request;　　　[2] overlined.　King Costus.
The grete see hadde he holy in his honde,
And alle the hauenes bothe est and west,
he welded hem alle ryght as hym lest;　　　19
Were thei marchavnt*is*, were thei maryneres,
Alle were thei thanne to hym as homageres.　21

This kyng in pees regned many yeers.　　　22
And be-cavse he was fayr and strong of boones,
he was weel belouyd of al his homageers;　　　He was belovd,
A noble man, þei seyde, he was for the nones,
Gracyovs in feeld, peesible[1] in wones,　　[1] orig. poisible?　26
ffree of his speche, large of his expens,
fful gladly with peynes wolde he dispens.　28

Was no lord be-syde þat wold do hym wrake,　29
ffor what man̄ that dede, he shulde it sone **wayle**;
Whan he gan veng^eavns to take,
Prayer as þan̄ wolde now a-vayle;
To many a kyngdam made he asayle,　　　33
And many a castell beet he ryght dow(n)
Whan̄ thei to his lawes wolde not be boun̄.　35

A good man̄ was he, this is the grovnd:　　36　was good,
Meke as a mayde, manful at nede,
Stable and ste[d]fast euer-more I-fovnd,
Strong man of hand, dovty man̄ of dede,　　　doughty,
helpere of hem þat to hym had hede[1];　[1] orig. nede　40
Wronge þingys tho wrovght he neuere,
Pytous of spyryt and mercyful was he euere.　42　and merciful.

Pees wolde he putte debate euere a-bove—　43
That vertu cleymed he oonly to hym-selve;
Al his noble werkys on-to pees and love
Were made as mete as ex on-to helve.　[1] were—twelve on erasure.
A-mong*is* alle the lordys, were there ten or twelve,[1]　47

Bk. I. Ch. 1. he was most worthy & eke most wys;
Synne hated he hertly, harlatrye & vyis. 49
fful grete. pyte on-to our' thowt it is 50
þat swecħ a trew man schuld hethen be.
But ryght þus, wrote þei þat wer' full wys,
Oute of þe harde thorn[y] brymbyl-tree
Growyth þe ffrescħ rose, as men may see; 54
So sprong our' lady oute of þe Iewys,
And kateryne of hethen, þis tale ful trew is. 56

Bk. I. Ch. 2. Ca^m. 2^m.

TOo cytes had þis kyng a-mong all other', 57
largest & grettest a-boue hem alle;
þe on cost of gold ful many a fother'
Or he had made it wyth tour' & wyth walle;
þe other' was made, as bokes sey alle, 61
A full longe tyme er he was bore,
In whecħ all kynges þoo crowned wore. 63
The fyrst hytȝ Amalech—in cypre it stant, 64
þe other' hytȝ Alysaunder'—in egypt it is.
þe same lond of cypre no-thyng dotħ waunt,
But is ful of plente & full of blys,
Off gold, syluyr, frute & men, I-wys, 68
A grete lond closyd wyth þe see a-bowte,
On þe northwest syde of surre, it is no doute. 70
Therfor' þis kyng ryght as for a keye 71
Of all hys kyngdame set hys town þer';

[1st hand] Who come to surre, mote come þat weye,
þer may no shyp[1] þis cours forbere, [1] MS. shyhp
Wer' it in[1] pees or ellis in wer'. [1] overlined. 75
It had a hauene ful huge & ful grete,
And castelle strong' wyth turrettis feete, 77
Open on[1]-to marchauntis, to alle þat wille come, [1] overlined.
Be-cause her' fredomys wer' large & fayr', 79
Both oute of' hethnes & of' cristyndome;

MS. Arundel.] *The cities Amalek and Alexandria.*

he was most worthi and most wys; *Bk. I. Ch. 1.*
Synne hated he hertely, harlotry and vys. 49
  ffful gret pyte on-to ovre thovght it is 50 King Costus
That swiche a man trewe shuld hethen be.
but ryght thus, wrot thei þat were ful wys,
Ovte of the hard, thorny brymbyl-tre
Groveth the fresh rose, as men may see; 54
So sprong oure lady ovte of þe iewys,   was St.
And kataryne of hethen, this ful trewe is. 56 Katharine's father.

Ca^{m.} Sec*un*d*u*m.   *Bk. I. Ch. 2.*

Too cytes had þis kyng a-mong*is* alle other, 57 His 2 chief cities were
  laargest and grettest a-boveṅ hem alle;
The oon cost of gold many a fother
Eer he hadde made it wyth tovr and w*yth* walle;
The other was maad, as book*is* seyṅ alle, 61
A ful longe tyme eer he was bore,
In wiche alle kyng*is* tho crovned wore. 63
  The firste hight Amalek—in Cypre it stant, 64 Amalek and Alexandria.
The other hight Alysavndre—in egypt it is.
The same lond of Cypre no-þing dooth it want,
But is ful of¹ plente and ful of blys, ¹ overlined.
Of gold, of silu*er*, frute and meṅ, I-wys, 68
A grete lond closed wyth þe see a-bovte,
On the North-west syde of surre it is, no dovte. 70
  Therfore this kyng ryght as for a keye 71
Of all his kyngdam set his tovṅ there;
ho comṅ to surre, mot come þat weye,   Amalek was the port of Syria.
There may no shyp this cours for-bere,
Were it in pees or ell*is* in werre. 75
It had an havene ful huge and ful gret,
And castel strong wyth turrett*is* feet, 77
  Open on-to marchavntys, to alle þat wil come, 78 Amalek was a free port.
Be-cause her fredames were large and fayre,
Bothe oute of hethenesse and of cristendome;

It was a place of¹ ful grete repayr'.
Vnder hym þer þe kyng¹ made a mayr', 82
To kepe his lawes þei shuld not fayle,
Too stuf it wyth men & eke wyth vytayle. 84
þus myght þis lord from Alisaunder' ryde, 85
In schyppes I mene, to þis grete cetee
And euyr on hys owe lordchippe a-byde—
ffor on¹ alle cuntres principale lorde was hee, ¹ r. of
Wer' it of felde, of town) or of see 89
Whech stode be-twyx þe grete cytees too,
All was it do þer' as he bad it doo. 91

The other' cytee, Alysaunder' be name, 92
On þe bordyr' of egypt it stant ful fayr',
A gret place, a large & of hye fame.
þei of egipt mote nedys repayr'
On-to þis cyte, thorow wey & thorow wayr', 96
If þei to affryk or to cartage goo ;
And þei of affryk þe same mote also, 98
If þei in egypte wyll bye or selle. 99

þedyr was seynt mark þe euangelyste
Sent be seynt petyr þer for to dwelle,
To prech hem þe gospell of our' lord cryste ;
he prechyd so ther' þat hem¹ alle twyst ¹ r. he hem 103
ffro all her' maumentrye & fals be-leue,
he mad hem in cryst for to be-leue. 105

he þat wyll know þis mor' plat & pleyn), 106
Rede Philo in hys book whech he dyd calle
' De uita theor[et]ica ' : þer schall he seyn)
þat thorow-oute þe cyte in towr' & in walle
It was þoo fulfyllyd wyth hermytes alle, 110
Monkys & prestys & swech holy men,
her' xxxᵗⁱ, her' xxᵗⁱ, her' ix., her' ten. 112

The cuntre all-abowte was full of þese men), 113
And ful of martires, ful of confessoures,
Of maydenes, wydowys & chast women)—

It was a place of ful gret rapayre.
Vndir hym there the kyng made a mayre,   82   *Amalek was ruled by a Mayor, under K. Costus.*
To kepe his lawes thei shuld not fayle,
To stuffe it wyth men) and eke wyth batayle (!).   84

Thus myght this kyng from alysavndre ryde   85
In shippes wyth mene to this grete Cytee
And euere on his owe lordship a-byde—
ffor ouer alle contres pryncypal lord was hee,
Were it of feeld, of town or of see   89
Whiche stood be-twyxe þe grete Cytees too,
Al was it wrought there as he bad it doo.[1]   [1] *wrought—doo on erasure.*   91

The other Cyte, Alysavndre be name,   92   *Alexandria*
On the bordour of Egypt it stant ful fayre,
A grete place, a large and of hey fame.
Thei of Egipte it[1] mote nedes repayre   [1] *overlined.*
On-to þis Cytee, þurgh weyes & thurgh wayre,   96   *was the port*
If þei to affryke or to Cartage goo ;
And thei of affrike the same mote alsoo,   98

If thei in Egipte wil bye or selle.   99   *and mart of Egypt.*
Theder was seynt Mark the Evangelyste
Sent be seynt petir there for to dwelle,
To preche hem þe gospell of oure lord cryste ;   *St. Mark preacht there.*
he preched so there þat hem alle twyste   103
ffro alle here mavnmentrie and her fals lawe,
he made hem in crist her[1] hertys for to drawe.   [1] *on erasure.*

he that wil knowe this more plat and pleyn),   106
Rede philo in his book whiche he ded calle   *See Philo, De vita theoretica.*
'De vita theoretica :' there shal he seyn)
That þorgh-oute the Cyte in tovr and in walle
It was tho fulfilled wyth hermytes alle,   110
Monkes and preestys and swiche hooly men),
here thretty, here twenty, here nyne, here ten).   112

The contre al abovte was ful of these men),   113
Al ful of martirs and ful of Confessovrs,   *Alexandria was full of Martyrs.*
Of maydenes, wedewys and chaast women)—

Who coude noumbyr all þe fayr' floures
þat growe in þe mede aftyr swete schowres,   117
þan myght he noumbyr hem—I trow not he may!
þer' wer' þei putte in full scharp asay,   119
These vessells of gold, martires I mene,   120
Wyth fyr' & wyth yryn I-slayn & I-brent,
In furnes of sorowe wer' þei mad clene;
Was non þat scaped, but or þat he went
he schuld be dede or turn hys entent.   124
þer was þe fyrst exercyse of dyuyn) scole,
Whech is a scyens þat longeth to noo foole.   126
ffor on pathenus, as seyth our' book,   127
ffull many a ȝer' red ther' wyth besy entent,
And aftyr hym clement þe scole vp toke,
Orygene was þe þirde aftyr þat clement—
Not clement of rome, but a-nother' þat us lent   131
Many a good coment & many a holy exhortacyon),
Most specyali in þat book whech is called stromatum.   133
Thys same Alysaunder whech I spak of now,   134
Was large, ryche, ful of puple eke;
ffor þat fame euery man þedyr drow,
Euery knyght & marchaunt gune it than seke.
þei thowt it was enow, qwan þei schuld speke,   138
A kyng to be lorde ouyr thys a-lone,
Thow he had not ellys longyng to hys trone;   140
Eke for þe grete welth þat was in þat wonis,   141
þei called her' kyng none other' name;
"Kyng of alysaundyr'," þei seyd, "a-lone he is,
he is a lord, he is worthy swech fame.
Mote euery tunge be doum & euery kne lame   145
þat our' noble lord neyther' loue ne drede;
And þei þat do it, well mote þei spede!"   147
Too hundred & fourty ȝer' aftyr crystys byrthe   148
Was euen & no mor' to þese gynges[1] dayes.   [1] r. þis kynges
he leuyth þus in ioye & in mekyll myrthe,

hoo covde novnbre alle the fayre flovrs
That growe in medewe after swete shovrs, 117
Than myght he nombre hem—I trowe not he may!
There where¹ thei put in ful sharp assay, ¹ read were 119

These vessellis of gold, martyrs I mene, 120 *The Martyrs in Alexandria were slain and burnt.*
Wyth feer and wyth yerw I-slayn and I-brent,
In furneys of sorwe were þei made clene;
Was now þat skaped, but er than he went
he shuld be ded or turne his entent. 124
There was the fyrste excersyse of dyuyne scole, *It had a School of*
Whiche is a scyens that longeth to no foole. 126 *Divinity,*

ffor on phatenus, as seyth oure book, 127 *under Pantaenus,*
fful many a yeer red there wyth besy entent,
And after hym Clement þe scole vp took, *Clement,*
Orygene was the thredde after þat Clement— *and Origen.*
Not Clement of Rome, but an other þat vs lent 131
Many a good coment an many an holy exortacyon, ¹ om. in MS.
Most specyaly in that book [whech is called stromatum].¹

This same alysavndre wiche I spak of nov, 134
Was large, ryche, ful of peple eke;
ffor that fame euery man theder drov,
Euery knyght and marchavnt gvnne it thanne seke.
They thovght it was I-novgh, whan þei shuld speke, 138
A kyng to be lord ouere this allone, *It had also a King, cald*
Thovgh he had not ellis longynge to his trone; 140

Eke for the grete welthe þat was¹ in þat wonys, 141
Thei called her kyng non other name; ¹ MS. he was
"Kyng of Alysavndre," þei seyde, "allone he is, *The King of Alexandria.*
he is a lord, he is worthi suyche fame.
Mote euery tovnge be dovn and euery kne lame 145
That ovre noble lord neyther love ne drede;
And thei þat doo it, weel mote þei spede." 147

Too hundyrth and fovrty yeer after crystis berthe 148 A.D. 240.
Was evene and [no] more to this kyngys dayes.
he lyueth thus in ioye and mekel merthe,

Bk. I. Ch. 2.
[1st hand]

And honourde swech goddes as longed to hys layes;
Or he wan his land he had sharpe a-sayes.   152
But to othir þing' we wyl go now playn,
To telle forth our' tale as þe cronycles seyn.   154

Bk. I. Ch. 3.

Ca^m. 3^m.

Almyty god þat althing' makyth growe,   155
Doth many mor' mervayles þan we can cast;
ffor who-so-euer men heryn[1] or ellis sowe,   [1] MS. herþ
It is sumtyme fyrst we wene shuld be last.
Our' witte on-to his witte is but a gnast',   159
It mote nede be þus whan he wil haue it so;
[fol. 6, b.]
[2nd hand]
All hys wyll only mote nede be do.   161

Whan thyng is ferthest from our' opynyon),   162
þane werkyth he hys wondres ryth at hys wyll:
Be-holde now þe spede & þe sauacyoun)
Of þe chyldryn of israel; god wold hem not spylle,
But to kepe hem in daunger' & miserye stille,   166
In whech þei wer' falle only for synne;
he halpe hem owte qwan þat þei cowde blyne.   168

If he had soner' holp hem, þei myth a went   169
It had not be goddys myght but her' owne dede.
þer-for chaunged he all her' entent,
he wold not help hem tyl þat þei had nede;
Whan þei wer' in dyspeyr' & myght noght spede,   173
þan sent he hys help & hys socour'—
þus doth our' lord, þus doth our' sauyour'.   175

Ryght in þis wyse wrowt our' lorde her':   176
he wold send a chyld ful on-lych to other'
To þese elde folk, whech lyued all in dwer'
To hafe any chyld, most specyaly þe modyr;
þe kyng had leuer' þan of gold a fothyr'   180
he myght be sekyr of [s]wych a new chaunce.
ȝacharye & Elysabeth stode in þis traunce;   182

And honovred suyche goddys as longed to his layes ;   *Bk. I. Ch. 2.*
Er he wan his lond he hadde sharp assayes.   152   K. Costus was a Heathen.
But to other þing we wil go nov playn,
To telle foorth ovre tale as the cronycles sayn.   154

Ca^{m.} tercium.

Bk. I. Ch. 3.

Almyghty god þat alle þing maketh growe,   155   Almighty God
Dooth many mo mervayles than we can cast ;
ffor what-so-euere men ereeth or ellys sowe,
It is somtyme first þat we wende shuld be last.
Ovre wyt on-to his wyt is but a knast,   159
It mote nede be thus whan he wil haue it soo ;   does what He will.
Al his wil oonly mote nede be doo.   161

Whan þing is ferthest fro ovre oppynyon,   162
Than werketh he his wondrys ryght at his wille :
Be-hold nov the speed and the saluacyon   He saved the Children of Israel.
Of the children of israel ; god wolde hem not spylle,
But to kepe hem in davnger and myserye stille,   166
In whiche thei were falle oonly for synne ;
he halp hem ovte whan þei covde blynne.   168

If he had sonnere holpyn hem, thei myght a went   169
It had not be goddys myght, but her owen dede.
Therefore chavnged he al here entent,
he wolde not helpe them tyl thei had nede ;
Whan thei wer' in dispeyre and myght not spede,   173
Thanne sent he his helpe and his sokovr—
Thus dooth ovre lord, thus dooth ovre sauyo*ur*.   175

Ryght in þis wise wrought oure lord here :   176
he wolde sende a chyeld ful on-liche to other   He resolvd to send a child to old folk, like K. Costus and his wife.
To þese olde folk, wiche leveden alle in dwere
To haue ony chyeld, most specyally þe moder ;
The kyng had levere than of gold a fother   180
he myght be sekyr of suche a newe chavns.
Ȝakarye and Elyȝabeth stoodyn in the same travns ;   182

28 God sends Katharine's old Parents a Child. [MS. Rawlinson.

Bk. I. Ch. 3.

So dede abraham wyth sarra, hys wyff— 183
sche conceyuyd not tyll sche was in age;
Ioachym & Anne had þe same lyff,
Maryes forth-bryngers, & þe same wage.
God can ful well make of swech a rage 187
A ful fayr' floode, blessed mote he be.
So kateryne is not a-lone in þis degre. 189
ffor god to hym-selfe þis mayden had I-chose 190
As for hys owyn spouse & for hys wyffe der';
Of swech[1] spek all crysten, as I suppose :   [1] r. wech
"God send vs part of her' good prayer';
Of all saue on sche is hym most nere ; 194
Sche may & sche can, & sche wyll alsoo
Pray to our' lord þat we may cume hym too." 196

Bk. I. Ch. 4.

Ca^{m.} 4^{m.}

Qwan godd, our' lord, wold þe seson schuld be 197
þat þis fayr' lady to lyth schuld be born),[1] [1] MS. forn)
[fol. 7] he ordeynd & sett it in swech a degre
þat of too folkes whech lustes had lorn),
Schuld þis mayde spryng as rose oute of thorn). 201
þis world wondred þat þis þing myght be soo,
who so elde a lady wyth chyld schuld now goo. 203
Many a man & woman at þis thyng low, 204
Sume of hem sayd, " it is but a lye,
þe kyng is ful febyll, þe qwen ful eld now:
Schall sche now grone, schal sche now crye?
schal sche in þis age in chyldebede lye? 208
þis thyng is not lykly," þus seyd þei alle,
ladyes in þe chaumbyr' & lordys in þe halle. 210
But þe tyme is come, sche be-gynnyth to grone, 211
Cryeth & wayleth as do alle women)—
ffor of þat penaunce was mary a-lone
Excused, & no moo, þus our' bokes ken)
Whech þat wer' wretyn of ful holy men). 215

So dede abraham wyth sara, his wyef— 183 *God sent a child to aged Sara, and to Joachim and Anna.*
She conceyved not tyl she was in age;
Ioachym and Anna hadden þe same lyef,
Maryes foorth-bryngeris, and the same wage.
God can ful weel make of swiche a rage 187
A ful fayre flood, blissed mote he be.
So kataryne is not alone in this degre. 189

ffor god to hym-self this mayde hath[1] I-chose   [1] r. had   *He chose St. Katharine for His wife.*
As for his owe spovse and for his wyef dere; 191
Of wiche spekyn alle crysten, as I suppose,
"God sende vs part of her good prayere;
Of alle saue of on she is most hym nere; 194
She may and she can, and she wil also
Pray to our lord that we may come hym to." 196

Ca^{m.} quartum.

Whanne god, oure lord, wolde þe seson shuld be 197
    That this fayre lady to lyght shuld be boorn,
he ordeyned it, and sette it in swiche a degre
That of tho[1] folkes wiche lustys had lorn,   [1] corrected; r. too   *When her parents are old,*
Shulde this mayde sprynge as Rose ovte of thorn. 201
The world wondred that þis thyng myght be soo,
hov so old a lady wyth chyeld shuld now goo. 203

Many man and woman at this þing lough, 204
Som of hem sayde, "it is but a lyȝe,
The kyng is ful febel, the qveen ful olde nov;
Shal she nov grone, shal she nov crye?
Shal she in þis age in chyeldbed nov lye? 208
This þinge is not likly," thus seyde þei alle,
ladyes in the chavnbre and lordys in þe halle. 210

But the tyme is come, she be-gynneth to grone, 211   *St. Katharine is born.*
Cryeth and waileth as doo alle women—
ffor of þat penavnce was Mary allone
Excused, and no mo, thus ovre bookis ken
Whiche þat were wretyn of ful hooly men. 215

Bk. I. Ch. 4.	Kateryne þei named þat fayrˀ mayd ȝinge.	
	herˀ faderˀ men called costus þe kyng,	217
	herˀ moderˀ þei seye sche hyght meliades—	218
	þe kynges dowterˀ sche was of ermenye,	
	Off bewte[1] sche had prys in euery prees [1] MS. brewte	
	Thorow-owte þe londe of alle sarcynrye.	
	Me lyst not in herˀ preysyng lengerˀ to tarye,	222
	Sche was full fayrˀ & full goode eke—	
	It is schewyd in hyrˀ dowterˀ, þat men now seke	224
	To be herˀ help in myschefe & in nede.	225
	But whan thre dayes werˀ pased & I-gon,	
	þis chyld for to hylle, to lulle & to lede	
	Too worthy ladyes werˀ ordeynd a-non,	
	And not only þei to trauayle þerˀ a-lone,	229
	But of otherˀ women a ful grete rowte,	
	Ryght for þis cause : to berˀ it a-bowte,	231
	To kepe it, to wasch it & for to clothe,	232
	To lyft it, to lull it & to fede it eke,	
	To bathe it, to wyp it & to rokke it bothe ;	
	þei had herˀ laburˀ newly be þe weke.	
	þus is it kept, it schuld not be seke.	236
[fol. 7, b.]	þe kyng had of it a comfort ful hye,	
	þe qwen coude not þer-fro kepe now herˀ hye.	238
	þus was it norched, þis nobyl goodly chylde,	239
	þis gracyous lady, tyll sche cowde goo.	
	Sche was fro hyrˀ byrth boþe mek & mylde,	
	Mercy fro þe tetys grew wyth hyr al-soo,	
	And lested wyth herˀ all herˀ lyffe þer-too.	243
	Sche was fulsone plesyd whan sche made mone,	
	No wondyr it is—þei hafe but hyrˀ a-lone.	245

Bk. I. Ch. 5.   Ca^m. 5^m.

Thus prouyd þis princesse euyrˀ morˀ & morˀ.   246
Sche was set to book, & be-gan to lerˀ
All þe letters þat werˀ leyd hyr be-forˀ.

St. Katharine's Birth and Upbringing.

Kataryne þei named that fayre mayde yinge.
hir fadir men calle Costus the kynge, 217
  hir modir þei seyde she hyghte meliades— 218
The kyngys dovter she was of [1] Ermenye, [1] overlined.
Of bevte she had preys in every pres
Thurgh-oute þe lond of al sarsynrye.
Me leste not in hir preysynge lengere to tarye, 222
She was ful fayr and ful good eke—
It shewed in hir dovghter, þat men nov seke 224

  To be her helpe in myschef and in nede. 225
but whan thre dayes were passed and I-gon,
The chyeld for to hille, to lulle and to leede
Too worthy ladyes were ordeyned a-non,
And not oonly thei to[1] travayle there allon, [1] orig. too 229
But of othere women a ful gret rovte,
Right for this cause: to bere it a-bovte, 231

  To kepe it, to wash it and for to clothe, 232
To lyfte it, to lulle it and to fede it eke,
To bathe it, to wype it and to rokke it bothe;
Thei had her labour newely be the weke.
Thus is it kepte, it shuld not be seeke. 236
The kyng hadde of it a confort ful heye,
The qveen coude not ther-fro kepe nov hir eyȝe. 238

  Thus was it norysshed, this noble goodly chield, 239
This gracyous lady, til she covde goo.
She was fro hir byrthe bothe meke and myeld,
Mercy fro the tetys grewe wyth hir also,
And lefte[1] wyth hir al hir lyef ther-too. [1] orig. lested? 243
She was ful sone plesed whan she made mone,
No wonder it is—thei have but hir allone. 245

       Ca^{m.} qvintum.

Thus proued this pryncesse euere more and more. 246
  She was set to book, and be-gan to lere
Alle the letteris þat were leyde hir be-fore.

Bk. I. Ch. 4.
Katharine's father is King Costus; her mother, Queen Meliades.

The babe has 2 Nurses, &c.

to wash, feed, and rock her, each for a week,

till she can walk.

Bk. I. Ch. 5.
Katharine is set to her books,

ffor of all þe scoler*is* þat ar now or wer',
Sche is hem a-boue; for neyther' loue ne feer' 250
Mad hyr to stynt whan sche be-gan to ken
þe lettyr*is* & þe wordys þat sche spelled then. 252

Sche had maystyres fro ferre þat wer' full wyse, 253
To tech her' of rethoryk & gramer' þe scole;
þe cases, þe nounbres & swych-maner' gyse:
þe modes, þe u*er*bes, wech long to no fole,—
Sche lerned hem swetly w*yth*-owte any dole, 257
Bothe þe fygures & þe co*n*sequence,
þe declynacyons, þe p*er*sones, þe modes, þe tens. 259

Among all oþ*er* a wyse man þer' was, 260
And ful sad þer-to, he was her' chaunsler',
Men called hym be name Mayster' Athanas;
he was suruyour' to all þat þer wer',
And as I seyd ere,[1] he payed her' hyer'. 264
he was an hye clerk & a souereyn, [1] MS. her ere; her crossed out.
All þe vij artes coude he ful pleyn. 266

And ouyr' þis lady was hys most cure, 267
þat sche schuld be occupyed all þe long day
In doctrine & stodye, saue i*n* mesure
Sume-tyme a-mong had sche hyr play.
Sume-tyme to hyr mayster' wold sche sey nay: 271
Whan he bad hyr pley, sche wold sit stylle;
To stody & goodenes inclined was her' wylle. 273

Sche lerned þe greke, sche lernyd þe latyn tunge, 274
sche lerned of natur' þe p*r*euy weys alle
[fol. 8] þat ony philosophyr' be hys doct*r*ine had runge,
sche knew þe effect*is* as þei schuld falle
Of all þe bodyes whech we þe planetes calle; 278
þis was thorow besynes of Athanas þe clerk,
Wech tended on-to hyr' & set hyr th*us* on werk. 280

God of hys g*r*ace, as seyth þe story, 281
Aȝens alle heretykys þat reygned þoo ther'
Wold all hys conquest & hys victory

ffor of [1] alle the scoler*is* þat arn nov or were,   [1] overlined.
She is hem a-bove; for neyther love ne fere   250
Made hir to stynt whan she gan to ken
The letteris and wordes þat she spelled then.   252

She hadde maystres fro fer þat were ful wise,   253
To teeche hir of retoryk and gramer the scole;
The cases, the novmbres and suche-man*er* gyse,
The modes, the verbeȝ, wiche longe to no foole,
She lerned hem sweetly wyth-ovte ony doole,   257
Bothe the figures and the conseqvens,
The declynac*i*ons, þe p*er*sonys, the modys, þe tens.   259

Among alle other a wysman ther was,   260
And ful sad ther-to, he was hir chavncelere,
Men called hym a name Mayster athanas;
he was surveour to alle þat there were,
And as I seyde er, he payed hem her heere.   264
he was an hygh clerk and a sovereyn,
Alle the .vij. artes covde he ful pleyn.   266

And on this lady was his most cure,   267
That she shulde be occupyed al the long day
In doctryne and studie, save in mesure
Somtyme a-monge had she hir play.
Somtyme to hir mayster wolde she sey nay   271
Whan he bad hir pleye, she wolde sytte stille,
To stody and goo[d]nes inclyned was hir wille.   273

She lerned the greek, she lerned the latyn tunge,   274
She lerned of nature the prevy weyes alle
That ony phylysophre be his doctryne had rvnge,
She knewe the effectes as þei shul falle
Of alle þe bodyes wiche we planetes calle;   278
This was thurgh besynes of athanas þe cleerk,   [1] on overlined.
Wiche tended on[1]-to hir and set hir thus on weerk.   280

God of his grace, as seyth þe story,   281
A-yens alle the heretykes þat regned tho there
Wold all his conqvest and his victory

Bk. I. Ch. 5.

and has masters in Grammar, &c.

Her Chancellor is Athanas,

who oversees all her teachers.

She learns Greek and Latin,

that she may get the victory over heretics.

Schuld be a-rered only be hyr'.
þerfor lern sor', þou ʒong goddys scoler'! 285
þou schall ouercome heresye & blaspheme
Thorow-owte all grek, thorow-owte all þi reme. 287

Ryght as [be]¹ .xij. ydyotis, seynt Austyn) seyth— ¹ om.
he meneth þe Aposteles, for þei not lerned wer'— 289
Thorow-owte þe werd was sowyn) our' feyth,
þat euery man may know & euery man ler'
Godd wold not wynn vs wyth wysdam ne feer', 292
But wyth holy boystysnesse, if I schuld sey soo:
Ryght þus, as me thynkyth, in þis caas hath he doo; 294

ffor whan þat hys chyrch was at gret neede, 295
he ordeynd þis lady for to ʒeue batayle
Ageyn all þe werd; þei schall hyr not ouyr' lede,
Ne alle her' argumentis schall not a-vayle;
Sche schal so be lerned þat all her' asayle 299
Schall fayl, & falle boþe cunnyng & bost,
Sche schall be myty wyth strenght of goost. 301

Caᵐ. 6ᵐ.

HEr' fader', þat sche schuld lern) þese artes alle, 302
þis nobyll lady, hys owyn) douter' der',
Ded mak a paleyse large & ryalle,
In whech he wold þat sche schuld ler'.
Boþe knytes & clerkes, all dwelt þei þer' 306
Whech wer' ordeynd to her' owyn) seruyse,
Now to make hyr' rest, now for to make hyr' ryse, 308

And eke new norture to tell hyr' & to tech. 309
Many maysters þer-for' þethyr wer' fett;
'As fer' as her' cunnyng myght strech & rech,
þei lerned þis lady wyth-owte any lett;
Alle her' wyttys wer' only on hyr sett. 313
ʒe may well suppose in ʒour' owne dome
Euer as sche grew, þe gretter' mayster' come. 315

Shuld been arrered oonly be here.
Therefore lerne sore, þou yov[n]ge goddys scolere! 285
þou shalt ouercome heresye and blaspheme
Thurgh-ovte aH grece, þurgh-ovte al þi reme. 287

Ryght as be twelue ydiotes, sent Austyn seyth— 288 *As 12 Idiots, the Apostles, founded the Faith,*
he meneth the apostellis, for thei¹ not lerned were—
Thurgh-ovte þe world was sowen ovr' feyth, ¹ overlined.
That every man may knowe, and every man may lere
God wulde not wynne vs wyth wysdam ne fere, 292
But wyth holy boistonesse, if I shulde sey soo:
Ryght thus, as me thynketh, in this cas hath he doo; 294

ffor whan þat his cherche was at gret nede, 295
he ordeyned þis lady for to yeve batayle *so God ordaind Katharine to do battle for the Church.*
A-geyn al the world; þei shal hir not ouere lede,
Ne alle her argumentys shal not a-vayle;
She shal so be lerned þat alle her assayle 299
Shal fayle, and falle bothe connyng and bost,
She shal be myghty wyth the strengthe of þe gost. 301

Ca^{m.} sextum.

Hir fadir, that she shuld lerne these Artes alle, 302 *Katharine's Father builds her a Palace,*
This noble lady, his ovne doughter dere,
Dede make a paleys large and royaH,
In wiche he wolde þat she shuld lere.
Bothe knyghtes and clerkys, alle dwelt þei there 306 *where her Teachers dwell.*
Wiche were ordeyned to hir owne seruyse,
Nov to make hir reste, now for to make hir to ryse, 308

And eke newe norture to telle here and to teche. 309
Many maystris therefore theder were fette;
As fer as her connyng myght stretche and reche,
Thei lerned this lady wyth-ovten ony lette;
Alle here wittes were oonly on her sette. 313
Ye may weel suppose in yovre owen dome,
Euere as she grev the grettere mayster come. 315

D 2

Bk. I. Ch. 6.	her' stodyes þer full craftily wer' I-pyght,	316
	Wyth deskys & chayeres & mech oþer ger'	
	Arayed on þe best wyse, & glased full bryght,	
	Euery faculte be hym-selue : for þei of gramer' wer'	
	Sett on þe west syde, & eke þei þat ler'	320
	Astronomye on þe est, ryght for þei schuld loke	
	Sumtyme on þe heuyn), sumtyme on) her' boke ;	322
	All þe other' artes be-twyx hem stode a-rowe,	323
	Ryght aftyr her' age & aftyr' her' dygnyte—	
	Euery man þat cam þer' myght well I-knowe	
	Whech was worthyer' & hye[r] of degre.	
	her' fadyr þe kyng seldom wold her' se,	327
	On-to þese clerkes he hath hyr' thus take	
	As thow he had hyr only now newly forsake—	329
	ffor lettyng of hyr lernyng dyd he þan soo.	330
	Sche wex fast in body, & lerned eke sore ;	
	Whan o mayster' was goo, a-noþir cam hyr too.	
	Thus chaungyng of maystirys & eke of lore	
	had þis noble mayde, sche lerned mych þe mor'—	334
	Ȝe may wete natur' louyth variaunce,	
	Sumetyme men stody, sumtyme þei daunce.	336
	Þe kyng dyd make þer for' her' a-lone	337
	A paleyse wallyd, ryght on þe sowth-syde	
	Open to þe sune : þer was her' trone—	
	þer is no swych now in þis werde wyde.	
	It was made for kateryne þer to a-byde	341
	Whan sche wold stody be hyr-selue sole.	
	In þe grete garden was most hyr' scole :	343
	It was fer a-wey fro euery-maner' wyght,	344
	It was made & ordeynd at hyr' owyn deuyse.	
	þer wold sche ly sumtyme, stody & wryght ;	
	It was sett full of trees, & þat in straunge wyse ;	
	þer' wold sche sytte, & þer wold sche ryse,	348
	þer was hyr walkyng & all hyr dysporte—	
[fol. 9]	Solitary lyff to stodyers is comfort.	350

hir stodyes there ful craftely were I-pyght, 316 *Bk. I. Ch. 6.*
Wyth deskes and chayer*is* and moche other gere
A-rayed on the best wyse, and glased ful bryght,
Euery faculte be the selue : for þei of gram*er* were
Sette on the west syde, and eke þei that lere 320
Astronomye on the Est, ryght for þei shuld loke
Somtyme on heuene, somtyme on her booke ; 322

The Studies of Katharine and her Teachers are well fitted up.

Alle the other artes be-twyxe hem stood on rowe, 323
Ryght after her age and after her dignyte—
Eue*ry* man that cam ther myght weel I-knowe
Wiche was wurthier and heyere of degre.
hir fadyr the kyng seeldom wolde hir see, 327
On-to these clerkys he hath hir thus I-take,
As þough he had hir oonly now newely for-sake— 329

ffor lettyng of hir lernyng dede he than soo. 330
She wex faste in body, and lerned eke soore ;
Whan on maystir was goo, a-nother cam hir too.
Thus chavngynge of maystres and eke of loore
had this noble mayden, she leerned moche þe moore— 334
Ye may wete weel nature lovyth varyaunce,
Somtyme men stodye, sumtyme thei davnce. 336

Katharine grows and learns, often chaunging her Masters and studies.

The kyng ded make there for hir allone 337
A paleys ryght weel walled, on the sovth syde
Open to the sonne : there was hir trone—
There is non suche now in this world wyde.
It was made for kataryne there to a-byde 341
Whan she wulde stodyen be hir-self soole.
The grete gardeyn was þe most hir scoole : 343

A Palace is built for her alone

to work in.

It was fer a-wey from eue*ry*-man*er* wyght, 344
It was made and ordeyned at hir owne devyse.
There wolde she lye somtyme, stody and wryght ;
It was set ful of trees, and that in strong wyse ;
There wolde she sitte, there wolde she ryse, 348
There was hir walkyng and alle hir disport—
Solitary lief to stodieres is confort. 350

She studies in the Garden.

Sche bar' þe key of þis gardeyn)—þer had it no moo; 351
Whan sche went in, sche schett it full fast;
It was speryd ful treuly went sche to or froo,
ffor of many thynges was sche sor' a-gast,
But most of inquietude—stody may not last 355
Wyth werdly besynesse ne wyth hys cure,
þe olde wyse sey þus, I ȝow ensure. 357

þe walles & þe toures wer' mad nye so hye, 358
fful couertly wyth arches & sotelly I-cast:
þer myght not cume in but foul þat doth flye;
þe ȝatis, as I seyd, wer' schett full fast,
And euer-mor' her'-selue wold be þe last; 362
þe key eke sche bar', for sche wolde soo.
þus leuyd þis lady in her' stody þoo. 364

Ca^m. 7^m.

Sche lerned þan) þe liberall artes seuen). 365
Gramer' is þe fyrst & þe most lyte;
he tellyth þe weye full fayr' & full euen)
who men schall speke, & who þei schall wryte.
Retoryk þe secunde is sett in þis plyte: 369
he doth ny þe same, saue þat he arayeth
hys maters wyth colourys & wyth termes dysplayeth. 371

þe thyrde sciens call þei dialetyk; 372
he lerneth men wyth-in a lythyll throwe,
If he be stodied þer is non to hym lyke,
þe trewth fro þe falshed þat techeth for to know.
Aftyr hym þan folowyth ryght be rowe 376
Arsmetryk, in whech þe cunnyng so stant:
Nowmbres schall þou know, þou schall not whant. 378

Thei tawt[1] her' also þe scyens of musyk,   [1] MS. tawter' 379
fful wel grownded was sche in þis melodye;
Sche had a mayster, þer' was none hym lyke,
he departyd þis scyens in thre wyth-outen lye:
In-to metyr, to ryme, & to armonye; 383

She baar the keye of þis gardeyn—þer had it no moo ;
Whan she wente in she shet it ful fast ; 352
It was sperd ful truly went she too or froo,
ffor of many thyngis was she sore a-gast,
But most of inquietude—stody may not last 355
With wordly besynesse ne with his cure,
The olde wyse sey thus, I yov ensure. 357

The walles and þe tovris were made vp so hyghe, 358 *Katharine's Garden is walld round.*
fful couertly wyth arches arn sotylly I-cast :
There myght not come in but foul that doth flighe ;
The ʒates, as I seyde, were shet ful fast,
And euere-more hir-selue wold be the last ; 362
The keye eke she baar, for she wold do soo.
Thus lerned this lady in hir stody thoo. 364

Ca^{m.} septimum.

Bk. I. Ch. 7.

She lerned thanne the liberal artes seuene. 365 *She learns 1. Grammar,*
   Gramer is the firste and the most lyght ;
he telleth the weye ful fayer and ful euene
hov men shal speke, and hov thei shal wryght.
Rethorik the secunde is sette in this plyght : 369 *2. Rhetoric,*
he dooth ny the same, saue that he arayeth
his materis with colovris and wyth termes displayeth. 371

The thredde scyens calle þei dialetike ; 372 *3. Dialectic,*
he lerneth men wyth-inne a lytil throwe—
If he be stodied, there is non to hym like—
Truthe[1] fro falshed that teecheth he for to knowe. [1] *on erasure.*
After hym thanne folweth ryght be rowe 376
Arsmetryk, in wiche the connyng soo stant : *4. Arithmetic,*
Noumbres shalt þou knowe, thou shalt not want. 378

Thei taught hir also the scyens of musyk, 379 *5. Music,*
fful weel grovnded was she in this melodie ;
She had a mayster, there was non hym lyke,
he departed this scyens in thre, wythovte lye :
In to metir, to ryme, and to armonye ; 383

40 Katharine knows as much as 310 wise men. [MS. Rawl.

Bk. I. Ch. 7.

Armonye is in voyse, in smytyng or wynde,
Symphonye & euphonye arn) of hys kynde. 385

[fol. 9, b.]
[1st hand]

In geometrye was þis lady lernyd also, 386
In euclidis bokys wyth his portraturys;
þat is a sciens—mech stody longeth per-too—
ffor to know þe letterys & þe figures;
Yf⁺ I speke þerof⁺, I xaƚƚ make forfetures 390
Agayn þis sciens, I can not of⁺ þat arte
But swech as he can þat makyth a carte. 392

In astronomye þis lady eke so hye steye, 393
Sche know þe strenght & þe stondyng⁺ styƚƚ
Of⁺ alle þe planetis þat regnen vp-on hey;
Whech ar' of⁺ goode wyƚƚ & whech ar' of⁺ iƚƚe,
Whech wyll help a mater & whech will it spille. 397
And þeis she lernyd both mor' & lesse,
Sche mowled not, I trow, in no ydylnes. 399

þus for her' lernyng⁺ had sche swech fame, 400
þat her' fader dede gader þorow-oute þe lond
Aƚƚ þe grete clerkys þat wer' of⁺ any name,
Ryth to þis entent, as I vnderstande,¹ ¹ MS. stonde?
To wete yf⁺ his douter dar' take it vnhand¹ ¹ r. on hand 404
To be apposyd of⁺ so many wyse men.
þei wer' gadred in þat place CCC. & ten. 406

[2nd hand]

Eche of hem schaƚƚ now do aƚƚ hys myght 407
To schew hys cunnyng—if any straung thyng
hath he lernyd hys lyue, he wyll now ful ryght
Vttyr hit, for hys name therby schaƚƚ spryng.
But þer was ryght nowt but kateryn þe 3yng 411
vndyrstod aƚƚ þyng & answerd per-too;
her' problemes aƚƚ sche hath sone on-doo. 413

"O good godd," seyd þeis¹ clerkes thane, ¹ MS. þe's 414
"þis mayd hath lerned mor' thyng in her' lyue
Than we supposyd, for mor' than we sche canne.
We woundyr who sche may our' argumentis dryue,
ffor hyr conclusyon) now in 3erys fyue 418

MS. Arundel.] *Katharine knows as much as* 310 *wise men.* 41

Armonye is in voys, in smytynge or wynde,
Symphonye and Euphonye arn of his kynde. 385

In gemetrie was þis lady lerned also, 386   6. Geometry, Euclid,
In eclydys book*is* wyth his portratures ;
It is a scyens—moche stody longeth ther-too—
ffor to knowe the letter*is* and the fygures ;
If I speke of it, I shal make forfetures 390
A-geyns þis sciens, I can not of that art
but suche as he kan þat maket a cart. 392

In astronomye þis lady eke so hey stey, 393   7. Astronomy.
She knewe the strengthe and the stondyng stille
Of alle the planetes þat regnen vp-on hey ;
Wiche are of good wil and wiche are of ille,
Wiche wil helpe a mater and wiche wil it spille. 397
And these she lerned bothe more and lesse,
She mused not, I trowe, in now Idelnesse. 399

Thus for hir lernyng had she suche fame, 400   The girl Katharine is so learned
That hir fadyr dede gaderyn þvrgh-ovte the lond
Alle the grete clerkys that were of ony name,
Ryght to this entent, as I vnderstonde,
To wete if his doughter dar take it on honde 404
To be apposed of so many wyse men.   that when 310 Examiners
Thei were gadered in þat place thre hundred and ten. 406

Eche of hem shal now doo al his myght 407
To shewe his connyng—if ony stravnge thing   question her,
hath he lerned hys lyve, he wil nov ful ryght
Vtter it, for his name thereby shal spryng.   [1] MS. þing.
but there was ryght novght but kataryn þe ying[1] 411
Vndirstood alle þing and answerde ther-too ;   she answers them all.
her problemes alle she hath soone on-doo. 413

"O good god," seyden these clerkys than, 414   The 310 Wise Men
"This mayde hath lerned more þing in hir lyue
Than we supposed, for more þan we, she kan.
we wunder[1] hov she may oure argumentis dryve   [1] MS. wurder
ffor her conclusyon, for in yeer*is* fyve 418

Bk. I. Ch. 7.
Cune we not lerne þat sche doth in one"—
Thus seyd þeis wysmen be row cuerychon. 420
Thei tok þan her' leue at þe kyng alle, 421
[fol. 10] home to her' cuntre, certeyn), will þei goo;
"þis mayd ȝour' doghtyr, lord," þei seyd, "sche schall
Be a woundyr woman, & sche may leue þer-too.
Of vs nedyth sche noght, we hafe not her' to doo, 425
Sche can þat we can, & þer-to mech more"—
þus seyd þei, certeyn), þe wyse þat ther' wore. 427
Thys noble kyng hath reward hem full weele, 428
ȝoue hem grete ȝyftys & grete liberte;
Lordes dede so þanne, clerkes had euery deel,
All þat þei spent, of þe liberalyte
And of þe bountyfnesse of swech lordes fre. 432
þus are þei rewardyd, & home euerych oone,
And kateryne in stody is left þus a-lone. 434

Bk. I. Ch. 8.
Ca^{m.} 8^{m.}

Qwan all was welle & sekyr, as sche wende, 435
þan cam deth to hows & dyd hys dute,
Of all her' ioye he made sone an ende:
ffor he hath take a-way hyr owyn) fadyr fre
And owte of þis werld hath ledd hym wher' he 439
Is in swech place as longyth on-to hym,
he is logged þer' wyth lordys of hys kyne 441
Whech deyd wyth-outen feyth, wyth-owt crystendome—
Kateryn is swech on, ȝet sche schall not be long. 443
Owte of all grece þe grete lordes come—
But þei had do soo, þei had do grete wrong;
All her' grete worchep oonly dyd honge 446
Vp-on þe noble kyng—he lyght þer' now ded;
þei closyd hym in clothe & aftyr-ward in lede, 448
Thei led hym to þe temple wyth solennite, 449
If wepyng & waylyng schuld be called soo.
þer' was noon oþer noyse than in þat cete

MS Arundel.] *Katharine's Father, Costus, dies.*

kvn we not lerne þat [s]he hath[1] dooth (!) in oon "— 419   *Bk. I. Ch. 7.*
Thus seyde these wys*e*men be rowe eu*e*rychon.   [1] overlined.

Thei took þanne her leue at the kyng alle,   421
hom to her contre, certeyn, wil þei goo ;   *go back home,*
" This mayde yovre doughter, lord," þei seyde, " she shalle
Be a wunder[1] woman, and she may leve ther-too.   [1] MS. wurder
Of vs nedeth she nought, we haue here nought to doo,   425   *as they can teach Katharine nothing.*
She can þat we can, and there-to moche more "—
Thus seyde thei, certeyn, þe wise þ*a*t there wore.   427

This noble kyng hath rewarded hem ful weel,   428   *They are well paid.*
yeve hem grete ȝeftes and grete liberte ;
lordes dede also[1] þanne, the[2] clerk*is* had eue*r*y deel   [1] corrected. [2] overlined.
Al þat þei spente, of there lyberalyte
And of there bovntyffulnesse—of the wiche lordys free   432
Thus are þei rewarded, and hom eue*r*y-choon,
And kataryne in stody is lefte thus allow.   434

      Ca^m· octauu*m*.   *Bk. I. Ch. 8.*

Whanne al was weel and sekyr, as she wende,   435
     Thanne cam deth to hovse and dede his dute,
Of al hir ioye he maad soone an ende :
ffor he hath take a-wey hir owen fadir fre   *Katharine's Father, Costus, dies.*
And ovte of this world hath ledde hym where he   439
Is in swiche place as longyn on-to hym,
he is lodged there wyth lordes of his kyn   441

Whiche deyden wyth-ovte feith, w*yth*-ovten crysten-
Kataryne is swiche on, yet she shal not longe.   [dom—
Ovte of al grece the gret lordys coom—   *The Lords of Greece come.*
But thei had do soo, þei had doon grete wronge ;
Al her grete wurshep oonly dede honge   446
Vp-on þe noble kyng—he lith nov there deed ;
Thei closyn hym in clooth and afterward in leed,   448   *Katharine's Father is coffind,*
     Thei led hym to þe temple wyth solennyte,   449   *taken to the Temple,*
If wepyng and waylyng shuld be called soo.
Ther was non other noyse thanne in þ*a*t Cite

But "welaway, alas! qwat schul we doo?
Our' lord is now gon), we gete hym no moo, 453
Who schall ber' þe crown), now he is deed?
he left vs non eyre for to be our' heed, 455
"But a ʒong mayde; what schal sche doo? 456
Sche is but a woman! ʒet, had sce weddyd be
Or tyme þat hyr fadyr went þus vs froo,
It had be mor' sekyrnesse & mor' felicyte.
þer is no mor' to sey, but sekyrly we 460
Are likely to be subiect on-to oþer londys;
We bounde sumtyme, now mote we suffyr bondys." 462

The noble qween eke, qwat sorow þat sche made 463
It is pyte to her', to telle & to rede;
þer cowde no solace hyr hert þat tyme glade,
þe teeres fell down) euer as sche ʒede.
þe ʒung lady kateryne hath chaunged her' wede, 467
And hyr' colour' eke is now full pale.
What schuld I of her' sorow make lenger' tale? 469

The kyng was leyd in a toumbe, made of golde & stones
fful ryaly, ʒe may wete, for he was her' kyng, 471
A-noynted eke wyth baume, þat neyþer flesch ne bones
Schuld rote ne stynke—swech was þe beryyng
In þat tyme to lordes; & mych other' thyng 474
Was seyd & do, whech nedyth not to rehers,
ffor happyly sume folk myght than be þe wers 476

To her' swech maummentrye & swych-maner' rytes. 477
þe lordes a-bode þer styll in þat same place,
Both dukys & erlys, byschoppys & knytes,
Thrytty dayes euyn)—for so vsage was.
þe dayes rone fast & be-gune to pace. 481
þe lordes þat þer wer', þei seyd þat her' kyng
Mote hafe a memoryall for any-maner' thyng, 483
And þat of swech lestyng whech schuld not fayle, 484
þus seyd þei all ryght wyth oon entent;
Pey[n]tyng & wrytyng & grauyng in entayle

but " weelaway, allas ! what shal we doo ? *Bk. I. Ch. 8.*
Oure lord is now goo, we gete hym no moo.   453 and bewaild.
ho shal bere the crovne, now he is deed ?
he lefte vs non other for to be oure heed,   455

" But a yovnge mayde ; what shal she doo ?   456
She is but a woman ! ȝet, had she wedded be   His folk wish
Or tyme þat hir fader went thus vs froo,   Katharine was married.
It had be more sekyrnesse and more felicite.
There is no more to seye, but sekirly we   460
Arn lykly to ben subiettys on-to other londes ;
We bounde somtyme, nov mote we suffre bondes."   462

The noble qveen eke, what sorwe þat she made, 463 The Queen sorrows.
It is pete of hir to telle and to[1] reede ;   [1] orig. om.
There coude no solas þat tyme hir hert glade,
The teeres fel doun euere as she yeede.
The yov[n]ge lady kataryn hath chavnged hir wede 467 So does Katharine.
And hir colovr, and eke is nowe ful pale ;
What shuld I of hir sorwe make a lengere tale ?   469

The kyng was leyd in a toumbe, made of gold and stones
fful ryally, ye may wete, for he was her kyng,   471
A-noynted eke with bavme, þat neyther flesh ne bones   The body of Katharine's Father is embalmd.
Shulde not rote ne stynke—swiche was the berying
In þat tyme to lordys ; and moche other thyng   474
Was þanne seyde and doo, wiche nedeth not to be (!) rehers,
ffor happely som folk myght thanne be the wers   476

To heere swiche maumentrye and suche-maner ryghtes.
The lordes a-bode there stille in þat same plaas, 478
Bothe dukys and erlys, bysshopys and knytes,
Thretty dayes euene—for soo vsage waas.
The dayes ronne faste and be-gonne to paas.   481
The lordes þat þer were, þei seyde þat her kyng   As a lasting Memorial to him,
Mote haue a memoryal for ony-maner thyng ;   483

And þat of swiche lestynge the Cite (!) shuld not faile,
þus seyde þei alle ryght wyth on entent ;   485
Peyntyng and wrytyng and gravynge in entayle

Bk. I. Ch. 8. It wyll wanyse & wast, roten & be brent.
þer-for' to þis ende are þei all consent : 488
þe grete cyte, whech her' lord dyd make,
Schall chaunge now hys name for her' lordes sake ; 490

It schall no lenger' hyght þus : þe gret amaleck, 491
hese name wyll þei turn) thorow-oute all þe cost ;
Who-so-euer þedyr come, wyth cart or wyth sek,
þei mote calle it now þe cetee famagost.
þus mad þei crye þan thorow-oute al þe hoost 495
þat all men of grece mote hafe it in mowthe,
[fol. 11] Dwelle he est' or west, dwell he north or sowthe. 497

And þis is her' cause, for þat cyte he made, 498
In þe same dwelt he most, þus seyd þei alle,
In þis cyte mych myrth & mych ioye he had,
In þis cyte to deth eke he down dede falle ;
ffor þeis same causes hys name ber' it schaH, 502
Euer whyll it on grounde stant, it schall neuer be lost,
But euer be in knowlech þe cyte of famagost. 504

þus it is called now & euer-mor' schall be, 505
Wyth a g. sett per' þe c. schuld stande ;
þe grete noble famagost þat stant on þe see
[1st hand] þus it is named þorw-out euery lande ;
þer walkyth many a foote, & werkyth many hande. 509
þus shal þe name of' wordy men sprede,
And shrewes shul sterue nameles, swech is her' mede. 511

Bk. I. Ch. 9. Ca[m]. 9[m].

The qwen sett a parlement at her' owe coste 512
Att alisaunder þe grete, to whech she wolde
Euery lorde þat held of' her' husbond[1] coste, [1] MS. husbondis
To þis parlement nedis goo or ryde shold—
But he come wylfully, he may be ful bold, 516
he schal be compelled. sche sent ferre & nye
ffor alle þe lordis, & no man wyst why. 518

It wil whanse and waste, roten and be brent.
Therefore to this ende arn) they alle consent: 488
The grete Cite, wiche her lord dede make,
Shal chavnge nov his name for her lordis sake; 490

the name of the city Amalek is

It shal no lengere hatte thus: the grete Amalek, 491
Is name wil þei turne thorgh-ovte al þe coost;
ho-so-euer come thedyr, wyth carte or wyth sek,
Thei mote nov calle the Cite ffamagoost.
Thus made thei cry thanne þurgh-ovte alle the oost 495
That alle men) of Grece mote haue [it] in movthe,
Dwelle he Est or west, dwelle he north or sovthe. 497

changed to Famagost,

And this is her cavse, for that Cite he made, 498
In þat same dwelled he most, thus seyde þei alle,
In this Cite meche merthe and meche ioye he hade,
In this Cite to deth eke doun) ded falle;
ffor these same cavses his name bere it shalle, 502
Euer whil it on) grovnde stant, it shal neuer be lost,
But euer be in knowleche the Cite famagost. 504

for he dwelt most there, and died there.

Thus is it called now and euere-more shal bee, 505
Wyth a G. set there C. shuld·stond;
The grete noble famagost þat stondyth on þe see
þus is it named þurgh-ovte euery lond;
There walketh many a foot, and werketh many an hond. 509
Thus shal þe name of wurthy men sprede,
And shrewes shul sterve nameles, suche is her mede. 511

The C of Costus is changed to G, in Famagost.

Ca^{m.} nouu*m.*

Bk. I. Ch. 9.

The qveen sette a parlement at hir ovne cost 512
At Alisavndre the grete, to wiche she wolde
Euery lord þat held of hir hovsbonde Cooste,
To þis parlement nedes goo or ryde sholde—
But he come wilfully, he may be ful bolde, 516
he shal be compelled. she sente fer and ny
ffor alle the lordes, and no man) wyste why. 518

Katharine's Mother summons a Parliament at Alexandria,

Bk. I. Ch. 9.	But why þat sche sette þe parlement in þat place?	519
	O cause þer was, for in þat same cite	
	Alle kynges of⁺ þat lond, as vsage was,	
	hadd receyued þe crowne wyth solennyte;	
	And for a costom long⁺ hold may nott brokyn be,	523
	But yf⁺ it turbel many men, þerfor' she held it þer.	
	Many lord & lady att þat parlement wer'.	525
	Anoþer cause þer was, for þe kynrode of⁺ her'	526
	had founded þis cete & refounded eke—	
	Be whom & be whos dayes, ȝe shal sone her',	
	Yf ye wyl be stylle & no man now speke	
	But I my-selue. Ȝe shal not nede to seke	530
	Mo cronycles or storyes; ȝe schal ler' of⁺ me	
	Alle þe lyne & þe lordes aftyr her' degre.	532
[fol. 11, b.] [2nd hand]	Ther was a lord sumty[m]e þat þe soudon was	533
	Of surre & of egipt, babel was hys name;	
	he beldyd alysaunder in þat same place,	
	he called it babilon, in haunsyng of hys fame,	
	þat it schuld not falle ne neuyr be lame—	537
	þis was hys wyll; & aftyr many a day	
	It was called babilon, sothly for to say,	539
	Not babilon a-lone, but babilon þe lasse,	540
	ffor differens of þe other' þat stant in þe est.	
	Who wyll owte egypt in to affryk passe,	
	Goo or ryd wheyder he wyll, þis wey is þe best.	
	þis was an othyr cause why þis gret fest	544
	Was hold in þat place: for her' ryall kyn	
	Owt of þis babell cam, boþe þe mor' & þe myn.	546
	The þird cause was þis, as seyth Athanas,	547
	Grettest of hem alle, as semyth on-to me:	
	þis same cyte in þe londe of egipt was,	
	In whech þer' reygned an-other' kyng þan he:	
	So was he called þan for diuersyte	551
	Kyng of alysaundyr a-lone, ryght for differens	
	Of þe kyng of egypt—þis is þe sentens.	553

But why that she sette the parlement in þat place? 519 *Bk. I. Ch. 9.*
Oo cavse there was, for in that same Cite
Alle kyng*is* of that lond, as vsage was,   *where the Kings of the Land were crownd,*
had receyved the crovne with solennyte;
And, for a custom longe holde may not broken be, 523
But if it turbe many men, therefore she helde it þere.
Many lord and lady at that parlement were. 525

A-nother cavse ther was, for the kynhod of hir 526 *and which her kindred had founded.*
had fovnded this Cite and refovnded it eke—
Be hom and in whos dayes, ye shal sone here,
yf ye wil be stylle and no man now speke
But I my-self. ȝe shal not nede to seke 530
Mo cronycles or storyes; ye shal lerne of me
Alle the lyne and þe lordes after her degre. 532

There was a lord somtyme þat þe sovdon was 533 *Sultan Babel built Alexandria,*
Of surre and of Egypte, babel was his name;
he byelded alisavndre in that same plas,
he called it Babilon, in haunsynge of his fame,   *and cald it 'Babylon the*
That it shuld not falle ne neu*er* be lame— 537
This was his wil; and after many a day
It was called babylon, soothly to say, 539

Not babylon allone, but babylon the lasse, 540 *Less.'*
ffor differens of other þat stant in the Est.
ho wil ovte of Egypte into affryke passe,
Goo or ryde wheder he wil, this w[e]ye is the best.
This was a-nother cavse why this grete fest 544
Was holde in that plaas: for hir ryal kyn̴
Ovte of þis babel cam, bothe the more and þe myn̴. 546

The thredde cause was this, as seyth athanas, 547
Grettest of hem alle, as semyth on-to me:
This same Cite, in the lond of Egypte was,   *It was in Egypt.*
In whiche there regned a-nother kyng þan he:
So was he called thanne for diu*er*site 551 *The king was cald 'King of Alexandria.'*
kyng of Alysavndre allone, rygh[t] for differens
Of þe kyng of Egypte—this is þe sentens. 553

Bk. I. Ch. 9.

Thys wote I well of Athanases resoñ,   554
Whech þat he makyth of þe fundacyoñ
Of þis same Alysandyr, whech oft w*yth* tresoñ
Was nye disceyuyd of many straunge nacyoñ.
But now wyll we leue all þ*a*t declaracyoñ,   558
And tell forthe of babel & of oþ*er* meñ
Whech long to þe kynred, mo þa*n* .ix. o[r] teñ.   560

Bk. I. Ch. 10.

Ca^m. x^m.

Thys same babell had a sone aftyr hym,   561
    Madagdal*us* he hyght, he was lord alsoo
Of þis babilon many ʒer'. & forth þe same kyñ
Reygned i*n* þ*a*t same place mo þa*n* on or too :
ffor hys sone hyght antioch*us*, þe story seyth soo,   565
Not antioch*us* þe grete of whech spekyth machabe,
But an-other be-fore, as ʒe schall sone se.   567

Thys antioch*us* had a soñ men cleped gorgalus,   568
A worþi ma*n* he was, of surre lord & syre.

[fol. 1ᶜ] he be-gate a sone, me*n* clepyd antioch*us* ;
And aftyr antioch*us* reygned i*n* þ*a*t empyre
hys sone seleuc*us*—he sett ryght i*n* a myr' ;   572
þe cyte me*n* clepe seleuce for hys owyñ fame,
And antyoche he beldyd i*n* hys faderes name.   574

þis is þe fyrst lyne of þis ych gorgal*us*—   575
ffor we mote turñ a-geyñ, if we truly telle.
þis same gorgale[1] ʒonger' soñ hyght mardemius,   [1] r. gorgalis
a manly ma*n* he was & of hert felle ;
Gret alysaundyr sprong of hy*m* as strem owt of welle :   579
ffor vn-to þis mardemy wedded was þis[1] fayr'   [1] r. þe
Melior', þe noble mayde, of macedonye þe ayr',   581
And of þis mardemye & meliore þe mayde   582
kam kyng phylyppe, fadyr to alysaunder' þe grete.
þus went þe secund lyne, as ou*r* aucto*ur* sayde,
Oute of gorgales yong[1] soñ—þe fyrst hat[2] we lete   585
But for a lytyll whyle ; for we wyll now trete   [1] r. yonger? [2] r. hat

This wote I weel of athanas resonı, 554 *Athanas writes of the founding of Alexandria.*
whiche that he maketh of fundacyonı
Of this same Alysaundre, whiche ofte w*yth* tresonı
Was ny disseyued of many stravnge nacyonı.
But nov wil we leue al that declaracyonı, 558
And telle foorth of Babel and of other menı
Wiche longe to the kynrede, mo than nyne or tenı. 560

Ca^m. decimu*m*. *Bk. I. Ch. 10.*

This same babel had a sone after hym, 561 *Babel's son Madagdalus succeeded him.*
Madagdalaus he hyght, he was lord also
Of þis babilonı many a yeer. and foorth þe same kyn
Regned in the same place mo thanne on or too :
ffor his sone hyght Antiochus, the story seyth soo, 565 *Then followd Antiochus I,*
Not antiochus the grete of whiche speketh Machabe,
But a-nother be-fore, as ye shal sone see. 567

This antiochus had a sone men cleped gorgalus, 568 *Gorgalus,*
A worthi manı he was, of surre lord and syre.
he be-gate a son men cleped antiochus ; *Antiochus II,*
And after þat antiochus regned in þat empyre
his sone seleucus—he set ryght in a myre ; 572 *and Seleucus.*
The cyte men clepen seleuce for his owe fame,
And Antioche he byl[d]ed in his faderis name. 574

This is þe firste lyne of þis iche gargalus— 575
ffor we mote turne a-geynı, if we trewly telle.
This same gorgale yovnger sone hight Mardemius, *Gorgalus's 2nd son Mardemius*
A manly man[1] he was and of hert felle ; ¹ overlined. 578
Grete alisavndre sprange of hym as strem ovte of welle :
ffor on-to this Mardemye wedded was þe fayre
Meliore, the noble mayde, of Macedony þe ayre, 581

And of this Mardemye and Meliore the mayde 582 *begat Philip, and he Alexander the Great,*
Kam kyng philip, fader to Alysavndre the grete.
Thus wente the secunde lyne, as oure avtour sayde,
Ovte of gorgalus yovnge sone—þe firste haue we lete
but a lytil while ; for I wyl nov trete 586

E 2

52 *Former Kings of Alexandria in Egypt.* [MS. Rawlinson.

Bk. I. Ch. 10.

Off þe woundres þat þis Alysaundyr' sowte in hys lyffe—
All hys labur' ȝet in euery mouth is ryffe. 588
he conquered þe kyng of pers whych dary hyght, 589
he toke arabe & fenice, & eke hys owyn cosyn
Antiochus, gorgalys sone, he ouyr-came be myght, [1] = wan
he whan[1] þis babylon from hym wyth gunne & engyne.
þer cessed þe name of babylon & for euyr gan lyne : 593
ffor he chaungyd it to hys, & þus he called it þan
" Alysandyr" aftyr hyme, be-cause he it wanne. 595

Ten cytes mad þis lord euen oute of þe grounde, 596
All .x. þei hafe is name, alysaundyr þei hyght ;
Too cytes he chaunged & kept hem hole & sounde,
Alysaundyr' he wolde þei schulde hyght be ryght.
In xij. ȝer' he wan þis worlde wyth ful grete myght. 600
Whan he schuld dey, he partyd hys londe on twelue,
Whech he had gouernd a-lone sumtyme hym-self. 602

To hys lordes ȝaue he hys londes for to holde ; 603
Surry & Alysaundir', ffenice & Palestyne
þat ȝafe he to seleucus, myghty man & bolde—

[fol. 12, b.] he was to þis alysaundyr of kyn ryght cosyn,
Of gorgalus bloode, as i seyde, of þe fyrst lyn, 607
At whech I þan left & now be-gynne a-geyn—
Alle þing may not be seyd at ones, as clerkys seyn. 609

Bk. I. Ch. 11.

Ca^{m.} xj^{m.}

Too & þirty ȝer' reigned seleucus þer'. 610
he had an eyr', aftyr hym kyng of þat place,
A noble man, þei called antiochus sother' ;
Twenty wyntyr' euene a-mong hem he was.
And aftyr had þe crown, þe sceptyr, & þe mace 614
hys sone, whech þei calle antiochus theos ;
he reygued .xv. ȝer'. & aftyr hym þan roos 616
A man þei call be name seleucus galericus ; 617
þer' reygned he .xx. wynter'. & þan seleucus garanne
Thre ȝer' bar' þe crown. & efte antiochus

Of þe wondres þat this alysavndre soovght in his lyef— *Bk. I. Ch. 10.*
Al his labour ȝet in euery movght is ryef. 588

he conqvered the kyng of perce whiche Dary hight, 589 who conquerd Persia,
he took arabe and fenice, and eke his owne cosyn Arabia, Phœnicia;
Antyochus, gorgalus soone, he ouere-cam be myght, [1 r. wan]
he whan[1] this babilon from hym with gvnne and engyn. took Babylon,
There cecyd the name of babilon and for euer gan lyn : 593 and changed its name to Alexandria.
ffor he chavnged it to his name, & þus he called it þanne
"Alysavndre" after hym, be-cause that he it wanne. 595

Ten citees made þis lord euene ovte of the grovnd, 596 Alexander had 12 cities
Alle ten þei haue his name, Alysaundre thei hyght; cald Alexandria.
Too Cytees he chaunged and kepte hem hool and sovnd,
Alisaundre he wold thei shulde hatte be ryght. [1 MS. lord]
In xij. yeer he wan this word[1] wyth ful grete myght. 600
Whanne he shuld deye, he parted his lond on twelue, On his death
Whiche he had gouerned a-lone somtyme hym-selue. 602

To these lordes yaue he his londys for to holde; 603
Surry and alysaundre, fenyce and palestyn he gave Syria, Alexandria, &c., to his cousin Seleucus,
That ȝaue [he] to seleucus, myghty man and bolde—
he was to þis Alisavndre of kyn ryght cosyn,
Of gorgalus blood, as I seyde, of the first lyn, 607
At wiche I thanne left and nov be-gynne a-geyn—
Alle þing may not be seyd at ones, as clerkys seyn. 609

Ca^{m.} vndecimum.   *Bk. I. Ch. 11.*

Too and thretty ȝeer regned seleucus there. 610
he had an Eyr, after hym kyng of þat plas, whose heir was Antiochus Sother:
A noble man, thei called Antiochus sothere;
Twenty wynter euene a-mong hem he was.
And after had þe crowne, the sceptre, and the mas 614
his sone, wiche thei calle antiochus theos; and his son was Antiochus Theos.
he regned there fyftene ȝeer. And after hym þan roos 616

A man thei calle be name seleuchus galericus; 617 Then came Seleuchus Callinicus,
There regned he xx wynter. and þanne seleucus garanne Seleucus Ceraunus,
Thre ȝeer bar the croun. and efte antiochus

7 *

54 Former Kings of Alexandria in Egypt. [MS. Rawlinson.

Bk. I. Ch. 11.

Wech is called þe grete; he reygned þanne
Sex & þirty wynter'—iewes ȝet' hym banne 621
ffor þe sorow þat he dede on-to her lond & hem
Whan he robbed þe temple at iherusalem. 623

The noble book of machabe wryghtyth hys dedys, 624
hys cruelnesse, hys[1] ire & hys tresoṅ eke, [1] MS. hyr
hys feyned repentauns—þer-for hys mede is
Sorow for synne: for qwan he was seke,
he askyd mercy, but not worth a leke. 628
he left a sone nye of þat same plyte,
Seleucus philophator men seyn þat he hyght; 630

he synnyd be hys doghtyr ful on-kyndely, 631
þer-for was he brent wyth þe bryght leuene;
In appollony of tyr' ȝe may rede þe storye
who many lordes wer' dede be vj. & be seuyṅ
ffor þei coude not gesse hys problemes euyṅ. 635
he reygned þer' xj. ȝer' wyth-owten any lees.
hys sone aftyr hym hyght antiochus epiphanes; 637

hys ȝeres wer' xj. & hys son hyght þus 638
Antiochus eupater'; he leued ȝer's too.
And aftyr hym sekyrly reygned demetrius;
Thre ȝer' he bar' þe crowṅ, þe story seyth soo.
Antiochus sedites kyng was þer' þoo 642
[fol. 13] Nyne ȝer' euyṅ; & aftyr hym reygned þer'
A-noþir kyng þei calle demetrius sother'. 644

Bk. I. Ch. 12.

Ca^{m.} xij^{m.}

IN hys tyme þe romaynes whon fro hym 645
Mech of hys londe, & eke þat gret cyte
Whech þat he helde, & so had all hys kyṅ,
I mene alysaundyr'; þei set þer' her' see.
þe romaynes dyd so, for he was fayṅ to flee 649
fforth in-to egypt; he held hym ryght þer'—
þus led he hys lyffe in sorow & in feer'. 651

Whiche is called the grete; he regned thanne
Sex and thretty wyntyr—iewes ȝet hym banne 621
ffor the sorwe þat he dede on-to her lond and hem
Whan he robbed the temple at Ierusalem. 623

and Antiochus the Great, who plunderd Jerusalem.

Bk. I. Ch. 11.

The noble book of Machabe wrytheth his dedys, 624
his cruelnesse, his ire and his treson eke,
his feyned repentavns—þer-for his mede is
Sorwe for synne: for whanne he was seeke,
he asked mercy, but not wurth a leeke. 628
he lefte a sone ny of the same plyght,
Seleucus philopator men seyn þat he hight; 630

Followd, Seleucus Philopator,

he synned be his doughter ful onkeendely, 631
Therefore was he brent wyth the lyght of [1] leuene;
In appolony of Tyre ȝe may rede the story   [1] overlined.
hov many lordys were ded be sexe and be seuene
ffor thei covde not gesse his problemes euene. 635
he regned there xj yeer wyth-ovtyn ony lees.
his sone after hym hight Antiochus epiphanes; 637

Antiochus Epiphanes,

his ȝeeris were eleuene. And his sone hight thus 638
Antiochus eupater; he leued ȝeeris too.

Antiochus Eupator,

And after hym sekerly regned Demetrius;
Thre yeer he bar the crovne, þe story seyth soo.

Demetrius,

Antiochus sedites kyng was there thoo 642
Nyne yeer evene; and after hym regned there
An other kyng þei called Demetrius sothere. 644

Antiochus Sidetes,

Demetrius Sother.

Ca^{m.} duodecimum.

Bk. I. Ch. 12.

IN his tyme þe Romaynys wonne fro hym 645
Meche of his lonnd, and eke the grete Citee
Wiche þat he held, and so had al his kyn,
I mene Alisavndre; thei sette þere here see.
The romaynis dede soo, for he was fayne to flee 649
fforth in to Egypte; he held hym ryght there—
Thus led he his lyef in sorwe and in fere. 651

The Romans then took Alexandria,

Bk. I. Ch. 12.	he lost all þe londes whych hys faderes wonne.	652
	ffour'-skore ȝer' euen) reygned þe romaynes þer',	
	And in þis seruage newly þus be-gunne	
	Reygned þe same kyng þe tyme of xij. ȝer'.	
	Alysaundyr', hys sone, þan dede þe crown) ber'	656
	Nyne ȝer' euyn. & þan demetrye, hys brother';	
	he reygned iiij. ȝer'. & aftyr hym an-oþir,	658
	Men calle hym in bokes antiochus griphus;	659
	he gouerned xij. ȝer' all þis forsayd londe.	
	In þᶜis iiij kynges tyme, myne auctour seyth þus,	
	All þis ilke cuntre to þe romaynes was bonde,	
	Tyll þat fortune turned so hyr honde,	663
	Whan helyus adrianus emperour' was of rome,	
	Whych weddyd hys doghtyr to on þei call phalone.	665
	þis phalon was sone on-to þe seyd demetrius:	666
	Be hym cam surry to ryght hold a-geyn),	
	And all her' subieccyon) to rome cessed þus.	
	Solaber was þe name of þe mayd, þei seyn),	
	Ryght soo hyght sche, þei þat hyr' þer' seyn)	670
	Seyn neuer swych an-oþir, þus seyd þei alle.	
	þis same phalon, summe men so hym calle,	672
	had a fulfayr' sune be þis same solaber',	673
	ȝoȝimus he hyght, kyng aftyr hys fadyr' he was.	
	And archenon, & archibelon reygned also þer';	
	þan aftyr antigonus, & þan cam claudace—	
	Sune aftyr fadyr', all reygned in þat place.	677
	þan aftyr borus, ryght þus haf I founde.	
[fol. 13, b.] [4th hand]	And þanne a-geyn claudace called þe secunde.	679
	þis same claudace, costus fadyr was,	680
	And þis same costus fadyr to kateryne.	
	Here may ȝe se of what men & of what place	
	Cam þis woman, þis lady, þis virgyne;	
	Here is[1] it schewyd hooly all þe lyne— [1] overlined.	684
	þus I be-hyte ȝou þat I schuld doo.	
	In þis reknyng myne auctour & I are too:	686

he loste alle þe londes wiche hys faderis wonne. 652
ffovre-skore ȝeer evene regned the romaynys there,
And [in] þis servage þus newely be-gonne
Regned þe same kyng the tyme of xij. ȝeere.
Alysavndre, hys sone, thanne dede þe crovne bere 656
Nyne yeer euene. And thanne demetrie, his brother;
he regned iiij. ȝeer. And after hym a-nother, 658

Men calle hym in bookis Antiochus Griphus; 659
he gouer[n]ed xij. ȝeer al this forseyd lond.
In this .iiij. kyngis tyme, myn Auctour seyth thus,
Alle þis eke contre to þe romaynis was bond,
Til þat fortune turned soo her hond, 663
Whan helyus Adryanus emperour was of rome,
Wiche weddyd his doughter to oon þei calle phalone. 665

This phalon was sone on-to þe seyd demetrius: 666
Be hym cam surry to ryght hold a-geyn,
And alle her subiectyon to rome cesyd thus.
Solaber was þe name of the mayde, þei seyn,
Right soo hyght she, þei that her þer seen 670
Seen neuer swiche a-nother, thus seyde thei alle.
This same phalon, sum men soo hym calle, 672

had a ful fayr sone be this same solaber, 673
Zoȝymus he hyght, kyng after his fader he was.
And Archenon, and Archibelon regned also ther;
Thanne after Antygonus, and þanne¹ cam claudas—
Sone after fadyr, alle regned in that plas. ¹ MS. þanned 677
Thanne after borus, ryght þus haue I founde.
And thanne a-geyn claudas called the secunde. 679

This same claudas, Costus fadir was, 680
And this same Costus fadyr to Kataryne.
here may ye see of what men and of what plas
Cam this woman, þis lady, this virgyne;
heere is shewyd holy al the lyne— 684
Thus I be-hight ȝou þat I shuld doo.
In this reknyng, myn auctour and I arn too: 686

marginalia:
652 Bk. I. Ch. 12. and kept it 80 years.
656 Its kings were Alexander, Demetrius,
659 Antiochus Grypus,
665 Phalon,
673 Zozymus, Archenon, Archibelon, Antigonus, Claudas I,
677 Borus,
679 Claudas II,
680 and then Costus, Katharine's Father.
684 In this line of kings I often differ from my author.

Bk. I. Ch. 12.	ffor he acordeth not wyt3 cronicles þat ben olde,	687
	But diuersyth from hem, & þat in many thyngis.	
	þere he acordyth, þer I hym hold;	
	And where he diuersyth in ordre of þeis kyngis,	
	I leue hym, & to oder mennys rekenyngis	691
	I 3eue more credens whech be-fore hym & me	
	Sette alle þese men in ordre & degre.	693
	Butte men wyll sey now & happely replye:	694
	"what menyth þis lyne & þis rehersayle,	
	To rekene so many men, & to multiplye	
	Noumbres and 3erys, whech may not a-vayle?	
	And eke us thynkyth, it doth sumwhat fayle,	698
	ffor, þow þei wer' men of grete lordschype,	
	þe kynrod of schrewys to godd is no worchepe."	700
	I answere here-to as do[th] seynt Ierome:	701
	"Crist cam of schrewys," he seyth, "for þis skylle,	
	þe principall cause qwy to þis werld he come:	
	To corect synneris, þat was his wylle—"	
	ffor many men þat synfull wer' & ille	705
	Are in his genelogie, 3e may hem þer' fynde.	
	My lady Kateryne stante in þis¹ same kynde. ¹ r. þe	707

Bk. I. Ch. 13.	Ca^m. 13^m.	
	Now to telle forth euen) as I fyrst sayde,	708
	þe lordys are come whech clepyd were.	
	A3ens þe parlement þe cite is arayd	
	With plente of vitayle and all odyr gere;	
	Men lakked ryth nowt þat wer' logged þere,	712
	Gret chepe had þei, all-maner vitayle—	
	It is stuffyd so be reson) it may not fayle.	714
	þe riall lordys wyt3 baron) & bacheler	715
	Are com now þedyr to do here servyse,	
[fol. 14]	Byschopis & clerkys to-gedyr in-fere,	
	þei wyll now schew here wyttys wyse—	
	þei schall haue nede or þat þei ryse;	719

MS. Arundel.] *The Parliament at Alexandria.* 59

ffor he a-cordeth not wyth cronyclys tho ben olde, 687 *Bk. I. Ch.* 12.
But diuerseth fro hem, and þat in many thyngis.
There he a-cordeth, ther I hym holde;
And where he diuerseth in ordre of these kyngis,
I leve hem,[1] and to other mennes rekenyngis [1] r. him 691
I ʒeve more credens whiche be-fore hym and me
Sette alle these men in ordre and degre. 693

But men wil sey nowe, and haply replye: 694 And I've told you Katharine's genealogy,
"What meneth this lyne in this rehersayle,
To rekne so many men, and to multiplie
Noumbres and ʒeerys, whiche may not a-vayle?
And eke thenketh vs, it dooth sumwhat fayle, 698
ffor, thou thei where men of grete lordshep,
The kynred of shrewys to god is no wurshep." 700

I answere her-to as dooth seynt Ierom: 701 to show you that as Christ came from shrews,
"Crist cam of shrewes," he seyth, "for this skyl,
The pryncypal cavse whi to this world he com:
To correcte synneris, þat was his wyll—"
ffor many men that synful were and ill 705
Arn in his genealogie, ye may hem þere[1] fynde. [1] MS. þerre
My lady Kataryn stant in þe same kynde. 707 so did St. Katharine.

Ca^m. 13^m. *Bk. I. Ch.* 13.

Now to telle foorth euene as I first sayde, 708
The lordes arn come wiche cleped where.
Aʒens the parlement the Cite is arayde Alexandria is well victuald for the Parliament.
With plente of vitaill and alle other gere;
Men lakked ryght nought þat were lodged there, 712
Grete chepe had þei, all maner of vitaile—
It is stuffed so be reson þat it may not fayle. 714

The ryal lordes with Barouns and Bachelere 715
Arn come nov thedir to don hir seruyse,
Bysshoppys and clerkys to-gedere in-fere,
Thei wil nov shewe her wyttys wyse—
Thei shal haue nede or than þei ryse; 719

Summe lordys are come eke homage to make,
And ladys many ryth for þe qwenys sake. 721
Þis mayde is crownyd, wyth aH þe observawns 722
Whech servyd þat tyme in stede of þe masse ;
Þei prayd to iupiter He schuld here avauns,
And to aH þe goddys, both more an lasse—
Þer was no god whech þei lete þoo passe ; 726
Þe lordys swore aH who þat þei schuld
Here servyse euyr sewe & here sutes holde. 728

Þanne be-gunne þe festes, I trow, gret I-now, 729
As in þat cuntre custome was þanne.
To lord & to lady, & to pouert lowe,
ffuH foyson was þere, to eueri man, 732
Many mo deyntys þan I rehers can ;   [1] om.; but so in MSS. Ar. 396 and 168. hale = tent.
Euery man had plente in hale [& in halle] ;[1]
Þoo men þat seruyd it, nedyd not hem to calle. 735

Swech rewle & ordinauns was þere I-had, 736
Þere was no ȝate warnyd to no-maner wyte,
But, þat euery man schuld be ryth glad,
Þei were kept opyn both day & nyth,
Þe bordes euer cured & þe mete dyth ; 740
whan on had his mele, in cam an-odyr;
Of syluyr wesseH þer was many a fothir. 742

No place was voyd, neydyr parlour nor chaumbyr, 743
But aH wer þei fuH of women or of[1] men ; [1] overlined.
Þe grete paleys þat stante at Alisaundyr,
It was fuH of puple, no man seyd "go hen !"
Saue reuerens was had ; lordes here ix her ten 747
Þus kept here astate ; þe cete eke aH-a-bowte
Was ffuH of gentylys wyth-inne & wyth-owte. 749

Lordes & ladyes þat wer þer of here kynne, 750
On-to þat feste come both on & odyr
And aH wer þei loggyd in fuH riaH Ine—
Sume wer of here fadyrs syde, summe wer of her modyr.
Of curtesye & gentylnesse, game & non othyr 754

MS. Arundel.] *Katharine's Coronation in Alexandria.* 61

Some lordes arn) come eke homage to make,
And ladyes many ryght for the qvenes sake. 721
 This mayde is corovned, wyth alle the observaunce 722 Katharine is crownd.
whic[h]e serued at þat tyme in stede of the masse;
Thei preyden) to Iubiter he shulde hir avaunce,
And to alle the goddes, bothe more and lasse—
Ther was non) god wiche thei do lete passe; 726
The lordes sworn) alle how þat thei shulde
hir scruyse euer sewe and hir sevtes holde. 728

 Thanne be-govnne the festis, I trowe, grete I-nowe, 729 Feasts are held.
As in þat contre custom was thanne.
To lord and to lady, and to povert lowe,[1] [1] MS. bowe
fful foyson was there, on-to euery manne,
Many mo deyntes þan) I rehers canne; 733
Euery man) had plente in hale and in halle;
Tho men) þat sewed[1] it, neded not hem) to calle. [1] r. served

 Swiche reule and ordynavnce was there I-hadde, 736
There was no yate warned to ony maner of whyght, All the gates are open.
But, that euery man shulde be ryght gladde,
Thei were kepte open bothe day and nyght,
The boordes euere cured and the mete dyght; 740
Whanne oon) had his meel, in can) an other;
Of siluer vessel ther was many a fother. 742

 No place was[1] voide, neyther parlovr ne chavnbre, 743
but alle were þei ful of men) and women); [1] overlined.
The grete paleys þat stant at Alysavndre, The Palace is full of folk.
It was ful of peple, no man) seyde "go hen)!"
Save reverens was had of lordes; here ix. here .x. 747
Thus kepte her astate; þe Cytee eke al a-bovte
Was ful of gentyllis wyth-inne and wyht-ovte. 749

 Lordes and ladyes þat were there of hir kyn) 750 Katharine's kin are royally lodgd.
And to þat feste com bothe oon) and other,
Also were thei lodged in ful ryaH In—
Some were of hir faderis syde, some were of hir moder.
Of curtesye and gentilnesse, game and noon) other 754

[fol. 14, b.]
[2nd hand]

Was þan her' carpyng, sauc summe spoke of loue;
Euery man spak of þing whech was to hys be-houe. 756

Iustys wer' þer', & þoo wyth þe best; 757
Sume had þe bettyr & sume had þe werr';
þe grete theatyr þer' had ful lytyll rest:
Euyr was þer fytyng, but þer was no werre;
Many noble men whech wer' come fro ferre, 761
In þat same place wer' asayd ych oon
As well in wrestyllyng as puttyng at þe ston. 763

And aftyr all þis is endyd & eke I-don, 764
Iustis, reuell[is] & festes gune to slake,
þei toke her' leue homward for to goon.
But ȝet or þei fully had her leue I-take,
Ech lord whech had þer' any lady & make, 768
Was ȝoue to courser's, of whech þe on
Was blak as cole, þe other' wythe as bon, 770

Wyth sadyll & brydyll of gold & of sylke; 771
Many moo rewardes eke þan I can now seye;
Sume wer' ȝoue mantellis wyght as þe mylk,
On whech wer' many a broche & many a beye.
þus ryd þei homwarde forth in her' wey; 775
þer' is[1] noght ellys now but "farwell & goo! [1] MS. it
I pray god be wyth ȝow." þus is þe parlement doo. 777

Bk. I. Ch. 14.   Ca^m. 14^m.

THys lady, as þe story euen forth telleth, 778
kepyth her' chambyr' & holdyth hyr' þus inne,
Wyth hyr modyr þe qwen as ȝet sche dwellyth;
her' bokes for to loke on can sche noght blyne—
Who-so-euyr lett hyr, he dothe full gret synne! 782
To offende hys lady, what wene ȝe it is?
þer was no man þat tyme þat durst do thys. 784

It was oonly hyr' ioye [&] all hyr' entent, 785
ffor hyr' hert þat tyme was set to nowt elles—
fful hye honour' þer'-by aftyrward sche hente!

Coronation Festivities and Gifts.

Was þanne her carpynge, saue some spoke of love; *Bk. I. Ch. 13.*
Euery maṇ spak of thyng wiche was to his be-ove. 756

Iustes were there, and tho with the beste; 757 *Jousts are held,*
Some hadde the bether and some were of herre (!);[1]
The grete Theatre ther had ful lytel reste: [1] w. o. h. on erasure.
Euere was there fytynge, but there was no werre!
Many noble meṇ whyche were come fro ferre, 761
In that same place were a-sayde iche ooṇ
As weel in wrestlyng as puttyng at the stooṇ. 763 *and wrestlings.*

And after[1] al thys is ended and eke I-dooṇ, [1] overlined.
Iustes, reuelle and festes gonne to slake,
Thei take her leve homward for to gooṇ.
But ȝet er thei fully [had] her leve I-take,
Eche lord wiche had there ony lady or make, 768
Was yove too courseris, of wiche the ooṇ *Coursers are given to the*
Was blak as cole, the other whyt as booṇ, 770 *guests,*

Wyth sadeH and brydeH of gold and of silk; 771 *with other presents.*
Many mo rewardys eke þaṇ I can now seye:
Some were yove Mantyllis white as the mylk,
On whiche were many a broche and many a beye.
Thus ryde thei homward forthe in her wey; 775
There is not ellis now but "fare wel and goo!
I prey god be with yov!" thus his the parlement doo. 777

Ca. 14.
Bk. I. Ch. 14.

This lady, as þe story euene foorth telleth, 778
Keept hir chavnbre and holdyth hir thus Inne,
Wyth hir moder the qveen as ȝet she dwelleth; *Katharine lives with her*
hir bookes for to looke on can[1] she not blynne— [1] MS. canse *Mother,*
ho-so-euere lette hir, he dooth grete synne! 782
To offende his lady, what wene ye he is?
Ther was no maṇ þat tyme that durste doo this. 784

It was oonly hir ioye and alle hir entent, 785
ffor hir herte þat tyme was sette to novght ellis—
fful high honour therby afterward she hent!

Bk. I. Ch. 14. Bothe wyght & wysdome owte of hyr' hert welles,
Euyn as þe streme rennyth fro þe welles. 789
Swych fayr' frute in stodye dyd sche fynde,
Wyth besy conceytes whech sche had of kynde. 791

Ther' was noo wyght þat in hyr' presence 792
[fol. 15] Durst onys touch of ony ille dede;
And if he dyd, he had hyr offens,
ffor euyr-mor he coude not aftyr spede;
As for to be hyr seruaunde, þat is no drede, 796
Sche hated not þe persone, but only þe synne;
Of uertuous spech coude sche not blynne. 798

Ther' was neuer wrong founde in þat may, 799
þe cors of hyr couernauns¹ was euer so clene, ¹ r. gouernauns
Boþe pryuy & aperte, at euery a-say,
Stedfast & stable was euer þis qwene;
Sche was a very seynt, truly, as I wene, 803
þow sche wer' not baptiȝed—so was cornelius;
hys prayer' was herde, scriptur' seyth þus, 805
Of our' lorde godd, or he baptiȝed wer', 806
And þer-for was Petyr sent vnt-to hym
þe articles of þe feyth hym for to ler';
he had feyth be-for, but it was dyme,
he was made to cryst a ful ryght lyme; 810
hys feyth was not cause of hys good werkes,
But hys werkes causyd feyth, þus seye þese clerkes. 812

Thys same lady eke, thow sche not baptiȝed wer', 813
Sche hauntyd holy werkys be steryng of þe spryght,
Whech made hyr of synne for to hafe fere
And to loue vertu, boþe day & nyght.
þe soule nedyth uertu as mech as yȝe lyght— 817
þis wote þei well þat feel experyens.
þis was þe cause þat her' noble presence 819
Was noryscher' of vertu & qwencher' of vyce. 820
ffor whan sche coud a-spye any mysdrawte
Of man or of woman, þat þei wer' nyce,

Bothe wit and wysdam oute of hir hert swelles (!),
Euene as [þe] strem renneth fro the welles. 789
Swiche fayr frute in stody dede she fynde,
Wyth besy conseytis wiche she hadde of kynde. 791

There was no wyght that in hir presens 792
Durste oones tovche of ony ille dede;
And if he dede, he had hir offens,
ffor euere-more he covde not after speede;
As for to be hir seruaunt, þat is no drede, 796
She hated not the persone, but oonly the synne;
Of vertuous speche covde she not blynne. 798

There was neuere wrong fovnde in þat may, 799
The cors of hir gouernavns was euere so clene,
Bothe preuy and apert, at euery assay,
Stedefast and stable was euere þis qveene;
She was a very seynt, trewely, as I weene, 803
Thov she were not baptysed—so was Cornelius;
his preyere was herd, scrypture seith thus, 805

Of oure lord god, er he baptised were. 806
And þerfore was petir sent on-to hym
The Articules of the feyth hym for to lere;
he had feyth be-fore, but it was dym,
he was made to cryst a ful ryght lym; 810
his feyth was not cavse of his good werkys,
but his werkys caused feith, thus seyn these clerkys. 812

This same lady eke, þovgh she not baptised were, 813
She havnted hooly werkys be strengthe (!) of þe spyryt,
Wiche made hir of synne for to haue fere
And to love vertu, bothe daye and nyght.
The sovle nedeth vertu as moche as the hyӡe lyght— 817
This wote þei weel that feele experiens.
This was the cavse that hir noble presens 819

Was norysshere of vertu and quenchere of vice. 820
ffor whanne she covde aspye ony mysdraught
Of man or of woman, that thei were nyce,

Bk. I. Ch. 14.

and studies.

No ill deed is spoken of to her.

No wrong is ever found in her.

Katharine does holy works, and fears sin.

Bk. I. Ch. 14.

ffor fer' or for lofe wold sche leue nawte,
But soone schuld þei fulwysyly be tawte; 824
" It may not be þus," sche sayd, " it is not honest;
A man, but he be reulyde, he is but a beest. 826

" What wene ȝe now whan ȝe trespace? 827
þow I not a-spye ȝow, I sey ȝow trulye,
þer is oon a-boue þat loketh on our' face,
And on all þe membrys of our' bodye;

[fol. 15, b.]
[4th hand]

Iff he ony fowle dede may in vs aspye, 831
He deynyth[1] our' seruyse—þis is my preue; [1] = dedeynyth
Sey clerkys qwat þei wyll, þus I be-leue. 833

" ffor wele I wote, a-boue Iupiter and alle 834
Is a mayster-rewler, & eterne he is; [1] euyr on the margin.
Vp-on þis werld qwat-so-euyr[1] schall be-falle,[2] [2] r. falle
ffalle qwan it schalle, he is euyr in blysse.
And þei þat loue vertu, schall not want, I-wysse, 838
Neuyr his gode lordschep; he may, as it is skylle,
Make goddes of men, qwan þat euyr he wylle." 840

þus wold sche sey, þat noble lady dere, 841
On-to her' servauntes, and hem all exhorte;
Sche was homly as þow sche wer' here fere.
þe dredfull & sekely wold sche coumfort;
Mery & glad was sche at eueri disport, 845
Sad eke þer-to qwan sche schuld sad be,
Godely of her' spech, of here expens fre. 847

Bk. I. Ch. 15.

Ca^m. 15^m.

What is a lond qwan it hath now hed? 848
þe lawes are not kept, þe lond desolate,
þe hertes hangyng and heuy as lede,
þe comonys grutchyng & euer at þe bate,[1] [1] r. debate
þere is kept non rewle, kept now astate. 852
þus seyde þe puple of surry alle-aboute,
" Our' kyng is now ded, oure lyth is nye owte. 854

ffor feer or for loue wulde she leue nawght,
But sone shuld þei ful wysly be taught ; 824
" It may not be þus," she seyde, " it is nought honeste ;
A man, but he be reuled, he is but a beeste. 826

She corrects all misdoing,

" What wene 3e now whan 3e trespace ? 827
Though I not aspye 3ov, I sey yow trewelye,
There is oon[1] a-bove þat looketh in oure face, [1] overlined.
And on alle the membris of oure bodye ;
If he ony fovlhed may in vs aspye, 831
he deyneth oure seruyse—this is my precue ;
Sey clerkys what they woH, thus I be-leue. 833

" ffor weel I wot, a-bove Iubiter and alle 834
Is a mayster-revlere, and eterne he is ;
Vp-on this world what-so-euere shal falle,
ffalle whan it shal, he is euere in blys.
And þei þat loue vertu shul not wante, I-wys, 838
Sithe of[1] his good lordshipe he may, as it is skyl, [1] overl.
Make goddys of men, whanne-so-euere he wyl." 840

saying that above Jupiter is a Ruler in eternal bliss.

Thus wolde she seyn, that noble lady deere, 841
On-to hir servantes, and hem alle exorte ;
She was homly as þough she were her feere.
The dreedful and seekly wolde she conforte,
Mery and glad was she at euery disporte, 845
Sad eke þer-to whan she shuld sad be,
Goodly of hir speche, of hyr expens fre. 847

Katharine comforts the humble and sick.

Ca^m. 15^m.   Bk. I. Ch. 15.

What is a lond whan it hath non hed ? 848
The lawes arn not kepte, the lond is desolate,
The hertys hangyng as heuy as leed,
The commouns grutchynge and euere at debate, 851
There is kepte no revle,[1] ne kepte noon astate. [1] orig. rewle
Thus seyde the peple of surry al a-bovte,
" Oure kyng is now ded, oure lyght is ny ovte. 854

The Syrian folk

"Oþir londys spoyle vs, & þat wyth-oute mercy,   855
We mote nede suffyr, we may now odyr doo;
þow we speke & calle and for help cry,
þer is no man gladly wyll cum vs to.
We haue allewey thoutȝ þat it schuld be so—   859
Wyth-owte a kyng how schuld a cuntre stand?
We haue lost for euyr oure name & oure land.   861

"We haue a qwen, sche comyth among no men,   862
Sche loueth not ellys but bokys & scole;
late all our' enmys in lond ryde or ren,
Sche is euer in stody and euermore sole.
þis wille turne vs all to wrake & to dole!   866
But had sche a lord, ȝit all mythe be wele.
O þou blynd fortune, how turnyst þow þi wheel!   868

"Now hye, now lowe; now he þat was a-boue   869
lyght low be-nethe, in car' & myschef eke,
And he þat supposyd to conqwer' now hys[1] loue,   [1] = ys
he schall noght haf hyr' of all þis next weke;
Sumtyme be we heyle, sume-tyme be we seke.   873
O very onsekyrnesse, o chaungand & variable!
þou werdly lyffe, for euyr art þou vn-stable!   875

"Who schall þis londe wyth-oute kyng now stande?   876
It was neuyr seyn ȝet þat þe sarsynrye
Was left a-lone vn-to a wommanes hande.
Sche must be weddyd, þis mayd, & þat in hye,
On-to sume kyng—our' lond may þus not lye.   880
ffy vp-on rychesse, but if þei worchep doo
To man þat weldyth hem—for þei ar mad þer-too.   882

"We schall far' ellys as þeise negardes doo,   883
ley vp her' gold & euyr wyll þei spare,
In all her' lyffe þei may not tend þer-too
To hafe any myrthe or ony welfare;
Ryght euyn þus now are we lyke to fare,   887
We schul haf rychesse & it schal do noo goode.
Godd forbede eke þat þis ryall blode   889

MS. Arundel.] *Katharine's folk want her to wed.* 69

"Other londis spoyle vs, and that wyth-ovte mercy, 855   Bk. I. Ch. 15.
We mote nedes suffer, we may now other doo;
Though we speke, and calle, and for help cry,
Ther is no man gladly wil come vs too.
We haue alwey thought þat it shuld be soo— 859
Wythoute¹ a kyng hov shulde a contre stonde?   ¹ oute overl.   grumble at having no
We haue lost for euere the name of oure londe.   861   King,

"We haue a qveen, she cometh a-mong no men, 862   but only a Queen, who
She loveth not ellis but bookys and scole;   loves books.
Lete alle oure enemys in londe ryde or ren,
She is euere in stody and euere-more soole.
This wil turne vs alle to wrake and to doole! 866
But had she a lord, yet al myght be wel.   She ought to marry.
O þou blynde fortune, how turnest þou þi¹ whel!   ¹ MS. þe

"Now hy, now lowe; now he þat was a-bove 869
Lyeth low be-nethe, in care and myschef eke,
And he þat supposed to conquere now is loue,
he shal not haue here of al þis nexte weke;   The Syrian folk say
Somtyme we be heyl, somtyme we be seeke. 873
O very onsekernesse, o chaunged (!) and varyable!
Thou worldly lyf, for euere art þou onstable! 875

"how shal þis lond wyth-ovte kyng now stande? 876
It was neuere seen ʒet þat þe sarsynrye
Was left allone on-to womans hande.
She must be wedded, þis mayde, and þat in hie,   that Katharine must
On-to som kyng—oure lond may þus not lye. 880   wed some King.
ffy vp-on rychesse, but if þei wurshep doo
To man þat weldeth hem—for þei arn made þer-too. 882

"We shul fare elles as these nygardes doo, 883
ley vp here gold and [euyr] whil¹ thei spare,   ¹ r. wil
In al her lyue þei may not tende þer-too 885
To haue oo myrthe or ony weelfare;   ¹ a word (nov?) erased before arn)
Ryght euene thus arn¹ we lykly to be brought in care (!),
We shul haue rychesse and it shal do no good.
God forbede eke þat this ryal blood 889

8 *

"Of our noble kyng schuld cesse þus in þis mayde! 890
We wyll require hyr on all-maner wyse
ffor to be wedded"—þus þe puple sayd;
"þer is noo reule in lorde ne in iustyse,
þei sett þe schyer, þe cessyons & þe cyse 894
Ryght as hem lyst; will for reson goth now—
þis gouernauns is no-thyng vn-to our prowe. 896

"And if we to batayle schuld vs enbrace, 897
Who schuld lede vs, who schall be our gyde?
A woman-kende neuyr ȝet able was
To reule a puple þat is so grete & wyde,
To sette þe standard þe wengys on þe syde; 901
And if we chese to captayn any oþer[1] lorde, [1] to be om.
Enuye & rancur wyll cause sone dyscorde." 903

Thys was her lay thorow-owte all þe londe, 904
"Why is our qwen þus long wyth-owte a kynge?"
Boþe hye & lowe all had þis on honde,
"Why is see vn-weddyd, þis ȝung, þis fayr thynge?
Sche is full wyse, sche is full lykyng, 908
Sche is ful able a husbond for to haue:
Sche mote so nedys, yf' sche wylle us saue." 910

Vp-on þis mater, euene wyth a comon asent, 911
Thei made a gaderyng wyth-oute autorite.
ffor serteyn lordes ryth sone haue þei sent,
That þei shal come þe common[1] profyth to se. [1] MS. comōn
Among hem alle þis was þan her decre: 915
Vp-on þis mater a lettir wylle þei wryte,
In most goodly wyse þei wyll þat lettir endyte, 917

In whech þei shal on-to her lady þe qwen 918
And to her moder, whech is her lady eke,
Wryte & pray þat þei wyl to hem seen,
As þei be ladies both mercyful & meke,
Thei suffyr no mor þe lordes þus of greke 922
Ouyr-ryde hem so, it was not þe old gyse.
The lettir, certeyn, was wrytyn in þis wyse: 924

"Of oure noble kyng shuld cece[1] thus in þis mayde! 890
We wyl requyre hir on aH-maner wyse
ffor to be wedded,"—thus þe peple sayde;
"Ther is no revle in lord ne in Iustyse,
They sette the shire, þe cessyons and the Cyse 894
Ryght as hem lest; wiH for resoun gooth now—
This gouernaunce is no-thing to oure prow. 896

"And if we to batayle shulde vs enbraas, 897
ho shal lede vs, ho shal be oure gyde?
A woman-keende neuere ȝet able waas
To reule a peple that is [so] gret and wyde,
To sette þe standard the wyngis on the syde; 901
And if we chese to oure captayn ony lord,
Envye and rancovr wil cause sone discord." 903

This was her lay thurgh-oute al the land, 904
"Whi his oure qveen thus longe wyth-oten a kyng?"
Boþe hey and lowe al had þis on hand, [1] MS. yovⁿge
"Why is she on-wedded, þis yovnge,[1] this fayre thyng?
She is ful wys, she is ful lykyng, 908
She is ful able an housbond for to haue:
She mote so nedes, if she wil vs saue." 910

Vp-on this mater, euene wyth a comon assent, 911
Thei made a gaderyng wyth-oten autorite.
ffor certeyn lordes ryght soone haue þei sent,
That þei shul come the comon profyte to see.
A-mong hem alle þis was thanne her decree: 915
Vp-on this mateer a lettere wil thei wryte,
In moost goodly wyse þei wil þat lettere endyte, 917

In whiche þei shal on-to her lady the qveen 918
And to hir moder, whiche is her lady eke,
Wryte and pray þat þei wil to hem seen,
As thei be ladyes mercyful and meke,
Thei suffre no more the lordis thus of greke 922
Ouere-ride hem soo, it was not the olde gyse.
The lettere, certeyn, was wreten in this wise: 924

[1] orig. cese

They want her father Costus's line continued,

and a Chief to lead them in battle.

The Syrians say that Katharine must get a Husband.

They resolve to write a Letter about

it to her and her Mother.

Ca^m. 16^m.

"On-to our' ladyes, þe elder & þe ȝonge,　925
Be it now knowe þat þorow alł surry-lond
Yt is seyd & spoke ny of' euery tonge,
þat þei wer' neuer sd lykly to be bonde
To oþer londes wheche haue þe hyer hond,　929
As þei ar' now. wherfor' to-gyder' þei crye
On-to yow, ladyes, þat ȝe wylł haue mercye　931

"Vp-on ȝour' men, vp-on ȝour' lordes eke :　932
þei maynot lyue but þei defended be.
Ȝour' hertys be so petouse & so meke,
Ȝe wyl not lete þis mater' slyde, parde.
What is a lord but yf' he haue mene ?　936
What is a puple but yf' þei haue a lord ?
loke euery kyngdam þorow-out alł þis world,[1]　[1] r. worl　938

"But yf' þei haue a man þat dar' wele fyte,　939
Thei ar' put vnder. it was not sene or[1] now　[1] orig. er
That surre & cipre, & þat ylde þat hyte
Cande þe rych, whech hath a see ful rowe,
Shuld be þus kyngles. to god we make a vowe,　943
[fol. 17]
[4th hand] We may not lyue þus long in rest & pes.
Of clamoure & cry wylł we neuer I-ses,　945

"But euer be-seke ȝou, as oure ladyes dere,　946
Ȝe wyl be gouernyd & werk be counsayle ;
Thynk' ȝe be to vs both leef & dere,　[1] overlined.
And þink' our' seruyse may ȝet[1] sumwhat a-vayle ;
Lete sum pete owt of ȝour' hertys hayle,　950
Suffyr ȝour' puple haue sum of her' desyre !
This was þe losse certayn) of men of tyre,　952

"Thei had no kyng, þerfor þei had no grace ;　953
Whan appolony was ded, fro hem passed & goo,
Euery man as þer his owe mayster was.
God forbede for euyr þat it were so
In surre-lond ! for þan were it vn-do.　957

MS. Arundel.] *The Petition to Katharine to marry.*

Ca^{m.} 16^{m.}

"Oon-to oure ladies, the oldere and the yov[n]ge,   925   *The Letter.*
be it now knowe þat thurgh al surry-lond
It is seyd and spoke ny of euery tovnge,
That thei were neuere so lykly to be bond   'Syria was never so
To other londes whiche han the heyere hond,   929   likely to be subjugated.
As thei arn now. wherefore to-gedir þei crye
On-to yov, ladyes, that ye wil haue mercye   931

"Vp-on ȝour men, vp-on ȝour lordes eke :   932   We Syrians
Thei may not lyve but þei defended be.
Yovre hertes ben so pytous and so meke,
Ye wil not lete þis mater slyd, hope we (!).
What is a lord but if he haue mene ?   936   want a Lord
What is a peple but if he haue a lord?
Loke euery kyngdam thurgh-ovte al þe word,   938

"But if thei haue a man that dar weel fyte,   939   to fight for us.
Thei arn put vnder. it was not seen er now
That surry and Cypre, and þat ylde¹ þat hyghte   ¹ orig. hylde   Syria, Cyprus, and
Cande the ryche, þat hath a see ful row,   Candia are kingless.
Shulde be thus kyngeles. to god we make a vow,   943
We may not lyve thus longe in reste and pees.
Off clamour and Cry wil not we sees,   945

"But euere be-seeke you, as oure ladyes, now heere (!),
Ȝe wil be gouerned and werke be counsayle ;   947
Thenketh ye be to vs bothe leef and dere,
And thenketh oure seruyse may yet somwhat avayle ;
Lete som pyte ovte of your hertys hayle,   950
Suffre yovre peple to haue somwhat of her desyre !
This was the losse certeyn of men of Tyre,   952

"Thei had no kyng, therefore thei had no grace ;   953   When Tyre lost Appolonius, the
Whan appolony was ded, fro hem passed and goo,   land was in anarchy.
Euery man as there his owne mayster wace.
God forbeede that euere it were soo
In surre-lond ! for thanne were it vndoo.   957

Bk. I. Ch. 16. It was neuer sene forsoth, ne neuyr schall be;
And if it wer', far'-wele þan¹ felicite! ¹ overlined. 959

"This we desyre now, schortly for to telle, 960
And þus desyrith all þe lond be-dene,
þis is conclusion of all our' gret counselle:
That oure ȝong lady mote nede weddyd bene.
Late here haue choys, sche is wyse, we wene; 964
Chois hath sche, for many on wold her' haue.
Deliuer þis mater, so god ȝour' soulys saue. 966

"This thing is all þat we wylle sey as now. 967
We aske a answere, and þat in hasty wyse.
We pray to god, to whom we alle mote bowe,
He sette ȝow soo and lede in swech a gyse,
That ryth to-morow, or ȝe owt of bed ryse, 971
And er¹ ȝe come owte in-to þe halle, ¹ corr. to or?
That ȝe desyre as we desyre now alle." 973

Bk. I. Ch. 17.   Caᵐ· 17ᵐ·

The qwene answeryd & wrot ryght¹ þus ageyn, ¹ overl.
Sche seyd, þis thyng all-gatys moste be do; 975
To lyue a-lone in stody, it was neuer seyn
That ony lady ony tyme dyd so.
Therfor her' wylle is fully sette þer-to 978
That her' dowter, qwen of þat empyre,
Schall be weddyd hastyly to sum syre. 980

[fol. 17, b.] And vp-on þis her' letter hath she sent 981
[1st hand] Ryth in þis forme & in þis-maner style:¹ ¹ MS. stylle
"The qween of' surry, of' cypre þat was brent',
Of' candy eke lady & of' many a myle,
Wyffe on-to costus whech but a lytyle whyle 985
Is passyd & ded, on-to her' puple she seyth:
She a-lowetȝ ful wele her' manhode & her' feyth; 987

"Sche wyl as þei wyll, & hath do many a day, 988
þat her' douter on-to sum kyng' shuld be
Maryed or wedded; she seyd ȝet neuer nay,

It was neuere seen for sooth, ne neuere shal bee ;
And if it were, farwel felycyte ! 959

"This we desyre now, shortly for to telle, 960
And thus desyreth al the lond be-dene,
This is the conclusyon of oure grete counselle :
That oure ȝounge lady mote nede wedded bene.
lete her haue choys, she is wis, we wene ; 964
Chois hath she, for many on wolde hir haue.
Delyuere this mater, so god ȝoure sovlys saue. 966

"This þyng is al[1] that we wil sey now. [1] orig now al 967
We aske an answere, and that in hasty wyse.
We pray to god, to whom we alle mote bow,
he sette ȝow soo and lede in swiche a gyse,
That right to-morwe, er ȝe ovte of your bed ryse, 971
And er ȝe come ovte in to þe halle,
That ye desyre as[1] we desire nov alle." [1] overlined. 973

Ca^{m.} 17^{m.}

The qveen answerde and wrot ryght þus ageyn, 974
She seyde, " this þyng algates mote be doo ;
To leue allone in stody, it was neuer seyn
That ony lady ony tyme dede soo."
Therfore hir wil is fully seet þere-too 978
That hir dovghter, queen of that empyre,
Shal be wedded hastyly to som grete syre. 980

And vp-on this hir letter hath she sent 981
Ryght in this foorme and in this-maner-stile :
"The qveen of surry, of Cypre þat was brent,
Of Candy eke lady and of many a myle,
Wyf on-to Costus whiche but a lytyl while 985
Is passed and ded, on-to hir peple seyth :
She alloweth ful weel her manhod and her feyth ; 987

"She wil as thei wil, and hath doo many a day, 988
That hir dovghter on-to som kyng shuld bee
Maryed or wedded ; she seyde ȝet neuere nay,

Marginal notes:
[fol. 18] Bk. I. Ch. 16.
We want' our Queen Katharine to wed.'
Bk. I. Ch. 17.
Her Mother agrees with the Syrians,
and writes to tell them so.
Katharine ought to marry some King.

But euer her' wylle hath be in to þis degre,
loke wher' ȝe wyll & whanne, for so wyl sche. 992
Sche wold ful fayn þat þis þing' wer' I-doo;
Yt had be fynyschyd ful long' tyme a-goo, 994

"Yf' it had ley in her' or in her' wylle. 995
Sche thynkyth certeyn reson þat þei sey:
To haue a kyng' it is ful goode skylle,
Be-cause a woman neithir can ne may
Do liche a man ne sey, it is no nay, 999
Go loke ȝour'-selue, for ȝe be wyse men alle.
My doutir, I trowe, on-to your' wyll shal falle. 1001

"She was neuer ȝete a-sayed in no degre 1002
Of' ȝow ne me ne of' no-maner with;
As in þis mater' sche seyd neuer nay ne ȝee,
We may not blame her' in no-maner plyth;
She doth to vs as ȝet no-thyng' but ryght, 1006
Ne non she cast', truly, as I suppose.
We wyll ful sone her' of' þis þing' appose. 1008

"Yf' she consent, þan haue we al I-doo. 1009
But þis same þing', certayn, touchith vs all,
It longyth nowtȝ only to on or too,
But all our' reme herto must we calle,
ffor grete perell ellys þerof' myth fall; 1013
Yt longyth to þe ferthest' as wele as to hem
þat dwelle her' ny. ȝe wote ful wele, her' em, 1015

[fol. 18] "The duke of' tyre, mote nede know þis þing', 1016
The duke of' antioche eke, her' owne cosyn;
If' we shul haue a lord or ellys a kyng',
þei mote consent, þei mote make þe fyn.
lete þis mater' no lenger slepe ne lyne! 1020
We wyll send oute now in all hastly wyse
þat euery man shal com in hese best gyse 1022

"On-to þis alisaundre, þer we dwelle as now; 1023
þei shal sey & her' alle þat euer þei wylle,

But euere hir wil hath be in this degree,
Looke where thei wil and whanne, for soo wil shee. 992
She wuld ful fayn that this thyng were I-doo;
It hadde be fynyshed ful longe tyme a-goo, 994

"If it had leyn in hir or in hir wille. 995
She thenkyth¹ certeyn resoun that þei say: ¹ MS. thenkyteh
To haue a kyng it is ful good skylle,
be-cavse a woman neyther can ne may
Doo lyche a man ne seye, it is no nay, 999
Soo¹ loke youre-selue, for ye be wise men alle. ¹ r. Go
My dovter, I trowe, on-to your wil shal falle. 1001

"She was neuere ȝet assayed in no degree 1002
Of yow, ne me, ne of no-maner wyght;
As in this mater she seyde neuere nay ne ȝe,
We may not blame hir in no-maner plyght;
She dooth to vs as ȝet no thyng but ryght, 1006
Ne non she casteth, trewly, as I suppose.
We wiln ful sone hir of this þing appose. 1008

"If [s]he consente, than haue we alle I-doo.
But þis same þing, certeyn, toucheth vs alle,
It longeth not oonly to oon or too,
but alle oure reem herto must we calle,
ffor gret pereH [ellys] ther-of myght falle; 1013
It longeth to the ferthest as [wel as] to hem
That dwellyn here ny. ye wote ful weel, here hem, 1015

"The duke of Tyre, muste nede knowe this thing, 1016
The duke of Antyoche eke, hir owyn cosyn;
If we shul haue a lord or ellis a kyng,
Thei mote conscente, thei mote make þe fyn.
lete þis mater no lenger slepe ne lyn! 1020
She wil sende oute now in hasty wyse
That euery man shal come in his beste gyse 1022

"On-to þis Alysavndre, there we dwelle as now; 1023
Thei shal sey and here aH [euer] thei wille,

Marginalia: Bk. I. Ch. 17. Katharine's Mother agrees that the Syrians ought to have a King, and thinks her Daughter will marry, if askt; [fol. 19 b. The next passages are out of order in the MS.; ll. 36—105 precede v. 1009.] but the whole Realm is concernd in the matter, so she will summon its chief men, to Alexandria

Bk. I. Ch. 17.
Ther' shall no man, to god I make a vowe,
Be lettyd for vs, speke he loude or stylle."
This was þe sentense of' þe qwenes bille. 1027
The puple red it & was ful wele a-payde,
"God saue our' lady,", wyth o voys þus þei seyde. 1029
Thus endeth þis boke of' þis clene uirgine, 1030
In whech her' byrth, her' kynrod & her' countre
Is declared, so as she wold enclyne
hir' gracious help to send on-to me.
Now ferthermor' a newe boke be-gynne wyl we, 1034
In whech we shall on-to hyr' worchep wryte,
So as we can in our' langage endyte, 1036
The grete conflicte be-twyx þe lordes & her' 1037
Ryth in þe parlement, whech was ful realy hold
At grete alysaunder—many a ful stout syre
On-to þat cite at þat tyme cam ful bold.
It wyl be long' or þat þis tale be told; 1041
þerfor I counsell þat we make her' a pause
And eke a-rest ryth euene at þis clause. 1043

Bk. II. Prol.
liber secundus. Prologus.

Loke whanne ȝe see þe sparkes fayr' & bryth 1
Spryng' fro þe fyre & vpward fast to goo,
ȝe may suppose be reson & be ryth
Summe fyre is nye, experiens telleth you soo;
þer go no sparkes neithir to ner' fro 5
But þer as fyr' is, þis se we ryth at eye.
In þis same maner of' þis same lady I sey: 7
þeis holy wordes, þeis holy dedes eke 8
[fol. 18, b.]
[4th hand]
Whech sche spake & vsed here lyuande,
Alle þoo were tokenys þat her' hert gan seke
Here gostly spouse, sche lefte not tyll sche fond
That blyssyd lord. sche knowyth not ȝit hys hand 12
As sche schall aftyr, but sche haue[1] tokenys gode; [1] r. hath
And all[2] of god sche knowyth not ȝit þe rode; [2] r. als? 14

A Parliament cald in Alexandria.

There shal no man, to oure god I make a vow,	*Bk. I. Ch. 17.*
Be letted for vs, speke he loude or stylle."	to discuss Katharine's
This was þe sentens of the qveenes bille. 1027	marriage.
The peple redde it, and was ful weel a-payede,	
"God saue oure lady" with oo voys thus thei sayde. 1029	
Thus endeth þis book of this clene virgine, 1030	
In whiche hir byrthe, hir kynred and hyr contre	
Is declared, soo as she wolde enclyne	
hyr gracyovs helpe to sende on-to me.	
Now ferthere-more a newe book begynne wil we, 1034	
In whiche we shal on-to hir wurshyppe wryte,	
So as we kan in oure langage endyte, 1036	
The grete conflicte be-twyxe the lordes and hir 1037	But as there's to be a dis-
Ryght in þe parlemente, whiche was ful ryaly holde	pute over it,
At grete Alysavndre—many a ful stoute sir	
On-to þat Cytee at þat tyme cam ful boolde.	
It wil be long er þat this tale be toolde; 1041	
Therfore I counseyll þat we make here a pavse	we'll end Book I. here.
And eke a reste ryght euene at this clause. 1043	
	[1] MS. Cam. 1m.

Liber secundus. Prologus.[1]

Bk. II. Prol.

Loke, whan ye see þe sparkes fayre and bryght 1	As sparks
Sprynge fro the fyre and vpward faste to goo,	
Ye may suppose be reson and be ryght	
Som fyre is ny, experyens telleth yow soo;	show that fire is nigh,
There go no sparkes neyther too ne froo 5	
But there as fyre is, þis see we ryght at eyȝe.	
In this same maner of this lady I seye: 7	
These hooly woordys, these hooly deedes eke 8	so Katha- rine's holy
Whiche she[1] spak[2] and vsed here lyuande, [1] overlined. [2] MS. spark	words show
Alle tho were tookenes þat hir herte gan seke	
hir goostly spovse, she lefte not tyl she fande [1] overlined.	that she is seeking
That blyssed lord[1]. she knoweth not yet his hande 12	Christ,
As shal she afterward, but she hath tookenes goode;	
And alle-soo[1] of god she knoweth not yet the roode; 14	
[1] soo overlined.	

Sche knowyth not crist, sche hath not herd his lore,   15
But ȝit þe fyre of charite & of loue
Brennyth in here, so þat euer more & more
Here hert is sette on oon) þat sytte a-boue.   [1] MS. dewe   [2] overlined.
I trowe þat dowe[1] þe qwech vp[2]-on crist dide houe   19
Whanne he was baptiȝed, had mad in hyr' hys nest.
This wote I wele, sche can not now haue rest,   21

But all hyr' spech is now to comend   22
þe grete vertu qwech we virginite
A-mongys [vs][1] name. who coude þanne a wende   [1] omitted.
That on þis vertu so dewly thynk' wold sche?
ffor swech exaumples want in þat cuntre;   26
Ther is no man desyryth sche be a mayde,
Sche mote be weddyd nedys, þus þei sayde.   28

And as we see, þe more is leyde to brenne   29
þe gretter fyre þer is, it is no dowte;
ffor drawe awey þe schydys fro it þen),
Sone wyll þe fyre be qwenchyd & be owte:—
þe more þis lady vertues is a-bowte   33
þe more þei grow, þei haue a full gode grownde.
Here cours, þei sey, as sercle it is rownd,   35

ffor eueri vertu folowyth ryth aftyr odyr: 36
Whan) on is come, he callyth ine his felaw;
þei loue to-geder as syster or as þe brothyr,
Ech of hem all his besynesse doth to draw,
Tyll all be come—ryth swech, lo,[1] is her' lawe,   [1] orig. so 40
Be-gynne ageyn) whan þou hast vsed þe last;
here serculed cours ryth þus, lo, haue þei cast.   42

Thys made here hate þese fleschly lustys alle,   43
ffor in þis sercle sche is so farre I-paste
þat from þat whele sche cast here not to falle;
here hert & þei be teyd so wondyr fast',
Of hem it hath take so swetly þe tast',   47
Thei are mette and mates, now & euer-more,
Thei are now bownd to-gedyr wondyr sore.   49

She knoweth not cryst, she hath not herd his lore, 15 *Bk. II. Prol.*
But yet þe fyre of charyte and of love — *though she knows Him not yet.*
Brenneth in hir, soo þat euere more and more
hir herte is sette on oon that sitteth a-bove.
I trowe þat dowe whiche vp-on cryst dede houe 19
Whan he was baptysed, had made in hir his nest.
This wote I weel, she can not now haue rest, 21

But al hir speche is now to comende 22 *She talks much of Virginity.*
The grete vertu whiche is vyrgynyte,
A-mong vs namely—who cowde thanne a wende
That on þis vertu so dewly thenke wulde she?
ffor swhyche exaunplys wante[1] in þat contre; [1] MS. wente 26
There is no man desyreth she be a mayde,
She mote be wedded, nedys thus, þei sayde. 28

And as we see, þe more is leyd to brenne 29
The grettere fyer þer is, it is no dowte;
ffor drawe a-wei þe shides fro it thenne,
Soone wil þe fyre be qvenched and be ovte:
The more this lady vertues is aboute 33
The more thei growe, þei haue a ful good grounde. *Her virtues grow:*
her cours the seyd sercle (!) it is rounde, 35

ffor every vertu folweth right after other: [fol. 18 b] 36
Whan on is come, he calleth in his felawe; *one brings another.*
Thei loue to-gedir as sister or as the brother,
Eche of hem alle his besynesse dooth to drawe,
Til alle be come—right swiche lo is her lawe, 40
Be-gynne a-geyn whan thou hast vsed the last;
her sercled cours right thus loo haue þei cast. 42

This made hir hate these fleshly lustys alle, 43 *Katharine hates fleshly lusts.*
ffor in þis sercle she is soo ferre I-paste
That from that wil (!) she casteth hir not to falle;
hir herte and thei be teyed so wunder faste,
Of hem she hath soo sweetly take þe taste, 47
They arn mette and mates now and euere-more,
Thei arn[1] now bounde to-gedere wonder sore. [1] overlined. 49

KATHARINE. G

Bk. II. Prol.

It acordeth fuH weel, me thynk, to here name 50
That vicyous lyfe in here schuld haue no place;
þeis latyn bokys, I suppose, sey þis same,
Here name, þei seyn, it is so fuH of grace
That synfuH lyfe it can distroy & race; 54
ffor þus it menyth, certeyn[1], it is no nay :   [1] orig. forsoth
Cata in grew, in englysch is þus to say 56

"Ouyr aH" or "aH," & ryne in oure langage 57
Sownd "fallyng," as who schuld sey, in here
Of synne & schame aH þe sory rage
Destroyd was, it neyhyd her' not nere.
þeis holy vertues were to here so dere, 61
þei putte a-wey of synne[s] aH þe flok';
þei are schyt owt & sche speryd þe lok'. 63

O noble lady, þat art now us aboue, 64
Suffyr oure tungys, þow þei vn-worthy be,
To telle þi lyfe, þi[1] langoure & þi[1] loue   [1] r. þe
þat þou had here in þi denoute secre,
To telle þe sorowe eke & þat aduersite 68
Whech wyth þi lordys þou suffyrd as a clerk'!
We wyH now streyte dresse vs to þat werk'. 70

Bk. II. Ch. 1.

Ca^{m.} 1^{m.}

Now is not ellys but ryde, go & ren, 71
   Messangerys are oute on hasty wyse
To calle to parlement alle-maner menne,
That þei come alle now in her' best gyse;
Clerkes must come, for þei be so wyse, 75
And lordes eke, be-çawse þei be strong'.
This gaderyng hardely was not taryd long'. 77

ffor, as I rede, wyth-inne wekys three 78
Thei be come thydir, & þat wyth gret pryde :
The prince of capadoce wytʒ a gret mene,
The erl of ioppen cam ryth be his syde—
[fol. 19, b.] [2nd hand] þer' myght men se who can best sytte & ryde; 82

It accordeth ful weel, me thenketh, to hir name 50 *Her name implies this;*
That vyciouse lyf in hir shuld haue no place :
These latyn bookes, I suppose, seyn the same,
hir name, þei seye, it is soo ful of grace
þat synful lyef it can distroye and race ; 54
ffor thus it meneth, certayn, it is no nay :
Catha in greu, in englyssh is to say 56 *Catha* means

"Ouere alle," or "alle," And ryne in oure langage 57 'over all,' *Ryne* means 'falling.'
Soundeth "fallyng," as we¹ shulde sey, in heer ¹ r. who
Of synne and shame al the sory rage [fol. 19]
Destroyed was, it neyhed hir not neer.
These holy vertues were to hir soo deer, 61
Thei put a-wey of synne[s] al the flook,
Thei arn shet oute and she spered the look. 63

O noble lady, þat art now vs a-bove, 64 Sainted Lady, let me tell thy Life and Love,
Suffre oure tounges, þhough thei onworthi be,
To telle thi lyef, the langure and the love
That þou hadest in thi devoute secree,
To telle the sorwe eke and that aduersite 68 thy Sorrow and Distress!
Whiche wyth thi lordes þou suffered as a clerk !
We wil now streit dresse vs to þat werk. 70

Cap. 1.¹ ¹ MS. Cap. 18 *Bk. II. Ch. 1.*

NOw is not ellis but ryde, goo and renne, 71
Massagerys arn oute on hasty wyse
To calle to parlement alle maner men,
That thei alle come now in her beste gyse ;
Clerkys muste come, for þei ben so wyse, 75 The Parliament
And lordes eke, be-cause thei be stronge.
This gaderyng hardyly was not taryed longe. 77

ffor, as I reede, wyth-inne wekes thre 78
Thei be come theder, and that wyth grete pryde : *meets in Alexandria.*
The prynce of Capadoce with a grete mene,
The Erlle of ioppen cam rydyng be his syde— *To it come the Earl of Joppa,*
There myght men see who can best sytte and ryde ; 82

G 2

þe prince of paphon is come þedyr allsoo, ¹ MS. &
þe duke of damask, wyth many [an]¹ oþer' moo ; 84

The duke of salence, þe duke of garacen, 85
þei wer' ther' reall, & eke so was he
þe erle of lymason—ful many strong men
had þei wyth hem, þese reall lordes thre.
þe amerell of Alysaundyr', wyth solennite 89
he hath receyuyd hem, he was a full strong syr'.
he is come also, þe noble duke of tyre. 91

Last of all þedyr' gan aproche 92
A worthy man, hyr owyn ny cosyn,
þei call hym þer' þe duke of Antioch ;
All þis mater' he schall now determyn,
þus wene þei alle, for owte of o lyne 96
Ar' þei come bothe ; he may ryght nowt wante,
hys wyll in her' hert ful sone schall he plante. 98

The day is come now whech assygned was ; 99
þe lordes are gadred to-gedyr all in-fer'.
þe lenghe of þe halle fully too hundyrd pace
So was it, certen, in wech þei gadered wer',
Syttyng in her' cownsell—þoo men þat wer' þer' 103
þei mett it hem-self, þei seyd it was soo—
Swech howses in þis werld ar not many moo. 105

A grete lorde was choso þer a-mongis hem alle 106
To tell hyr¹ wylle—" speker'," he² sey, he was, ¹ r. her ² r. þei
I wot not veryly what þat men hym calle.
he went ful esyly forth a ful soft pas
Tyll he was come ryght be-for þe face 110
Of þis meke lady, & þan þus he seyd :
" Myn souereyn lady, ȝe schull not be dysmayde, 112

" Ȝe schall forȝeue, & þat I pray ȝow her', 113
Thow I to ȝow sey treuth, as I must nede.
I am a seruaunt, for I hafe take wage & hyr'

The prynce of paphon̄ is com̄ thedir also,
The duke of Damaske, wyth many other mo ;   84 the Duke of Damascus, &c.,
The duke of salence, the duke of Garaencen,   85
Thei were there ryal, and eke so was he,
The Erlle of lymason̄, with ful many strong men
had thei with hem, [þese] ryal lordes thre.
The amyrall of Alysaundre, with solennyte   89
he hath receyued hem̄, he was a ful straunge syre.
he is come also, the noble duke of Tyre.   91

Laste of alle theder gan̄ approche   92
A worthi man̄, hir owne ny Cosyn,
Thei calle hym there the duke of Antioche ;   the Duke of Antioch, &c.
Al this mater he shal now determyn,
Thus wene thei alle, for ovte of oo lyn̄   96
Are thei come bothe, he may ryght novght whant,
his wyl in [her] herte ful sone shal he plant.   98

The day is come now whiche assigned was ;   99
The lordes arn̄ gadered to-gedyr alle in-feere.
The lengthe of the halle fully too hundir paas   The Hall is 200 paces long.
So was it, certeyn̄, in whiche thei gadered were,
Sittynge in her counseyl—tho men̄ þat were there 103
Thei mette it hem-selue, þei seyde it was soo—
Swhiche hovses in þis world arn̄ not many moo.   105

A grete lord was chose there a-mong hem alle [fol. 216. In the MS. vv. 176— 245 precede 106—175.] A Speaker is chosen.
To telle her wil—"spekere," þei seyn, he was,
I wot not veryly what þat men̄ hym calle.
he went ful esyly foorth a ful soft paas
Til he was come ryght be-foorn̄ þe faas   110
Of þis meke lady, and þanne thus he sayde :
"My souereyn̄ lady, ye shul not be dismayde,   112 He addresses Katharine.

"Ye shal foryeue, and þat I prey yow here,   113
Thow I to yow sey treuthe, as I muste nede.
I am a seruant, and haue take wage in fere[1]   [1] MS. orig. for I h. t. w. and here

Of yow, my lady, & þat in many stede;
I am chose eke þe nedys for to bede 117
Of all your reume, of lordys & of othyr—
I except ryght noon, for certenly ȝour modyr 119

"As in þis case is ryght on of heme. 120
Sche wyll & þei, þat ȝe, my lady der,—
So wyll my lord þe duk of tyr, ȝour hem,
I sey not fals, for he is present her—
What schuld I lenger hyde now my mater, 124
Ȝe must now leue your stody & ȝour bokys
And tak your solace be feldys & be brokys. 126

"T[h]ynk on your kyn, thynk on your hye lyne; 127
If ȝe lef þus, þe elde auncetrye
Schall fayle in ȝow. Þer is no dyuyne
Ne phylysophre her wyll sey þat I lye,
ffor I sey þus: on-to our goddys hardylye 131
It is not plesaunce þat ȝe schuld þus doo;
It pleseth hem bettyr, & ȝe consent þer-too— 133

"And eke ȝour puple—þat ȝe a husbond haue, 134
A real lorde, whech may us alle defende.
Þe goddys ffrenchep if ȝe wyll kepe & saue,
On-to þis purpose ȝe mote nede condescende;
Ȝour puple gretly þer-by schuld ȝe mende. 138
Excuseth not þat wyll noght be excusede,
Ther is swech choys, it may not be refusede. 140

"What lord is þat, if onys he myght yow see, 141
But he wold hafe ȝow? mech mor, dar I sey,
If he knew your cunnynge, as now do we,
he wold desyr ȝow in all-maner weye;
hys crown, hys kyngdam wold he rather leye 145
þan he schuld want your noble wyse presence—
Who se yow onys, desyryth not ȝour absence. 147

"Ther-for, lady, ȝour seruauntis are now her 148
Be-sekyng [yow][1] þat ȝe wyll of ȝour grace   [1] om.

Of yow, my lady, and that in many stede ;
I am chose eke the nedes for to bede 117
Of alle youre reem, of lordes and of othir—
I excepte ryght now, for certeynly your modir 119

Bk. II. Ch. 1.
All her lords, and her Mother

"As in þis caas is ryght oon) of hem. 120
She wil and thei, þat ye, my lady deere,—
Soo wil my lord the duke of Tire, your eem),
I sey not fals, for he is present heere—
What shuld I lengere now hyde my matere, 124
Ye must now leue your stody and your bookes
And take yowre solace be feeldes and be brookes. 126

and Uncle,
want her to leave her books,

"Thenke on yovre kyn), thenke on) your hei lyne ; 127
If ye leue thus, the old auncetrye
Shal fayle in yow. ther is no dyuyne
Ner philysophere here wil sey þat I now lyʒe,
ffor I sey thus : on-to ovre goddys hardylye 131
It is now) plesauns that ye shuld thus doo ;
It pleseth hem better, and ye consente ther-too— 133

"And [eke] your puple—that ye an husbond haue, 134
A ryal lord, whiche may us alle defende.
The goddys frenshepe if ye wil kepe and saue,
On-to this purpos ye mote nede condescende ;
Youre puple gretly therby shul ye mende. 138
Excuseth not that wil be not excused,
There is swyche choys, it may not be refused. 140

and take a Husband.

"What lord is that, if ones he myght yow see, 141
But he wold haue yow ? moche more, dar I seye,
If he knewe your connyng, as doo we,
he wolde desyre yow in al-maner weye ;
his crovne, his kyngdam) wolde he rather leye 145
Than he shulde whante your noble wyis presens—
Ho see yow ones, desyreth not your absens. 147

Any Lord will be too glad to have her.

[fol. 22]

"Therfore, lady, yovre seruauntys arn) now here 148
Be-sekynge that ye wil of yovre grace

Bk. II. Ch. 1. Ope ȝour' eres & lyst to our' prayere —
ffor þis cause only came we to þis place
Ryght all in-feer'. ȝe may vs graunte solace,　　152
Or peyne & sorow, ryght as ȝe lyst to chese ;
Ȝour' answer', lady, schall cause on of þese."　　154

Bk. II. Ch. 2.　　　　　　　Ca^m. 2^m.

Fvl a-stoyned & all a-basched sore　　155
　　was þis lady, whan sche herd hym than.
"O noble godd," thowt sche, " þat I now were
No qwen, ne lady! for I ne wote ne can
Voyde þe sentens of þis ilke wyse man ;　　159
My priuy counsell whech I hafe bor' long,
Now must it owte, & þat thynkyth me wrong.　　161

" ffor if I schewe þat I so long hafe bor',　　162
þe priuyest poynt of my perfeccyoun,
Me thynkyth swyrly þan þat I hafe lore
þe hye degre of my deuocyoun).
Whan veynglorye comth, uertu is þan gon) ;　　166
Vertu serueth to plese godd only,
And not þe puple — ryght þus redd hafe I.　　168

" If I concelle my counsell, þan schall I falle　　169
In indignacyon) of all my puple her' ;
If I denye her' askyng in þis halle
And tell no cause, I put hem mor' in dwer'.
Whech þing I do, I fall euyr in dawngere.　　173
Ȝet wondyr I sore þat my hert is sett
On swech a poynte, þat I can not lett,　　175

" And ȝet it is ageyns myne owyn lawe,　　176
Whech I am swor' to kepe & to defende !
My mynd it faryth ryght as on þe wawe
A grete schyppe doth : for [whan]¹ he best wende　　¹ om.
To be escaped, þan comth þe wawys ende,　　180
he fyllyth þe schyppe & forth a-non) is goo.
On-to þis poynt I drede I am browte too.　　182

The Speaker asks Katharine to marry.

Open your eeris and leste to oure prayere— *Bk. II. Ch. I.*
ffor þis cavse oonly com we to þis place *Will she not grant their wish?*
Right alle in-fere. ye may graunte vs solace, 152
Or peyne or[1] sorwe, ryght as ye leste to chese ; [1] r. &
Youre answere, lady, shal ben oon of these." 154

Ca[m.] secundum.[1] [1] MS. tercium *Bk. II. Ch. 2.*

FvH astoyned and al abashed soore 155 *Katharine is abasht.*
was þis lady, whan she herde him[1] pan. [1] MS. hem
" O noble god," thought she, " that I now whore
No qveen ne lady! for I ne wot ne can   *She wishes she wasn't a Queen.*
Voyde the sentens of þis ilke wyse man; 159
My preuy counseyH whiche I haue bore longe,
Now muste it ovte, and that thengeth me wronge. 161

"ffor if I shewe þat I soo longe haue bore, 162
The preuyest poynt of my perfectyon,
Me thenketh suerly þanne þat I haue lore
The hey degree of my deuocyon.
'Whan veynglory cometh, vertu is þan goon; 166
Vertu seruyth to plese god oonly,
And not the puple—oonly ryght thus red haue I. 168

" If I conseH my counseH, than shal I falle 169 *Katharine thinks she must answer her people's request,*
Into[1] the indignacyon of alle my puple here ; [1] to overlined.
If I denye her askynge in this halle
And telle no cause, I putte hem more in dwere.
Whiche þing I doo, I falle euere in daungere. 173
Yet wondre I sore þat myn hert is so[1] sette [1] overlined.
On swiche a poynt, that I can not lette, 175

" And yet it is ageyn my owne lawe, [fol. 20 b.] 176
Whiche I am swore to kepe and to defende!
Myn mende it fareth ryght as on þe wawe
A grete shyp dooth : for whan he best wende
To be skaped, than cometh the wawes ende, 180
he filleth the ship and forth anon is goo.
On-to this poynt I drede I am brought too. 182

Bk. II. Ch. 2.

"I supposed ful welle to leue now at myn) ese : 183
Now must I leeue my stody & my desyre,
My modyr, my kyn, my puple if I wyll plese ;
I most leeue stody & wasch my boke in myre,
Ryde owte on huntyng, vse all new a-tyre ! 187
Godd, þou knowyst my preuy confessyon),
I hafe made all a-nothyr professyon) ! 189

"If I myght kepe it, I schall ȝet, & I may, 190
Contynue þe same, to godd I make a vowe.
Schuld I now chaunge my lyffe & myn aray,
And trace þe wodes a-bowte undyr þe bow?
I loued it neuyr, who schuld I loue it now ?" 194
Þus thowt þis mayde be hyr-self a-lone,
And aftyr softly wyth syhynge gan sche grone. 196

Sche spak þan lowde, þei myght her' at onys : 197
"Gramercy, lordes," sche seyd, "of your good wylle !
Ȝe sey, ȝour' feldys & your' wonys
Are in poynt for me to scatyr & spylle,
But if I take a lorde now me vn-tylle 201
Whech may put all þis in gouernaunce ;
Þan schuld ȝe hafe boþe rest & abundaunce. 203

"I suppose weele þat it schulde be soo. 204
Ȝet wyll ȝe graunte, parde, of curtesye
þat syth þis þing muste nedys goo þer-too,
þat I my-selfe, in whom) all þis doth lye,
May hafe a-vysement. I am not schape to flye, 208
Ne to fle neyther' ! me þinkyth, ȝe euerychon)
haue ful gret hast, & I haf ryght non). 210

"I am but ȝunge, I may full weell a-byde, 211
Þus schuld ȝe sey to me if I had hast.
lete all þis mater' as for a whyle now slyde,
Tyll mo ȝerys of myn age be past ;
þer'-whyles wyll I boþe lok & tast[1]   [1] r. cast? 215
Wher' I wyll sett me, & telle yow myn a-vys.
I wold noght men seyd I wer' hasty or nyce. 217

"I supposed ful wel to leue now at myñ eese : 183
Now must¹ I leue my stody and myñ desyre,   ¹ MS. musty I
My modir, my kyñ, my peple if I wil plese ;
I muste leue stody and wasſh myñ book in myre,
Ryde ovte on huntynge, vse al newe a-tyre ! 187
God, þou knowest my preuy confessioñ,
I haue made al a-nother professyoñ ! 189

"If I myght kepe it, I shal yet, and I may, 190
Contynue the same, to god I make a vovgh.
Shulde I now chaunge my lyf and myñ aray,
And trace þe wodes abovte vndir the bow ?
I loued it neuere, how shuld I loue it now ? " 194
Thus thought this mayde be hir-selue allone,
And after softly with syhynge gañ she grone. 196

She spak thañ loude, þei myght here at oones : 197
"Gromercy, lordes," she seyde, "of your good wil !
Ye seye, youre feeldes and your wones
Arn in poynt for me to scatyr and spyl,
But I take a lord now me oñ-tyl 201
Whiche may putte al þis in gouernaunce ;
Thanne shuld ye haue bothe rest and abundaunce. 203

"I suppose weel þat it shuld be soo. 204
Yet wil ye gravnte me of your curtesye
That, sith þis thyng muste nedes goo ther-too,
That I my-self, in whom al þis dooth lye,
May haue avisement. I am not shape to flye, 208
Ne to flee neyther ! me thenketh, ye euerychoñ [fol. 21]
haue ful grete hast, and I haue ryght nooñ. 210

"I am but yovng, I may ful wel a-byde, 211
Thus shuld ye seye to me if I had hast.
let al this mater as for a whyle now slyde,
Til mo ȝeerys of myñ age been past ;
There-whiles wil I bothe lokeñ and tast 215
Where I wil sette me, and telle yow myñ avys.
I wolde not meñ seyde I were hasty or nys. 217

Marginal notes: Bk. II. Ch. 2. — tho' she doesn't want to give up her studies, and take to hunting. — She never liked hunting. — Katharine asks her people for time. — She is quite young.

Bk. II. Ch. 2.
"ffor hasty schall I noght be in þis mater'; 218
I sewyr' ȝow her', I wyll noo husbond take
But if I telle my frendys whech be her',
lest þat I renne in daunger' & in wrake.
What schuld I lenger' to ȝow tale now make? 222
Tyme goth fast, it is full lyght of lope,
And in a-bydyng men seyn þer lyghte hope. 224

"Thus schall we bope wyth a-vysement werk; 225
Best it is, me þinkyt, þat we do soo.
late þe puple for a whylle iangyll & berk,
Spek at her' lust—so are þei won to doo;
þe choys is myne, I mote consent þer'-too. 229
[fol. 21, b.]
[1st hand]
Tyme of' a-vysement to haue I pray yow—
Thys is all & sum þat I wyll sey as nowe." 231

Bk. II. Ch. 3.
Ca^m. 3^m.

Than ros a lord, a man of' gret statur', 232
A rych man eke þei sey þat he was;
hys wordes wer' taut hym wyth ful besy cur'
Of' a clerke þere, þe mor' & eke þe lasse—
hys wytte was not sufficient as in þis cas 236
To speke in þis mater', ryth þus he þouth.
"Myn owe lady," he seyde, "it is ful der' a-bowth 238

"The absens of' your' fader now in þis land: 239
I haue lost my-selue, & so haue oþir' moo,
A þousand pownd þat was þoo in my hand,
Whan þat he deyed & went vs þus froo;
The same haue oþir men, I am sekyr it is soo. 243
We ar' come heder to her' now your' entent
In þis mater', & ȝe haske a-vysement! 245

"Ȝe myth a be vysyd, lady, wele I-now 246
long' or þis tyme, if' ȝe had lyste;
In long' a-bydyng' is ful lytyl prowe—
All þat euer I mene I wold þat ȝe wyste.
It is mor' sykyr a bryd in ȝour' fyste 250

Katharine craves Delay.

"ffor hasty shal I not be in this matere ; 218
I sewer you heere, I wyl noƜ housbond take
But if I telle my freendes whiche be here,
lest þat I renne in daunger and in wrake.
What shuld I to yow lengere tale now make ? 222
Tyme gooth faste, it is ful lyght of lope,
And in a-bydyng menƜ seynƜ there lyeth hope. 224

Bk. II. Ch. 2.
She won't marry without advice.

"Thus shal we bothe wyth avysement werke ; 225
Best it is, me thenketh, þat we doon soo.
late þe peple for a while iangle and beerke,
Speke at her lust—soo arnƜ thei wont to doo ;
The chois is mynƜ, I mote consente ther-too. 229
Tyme of avysement to have I pray yow—
This is al and sum þat I wil sey as now." 231

She begs for delay.

Ca^{m.} tercium.

Bk. II. Ch. 3.

Thanne ros a lord, a manƜ of gret stature, 232
A ryche manƜ eke þei seynƜ that he was ;
his wordes were taught hymƜ wyth ful besy cure
Of a clerk there, the more and eke the las—
his wyt was not sufficient as in þat cas 236
To speke in this mater, ryght thus he thought.
"MynƜ owne lady," he seyde, " it is ful deere abovght, 238

A rich lord

"The absens of your fadir now in this land : 239
I haue lost my-self, and soo haue other moo,
A thousand povnd þat was tho in mynƜ hand,
WhanƜ þat he deyed &¹ wente vs thus froo ;   ¹ overlined.
The same haue other menƜ, I amƜ seeker it is soo. 243
We arnƜ come now heder to here youre entent
In this mater, and ye aske avysement ! 245

tells Katharine he's lost £1000 since her Father died.
So have others.

"Ye myght a be avysed, lady, weel I-now [fol. 22] 246
longe er þis tyme, if ye had lest ;
In longe a-bydynge is ful litel prow—
Al þat euere I meene I wolde þat ye west.
It is more sekyr a byrd in your fest 250

A bird in the hand is worth

Bk. II. Ch. 3. Than to haue iij. in þe sky a-boue,
And mor' profetabyl to your' be-houe. 252

"The gray hors, whyl his gras growyth, 253
May sterue for hunger, þus seyth þe prouerbe.
Euery wyse man as weele as I now knowyth
The sore may swelle long', or þe herbe
Is growe or rype—a grete clerke of[1] viterbe 257
Seyd so sumtyme & wroot it in hys boke.
We haue ful grete nede to spy[e] & to loke 259

"That we may[1] haue a kyng' to rewle us & yow, 260
To gouerne þe lawe þat it' shuld not erre,   [1] mow expunged.
To be to traytourys both cruel & row,
To lede þe lordys whan þei go to werre.
ffro ȝour' kend þis gouernauns is full ferre, 264
Your' blod is not so myty for to abyde
To se man be slayn be ȝour' owyn[1] syde,   [1] overlined. 266

[fol. 22.]
[2nd hand]

"To se þe boweles cut oute of hys wombe 267
And brent be-for' hym, whyll he is on lyue,
To se man[1] serued as þei serue a lombe,   [1] MS. men corr.?
Thorow-oute hys guttys boþe rende & ryue,
To se hem draw oute be four' & be fyue. 271
ȝour' pytous hert myght not se þis chaunce,
ffor it wold mak yow to fall in a traúns. 273

"Ther-for' it is best to ȝow, þus we þink, 274
To take a lord þat may suffyr all thys,
Whech may se men flete & also se hem synk,
Suffyr hem to smert whan þei do a-mys,
Whan þei do weell to hafe reward & blys. 278
Ryght þus I mene, I mak no lenger' tale;
But ȝe do þus, gretter' growyth our' bale." 280

Bk. II. Ch. 4.

Ca[m]. 4[m].

Thys lady answerd on-to þis lord a-geyn: 281
"My faderes absence is mor' greuous to me

> Than to haue three in þe sky a-boue,
> And more profytable to youre be-houe. [fol. 22 b.]   252
>
> "The grey hors, whil his gres groweth,   253
> May sterue for hunger, thus seyth the prouerbe.
> Euery wysman as wel as I now knoweth
> The soor may swelle longe er the herbe
> Is growe or rype—a grete clerk of viterbe   257
> Seyde soo somtyme and wrote it in his booke.
> We haue ful grete nede to spye and to looke   259
>
> "That we may haue a kyng to revle vs and yow,   260
> To gouerne the¹ lawe that it shuld not erre,   ¹ overlined.
> To be to traytouris bothe cruel and row,
> To lede þe lordis whan thei goo to werre.
> ffro youre kende this gouernauns is ful ferre,   264
> Youre blood is not so myghty for to a-byde
> To see men¹ slayn be youre owen syde,   ¹ r. man   266
>
> "To see þe bowailes cutte oute of his wombe   267
> And brent be-fore hym, whil he is on lyve,
> To see men be serued as thei serue a lombe,
> Thurgh-oute his guttes bothe rende and ryue,
> To see hem drawe oute be foure and be fyue.   271
> Youre pytous herte myght not see þis chaunce,
> ffor it wolde make you to falle in a traunce.   273
>
> "Therfore it is best to yow, thus we thenke,   274
> To take a lord that may suffre al þis,
> Whiche may see men fleete and also hem synke,
> Suffre hem to smerte whan þei doo a-mys,
> Whan þei doo wel to haue reward and blys.   278
> Ryght thus I mene, I make no lengere tale;
> But ye doo thus, grettere groweth oure bale."   280

Cam. quartum.

> This lady answerde on-to þis [lord] ageyn: 281
> "My faderis absens is more grevous to me

Sidenotes: Bk. II. Ch. 3. — three in the sky. — The Syrians want a King. — Katharine cannot see men boweld like a lamb. — She must have a Husband to punish offenders. — Bk. II. Ch. 4.

þan to ȝow alle, þis dar' I sauely seyn).
And thow he leuyd, he wer' no mor', parde,
But o man—wyth-oute men what myght he 285
Doo or sey but as o man a-lone?
What nedyth ȝow now for to make swech mone 287

"ffor losse of o man? ȝe coude, whyll he was here, 288
Defende ȝour'-self, thow he wyth ȝow not ȝede:
ȝour' ennemyes alle ȝe put in full grete dwere,
Þan wer' þei kept full low, in full grete drede.
My lord my ffadyr whan dyd he ȝow lede? 292
Not many ȝerys be-for þat he went hens.
As ȝe[1] dyd þan, dothe now in hys absence! [1] MS. ȝed 294

"ȝe chose a capteyn) þoo, so may ȝe now, 295
To whom obeyd as in þat iornay
Euery lord, loked he neuyr so row,
Þei durst not onys to hym þan sey nay.
Goode serys all, of pacyens I ȝow pray; 299
Why may ȝe not do now as ȝe dyd þanne?
What nedyth ȝow þus to gruch & to banne? 301

"ȝe sey it is lost, all þat was sume-tyme 302
Wonne wyth swerde. I wote as weell as ȝe,
þat many a theft & many a gret cryme
Was hyd fro hym be craft & sotelte,
And sume wer' punychyd—he wold it schuld so be— 306
And ȝet of[1] þis punchyng oft he knew ryght nowt.
May it not now in þe same case be wrowte? [1] MS. of of 308

"I vouch-saue, ȝe ryd & eke ȝe renne 309
To seke ȝour' enmyes whech do ȝow þis wrong,
Distroye her' cuntre, her' howses down) ȝe brenne,
Þe traytours eke be þe nek ȝe hem hong—
What word seyd I euyr, eyther' schort or long, 313
Schuld let ȝour corage? I pray ȝow tell me now.
Be good to me ryght as I am to ȝow." 315

Katharine argues against a Husband.

Than to yow alle, this dar I sauely seyn! \
And thow he leued he were no more, weel kenne ye, \
But oo man. wyth-oute men, what myght he   285 \
Doo or seye, but as oo man allone? \
What nedeth yow now for to make swiche mone   287

Katharine urges that her Father was only one man.

"ffor losse of oo man? ye covude, whil he was heere, 288 \
Defende your-selue, though he wyth yow not yede; \
Your enmyes alle ye putte in ful grete dwere, \
Thanne were thei kepte ful lowe in ful grete drede. \
My lord my fadir whanne dede he[1] yow leede?   [1] overl. 292 \
Not many yeeres be-fore that he wente hens. \
As ye dede thanne, dooth now in his absens!   294

His people fought without him,

"Ye chose a captayn tho, so may ye doo now,   295 \
To whom obeyed as in that iornay \
Euery lord, looked he neuere soo row, \
Thei durst not oonys to hym þanne sey nay. \
Good sirs alle, of pacyens I yow pray,   299 \
Whi may ȝe not doo now as ȝe did þanne? \
What nedeth yow thus to grotche and banne?   301

under a chosen Captain,

"Ye seye it is lost, al that was sumtyme   302 \
Wonne with swerd. I wot as weel as ye, \
That many a theft and many a grete cryme \
Was hid fro hym be crafte and sotylte, \
And somme were punyshed—he wolde it shulde so bee— \
And yet of this punyshyng ofte he knew ryght nought. \
May it not now in this same wyse be wrought?   308

and punisht criminals, without him.

"I vowche-saf, ye ryde and eke ye renne   309 \
To seeke youre enmys whiche doo yow þis wrong, \
Destroye her contres, her houses doo ye brenne, \
The traytoures eke be nekke þat ye hem hong. \
What woord seyde I euere, eyther short or long,   313 \
Shulde lette yowre corage? I pray yow telle me now. \
Beeth good to me, ryght as I am to yow."   315

Why cannot they do so now?

KATHARINE.

Than ros a reall, a rycħ lord þer-wyth-alle, 316
þei called hym clarus, prince of capados ;
Vp-on hys knees a-noon he gan down falle,
"Madame," he seyd, "ȝour conseytes are full clos ;
ȝour name is spronge, ȝour cunnyng & ȝour los— 320
All þeis are know, þei may not now be hyd ;
And ȝet ȝe may neyther doo ne byd 322

"As may a man. ȝour fadyr—godd hafe hys sawle[1]— 323
As seyd þis lord, is ded & go vs froo ;   [1] orig. sowle
What-so-euyr men crye or elles gaule,[2]   [2] calle expunged.
We are full lykly to falle in care & woo.
Come now who schall, he is I-pased & goo, 327
And ȝe be left for to be our qween.
It lykyght vs weel þat it schuld so been, 329

"But ȝet þe chaunge is wondyr-full, me think : 330
ffor a man, a woman now we haue,
And þat a mayde ! it may in no wey synk
In our hertys þat ȝe myght vs saue—
I schall sey truthe, thow ȝe þink I raue. 334
ȝe wyll wepe, & ȝe ȝour fyngyr kytte :
Who schuld it þan setyll in our wytte 336

"ȝe myght redresse all þat was now spoke ? 337
A kyng is ordeynd ryght to þis entent :
To kepe hys castelys, þat þei be not broke,
To kepe hys puple, þat it be not schent.
Now is þis werk all othyr-wyse I-went ; 341
To kepe all þis, a woman is not strong enow,
We must enforce us þer-for to kep ȝow. 343

"And thow ȝe be þe fayrest þat beryth lyffe— 344
ffor so wene I, & so wene many moo—
It wyll be-come ȝow full welle to be a wyffe,
Myn owne lady, & ȝe wold enclyne þer-too,
To bryng forthe frute, eyther on or too— 348

MS. Arundel.] *Katharine is urgd to marry, by Clarus.* 99

Ca^{m.} qui*n*tu*m*. *Bk. II. Ch. b.*

Thanne ros a rial, a ryche lorde eke w*yth*-alle, 316   Clarus,
   Thei called hy*m* Clarus, prynce of Capados;   Prince of Cappadocia,
Vp-on his knees a-noo*n* he ga*n* dou*n* falle,
" Madame," he seyde, " yo*ur* conseytes ar*n* ful cloos;
Youre name is spronge, youre connyng and yo*ur* loos— 320
Alle these ar*n* knowe*n*, thei may not now be hid;
Yet may ye neyther doo ne bid   322

" As may a ma*n*. yo*ur* fadir—god haue his saule— 323   tells Katharine
As seyd þis lord, he is ded and goo*n* vs fro;
What-so-eu*er*e me*n* crye or ellys gaule,
We ar*n* ful lykly to falle in care and woo.
Come now hoo shal, he is passed and goo,   327
And ye be left for to be*n* oure qvee*n*.
It liketh us weel þ*a*t it shuld so be*n*,   329

" But yet the chaunge is wundirful, we thenke: 330
ffor a ma*n*, a woma*n* now we haue,   that she is only a Maiden,
And þ*a*t a mayde! it may in no weye senke
In oure hertis þ*a*t ye myght vs saue—
I shal sey yow treuthe, thow ye thenke I raue. 334
Ye wil wepe, and ye yo*ur* fynger kytte: and 'll cry if she cuts
how shulde it thanne satel in oure witte   336   her finger.

" Ye myght redresse al that was now spoke? 337
A kyng is ordeyned ryght to þis entent:
To kepe his Castell*is*, þ*a*t þei be not broke,
To kepe his puple, that þei be not shent.
Now is this werke al other-wyse I-went;   341
To kepe aH this, a woma*n* is not strong I-now,   She can't guard her
We muste enforce vs therfore to kepe you.   343   people.

" And though ye be the fayrest þat bereth lyf— 344
ffor soo wene I, and soo wene many moo—
It wil be-come yow ful weel to be a wyf,
My*n* owe*n* lady, and ye wolde enclyne þ*er*-too,   Moreover, they want
To brynge foorth frute eyther oo*n* or too—   348   her to have Children:

H 2

It schuld plese vs thow þat ȝe had twelue!
It schuld plese ȝour modyr & eke ȝour-selue. 350

"All ȝour rychesse, what schall it vs a-vayle 351
hyd in ȝour cophyr & kept now þus clos?
ȝe may[1] þer-wyth make plate & mayle.   [1] r. myght
I dar well sey, þe lond of capadoos,
If ȝe had on whech myght ber up ȝour loos, 355
Wold pay a raunson wyth full good entent,
So þat ȝe wold on-to þis þing consent. 357

"And thow ȝe be þe wysest of þis worlde, 358
ȝet haue ȝe not o þink[1] þat ȝe waunte—   [1] r. þing
Ther-of ȝour-self wyll ber me recorde:
Natur can not ne wyll not, parde, plante
Myght & strength in women, for þei it waunt; 362
In stede of strength, of natur þei hafe beute.
Thow ȝe be fayr & wyse, ȝet want ȝe 364

"Bodyly strength wer-wyth ȝe schuld oppresse 365
Thoo wykkyd dedys whech reygne now ful ryue;
Wyth deth & vengeaunce schuld ȝe þoo so[1] dresse,   [1] overl.
Wer it in man, in mayden or [in] wyffe.
I tell ȝow sekyr, þis is a kyngys lyffe; 369
he may not hafe hys worchepe all wyth ese,
Sume of hys puple oft he must dysplese. 371

"Theyse þingis fall not, vs þinkyth, to ȝour persone. 372
Wherfor we wyll, & ȝe consent þer-too,
Ordeyn a meen: ȝe schall not lyue a-lone,
Spowseles I mene, as ȝe ȝet euyr hafe doo.
þis is our erand, my tale is fully doo. 376
Sped þis mater, hold vs not long suspens!
þan is it weele wared, boþe labur & our expens." 378

Ca[m]. 6[m].

"GRamercy, syr," to hym þan seyd þe qween; 379
"Be þe tendyrnesse þat ȝe to me haue

MS. Arundel.] *Katharine is urgd to marry, by Clarus.*

It shulde plese vs though þat ye had twelue!   *Bk. II. Ch. 5.*
It shulde plese y*our* moder and eke y*our* owne selue.   350   twelve, if she likes.

"All y*our* rychesse, what shal it vs avayle,   351
hyd in y*our* Cofer and kept now thus clos?
Ye myght ther-wyth make plate and mayle.
I dar weel seyn, the lond of Capados,
If ye had oon swiche myght bere vp y*our* loos,   355
Wolde paye a raunsom with ful good entent,
So þat ye wolde on-to this thyng consent.   357

"And thow ye be the wysest of this world,   358   Tho' Katharine is wise,
Yet haue ye not oon thyng that ye wante—
There-of y*our*-selue wil bere me record:
Nature can not ne wil not trewely plante
Myght and strengthe in women, for thei it wante;   362   she has no bodily strength
In stede of strengthe, of nature þei haue bewte.
Thow ye be fayr and wys, yet wante ye   [fol. 26]   364

"Bodyly strengthe wherwyth ye shulde oppresse   365
Tho wykked dedes whiche regne now ful ryff;   to punish ill deeds with death.
With deth and vengaunce shulde ye tho soo dresse,
Were it in man, [in] mayden or in wyf.
I telle yow sekyr, this is a kynges lyf;   369   A King is wanted.
he may not haue his worshyp al with ese,
Some of his puple ofte he muste displese.   371

"These thyng*is* falleth not, vs thenketh, to ȝo*ur* persone.
Wherfore we wil and consente ther-too,
Ordeyne a mene ye shal not leue allone,   Her people desire her marriage.
Spousele (!) I mene, as ye ȝet eu*er*e haue doo.
This is oure erande, my tale concludeth soo.   376
Spedeth this mater, holdeth vs not longe suspens!
Thanne is it weel wared, bothe labo*ur* and expens."   378

      Ca^{m.} sextu*m*.   *Bk. II. Ch. 6.*

"GRomercy, sere," to hym than seyde the qveene,   379
    "ffor the tendernesse þat ye to me haue.

3e loue me weell, & þat is now I-sene,
3e loue my worchep, my londys wold 3e saue.
I thank 3ow, syr'; I sey not þat 3e raue, 383
But wysely spek aH þat 3e haue told,
And for þis talkyng I am to 3ow behold. 385

"But euyr me thynkyth, whan I a-vyse me weell: 386
If it so streyt wer', as 3e sey, wyth 3ow—
Whech dyssese wold lek me neuyr a deell:
ffor if it wer' þus as 3e pretendyn now,
3e schuld not hafe neyther' feld ne plow 390
In no pes, if it wer' all as 3e sey.
þerfor me thynkyth 3e walk no trew wey. 392

"And as for conquest', seres, car' 3e ryght nowte! 393
3our' lordchepys frely wune wer' to 3our handys
Or 3e coude goo & or þat 3e wer' wrowte;
3e fawte neuyr 3et for tounnes ne for no landys.
Wher' ar 3our prisoneres whech 3e led in bandys? 397
þer was no werr' syth þat I was bore,
But on our' borderes, & 3e car' not þer-fore— 399

"ffor we fynde þe sowdyoures þat be ther' 400
3e pay ryght not, ne nowte I coueyte 3e doo.
Pluk vp 3our' hertes, & be no-þing in fere!
Arme 3ow not, but if we send 3ow too;
3e dwelle in pees, & so do many moo. 404
Pleyn 3ow nowte on-tyll 3e fynd greuaunce!
3e sey al-so þat I wold falle in traūns 406

"If domys wer' kepte euene as þei schuld be, 407
And peynes 3oue to hem þat schuld be ded;
I am a woman, þerfor it semyth not me
Ouyr swech bochery for to hold my hed,
Myn hert wold drupe heuy as any led 411
ffor very pyte—þus 3e gune replye,
Ryght for 3e wold I schuld be wedded in hye. 413

MS. Arundel.] *Katharine argues against her Marrying.* 103

Ye loue me well, and that is now I-seene   *Bk. II. Ch. 6.*
My loue, my londes, my worshyp if ye wolde saue.   Katharine thanks Prince
I thanke yow, sir; I sey not [þat] ye raue,   383   Clarus of Cappadocia.
But wysely speke al that ye haue toold,
And for this talkyng I am to yow be-hoold.   385

"But euere me thenketh, whaɳ I vise me weel: 386   Katharine says Prince Clarus has
If it so streyt were, as ye seyɳ, wyth you—
Whiche disese wolde lyke me neuere a deel.
ffor if it were thus, as ye pretende now,
Ye shulde haue neyther feeld ne plow   390
In no¹ pees, if it were al as ye say.   ¹ no expunged
Therfore me thenketh ye walke no trewe way.   392   exaggerated.

"And as for conqvest, seres, care ye ryght noght;   393
Youre lordshipes freely wonne were to your handes
Eer that ye cowde goo, eer thanne ye were wrought;
Ye faute neuere ʒet for townes ne for landes.
Where arɳ your presoneris whiche ye leyde in bandes?   397
There was no werre syth that I was bore,   No war has come in her
But on ovre bordouris, and ye care not þerfore—   399   life.

"ffor we fynde the sowdyouris tho been there   400   She pays the Soldiers.
Ye paye ryght nought, ne nought I coveyte þat ye doo.
Pluk vp your hertis, and be no-thyng in fere!
Arme yow nought, but if we sende yow too;
Ye dwelle in pees, and so doo many moo.   404   Her people live in peace.
Pleyne yow nought vn-til ye fynde grevaunce!
Ye sey also þat I wolde falle in travnce   406

"If domes were kepte euene as they shuld bee,   407
And peynes youe to hem þat shulde beɳ deed;
I am a womaɳ, therfore it semeth not mee   And as to her not being able
Ouere swiche bocherye for to holde myɳ heed,   to punish ill-doers,
Myn herte wolde droupe heuy as ony leed   411
ffor very pyte—thus ye gunne replye,
Ryght for ye wolde I shulde be wedded in hye.   413

" her-to I answerᵖ as ȝe mote nede sey alle : 414
A kyng, ȝe wote weell, hath so gret powerᵖ
Ouyr hys puple, þat whom he wyll he schall
To mak hem fre or make hem prysonerᵖ ;
he may graunt lyffe to hem þat be in dwerᵖ 418
And ek in hope for to be hang & drawe—
þus may he doo, he is a-boue þe lawe. 420

" Than I my-selue, ratherᵖ þan I schuld swoune, 421
Myght graunt hem lyffe, thow þei not worthy werᵖ ;
þus dyd my fadyr full often in þis town—
loke wel a-bowte, for sume of hem be herᵖ
Whech werᵖ þus saued, I am no-þing in dwerᵖ, 425
I a-lowe ȝourᵖ motyues whan þat þei be owte.
I meruayle also þat ȝe consydyr nowte 427

" That for be-cause a kyngys gentyll hert 428
hath swech fredam growyng ryght wyth-Inne
Whan he may not se men blede or smert,
þerfor hys deputees, þe morᵖ & ek þe mynne, 431
Schuld punysch þoo schrewys þat can not cese ne blynne
Of herᵖ euyl dedys—ilk day ȝe may þis se ;
It nedyth not herforᵖ to legge auctorite. 434

" Swech deputees, serᵖ, hafe we many & fele 435
þat of swech materys nedys most hem melle ;
What man þat sle, fyght, robbe or stele,
Ourᵖ offyceres full sekyrly schull hem qwelle,
Nay not þei, but þe lawe þat is so felle, 439
he sleth þis meny—þei ar in þis cas
Seruuantys to lawe, þe morᵖ & ek þe las. 441

" All herᵖ powerᵖ, ȝe wote weell, of us þei haue, 442
As þei had euyr in my fadyres lyffe.
let hem deme, lette hem spylle & saue,
þis longyth to hem, I kepe not of þis stryffe ;
Be it to man, be it to mayde or wyffe 446
þat do a-mys, be hem þei dampned bene :
I schall be to iuges boþe kyng & qween)." 448

"her-to I answere as ye mote nedes sey alle : 414
A kyng, ye wote weel, hath so grete powere
Ouere his puple, that whom he wil he shalle
To make hem free or make hem presonere ;
he may graunte lyf to hem þat be in dwere 418
And eke in hope for to be hange and drawe—
Thus may he doo, he is a-bove the lawe. 420

"Than I my-self, rathere than I shulde swowne, 421
Myght graunte hem lyf, though þei not worthi were;
Thus dede my fadir ful often in this towne—
looke weel abowte, for somme of hem ben here
Whiche were thus saued, I am no-thyng in dwere, 425
I allowe your motyues whan that thei ben ought.
I merueyle also that ye conceyue nowt 427

"That for be-cause a kyngis gentil herte 428
hath suche fredam growyng ryght wyth-Inne
That he myght not see men blede or smerte,
Therfore his deputes, the more and eke the mynne,
Shulde punyshe the shrewes þat can not cece ne blynne
Of her euele dedys—ilke day ye may this see ;
It nedeth not hyrfore to allege auctoryte. 434

"Swiche deputes, syr, haue we many and feele 435
That of suche materis nedes muste hem melle ;
What man that slee, fyghte, robbe or steele,
Oure offyceris ful sekerly shul hem quelle,
Nay not thei, but the lawe that is soo felle, 439
he sleth this meny that (!) are in this cas.
Seruauntes to lawe, the more and eke þe las, 441

"Al her power, ȝe wote weel, of vs thei haue, 442
As thei had euere in my faderis lyf.
lete hem deme, lete hem spylle and saue,
This longeth to hem, I kepe not of þis stryf ;
Be it to men, be it to mayde or wyf 446
That doo a-mys, be hem þei damned bene :
I shal ben to iuges bothe kyng and qveene." 448

Ca^m. 7^m.

The erle of Iaff, was called syr ananye, 449
he stode up þan & to þis lady sayde,
Aȝens hyr answer' he gan ryght þus replye:
"It is full perlyous," he seyd, "to be a mayde
And eke a qween): ȝe may be full sone a-frayde 453
If any rysyng or ony scisme wer' sterde.
ffor of a kyng men wold be more ferde 455

"Than þei of ȝow ar', it is no dowte. 456
þe puple erryth—be-hold ȝe not who fele
Thorow-owte ȝour' londe in euery town) a-bowte
Renn as woodemen? ȝe may it not consele,
þei fyght, þei flyght, þei robbe & þei stele. 460
All þis aray, me thynkyth, ȝe sett at nowte,
It faryth as ȝe of all þis þink[1] ne rowte.   [1] r. þing 462

"Ȝe sett mor', be godd þat sytt a-boue, 463
Be on old boke, & eke mor' deynte haue,
þan be werr' or iustys, lust or elles loue.
Men sey, þei schall bryng ȝow to ȝour graue!
What do ȝour bokys? parde, þei wyll not saue 467
Neyther' man ne best; þei dull a manny[s] mende,
Apeyr' hys body, hys eyne þei make blynde. 469

"he þat taute [yow] fyrst þis scole, I pray 470
he mote be hangyd, I trow he is worthy!
he hath ȝow browte & put in swech aray
þat myrth & ioye ȝe late hym)[1] slyde forby;   [1] r. hem
Euyr at bokes ȝe sytte, knele & lye. 474
Alas, madame, who lese ȝe ȝour' tyme!
I wepe so sor', I may no lenger' ryme. 476

"ffor goddys lofe, & for ȝour' puples sake, 477
Chaunge now ȝour' lyff & let ȝour bok be stylle,
loke no lenger' vp-on þoo letteres blake!
ffor, be my trowth, stody schall ȝow spylle.
Tend on-to myrth, tak a lord ȝow tylle! 481

MS. Arundel.] *Katharine is again urgd to marry.*

Ca^{m.} septimu*m*.

The Erl of Iaf, was called ananye,   449   Earl Ananias of Joppa tells Katharine
he stood vp thanne and to this lady sayde,
A-yens hir answere he gan ryght thus replye:
"It is ful p*er*illous," he seyde, "to be a mayde
And eke a qveen; ȝe may be ful sone afrayde   453
If ony rysynge or ony sisme be sterde.
ffor of a kyng meñ wolde be more a-ferde   455

"Thañ þei of yow are, it is no dowte.   456
The puple erreth—be-hoold ye not how fele   *that her people*
Thurgh-ovte youre lond in euery[1] touñ a-bowte   [1] MS. eue'y
Renne as wode meñ? ye may it not consele,
Thei fyght, þei flyght, thei robbe and þei stele.   460   *fight, rob and steal, and she disregards it.*
Al this aray, me thenketh, ye sette at nowt,
It fareth as ye of al this þing ne rowt.   462

"Ye sette more, be god þat sytteth a-boue,   463   *She cares more for an old book than for war or love.*
Be an olde book, and eke more deynte haue,
Thañ be iustes or werre, lust or ell*is* loue.
Meñ seyñ, thei shal brynge you to y*our* graue!
What doo y*our* bookys? sekirly thei wil not saue   467
Neither mañ ne beeste; thei dulle a mannys mende,
A-peyre his body, his eyne thei make blynde.   469

"he þat taught yow first þis scole, I pray   470
he mote be hanged, I trowe he is worthy!
he hath you browght and put in suche aray
That myrthe and ioye ye late heñ slyde forby;
Euere at bookys ye sitte, knele and ly.   474   *She's always at her books.*
Allas, madame, how lese ye y*our* tyme!
I wepe so sore, I may no lengere ryme.   476

"ffor goddys loue, and for youre puples sake,   477
Chaunge now y*our* lyf and lete youre book be stille,   *Let 'em be!*
Looke no lengere vp-on tho letterys blake!
ffor, be my wytte, stody shal yow spylle.
Tende on-to myrthe, take a lord yow tille!   481   *Marry, and*

Bk. II. Ch. 7. þan schal ȝour body be full heyll & qwert,
And mech̄ mor' ese schull ȝe haf at hert." 483

Bk. II. Ch. 8. **Ca**^{m.} **8**^{m.}

"ȜE wold allgate þat I schuld wedded be, 484
Ryght for þis skylle, ȝe sey, men drede me nowte;
If any scysme wer' reysyd in þis cuntre,
[fol. 25]
[1st hand] It wer' not likly be me for to be browt'
To ony good end, men sett at me ryth nowt; 488
Ȝe shuld drede mor' a man þan ȝe do me.
And I sey þus: I knowe as wele as ȝe, 490

"A man a-lone, be he neuer so wyse 491
Ne eke so strong', he may no mor', I-wys,
But euyn as I may; hys puple shal be nyse
And eke euele tetched; þe power' is not his
To amend a-lone all þat is a-mys: 495
his lordes must help to his gouernayle,
And elles his labour' it wil lytyl a-vayle. 497

"help ȝe on your' syde as I shal on myn! 498
loke ȝe be trew on-to my crowne & me,
lete no treson in ȝour' hertys lyn:
Than schal þis lond ful wele demened be.
O noble god, who grete felicite 502
Shuld be wyth vs, if' we wer' in þis plyth!
We myth sey þan, our' leuyng' wer' ful ryght. 504

"Wyl ȝe¹ now her' who puple may make her' kyng' 505
To erre sumtyme & sumtyme to do a-mys? ¹ MS. we
Ryth be ensaumple shal I proue þis þing'.
Ther' was a kyng' her'-be-syde, I-wys,
ffer' in þe est', þat lyued in ioy & blys, 509
In babilony euene,¹ nabugodonosor he hyth. ¹ r. I mene?
his puple made hym to do a-gayn þe ryth. 511

"ffor he had with hym in maner of' a preest 512
A ful goode man & of' grete abstinense—
fful preuy þingis bar' he in his breest,

Thanne shal youre body ben ful heil and qvert, — *be healthy* 483
And moche more eese shul ye haue at hert." — *and happy!*

Ca^{m.} octauu*m*. — Bk. II. Ch. 8.

"YE wolde algate þat I shulde wedded be, 484 — *Katharine answers*
Ryght for this skyl, ye sey, men drede me nought; — *the Earl of Joppa.*
If ony sisme were reysed in this contre,
It were not lykly be me for to be brought
To ony good ende, men sette me at ryght nought; 488
Ye shulde drede more a man þan ye doo me.
And I seye thus: I knowe as weel as yee, 490

"A man allone, be he neue*r*e so wys [1] — *A King alone*
Ne eke so strong as[1] eue*r* was ony in world þis,
What may he doo but as I? hys puple shal be nys
And eke euel tetched; the power is not his — *can't mend all that's*
To amende allone al that is a-mys: 495 — *amiss.*
his lordis muste helpe to his goue*r*nayle,
And ellys his labour it wil lytyl avayle. 497

"helpe ye on youre syde as I shal on myn! 498
Looke ye be truwe on-to my crowne and me, — *If her Lords*
lete no treson in yowre hertys lyn: — *'ll be true to her,*
Than shal this lond ful weel demened be.
O noble god, how gret felicyte 502 — *all will go well.*
Shuld be wyth vs, if we were in this plyght!
We myght sey þanne, oure leuyng were ful ryght. 504

"Wyl ye now here how puple may make her kyng 505 — *People often make Kings*
To erre somtyme and somtyme to doo a-mys? — *err.*
Ryght be exauample shal I proue this thyng.
There was a kyng heere-be-syde, I-wis,
ffer in the Est, that leued in ioye and blys, 509
In babylon euene, Nabuchodonosor he hyght. — *Nebuchadnezzar*
his puple made hym to doo a-geyn the ryght. 511

"ffor he had wyth hym in mane*r* of a preest 512
A ful good man and of grete abstynence,
fful preuy thyng*is* bar he in his breest,

---
[1] as ff. till 493 as I, on erasure; orig. he may no more I-wys

he coude tell all of¹ derth &¹ of¹ pestilence.   ¹ overlined.
O þing¹ þer was in whech he dede offence: 516
he worchiped not swech goddes as we doo—
Danyel he hyth. but a-mong lyones too   518

"Was he putt, ryth for þe puple so wolde;   519
The kyng¹ durst not wythstand hem in þat cas,
he must do soo, þow he wold or nolde.
fful sor' repentaunt aftyr-ward he was:
[fol. 25, b.]
[2nd hand]
ffor danyell was saued ryth be goddys grace,   523
Whech god he seruyd—god wold I myght hym know,
þat noble godd þat made hys myght so growe   525

"In swech lowe puple! her' may 3e see & ken: 526
ffor puples crying a kyng may oftyn erre;
þe woode opynyon of swech fonned men
Makyth a lord oft-tyme to do þe werr',
To make hym meuyd, to sett him¹ oute of herr'—   530
ffy on her' cry, qwan þei no reson hafe!   ² MS. hem
3e sey alsoo, for þat 3e wold me saue,   532

"I must leue book, I must leue stody eke.   533
My bokes, seres, godd help, what greue þei 3ow?
þis werdly gouernaunce wer' not worth a leke,
Ne wer' þeis bokes; þei ar' to mannes prow
ffull necessarye, for our' myndys ar' swech now: 537
It slydyth forby all þat euer þei know,
And be our' bokes a-geyn full fast þei grow.   539

"Who schuld we wete þat þe fyrst man of all   540
had hyght Adam, & eke hys wyff eue,
Saue þat in a booke, whech genesis þei calle,
I sey it onys wrete, & red it on a eue?
3et is þat book not of our' be-leue   544
Receyued as 3et—me þinkyth it mut nede,
Be-cause he tellyth þe be-gynnyng & þe dede   546

"Of our' olde ffaderes. who schuld eke know   547
þe worthy conquestys of elderys þat wer' her',

he cowde tell al of derthe and of pestilence.
Oo þing ther was in wiche he dede offence: 516
he wurshiped not swiche goddys as we doo—
Danyel he hight. but a-mong leones too 518

" Was he put, right for the puple soo wolde; 519
The kyng durst not withstonde hem in þat cas,
he muste doo soo whedyr he wolde or nolde.
fful sore repentaunt afterward[1] he was: [1] ward overlined.
ffor Danyel was saued ryght be goddys gras,   [2] I m. overl. 523
Whiche god he serued—god wulde I myght[2] hym knowe,
That noble god þat maad his myght so growe 525

" In swiche lowe puple! heere may ye see and ken:
ffor puples cryeng*is* men may often erre; 527
The wood oppynyon of suche fonned men
Maketh a lord often-tyme to doo the werre, 529
To make hym to be meved and sette hym oute of herre—
ffy on her cry, whan thei no reson haue!
Ye sey also, for that ye wolde me saue, 532

" I muste leue book, I muste leue stody eke. 533
My book*is*, seers, god help, what greue þei yow?
This wordly gouernauns were not wurth a leke,
Ne where[1] these book*is*; thei arn to mannys prow   [1] r. were
fful necesarye, for oure myndes arn suche now: 537
It slydeth forby al þat euere thei knowe,
And be oure bookys a-geyn ful faste thei growe. 539

" how shul we wete þat þe first man of alle 540
had hyght Adam, and eke his wyf Eue,
Saue in a book, genesis thei calle,
I seye it oones wretyn, and red it on an Eue?
Yet is that book not of oure be-leue 544
Receyued as yet—me thenketh it muste nede,
Be-cause he telleth the be-gynnyng and the dede 546

" Of oure olde fader*is*. hoo shulde eke knowe 547
The wurthy conqvest*is* of elderes that wer heere,

Bk. II. Ch. 8.

If bokes teld hem not only be rowe?
We can for-gete þat we dyd þis ȝer'!
Wherfor' our' bookes tell to vs ful cler' 551
Swech-maner' þinges as we had for-ȝete.
Ȝour' opynyon þer-for', ser', now must ȝe lette. 553

"ffor goddys lawe ne ma*n*nys schuld not be know, 554
Ne wer' our' bokes, þis dar' I sauely say;
Our' preestes arn fayn) to loke hem be row
A-geyn a feest, a-geyn an holyday,
Wha*n* þei wyll pre*c*he of any swech aray, 558

[fol. 26]   Eyther' of Iubiter, or neptune, hys brothyr.
leue we þa*n* þis mater' & carp of sume othyr! 560

"Blame not swech þing þat stant i*n* full grete stede; 561
Curse not my mayster', for þa*n* wyll I be wroth!

[5th hand] It semyth ȝou bettir for to bydde ȝour' bede
Than to sey swech wordes! eke it is ful lothe
To me, to sey þus, but only for myn) othe 565
Whech þat I made to meynteyn) al-maner þing
Whech longe to our goddis and to her offring." 567

Bk. II. Ch. 9.

Ca^m. 9^m.

Than spake a lord, þei called ser hercules, 568
The prince of paphon), of þat gret cuntre—
Eue*r*y man satt' stille and held his pees
To her þe speche, þe tale whech þat he
Be-gan to telle; for his auctorite 572
Was þoo ful gret, in special for his age.
his wordes wer acordyng to his visage. 574

Thus he be-gan: "it is bettir, my lady dere, 575
In swech a caas, whan it mote nedis be doo,
To do it at onys, þan for to lyue in dwere
And for to a-byde eythir ȝer or too.
Take ȝe no heed, consyder ȝe not þer-too 579
Who ouyde seyde & wrote it in his booke:
'Whan þing is newe, be war be tyme and looke 581

If bookys tolde hem not oonly be rowe?
We can forgete þat we dede this yere;
Wherefore oure bookys telle to us ful clere 551
Swiche-maner þing*is* as we had for-yeet.
Youre oppynyoɯ therfore, sere, now must ye leet. 553

" ffor goddis lawe ne mannys shuld not be knowe, 554 *of God's law, and man's.*
Ne were oure bookys, this dar I sauely say;
Oure preestes arɯ fayɯ to looke hem be rowe
A-geyɯ a feste, a-geyɯ an holy day,
Whaɯ thei wil p*reche* of ony suche aray, 558
Eyther of Iupiter, or Neptune, his brother.
leue we thanne þis mater and carpe of soɯ other! 560

" Blameth not suche þing þat stant in ful gret stede; 561 *Do not blame books.*
Curse not my mayster, for þanne wil I be wroth!
It semeth yow bett*er* for to bydde yowre bede
Thanne seye swiche wordys!—eke it is ful looth
Soo (!) me to sey thus, but oonly for myɯ ooth 565
Whiche þ*at* I made to may*n*teyɯ aH-man*er* thyng
Whiche longeɯ to oure godd*is* and to her offeryng." 567

Ca*m.* nonu*m.*   *Bk. II. Ch. 9.*

Thanne spak a lord, þei calle s*i*r hercules, 568 *Hercules, Prynce of Paphon,*
The prynce of paphoɯ, of þat grete contre—
Eu*er*y man sat stylle and helde his pees
To here the speche, þe tale whyche þat hee
Be-gaɯ to telle; for his auctoryte 572
Was tho ful grete, in specyal for his age.
his wordys were a-coordynge to his vysage. 574

Thus be-gaɯ he: "it is better', my lady dere, 575 *tells Katharine she'd better get married at once.*
In suche a cas, whaɯ it must nedes be doo,
To doo it at oones thanne for to leue in dwere
Or for to abyde ether on yeer or too.
Take ye non heed, consydere ye not ther-too 579
how ouyde seyde and wrote it in his book:
' Whaɯ thyng is newe, be war be tyme and look 581

"'ffor to amende it; for medecyn comyth ouyr-lathe¹ 582
Whañ þat þe man his² ded and hens I-goo,   ¹ r. late ² r. is
And with his frendes born oute at þe gate'?
ȝour' londes, lady, if ȝe take heed þer-too,
ly fer a-sunder, for fro þis cuntre, loo,   586
Whech we be Inne, rith on-to famagost
Is many a myle; who schuld ȝe with ȝour host   588

"Ryde sweche a way? and if þat ȝe schuld sayle,   589
It wold yow fese þe salt water rowe,
ȝour' hert wold drede wyth-outyn ony fayle—
That I sey now, me þinkyth it for your' prow.
The lond of¹ cipre, þat I cam þorow now,   593
Is eke ful ferr'.   it mute nedes be a man
Whech schal wil, & eke þat may & can,   595

"Do al þis labour', both in flesch & gost,   596
Ryde & seyle, labour' to se his lande,¹   ¹ orig. londe
Sumtyme her', sumtyme at famagost—
þus shal he gouerne þe lond, þe see, þe sand.
Þan may ȝe haue your' bokes in your' hond   600
And stody ȝour' fille, it shal not greue us.
Me þinkyth sewyrly þat ȝe shul[d] wil þus!   602

"ȝe shul[d] desyr' to be mor' at ȝour' ese,   603
To weld ȝour' leyser' as ȝe desyr' to haue;
þer is mech þing¹ þat doth ȝou of[t]¹ displese,   ¹ MS. oft
Whech shuld not þan.   þerfor, if¹ ȝe wil saue
Your' owne astate, & þus no lenger waue   607
Both too & fro, doth be our' counsayle;
In tyme comyng¹ it may ȝow mech avayle."   609

Ca^m. 10^m.

"Gramercy, ser', of¹ your' goode counsayle!"   610
 þus seyd þe qween, "if¹ ȝe be as ȝe wer',
ȝour' myth & cunnyng¹ may vs mech avayle,
&, as me þinkith, no man shal vs der',
On paphon or cipre shal þer be no wer'   614

Katharine is once more urgd to marry.

"'ffor to amende it; ffor medecyn comyth ouere-late
Whan þat the man is deed and hens I-goo 583
And wyth his freendis boorn oute at þe gate?'
Youre londes, lady, if ye take heed ther-too,
lye fer a-sondre, for fro this contre, loo, 586 *Her lands lie far asunder.*
Whiche we be Inne, ryght on-to famagost
Is many a myle; how shuld ȝe wyth your oost 588

"Ride swiche a weye? and if ye shuld sayle, 589 *How can she ride, and sail, and be everywhere?*
It wulde yow fese, that salt water row,
Your herte wolde drede wyth-outen ony fayle—
That I seye now, me thenketh it for your prow.
The lond of Cypre, that I cam thorgh now, 593
Is eke ful ferre. it muste nedes ben a man *A man is needed*
Whiche shal haue will,[1] and eke þat may and can 595 [1] overl.

"Doo al this labour, bothe in flesh and goost, 596
Ride and sayle, laboure to see his lande,
Somtyme here, somtyme at famagoost—
Thus shal he gouerne the lande, the see and þe sande. *to govern,*
Thanne may ye haue your bookys in youre hande 600 *while she may study her books.*
And stodyen yowre fylle, it shal not greuen vs.
Me thenketh suerly þat ye shulde wiln thus! 602

"Ye shulde desyre to be more at youre Eese, 603
To welde your leyser þat ye desyre to haue;
There is moche thyng þat dooth yow ofte displese
Whiche shulde not þanne. therfore, if ye wil saue *The Prince urges Katharine to marry.*
Youre owne astat, and thus no lengere waue 607
Bothe too and fro, dooth be oure counsayle;
In tyme comynge it may yow moche avayle." 609

Cam. decimum.

"GRomercy, sir, of youre good counsayle!" 610 *Katharine answers Prince Hercules of Paphon.*
Thus seyde the queen, "if ye be as ye were,
Youre myght and cunnynge may vs moche avayle
And, as me thenketh, no man shal vs dere, *She praises his rule of Cyprus,*
On paphon or Cypre shal there be no werre 614

Bk. II. Ch. 10. Whil þat ȝe lyue, her-of¹ I drede ryth nowth.
Now wold god so, it wer' ful der' I-boute 616

"Vp-on my body, in cas þat it stood soo 617
Thorow all my lond as it in cipre stant!
I mith þan stody, þan myth I tend þer-to
And al my wil¹ þerof¹ now I want. ¹ haue om. ?
ȝe shuld plese god, if¹ ȝe wold set & plant 621
ȝour' knythly maneres in yong¹ men þat be her',
To lern hem iust; I wolde wele qwite ȝour' h^rere. 623

[fol. 27]
2nd hand]
" Of þat gret godd ek whech goucrneth all batayle, 624
Mars I mene, whos knyght ȝe hafe be founde,
ȝe schall haf worchep, thow ȝe hafe non auayle,
To tech hem holde þe schaftes þat be rounde.
Wyth ȝour' praysyng my tale schuld mor' abunde 628
But þat we schuld noght preyse men in presence.
Than in ȝour' londe I lak not now þe absence 630

"Of my lorde my ffadyr; it is noght gretly a-spyede 631
hys deth wyth yow. I sette cas ferthermor'
þat if I wer', as ȝe wolde, now newe a-lyede,
Weddyd I mene, what schuld þan ȝour' sore
Therby be esed ? þat man is not ȝet bore, 635
Wer' he neuyr so wys, manfull or stronge,
Of hert fell, of body broode & longe, 637

"That myght at onys be in all þese places 638
Whech ȝe spak of ryght now in ȝour' tale;
Thow he had plentiuously all þe grete graces
Whech kepe a man fro byttyr peynes bale
And saue hym harmles, as wyth-Inne þe wale 642
Of a strong schyppe a man is bor' a-lofte,
ȝet myght he noght, rode he neuyr so softe, 644

" Be in too places at onys. for ryght as a stone, 645
Whan he is layd in hys naturall place,
May not þat tyme be founde but þer a-lone

Whil þat ye leuen̄, her-of I drede ryght nought.   *Bk. II. Ch. 10.*
Now wolde god so, it were ful dere I-bought   616

"Vp on̄ my body, in cas that it stood soo   617
Thurgh̄ al my lond as it in Cypre stante!
I myght þanne stody, thanne myght I tende ther-too
And haue¹ al my wil ther-of now I wante.   ¹ A. h. on erasure.
Ye shulde plese god, if ye wolde sette or plante   621   and wishes he'd teach her young Syrians
Youre knyghtly maners in yonge men̄ tho ben̄ her',
To lerne hem Iusten̄; I wolde weel quyte your hyre.   623

"Of þat grete god eke whiche gouerneth al batayl̄,   624
Mars I mene, whos knyght ye haue be founde,
Ye shal haue wurship, thow ye haue not avayle,
To teche hem̄ hoolde the shaftes tho ben̄ rovnde.   to handle their spears.
With youre preysyng my tale shuld more abounde   628
But þat we shulde not preyse men̄ in presens.
Than in yowre lond I lakke not now the absens   630

"Of my lord, my fader; it is not gretely aspyede   631
his deeth with ȝow. I set cas ferthermore
That if I were, as ye wolde, now newe allyede,
Wheddede I meene, what shuld thanne your soore
Therby ben̄ esed? þat man̄ is not yeet bore,   635   No one man
Were he neuere soo wys, manful or strong,
Of herte fel, of body brood and long,   637

"That myght at oones be in al̄ these places   638
Whiche ye spak of ryght now in your tale;
Though he hadde plentyuously al̄ þe grete graces
Whiche kepe a man̄ from alle þe bitter peynes bale
And save hym̄ harmles, as with-inne the wale   642
Of a stronge ship a man̄ is bore a-loft,
Yet myght he not, rood he neuer so soft,   644

"Be in to places at oones. for ryght as a ston̄,   645   can be in two places at once,
Whan he is leyd in his natural place,
May not at that tyme be founde but there alon̄

Wher' he was leyd, ryght so in þis cas ;
O man may not be in dyuerse place, 649
And þat at ones, for' be our' phylosophye
It is condempned as for an heresye. 651

" Therfor' ryght thus we conclude our' clause : 652
Euery body hath hys naturall rest,
Aftyr hys kende or aftyr hys priuy cause, [1 on the margin.
Whech þat¹ þe goddes ryght euene as hem lest
haue departyde. to opyne thus þan holde I best : 656
he þat is her', he is her', & noo-wher' ellys—
Example lo I mene : who-so-euyr þat dwelles 658

" At grete Alysaundyr', he dwelleth not in famagost. 659
þan must euery man nedys hym-self remeue
And cary hys men thorow-owte all þe coost,
Ete at noone, rest [hym]¹ eke at eue [¹ om.
her' & þer' as hys iornay wyll preue. 663
Ryght so may I, thow I a woman be ;
þan in ȝour argument me thynkyth noo difficult." 665

Cam. 11m.

The duk of damasko was wroth wyth þis answer', 666
he stode up tho & þus he gan to sey :
" In my ȝong age ryght thus dyd I ler' :
þe pupyll must nedys on-to þe kyng obeye,
loue hym & drede hym euyr tyll þei deye, 670
ffor þei ar' bounde full sor' thus to do ;
And we wyll euyr hertly bowe þer-too. 672

" So is a kyng swor' eke ful depe 673
To loue hys pupyll, be þei heye or lowe,
Ryght & trowth amonge hem alle to kepe,
So þat noo wrong schuld hem ouyr-throwe.
þus ar' ȝe swor', madame ; ȝe it know, 677
Bettyr þan I, qwat is to breke an othe—
Reson may not ne schall not make ȝow wroth. 679

MS. Arundel.] *Katharine doesn't need a Husband.*

Where he was leyd, ryght soo in this cace ; *Bk. II. Ch. 10.*
Oo man may not be in dyuers place, 649
And that at oones, for be oure philosophie — as natural philosophy
It is condemned as for an heresye. 651 teaches;

"Therfore ryght thus we conclude oure clause : 652
Euery body hath his natural reste,
After his kynde or after his preuy cause,
Whiche that þe goddys ryght as hem leste
haue departed. to opyne thus than holde I beste : 656
he þat is here, he is here, and noo-where ellys—
Exaunple loo I mene : hoo-so-euere þat dwellys 658

"At grete Alysaundre, he dwelleth not in famagost. 659
Than muste euery man nedes hym-self remeue — man must move himself when he wants to get to another place;
And carye his men thurgh-oute al the oost,
Ete at noon, eke reste hym at eue
heere and there as his Iorney wil preue. 663
Right soo may I, thow I a woman be ; — so she, Katharine, can do the same.
Thanne in youre argument me thenketh noon difficulte."

Ca^{m.} vndecimum.   *Bk. II. Ch. 11.*

The duke of Damask was wroth wyth þis answere, 666 The Duke of Damascus
he stood vp tho and thus gan he to seye :
"In my yonge age ryght thus dede I lere :
The puple must nedes on-to the kyng obeye,
Loue hym and drede hym euere tyl thei deye, 670
ffor thei arn bounde ful sore thus for to doo ;
And we wyl euere hertely bowe ther-too. 672

"Soo is a kyng sworn eke ful depe 673 reminds Katharine that she swore
To loue his puple, be thei heygh or lowe,
Right and treuthe a-mongis hem alle to kepe,
Soo that no wrong shulde hem ouere-throwe.
Thus arn ye sworn, madame, ye it knowe ; 677
Better þan I ȝe [1]wot what[1] it is to breke an ooth— [1] overl.
Reson may not ne shal not make yow wrooth. 679

"Ȝowrᵉ othe was þis, if ȝe remembyrᵉ ȝow welle : 680
To ordeyn so for londe, for man & townⁿ),
þat alle þese þingys at euery tyme & seele
Schuld be redressed, be it vp or downⁿ),
ffor þat þei longe alle on-to ȝourᵉ crownⁿ). 684
Þis othe may ȝe notᵗ saue non otherᵉ wey
But if ȝe wyll on-to ourᵉ wyll obeye, 686

"ffor to be weddyd on-to sume worthy man. 687
Wherᵉ is no lorde, þer is no lawe, men say.
Now, be my trowth, in no wey þink I can
þat ony woman, if þer come a fray,
Schuld sese vs sone, & specyaly a may. 691
Ȝe berᵉ vs downⁿ) wyth ȝourᵉ philosophye ;
But at þe last ȝe must bowe, hardylye." 693

Bk. II. Ch. 12.   Caᵐ. 12ᵐ.

"SEr'," seyd þe qwenⁿ), "ȝe make now swech a skyll 694
Ryght in ȝour tale whech ȝe enforsed now,
þat I wold thus, & þat it werᵉ my wylle,
þat ȝe no gouernauns had. & I sewyrᵉ ȝowe,
I thowte it neuyrᵉ ; it werᵉ not to my prow. 698
ffor thowe it¹ schuld noye alle ourᵉ oost,   ¹ MS. I
Thys wote I well, it schuld towch me moste. 700

"I kepe, & schall, myn othe whech I made, 701
Tyll þat I deye I schall it neuyr breke.
Ȝe may wel carpe & in ȝour langage wade,
New wordes reherse & new resones speke,
Whech werᵉ rehersyd & haue herᵉ answers eke ; 705
Me lyst not for to remembre swech thynk¹ a-geynⁿ). ¹ r. thyng
But thus mech, serᵉ, to ȝow darᵉ I seynⁿ) : 707

"As for my ffadyrᵉ, he left ȝow in rest & pes, 708
And in noo debate, ne lykely for to be ;
If þerᵉ ryse ony, ȝe may ȝourᵉ-self it ses,
And but ȝe do, ȝe be on-trewe to me,
Not to me oonly, but to þe mageste 712

"Youre ooth was þis, if ye remembre yow weel: 680 *Bk. II. Ch. 11.*
To ordeyne soo for the lond, for man and town, *an oath to redress all her folk's wrongs;*
That alle þese þing*is* at eu*er*y tyme and seel
Shulde be redressed, be it vp or down,
ffor that thei longen alle to yo*ur* crown. 684
This oth may ye not saue non other weye *and this she cannot do*
But if ye wil on-to oure wil obeye, 686

"ffor to be wedded on-to som wurthy man. 687 *unless she weds some worthy man.*
Where is no lord, there is no lawe, men say.
Now, be my sothe, in no weye thenke I can
That ony woman, if there come a fray,
Shulde cece vs soone, and specyally a may. 691
Ye bere vs doun with youre phylosophie;
But at þe last ye muste bowe, hardylye." 693

"SEre," seyde the queen, "ye make now suche a skyl *Katharine answers*
Ryght in yo*ur* tale whiche ye enforced now, 695
That I wolde thus, and also[1] it were my wyl, [1] *on erasure.*
That ye no gou*er*nance had. I sewer you,
I thoughte it neu*er*e; it were not to my prow. 698
ffor thow it shuld noyen al oure oost,
This wote I weel, it shuld touche me moost. 700

"I kepe, and shal, myn ooth whiche I made, 701 *that she will keep her oath.*
Til þat I deye I shal it neu*er*e breke.
Ye may weel carpe and in yowre langage wade,
Newe woordys reherse and newe resouns speke
Whiche where rehersed and haue her answere eke; 705
Me leste not for to remembre swiche þing ageyn.
But thus moche, sir, to yow dar I seyn: 707

"That, for my fader lefte yow in reste and in pees 708
And in no debate, ne lykly for to bee,
If there ryse ony, ye may youre-seelf it cees; *If any quarrels rise, it is the Duke's duty to stop them.*
And but ye doo, ye ben on-trewe to me,
Not to me oonly, but to the maieste 712

Bk. II. Ch. 12. Of my crown, & gylty for to deye.
A-vyse ȝow bettyr whan þat ȝe lyst to seye!" 714

Bk. II. Ch. 13. Caᵐ. 13ᵐ.

A Gret clerk þoo stod up be hym-selue, 715
þat was fful scharp in wytte, as I wene;
In þis mater' he thowte þoo for to delue
A lytyll depper', per-for vn-to þe qwene
Thus he spake: "þese lordes all-be-dene 719
þei can not, lady, a-spye as ȝet ȝour' art,
Who pregnantly ȝe can kepe ȝour' part. 721

"Ȝe arn lerned, & so be þei nowte; 722
It is less wondyr' thow þei concluded be.
But euyr wondyr I gretly in my thowte,
Ȝe sett no mor' be þat hye degre,
Grettest of all, I mene þe regalte. 726
Who schuld preys it but ȝe? I supposyd,
Aftyr' þe name wyth wech ȝe ar' losed, 728

"That ȝe wold enhaunse þis ilk degre 729
Most of all wommen. what eylyth now ȝour wytte?
I am in poynt to leue it is noght ȝe.
þis mater', lady, on-to myn hert it sytte
So sor', I-wys, me thynkyth it wyll it kytte. 733
Ȝe drynk so sor', I trowe, of poetrye,
And most in specyale of hym, valerye, 735

"Whech wold, it semyth, þat no man wedded schulde be,
he counseled so to on ruffyn, ȝe know it welle, 737
ȝa ouyrwelle—what nede is for me
ffor to reherce þe sorow, þe langwor' euerydelle
Whech þat longyth vn-to þat fykell whelle 740
Of spousalye, as wrytyth þis hold clerke,
Valerye, þe moost in þis forsayd werke. 742

"But thow in þe por' be often) swech myschauns, 743
It is not þus in swech grete mageste
Wyth whech we wolde ȝow, lady, now avauns.

Of my crowne, and gylty for to deye.
A-vyse yow better whaɴ ye leste to seye!" 714

Ca^{m.} duodecimu*m*.

A grete clerk tho stood vp be hym-self, 715
That was ful sharp in witte, as I wene;
In [t]his mater tho he thought for to delf
A lytil deppere, therfore on-to the queene
Thus he spak: "these lordes alle be-dene 719
Thei can not, lady, a-spye as yet yo*ur* art,
how pregnauntly ye kaɴ kepe youre part. 721

"Ye arɴ lerned, and so be thei nought; 722
It is lesse wondir thow thei concluded bee.
But eue*r*e wonder I gretly in my thought,
Ye sette no more be that heye degre,
Grettest of alle, I meene the regalte. 726
hoo shulde preyse it but ye? I supposed,
After the name with w^hyche ye arɴ losed, 728

"That ye wolde enhaunce this ilke degre 729
Moost of alle womeɴ. what eyleth now yo*ur* wyt?
I am in poynt to leeue it is not yee.
This mater, lady, on-to myɴ hert it syt
Soo sore, I-wys, me thenketh it wil it kyt. 733
Ye drynke so soore, I trowe, of poetrye,
And most enspecial of hyɴ, Valerye, 735

"Whiche wolde, it semyth, þat no maɴ wedded shuld be,
he counseiled soo to on ruffyn, ye knowe it weel, 737
Ya oue*r*ewel—what nedeth it for me
ffor to reherce the soorwe, the langour eue*r*y deel
Whiche þat longeth on-to þat fekel wheel 740
Of spousayle, as wryteth þis olde clerk,
Valery, the moste in this forseyd werk. 742

"But thow in the pore be ofteɴ suche myschaunce, 743
It is not thus in swiche maieste
Wyth whyche we wolde you, lady, avaunce.

Bk. II. Ch. 13. And euyr contrarye on-to our wylle are ȝe.
Thynk ȝe not what ȝe seyd wole late, parde? 747
Ȝe spake not long sythe & seyd ryght euen þus:
Ȝe wold, ȝe seyd, haue on to gouern vs. 749

"What schuld he be but he wer a kyng? 750
Þer may no man gouern þis grete reem
But swych a man þat is able in all þing
To wedd ȝow;—& for my lord ȝour Em
May not wed ȝow neyther in wecch ne drem, 754
Therfor he may not her as in þis place
Ber noo crown, for it stant in ȝour grace 756

"Who schall it ber, it longeth on-to ȝour ryght. 757
Syth ȝe haue graunted þan þat we schall haue
A gouernour to sett vs in good plyth,
Þan haue ȝe graunted all þat euyr we craue;
And fro þis purpos efte ȝe turn & wane, 761
And sey ȝe wyll no husbonde haue as ȝitte!
Be-holdeth now wysely if so be þat ȝour wytte 763

"Be stedefastly I-sett euyr vp-on o poynt? 764
Me thynkyth nay, ȝe changen too & froo,
Now wyll ȝe, now ar ȝe in an other ioynte
And þan wyll ȝe not. who schuld we come þer-too
To know your purpos, whan ȝe vary soo? 768
lat vs know pleynly, lady, what ȝe mene;
We be ȝour men, þinkyth ȝe be our qwene." 770

Bk. II. Ch. 14. Ca^{m.} 14^{m.}

"SEr," seyd þe qwene, "ȝe be lordes fele, 771
And wyse also: what nedyth ȝow þus to care,
Whan ȝe be ȝung, lusty, & in good hele;
Eke ȝour countres beth as now not bare
Neyther of corn, of men, ne of welfar? 775
But to ȝow, syr, I woundre mych mor than ȝe—
ffor ȝe sey in þis mater ȝe hafe meruayle of me; 777

[MS. Arundel.] *Katharine is still again urgd to marry.*

And euere contrarye on-to oure wil arn) ye.   *Bk. II. Ch. 12.*
Thenke ye not what ye seyde wol late newele?   747   She has promist her
Ye spak not longe syth and seyde ryght thus: folk some one to govern
Ye wulde, ye seyde, haue oon) to gouerne vs.   749   them.

"What shulde he be but he were a kyng?   750
There may no man) gouerne this grete reem
But swhiche a man that is able in al þing
To wedde yow;—and for my lord youre eem)[1]   [1] orig. heem   This must be her husband.
May not wedde yow neyther in wetche ne in dreem,   754
Therfore he may not here in þis plas
bere no crowne, for it stant in youre gras   756

"ho shal it bere, it longeth on-to your ryght.   757
Syth that ye haue graunted thanne that we shal haue
A gouernour to sette vs in good plyght,
Thanne haue ye graunted al þat euere we craue;
And fro this purpos efte ye turne and waue,   761   But she says she won't
And seye ye wil now) housbond haue as yit.   have a husband.
Be-holdeth now wysly if soo be þat youre wyt   763

"Be stedfastly set euere vp-on) oo poynt?   764
Me thenketh nay, ye chaungen too and fro,
Now wil ye, now arn ye in a-nother ioynt
And thanne wil ye nought. how shuld we come þer-too
To knowe youre purpos, whanne ye varye soo?   768   Why does she vary so?
Lete vs knowe pleynly, lady, what ye meene;
We ben) youre men, thenketh ye ben) oure queene."   770

Ca^{m.} 13^{m.}   *Bk. II. Ch. 13.*

"SEre," seyde the queen), "ye be lordes fele,   771   Katharine
    And wyse also: what nedeth yow thus to care,
Whan) ye be yonge, lusty, and in good hele;
Eke youre contrees beth as now not bare
Neyther of corn, of men, ne of weelfare?   775
But to you, sir, I wonder moche more than) ye—
ffor ye seyn) in this mater ye haue merueyle of me;   777

" And wher' ȝe sey þat I wold now disseyue 778
Wyth my termes my lordes whech I loue,
I pray ȝow hertly þat ȝe wyll noght conceyue
Of me swech þing. for truly, it wold not proue ;
Swech iapes to make wer' not to be-houe, 782
Neythyr to me ne to non other' wyght ;
To be a dysseyuour' it is a grett dispyte. 784

" Ȝe sayd eft-sone þat I dyspyse a kyng, 785
Eke þat astate I trede all vndyr fote.
Thow I be not enclyned to ȝour askyng,
As for to be weddyd whan I schall, godd wote,
Ȝet am I come bothe of þat stok & rote— 789
I may not hyde it, for it is know so wyde—
Bothe on my faderes & on my moder's syde. 791

" Schuld I þan dyspyse þat hye degre, 792
Whech þat is ordeynd be goddys prouidens,
Whech is eke come be descense to me ?
Godd forbede in me þat gret offens,
Or þat I wer' founde in swech neclygens ! 796
I wote full weele, a kyng is all a-boue
Ouyr hys legys, both in fer' & loue ; 798

" And þei be to hym as it wer' botraces, 799
To schoue & holde fast & stedefastly,
To mey[n]ten ryght a-geyn all wrong traces ;
A kyngis myght full small is hardyly
Wyth-oute swech help, ȝe wote as weel as I. 803
But þat ȝe lyst to seye as for ȝour' part.
Þan semeth it, ser', þat I vse treuly myn art, 805

" And not pretende in no-maner' terme 806
Non othyr sentens þan þe terme schuld haue,
But vse my langage stabyly & ferme ;—
Myn entent is swech, so godd me saue,
And euyr schall be, I trow neuyr to waue 810
ffro þat purpos whylys þat I am her'—
Þis is my mynde, if ȝe wyll it her'. 812

MS. Arundel.] *Katharine answers the Clerk.*

" And where ye sey þat I wolde now disceyue 778 *Bk. II. Ch. 13.*
With my termes my lordes whiche I loue, *says she never meant to deceive her lords,*
I pray you hertily þat ye wil not conceyue
Of me swiche þing. for treuly, it wil not proue ;
Swiche iapes to make where not to be-houe, 782
Neyther to me ne to noon other whygt[1] ; [1] corrected.
To be a disceyuour[2] it is a gret disspyght. [2] orig. diss 784

" Ye seyde eftsone þat I despise a kyng, 785 *or despise a King.*
Eke þat astate I trede al vnder fote.
Thou I be not enclyned to your askyng
As for to be wedded whanne I shal, god wote,
Yet am I come bothe of þat stok & rote— [1] MS. a 789
I may not hyde it, for it is knowe soo wyde—
bothe on my faderis and on my moderis syde. 791

" Shulde I thanne despyse that heigh degree, 792 *She reverences Royalty.*
Whiche þat is ordeyned be goddys prouydens,
Whiche is eke come be discens on-to me ?
God forbede in me þat grete offens,
Or that I were founde in suche neglygens ! 796
I wot ful weel, a kyng is al a-boue *A King is over his lieges*
Ouere his lyges, bothe in fere and in loue ; 798

" And thei ben[1] to hym as it were boteras, [1] orig. bo 799 *and they are a buttress to him to maintain Right.*
To shoue and holde faste and stedefastly,
To mey[n]teyn ryght a-geyn alle wrong tras ;
A kyngys myght ful smal is ha[r]dyly
With-outen swiche helpe, ye wote as weel as I. 803
But that ye list to seye as for your part. [1] corr. to sir
Thanne semeth it, ser,[1] þat I vse treuly myn art, 805

" And not pretende in no-maner terme 806
Non other sentens thanne the terme shuld haue,
but vse my langage stabely and ferme ;—
Myn entent is suche, soo god me saue,
And euer shal bee, I trowe neuer to waue 810
ffro þat purpos wils that I am heere—
This is myn mende wyth-oute ony feere. 812

Bk. II. Ch. 14.

"3e list also me efte to repreue : 813
ffor I graunted 3ow to haue a gouernour',
Therfor' 3e sey, ffully I 3aue 3ow leue
To haue a kyng, lord of town & toure.
lett be 3our' sophym! 3our termes ar' but sour'! 817
ffor thow 3e bryng forth alle 3our hool bunch,
3e schall not mak an elue of a vnch. 819

"I sett cas a man hath 3oue to 3ow a best, 820
It folowyth not þer-of þat he 3aue 3ow an ox ;
he may as weell paye þe mor' as þe lest,
he may chese to 3eue 3ow a hors or a fox.
3our termes come owte of þat sotyll box 824
Of Aristoteles elenkes, made in swych wyse
Who so þat lerneth hem, he schall seme wyse. 826

" So graunted I to 3ow to haue 3our' choys fre 827
To chese a duke whech þat schuld lede 3ow,
Not for to haue no (!) gouernauns vp-on me,
But to my byddyng he must lowte & bowe.
All þis entent 3et eft I new alowe, 831
Thus schull 3e haue 3our wylle, & I schall haue myne ;
ffor of myn answer', ser', her' is þe fyne." 833

Bk. II. Ch. 15.

Cam. 15m.

"MAdame," quod þe erle þoo of lymasones, 834
"Alle these lordes þat now her' sitte
Wondyr' full sor' of 3our grete resones,
þei wayle eke þat 3e haue swech a wytte ;
3our' wordes ar' scharpe, þei can bynde & kytte. 838
But had 3e ben as other' wommen ar',
þan schuld 3e a ferde as other' wommen far'. 840

"3our' scole wyll schath vs, I-wys, we skape it nowte. 841
We hoped of 3ow to haue had sume grete empryse,
But all is turned no-þing as we thowte.
In many materes men may be ouyr'-wyse !
3our' conceytes, madame, set hem in sume syse ; 845

Ye liste also me efte to repreue, 813
ffor I graunted yow to haue a gouernour,
Therfore ye sey, fully I yaue you leue
To haue a kyng, lord of toun and tour.
late be youre sophym! your termes arn but sour! 817
ffor thow ye brynke foorth al your hool bunch,
ȝe shal not make an elne of an vnch. 819

She agreed that her people should have a Governor.

"I sette cas a man hath youe to you a beeste, 820
It folweth not therof þat he yaaf yow an[1] oxe;
he may as weel paye the more as the leeste,
he may chese to yeue yow an hors or a foxe.
Youre termes come oute of þat sotil boxe 824
Of aristoteles elenkes, made in suche gyse
ho-so þat lerneth hem, he shal seme wise. 826

[1] MS. and

"Soo graunted I yow to haue your choys free 827
To chese a duke whiche þat shulde leede yow,
Not for to haue gouernauns vp-on mee,
But to myn biddyng he muste lowte and bowe.
Al this entent yet eft I newe allowe, 831
Thus shul ye haue your wil, and I shal haue myn;
ffor of myn answere, sir, this is the fyn." 833

But by that she meant a Duke under her, not a husband.

Ca[m]. 14[m].

Bk. II. Ch. 14.

"Madame," quod the Erl tho of lymasones, 834
"Alle these lordes that now here sitte
Wondyr ful soore of youre grete resones,
Thei wayle eke þat ye haue swiche a wytte; 837
Youre wordes arn sharpe, thei can bynde and knytte (!).
But had ye ben as other women are,
Thanne shulde ye a ferde as other women fare. 840

The Earl of Lymasons

"Youre scoole wil scathe vs, I-whis, we scape it nowht. 841
We hopyd of yow haue had som grete empryse,
But al this turned no-thyng as we thought.
In many maters men may ben ouere-wyse! 844
Your conseytes, madame, sette hem in som syse,[1]

begs Katharine not to be overwise,

[1] MS. fyse

ffor loue of godd, whech is our' gouernowr',
Accepte our' wyttes & leue sume-what of ȝour'! 847

"We may weel doo ryght as ȝe sayn), 848
Chese vs now a leder', if þat we lyst,
Whech schall be to vs in maner' of a cheuetayn).
But in þis lond it was ȝet neuyr wyst; 851
he myght be swech parauentur' þat he schuld fro ȝour' fyst
Drawe mech of ȝour' lande euyn vn-to hym—
A-vyse ȝow ryght weele, þis mater' is full dym! 854

"Eke, thow we peyned vs alle hym to plese, 855
he schuld noght lyke vs, certeyn, lyuyng ȝow;
Our' hertes schuld not haue no rest ne no ese,
But he wer' lorde ryght as ȝe be, lady, now.
It is full harde a-geyn wylle to bowe. 859
he cowde not be chose eke a-mong ony of vs;
And hard it is to leue in langour' thus." 861

Ca^m. 16^m.

Than) answeryd schortely þat fayre swete may: 862
"Sere erl," sche sayde, "ȝe may full wele tryst,
þere is but o poynt to qwech I sey nay;
And my cawse is þis: I haue ȝit no list
þat ony man my maydynhod schuld twyst, 866
But if I knew better what þat he were.
Thus say I now, & þus sayde I ere: 868

"I wyll abyde tyll better tyme may come, 869
A ȝere or two, tyll þat I elder be;
ffor to wedde ȝit me thynk' it full sone;
And to ȝour' gouernawns þus I demene me.
Iff ȝe lyst not to haue on, I graunt ȝow two or thre, 873
Whych men may gouerne wyth-owtyn enuye.
I profyr ȝow reson), what-so-euer ȝe crye." 875

ffor loue of god, whiche is oure gouernoure,
Accepte oure wittes and leue som) of your! 847 *Bk. II. Ch. 14.*

"We may weel doo ryght as ye seyn), 848 *but to adopt her people's views.*
Chese vs now a leedere, if that we lyst,
Whiche shuld be to vs in maner of a cheuentayn).
But in this lond it was neuer yet wist; 851
he myght be swiche paraventure þat he shuld fro your fyst
Drawe meche of your lond euene on-to hym)—
Avyse yow ryght weel, this mater is ful dym)! 854

"Eke, thow we peyned vs alle hym) to plese, 855 *No Governor under her 'ud please her folk:*
he shuld not lyken) vs, certeyn), lyuyng yow;
Owre hertes shulde haue non) reste ne non) ese,
But he were lord ryght as ye be, lady, now.
It is ful hard a-geyn) the wil to bow. 859 *her Husband would.*
he cowde not be chose eke a-mongis ony of vs;
And hard it is to lyue in langour thus." 861

Ca^{m.} 15^{m.}

Bk. II. Ch. 15.

Thanne answerde shortly þat fayr swete may: 862 *Katharine declares she'll*
"Sir Erl," she seyde, "ȝe may ful weel tryst,
There is but oo poynt to whiche I sey nay;
And my cause is thys: I haue no lyst *not marry any man till she knows what he is.*
That oony man) my maydenhod shuld twyst, 866
But if I knowe beter what þat he were.
Thus sey I now, and thus seyde I heere:[1] [1] = ere 868

"I wyl a-byde til beter tyme may come, 869 *She'll wait a year or two.*
A yeer or too, til that I ooldere bee;
ffor to wedde yet me thenketh it ful sone;
And to yowre gouernauns thus I demene me.
If yee lyst not to haue oon), I graunte you too or thre, 873
Whiche men) may gouernen) withouten) enuye.
I profere yov reson), what-so-euere ye crye." 875

K 2

132   Katharine is again urgd to marry.   [MS. Rawlinson.

Bk. II Ch. 17.   Ca^{m.} 17^{m.}

Than spak þe amiraȞ of gret Alisawndre,   876
Thus he gan sey ryght in þis manere :
"ȝoure wordis to ȝour wysdom) are but slaundre,
Thus thynk^t ȝour frendis aȞ þat sytte here.
Loke þat ȝe þrow not now aȞ in þe mere!   880
Loke þat ȝe lese not now ȝour gret namyd lose,
Whan þat ȝe may so heyly it endoos!   882

"Who honoure ȝe ȝour' owne grete astate!   883
Why hate ȝe now þat ilk lady must haue?
Wherfore haue ȝe swech þing in hate
That may ȝoure londes & eke ȝour-self saue?

[fol. 30, b.]   Yf ȝe wer' not my lady, I wold wene ȝe raue;   887
[1st hand]   ffor yf aȞ þeis conseytes had come of^t wyt,
Mo folk þan ȝe wold haue usyd it.   889

"Men seyn, madame, þat he maddyth mor'   890
þat doth lich no man, & is mor' out^t of^t herr',
þan is a foole þat can not se be-for'
Ne can not knowe þe best fro þe werr'.
Be ye[1] war' be-tyme þat ȝe no lenger' erre;   [1] MS. þe   894
Schape not your'-self^t ne your' lond to schend,
Thynk now be-tyme what shal be þe ende!   896

"ȝe wote þat I am keper of^t þis grete cite,   897
And in þis same cite as now standyth it soo :
þer is many a man & many dyuerse degre,
Both cristen & hethen, frely com þer-too :
I woote not sumtyme what is best to doo,   901
I dweȞ her' soo in swech-maner drede,
I knowe not my frend whan I haue nede.   903

"I se also her' an othir grete myscheffe,   904
In ȝow, madame, & ȝe lyst to her' :
ȝe be to euery man both deynty & leffe,
& ȝe no man cownt not at a per'.
It wyȞ not proue, swech solen daunger';   908

Caᵐ· 16ᵐ·

Thanne spak the amreɫɫ of grete Alysaundre, 876
Thus he gan seyn right in this manere:
"Youre woordis to *your* wysdam arn but slaundre,
Thus thenken youre freendys alle that sitten here.
Looke þat ye throwe not now al in the meere! 880
Looke that ye lese not youre grete named loos,
Whanne that ye may soo heyly it endoos! 882

"how honoure ye *your* owne grete astate! 883
Why hate ye now that ilke lady muste haue?
Wherefore haue ye swiche thing in hate
That may youre londes and eke *your*-self saue?
If ye were not my lady, I wolde wene ye raue; 887
ffor if alle these conseytes had come of wyt,
Mo folkys than ye wold haue vsed it. 889

"Men, madame, seyn[1] that he maddeth more [1] corr. 890
That dooth liche no man, and is more oute of herre,
Than is a fool that can not see be-fore
Ne kan not knowe the beste fro the werre.
Be ye war be-tyme that ye noo lengere erre; 894
Shape not youre-self ne youre lond to shende,
Thenke now be-tyme what shal be the ende! 896

"Ye wot þat I am kepere of this grete Cytee, 897
And in this same Citee as now standeth[1] soo: [1] corr.
There is many a man in many dyuers degree,
Bothe crystene and ethen, freely come ther-too:
I wote not somtyme what is best to doo, 901
I dwelle heere soo in swhiche-maner dreede,
I knowe not my freend whan I haue neede. 903

"I see here also[1] a-nother grete myschef [1] overlined. 904
In you, madame, and ȝe listen to heer':
Ye be to euery man bothe deynte and leef,
And ye no man counte the valu of a pere.
It wil not proue, swiche soleyn daungeere; 908

1 2 ✱

Thinke on othir þat haue abyden longᵗ,
And at þe lastᵗ þei haue walkyd wrongᵗ." 910

Caᵐ· 18ᵐ·

"And dede þei so," seid þis noble qwene, 911
"So shal I not, wyth grace ofᵗ god aboue;
My wyttes, I telle ȝou, no-þingᵗ besy been
I[n] swech materᵖ, neythir to lust ne to loue—
ffy on þo hertes þat euer on swech þing houe! 915
Dred yow not ofᵗ me in þis materᵖ,
Beth not a-ferd tyl ȝe morᵖ þingᵗ herᵖ. 917

"And as for yourᵖ puple þat amonges you dwell, 918
haue ȝe not powerᵖ & ful auctoryte
To put out hem whech beth ofᵗ hert so fell,
Or hem þat use falshed or sotylte,
Be whech ourᵖ rewme happyly harmed myth be? 922
Syth þat ȝe may, whi do ȝe not yourᵖ dede?
þe[i] þat lett yow, arᵖ worthy to be dede. 924

"Ȝe arᵖ a man large & grete ofᵗ bones; 925
Yfᵗ yourᵖ hert be as ȝourᵖ grete body is,
Ȝe ar ful lyckly to do morᵖ note at onys
Than othir thre men. a schame for soth it is
That swech a man schuld ferᵖ ony ofᵗ his, 929
Whan þat he may correct hem hym-selue;
I wold ȝeue¹ ȝe alone shuld oppresse twelue!" ¹ r. wene 931

Caᵐ· 19ᵐ·

An othir duke gan þan to approche, 932
Ser clamadourᵖ þei calle his ryth name,
A worthi man & duke ofᵗ Antioche,
þe qwenes cosyn, a lord ofᵗ ful grete fame.
"þei þat lerned you, ar ful mech þe¹ blame ¹ r. to 936
As in my conseyt," þus seyd he to þo qwene,
"ffor ofᵗ swech wytt & ofᵗ swech cunnyngᵗ ȝe been 938

Thenke other that haue abeden longe,   910
And at the laste thei haue walked wronge."

Ca^{m.} 17^{m.}

"And dede thei soo," seyde this noble queen,   911
"Soo shal I not, wyth þe grace of god aboue;
My wittis, I telle you, no-thyng besy been
In swiche mater, neither to lust ne to loue—
ffy on tho hertis þat euere on suche þing¹ houe!   915
D ede you not of me in this matere,   ¹ MS. þingis
beth not aferd til ye more þing here.   917

"And as for your puple that a-mong yow dwelle,   918
haue ye not power and ful auctoryte
To putte oute hem wiche been of herte soo felle,
Or hem þat vsen falshed or sotilte,
In whiche oure reem happely harmed myght be?   922
Syth þat ye may, whi doo ye not youre offys¹?   ¹ corr.
They þat lette yow, arn wurthi deed, be thei neuer so wys.

"Ye arn a man large and gret of bones;   925
If your herte be as youre grete body is,
Ye arn ful likly to doo more note at oones
Than other thre men. a shame forsothe it is
That swiche man shuld fere ony of his,   929
Whan ye may correcte hem youre-selue;
I wol wene, ye allone shuld oppresse twelue!"   931

Ca^{m.} 18^{m.}

An other duke gan thanne to approche,   932
Syr Clamadour' thei calle his ryght name,
A worthi man and duke of Antioche,
The queenes cosyn, a lord of ful grete fame.
"Thei that lerned yow, arn ful moche to blame   936
As in myn consceyte," thus seyde he to the queen,
"ffor of swiche wyt and of swiche con[n]ynge ye been,   938

Bk. II. Ch. 19.

"It passith our' wittis, þer is no mor' to say; 930
lych to an egle ȝe flye vs all a-boue.
ȝete in as mech as ȝe be ȝet a may,
And eke a qwene, it fallyth to ȝour' be-houe
To fostre hem whech ȝou drede & loue, 943
Despise hem nowt, þouȝ þat þei be dulle,
Noutȝ lich to ȝou—for ȝe be in þe fulle, 945

"As I suppose; I pray god as for me, 946
Grow ȝe no hier', ȝour' wyt is hye I-now.
Than, þow our' wytt be not in swech degre,
ȝet our' good wyll must ȝe nedes a-low.
What shal men ellys wryte & sey of¹ yow: 950
þat ȝe dysdeyne þe pore creature
And hauns your' witt out of¹ all mesur'. 952

"What þing¹ letteth yow þat ȝe wil not us leue, 953
& be we your' men & your' seruauntis alle!
ȝour' counsayl, lady, whech shal ȝow not greue,
ȝe shuld tel us, for it may so falle
þat þe better end þat mater schalle 957
Be browt to—for þe mo wyse hedes þer be
In ony mater', þe better is it, as þinkyth mee." 959

Bk. II. Ch. 20.

Ca^m. 20^m.

"Cosyn," sche seyd, "ȝe preyse sor' a kyng¹. 960
But I wold wete of¹ you þe cause qwy
þat o man a-boue many shal haue gouernyng¹,
To byd & commaund, send both ferr' & nye;
What is þe cause þat he hath swech maystry 964
Ouer all men, & no man hath ouer hym—
he his lord of¹ lond, of¹ body & of¹ lym? 966

[fol. 31, b.]
[2nd hand]

"In elde tyme, for stryff & for þe bate¹   ¹ r. debate 967
Amongys þe puple þat reygned to & froo,
And for to staunch bothe enuye & hate,
ffor to haue reule, þei wer' compellyd þer-too
To chese a leeder', hem for to gouerne thoo— 971

"It passeth oure wyttis, there is no more to say; 939   *Bk II. Ch. 18.*
Lyche on-to an Egle ye flye us alle a-boue.   The Duke of Antioch says
Yet in as moche as ye been a may
And eke a queen), it falleth to yo*ur* be-houe
To fostre hem whiche yow drede and loue, 943
Despyse hem not, though þ*at* þei be dulle,   Katharine ought to
Not lyche to yow—for ye be in the fulle, 945 hear others,

"As I suppose, I prey god as for me, 946
Growe ye now heyere, youre wyt is heye I-nowe.
Thanne, thow oure wyt be not in suche degre,   especially her men,
Yet oure good wil muste ye nedes allowe.
What shal men wryte ell*is* and sey of yowe? 950
That ye disdeyne the poere creature
And haunce youre wyt oute of all mesure. 952

"What þing letteth you þ*at* ye wil not vs leue, 953
And be we youre men and yo*ur* seruauntys alle!
Youre counseil, lady, whiche shal you not greue,   and tell them her mind.
Ye shulde telle vs, for it may soo falle
That þe better eende the mater shalle 957
Be browt too—for þe moo wyse heedes ther be
In ony mater, the better it is, as thenketh me." 959

Ca^m. 19^m.   *Bk. II. Ch. 19.*

"COsyn," she seyde, "ye preyse sore a kyng. 960   Katharine puts the question how there came to be kings,
But I wolde wete of you þe cause whi
That oon man a-boue many shal haue gou*er*nyng,
To bidde and com*m*avnde, sende bothe fer and ny;
What is the cause that he hath swiche maystry 964   with such extravagant power?
Ouere alle men, and no man hath oue*r*e hym—
he is lord of lond, of body and of lym? 966

"In oolde tyme, for stryf and for debate, 967
A-mong*is* the puple that regned too and froo,
And for to staunche bothe enuye and hate,
ffor to haue reule, thei were compelled þ*er*-too
To chese a leedere, hem for to gouerne thoo— 971

| Bk. II. Ch. 20. | þis was þe cause why þei chose a kyng ; | |
| | þei schuld ellys a streue for many a thyng. | 973 |

"ffor qwan þer is not ellys but per & pere, 974
þer is non as than wyll do for othyr,
On seyth her', an other' seyth it schall be þer' ;
þis stryffe it fallyth be-twyx brother' & brother,
Ageyn þe sune sumtyme stryuyth þe modyr. 978
Than wer' þei chose ryght for þis entent,
To bryng in reule þing þat was wrong went. 980

"Summe wer' chose for wysdam & for wytt, 981
Summe for strenght, summe for humanyte—
þat I sey treuth, cronycles wytness it.
So þan a kyng as in auctorite
Excellyth hys puple—for þer be as wyse as he 985
Oft-tyme seyn) ryth wyth-inne hys londe.
Þan may 3e se þat all þis seruyle bonde 987

"Came oute of fredam—þe puple was sume-tyme fre 988
And had noo lord, but ych man reuled hym-selfe.
Þus cam þei þan oute of her' liberte,
Be her' fre choys ten of hem or twelue
Wer' draw a-wey, þei schuld noo lenger' delue 992
Ne do no labour', but reule þe cuntre a-bowte ;
And to her' heed hem-self 3et must [þei]¹ lowte. ¹ om. 994

"But for 3e wyll allgate know myn hert, 995
Whath þat I thynk, I tell 3ow platt & pleyn) :
þer schall neuyr man, be he neuyr so smert
Ne eke so st[r]ong, wynne me, þat is to seyn)
haue me to spowse—I wyll no lenger' feyn)— 999
But if he be so strong hym-self a-lone
þat he be able to fyght wyth all hys fone. 1001

"Thys is þe ende, & þis my wyll now is, 1002
let vs no mor' as in þis mater' speke.
So god my soule bryng on-to hys blys,

This was þe cause whi þei chose a kyng;
Thei shulde ellis a streuen for many a thyng. 973 *Kings were chosen*

"ffor whanne there is not ellis but peere and peere, 974
There is non as than wil doon for other,
Oon seyth here, another seyth it shal be there;
This stryf it falleth be-twyxe brother and brother,
A-geyn the sone somtyme stryueth þe moder. 978
Thanne were thei chosyn ryght for þis entent, *only to set wrong, right.*
To brynge in rewle thyng þat was wrong went. 980

"Some were chosyn for wysdam and for wyt, 981
Some for strengthe, and some for humanyte—
That I sey treuthe, cronyclys witnesse it.
Soo thanne a kyng as in Auctoryte
Excelleth his puple—for there been as wys as he 985
Ofte-tyme seyn ryght wythinne his loond.
Thanne may ye see þat all this seruyle boond. 987

"Cam oute of fredam—the puple was sumtyme free 988 *Folk were first free,*
And had no lord, but iche man reuled hym-selue.
Thus cam thei thanne oute of her liberte,
Be her fre choys ten of hem or twelue *and then gave up their liberty.*
Were drawe a-wey, þei shuld no lenger delue 992
Ne doo no labour, but reule the contre aboute;
And to her hed hem-selue yet muste þei loute. 994

"But for ye wil algates knowe myn herte, 995
What þat I thenke, I telle yow plat and pleyn: *She then speaks out her mind;*
There shal neuere man, be he neuere so smerte
Ne eke so strong, wynne me, þat is to seyn *she will never wed.*
haue me to spouse—I wil no lenger feyn— 999
But if he be soo strong hym-self allone
That he be able to feyghte with alle his fone. 1001

"This is the eende, and this my wil now is, 1002
Lete vs no more as in this mater speke. *Let no more be said to her about Marriage.*
Soo god my soule brynge on-to his blys,

Bk. II. Ch. 20.

þis couenaund made ne schall I neuyr breke.
Ȝe may well carp, stryue, clatyr & creke ;   1006
Whan all is doo, þis schall be þe ende ;
Ȝour wordys þerfor' lett hem fall fro meende."   1008

Bk. II. Ch. 21.
Ca^m. 21^m.

Than was þer' woo & waylyng eke enowe,   1009
  þei morned alle & made mekyl mone
Whan þat þei sey wher'-to þe mater' drowe,
Carefull wytys wer' þei than ilkone.
Þe qween, hyr' modyr, gan to syghe & grone,   1013
Sche seyd : " doghtyr, þis is noght ȝour avayle,
Put not ȝour purpos in swych grete perayle !   1015

" Ȝour dotyng-dayes, I trow, now be come !   1016
What wold ȝe hafe ? wote ȝe qwat ȝe say ?
Thorow-oute þis werlde, in grece ne in rome
Is no swych man[1] þat þis thyng do may,   [1] r. woman ?
Schuld kepe a londe of so gret aray   1020
And he a-lone. what wene ȝe for to hafe ?
It is inpossible þat ȝe desyr' and crafe.   1022

" A-vyse ȝow bettyr, & take an other' day,   1023
Tyll þat ȝour wytte is chaunged & ȝour thowte !
Is ȝour wysdam now turned to swech aray
ffor to desyr' swhych þing as is nowte ?
Cursyd be þei þat ȝow her'-to browte,   1027
On-to þis errour' to do as no man dothe ;
þat euery poynt þei varye fro þe sothe."   1029

Bk. II. Ch. 22.
Ca^m. 22^m.

" Madame," sche seyd, " þis þing wech I schall doo
  I not who sett it in myn hert, treuly.   1031
It is so fast, I may not fle þer-froo,
It cleuyth so sor', it wyll not slyde for-by,
Wheythyr' I goo, sytte, knele or elles ly ;   1034
ffor noo counseyll I may it not for-sake,
Ne for noo crafte a-wey I can it schake."   1036

This conuenaunt made shal I neuere breke.
Ye may weel karpe, stryue, clatere, and creke [1] ; 1006
Whanne al is doo, this shal be the ende ;   [1] MS. treke
Youre wordis therfore lete hem falle fro meende." 1008

Ca^m. 20^m.

Thanne was ther woo and weylþyng eke I-now, 1009
  Thei moorned alle and made mekel mone
Whan þat þei saugh wherto the mater drow,
Careful wyght*is* were thei thanne ilkone.
The queen, hir moder, gan to sey and grone, 1013
She seyde : " doughter, þis is not youre avayle,
Putte not youre purpos in swiche grete p*er*ayle ! 1015

" Youre dotynge-dayes, I trowe, now be come ! 1016
What wolde ye haue ? wote ye what ye say ?
Thurgh-oute this world, in grece ne in Rome
Is noon swiche man þat þis thyng doo may,
Shulde keepe a lond of soo grete aray 1020
And he allone. what wene ye for to haue ?
It is impossible that ye desyre and craue. 1022

" Avyse yow bettere, and take another day, 1023
Til þat youre wit is chaunged and youre thought !
Is youre wysdam now turned to swiche aray
ffor to desyre swyche þing as is nought ?
Cursed be thei that you here-to han brought, 1027
On-to this errour to doo as no man dooth !   [1] corr.
What[1]-euere thei poynt, ye varye euere for[1] sooth." 1029

" MAdame," she seyde, "this thyng whiche I shal doo
  I not hoo seet it in myn herte, truly. 1031
It is soo fast, I may not flee ther-froo,
It cleueth soo sore, it wil not slyde forby,
Whether I goo, sytte, knele or ellys ly ; 1034
ffor no counseH I may it not for-sake,
Ne for [no] craft a-wey I can it shake." 1036

Caᵐ. 23ᵐ.

Than wept þe qweeñ & was in carᵉ & woo, 1037
And to þe lordes sche sayd : "all is I-lorñ,
What schall we say, what schall we speke or doo?
I wayle þe tyme þat euyr sche was borñ.
hyr hert is harde & tow as is¹ þe thorñ,   ¹ overlined. 1041
hyr wytte is sett so hye I wot not qwerᵉ ;
þer is no man þat may hyr herᵉ answere. 1043

"What sey ȝe, cosyñ, lord & duk of tyrᵉ? 1044
What comyth herof? can ȝe owte fertherᵉ say?
ffor as wyth me, dunne is in þe myre,
Sche hath me stoyned & browte me [to] a-bay.
Sche wyll not wedde, sche wyll be styll a may! 1048
It schall cause my deth, but mech sonerᵉ, loo,
Be-cause I leue þus in swech carᵉ & woo." 1050

Caᵐ. 24ᵐ.

Than roos þis lord, em to þe qweeñ, 1051
Gaufroñ he hyght, he was herᵉ omagerᵉ,
And duke of tyre—mech þing had he seeñ,
he had passed eke many a grete daungerᵉ ;
he was þe next of hyrᵉ kynrod therᵉ, 1055
he myght morᵉ boldly sey all hys entent.
"Madame," he seyd, "a þing þat was neuer ment 1057

"What ayles ȝow þat ȝe desyrᵉ so sore, 1058
And ȝe so ȝung, & wys woman alsoo?
A þing þat lawe for-bedyth euyr-morᵉ ;
Naturᵉ eke wyll ȝeue no leue þer-too—
þis ȝe desyrᵉ, ȝe wyll not twynn þer-froo. 1062
What is ȝourᵉ wyll? I wolde wyte qwat ȝe mene.
Wyll ȝe ȝourᵉ bodye fro alle men kepe clene? 1064

"What boote was it to vs þat ȝe werᵉ borñ, 1065
If þat ȝe wyll not do ryght as þei dede,
I mene ȝourᵉ ffadyr & modyr ȝow be-forñ?

Ca^{m.} 21^{m.}

Thanne wepte þe queen) and was in care and woo, 1037 — Her Mother weeps,
And to the lordes she seyde : "al is I-lorn),
What shal we say, what shal we speke or doo?
I wayle the tyme that euere she was born).
hir herte is hard and tough as is the thorn), 1041
hir wyt is sette so hye I wot not where;
There is no man) that may here hir answere. 1043

"What seye ye, cosyn), lord and duke of Tyre? 1044 — and appeals to the Duke of Tyre.
What cometh here-of? can) ye owte ferthere say?
ffor as wyth me, dun is in the myre,
She hath me stoyned and brought me to a bay.
She wil not wedde, she wil be stylle a may! 1048
It shal cause my deeth, but meche sonnere loo,
Be-cause I leue thus in suche care and woo." 1050

Ca^{m.} 22^{m.}

Thanne ros the lord, een) on-to the queen), 1051 — Gaufron, Duke of Tyre, her Uncle,
Gaufron) he hyght, he was hir homagere,
And duke of Tyre—moche þing he had seen),
he had passed eke many a gret daungere;
he was the nexte of hir kenerede there, 1055
he myght more boldely seyn al his entent.
"Madame," he seyde, " a thyng þat was neuere ment, 1057

"What eyleth you þat ye desire soo sore, 1058 — argues with Katharine.
And ye so yong and wyse woman) alsoo?
A þing þat lawe forbedeth euer-more;
Nature eke wil yeue no leue ther-too—
This ye desyre, ye wil not twynne therfroo. 1062
What is youre wil? I wold wete what ye mene.
Wyl ye youre body fro alle men) kepe clene? 1064 — Does Katharine mean to keep herself from men?

"What boote was it to us þat ye were born), 1065
If þat ye wil not doo ryght as thei dede,
I mene youre fader and moder yow be-forn)? — How would she be here

3e had not come ne sote (!) now in þis stede,
had not 3our modyr' wyth mech care & drede   1069
Browt 3ow forth & to þis lyght 3ow bore.
ffolow 3e þe steppys of hem þat went be-fore!   1071

"3e do wrong ellys on-to þo chyldryn alle   1072
Wech 3e ar' lykly to bryng forthe & bere.
Wʰat desese & what myschefe may falle
But if 3e do þus, I trow your'-self wot ner'.
To put all þis thyng oute of drede & fere,   1076
And þat þis synne in 3ow schuld not be sene,
A kynges doghtyr to dey bothe mayd & qween,   1078

"I counsell 3ow þis, & 3e receyue it wold: 1079
To fle þis chauns of feyned chastite.
hewe not so hye but if 3e may it holde,
Desyr' no thyng þat may not goten be—
Lerneth þis lesson, if þat 3e lyst, of me;   1083
Sche is not born, me thynkyth, þat myght wynne
To grype a degre so grete as 3e be-gynne."   1085

Cam. 25m.

"VNcle," sche seyd, "& þat wer' me full lothe   1086
To clyme so hye þat I myght not come down;
ffor, as I wene, þat mater' wold greue us bothe,
And lese our' londe be cyte & eke be town;
It wer' destruccyon eke to our' crown.   1090
God he lede vs þat we come not ther',
To ley our' worchep so lowe vndyr brere!   1092

"But for 3e say, to me it schuld be ioye   1093
To hafe a lord schuld gouern both 3ow & me,
I sey 3ow nay, it schulde be but a-noye
On-to myn hert. for if it wer' so þat he
Wer' louyng & gentyll, & all hys hert on me,   1097
þat he louyd me & I hym best of alle,
What sorow, hope 3e, on-to myn hert schuld falle 1099

[MS. Arundel.] *Katharine is again urg'd to marry.*

Ye had not come ne sete now in þis stede,		*Bk. II. Ch. 22.*
had not yo*ur* moder with moche care and drede	1069	If her Mother hadn't
Brought yow foorth and to this lyght you bore.		brought her forth?
ffolwe ye þe steppys of hem þat wente be-fore!	1071	
" Ye doo wrong ellis on-to tho children alle	1072	Chastity is a sin against the unborn, and impossible.
Whiche ye arn lykely to brynge foorth and bere.		
What disese and what myschef may falle		
But if ye thus doo, I trowe youre-self wot neere,		
To putte alle these thyng*is* in dreed and¹ fere.	1076	
And þat þis synne in yow shuld not be seene,	¹ orig. and in	
A kyng*is* doughter to dey bothe mayde and queene,	1078	
" I counseill you thus, and ʒe¹ receyue it wolde :	1079	She should give up this feignd chastity.
To flee this chauns of feyned chastyte.	¹ overlined.	
hewe not so hye but if ye may it holde,		
Desyre no thyng that may not goten be—		
Lerne this leson, iff þat ye list, of me ;	1083	
She is not bore, me thynketh, that myght wynne		
To gryppe of degree so grete as ye be-gynne."	1085	

Ca^m. 23^m.   *Bk. II. Ch. 23.*

" Vncle," she seyde, " and that were me ful looth	1086	Katharine answers her Uncle.
To clymbe so hye that I myght not com doun ;		
ffor, as I wene, that mater wolde greue vs booth,		
And lese oure lond be Cyte and be toun ;		
It were grete destruccyon eke to oure croun.	1090	
God he lede vs that we come not there,		
To ley oure wurshype soo lowe vnder brere !	1092	
" But for ye sey, to me it shulde be Ioye	1093	Katharine says,
To haue a lord shulde goue*r*ne bothe yow and me,		
I sey yow nay, it shulde be but a-noye		
On-to myn herte. for if it were soo þat hee		
Were lovyng and gentyl and al his herte on me,	1097	If she lovd her Husband,
That he loued me and I hym beste of alle,		
What sorwe, hope ye, on myn hert shuld falle	1099	

KATHARINE.   L

Katharine answers Prince Baldake. [MS. Rawlinson.

Bk. II. Ch. 25.

"If þat he deyd or ellys wer' slayn) in felde,   1100
And I for-go þat þing þat I loued best?
It myght fall also, thow it hap but selde,
þat þis loue be-twyx vs too myth brest
And part a-sundyr'—þis wer' a full hard rest   1004
On-to our' hert! þer-for', to put alle oute of dowte,
I wyll not enter', wyll[1] I may kepe me owte.   [1] = whil   1106

"What counsell 3e me swech game to be-gynne   1107
Whech is not stedfast', in lowe ne in astate?
In all her' gladeness sorow is euyr wyth-inne,
And wyth her' plesaunce eft medeleth debate.
þer-for' þat lyfe I dispyce & hate   1111
þat hath noo sewyrte, but euyr is variable;
I wold hafe lyffe & loue[1] þat euyr is stable."   [1] MS. lond

Bk. II. Ch. 26.   Ca^m. 26^m.

"O Mercy godd," seyd þe gret baldake—   1114
he was þoo lord & prince of palestyne—
"Þer' may no man my lady grype ne take,
her' craft is swech, we may her' not enclyne;
þer is no philosophyr' ne ek noo diuine   1118
Whech sche dredyth, hyr' termys be so wyse;
What-euyr we say, sche 3euyth of it no pryce.   1120

"I sey 3ow, madame, as it is seyd be-fore: 1121
We want a leeder', if we owte schuld doo.
Be-thynk 3our-self, fro tyme þat 3e wer' bore
To gorgalus tyme—thre hundred 3er' & moo
It is, certeyn), & 3et stod it neuyr soo   1125
As it' stant now, madame, in no lond of 3our'.
Of þing þat 3e reioye we schall hafe langour'."   1127

Bk. II. Ch. 27.   Ca^m. 27^m.

"Qwat wold 3e hafe?" seyd þis noble qween),   1128
"haue 3e not 3oue to me bothe crown) & londe?
I am 3our lady, my subiectis all 3e been).

"If þat he deyed or ell*is* were slayn̄ in feeld, 1100
And I for-goo þat thyng that I loued beste?
It myght falle soo, though it happed but seeld̄,
That this loue be-twyxe vs to myght breste
And parte a-sondre—this were a ful harde reste 1104
On-to oure herte! therfore, to putte all oute of dowte,
I wyl not entre whil I may kepe me oute. 1106

"What counsell ȝe me suche game to be-gynne 1107
Whiche is not stedfast, in lowe ne in astate?
In al her gladnesse sorwe is eu*ere* w*yth*-Inne,
And wyth her plesauns efte medeleth debate.
Therfore that lyf I despyse and hate 1111
That hath no suerte, but eu*ere* is varyable; ¹ MS. lond
I wolde haue lyf and loue¹ that eu*ere* is stable." 1113

Ca^m. 24^m.

"O Mercyful god," seyde the grete baldake— 1114
he was tho lord and prynce of palestyn—
"There may no man my lady gripe ne take,
hir craft is suche, we may hir not enclyn̄;
There is no philisophre ner eke dyvyn̄ 1118
Whiche she dredeth, hir termes be so wys;
What-eu*ere* we say, she yeueth of it no prys. 1120

"I sey yow, madame, as it is seyde be-fore: 1121
We wante a leedere, if we owte shulde doo.
Be-thenke yo*ur*-self, fro þat tyme that ye were bore
To gorgalus tyme—thre hundred yeer and moo
It is, certeyn̄, and yet stood it neu*ere* soo 1125
As it stant now, madame, in no lond of youre.
Of thing þat ye reioe we shal haue langoure." 1127

Ca^m. 25^m.

"What wolde ye haue?" seyde this noble queen̄, 1128
"haue ye not youe to me bothe croune and loonde?
I am youre lady, my subiectis alle ye been̄.

I wot full wele what longyth to þe bonde
Of regalte whech I hold in myn honde. 1132
ffor every werk, sothely, it stant in too :
In good councell & eke in werkyng alsoo. 1134

"The wytt & councell, syr', þat schall be our', 1135
We schall telle who we¹ wyll hafe it wrowte ; ¹ MS. ȝe
And al¹ þe labour' & werke þat schall be ȝour'— ¹ MS. all?
Ȝour' grete lordchype ȝe schul noȝt haue for nouȝ !
Þe lond of palestyne it was neuyr to ȝow boute, 1139
It was ȝoue ȝour' elderes ȝow be-fore
To serue my crown : & þer-to be ȝe swore." 1141

Cam. 28m.

Than spake a-nothyr, lord of nychopolye, 1142
he seyd wordys whech sempt full wyse—
hys name was called þoo syr' Eugeny—
To þe qween he spake þan ryght on þis wyse :
"Þe estate of regalte is of swych a pryce, 1146
Ther may no man, sothly, to it atteyne
But if he hath both power' & wytte, certeyne. 1148

"Therfor sey I ȝett þat we nedys muste 1149
Be rewled be on whech þat hath þeis too,
Boþe wytt in sadnesse, & power' eke in lust,
And elles our' reule sone wyll breke in-two.
As other' londys ar' reuled, let vs be reulyd soo ; 1153
Let vs suppose þei be as wyse¹ as we. ¹ MS. as wyse as wyse
for þus he wrytyth, þe astronomer' tholome : 1155
¹ MS. neybour)
"'Who-so wyll not doo as hys neybour[s]¹ werk, 1156
Ne wyll not be war' be hem whan þei do amys,
Of hym schul other' men boþe carp & berke,
And sey, be-holde þis man, lo [he]¹ it is— ¹ om.
Wheythyr he do weel or wheyther' he do amys. 1160
he wyll none exaumple of other' men i-take,
Exaumple to othyr' mene he schall be for þat sake. 1162

[MS. Arundel.] *Eugenius urges Katharine to marry.* 149

I wot ful weel what longeth to the boonde
Of regalte whiche I holde in myn honde. 1132
ffor euery werk, soothly, it stant in too:
In good counseH and eke in werkyng also. 1134

"The wyt and counseH, syr, þat shal ben oure, 1135
We shal telle how we wil haue it wrought;
And al the labour and werk that shal be youre—
youre grete lordshepe ye shul not haue for nought!
The lond of palestyn it was neuere to yow bought, 1139
It was yove youre olderis[1] here-be-fore   [1] orig. elderis
To serue my croune: and ther-to be ye swore." 1141

Bk. II. Ch. 25.
all work needs 1. counsel, 2. carrying-out.
She'll do the counsel.
The lords should do the carrying-out.

Ca[m]. 26[m].

Bk. II. Ch. 26.

Thanne spak a-nother, lord of Nychop[o]ly, 1142
he seyde wordys whiche sempte ful wise—
his name was called tho syr Eugeny—
To the queen he spak þanne ryght on þis gyse:
"The astate of regalte is of suche apryse, 1146
There may no man, sothly, to it atteyne
But he haue bothe pouer and wytte, certeyne. 1148

"Therefore sey I yet that we nedes must[1] [1] or. muste 1149
Be rewled be on whiche þat hath these too,
Bothe witte in sadnesse, and pouer in lust,[1]   [1] or. luste
And ellis oure rewle shal breke and asunder goo.
As other londes arn reuled, lete vs be reuled soo; 1153
Lete vs suppose thei be as wys as we.
ffor thus he wryteth, the Astronomer tholome: 1155
       [1] MS. neybour
"'ho-so wil not doo as his neybour[s][1] werke, 1156
Ne wil not be war be hem whan thei doo amys,
Of hym shul othere men bothe carpe and berke,
And sey, beholde this man, loo he it is—
Whether he doo weel or wheder he doo other-wys. 1160
he wyl non example of other men I-take,
Exaumple to other men he shal be for þat sake. 1162

Sir Eugenius of Nichopolis
then argues with Katharine.
A ruler needs not only wit, but power.
The example of other nations should be followd.

Bk. II. Ch. 28.

"'All oþir' mene schul be war' be hyme,   1163
ffor þei schul se & fele in hem-selue
þat hys werkys wer' bothe derk & dyme.'
Therfor', madame, what schuld I lenger' delue
In þis mater'? me thynkyth, ten or twelue   1167
Schuld ȝeue exau*m*ple, rather' þa*n* schall oone.
Ȝe haue my mocyo*n*, for my tale is doone."   1169

Bk. II. Ch. 29.

Ca^{m.} 29^{m.}

The qwee*n* full sadly answerd to þis lord: 1170
"I wold wyte," sche seyd, "of ȝow, whyll ȝe be her',
And alle, I trowe, to-gyder' mote a-corde:
If þat I dede þis tyme at ȝour' prayer',
To leue my wyll & put me in daunger',   1174
I sett cas, þe man whech þat I schall chese
To be ȝour' lord, þat he haue non of þese,   1176

"That is to sey neythyr wytte ne strength,[1]   [1] orig. strengh
What sey ȝe now, who schall reule ȝow tha*n*,   1178
Ȝour' londys þat ly so fer' in brede & length?
þe febyll may nott, þe fool eke ne ca*n*
Demene swych þing; þa*n* wyll ȝe curs & bane   1181
þat euyr wer' ȝe subiectys to swech a foole,
And to ȝour' hert it wolde be full grete dole.   1183

"Ȝe schuld be fay*n* þa*n* for to reule hyme,   1184
To cou*n*cell & rede þat he do not amys.
þis wer' noo worchepe to me ne to my ky*n*!
And sekyrly, a full grete cause it is
þat I wedde nowte, for owte of ioye & blys   1188
Schuld I þa*n* passe & make my-selue a thralle.
held me excused, for sykyrly I ne schalle.   1190

"ffor syth ȝe sey þat I am now so wys,   1191
Than haue I o þing whech lo*n*geth to regalte.
þer is no man but if he be ouyr-nys,
But if[1] he wyll sey & held wyth me   [1] if on the margin.
þat it is bettyr, wha*n* it no*n* other' wyll be,   1195

MS. Arundel.] *Katharine again refuses to marry.* 151

"' Alle othere men shul be war be hym), 1163 *Bk. II. Ch. 26.*
ffor thei shul see and fele in hem-selue
That his werkys were bothe deerke and dym.'
Therfore, madame, what shulde I lenger delue
In thys mater? me thenketh, ten or twelue 1167
Shulde yeue exaumple rathere þan shal oon. rather than
Ye haue myn mocyon, for my tale is doon." 1169 one woman's whims.

Cam. 27. *Bk. II. Ch. 27.*

The queen ful sadly answerde to this lord: 1170 Katharine answers Sir
"I wolde wyte of yow," she seyde, "whil ye ben here, Eugenius of Nichopolis.
And alle, I trowe, to-gedere mote acord:
If þat I dede this tyme of youre prayere,
To leue my wyl and putte me in daungere, 1174
I sette cas, the man whiche þat I shal chese
To be youre lord, þat he haue noon of these, 1176

"That is to sey neyther witte ne strengthe, 1177 Suppose she marries a
What sey ye now, hoo shal reule you than, stupid or weak man,
Youre londes þat lyn soo fer in brede and lengthe?
The feble may not, the fool eke ne kan
Demene suche þing; than wil ye curse and ban 1181 her folk 'll curse him.
That euere were ye subiectis to swyche a fool,
And to youre hertis it wold been ful gret dool. 1183

"Ye shulde be fayn thanne for to reule hym, 1184 They'd have to rule him.
To counseyll and rede that he dede not amys.
This were no worshep to me ne to my kyn!
And sekyrly a ful gret cause it is
That I wedde not, for oute of Ioye and blys 1188
Shulde I thanne passe and make my-self a thral.
helde me excused, for sekyrly I ne shal. 1190 She will be free.

'ffor syth ye sey that I am now so wys, 1191
Thanne haue I on thyng whiche longeth to regalte.
There is no man, but he be ouere-nys,
But he wyl sey and helde wyth me
That [it] is better, whanne it no other wil bee, 1195

152 *Katharine is again urgd to marry.* [**MS. Rawlinson.**

Bk. II. Ch. 29.
To chese þe on þan for to want bothe.
Chese ȝe now; we be no lenger wrothe." 1197

Bk. II. Ch. 30. Ca^m. 30^m.

ȝEt gan to knele eft be-for þe qweenꝺ 1198
Bothe mayster & duke of Athenes þat cyte;
Mayster he was in scole & long had beenꝺ,
And duke I-chose be þe puple þoo was he—
ffor her choys þer as þan was fre 1202
To haue qwat man, whech hem lyked to heed.
Þus in hys tale be-gan he [in] þat steed : 1204

" We supposyd, lady, euyr on-to þis tyme 1205
þat ȝe had come of þat gentyll bloode
Of ȝour modyr, descendyd downꝺ be lyne,
And of ȝour fadyr þat was ful gentyll & good.
But our opynyonꝺ is chaunged & our moode, 1209
ffor, as it semyth, ȝe ar no-þing of kyne;
And if ȝe wer, ȝe coude not cese ne blyne 1211

" To folow þe steppes of ȝour elderys be-for, 1212
As graynꝺ reall growynꝺ oute of her groundeꝺ—
ffor natur wolde, thow ȝe þe reuers had swore,
þat ȝe wer lych hem, certeynꝺ, in euery stownnde ;
And in our Philosophye, I hope, þus it is founde 1216
þat naturaly þe braunch oute of þe rote
Schall tak hys sauour, be it sour or swote. 1218

" ffferthermore ȝet sey our bokys þus : 1219
' þat euery lych hys lych he schall desyre.'
Be all þese menes it semeth þan to vs :
Eyther ȝe cam neuyr duly to þis empyr,
Or ellys ȝour hert dyspysyth ioye as myr. 1223
I can no mor, I speke on-curteslye,
I may not chese, I am so vexed, trulye." 1225

To chese the on) than for to wante bothe.
Chese ye now; we be no lengere wrothe." 1197

Ca^m. 28^m.

Yet gan to knele efte be-fore the queen), 1198 *The Duke of Athens argues with Katharine.*
Bothe mayster and duke of athenes þat citee;
Mayster he was in scole and longe had been),
And duke I-chose be the puple tho was hee—
ffor her choys there and thanne was free 1202
To haue what man), whiche hem lyked to hed.
Thus in his tale be-gan) he in that steed: 1204

"We supposed, lady, euere on)-to this tyme 1205
That ye had come of that gentyl blood
Of youre moder, descendet doun) be lyne,
And of your fader þat was ful gentil and good.
But oure oppynyon) is chaunged and oure mood, 1209
ffor, as it semeth, ye arn) no-thyng of kyn);
And if ye were, ye cowde not sece and blyn) 1211

"To folwe þe steppes of youre olderis be-forn), 1212 *Katharine will not follow her elders.*
As greyn) real growen) oute of her grounde—
ffor nature wolde, þough ye the reuers had sworn),
That ye were lyche hem in euery stounde;
And in oure philosophie, I hope, thus is it founde 1216
That naturally the braunche oute of þe rote
Shal take his sauour, be it soure be it swote. 1218

"fferthermore yet seyn) oure bookis thus: 1219 *Like ought to follow like.*
'That euery liche his lyche shal desyre.'
Be alle these menes it semeth þan to vs:
Eyther ye cam neuer dewly to þis empyre,
Or ellis youre herte despiseth ioye as myre. 1223
I can no more, I speke on-curteysely,
I may not chese, I am) so vexed, trewly." 1225

Ca^m. 31^m.

ON-to þe duk þus answerd þoo þe qween): 1226
"ʒe make a reson) of ful gret apparens,
ʒe schew full wele wher' þat ʒe hafe been):
In þe grete nest of bysy dylygens,
Wher' stody & wytt is in experiens, 1230
I mene Athenes—of wysdam it beryth þe key;
Who will oute lerne, lat hym tak þidyr þe wey. 1232

"But neuyrþelasse, thow þat ʒe be endewyd 1233
Wyth werdly wysdam & can all þing pleynly,
So þat ʒe may wyth no sophym be pursewyd:
ʒet to ʒour motyff answer' þus may I,
And voyd ʒour' resoun) well & pregnantly, 1237
If ʒe wyll her' & take entent to me.
ffor if men take heed, oft-tyme þei may se 1239

"Owte of a tre growyng dyuerse frute, 1240
And þat same tre þat sumetyme bar' þe grene,
Now bereth he reed or qwyte, of dyuerse sute.
Be þis example pleynly þus I mene:
My modyr is, & so am I, a qween), 1244
In þis we a-cord; & þat I am a may,
In þat we dyuerse, I can not per-to sey nay. 1246

"It semeth me þat lych a griff am I, 1247
I-planted be god vp-on an elde stoke,
Of an oþer kynde, an othyr sauour' hardyly;
And euene as be miracle þe elde blok,
Wech is clouyn) in four' wyth many a knok, 1251
Schall rather' folow þe gryff, þan þe gryff hym,
So faryth it be me & be my elder' kyn): 1253

"Thei schul rather' consent to leue all sole 1254
As I do now, þan schall I¹ folow hem).   ¹ r. I schall
ffor certeynly, I kepe not of þat scole
Wher' þat her' ioye is, but lych a drem)
ffarwell ffadyr, ffarwell modyr & eem, 1258

Ca^{m.} 29^{m}.

O N-to the duke þus answered tho þe queen): 1226
  " Ye make a reson of ful grete apparens,
Ye shewe ful weel where þat ye haue ben),
In the grete neste of besy diligens,
Where stody and wytte is in experiens, 1230
I mene athenes—of wysdam it bereth the keye ;
ho wil owte lerne, lete hym take thedir þe weye. 1232

"But neuerthelesse, thow þat ye be endwed 1233
Wyth werdly wisdam) and kan) aH thyng trewly,
Soo þat ye may with no sophym) be pursewed :
Yet to youre motyf answere thus may I,
And voyde youre reson) weel and pregnauntly, 1237
If ye wele here and take entent to me.
ffor if men) taken heed, often-tyme may þei see 1239

"Oute of oo tre growyng dyuers frute, 1240
And þat same tree that somtyme baar the grene,
Now beryth he reed or white, or of dyuers sute.
Be þis exaumple pleynly thus I mene :
My moder is, and so am I, a queene, 1244
In this we a-coorde ; and in þat I am a may,
In that we dyuers, I can) not ther-to sey nay. 1246

"It semeth me þat liche a gryf am I, 1247
I-planted be god vp-on) a old stok,
Of another keende, a-nother savour hardyly ;
And euene as be myracle þe olde blok,
Whiche is clouen) in foure with many a knok, 1251
Shal rathere folwe the gryffe, than) þe gryffe hym),
Soo fareth it be me¹ and be myn) oldere kyn): ¹ overlined. 1253

"Thei shul rathere consente to lyve al soole 1254
As I doo now, than) I shal folwe hem.
ffor certeynly I kepe not of þat scoole
Where þat her ioye is, but lyke to a drem)
ffar-weel, fadir, farweel, moder and em), 1258

156 Four Reasons for Katharine's Marriage. [MS. Rawlinson.

Bk. II. Ch. 31. Whan þat her' counsell is not profitable;
I take swych lyffe, I hope is ferm & stabyll."   1260

Bk. II. Ch. 32.   Ca^m. 32^m.

Qwan þei had sayd all þat euyr þei coude,   1261
þei went a-sundre & parted for a space;
Comound her wyttys styll, & no-þing lowde,
Euyr [h]opyng & lokyng aftyr grace
Of þis same mayde, if þei it myght purchase,   1265
And at a day sette þei cam to-gedyr a-geyn,
To haue an answer' of hyr plat & pleyn.   1267

Thei chose a clerke to telle her' alders tale,   1268
Whech was full wys & of full grete cunnyng—
ffor uery stody hys vysage was full pale,
Alle hys delyte & ioye was in lernyng;
Be alle her' consent he had enformyd a thyng   1272
Whech he wyll vttyr if he may owte spede,
And all is lost but sche þer-to take hede.   1274

"ffour þinges," he seyde, "madame, be in ȝow,   1275
Whech schuld excite ȝow wedded for to be;
If ȝe commaunde, I wyll declar' hem nowe.
þe fyrst of hem is þat grete dygnyte
Of ȝour bloode ryall—I trow þat þer non be   1279
In all þis werld whech is so hye a-lyed.
þe secunde also may be sone a-spyed,   1281

"ffor it is open to euery mannes eye: 1282
I mene ȝour beute—god mot it preserue!
þer lyuyth no man þat euer fayrer' syȝe—
Euyr lest it tyll tyme þat ȝe sterue!
þat blessed lady whech we clepe mynerue,   1286
Sche hath ȝoue ȝow þe thryd þat I of sayde:
Whech is cunnyng; it is so on ȝow layde,   1288

"It may not fall fro ȝow be no weye.   1289
And eke þe fourt is þe gret rychesse
Whech þat ȝe welde, I can not tell ne seye,

Whan her counseH is not profytable ;   [1] orig. his
I take swyche lyf, I hope, as is[1] firme and stable."   1260

Ca^{m.} 30^{m.}

Whanne thei had seyd al that euere þei cowde,   1261
 Thei went a-sundre and parted for a space ;
Comouned her wittis stylle, and no-thyng lowde,
Euere hopyng and lookynge after grace
Of this same mayde, if thei myght it purchace,   1265
And at a day sette thei come to-gedyr a-geyn,
To haue an answere of hir plat and pleyn.   1267

Thei chose a clerk [to telle] her alderis tale,   1268
Whiche was ful wys and of ful grete connynge—
ffor very stody his face was ful pale,
Al hys delyte and ioye was in lernynge ;
Be al her consent he had enformed a þinge   1272
Whiche he wil[1] vttere if he may owte speede,   [1] MS. wild
And al is lost but she therto take heede.   1274

"ffoure þingis," he seyde, " madame, ben in yow,   1275
Whiche shulde excite you wedded for to bee ;
If ye comaunde, I wil declare hem now.
The firste of hem is þat grete dignyte   [1] not—she over erasure.
Of youre blood rial—I trowe that not boorn his she[1]   1279
In al þis world wich is so hy allyed.
The secunde also may bee ful soone aspyed,   1281

"ffor it is open to euery man-is eyȝe :   1282
I mene youre beute—god mote it preserue !
Ther leueth no man that euere fairere seyȝe—
Euere leste it til tyme that ye sterue !
That blyssed lady whiche we clepe mynerue,   1286
She hath youe yow the thredde that I sayde :
Whiche is connynge ; it is soo on yow layde,   1288

" It may not falle fro yow be no weye.   1289
And eke the fourthe is the grete rychesse
Whiche þat ye welde, I can not telle ne seye,

Bk. II. Ch. 29.

Bk. II. Ch. 30.

Katharine's lords depart,

commune,

and assemble again for her answer.

They choose a Clerk to argue for them.

The Clerk urges Katharine to marry,

1. for her high lineage,

2. for her beauty,

3. for her knowledge,

4. for her riches.

ffor, as I suppose, no man may hem gesse.
Suffyr me, lady, my resones to expresse, 1293
So þat þei may be on-to ȝow plesaunce,
And eke ȝour puple, I hope, it schuld avaunce. 1295

"The fyrst of alle, as I seyd be-for', 1296
Is ȝour bloode, ȝour reall stok & lyne,
Owte of whech ȝe wer be-gote & bore :
þis schuld ȝour hert boþe drawe & enclyne
ffor to spede our purpos well & fyne. 1300
Wote ȝe nott welle of what lordes ȝe came?
Kyng alysaundyr, þat all þis werld wan, 1302

"Was of ȝour kyn, & so was þat noble kyng 1303
Whech[1] made þis cyte, babel I mene be name,
Eke many an other þat her in her lyuyng   [1] þat crossed out after Wh.
Wer enhaunshed hyely wyth gret fame.
Take heed her-to, for goddys sake, madame ; 1307
Syth þei weddyd wer & ech on had a make,
Dothe ȝe þe same, for ȝour kynrod sake! 1309

"On þe other syde of ȝour bryte beute 1310
þus dar I say, & I dar stand þer-by :
þer is no man þat euyr wyth eye ȝet see
Swech an othyr as ȝe be, hardyly.
I flatyr not, I am non of þoo, sewyrly ; 1314
It is not presyd in noo book þat I rede.
þan sey I thus þat natur wyth-oute drede, 1316

"Whan sche wyll peynt, þer can no man do bettyr. 1317
ffor sche schapyth parfytely all þat euer sche dothe,
Sche is vndyr godd made be patent lettyr
hys vycere generall, if I schall sey sothe,
To ȝeue mankynd bothe nase, eye, & tothe 1321
Of what schape þat hyr lykyth to ȝeue,
And of hyr werk no man hyr to repreue. 1323

"Sche hath ȝoue, lady, ryght on-to ȝour persone 1324
Ȝour bryght colour & fayr schap eke wyth-alle,

ffor, as I suppose, no man may hem gesse.
Suffre me, lady, my resones to expresse, 1293
Soo þat þei may bee on-to you plesauns,
And eke youre puple I hope it shuld avauns. 1295

"The firste of alle, as I seyde before, 1296 *The Clerk enlarges on these points.*
Youre blood, youre ryal stook and lyne,
Oute of whiche ye were be-gote and bore,
This shulde youre herte bothe drawe and enclyne
ffor to spedyn oure purpos weele and fyne. 1300
Wote ye not weel of what lordes ye cam?
Kyng Alysaundre, that al thys word wan, 1302 *Alexander*

"Was of youre kyn, and so was þat noble kyng 1303 *was of Katharine's kin.*
Whiche made þis citee, babel I mene be name,
Eke many an other in er lyuyng
Were enhaunced hyly wyth ryght grete fame.
Taketh heed her-to, for goddys sake, madame; 1307
Syth thei wedded were and iche had a make,
Dooth ye the same, for youre kenredes sake! 1309 *She should marry.*

"On the other syde of youre bryght beute 1310
Thus dar I seye, and I dar stande ther-by:
There is[1] noman that euere with eye yet see [1] overlined. *She is very beautiful.*
Suche an other as ye be, hardyly.
I flather not, I am noon of tho suerly; 1314
It is not preysed in ony book þat I reede.
Thanne sey I thus þat nature with-oute dreede, 1316

"Whanne she whil poynte, þer can no man doo better.
ffor she shapeth parfyghtly al þat euere she dooth, 1318 *Nature has given her*
She is vnder god made be patent letter
his viker general, if I shal sey sooth,
To yeve mankeende bothe nase, eye and tooth, 1321
Of what shap þat hir lyketh to yeue,
And of hir werk no man hir to repreue. 1323

"She hath youe, lady, ryght on-to youre persone 1324
Youre bryght colour and fayr shap ryght wyth-al, *colour and shape,*

To þis entent ȝe schuld not leue a-lone,
But wyth charyte departe þis ȝyfte ȝe schall.
But ȝe do þus, ȝe may sone haue a fall, 1328
ffor sche may take þing þat sche ȝafe, certayn),
And doth allday fro hem þat ar' dysdayn), 1330

"Whech can not thank hyr' of hyr hye grace. 1331
þerfor', madame, taketh heed her-to, I pray,
lese not ȝour holde, lese not ȝour purchase,
lete mekenesse dwelle wyth swych a fresch may!
þan schall we sykyrly of ȝow syng & say 1335
þat all is well, ryght as we wold it haue.
fferþermor', so godd my sowle mote saue, 1337

"I trow, þow natur' had coupled in o persone 1338
All hyr ȝyftis—as, if sche wyll, sche kan),
Than trowe I welle ȝe haue hem all a-lone.
Of ȝour' charyte þan take to ȝow sume man),
lete hym haue parte of swech þing as ȝe han)! 1342
Swech goodely ȝyftis wold not euer be hyd—
If natur' wer' her', þe same sche wold byd. 1344

"And for þe thryd poynt in whech I ȝow commende,
Whych is ȝour wysdam & ȝour gret lernyng: 1346
Ȝour' wyttys ar' swech, þer can no man amende
Ȝour' conceytes hye, for, if ȝe had a kyng,
he myght ful well trost in ȝour cunnyng, 1349
Thow he hym-self had not as ȝe haue.
And as me þinkyth, ȝour soule can ȝe not saue 1351

"But if ȝe comoun) þis ȝyfte to other' mene— 1352
It is not ȝoue ȝow to haue it all a-lone.
þe fyrst meuer', as our' bokes vs ken),
Whech syttyth a-boue þe sterrys in hys trone,
he ȝeuyth sume man more wysdham be hys one 1356
þan haue xx^{ti}, only for þis entent
þat he to other' schall comon) þat godd hym sent. 1358

To this entent ye shulde not lyue allone,
But with charyte departe this yifte ye shal.
But ye doo thus, ye may soone haue a fal, 1328
ffor she may take thyng that she yaf, certayn,
And dooth al day fro hem þat arn dysdayn, 1330

"Whiche can not thanken hir of hir hy grace. 1331
Therfore, madame, taketh heed hir to, I you¹ pray, ¹ on eras. Katharine
lese not youre hold, lese not youre purchace,
lete mekenesse dwelle with suche a freshe may!
Thanne shal we sekerly of you syng and say 1335
That al is weel, ryght as we wold it haue.
fferthermore, so god my sowle mote saue, 1337

"I trowe, though nature had complet in oon persone
Alle hir yeftes—as, if she wil, she can, 1339
Than trowe I weel ye haue hem all allone.
Of yowre charyte þanne take to you som man, *should share her gifts with*
lete hym haue part of suche þing as ye hane! 1342 *a Husband.*
Swiche goodly yyftis wolde not euer ben hyd—
If nature were here, the same she wold byd. 1344

"And for the thredde poynt in whiche I yow commende,
Whiche is youre wysdam and youre gret lernynge: 1346 *She is very wise.*
Youre wittis and swhiche, there can noo man amende
Youre conseytes hye, for, if ye had a kyng,   *A King could trust her.*
he myght ful weel trost in youre conyng, 1349
Thow he hym-self had not as ye haue.
And as me thenketh, youre soule can ye not saue 1351

"But if ye comoun thys yifte to other men— 1352 *If she doesn't marry,*
It is not youe you to haue it allone.
The first meuere, as oure bookis us ken,
Whiche sitteth a-boue the sterris in his trone,
he yeueth som man more wysdam be his oone 1356
Thanne haue twenty, oonly to this entent
That he to other shal comoun þat god hym sent. 1358

| Bk. II. Ch. 32. | "Take heed herto, for perell*is* þat may falle | 1359 |

If ȝe dysplese þat meuer' whycħ sitt a-boue ;
hys ȝyft*is* fro ȝow draw a-wey he schaħ—
þat I spek now, I sey it of very loue,
And, as me þinkyth, mecħ to ȝour' be-houe. 1363
þe fourt poynt of theyse & last of alle,
Is þe rychesse whecħ is on-to ȝow falle. 1365

" Ȝe be so rycħ þe werld woundyrth of it. 1366
What schall ȝe do w*yth* alle þis welth a-lone ?
I sey of þis as I seyd of ȝour' wytt :
þei wer' I-gr*a*unted of godd to ȝour' p*er*sone
þat ȝe schuld part all þis welth & woone ; 1370
þat schall ȝe best [do]¹ if ȝe take a kyng.   ¹ om.
her' is my tale, her' is myn askyng." 1372

| Bk. II. Ch. 33. | Ca^{m.} 33^{m.} |

Than answerd sone þat swet gr*a*cyous wyght, 1373
   And to þis mayster sche seyd þus a-gayn :
"Ȝour' comme*n*dacyo*n* whecħ ȝe dyd endyth,
If it be soth as ȝe sayd plat & playn,
Schall cause me, þer is no mor' to sayn, 1377
To plese þat lord w*yth* all hert & mynde
þat i*n* hys ȝyftis hath be to me so kynde 1379

" And sent me graces whech oþ*er* wome*n* want. 1380
Ȝe seyd efte : for þat I am so fayr'
And eke so wys & rycħ as ȝe warant,
þerfor' me must purpos to haue a ayr',
To chese an husbond good & debonayre. 1384
A-vyse ȝow, syr', what þat ȝe haue sayde ;
We wyll not lyght lower' þa*n* ȝe vs layde. 1386

" Ȝe haue sett our' loos a-boue so hye, 1387
We pase all wome*n* þat now formed are.
And on ȝour' grou*n*de a-geyn I þus replye :
I wold know to me who þat worthy ware.
þis is ȝo*ur* argument, þis is ȝo*ur* owne lare 1391

Katharine answers the Clerk's Argument.

"Take heed her-to, for periḻ that may falle,   1359   *Bk. II. Ch. 30.*
If ye displese that meuere whiche sit a-boue ;
his yiftes fro you drawe a-wey he shalle—   *God may withdraw*
That I speke now I sey it[1] of very loue,   [1] overlined.   *His gifts from her.*
And, as me thenketh, moche to youre be-houe.   1363
The fourthe poynt of these and last of alle,
Is the rychesse whiche is oⁿ-to yow falle.   1365   *Katharine has such riches,*

" Ye be so ryche the world wondreth of it.   1366
What shal ye doo wyth al this welthe allone?
I sey of this as I seyde of youre wit :
Thei were I-grauntid of god to youre persone
That ye shuld parte al this welthe and wone.   1370   *that she should share them with a Husband.*
That shal ye best doo if ye take a kyng.
here is my tale, here is myⁿ askyng."   1372

Caᵐ. 31ᵐ.   *Bk. II. Ch. 31.*

Thanne answerde þat swete gracyous whigt,   1373   *Katharine answers the wise Clerk.*
And to this mayster she seyde thus a-geyⁿ :
" Youre commendacyoⁿ whiche here now ye endyght,
If it be sooth as ye seyde plat and pleyⁿ,
Shal cause me, there is no more to seyⁿ,   1377
To plese that lord with al myⁿ herte and mynde
That in his yiftes hath beeⁿ to me so kynde   1379

" And sente me grace whiche other womeⁿ wante.   1380
Ye seyde efte : for þat I am so fayre   *As he has made her out to be perfection,*
And eke so wys and ryche as ye warante,
Therfore me muste purpos to haue an ayre,
To chese an husbond good and debonayre.   1384
Avise you, sir, what that ye haue sayde ;
We wil not lyght lower thaⁿ ye vs layde.   1386

" Ye haue sette oure loos a-boue so hye,   1387
We passe alle womeⁿ þat now foormed are.
And on your grounde a-geyⁿ I thus replye :
I wulde knowe to me hoo worthy ware.
This is your argument, this is your owne lare   1391

M 2

þat I am worthyest lyuyng of all women :
þan must I hafe þe worthyest of all men),   1393

"It folowyth full euene ryght of[1] ʒour tale,   1394
If ʒe take heed. I pray ʒow wher' dwellyth he,
So wyis, so fayr', so rych wyth-outen bale,
And of swech lynage born) as we be ?
But if ʒe fynde swech on, ʒe may leue me   1398
I wyll noon[1] haf ; þer-for' loke well a-boute !—
þe mor' ʒe plete, þe mor' ʒe stand in doute.   1400

"But ʒe wyll wyte allgate what I desyr' :   1401
I schall dyscriue myn) husbond whom I wyll hafe.
A-boue all lordes he must be, wyth-oute pere,
Whom he wyll to spylle or elles to saue ;
he must be stable, & neuyr turn) ne waue   1405
ffro noo purpos þat he set hym on—
But he be swech, husbond schall he be none   1407

"As on-to vs, whom ʒe hafe so commended.   1408
he must be wyis alsoo, þat he knowe all,
Euery þing þat it may be a-mendyd
And reryd a-geyn), or it fully fall.
If þer be swech on), receyue hym sone we schall, 1412
And ellys, sekyr, we wyll haue husbond none.
loke well a-boute if ʒe can fynd swych on) !   1414

"fferþermor' ʒet must he haue swech myght   1415
þat hym nedyth no help of no creature,
But he hym-self be suffycyent to do þe ryght ;
And euer hys myght demened wyth mesure.
If þat ʒe wyll swech on me ensure,   1419
I wyll hym hafe, I schall neuer sey nay.
Herkenyth also more what I wyll say :   1421

"I wold eke þat he schuld be so rych   1422
þat hym neded not of oþir mennys goode ;
No lorde in erthe I wold haue hym lych ;

---

[1] MS. oft
[1] MS. now

That I am wurt[h]yest lyuyng of alle women: *Bk. II. Ch. 31.*
Than must I haue þe wurt[h]yest of aH men,   1393   she must have a perfect Husband.

"It folweth ful euene ryght of youre tale,   1394   But where is a Husband worthy of her to be found?
If yee take heed. I prey yow where dwelleth he,
So wys, so fayr, so ryche wyth-oute bale,
And of swyche lynage born as we bee?
But if ye fynde suche oon, ye may leue me   1398
I wil noon haue; þerfore looke weel a-boute!—
The more ye plete, the more ye stonde in doute.   1400

"But ye wil wete algat*is* what I desyre: 1401
I shal discrie myn husbonde whom I wil haue.
A-boue alle lordes he muste be and w*y*t*h*-oute pyre,[1]   [1] corr.   He must be peerless,
Whom he wil to spille or ellis to saue;
he muste be stable, and neuere turne ne waue   1405
ffro no purpos that he sette hym up-on—
But he be swiche on husbond, myn shal he be noon,   1407

"As on-to vs, whom ye haue so commended.   1408
he must be wys also, that he knowe al,   most wise,
Euery thyng that it may be mended,
And rered ageyn, or it fully fal.
If there be swiche on, receyue hym soone we shal,   1412
And ellys, sekyr, we wil haue husbond noon.
looke weel a-bouthe if ye can fynde swiche oon!   1414

"fferthermore yet muste he haue suche myght   1415   most mighty,
That hym nede non helpe of other creature,
But he hym-self be suffycyent to doo ryght;
An euere his myght demened wyth mesure.
If that ye wil swiche on me ensure,   1419
I wyl hym haue, I shal neuere sey nay.
herkeneth also more what I wil say: 1421

"I wil eke þat he shal be so ryche   1422   most rich,
That hym nedeth not of other mannys good;
No lord in erthe I wulde haue hym lyche;

I desyr' eke he schuld be so large of goode,
ffre of hert & manfull eke of moode, 1426
þat, what man onys asked hym any þing,
he schuld hem graunte mor' þan her' askyng. 1428

"he must be fayr' also, he whom I desyre, 1429
So fayr' & amyable þat he must pase me;
ffor syth he schall to me be lord & syr',
It is good resoun) þat hys schynyng ble
Pase hyr colour' whech schall hys seruaunt be, 1433
And on-to hys lordchype boþe seruaunt,[1] spouse & wyffe.
fferþermor' ȝet schall þis lordes lyff   [1] to be om.? 1435

"Be eterne—elles all þis is nowte, 1436
All þat is sayd, but he haue þis;
ffor syth he schall wyth so gret labour' be sowte,
As me semeth, þe game went sor' a-mys,
Whan all wer' well & all in ioye & blys, 1440
Sodenly to fayle & falle fro swech welth.
þerfor I tell ȝow, I dysyr' þat hys helthe, 1442

"hys age, hys strength, þat all þeis fayl neuyr, 1443
But euermor' lest, for sorow þat it wold make
To me whech-tyme þat we schuld dysseuyr—
ffor other' lord wold I neuer-mor' take,
But wepe & morne all in clothys blake. 1447
þer-for ȝe schull me warant he schall not deye,
þis lord to whom ȝe wold me newe alye: 1449

"And þan consent I to all þat euer ȝe craue, 1450
Elles nowt. wene ȝe þat I wold fare
As many other' do, & haue as þei haue,
lych to my modyr, þe sorow, þe wo, þe care
Whech sche had, whan þei departed ware, 1454
My lord my fadyr & eke my lady a-sundyr?
þat I fle þis, me þinkyth it is no woundyr!" 1456

I desyre eke he shulde bee so large of food,   *Bk. II. Ch. 31.*
ffre of herte and manful eke of mood,   1426   most liberal,
That, what man asked hym oones ony thyng,
he shulde hem graunte more than her askyng.   1428

"he muste be fayr also whom I desyre,   1429   most fair and amiable.
Soo fayre and amyable that he muste passe me;
ffor sith he shal to me be bothe lord and syre,
It is good reson that his shynyng blee
passe hir colour whiche shal his seruaunt bee   1433
And on-to his lordshype bothe seruaunt, spouse and wyf.
fferthermore yet shal this lordys lyf   1435

"Ben eterne—ell*is* al this is nought   1436   immortal,
Al þat is seyde, but if he haue this;
ffor sithe he shal with soo grete labo*ur* be sought,
As me semeth, the game wente sore amys,
Whan al were weel and al in Ioye and blys   1440
Sodey[n]ly to fayle and falle fro swiche welthe.
Therfore I telle you, I desyre that his helthe,   1442

"his age, his strengthe, that alle these fayle neu*er*e,   and ever vigorous.
But eu*er*e-more leste, for sorwe þat it wolde make   1444
To me whiche-tyme þat we shulde dissceu*er*e—
ffor other lord wolde I neu*er*e-more take,
But wepe and moorne al in clothys blake.   1447
Therfore ye shul me warrant he shal not deye,   When a man like this can
This lord to whom ye wolde me newe alleye: 1449   be found,

"And than consente I to al þat eu*er*e ye craue,   1450   Katharine 'll marry him; else not.
Ell*is* nought. wene ye that I wold fare
As many other doo, and haue as[1] thei haue,   [1] as corrected.
lyche to my moder, the sorwe, þe woo, þe care
Whiche she had, whan thei departed ware,   1454
My lord my fadyr and eke my lady a-sunder?
Thou I flee this, me thenketh it is no wonder!"   1456

Whan sche had seyd þese wordes all a-lowde   1457
And vttyrd hyr conceyte pleynly to hem alle,
þer was no man as þan þat him kepe cowde
ffro wepyng teres—full sor' þei gun down falle.
hyr modyr fel down as rownd as any balle,   1461
ffor very sorow sche swounyd in þat place,
ffor now sche seeth þer is non othyr grace.   1463

Sche was lyft vp & comforted new a-gayn,   1464
And at þe last, whan sche had caut wynde,
"Alas," sche seyd, "sorow hath me nye slayn!
Wher' schall we seke, wher' schall [we] swych on fynde?
My dowtyr, I trowe, hath not well her' mynde,   1468
Sche wote not what sche seyth, sche is so made!
Who may it be? wher' may swech on be halde?   1470

"As sche desyryth it is not parde! possible,   1471
Ther is non swech, þan schall sche neuer haue non;
Neuyr deye, neuer seke, he must be inpassible!—
We may well see sche scornyth vs echon.
Go we fast hens, let hyr haue it a-loon!   1475
Worchep & rychesse sche schall ful soone lese,
No defaute in vs, for we may not chese."   1477

Thus wayled þe lordes as þei sote be-deen,   1478
Cursyng hyr maysterys, cursyng her' bokes alle:
"Alas," þei seyd, "þat euer any qween
þus schuld be comered! our' worchep is down falle!
God send neuyr rem kyng þat wereth a calle!   1482
We pray godd þat he neuyr woman make
So gret a mayster as sche is, for our' sake."   1484

Thus wyth wo, mych care & grucchyng   1485
þei parte a-soundyr, ech man on-to hys home
þei goo or ryde or sayle at her' lykyng;

Caᵐ. 32ᵐ.

Whan she had seyd these wordys alle allowde 1457
And vtteryd hir conseyte pleynly to hem alle,
There was no maɲ as þanne þat hym kepe cowde   *Katharine's Lords weep;*
Fro weepyng teeres—ful sore thei gunne douɲ falle.
hir moder fel douɲ as round as ony balle,   1461
for very sorwe she swouned in that place,
ffor now she seeth ther is nooɲ other grace.   1463

She was lyfted vp and comforted newe a-gayɲ,   1464
And at the laste, whaɲ she had caute wynde,
"Allas," she seyde, "sorwe hath me ny slayɲ!
Where shal we seeke, where shal we swyche ooɲ fynde?
My doughter, I trowe, hath not weel hir mynde,   1468   *her Mother thinks she's mad:*
She wot not what she seyth, she is soo mad!
how may it bee? where may swiche oon be had?   1470

"As she desireth it is not trewely possible,   1471
There is nooɲ suche, thaɲ shal she neuere haue nooɲ;   *no immortal man can be found.*
Neuere deye, neuere seek, he muste bee impassible!—
We may weel see she skorneth vs eche ooɲ.
Go we fast hens, lete hir haue it allooɲ!   1475
Wurshipe and rychesse shal she ful soone lese,
No defaute in vs, ffor we may not chese."   1477

Thus weyled the lordes as þei sete be-deene,   1478
Cursyng hir maysteris, cursyng hir bookis alle:
"Allas," thei seyde, "that euere ony queene
Thus shuld be comered! oure wurshype is douɲ falle!
God sende neuere reem a kyng that wereth a calle!   1482
We prey god þat he neuere woman make
Soo grete a mayster as she is, for hir sake."   1484

Thus wyth woo, meche care and grutchynge   1485   *The Parliament breaks up. Its members grumble.*
Thei parte a-sondre, iche maɲ to his hom
Thei goo or ryde or sayle as here lykynge;

170 Capgrave asks the Holy Ghost's Help. [MS. Rawlinson.

Bk. II. Ch. 34.
ffor wyth þe qween wroth þei are echon.
Sche is now left for hem to dwell a-lon ; 1489
Sche may stody, rede, reherse, & wryght.
þus is þe parlement fynchyd, & euery wyght 1491
Is in drede & leueth wyth hert suspens, 1492
lokyng alwey aftyr new chaungyng ;
Alle her' wyttes & all her' grete expens
Are now but[1] lost. & her' schall be þe endyng   [1] on the margin.
Of þis same boke, whech tretyth of þe pletyng 1496
Be-twyx þis qween & all hyr lychemen.
God send vs parte of hyr prayer'. AmEN. 1498

Bk. III. Prol.
Liber iij. (Prolog.)

Sith no man may her' in þis lyffe present   1
  Doo no good dede, but he enspyred be
Of þat goste whech fro þe omnipotent
ffader of heuyn & fro þe sune so fre
Is sent to us, ryght so be-leue now we   5
þat [it] is best þat we our' labour' commende
On-to þis gost, if we wyll haue goode ende.   7

ffor I haue tolde ȝow schortly, as I can,   8
þe byrth, þe kynrod, þe nobyllhed of þis mayde,
þe gret disputyng of lordes who it be-gan,
And eke hyr answer', what sche to hem sayd ;
þis haue I pleynly now be-for ȝow layde   12
In swech ryme, as I coude best deuyse—
Schall neuyr man lese no labour' ne no seruyse   14

Whech þat he doth on-to þis noble qween ;   15
And now hens-for-warde schall be my laboure
To tell of hyr be ordre & be-deen
Who sche was wonne to crist, our' sauyour',
Who meruelously he entred to hyr toure   19
I mene daun adryan þe munke, whech our' feyth
ffyrst to hyr tawte, as þis cronycle seyth.   21

MS. Arundel.] *Capgrave asks the Holy Ghost's help.* 171

ffor w*yth* the quee*n* wroth thei are iche oo*n*.   *Bk. II. Ch. 32.*
She is now left for hem to dwelle allo*n* ;   1489
She may stody, reede, reherce and write.
Thus is the p*ar*lement fynyshed, and eue*r*y whyte   1491   The meeting of the Parliament has
    Is in dreed and lyueth w*yth* hert suspens,   1492   been in vain.
lookyng alwey after newe chaungynge ;
Alle her wytt*is* and alle her grete expens
Ar*n* now but lost. and [here] shal be the endynge
Of this same book whiche treteth of þe pleytynge[1]   1496
Be-twyxe the quee*n* and alle hir lygeme*n*.   [1] MS. pleyntynge
God sende vs part of hir prayere, amen.   1498

       Lib*er* iij. Ca^{m.} primum.[1]   [1] r. Prolog.   *Bk. III. Ch. 1.*

Sith noo man may here in this lyf p*re*sent   1
   Doo no good dede, but he enspyred bee
Of þ*a*t goost whiche fro the omnypotent   To the Holy Spirit
ffadir of heuene and fro the sone soo free
Is sent to vs, ryght soo be-leue now we   5
That it is best that we oure labour commende   I commend my work.
On-to this goost, if we wil haue good eende.   7

ffor I haue tolde yow shorthly, as I ka*n*,   8   I've told you of Katharine's birth,
The berthe, þe kynrede, þe noblehed of þis mayde,
The grete disputynge of lord*is* hov it be-ga*n*,
And eke hir answere, what she to hem sayde ;   and her refusal to
This haue I pleynly now be-fore yow layde   12   marry;
In swiche ryme as I cowde beest deuyse—
Shal neue*r*e ma*n* lese labour ne scruyse   14

Whiche that he dooth on-to this noble queen ;   15
And now hens-forthward shal ben my labo*ur*   now I'll tell you
To telle of hir be ordre and be-deen
how she was wonne to cryst, oure saueour,   18   how she was won to Christ.
how meruelyously[1] he entred in to hir tour   [1] or. merueylously
I mene daun Adrya*n* the monke, whiche oure feyth
ffirst to hir taught, as this cronycle seyth.   21

And if ȝe dowte, ȝe reders of þis lyffe, 22
Wheyþer' it be sothe, ȝe may well vndyrstande :
Mech þing hath be do whech hath be ful ryue
And is not wretyn ne cam neuer to our' hande,
Mech þing eke hyd in many dyuerse lande ; 26
Euene so was þis lyffe, as I seyd in þe prologe be-for',
Kept all in cage, a-boute it was not bore. 28

Now schall it walk wyder' þan euyr it dede, 29
In preysyng & honour' of þis martir Katerine ;
hyr lyff, her' feyth, hyr passyon) schall neuer be dede
Whyll þat I leue, I wold fulfayn) enclyne
hyr holy prayer' to be my medycyne 33
And eke my tryacle a-geyns þe venym foule
Whech þat þe deuyll hath þrowyn) on my soule. 35

I dresse me now streyt on-[to] þis werk. 36
Thow blyssyd may, comfort þou me in þis !
Be-cause þou wer' so lerned & swech a clerk,
Clerkes must loue þe, reson) for-sothe it is !
Who wyll oute lerne, trost to me, I-wys, 40
he dothe mech þe bettyr if he trost in þis may.
Þus I be-leue, & haue do many a day. 42

Cam. 1m.

Ther' was an hermyth, as elde bokes telle, 43
  A munke, a man of ful hye grace & fame ;
Be þe see, þei sey, sett was[1] þoo[2] hys celle— [1] MS. wall
Adryane, I rede þat it was hys name ;   [2] overlined.
hys knelyng had made hys knes full ny lame ; 47
A prest he was eke, sothely, as I fynde,
he had a chapell in whech he song & dynde, 49

Slepe & welk—for other' hous had he non). 50
Þis man knew þe counsell of þis mayde
ffyrst of alle—for Athanas, of whom long a-gon)
We spoke be-for, was not þan arayde
Ne eke a-noynted wyth baytym ne assayde 54

And if ye doughte, ye rederes of this lyf,   22   *Bk. III. Ch. 1.*
Whether it be sooth, ye may weel vndirstande :
Moche thyng hath be doon whiche hath beṅ ful ryf
And is not wretyn ne cam neuere to oure hande,
Moche þing hid eke in many dyuers lande ;   26
Euene so was this lyf, as I seyde in the prolog before,
Kepte al in cage, a-boute it was not bore.   28

Now shal it walke wydere than euere it dede,   29   *Her fame shall spread ever wider.*
In preysyng and honour of ·this mayde Kataryne ;
hir lyf, hir feyth, hir passyoṅ shal euere-more sprede
Whil þat I leue, I wolde ful fayṅ enclyne
hir holy preyere to be myṅ medecyne   33
And eke my treacle a-geyns the venyṁ foule
Whiche that the deuele hath throweṅ on my soule.   35

I dresse me now streyt on-to this werk.   36
Thou blyssed may, comforte þou me in this !   *Blessed Maiden, strengthen me in my work!*
Be-cause þou were so lerned and swiche a clerk,
Clerkys muste loueṅ þe, resoṅ forsothe it is !
Who wil owte lerne, troste to me, I-wys,   40
he dooth moche þe bettere if he truste in þis may.
Thus I be-leue, and haue doo many a day.   42

     Ca^{m.} secu*n*du*m*.¹   ¹ r. primum.   *Bk. III. Ch. 2.*

There was an Ermyte, as olde bookys telle,   43   *There was a hermit named Adrian.*
   A monke, a man of ful hey grace and fame ;
Be þe see, thei seyṅ, set was tho his celle—
Adryan, I rede that it was his name ;
hys kneelynge had maad his knees ful ny lame ;   47
A preest he was eke, soothly, as I fynde,
he had a chapel in whiche he song and dyṅde,   49

Sleep and welk—for 'other hous he had nooṅ.   50
This maṅ knew the counseiłł of þis mayde   *This monk Adrian first converted Katharine.*
ffirste of alle—for Athanas, of whom longe agooṅ
We spoke before, was not þaṅ arayede
Ne eke anoynted w*y*t*h* bapteṁ ne assayede   54

Wyth goddys scorge; for he was turned be hyr',
And sche conuertyd be miracle, as ȝe schul here. 56
This man was ordeynd lyche, I vndyrstande, 57
To seynt Ioseph our' lady to lede & gyde·
ffor euene as Ioseph in to egypte lande
Went wyth our' ladye, euermor' be hyr syde
So was þis Ermyte þan in þat tyde 61
A bodyly leder to þis gostly werke,
Whech-tyme þat cryst þis noble mayd schulde merk 63
Wyth hys crosse to make hyr strong & stabylle 64
A-geyns þe flesch, a-geyns þe affluens
Of wordly delyte, & make hyr' to hym abyll,
Bothe spouse & wyffe; whech feestly dylygens
Was wroght so wondyrly, it paseth experiens 68
Of wordly men. wherfor' I am a-gast
To spek þer-of, knowyng it passeth þe gnast 70
Of my cunnyng, but þat I leue in hope 71
þat thorow þe prayer' of hyr & adryane
I schall haue myght & strength eke to grope
Thys holy mater', to telle forth of þis man
Who þat he lyuyd & who he vytail wan. 75
ffor on-to town wolde he neuyr aproche,
But tyllyd hys londe heye up-on a roche. 77
Sumetyme of schyppes þat ryden þer' fastby, 78
had he comfort of mete & eke of drynke.
Sexty ȝer' þis lyffe he led, sothely,
þat neuyr went he a-way fro þat brynke.
þus party wyth elmesse, party wyth hys swynke, 82
Alle blyssydly in abstinens & prayer'
þis lyffe led he, þis ermyte or þis frere— 84
ffor frere was name þan to all crysten men 85
Comon, I rede, & ermytys wer' þei called
þat dwelt fro town, mylys sex or ten,
Wer' þei growen, wer' þei bar' or balled;
Be-cause þei wer' eke all soole I-walled, 89

Wyth godd*is* scourge ; for he was turned be hir,   *Bk. III. Ch. 2.*
And she conue*r*ted be myracle, as ye shul here.   56

This ma*n* was ordeyned liche, I vndirstonde,   57
To seynt Ioseph oure lady to lede and gyde :   He led her as Joseph led
ffor euene as Ioseph in to Egipte londe   St. Mary into Egypt.
Wente w*yth* oure lady, eue*r*emore be hir syde,
Soo was this ermyte thanne in that tyde   61
A bodyly leedere to þis goostely werk,
Whiche-tyme þ*a*t crist þis noble mayde shuld merk   63

Wyth his cros to make hir strong and stabil   64
A-geyns the flesh, a-geyns the affluens
Of wordly delyte, and make hir to hym abil,
Bothe spouse and wyf ; whiche feestly dylygens
Was wrought so wonderly, it passeth expe*r*iens   68
Of wordly me*n*. wherfore I am a-gast
To speke ther-of, knowynge it passeth þe gnast   70

Of my*n* connynge, but þ*a*t I leue in hope   71
That thurgh the prayere of hir and Adria*n*   Thro' his prayer and Katharine's
I shal haue myght and strengthe eke to grope
This holy mater, to telle foorth of this ma*n*   I'll tell you about him.
how þ*a*t he leued and how þ*a*t he vitayl wa*n*.   75
ffor on-to tounne wolde he neue*r*e approche,
But tilled his lond hey vp-on a roche.   77

Somtyme of shippys þ*a*t rede*n* there faste-by   78
he had conforte of mete and eke of drynk.
Sexty yeer he ledde this lyf soothly,   Adrian livd 60 years on a rock.
That neue*r*e wente he away fro that brynk.
Thus party w*yth* elmesse, party wyth swynk,   82
Alle blyssedly in abstinens and prayere
This lyf led he, this ermyte or this frere—   84

ffor frere was name thanne to alle cristene me*n*   85   Friars who dwelt 6 or 10
Comou[n],[1] I rede, and ermytes were thei called   [1] n erased.   miles from a town were cald Hermits.
That dwelled fro tow*n* myles sexe or tee*n*,
Were thei growe*n*, were thei bare or balled ;
Be-cause thei were eke al sool I-walled,   89

176 Of the Penance of the monk Adrian. [MS. Rawlinson.

Bk. III. Ch. 1. Sume men called hem munkys, wyth-owte drede—
ffor þeis wordes, munke & soole, ar on, as we rede. 91

Bk. III. Ch. 2.   Ca^m. 2^m.

Whan þis ermyte was fall (!) stope in age, 92
    And myght not byd hys bedys as he was wont,
Þan wold he goo forthe a grete passage,
Ryght be þe see, on stones scharp & blunte,
And euyr hys body wold he chyde & runte : 96
" What eylyth þe now, why art þou so sone oute
Of holy prayer, of werkes þat be deuoute ? 98
" Now god," he seyd, " þat sytthest hey in trone, 99
ffor-ȝeue it me þat I do not so weell
As I was wone ! my body is cause a-lone,
And not my soule, ful sykyrly þis I feele ;
I may not wake ne fast neuyr a dele, 103
I can no mor—all þis defaute is myne ;
If any goodenes haue I, lord þat is þin. 105

" Demene[1] not me, lorde, aftyr my febyll myght,   [1] r. Deme?
But aftyr [my] wylle, þat euyr desyreth[1] in on   [1] MS. sesyreth
Wyth blessed dedes to be a-lowed in þe syte
Of þi mercy ! for þowȝ my myght be gon,
Ȝet is my soule as stable as any ston, 110
And euyr schal be, as I can best deuyse,
In þi drede & eke in þi seruyse." 112

Vn-nethys had he ended hys oryson, 113
he saw a syght, a meruelous þo, he þowte.
ffor as he walkyd þe strondes up & down,
he fond a þing whech he had long I-south,
A blessed syght on-to hys eye was browte : 117
A qween he sey, of vysage & stature,
Pasyng full mech alle erdely creature, 119
All hyr aray a-cordyng eke þer-too, 120
So bryght a corown, so bryte clothys eke !
he wot not what hym is best to do ;

[MS. Arundel.] *Of the Penance of the monk Adrian.* 177

Some men called hem monkes wyth-outen dreed—   *Bk. III. Ch. 2.*
ffor this woord monk and sool are on, as we reed.   91

           Ca^{m.} tercium.   *Bk. III. Ch. 3.*

Whanne this ermyte was fer stope in age,   92   When Adrian couldn't pray,
    And myght not bydden his bedes as he was wont,
Thanne wolde he gon foorth a grete passage
Ryght be the see on stones sharp and blont,   he walkt on the stony
And euere his body wolde he chyde and ront :   96   shore,
" What eyleth the now, why art þou soo sone oute
Of holy preyere and of werkys that ben devoute ?   98

    " Now god," he seyde, " þat sittest hyest in throne,   99
ffor-yeue me þat I doo not soo wel
As I was wont ! my body is cause allone   and told God that his body
And not my soule, ful sekerly this I feel ;   was at fault, not his soul.
I may not wake ne faste neuere a deel,   103
I can no more—al this defaute is myn ;
If ony goodnesse haue I, lord, þat is thyn.   105

    " Deme[1] not me, lord, after my febyl myght,   [1] orig. Demene
But after my wyl, þat euere desireth in oon   107
Wyth blyssed dedes to be allowed in the sight
Of thi mercy ! for though my myght be goon,
Yet is my sowle as stable as ony stoon,   110
And euere shal be, as I can beste deuyse,
In thi dreed and eke in thi seruyse."   112

    Vnnethes had he eended his oryson,   113
he saugh a sight, a meruelyous tho, he thought.
ffor as he walked the strondes vp and doun,   As Adrian is on the sea-
he fond a þing whiche he had long I-sought,   shore,
A blyssed sight on-to his eye was brought :   117
A queen he sawe, of vysage and of stature   he sees the Virgin Mary.
Passyng ful meche aH erthely creature,   119

    Alle hir array acordyng eke ther-too,   120
Soo bryght a coroun, soo bryght clothes eke.
he wot not what hym is best to doo ;

he is not febyll, he is no lenger' seke,
hys blode is come a-geyn on-to hys cheke, 124
hys eyne haue caute of new coumfort a lyght,
hys body is ʒonthyd, he þinketh hym-self ful lygth. 126
Than gan þis ermyte stalk¹ ny & nye, ¹ r. stalken 127
To se þis syght, þis selcowth new þing.
"O benedicite!" he seyd, "mech meruayle haue I,
þat þis lady fresch & fayr' & ʒyng
Is come so sodenly hydyr in þis morownyng, 131
And schyppe ne boote ne can I now her' see,
Neyther' on lond ne fletyng on þe see." 133
Thus merueylyng be-twyx ioye & drede 134
A full softe pase on-to hyr-ward he went;
ffor, as hym thowte, sche also to hym ʒede.
But sche spake fyrst wyth full meke entent:
"Brothyr," sche sayde, "þe lord omnipotent, 138
Whech made þe heuyn, þe watyr, & þe londe,
he saue ʒow euyr & blysse ʒow wyth hys honde!" 140
The ermyte þan on-to our' lady sayde: 141
"Gramercy, madame! & he kepe ʒow alsoo
ffro all myshap, þat ʒe be not a-frayde
Of noo dysese, but euyr wyth-owten woo!
I prey to godd, ʒe mote be on of thoo 145
Whech þat schall dwelle wyth hym in hys blys,
Wher' may no ioye ne no solace mys." 147
"Good syr'," seyd sche, "I wolde ʒow pray full fayn 148
To do a massage fro me vn-to a whyte
Whech þat I loue & trost, ʒe may hyr sayn—
So doth my sone, for werkys þat be ryght
Whech þat sche vsyth, þat mayde fayr' & bryte. 152
And ʒe, syr', our' massanger' I wold ʒe were,
Our' wyll & our' wordes to þis lady for to bere." 154
"O mercy, godd!" seyd þoo þis adryan, 155
"What, wold ʒe now I schuld forsak my celle,
fforsake my seruyce & to be ʒour' man?

he is not feble, he is no lengher seeke,
his blood is come a-geyn on-to his cheeke, 124
his eyne haue caute a newe comfort of lyght, [1 The 4 last words on erasure.]
his body is yongthed, he thenketh, and strenghed in myght.[1]

Than gan this ermyte stalke ny and ny, 127 *He draws nigh to her.*
To see this sight, this selkouth newe thyng.
"O benedicite!" he seyde, "moche merueyle haue I
That this lady fresh and fayr and ying,
his come soo sodeynly hedir this mornyng, 131
And ship ne boot ken I noon her to be[1] [1 ken—be on erasure.]
Neyther on lond ne fletyng on the see." 133

Thus merueylyng be-twyxe Ioye and dreed 134
A ful soft paas on-to hir he went;
ffor, as hym thought, she also to hym yeed.
But she spak first wyth ful meke entent:
"Brother," she seyde, "the lord omnipotent, 138 *She blesses him.*
Whiche made þe heuene, þe water, and þe lond,
he saue yow euere and blysse yov wyth his hond!" 140

The ermyte thanne on-to oure lady sayde: 141
"Gromercy, madame, and he kepe you also *Adrian thanks the Virgin Mary.*
ffro al myshap, that ye be not afrayed
Of no disese, but euere with-oute wo!
I prey to god ye mote ben on of tho 145
Whiche shal dwelle wyth hym in his blis,
Where may no ioye ne solas mys." 147

"Good sir," seyde she, "I wolde you prey ful fayn 148 *She asks him to be her messenger to a Maiden.*
To doo a masage fro me on-to a whight
Whiche þat I love and truste, ye may hir sayn—
Soo dooth my sone, for werkys tho be ryght 151
Whiche þat[1] she vseth, þat mayde fair and bryght. [1 MS. þo?]
And ye, sir, oure masager I wolde ye were,
Oure wyl and oure wordis to þis lady for to bere." 154

"O mercyful god," seyd tho þis Adryan, 155
"What, wolde ye now I shulde forsake my celle,
ffor-sake my scruyse and to be your man?

I haue made couenaunt euyr' her' to dwelle
Whyl þat me lestys, brethe, flesch & felle, 159
Tyl ihesu wyll fecch me, þat was maydenys sone.
Spek not þer-of, for it may not be don!" 161

Ca^m. 3^m.

Than sayd þat mayde a-geyn on-to hym: 162
"Art þou a-vysed what þou hast seyd to me?
þou prayed full late, whyll þe nyte was dyme,
þat god hym-self no-þing wrothe schuld be
Wyth þin age ne wyth þi febylte; 166
;þou prayed eke hys modyr, I herd it, loo,
Sche schuld be mene ryght be-twyx ȝow too. 168

"I am sche to whom þat þou so ofte 169
Wyth pytous noys hast cryed boþe day & nyght
þat I schuld help þi dulnes for to softe.
þer-for I wyll þou force þe wyth þi myghte
To be my massanger', & eke my gostly knyth, 173
On-to þat lady whom I loue full wele—
ȝet hath sche of me knowyng neuer a deele. 175

"Therfor' busk þe to Alysaundyr' for to goo, 176
On-to þat cyte whech men called sume-tyme
Grete babell—þer be swych no moo
In all þis werld, þus seyth euery pylgryme.
What schuld I lenger' tary in my ryme? 180
þou schalt fynde þer' a qween full reall,
And on-to hyr' bodyly[1] speke þou schall.   [1] r. boldly? 182

"Sey ryght thus: 'þe lady, boþe modyr & mayde, 183
Gretyth hyr[1] well, & þat in goodely wyse,   [1] r. þe
Ryth be me, for sche both comaunde & prayde
þat I schuld doo to hyr þis goode seruyse.'
þus schall þou sey, ryth as I deuyse— 187
Sche schall make straung & be a-stoyned sor',
leue not þis massage for þat cause neuer-þe-more! 189

I haue made convenaunt euere here for to dwelle
Whil þat me lesteth breth, flesh and felle,   159   Adrian says he has vowd to live on his rock.
Til ihesu wil fetche me, þat was maydenes sone.
Speke not ther-of for it may not be done!"   161

Ca^{m.} quartum.   *Bk. III. Ch. 4.*

Thanne seyde þat mayden a-geyn on-to hym: 162   The Virgin
"Art thou avysed what þou hast seyde on-to me?
Thou preyed ful late, whan the nyght was dym,
That god hym-selue no-þing wrooth shulde bee
With thyn age ne wyth thi febilte;   166
þou preydest eke is moder, I herde it loo,
She shuld be mene ryght be-twyxe yow too.   168

"I am she to whom þat thou soo ofte   169   tells Adrian who she is,
Wyth pytous voys hast cryed bothe day and nyght,
That shulde helpe thy dulnesse for to softe.   and that he is
Therfor I wil þou force the wyth thi myght
To be my masager, and eke my goostly knyght,   173
On-to that lady whom I loue ful weel—
Yet hath she of me knowyng neuere a deel.   175

"Therfore buske the to Alysaundyr for to goo,   176   to go to Alexandria,
On-[to] that citee whyche men called som-tyme
Grete babel—there be suche no moo
In al þis world, þus seyde euery pilgryme.
What shuld I lengere tarye in myn ryme?   180
þou shalt fynde there a queen ful real,
And on-to hir bodyly spekyn þou shal.   182

"Sey ryght thus: 'the lady bothe moder and mayde   and greet Katharine
Greeteth hir[1] weel, and that in goodly wise,   [1] r. þe   184   from her.
Right be me, for she bothe commaunde and prayde
That I shuld doo to hir this good seruyse.'
Thus shalt þou seyn, ryght as I deuyse—   187
She shal make straunge and be astoyned sore,
Leue not þis masage for þat cause neuere the more!   189

"It is not goo now but a lytyll whyle 190
Syth þat þis lady was wyth hyr counsayle,
In whech þer was ordeynyd many a wyle
And many a mene, & spent mych trauayle,
To do hyr wedde; but it myght not a-vayle. 194
ffor I my-selue haue ordeynd hyr' a lorde,
To whom sche schall in clennesse well a-corde. 196

"Eke þat þou schuld þe mor' deynte haue 197
To do þis massage & all þis grete labour',
I wyll þe tell pleynly, I wyll not waue,
I wyll not varye, but the lynage,[1] þe honour',   [1] MS. lynager)
The vertu, þe occupacyon of þis swete flour' 201
þou schalt it knowe be informacyoun of me,
Boþe hyr goodenes, hyr' cunnyng & hyr' degre. 203

"ffyrst of alle þou whyte[1] sche is a whem,[2]   [1] r. wyte 204
A rych, a reall, a wys, & eke a fayr'—   [2] r. qwem)
ffor in þis werlde swech no moo þer been);
Sche hath no chylde ne sche hath non ayr',
ffor, if sche leue, sche schall loue bettyr þe hayr' 208
Than any[1] reynes, aftyr þat sche be drawe   [1] corr. from ony
On-to my seruyse & to my sunnes lawe. 210

"Sche is also, in sothenesse, a ryth grete clerke, 211
And eke a sotyll, in alle þe seuyn scyens;
þat schewyd sche welle boþe wyth worde & werke
In þe parlement, wher' was grete expens
Of werdly rychesse, & eke grete dylygens 215
Of werdly wytte to make hyr' wedded be;
But þei sped not. a heyer' lord of degre 217

"Schal be hyr' spouse, whom sche ȝet not knowyth; 218
Sche must for-ber' fyrst mech þing, certayn,
I mene þe rychesse in which sche now flowyth;
ffor of pouert schall sche be as fayn
As euyr sche was of rychesse, sothe to sayn, 222
Or of ony welth or ony grete honour'.
I schall be to hyr a coumfortour' 224

"It is not goo now but a lytel while 190
Sith that this lady was with hir counsayle,
In whiche ther' was ordeyned many a wyle
And many a mene, and spente moche trauayle,
To doo hir be¹ wedde; but it myght not avayle. ¹ overd. 194

ffor I my-self haue ordeyned hir a loord,
To whom she shal in clennesse weel acoord. 196

"Eke þat þou shuldest þe more deynte haue 197
To doo this massage and al þis grete labour,
I wyl the telle pleynly, I wil not waue,
I wil not varye, but the lynage, the honour,
The vertu, þe occupacyon of þis swete flour 201
Thou shal it knowe be informacyon of me,
Bothe hir goodnesse, hir connynge and hir degree. 203

"ffirste of alle þou wite she is a queen, 204
A ryche, a real, a wys, and eke a fayre—
ffor in þis world no mo swiche ther been;
She hath no chyld ne she hath noon¹ ayre, ¹ MS. noon
ffor, if she leue, she shal loue bether þe hayre 208
Than ony regnes, after þat she be drawe
On-to my seruyse and on-to my sones lawe. 210

"She is also, in soothnesse, a right grete clerk, 211
And eke a sotil, in alle the scuene scyens;
That shewed she weel bothe in word and werk
In the parlement, where was gret expens
Of woordly ryches, and eke grete diligens 215
Of woordly wytte to make hir wedded to bee;
But þei sped not. An hyere lord of degree 217

"Shal ben hir spouse, whom she yet not knoweth; 218
She must for-bere first moche þing, certayn,
I mene the rychesse in whiche she now floweth;
ffor of pouerte shal she ben as fayn
As euere she was of rychesse, sooth to sayn, 222
Or of ony welth or ony grete honour.
I shal ben to hir a comfortour 224

MS. Arundel.] The Virgin tells Adrian about Katharine. 183

Bk. III. Ch. 4.

She has provided a Husband for Katharine.

The Virgin tells Adrian that Katharine is a Queen,

who knows the 7 Sciences;

but she must give up her riches.

Bk. III. Ch. 3.

"In all her' nede, whan þat sche schall fyght 225
A-geyns þe heresye of philosophye;
Of all her' resones sche schall rek but lyght,
Thow þei her' sophymes sotyly multyplye;
Sche schall asoyle hem & a-geyn replye 229
So myght[i]ly, þat þei schul lese her' art,
And sche schall drawe hem to be in goddis part. 231

"ffor aftyr me, I tell þe sykyrlye, 232
þer was neuer swech an other' lady lyuande
þat wyth-owte ensaumple cowde leue parfytely,
As sche hath now newly take on hande
So holy a lyffe. þerfor', þou vndyrstande, 236
Sche schall haue eke as gloryous [a] hende
As euyr had woman þat lyued her' in kende." 238

Bk. III. Ch. 4.

Ca^{m.} 4^{m.}

Whan þat our' lady had seyd all þis þing, 239
þis ermyte fell to grounde plat & pleyn,
he was a-ferd & raueched in swownyng.
And sche full mekely lyft hym vp a-geyn,
"Be not a-ferd," sche gan þoo to hym seyn. 243
And he answerd: "gramercy now, madame.
ffor-gyfe me now! in þat I was to blame 245

"That I knew not crystis moder' der', 246
But all wytles, rekles & boystous
Was I, lady, full late in myn answer'.
Ʒe may well se my wytte is komerous,
Ʒour comyng was to me so meruelous 250
My wytt was goo þan, I sey ʒow veryly.
My lordes moder', myn aduocate, my mary, 252

"And I her' seruaunt, & euyr' hath be & cast!¹ 253
Allas, allas! & it is wrete full pleyn   ¹ so all MSS.
A hard þing of whech I am a-gast:
'Who wyll not know, schall be for-gete, certeyn.'
þis is my thowght, my lady souereyn, 257

"In al hir nede, whan þat she shal fyghte 225
A-geyn the heresye of philosophie;
Of alle her resones she shal rekken but lyghte,
Thou þei her sophems sotyly multyplie;
She shal a-soyle hem and ageyn hem replye 229
Soo myghtyly, þat þei shul lese her art,
And she shal drawe hem to be in goddis part. 231

The Virgin will enable Katharine to confute all her opponents.

"ffor after me, I telle the sekerly, 232
Ther was neuere suche another lady lyuande
That wyth-outen exaumple cowde lyue so parfyghtly
As she hath now newely take on hannde
Soo hooly a lyf. therfore, þou vndirstande, 236
She shal haue eke as gloryous an eende
has euere had woman that leued here in keende." 238

Ca^{m.} qvintum

Bk. III. Ch. 5.

Whan þat oure lady had seyde al þis thynge, 239
This ermyte fel to grounde plat and pleyn,
he was a-fered and rauyshed in swownynge.
And she ful mekely lift hym vp a-geyn,
"Be not afered!" she gan tho to hym seyn. 243
And he answerde: "gromercy now, madame.
ffor-yeue me now! in þat I was to blame 245

Adrian swoons.

He begs the Virgin's forgiveness for not knowing her.

"That I knew not cristes moder deere, 246
But al wytteles, rekles and boystous
Was I, lady, ful late in myn answere.
Ye may weel see my wytte is comorous,
Youre comyng was to me soo meruelyous, 250
My wytte was goo whan I sey you, verely.
My lordis moder, myn aduocate, my mary, 252

"And I hir seruaunt, and euere haue be chast! 253
Allas, allas! and it is wreten ful pleyn
An hard þing of whiche I am a-gast:
'Who wil not knowe, shal be forgete, certeyn.'
This is my thought, my lady souereyn, 257

He is her servant.

Be-cause þat I so recles was full late,
þat ȝour' loue schuld now turn to hate. 259

"Therfor' ȝour' grace wyth pytous voys I pray 260
To punch & snybe, ȝour-self as ȝe lest,
And I am redy euermor' nyght & day
To be obedyent ryght at ȝour request,
To do ȝour massage, so as I can best. 264
But sewyrly, þis gret cyte large
Of whech ȝe spoke whan ȝe dyd me charge, 266

"I know it noght, ne eke þe wey þer-to, 267
I haue not herd but lytyll of it, certaynd.
But as ȝe wyll, ryght so mote I do;
To fulfyll ȝour' byddyng myn hert is ful fayn;
þow I for werynesse dey or elles be slayn, 271
I schall go thedyr. ȝet hafe I full mech care
Of wylsom weyis or þat I come þar', 273

"ffor, as I wene, many a wyldyrnesse 274
Is in þat wey, & many a wyked beest.
ȝet schall I forward hastly now me dresse;
I trost on ȝow þat ȝe schull at þe leest
Ordeyn for me þat I be noght a-reest, 278
But vndyr ȝour' wyng & ȝour proteccyon
May be þis vyage & þis progressyon." 280

Ca^m. 5^m.

Than seyd þe qween on-to hym a-geyn: 281
"Well may þou blys þat lord þat boute vs alle,
þat he be the wold send or elles seyn
þis reall mater', & eke þer-to þe calle!
Go now þi wey, þou may not stumble ne falle 285
Whan swech a leder' is to þe a gyde.
But whan þou comst wyth-in þoo ȝatis wyde, 287

"Whom-euer þou mete, if he spek to þe, 288
Spek not a-geyn in no-maner' wyse:
I tell þe why: þe hye noble secre

Adrian is to start for Alexandria.

Be-cause þat I soo rekles was ful late,
That youre loue shulde now turne to hate. 259

 "Therfore youre grace wyth pytous voys I pray 260
To punyshe and snebbe, youre-self as ye lest,
And I am redy euere-more nyght and day
To be obedyent ryght at youre request,
To doo youre massage soo as I can best. 264
But suerly, this grete cyte large
Of whiche ye spoke whan ye dede me charge, 266

 "I knowe it nought, ne eke the weye þer-too, 267
I haue not herd but lytil of it, certayn.
But as ye wil, ryght soo mote I doo;
To fulfille your byddynge my herte is ful fayn;
Though I for werynesse dey or ellis be slayn, 271
I shal goo theder. yet haue I ful moche care
Of wylson weyes, er thanne I com thare, 273

 "ffor, as I wene, many a wyldernesse 274
Is in þat weye, and many a wykked beste.
Yet shal I forward hastyly me dresse;
I truste on you þat ye shul at the leste
Ordeyne for me þat I be nought a-reste, 278
But vndyr your wenge and youre proteccyon
May be this viage and this progression." 280

Marginalia: Bk. III. Ch. 5. Adrian tells the Virgin he will do all she wishes. Adrian knows not the way to Alexandria, but he will go there, trusting to the Virgin.

Ca^{m.} sextum.

Thanne seyde the queen on-to hym a-geyn: 281
 "Weel may þou blysse þat lord that bought vs alle,
That he be the wold sende or ellis seyn
This ryal mater, and eke þer-to the calle!
Goo now thi weye, þou may not stomble ne falle 285
Whan swiche a leedere is to the a gyde.
But whan þou comest with-inne tho yates wyde, 287

 "Whom euere þou mete, if he speke to the, 288
Speke not ageyn in no-maner wise!
I telle the whi: þe hye noble secree

Marginalia: Bk. III. Ch. 6. She bids him start at once, and speak to no one he meets.

To whyche þou schall do labour' & seruyse,
If vnworthy herd it, þei myght it dyspyce.   292
Eke þi-self þi mouth must þou spere,
And kepe þi wordys only for þis mater'.   294

"So schall þou goo thorow þat grete cyte,   295
Tyll þat þou come on-to þe paleys reall
Whech þat he made, costus þe kyng so fre,
Both dych & hylle, doungon, tour', & wall.
Many a knyth & many a sqwyer' þou schall   299
ffynd þer' & se, þe gates for to kepe :
Be not a-ferde, my son schall þe kepe   301

"ffro all her' manace & all her' grete daunger'.   302
Blesse þe well, & eke my sones name
Ryght in þi forhed loke þou crouch & bere :
þan no man schall haue power' þe to blame
Ne eke to lett þe, tyll þou come at þat dame.   306
And wher' sche dwellyth, now wyll I þe say :
þou schall goo forthe & passe all þat a-ray,   308

"Tyll þat þou see wallys fayr' & newe ;   309
And at [a] posterne, smalle of forme &[1] schap—   [1] MS. & of
On-to þat same loke þat þou fast sewe ;
þer nedyth þe noght neyther' ryng ne rap,
þe gate schall ope[n] lygtly at a swap ;   313
þou schalt' enter' & fynd þat swet may.
Whech schall to hyr be full grete a-fray,   315

"ffor sche schall wondyr' who þat ony man   316
Myght enter' to her' in to þat pryuy place ;
hyr booke, hyr stody schall sche leue ryght than
And loke on þe wyth full sobyr face.
haue þou no fer' in no-maner' cace   320
Of hyr qwestyouns ne of hyr apposayle,
I schall enforce þe soo þou may not fayle   322

"To ȝeue hyr answer' to euery questyoun.   323
So sayd my sone to hys aposteles twelue :

To whiche þou shalt doo labour and seruyse,
If onwurthi herde it, þei myght it despyse. 292
Eke thi-self thi mouth must þou spere,
And kepe thi woordis oonly for this matere. 294

" Soo shalt þou goo thurgh that grete citee, 295
Til þou come on-to the paleys real
Whiche þat he made, Costus the kyng soo free,
Bothe dyche and hyll, dongeon, tour, and wal.
Many a knyght and many a sqwyer þou shal 299
ffynde there and see, the gates for to keepe:
Be nought a-ferde, my sone shal defende þe fro all þe heepe,

" ffro her manace and al her grete daungere. 302
Blysse þe weel, and eke myn sones name
Ryght in thi forhed looke þou crosse and bere:
Than no man shal haue pouer the to blame
Ne eke to lette, til þou come at þat dame. 306
And where she dwelleth now wil I the say:
Thou shal goo foorthe and passe al þat aray, 308

" Til þat þou see walles fayre and newe; 309
And at a posterne smal of foorme and shap—
On-to that same looke þat þou faste sewe,
There nedeth the not neyther rynge ne rap,
The gate shal open lightly at a swap; 313
Þou shal entre and fynde the swete may.
Whiche shal be to hir ful grete afray, 315

" ffor she shal wondir hough þat ony man 316
Might entre to hir in þat preuy place;
hir book, hir stody shal she leeue ryght than
And looke on the with ful sober face.
haue þou no fer in no-maner cace 320
Of hir questyons ne of hir apposayle,
I shal enforce þe soo þou may not fayle 322

" To yeue hir answere to euery questyon. 323
Soo seyde my sone to his apostellis twelue:

Bk. III. Ch. 6.

The Virgin Mary tells Adrian how to find Katharine in Alexandria.

The postern

gate will open, and he will find

Katharine studying.

'Whan ȝe stand,' he seyd, 'be-for þe dome
Of many tyrauntys, & ȝe a-lone ȝour-selue,
Thow þei ȝow calle lollard, whych or elue,   327
Beth not dysmayd, I schall gyue ȝow answere,
Þer can no man swech langage now ȝow lere.'   329

"Ryght so schall þou haue in þi langage   330
Swech wonder termes þat sche schall stoyned be,
Cryst schall endewe þin eld[e] rekeles age
Wyth eloquens whech full meruelous, trost me,
Schall be to þe, & most specyaly sche   334
Schall lyste ful sore aftyr þis new doctrine,
Alle her wyttys þer-to wyll sche enclyne.   336

"No wondyr it is, for my sone, in sothenesse,   337
hath chose hyr specyaly aboue all oþer lyuande,
ffor hyr uertew & for hyr grete clennesse,
he wyll wedd hyr in schort tyme comande;
Þou schall be massanger & tak þis werk on hande: 341
Þou schall brynge her euene vn-to þis place
Þi-selue a-lone wyth-owtyn othyr solace.   343

"Thys same tokne schall þou to hyr bere: 344
ffor if sche enqwyre who þe þedyr sent,
Þe same lord, sey a-geyn to hyr,
Whom þat sche chees syttyng in parlement,
ffor whech choys sche was full nye I-schent   348
Of hyr lordes, so as þei þan durst;
Sche toke þe bettyr & forsok þe wurst.   350

"Wyth-inne her stody þus schall þou hyr fynde.   351
Be not a-ferd of hyr sotell cunnyng,
Þou schall not fayle of answer to þe kynde
Of all hyr wytte & all hyr stodying.
Go now forth fast, & hedyr sone her bryng,   355
Gyrde þe sore & tuk vp well þi lappe,
Tak wyth þe þi staffe & ek þi cappe!"   357

'Whan ye stande,' he seyde, 'be-fore the doom
Of many tyrantis, and ye allone your-selue,
Though thei you calle lollard, wytche or elue, 327
Beth not dismayed, I shal geue you answere,
Ther can no man swiche langage now you lere.' 329

"Right soo shal þou haue in thi langage 330
Swiche wonder termes þat she shal stoyned be,
Criste shal endwe thyn old rekles age
With eloquencye whiche ful merueylous,[1] troste me,
Shal be to the, and most specyally she 334
fful sore after this newe doctryne
Alle hir wittes ther-to wil she enclyne. 336

"No wonder it is, for my sone, in soothnesse, 337
hath chosyn hir specyally a-boue all other lyuande,
ffor hir vertu and for hir clennesse,
he wyl wedde hir in short tyme comande;
þou shalt be massager and take this werk on hande: 341
Thou shal bryngen hir euene on-to þis place
Thi-self allone with-outen other solace. 343

"This same tookne shalt thou to hir bere: 344
ffor if she enquere hoo the thedyr sent,
The same lord, sey ageyn to here,
Whom þat she chees syttyng in parlement,
ffor whiche she was ful ny I-shent 348
Of hir loordis, soo as thei thanne durst;
She took þe better and for-sook þe wurst. 350

"With-Inne hir stody thus shal þou hir fynde. 351
be not aferde of hir sootyl connynge,
þou shalt nought fayle of answere to þe kynde
Of all hir witte and al hir stodyinge.
Goo now foorth faste and heder soone hir brynge, 355
Girde þe soore and tukke vp weel thi lappe,
Take wyth þe thy staf and eke thi cappe!" 357

[1] MS. mermeylous

Christ will give Adrian eloquence to speak to Katharine,

whom He will soon wed,

and who is the Lord whom she chose in her Parliament.

Adrian is to start at once.

192 *Adrian finds Q. Katharine in Alexandria.* [MS. Rawlinson.

Bk. III. Ch. 6.   Ca^{m.} 6^{m.}

Thus goth þis ermyte forth ryght in hys way,   358
Trostyng on gydes swech as long to heuen;
ffor thow he now aungellys þoo herd ne say,
Wyth-oute dowte, her' ledyng browte hym euene
On-to þis cyte, long or it was euyne,   362
Nowt þat same day, but aftyr a full long whyle,
Whan he had go & rune full many a myle.   364

Thus wyll god wyth ful onlykly þing,   365
As to þe werld, werk whan þat hym leest;
he chesyth sume-tyme on-to hys hye werkyng
ffull febyll & sekely, & a-wey can kest
þe strong & wyse—poule seyth þis best   369
In hys epistoles, who þat wyll hem rede.
Ryght þus dede he her', wyth-outen drede.   371

fful on-likly was þis man to þis massage,   372
But þat god chese hym of hys goodenesse.
he is now goo forth in hys vyage,
Be hyllys[1] & pleyn, felde & wyldyrnesse;   [1] r. hyll?
he is now come wher' as þis emperesse   376
Satte in her' gardeyn, stodying þan ful sore;
Sodenly enterd set he is hyr be-for'.   378

fful sore a-stoyned wer' þei þan both-twoo,   379
þe on for meruayle of hyr' hye beaute,
The other' was marred, if we schuld sey soo
þat sche a man so sodeynly þer gan se
Be-for hyr knele now ryght in hyr secre.   383
As, if ȝe wyll þis conceyt here mor' pleyn,
þe ermyte in hys wytte was a-stoyned, certeyn,   385

ffor he fond hyr þan lenyng on a booke,   386
In sad stodye, ful solitarie all a-lone,
And often a-mong to heuene gan sche look;
But swych beute sey þis man neuyr none
As now he setho in þis same persone,   390

Ca^m. septimum.

Thus gooth this Ermyte foorth right in his way, 358   *Adrian is led by heavenly Guides to Alexandria.*
Trustynge on gydes swiche as longen to heuene;
ffor though he non Aungell*is* tho herde ne say, [1] *w.—st. on eras.*
W*yth*-oute doute, here leedynge w*yth* ful myelde steuene[1]
Brovght hym to the citee longe be-fore[2] euene,   [2] *all this on eras.*
Nought that same day, but after a ful long while,
Whan he had goo and ronne ful many a myle. 364

Thus wil god w*yth* ful onlykly thyng, 365
As to the world, werke whan that hym lest;
he cheseth somtyme on-to his hey werkyng
fful febyl and sekely, and awey can kest
The strong and wyse—paule seith þis best 369
In his epystoles, hoo þ*at* wil hem reede;
Ryght thus dede he here, w*yth*-outen dreede. 371

fful onlykly was this man to this massage, 372   *He finds Katharine*
but þ*at* god chees hym of hys goodnesse.
he is now goon foorth in his viage,
Be hilt and pleyn, feeld and wildernesse;
he is now come where as this empresse 376
Saat in hir gardeyn, stodyenge ful sore;   *studying in her garden.*
Sodeynly entred set is he hir before. 378

fful soore a-stoyned were thei þanne bothe-too, 379
The on for meruayle of hir hy bewte,
The other was marred, if we shulde sey soo,   *She is astonisht to see him kneeling before her.*
That she a man soo sodeynly there gan see
Be-fore hir knelynge ryght in hir secree. 383
As, if ȝe wiln this conseit heere more pleyn,
The ermyte in his witte was astoyned, certeyn, 385

ffor he fond hir thanne leenynge on a book, 386
In sad stodye, ful solitarie al alone,
And ofte a-monge to heuene gan she look;
but suche beaute saugh this man neu*er*e noone   *Adrian has never seen*
As nough he seeth in this same p*er*sone, 390

Bk. III. Ch. 6. Saue ouṛ lady—blessed mot sche be!—
So bryght & sc[h]ynyng was þoo hyṛ fayṛ ble. 392
"A, meruelous gödd," thowth he in hys mynde, 393
"Wend I neuer a seyn swech creatouṛ lyuyng!
I trow, in erde as in womannes kynde
Is non so bryght, so beuteuous in all þing.
Blessed be iheṣu, þat hye heuyn-kyng, 397
þat me sent hedyr to se þis creature!
ffor aftyr ouṛ lady sche passeth wyth-oute mesure 399
"Alle oþer women." And wyth þis þouth a-non 400
Sche lokyd on hym, & was a-stoyned sore
Who þat he myght ouyr þoo wallys of ston,
þis olde man, clyme, or ellys if he wore
Crope thorow þe ȝate? þan meruelyth sche more, 404
Syth þat hyr-self had be þeṛ last,
ffor sche baṛ þe key, & sperd it wondyr fast. 406
Wyth þis same stoynyng hyr bloode gan to renne 407
Mech moṛ frescheṛ þan it was be-fore,
In cheke & forhed newly doth it brenne;
And if sche fayṛ & bryght wer be-fore,
It is a-mendyd a hundred parte more 411
As to hys syght, þis olde ermyte lame.
he knelyth down & seyth "all heyll, madame." 413

Bk. III. Ch. 7. Ca^{m.} 7^{m.}

Sche ryght þus a-geyn on-to hym sayde: 414
"Good syṛ, tell me who may þis be—
ffor of ȝouṛ persone be we soṛ dysmayde—
þat we so sodenly ȝow in ouṛ presence see,
I-come þus a-lone wyth-owte oþer menee? 418
þis ask we fyrst, for sekyr, wete we[1] must; [1] MS. wṣ?
Wheythyr þis is truthe or apparens, it schall be wust. 420
"What-maneṛ mane myght make ȝow so maisterlye 421
To clyme ouṛ wallys whech are so hye?
I trow, be enchaun[t]ment, or be nygromancye

Saue oure lady—blyssed mote she be !—
Soo bryght and shynynge was tho hir fair blee. 392
" O merueyleous god," thought he in his mynde, 393
" Wende I neuere a seen) swiche a creature lyuynge.
I trowe, in erthe as in womans kynde
Is noon soo bright, soo bewtyvous in al thynge.
blyssed be ihesu, þat hy heuene-kynge, 397
That me sente heder too see this creature !
ffor after oure lady she passeth wyth-oute mesure 399
" Alle other women)." and wyth this thought a-noon) 400
She loked on) hym), and was a-stoyned sore
how þat he myght ouere tho walles of stoon),
This olde man, clymbe, or ellis if he wore
Crope thurgh the yate ? thanne merueyleth she more, 404
Sith that hir-self had been) there last,
ffor she baar the keye, and spered it wonder fast. 406

Wyth this same stoynenge hir blood gan) to renne 407
Meche more freshere than it was be-fore,
In cheke and forhed newely dooth it brenne ;
And if she fayr and bryght were hoore,[1]   [1] = ore, on er. (or. before)
It is a-mended an hundird part more 411
As to his sight, this olde ermyte lame.
he kneleth doun and seith " al heil, madame." 413

Marginalia:
Bk. III. Ch. 7.
so lovely a lady as Katharine.
She wonders how he, so old, could climbe over her walls.
Adrian says "All hail !" to her.

Ca[m.] octauu*m.*

S he right thus ageyn) on-to hym sayde : 414
" Good sir, telle me how may this bee—
ffor of your persone be we sore dismayde—
That we soo sodeynly you in oure presens see,
I-come thus alone wyth-outen other menee ? 418
This aske we first, for sekyr weten) we must,
Whedir this is truthe or apparens, it shal be wust. 420

"What-maner man[1] myght make yow soo maisterlye 421
To clymbe oure wallys whiche arn soo hye ?   [1] overlined.
I trowe, be enchauntement or be nygramauncye

Marginalia:
Bk. III. Ch. 8.
She asks him to explain how he came.
Katharine asks Adrian who enabled him to climb over her walls.

O 2

Are ȝe entyrd now her' be-for' our' yȝe.
We wyll wete þis þing, be ȝe neuyr so slye, 425
Who ȝaue ȝow hardynesse for to be so bolde
Wyth-owte our' [leue] to entre to owr' holde? 427

"ffor of all þe lordes & knytys þat we haue 428
Is non so hardy but we ȝefe hym leue,
But if he wyll reklesly hys lyff laue,
Onys to entre, neyþer morow ne eue,
Our' priuy secre. þer-for is it repreue 432
On-to ȝour age to tak swech þing on ȝow;
It wyll not fall happyly on-to ȝour' prow. 434

"Ther-for' now tell me schortly in a clause: 435
Who ȝaue ȝow boldenesse to do þis grete folye?
Sekyr may ȝe be we wyll wete þe cause,
And euery mene þorow whech ȝe wer' hardy,
Perauentur' if treson be found in our' meny. 439
þis schall ȝe telle, or ȝe fro vs weende;
Ȝe gete of vs elles no ryght fayr' ende." 441

Ca^{m.} 8^{m.}

BE þis was þe erymyte coumforted a-geyn), 442
ffor wyth bolde spech he ȝaue þis answere
And wyth manly voys þus gan he seyn):
"Sche þat me sent is gretter', if ȝe wyll lere,
Than ony lady in erde þat dwellyth her'; 446
And eke þe lest þat longyth to hyr bour'
Is more of astate þan kyng or emperour'. 448

"Eke for ȝe ween) þat ȝe be so fayre, 449
So rych in welth as it is seyd, certayn),
Ȝet may ȝe not to hyr' beaute repayr',
Ne neuyr ȝe schall, sothly dar I sayn).
Boþe hyr & ȝow wyth eyne haf I seyn, 453
I may þe mor' boldely mak þis commendyng:
Sche paseth ȝow, certayn, in all-maner þing. 455

Arn ye now entred here be-forn oure eye.
We wyl wete this thyng, be ye neuere soo slye, 425
hoo yaf yow hardynesse for to be so bold,
Wyth-outen oure leeue to entre in to oure hold? 427

"ffor of alle the lordes and knyghtes þat we haue 428
Is noon so hardy, but we yeue hym leeue,
but he wil reklesly his lyf laue,
Ones to entre, neyther morwe ner eue,
Oure preuy secree. therfore is it to[1] repreue [1] overlined. 432
On-to youre age, to take suche thyng on you;
It wil not falle happyly on-to youre prow. 434

"Therfore telle me shortly now in a clause: 435
ho yaue you boldenesse to doo this gret foly?
Sekyr may ye bee we wil wete þe cause,
And euery mene thurgh whiche ye were hardy,
Perauenture if treson be founde in oure meny. 439
This shal ye telle, er ye fro vs wende;
Ye gete of vs ellis no[1] right fayr ende." [1] or, no good 441

Marginalia:
Bk. III. Ch. 8.
None of Katharine's lords would come into her private retreat.
Who has let Adrian in?
Has any of her household been a traitor?

Ca[m.] nouu[m].

Bk. III. Ch. 9.

BE this was the ermyte comforted ageyn, 442
ffoorth with bold speche he yaf this answere
And with manly voys thus gan he seyn:
"She þat me sente is grettere, if ye wil lere,
Than ony lady in erthe þat dweleth here; 446
And eke the leest þat longeth to hir bour
Is more of astate than kyng or emperour. 448

"Eke, for ye wene þat ye ben soo fayre, 449
Soo ryche in welthe as it is seyd, certayn,
Yeet may ye not to hir bewte repayre,
Ne neuere ye shal, soothly dar I sayn.
I haue you bothe seen, ther-of I am ful fayn, 453
I may the more boldely make þis commendyng:
She passeth you, certeyn, in al-maner good thyng. 455

Marginalia:
Adrian says the highest Lady sent him.
A Lady who is more beautiful than even Katharine,

"Eke hyr grete power' þat is spred so fer', 456
Sche may doo what þat euer sche lyst;
ffor be ȝon ȝate whech ȝe dyd sper'
Sche browte me in, sekyr, or I it wyst.
If sche be wrothe, no man skapyth hyr fyst; 460
þer-for' a-vyse ȝow, lady, what ȝe wyll say,
lest þat my lady turne fro ȝow a-way." 462

Ca^{m.} 9^{m.}

Than gan þe qween merueyle of þis word, 463
Mor' þan sche dyd euyr hyr lyue be-fore
Of ony mater. cryst had made hys horde
Or þis ermyte cam, & leyd hys grete tresour'
Ryght in hyr hert emprended full sore; 467
ffor þowȝ he sent þe ermyte as hys massanger',
Or þe ermyte cam crist hym-self was ther'. 469

Ryght as gabriell, whan he fro heuene was sent 470
On-to our lady to do þat hye massage,
In to naȝareth in forme of man[1] he went, [1] MS. o man?
ffayr' & fresch, & ȝong eke of age,
But er' that he cam on-to þis maydes cage, 474
Cryst was ther', as we in bokes rede:
Ryth so dyd he her'; if we wyll take hede. 476

But þowȝ god wer' come as þan to hyr hert, 477
It was fer' as ȝet fro hyr knowlechyng.
þer-for' wyth wordes þat wer' full smert
Sche turneth a-geyn on-to þe same þing
Whech we left er', & þus in apposyng 481
Sche þus procedyth, sey[i]ng to þis man:
"Who may ȝour' lady be so worthy woman 483

"As ȝe commende now in ȝour tale to me 484
Of hyr hye worchepe & also of hyr wytte?
þe worthyest of all women we ween þat we be,
We herd neuyr of non worthyer' ȝytte.
Wher' lyghte hyr londe, we wold fayn know itte; 488

"Eke hir grete power þat is spred soo fer,   456
She may doo what that euere she lyst;
ffor be youre yate, whiche ye dede sper,
She brouthe me in, seker, er I it wyst.
If she be wroth, no man skapeth hir fist;   460
Therfore avyse yow, lady, what ye wyl say,
lest þat my lady turne fro you a-way."   462

Ca^{m.} decimu*m*.

Thanne gan the queen meruayle of þis woord,   463
    More than she dede euere hir lyf before
Of ony mater. crist had maad his hoord
Er this ermyte cam, and leyde his gret tresore
Ryght in hir herte emprended ful soore;   467
ffor though he sente the ermyte as his massanger,
Er the ermyte cam, cryst hym-self was there.   469

Right as gabriel whanne he froo heuene was sent   470
On-to oure lady to doo that hye massage,
In to naȝareth in foorme of a man he went,
ffayr and fresh, and yong eke of age,
But er that he cam to this maydenes cage,   474
Crist was there, as we in bookys rede:
Right soo dede he here, if ye wil take heede.   476

But though god were com as þanne to hir herte,   477
It was fer as yet fro hir knowlechynge.
Therfore wyght[1] woordys tho were ful smerte,   [1] = wyth
She turned a-geyn on-to the same thynge
Whiche we lefte ere, and thus in apposynge   481
She þus procedeth, seyng on-to this man:
"how may youre lady be so worthi a woman   483

"As ye comende in youre tale now on-to mee   484
Of hir hygh wurship and also of hir wyt?
The wurthyest of alle women we wene þat we bee,
We herd neuere of noon worthiere yit.
Where lygħt hir lond, we wolde fayn knowe it;   488

Who is her' lorde, or wheyther' is sche lorde-lees?
ʒe telle vs þingys whech we holde but lees. 490
"Wheythyr' is þat dame lyuyng in spousayle, 491
Or leuyth sche sool as we do now?
If sche be weddyd, sykyrly sche may fayle
Mych of hyr wyll, for sche mote nedys bowe
On-to hyr lord, loke he neuer so row; 495
And if sche lyue be hyr-self a-lone,
Þan may sche make full oft mech mone 497
"Ryght for vexacyon of hyr' lordes a-boute— 498
þis know we well, we are vsed þer-to.
Þer-for, goodeman, put vs oute of doute,
Tell vs þe soþe, be it ioye or woo
Whech þat þis lady most is vsed too; 502
And we wyll þank & rewarde ʒow eke
Wyth swech plente þat it schall ʒow leke." 504

Ca^{m.} 10^{m.}

"I-wys, madame," seyd þis ermyte þoo, 505
"þe grete lordscheppe of my lady souereyn
Is spredd ouyr heuyn, & ouyr erd þer-too,
And ouyr þe see eke, sothely to seyn;
Þer comyth noo sune, no dewys ne no reyn 509
But be comaundement of hyr lord & hyr desyre—
Swech is hyr myght & all-so hyr powere. 511

"hyr ladyschepe eke þer-to is so strong 512
And euyr so stedfast, þat it may not fayle,
Þer may no man, treuly, do hyr wrong;
ffor þowʒ þei doo, þei lese her' trauayle.
Þer may no myght a-geyn hyr myght a-vayle, 516
hyr lord & sche, þei lyue in full grete pees,
Wyth many mylyons of men & mekyll prees. 518

"he is hyr lord, & eke to hym sche is 519
Moder' & noryse, ʒet is sche a mayde—
lord & sone boþe to-gedyr I-wys,

Adrian tells Katharine of the Virgin.

hoo is hir lord, or wheder is she lordles?
Ye telle vs thyng*is* whiche we holde but lees. 490 *who this noblest of women is.*

"Whedir is þat dame leuynge in spousayle, 491 *Is she married, or single?*
Or leueth she sool as we doo now?
If she be wedded, sekerly, she may fayle
Myche of hir wyl, for she mote nedes bow
On-to hir lord, looke she neu*er*e soo row; 495
And if she lyue be hir-self allone,
Thanne may she make ofte ful moche mone 497

"Right for vexacyon of hir lordes a-bowte— 498 *If she's single, her lords must worry her.*
This knowe we weel, we arn vsed ther-too.
Therfore, goodeman, put vs oute of dowte,
Telle vs þe sooth, be it Ioye or woo, [1] *3 last words on eras.*
Whiche þat this lady most absenteth hir froo[1]; 502
And we wil thanke and reward yow eke
Wyth swhiche plente þat it shal yow leke." 504

Ca^{m.} vndecimu*m*.

"I-wys," madame," seyde this ermyte thoo, 505 *Adrian says his Lady has Lordship over heaven, earth, and sea.*
"The gret lordship of my lady sou*er*eyn
Is spred ou*er*e heuene, and ouere erthe þ*er*-too,
And ou*er*e the see eke, soothly for to seyn;
Ther cometh noon sonne, no dewes ne no reyn 509
But be co*m*maundement of hir lord and hir desire—
Swiche is hir myght and also hir powyre. 511

"hir ladyship therto eke is soo strong 512 *Adrian's Lady is so strong,*
And euere soo stedfast, þat it may not fayle,
Ther may no man, trewely, doo hir wrong;
ffor þough þei doo, thei lese her travayle.
There may no wyght ageyn hir myght p*r*e[u]ayle, 516 *that no one can prevail against her.*
hir lord and she, thei leue in ful grete pees
Wyth many myllyons of men and meche prees. 518

"he is hir lord, and eke to hym she is 519 *She is the Mother of her Lord,*
Moder and norse, yet is she a mayde—
lord and sone bothe to-gedyr I-wys,

Bk.III.Ch.10.	Þis longyth to hym, & ȝet ist,[1] as I sayde—	[1] = is it
	leuyth my tale & beth no-þing dysmayde—	523
	ffor sche is modyr & also clene virgyne;	
	Þis schall ȝe know aftyr well & fyne."	525

Bk.III.Ch.11.   Ca^{m.} 11^{m.}

"SEr'," seyd þe qween, "now merueyle I ful sore   526
 ffor ȝe precħ of þis hye degre
Of þis same lady; for ȝe seyd þis more
Sche passyth all other' in very felycite
Whecħ þat be her' now or euyr-mor' schall be :   530
Þan wondyr we sore þat sche sent vs here
So euyll arayd, so sympyll a massengere.   532

"ffor to hyr astate it had be full conuenient   533
To send moo men, & not send on a-lone,
Wher' sche so many hath at hyr comaundement;
Eke, as me þinkyth, to swecħ a grete persone
Schuld long, all seruauntes þat ar' in hyr wone   537
To clothe mor' clenly, for worchyp of hyr hous;
ffor, syr', ȝour clothyng semeth not ryght precyous!" 539

Bk.III.Ch.12.   Ca^{m.} 12^{m.}

"MA-dame," seyd he, "if ȝe wold me leue,   540
  I wold tell ȝow pleynly þe cause & why
To mak me massenger' dyd þis lady meue.
ffor þow þat sche hafe many mylyons of meny,
Sche is in hert neuer þe hyer', hardyly ;   544
And swecħ as sche is, ar' hyr seruauntes, lo ;
ffor all þat loue hyr þei must do ryght so.   546

"Ȝe wote well, madame, for mych þing ȝe know,   547
Þat gostly aray passeth in souereyn wyse
Bodyly dysgysyng, in hye & in lowe ;
Þe sete of uerteu is sett in swycħ asyse,
Euen as þei witnesse, clerkes þat be wyse,   551
Þat treuth is fayrer' be many degrees
Þan euer was cleyn, þe fayr' lady of grees.   553

This longeth to hym, and yet eft, as I sayde, *Bk.III.Ch.11.*
leueth my tale and be no-thyng dismayde! 523
ffor she is moder and also clene virgyn; *and yet a Virgin.*
This shal ye knowe after weel and fyn." 525

Ca^{m.} duodecimum. *Bk.III.Ch.12.*

"SEre," seyde the queen, "now merueyle I ful soore. *Katharine wonders why*
ffor ye soo preche of this hy degree 527 *so great a Lady*
Of þis same lady; for ye seyde this more
She passeth alle other in very felycyte [1] MS. er
Whiche þat ben here now or[1] euere-more shul be: 530
Thanne wonder we soore that she sente us here *sent so poor a Messenger.*
Soo euel arayed, soo symple a massangere. 532

"ffor to hir astate it had be conuenyent 533
To a sentte mo men thanne to sende oon alone, *She should have sent many,*
Where she soo many hath at hir comavndement;
Eke, as me þenketh, to suche a grete persone
Shuld longe, alle seruauntis þat arn in hir wone 537
To clothe more clenly, for wurship of hir hous; *grandly clad.*
ffor, sir, youre clothynge semeth not ryght presyous." 539

Ca^{m.} 13^{m.} *Bk.III.Ch.13.*

"MAdame," seyde he, "if ye wolde me leue, 540 *Adrian tells Katharine*
I wulde telle you pleynly the cause and why
To make me massanger dede this lady meeue.
ffor though þat she haue many myllyons of meny,
She is in herte neuere the hyere, hardyly; 544
And suche as she is, arn hir seruauntis, loo;
ffor alle tho louen hir, thei must doo right soo. 546

"Ye wete weel, madame, for meche thyng ye knowe,
That goostly aray passeth in souereyn a vyse[1] [1] orig. wyse *that spiritual clothing is far*
Bodily dysgysynge, in hy and in lowe; *above bodily.*
The sete of vertu is set in suche assyse,
Euene as thei witenessen, clerkys þat be wyse, 551
That truthe is fayrere be many degrees
Than euere was Eleyne, the fayre lady of grees. 553

204 Adrian tells Katharine of the Virgin. [MS. Rawlinson.

"Therfor þat lady þat me to ȝow now sent, 554
Desyreth mor' gostly inwardly aray
þan golden clothys spred on bodyes gent.
And ferthermor' ȝet boldly dar I say,
Sche hath be-fore hyr in hyr paleys ay 558
Many a thowsand wyth faces bryght & schene,
Swech as in erde ȝet neuyr wer' sene. 560

"Sche sayde to me, þat hye noble qwene, 561
þat my seruyce plesyd hyr so weele
þat sche wold send me wyth þis aray mene
To sey hyr wyll on-to ȝow euery dele.
And be þis processe may ȝe see & feel: 565
If ȝe wyll þis ladyes ffrenchyp now wynne,
ffro werdly delyte mote ȝe part & twynne. 567

"ffor erdely welthys sett my lady at nowte, 568
þerfor' hyr seruauntes schull not haue;
Who-so hyr' loue, holy mote be her' thowte
Wyth deuoute lyuyng her sowles to saue;
þe mor' þei forsake her', þe mor' may þei craue 572
Whan þat þei come þer' her' lady is,
To hyr regyon wher' þei dwell in blys. 574

"But, lady, to þe purpos now wyll we goo: 575
Thys blessed qween a tokne dyd me take
Whan sche me sent ȝour' reuerens on-to;
þus sayd sche þan: 'my messenger' I þe make
On-to ȝen maydyn; sche may it not forsake 579
þe tokne I take þe, so enpre[n]ded it[1] is [1] overlined.
On-to hyr hert sche can it not mys.' 581

"Thys is þe tokne þat ȝe syttyng in parlement, 582
Wyth princes, dukes & erles in-fere,
þis was ȝour answer' & þis ȝour entent:
Ȝe wold no lorde ne kyng haue, but if he were
So strong, so myghty þat he had neuyr fere, 586
So fayr', so gentyll þat no man wer' hym lych,
So enduyd wyth good þat no man wer' so rych; 588

"Therfore þat lady that me to yow now sente,   554   *Bk.III.Ch.13.*
Desireth more goostly inwardly aray   His Lady
Thaw gooldew clothes sprede on bodyes gente.   (the Virgin
And ferthermore ȝet boldely dar I say,   Mary)
She hath beforw hir in hir paleys ay   558   has Angels in
Many a thousand with faces bryght and shene,   her service,
Swiche as in erthe yet neuere were seene.   560

"She seyde to me, þat hy noble queene,   561   yet she chose
That my seruyse plesed hir so weel   lowly him
That she wolde sende me with þis aray mene
To sey hir wil on-to yow euery deel.   to tell Katha-
And be this processe may ye see and feel: 565   rine her will.
If ye wil this ladyes frenshyp now wyne,
ffro wordly delyte mote ye parte and twynne.   567

"ffor erthely welthes set my lady at nought,   568
Therfore hir seruauntes shul not haue;
ho-soo hir loue, holy[1] mote be her thought,   [1] orig. hooly.
With deuoute lyuynge her sowles to saue;
The more thei forsake heere, the more mon þei craue 572 Adrian tells
Whanne that þei come there her lady is,   Katharine
To regyow where thei dwelle in blys.   574

"But, lady, to þe purpos now wil I goo: 575
The blissed queew a tooken dede me take   that the
Whan she me sente your reuerens on-too;   Virgin bade
Thus seyde she: 'my massanger I the make   him
On-to yone mayden; she may it not forsake   579
The tokew I take the, soo enprended it is
on-to hir herte, she can it not mys.'   581

"This is the tokene þat ye sittyng in parlement, 582   remind her
With pryncys, dukes and Erlis in prees there,[1] [1] in p. th. on er. of her answer
This was ȝour answere, and þis is[2] youre entent, [2] overl. in her Parlia-
Ye woolde no lord ne kyng haue, but if he were   ment,
Soo strong, soo myghty þat he had noo fere,   586
Soo fayr, soo gentel that no maw were hyw lyche,
Soo endued wyth good þat no maw were so ryche;   588

Bk.III.Ch.12. " Thys was at þat tyme, lady, ȝour desyre   589
þat þis lorde whecħ þat ȝe wold haue
Schuld lyue euermore, neuyr wyth watyr ne fyre
Be dreynt ne brent, but euyr hym-selfe saue ;
Ȝe wold be wyth hym euyr, & neuyr fro hym waue.   593
Þis was ȝour wyll, & fullfyllyd schall it be,
My lady sent ȝow bode, if ȝe wyll folow me.   595

" ffor þis same lord whecħ wyth my lady is,   596
he hathe alle þese, mor' pleynteuously, I telle,
Þan ony man in þis world may þink, I-wys ;
ffor of alle uertues he is þe very welle.
Come ȝe forth wyth me hom to my celle :   600
And if ȝe fynde my wordes be vnstable,
A-noþir day a-rest me be ȝour' constable !   602

" Ȝe schull hafe hyr lord & hyr sone eke,   603
A gracyous lynage þat may noght mys,
A merueylous kynrode, to lerne if ȝe leke ;
he is hyr lorde, sche hys modyr is ;
he is hyr sone & sche mayde, I-wys ;   607
he made hyr, sche bar' hym in hyr wombe,
Þe synnes of þe werld he clensyth, þis lombe."   609

Bk.III.Ch.13.   Ca^{m.} 13^{m.}

Than was þis mayden sor' marred in mynde—   610
Men myght se in hyr colour', in cheke & in pytte
So ran hyr bloode, so changed hyr kynde—
ffor neuyr was sche or now put in þis wytte ;
Sche is in swecħ a traws, wheyther' sche stant or sytte   614
Sche wote not hyr-selue ; sche is in swecħ cas,
ffor to sey a sotħ, sche wote not wher' sche was.   616

Be-twyx too þingys so is sche newly falle,   617
Whecħ sche schall leue or whecħ sche schall take.
If sche leue hyr lawe whycħ hyr lordes alle

"This was at that tyme, lady, youre desyre   589   *Bk.III.Ch.*13.
That þis lord whiche þat ye wolde haue   that she must
Shulde leuen euere-more, neyther wyth water ner fyre   have a Lord
                                                       immortal.
Be dreynt ne brent, but euere hym-self saue ;
Ye wolde[1] be with hym euere and neuere fro hym wauc. 593
This was your wil, and fulfillyd shal it bee,   [1] overl.
Mi lady sente ʒow bode, and ye wil folwe mee.   595

"ffor þis same lord whiche with my lady is,   596   This Lord
he hath alle these, more plentevously, I you telle,   is with the
                                                       Virgin.
Than ony man in þis world may thenke, I-wys ;
ffor of alle vertues he is the very welle.
Come ye foorth with me hom to my celle :   600   Katharine
and if ye fynde my woordys be vnstable,   must come
                                                       and see Him.
A-nother day areste me be youre constable !   602

"Ye shul haue hir lord and hir sone eke,   603   Katharine
A gracious lynage that may not mys,   shall have
                                                       the Virgin's
A merueylous kynrede, to lerne if ye lyke ;   Lord and
                                                       Son,
he is hir lord, she is moder his[1] ;   [1] m. h. on er.
he is hir sone and she mayden, I-wys ;   607
he made hir, she bare hym in hir wombe,
The synnes of þis world he clensed, þis lombe." 609   who washes
                                                       away the sins
                                                       of the world.

Ca[m.] 14.   *Bk.III.Ch.*14.

Thanne was thys mayden sore marred in mende—   610
Men myght see in hir colour, in cheke and in pyt
Soo ran hir blod, soo chaunged hir kende—
ffor neuere was she er now put in this wyt ;
She is in swiche a trauns, whether she stant or syt 614 Katharine is
She wot not hir-selue ; she is in suche caas,   in a trance.
ffor to sey a sooth, she wyst not where she was.   616

Be-twyx too þingis soo is she newly falle,   617
Whiche she shal leue or wyche she shal take.
If she leue hir lawe whiche hir lordis alle

hold at þis tyme, & now it forsake,
ffalle to a newe for a straunge lordes sake, 621
Sche seeth not what pereH in þis mater' is.
But for þe ermyte spake of þis lordes blys, 623

hys wordes haue enclyned now ful sor' hyr þowte 624
þat sche schall haue a þing long desyred.
Alle hyr goddys & hyr goode set sche at nowte,
So sor' is hyr hert wyth þis loue I-fyred,
It schall no mor', sche cast, wyth þe werld be myred. 628
þer-for' to þe ermyte eft sche gan þus seye :
"All ȝour informacyon I ber' well a-weye, 630

"Saue þat of o þing grete merueyle I ber'. 631
Ȝe seyd me ryght now whan ȝe told ȝour talle,
þat þis grete lady, if I wolde lere,
Bar' a noble chyld wyth-outen any bale,
And ȝet sche is a mayden at asay & sale. 635
þis same mater' is a-geyn¹ kynde ; [1] r. ageynis
What, wene ȝe, ser', þat I wer' so blynde 637

"þat I cowde not vndyrstand of generacyon 638
þe preuy weyes? þowe I now excersy[c]e
hafe had in my lyffe of swech occupacyon,
Ne neuyr wyll haue, be þat hye iustyce
Whech ȝe to me now newly gan deuyse, 642
Ȝet know I wele, & ilk¹ man it knowyth, [1] r. ilka
Who wyll ha chylde, seed sume-tyme [he] sowyth." 644

Ca^m. 14^m.

"Wyth-outen seed, lady, or wyth-outyn synne 645
May god make a man, & so he dede or now.
ffor if we at Adam or at Eue be-gyne,
It is full pleyn for to schew on-to ȝow :
ffor whan þat same Adam sleept in a swow, 649
Our' lord owte of hys syde þan made Eue.
þan be þis ensaumple pleynly may ȝe preue : 651

holde at þis tyme, and an other make,[1]   [1] an o. m. on er.   *Bk.III.Ch.14.*
ffalle to a newe for a straunge lordys sake,   621
She seeth not what pereH in this mater is.
But [for] the Ermyte spak of þis lord of blys,   623

his woordys haue enclyned now ful soore hir thought 624
That she shal haue a þing longe desyred.
Alle hir goddis and hir good set she at nought,   *Katharine counts her*
Soo sore is hir herte with þis loue I-fyred,   *Gods as nothing.*
It shal no more, she casteth, wyth þe world be myred. 628
Therfore to the ermyte efte she gan þus seye :
"Alle your informacyon I bere weel a-weye,   630

"Saue þat of oon þing grete merueyle I bere.   631
Ye seyde me right now, whan ʒe told your tale,   *She asks Adrian*
That þis grete lady, if I wolde lere,
Bar a noble chyld wyth-outen ony bale,   *how his Lady can have a*
And yet she is a mayden at a-say and sale.   635   *child, and yet be a Virgin.*
This same mater is a-geyns kynde ;
What, wene ye, sir, þat I were so blynde   637

"That I cowde not vndirstonde of generacyon   638
The preuy weyes ? though I not excercyse[1]   [1] or. excersyse
haue had in my lyf of suche occupacyon,
Ne neuere wil haue, be þat hey Iustyse
Whiche to me now newly ye gan deuyse,   642
Yet knowe I weel, and ilke man knoweth,   *Children come from*
hoo wil haue a child, seed somtyme he soweth."   644   *seed.*

Ca^{m.} 15^{m.}   *Bk.III.Ch.15.*

"Wyth-outen seed, lady, or wyth-outen synne   645   *Adrian explains,*
May god make a man, and soo he dede er now :
ffor if we at Adam or at Eue begynne,
It is ful pleyn for to shewe on-to yow :
ffor whan þat same Adam slepte in a swow,   649   *that as God made Eve out*
Oure lord oute of his syde þan made Eue.   *of Adam,*
Thanne be þis example pleynly may ye preue :   651

Bk.III.Ch.14.	" Syth þat he made a uirgyn of a man,	652
	he was of power eke for to make	
	A man of a uirgyne—þus he werk can,	
	þis gracyous lorde whech ȝe to make	
	Chosen in ȝour parlement. ȝet for ȝour sake	656
	A-nother demonstracyon in þis same mater	
	I wyll to ȝow schewe, if ȝe wyll it here.	658
	" Þer may no man, if we take good hede,	659
	Preue be any reson who all þing be-gan;	
	Speke we now of creatures & leue þe godhede,	
	þe sune & þe mone, þe bryght & þe wan,	
	Of her be-gynnyng þer can nowe no man	663
	haue no remembrauns ne tell in what plyght	
	þat þei wer made, eyther day or nyght.	665
	" Than, syth no man may of þese erdely werkis	666
	Tell þe pryuy cause, no wondyr is, certeyn,	
	þat þei of feyth schull¹ tell ony merkys ; ¹ r. schuld not	
	ffor feyth is not prouable, as clerkys seyn.	
	Þer-for our wyttes must be fful beyn	670
	To leue swech þingys þat we can not proue—	
	lete argumentys walk, þei ar not to our be-houe."	672

Bk.III.Ch.15.	Cam. 15m.	
	"What aylyd þat lord þat all myght hadde,	673
	In our frele natur hym for to clothe,	
	To leue þe bettyr & þus take þe badde,	
	Or ellys at hys lykyng to kepe styll hope?	
	Was he wyth mankynde euer or now wrothe,	677
	Was he euyr offendyd? we wolde wete fayn	
	What ȝe to þis mater now can vs sayn."	679

Bk.III.Ch.16.	Cam. 16m.	
	"For myschef, madame, þat man fell in	680
	Whan Adam þe appyll ete in paradys,	
	Wold þis lord in erde lowly take hys ine,	

Adrian explains Mary's Virginity.

"Sith þat he made a virgyn of a man,   652   *Bk.III.Ch.15.*
he was of power eke for to make   *so He can make a man*
A man of a virgyne—thus he werke can,   *out of a Virgin.*
This gracyous lord, whiche ye not slake[1]   [1] n. s. on er.
To chesyn in youre parlement. ȝet for ȝour sake   656
A-nother demonstracyon in þis same matere
I wil to yow shewe, if ye wil it heere.   658

"There may no man, if we take good heed,   659   *Moreover, no one can explain how*
Prouen be ony reson how alle þingis be-gan;
Speke we of creaturis and leue the godhed,
The sonne and the mone, þe bryght and þe wan,   *the Sun and Moon were*
Of her begynnynge ther' can now no man   663   *made.*
haue in[1] remembrauns and telle in what plyght   [1] r. no
That þei were made, eyther day or nyght.   665

"Than sith that no man may of these erthely werkys   666
Telle þe preuy cause, no wonder is, certeyn,
That þei of feith shulde telle ony merkys;
ffor feith is not prouable, as clerkis seyn.   *Faith is not provable.*
Therfore oure wittes musten ben ful beyn   670
To leue suche þingis that we can not proue—   *Let arguments be.*
lete argumentys walke, þei arn not to oure behoue."   672

"What eyled that lord þat al myght hadde,   673   *Katharine asks why*
In oure freel nature hym for to clothe,   *Christ took man's worse*
To leue the beter and thus taken the badde   *nature.*
Or ellys at his likyng to kepe stille bothe?
Was he with mankeende euere or nought wrothe,   677
Was he euere offended? we wulde wyte fayn
What ye to þis mater now can vs sayn."   679

Ca{m}. 16{m}.   *Bk.III.Ch.16.*

"For myschef, madame, þat man fel to[1] then   680   *Adrian answers: To*
Whan Adam the Appel eete in paradys,   [1] to on er.   *undo the mischief done by*
Wulde this lord in erthe louly take his en,[2]   [2] orig. in   *Adam's apple-eating,*

P 2

Not leuyng þat place full of delys,
But boþe her' & ther' at hys deuys 684
he dwelt, as we leue, our' soules to lech—
þis semyth to ȝow full wondyrfull spech! 686

"And þat same lord, as nobyll marchaunt, 687
hys blood for our' synne on crosse wold spylle.
Of þat same deth we may make a-vaunt,
It waschyth from vs alle þat we dede ille.
Of our' feyth, lady, þis is þe grettest bylle, 691
þat cryst hys bloode payed for' our' synnes alle;
Best of all marchauntis þer-for' we hym calle." 693

Ca^{m.} 17^{m.}

"Who may ȝe couple now þat ȝe[1] haue sayd? 694
he is lord of all, eyr', watyr & londe, [1] MS. we
lyuyng in pees wyth hys modyr & mayde;
her-too þus ȝe adde þat he is so bonde
þat he suffrede to be slayn wyth wykkyd honde— 698
Who can ȝe a-cord þat þis gret possessyoun
Schuld long on-to hym, & eke þis strong passyon? 700

"Who may þat lord lyuyn euyr & ay 701
Whan he is coupled of contraries too?
ffor of man & godd hys persone, as ȝe say,
hath take resultauns, & ȝet sey ȝe moo
he is boþe etern & temporall, loo. 705
lok if ȝour' spech be now no heresye!
þis wote I weel þat[1] it offendyth phylosophye." [1] to be om.

Ca^{m.} 18^{m.}

"To þese questyouns þus I answere: 708
ffor it paseth nature & all hyr scole.
Natur' fayleth whan we feyth lere,
ffor our' be-leue standyth so sole, 711
Wyth þeis argumentis whech are full of dole[1] [1] = Lat. dolus
Wyll sche not medelle be no-maner' preue—
Ther' wer' no mede þan in our' be-leue. 714

Adrian explains Christ's becoming Man.

Not leuynge that place ful of delys,
But heere and there at his deuys 684
he dwelt, has we leue, oure soulys to leche—
This semeth to yow ful wondirful speche! 686

"And that same lord as a noble marchaunt 687
his blood for oure synne on crosse wolde spylle.
Of þat same deeth we may make avaunt,
It washeth from vs al þat we dede Ille.
Of oure feyth, lady, this is the grettest bille, 691
That cryst his blood payed for oure synnes alle;
Best of alle marchauntis therfore we hym calle." 693

and to spill His own blood to cleanse us.

(Questio.)

"How may ye couple now that ye haue seyde? 694
he is lord of all, Eyr, water, and londe,
leuyng in pees with his moder and mayde;
her-too thus ye adde[1] that he is soo bonde   [1] or. hadde
That he suffred to be slayn wyth wykked honde. 698
how can ye acoorde that this grete possessyon
Shulde longe on-to hym, and eke þis stronge passyon? 700

"how may that lord leuen euer and ay 701
Whan he was coupled of contraries too?
ffor of man and god his persone, as ye say,
hath take resultans, and yet sey ye moo
he is bothe eternal and temporall alsoo. 705
looke if ȝoure speche be now noon heresye!
This wote I weel þat it offendeth philosophie." 707

Katharine asks how Christ can be Lord of all, and yet slain by wicked hands; how be both eternal and mortal.

Ca^{m.} 17^{m.}

"To these questions thus I answere: 708
ffor it passeth nature and al her scoole.
Nature fayleth whan we feyth leere,
ffor oure beleue standeth soo sole,
With these argumentis whiche arn ful of dole 712
Wil she not medele be non-maner preue—
There were no mede thanne in oure beleeue. 714

Adrian tells her. Belief doesn't trouble about arguments.

"Therfor, lady, if ʒe wyll lerne þis þing, 715
ʒe schall mech bettyr whan ʒe ʒour groundys haue.
ffor of oo poynt I geue ʒow full warnyng:
ʒe can neuyr grace of ʒour lorde craue,
Ne ʒour soule eke schul ʒe neuyr saue, 719
But if ʒe forsake for euyr ʒour elde be-leue
And trow swech þing as ʒe can not preue. 721

"Who knew ʒe þat costus, kyng of þis londe, 722
Was fadyr on-to ʒow? & what euydens haue ʒe
þat ʒe wer' bounden) sumetyme wyth a bonde,
Armes, bodye, bak, legges & kne,
layde þus in cradyll as¹ chyldyr are, parde? ¹ MS. all 726
Of all þeis þingys can we make no preue;
Wherfor' full mekely we must hem be-leue. 728

"So schall we be-leue all-maner' þing 729
Whech þat our lord comaundeth [on]-to vs;
ffor þat same lorde þat all hath in weldyng,
Our blessed god, our sauyour ihesus,
Whan þat he byddyth þat we schall do þus, 733
Suffyseth us as þan to be obedyent;
ffor but if we be, I holde vs but schent. 735

"ʒet, for ʒe argue be ʒour demonstracyoun) 736
þat þis same doctrine schuld be contrarius,
Be-cause þat I seyd in my declaracyon)
Who þat blessed lord whech is full delycyous,
I mene ihesu our sauyour, of all most vertuous, 740
þat he schuld be god & man eke in-fere:
Of þis same doctryne example may ʒe lere; 742

"And for ʒe dowte eke of þis coupelyng, 743
þat we two natures in cryst sey & prech,
I wyll preue þis be ʒour own felyng,
And ʒe ʒour-selue ʒour owne selue schall teche,
Myn arbytrour' I make ʒour owne tung & speche: 747
ffor wyth-inne ʒour-selue, if ʒe¹ take heede, ¹ MS. we
Two natures haf ʒe, wyth-outen any drede, 749

"Therfore, lady, if ye wil lerne this thyng,   715
Ye shal moche beter whan ye youre groundis haue.
ffor of oon poynte I geue you ful warnyng :
Ye can neuere grace of youre lord craue,
Ne youre soule eke shal ȝe neuere saue,   719
But ye forsake for euere your olde beleue
And trowe swhiche þinge as ye can not preue.   721

Katharine must believe what can't be proved.

"how knewe ye that Costus, kyng of þis lond,   722
Was fadir on-to you? and what euydens haue yee
That ye were bounden somtyme with a bonde,
Armes, body, bak, leggis and knee   [1] as & c. on er.
Leyde thus in cradel as[1] children arn, ye mowe see?   726
Of alle these thyngis can we make no preue ;
Wherefor ful mekely we must hem beleeue.   728

"Soo shal we beleue al-maner thyng   729
Whiche þat oure lord commaundeth to vs ;
ffor þat same lord that al hath in weeldyng,
Oure blissed god, oure saueour ihesus,
Whanne þat he byddeth þat we shal doo thus,   733
Suffyseth vs as thanne to be obedyent ;
ffor but if we bee, I holde vs but shent.   735

We must believe what Christ tells us to.

"Yet, for ye argue be youre demonstracyon   736
That this same doctryne shuld be contraryous,
Be-cause that I seyde in myn declaracyon
how þat blissed lord whiche is ful delicyous,—
I mene ihesu, oure saueour, of alle most virtuous,—   740
That he shulde be god and man eke in fere :
Of this same doctrine exaumple may ye leere ;   742

But that He is God and man, and

"And for ye doute eke of this coupelynge,   743
That we too natures in cryst sey and preche,
I wil proue this be youre owyn feelynge,
And ȝe youre-self youre owne self shal teeche,
Myn arbitrour I make ȝoure owne tunge and speche :   747
ffor with-inne youre-seelf, if ye take heed,
Too natures haue ye, with-outen ony dreed,   749

has two contrary natures, you may judge, for you have two natures,

Bk.III. Ch.18.

"Whech contrarye be; I preue it be þis skyll: 750
ffor þat þe on desyreth, þe other' wyll nouth;
Contrarye pan be þei, þese too, in wyll,
In desyre, in werkyng, in appetyte, in thowth.
Ryght so in þat lorde þat vs alle hath bouth 754
Bethe too kyndes & wylles eke too,
Bothe in oo persone—our' feyth seyth ryght soo. 756

"Now wyll we declare on-to ȝour' reuerens 757
Who god is eterne & wyth-outen ende.
ffor if ȝe loke wysely, þat same sentens
Schul ȝe haue in ȝour' bokes þat trete of kende;
þei determyn þus, if ȝe haue mende: 761
All þing þat is made be-gynnyng must haue;
And for þei fro þat heresye schuld hem saue 763

"Whech two begynnynges puttyth in kynde, 764
þer-for on hafe þei chose, & þus þei hym calle
'þe fyrst meuer',' if I[1] haue mynde;   [1] r. ȝe
Of whych meuer' oþer' causes alle
her' oryginall spryng both haue & schall, 768
All þat haue ben, & euer-mor' schul be.
Of ȝour' owyn bokes þis is þe decre." 770

Bk.III. Ch.19.
Ca^m. 19^m.

Whan adryan þe ermyte þese wordes had herde, 771
Assoyled alle þese qwestyouns, & many moo,
On-to þe lady þus he last answerde:
"Madame," he seyth, "if ȝe wyll now goo
And walk forth wyth me, non but we two, 775
þis lord schall ȝe see, þis lady schall ȝe speke;
howses schall ȝe haue þer' schull neuyr breke." 777

These wordes went so depe, sche left bokes alle; 778
So a-stoyned sche was, sche wot not veryly
Wheyther' sche schall þis ermyte a man now calle
Or ellys an aungell, come down fro hye.
ffor hys clothys to hys wordes ar' full on-lykly, 782

"Whiche contrarye be ; I preue it be þis skyl : 750 *Bk.III. Ch.17.*
ffor þat þe oon desyreth, the other wil nought ;
Contrarye thanne be þei, these too, in wil, *each striving against the other.*
I[n] desyre, in werkyng, in appetite, in thought.
Right soo in that lord þat vs alle hath bought 754
Beeth too keendes and willes eke too,
Bothe in oo per̃sone—oure feith seyth right soo. 756

"Now wil we declare on-to youre reuerens 757
how god is eterne and with-outen ende. *God is eternal,*
ffor if ye looke wysly, þat same sentens
Shul ye haue in youre bookes þat treete of keende ;
Thei determyn thus, if ye haue meende : 761
Alle þing þat is made, begynnyng must haue ; *because all things spring*
And for thei fro that heresye shuld hem saue 763 *from Him,*

"Whiche too begynnyngis putteth in keende, 764
Therfore oon haue thei chose, and thus þei hym calle
The firste mouere, if ye haue meende ; *the First Mover.*
Of whiche mouere other causes alle
her oryginal spryng bothe haue and shalle, 768
Alle þat haue ben and euere-more shal bee.
Of youre owne bookys that is the decree.[1] " ¹ MS. degree 770

Ca^{m.} 18^{m.}

Bk.III.Ch.18.

Whan Adryan the ermyte þese wordis had herde, 771 *Adrian asks Katharine*
Asoyled alle these questions and many moo,
On-to the lady thus he at last answerde :
"Madame," he seyth, "if ye wil now goo *to go with him,*
And walken foorth wyth me, noon but we too, 775
This lord shal ye see, this lady shal ye speke ; *see Christ,*
howses shal ye haue, thei shal neuere breke." 777 *and talk to the Virgin.*

These woordys wente soo deepe, she lefte bookys alle ;
Soo astoyned she was, she wote not verely 779 *Katharine thinks*
Whether she shal this ermyte a man now calle *whether she shall trust*
Or ellis an aungell, come doun fro hy. *Adrian.*
ffor his clothis to his woordis and ful onlykly, 782

An olde man & hor' clade in clothys bare,
A wyse man, a well a-vysed & a ware ; 784

A man lych a begger whan men hym see, 785
A man lych a doctour' whan þei hym here ;
ffew wordes & wyse & full of sentens had hee,
he semyth not so wyse be aray ne chere
As þis lady hath preuyd in dyuers manere. 789
Wherfor' aftyr hys counsele, certeyn, sche wyll do,
No man schall lett hyr, for sche wyll soo. 791

ffor a-noon as þe ermyte buskyd hym to fare 792
fforth in hys iornay, sche folowyth a-pace.
All lordes & knytes þat in þe castell war',
þei herd not, þei sey not of all þis solace ;
Ne thorow-oute þe cyte as þei gun trace, 796
Was no man a-spyed hem, but as inuisible
þei passed forby. ryght so seyth our' byble 798

Of þe men of sodom a-boute loth-is hous, 799
Who þei neyther dores ne ȝates myght fynde :
Godd smet hem þoo wyth a sekenes meruelous—
It is called acrisia, it maketh men seme blynde
As for a tyme, for sykyr all her' mynde 803
Schall be so a-stoyned þat þei schull not see
þing þat in her' hand vp hap þan bee. 805

So was all þe cyte a-stoyned ryght þan, 806
Be goddes prouidens fully, as we wene.
Lete hem curse now, lett hem chyde & banne,
No man knowyth now whedyr is þe qweene.
þus goo þei forth walkyng be-deene, 810
Tyll þei come to þe stronde wher' þat hys hous,
þis ermyte I mene, þis man meruelous, 812

Was won for to stande—but all is a-goo ; 813
þer' is no home, all[1] is wylldyrnesse.   [1] orig. all þis
he wayled, he loked, he went too & froo,

An olde man and an hore clad in clothis bare,
A wisman and a weel avysed and a ware ; 784

A man liche a beggere whan men hym see, 785
A man liche a doctoure whan men hym here ;
ffewe woordis and wyse and ful of sentens had hee,
he semed not [so] wys be aray ne be chere
As this lady hath proued in dyuers manere. 789
Wherfore after his counsell, certeyn, she wil doo, *Katharine*
No man shal letten hir, for she wil soo. 791

ffor a-noon as the ermyte busked hym to fare 792
fforth in his iornay, she folwed a-paas. *follows Adrian.*
Alle loordis and knyght*is* that in þe castel ware,
Thei herd not, thei sey not of al this solaas ;
Ne thurgh-oute the Citee as þei gun traas, 796
Was noo man aspyed hem, but as inuysible *They pass invisibly from*
Thei passed forby. right soo seyth oure bible 798 *Alexandria.*

Of the men of sodom a-bowte loth-is hous, 799
how thei neyther dores ner yates myght fynde : [1] MS. Soo
God[1] smette hem tho with a sekenesse merueylous—
It is called Aurisia,[2] it maketh men þat sen, blynde
As for a tyme, for sekyr al her mynde [2] r. acrisia 803
Shal ben soo astoyned þ*a*t þei shul not see
Thyng þat in her hand up hap than bee. 805

Soo was al that Citee astoyned right þanne, 806 *The Citizens know not where their Queen has gone.*
Be goddis prouidens fully, as we wene.
lete hem curse now, lete hem chyde and banne,
Noo man knoweth now whyder his the queene.
Thus gon thei foorth walkyng be-dene, 810
Til thei come to the stronde where that his hous,
This ermyte I mene, þis man m*er*ueylous, 812

Was wont for to stonde—but al is a-goo ; 813 *Adrian cannot find his Cell. It has vanisht.*
There is noon hom, al is wildernesse.
he wayled, he looked too and froo,

BK.III.Ch.19.	he cast þe cuntre, but he coude not gesse.	
	þus is he lefte in car' & heuynesse.	817
	"Good lord," he seyth, "wyth me do what þou lest,	
	But, as þou hyght me, coumforte my gest!"	819
	In who long tyme or in who many dayes	820
	þat þei fro Alysaunder' went to hys celle,	
	It is full harde to telle; for sewyrly, þo wayes	
	Wer' so meruelous, we can not wyth hem melle.	
	þer-for of þis mater' no mor' wyll I telle;	824
	But he made hem myghty þis iornay to take	
	þat be þe aungell led Abacuc to þe lake.	826
	Thus mornyth þis man, þus turneth he a-boute,	827
	he lokyth euery coost sekyng hys celle,	
	he is falle now sodeynly in full grete doute;	
	ffor all hys sorow, sothely for to telle,	
	Was for þis lady wher' sche schall dwelle;	831
	þus seyd he to hym-selue: "sche schall ween, I were	
	A fals deceyuoure, a ontrewe massanger'."	833

BK.III.Ch.20.   Ca^{m.} 20^{m.}

	The wheen a-spyed be þe ermytes face,	834
	ffor uery uexacyouw who he chaunged moode;	
	"Good syr'," sche seyd, "I pray ȝow of ȝour' grace,	
	haue we any tydynges othyr but goode?	
	þat ȝe ar' turmentyd I se be ȝour' bloode.	838
	Telle me what doute þat ȝe stand now Inne;	
	Councell ha ȝe non but me, mor' ne þe myn[n]e."	840
	"Madame," he seyd, "her' left I myn hous	841
	Whan I went for ȝow, as I was sent,	
	And now þe cuntre to me is meruelous,	
	Alle is a-goo, I-drenchyd or I-brent.	
	I must seke a new hous, for myn elde is schent.	845
	I had neuyr þowth myn herborow to chaunge:	
	Now mote I nedys, & þat schall be straunge."	847

he caste the contre, but he cowde not gesse.
Thus is he lefte in care and in heuynesse. 817
"Good lord," he seyth, "w*yth* me doo what þou leste,
But, as þou hight me, comforte my geste!" 819

In how longe tyme or in how many dayes 820
That þei fro Alisaundre went to his celle,
It is ful hard to telle; for suerly, tho wayes
Were soo m*er*ueylous, we ca*n* not w*yth* hem melle.
Therfore of this mater no more wil I telle; 824
But he made hem myghty this iornay to take
That be the aungeH led Abacuk to the lake. 826

Christ enables Adrian and Katharine to travel.

Thus morned þis ma*n*, thus turned he aboute, 827
he looked eue*ry* coost thus seekyng his celle,
he is falle now sodeynly in ful gret doute;
ffor alle his sorwe, soothly for to telle,
Was for this lady where she shal dwelle; 831
Thus seyde he to hym-self: "she shal wenen, I were
A fals disseyuere and noo*n* trewe massagere." 833

Adrian looks in vain for his Cell.

Ca*m*. 19*m*.

The queen aspyed be the ermyt*is* face, 834
ffor very vexacyo*n* how he chaunged mood;
"Good sir," she seyde, " I pray you of youre grace,
haue we ony tydyng*is* other tha*n* good?
That ye ar*n* tormented I see be yo*ur* blood. 838
Telle me what doute ye stonde now Inne; ¹ overlined.
CounceH haue ye¹ no*n* but me, the more ne þe mynne." 840

Katharine asks what troubles Adrian.

"Madame," he seyde, "heere lefte I my*n* hous 841
Whan I wente for yow, as I was sent,
And now the contre to me is m*er*ueylous,
Al is a-goo, I-drenched or I-brent.
I must seeke a newe hous, for my*n* oold is shent. 845
I had neue*re* though[t] my*n* herberwe to chaunge:
Now mote I nedes, and that shal be straunge." 847

He cannot find his Cell.

Tho sayd þe wheen҆ to þe man a-gayn҆ : 848
" þat lady þat sent ȝow for to fech me,
Sche is so gentyll, so trew, as ȝe sayn҆,
Sche wyll not suffyr vs in þis aduersyte
To be lost or deuoured in þis straung cuntre. 852
Trost we vp-on hyr & hyr gentylnesse,
ffor in good hope lyghte sumtyme sykyrnesse." 854

" Now euyr be ȝe wele ! " seyd þe ermyte, 855
" Ȝe hafe set ȝour trost hyer҆ þan my-selue ;
Thow ȝe be entered in to þe feyth but a¹ lyte, ¹ overlined.
Ȝe wyll pace in schort tyme oþer҆ ten or twelue.
Beth not a-ferde, of best ne of elue, 859
ffor þat same lady whos son ȝe chees,
Sche schall vs saue, I leue soo douteles. 861

" But all my þowth is now for my celle. 862
Schall I now grubbe & mak all newe a-geyn҆ ?
Schall I now delue & make me a welle ?
My myght is I-goo, sothely for to seyn҆.
To chaunge my dwellyng was I neuyr fayn҆. 866
þis is my grucchyng, lady, þis is my care ;
But for ȝour coumfort well mote ȝe fare ! " 868

Godd suffered þis man to falle þus in trauns 869
þat he schuld not hym-selfe magnyfye
Of so grete sytys & of swech dalyauns
Whech þat he had wyth our҆ ladye.
It is þe vse of our҆ lord to lede men hye 873
ffro full low degre, as dauid fro þe schepe
Was led to þe kyngdam, if we take kepe. 875

Caᵐ· 21ᵐ·

IN all þis feer҆ whech þe ermyte hadde, 876
Euyr was þis qween coumfortour to hys age ;
þe mor҆ he heuy was, þe mor҆ was sche gladde,
And euyr wyth full goodely, full trosty langage
Sche seyd on-to hym : " lete ȝour҆ heuynesse swage ! 880

Tho seyde the queen to the man ageyn : 848
"That lady that sente yow for to fetche me,
She is soo gentyl, soo trewe, as ye seyn,
She wil not suffre us in this aduersite
To be loost or deuoured in this straunge contre. 852
Truste we up-on hir and hir gentilnesse,
ffor in good hope lygth somtyme sekyrnesse." 854

Katharine bids Adrian trust in the Virgin Mary.

"Now euere be ye weel," seyde the ermyte, 855
"Ye haue sette yowre trost heyere than my-selue ;
Thow ye be entred in to the feyth but a lyte,
Ye wil passe in short tyme other ten or twelue.
Beth not a-feerd, of beste ne of elue, 859
ffor that same lady whos sone ye ches
She shal vs saue, I leeue soo douteles. 861

"But al my thought is now for my celle. 862
Shal I now grubbe and make al newe agayn?
Shal I now delue and make me a welle?
My myght is I-goo, soothly for to sayn.
To chaunge my dwellynge was I neuere fayn. 866
This is my grutchyng, lady, this is my care ;
But for youre comforte weel mote ye fare!" 868

He tells her he is too old to build a new Cell.

God suffred þis man to falle thus in trauns 869
That he shulde not hym-self magnyfye
Of soo grete syghtes and of swiche dalyauns
Whiche that he had with oure ladye.
It is the vse of oure lord to leede men hye 873
ffro ful lowe degree, as dauyd fro the sheep
Was leed to the kyngdam, if we take keep. 875

God lets him grieve, to prevent his being puft up.

Cam. 20m.

IN aH this feer whiche the ermyte hade, 876
Euere was the queen confortour to his age ;
The more he heuy was, þe more was she glade,
And euere with ful goodly and ful trosty langage
She seyde on-to hym : "lete your heuynesse swage ! 880

Katharine cheers him.

Lete it be lost þat lost now wyll be!
But trewly I telle, a solempne þing I se: 882

"Euene ʒondyr a-boue, ser', se ʒe nowth 883
þe woundyrfull wallys schy*nn*yn*g* as sune?
Swech a-nother' þing was neuyr wrowte,
þer was neuyr swech þing i*n* erde be-gune; 886
þe stones ar' bryght, þe roues[1] ar' not down*m*.[2]   [1] MS. rones
Loke vp, man, meryly! se ʒe noght ʒo*n* syght,   [2] r. du*n*ne
þe castell ʒondyr whech schynyth so bryght?" 889

The ermyte be-helde, but he sey nowth, 890
Neyther' wall ne ʒates, & þo sorow ga*n* he make;
"Lady," he seyde, "in blessed tyme wer' ʒe browte
On-to þis grou*n*de, ʒou*r*' spouse for to take!
he hath do now mor' for ʒour sake 894
þan I hafe felt all my lyffe leuaunde;
ʒe be mor' worthy, as I vndyrstande." 896

Tho wept he full sore, & sone þa*n* he say 897
þat same vysyo*n*, but sor' a-stoyned he was:
hys chapell was turned all i*n* oþer' way:
ffor þis whech he sethe, is brygter' þan glas,
þe oþir was elde, all growy*n* wy*th* gras; 901
hys elde hous was lytyll, þis new is large.
þa*n* ʒafe he þe mayde*n* a full grete charge, 903

Th*us* seyd he to hyr: "madame, now goo ʒe 904
On-to ʒon castell, on-to ʒon toure!
Trostyth no lenger' of þe ledyng of me,
ffor I am not worthy to prese to þat bour'.
God gra*u*nt þat I may be ʒour' successour', 908
þat I may sume-tyme come to þat place!
If ʒe may, I pray ʒow, aske [ʒe] me þat grace!" 910

Tha*n* went þe mayden forth be hyr one, 911
Desyryng sor' to se þis goodely place.
But Adrya*n* folowyd, wha*n* sche was gone—

lete it be lost that lost now wil bee!
But trewly I telle yov,[1] a solenne thyng I see,   [1] overl. 882

"Euene yonder aboue, [ser'], see ye nought   883 Katharine sees the Heavenly City.
The wonderful walles shynyng as the sonne?
Swiche a-nother thyng was neuere wrought,
There was neuere swiche thyng in erthe be-gunne.
The stones arn bryght, the roues arn not dunne.   887
look vp, man, meryly! see ye not yone sight,
The castel yonder whiche shyneth soo bryght?"   889

The ermyte be-held, but he sey nought,   890 Adrian cannot see it at first,
Neyther wal ne yates, and tho sorwe gan he make;
"lady," he seyde, "in blyssed tyme were ye brought
On-to this ground, youre spouse for to take!
he hath do more now for youre sake   894
Than I haue felt al my lyf lyuande;
Ye be more worthi, as I vndirstande."   896

Tho wepte he ful soore, and sone than he say   897 but afterwards does so,
That same auysyon, but soore he astoyned was:
his chapel was turned al in other way:
ffor this whiche he seeth, his brytere þan glas,
The other was olde, growen wyth gras;   901
his olde hous was litel, þis newe is large.
Than yaf he the mayden a ful grete charge,   903

Thus seyde he to hir: "madame, now goo yee   904 and bids Katharine go there.
On-to yone castel, on-to yone toure!
Trosteth no lengere of the leedyng of mee,
ffor I am not worthi to prese to þat boure.
God graunte that I may be youre successoure,   908
That I may somtyme come to þat place!
If ye may, I prey you aske ye that grace!"   910

Than wente the mayden foorth be hir oone,   911 She sets out.
Desyryng sore to see this goodly place.
But Adryan folwed, whan she was goone—   Adrian follows Katharine
KATHARINE.   Q
1 8

Oute of hyr hardynesse he gan hym purchace
On-to hys coumfort now a new solace. 915
But whan þei wer' come at þe ȝatys wyde,
þer' wer'[1] þei receyuyd on euery syde   [1] MS. wher), h expunged
Wyth swech-maner' persones of face & of clothyng 918
We can not speke it. I trow þei told it nowte—
ffor þei þat ar' lyfte to swech mysty þing,
þei telle what þei sey whan þei wer' þidyr broute,
But þei can not expresse her' wyll ne her' þowte 922
In whech þei hade þat manere solace—
It is a-nothyr langage þat longyth to þat place. 924

But þese too persones, as many other moo, 925
Wer' lyft vp in soule swech sytes for to see.
Seynt poule hym-selue was on of þoo
þat was þus I-raueched; ȝet dowted he
Wheythyr hys body, or nowte, wer' in þat secree. 929
But þis doute I not þat þe body of þis mayde
Was in þat temple wher' sche was arayde 931

Wyth holy baptem & anoy[n]ted eke 932
Wyth holy crisme, as our' lord wolde—
No man may be baptyȝed, if we treuly speke,
But þei haue a body, be þei ȝong or olde. 935
þus sey[1] þe elde[2] bokes, þer-of ar' we bolde :   [1] orig. seyth, th expunged. [2] MS. olde?
God may do what-euyr hym lyst,
And dothe mech þing whech is not wyst. 938

Thus ar' þei receyuyd in þe fyrst warde; 939
But aftyr mech bettyr, & of worthyer' men,
Whan sche to þe secunde cam; whech sauoured [a]s narde,
Nay, mech swettyr. þer' met sche mo þan ten
Of hundredes I mene, but non can sche ken, 943
þei wer' other'-maner persones þan sche had seyn.
But all þese in-fere on-to hyr gan seyn: 945

"Wolcom, syster', on-to þis holy place! 946
Wolcom to our' lorde whech hath ȝow chose
ffor to be hys spouse, ryght of hys grace!

Oute of hir hardynesse he gaṅ hym purchace
On-to his comforte a newe solace. 915
But whan thei were come at þe yates wyde,
There were thei receyued on euery syde 917

Bk.III. Ch.20.
to the Heavenly City.

With swiche maner persones of face & of clothyng 918
We can not speke it. I trowe thei tolde it nought—
ffor þei þat arn lyfte to swiche mysty thyng,
Thei telle what þei sey whan thei were thedir brought,
But þei can not expresse her wil ne her thought 922
In whiche thei hadde that-maner solace—
It is a-nother langage þat longeth to þat place. 924

They are welcomd by Celestial Beings.

But these too persones, as many other moo, 925
Were lyfte vp in soule swiche sightis for to see.
Seynt poule hyṅ-selue was oon of thoo
That was thus I-rauyshed; yet[1] douted hee
Whethir his body, or nought, were in þat secree. 929
But this doute I not þat the body of this mayde
Was in þat temple where she was arayde 931

[1] MS. þat

(Katharine is bodily in the Temple

With holy baptem) and anoy[n]ted eke 932
With hooly crysme, as oure lord wolde—
No maṅ may ben baptised, if we truly speke,
But thei haue a body, be thei yonge or olde.
Thus seyṅ the olde bookis, ther-of arṅ we bolde: 936
God may doo what-soo-euere hym lyst,
And dooth meche thyng whiche is not wyst. 938

where afterwards she is baptized and anointed.)

Thus arṅ thei receyued in þe firste warde; 939
But after moche better, and of wurthiere meṅ,
Whaṅ she to the secunde cam; it sauoured as narde,
Yaa,[1] meche swettere. there mette she mo than ten
Of hundredes I mene, but nooṅ kan she keṅ; 943
There were other-maner persones þan she had seyṅ.
But alle these in-feere on-to hir gan creyṅ (!): 945

[1] on er.

Worthier Beings greet them in the Second Ward.

"Welcoṅ, suster, on-to þis hooly place! 946
Weel-come on-to oure lord whiche hath you chose
ffor to be his spouse, ryght of his grace!

Katharine is welcomd

Bk.III Ch.21.
    Wolcome, of clennesse uery swete rose!
ffor ȝour' virginite, wyth-owte ony glose,   950
Schal we receyue ȝow," & thus forth þei hyr lede,
These gostly folkys in wondyrfull wede,   952

Tyl þei to þe temple cam). but þer' was a syght!   953
þer' came kynges, þer' cam emperoures,
þer' cam a meny wyth habytes so bryght,
It is not possible to erdely successoures
To expresse þoo fresch, þoo gay coloures;   957
Sche sey hem þan in her' goodely aray—
We leue in hope to se hem) an othyr day.   959

Thei led hyr þoo forthe a full softe pace   960
On-to þe barres of þe temple-ȝate,
hyr wolcomyng at þat tyme, swech þoo it was:
"Wolcom our' syster', wolcom our' mate!
As ȝe be now, wer' we full late,   964
ffor sumtyme had we bothe flesch, fell & bonys;
As ȝe hafe now, had we all ones."   966

Vp-on her' habytes certen tokenes þei ber',   967
Sum man oo tokyn), sume man an other' bare:
Aftyr þe passyones whech þei suffred here
So wer' þei merked wyth tokenes full bare;
þoo toknes wer' sett [t]her'[1] ryght to declare   [1] MS. her)   971
þat men had þei be & wyth grete distresse
Oute of þis herde com to þat holynesse.   973

But whan þis lady to þe dore was browte,   974
Sche loked in; hyr' leders louted alle.
Sche herd þer' melodye, as to hyr thowte
Sche herd neuyr swych. þer'-for' is sche falle
Down) all in trauns—þer was neuyr man, ne schalle,   978
þat may susteyn) in body swech heuynly blysse;
ffor who schall it susteyn), must dye fyrst, I-wys.   980

Oute of hyr traunce whan sche was wakyd,   981
Sche folowyd forth þan to þat noble place.

MS. Arundel.] *Katharine at the Heavenly Temple Gate.* 229

Wolcome, of clennesse very swote rose! Bk.III.Ch.20.
ffor youre virginite, with-outen ony glose, 950 for her Virginity.
Shal we receyue you," and thus foorth thei hir leede,
These goodly folk*is* in wonderful weede, 952

Til thei to the temple cam. but þere[1] was a syght! 953
There come kyng*is*, there come empe*r*our[i]s, [1] MS. þerre Holy Martyrs, in
There come a meny with habit*is* soo bryght kingly attire,
It is not possible to erthely successourys
To expresse tho fresh, tho gay coloures; 957
She sey hem thanne in her goodly aray—
We leue in hope to see hem a-nother day. 959

Thei ledde hir tho foorth a ful soofte paas 960 lead Katharine to the
On-to the barres of the temple yate, Temple gate,
hir weelcomyng at that tyme, swiche tho it waas:
"Weelcome oure suster, weelcome oure mate! welcoming her.
As ye be now, were we ful late, 964
ffor somtyme hadde we bothe fell, flesh and bones;
As ȝe haue now, had we alle oones." 966

Vp-on her habites certeyn tookenes þei bere, 967
Som man oo tookne, som man an other baar:
Affter the passyons whiche thei suffred heere
Soo were thei marked w*yth* tooknes ful yaar;
Thoo tooknes where sette there ryght to declaar 971
That men had thei been and with gret distresse
Oute of this erthe come to that holynesse. 973

But whan this lady to the dore was brought, 974
She looked in; hir leeder*is* lowted alle. She looks in and swoons.
She herde there melodye, as hir thought
She herde neue*r*e swiche. therfore is she falle 977
Doun alle in a trauns—there was neue*r*e man, ne shalle,
That may susteyne in body swiche heuenly blis;
ffor ho shal it susteyne, must firste deyn, I-wys. 980

Oute of hir trauns whan she was waked, 981
She folwed foorth þanne to þ*a*t noble plaas.

1 8 *

Þan sey sche our' lord, wheche all þing makyd,
Whech had called hyr to þat noble grace,
Sittyng full reall—but up-on hys face 985
Durst sche not loke for no-maner' þing,
So was sche a-ferde at hyr fyrst comyng. 987

Than wyst sche wele it was more þan man 988
þat sche had sowte & now sche hath it founde;
ffor wyth all þe wytt þat sche gadyr kan, [1] MS. hys; r. on hym this
Dar' sche noght fyxe hyr' eye in [t]hys[1] stounde,
But euyr sche in poynt is to falle on-to þe grounde— 992
hyr body is cause, it must be claryfyed,
And all þe carnalyte fully puryfyed, 994
Or sche swech þinges eyther' fele or grope. 995
Thus is þis mayden all in heuynesse
left, & leyd in maner' of wan-hope;
ffor þat same lord whech of hys goodenesse
lyst for to chese hyr as a specyall spousesse, 999
Now is so straunge sche may noght hafe þat grace
To come sumewhat nyher & se hys face. 1001

Ca^{m.} 22^{m.}

Tho cam our' ladye & left hyr' up sone; 1002
þus sayd sche te hyr: "be of good comforte!
Ʒour' heuynes is pased, ʒe hafe ʒour' bone,
All þis grete heuynesse schall turn to dysporte.
I sent aftyr ʒow þat ʒe schuld resorte 1006
On-to þis howsolde, for ʒe schall hafe þis grace,
Next me a-forn all women to be[1] in þis place. [1] om. to be?

"Therfor' come forthe now, for I wyll ʒow lede 1009
Ryght to my sone, on-to þat mageste."
Both maydes in-fer' þus forthe þei ʒede.
But þis noble adriane, at þat tyme wher' was he?
Myn auctour' telleth noght; but sekyr may ʒe be, 1013
he had blysse enowe assygned to hys parte,
he had so mech he was lothe to departe. 1015

Katharine dares not look on Christ's Face.

Thanne sey she oure lord, whiche al thyng maked,
Which had called hir to þat noble graas,
Sittyng ful riaH— but vp-on his faas   985
Durst she not looke for no-mane*r* thyng,
Soo was she afered at hir first comyng.   987

Katharine sees Christ, but dares not look on His Face,

Thanne wiste she weel it was more than man   988
That she had sought, and now she hath it founde ;
ffor with al the witte that she gadre can)
Dar she not fyxen hir eye in this stounde,
But eue*re* she in poynt is to falle on-to the grounde— 992
hir body is cause, it muste be claryfyed
And al the carnalite fully puryfied,   994

Er she swiche thyng*is* eyther feele or grope.   995
Thus is my mayden) al in heuynesse
left, and leyd in mane*r* of wanhope ;
ffor þat same lord wiche of his goodnesse
lest for to chese hir as a special spousesse,   999
Now is so straunge she may not haue þat *grace*
To come somwhat nyhere and see his blissed face.   1001

though He had chosen her for His Bride.

Ca^{m.} 21^{m.}

Tho cam oure lady and lift hir vp soone ;   1002
Thus seyde she to hir : " be of good comforte !
Youre heuynesse is passed, ye haue yo*ur* boone,
Al this grete heuynesse shal turne to disporte.
I sente after you that ye shuld resorte   1006
On-to this houshold, for ye shul haue þis grace,
Nexte me a-forn) alle women) to bee in this place.   1008

The Virgin Mary comforts her.

" Therfore come foorth now, I wil yow leede   1009
Right to my sone, on-to that mageste."
Bothe maydenes in-fere thus foorth þei yeede.
But this noble Adryan, at þat tyme where was hee ?
Myn auctour telleth not ; but sekyr may ye bee   1013
he had blisse I-now assigned to his part,
he had so moche he was ful looth thens-wart.¹   ¹ on er.   1015

The Virgin Mary takes Katharine

Thus aɼ þese ladyes euen on-to þe trone 1016
Of ouɼ lord allmyghty walked forthe a-pace,
Wyth-outen othyr[1] company, þei went þoo a-loone—
Perauentuɼ otheɼ folk stood not in þat grace, [1] omit othyr
So ny þat mageste, so ny goddys face 1020
To approch at þat tyme; it was a specyalte
Ordeyned of purpos at þis solemnyte. 1022

Ouɼ lady had þe wordes whan sche cam þeɼ; 1023
" Sune," sche seyth, " & makeɼ of all-maner þing,
I hafe browte [a] mayde her in full grete fere,
þe spouse whech þou louyst, heɼ I hyr bryng,
Sche desyryth þat þou schalt now wyth a ryng 1027
Despouse hyɼ to þi-self for euyr-more—
þis is hyɼ desyre, & hath be full ȝore." 1029

Ouɼ lord spake a-geyn) mysty wordes too, 1030
Whech þat þis mayde full heuy þoo made;
" Modyr," he seyth, " ȝe know ȝour-self, loo,
þe cause þat þis company in ioyes þus wade
Is þe look of my-selfe, whech dothe hem glade; 1034
ffor þei þat hafe þat, þei nede noo othyr þing.
But þei þat schul hafe þis gracyous syght lestyng, 1036

" ffull clene must þei be in body & in gooste, 1037
Wasched fro all synnes þat be fowle & derk.
Of swech hafe I her, ȝe see, a grete hoste,
Clensyd wyth my blode & merkyd wyth my merk—
All þis was my labouɼ & my bysy werk 1041
Whan I in erde was to bye mankynde,
Wech þat I fynde full oft to me onkynde. 1043

" Wherfor, modyr, þus I answer on-to ȝow: 1044
þis mayde may not hafe as now þat grace
Whech þat ȝe aske for hyr sake now,
I mene þe vysyon), þe syght of my face;
lete hyr goo clense hyɼ, lete hyr goo purchase 1048
þe holy baptem, þan hath sche my merke;
Bryng hyr þan to me, & I schall hyr merke 1050

Thus arn these ladies euene on-to the trone 1016 *Bk.III. Ch.21.*
Of oure lord almyghty walked foorth a-pace :   to Christ's throne,
Wyth-outen other company thei wente tho allone—
Perauenture other folk stood not in þat grace,
Soo ny that mageste, soo ny goodis face 1020
To approche at that tyme ; it was a specialyte[1]   [1] or. specialte
Ordeyned of purpos at this solennyte. 1022

Oure lady had the wordis whan) she cam there ; 1023
" Sone," she seyth, " and makere of al-man*er* thyng,   and says she brings Him a Bride who wishes to wed Him.
I haue brout a mayde here in ful grete fere,
Thi spouse whiche þou louest, here I hir bryng,
She desireth þat þou shalt now w*yth* a ryng 1027
Despouse hir to thi-self for eu*er*e-more—
This is hir desire, and hath been) ful ȝore." 1029

Oure lord spak ageyn) mysty woordis thoo, 1030
Whiche þat this mayde ful heuy tho made ;
" Modir," he seyth, " ye knowe youre-self, loo,   Christ says
The cause that þis company in ioyes thus wade
Is the looke of my-self, whiche dooth hem glade ; 1034 that all with Him
ffor þei þat haue that, thei nede noon other thyng.
But thei þat shul haue this gracyous sight lastyng, 1036

" fful clene muste þei bee in body and in goost, 1037 must be pure of sin.
Washed fro alle synnys that been foule and derk.
Of swiche haue I here, ȝe see, a grete oost,
Clensyd w*yth* my blood and m*er*ked w*yth* my merk—
Al this was my labo*ur* and my besy werk 1041 Christ tells
Whan) I in erthe was to b[e]ye mankeende,
Whiche þat I fynde ful ofte to me onkeende. 1043

" Wherfore, moder, thus I answere on-to yow : 1044 His Mother that Katharine mustn't see His face
This mayde may not haue as now þat grace
Whiche þat ye askyn) for hir sake now,
I mene the visyon), the sight of my face ;
lete hir goo clense hir, lete hir goo purchace 1048
The holy baptem, than hath she my merk ;   till she's baptized.
Brynge hir þanne to me, and I shal hir caerk (!)[1] [1] on. er.

234 Christ orders Katharine to be baptized. [MS. Rawlinson.

Bk.III.Ch.22.

Wyth swech a tokne þat neuyr mayde but ȝe 1051
had it so specyaly. lete þis þing be doo;
A prest hafe ȝe redy & a man, parde,
Bothe in flesch & goost: lete hym goo þer-too,
Performe he schall þis werk wyth hys handys too. 1055
Myn aungellis wyll I noght occupye wyth þis dede,
It longyth to mankynd, wyth-outen drede; 1057

"And ȝet þowȝ we myght of our' hye power' 1058
Graunte on-to aungellis þis specialtee
þat þei schuld baptiȝe men in erde here,
ȝet wyll we noght þat þei occupyed schuld bee
Wyth swych-maner' offyce as to humanyte 1062
longyth, & schal longe, as for most ryght.
Go now & baptiȝe þat noble wyght!" 1064

Than spake our' ladye, to swage hyr heuynesse: 1065
"Beth not discomfortyd in no-maner' weye
Wyth my sones wordes! for, in sykyrnesse,
ȝe must to hys byddyng ful buxumly obeye.
It is a goodely vsage, sothely to seye: 1069
Who schal be weddyd on-to duke or kynge,
Be-for hyr weddyng to hafe a bathynge, 1071

"ffor to mak hyr swete, for to make hyr clene— 1072
Ellys myght sche renne in ful grete offens.
Be þis example on-to ȝow I mene,
Do ȝe ȝour' deuer', do ȝour' dylygens
ffor to plese ȝour' lorde! a-non goo we hens 1076
In to ȝon chapell to ȝour baptistery;
Aftyr ȝour waschyng ȝe schal be full mery." 1078

Bk.III.Ch.23.

Cam. 23m.

Thus ar' þei walked, þe mayden & þe qween, 1079
In to þis chapell on þe mynster' syde.
þer' fond þei redy a funt, as I wene,
Wyth watyr, & wyth[1] crisme in a vessell wyde. [1] omit wyth
Adriane is called fro þe puple a-syde, 1083

MS. Arundel.] *Christ orders Katharine to be baptized.* 235

"With suche a tookne that neuere mayde but yee   1051   *Bk III. Ch.*21.
had it soo specyaly.   lete this thyng be doo;
A preest haue ye redy, and a man þat loueth me,   A priest of earth,
Bothe in flesh and in goost: lete hym þer-to goo,[1]   [1] on. er.
Perfoorme he shal þis werk wyth his handis too;   1055
Myn aungellis wil I not occupye wyth þis dede,   not an angel,
It longeth to mankeende, with-outen ony[1] drede;   [1] overl.

"And yet though we myght of oure hy powere   1058
Graunte on-to aungellis this specyalte
That thei shulde baptise men in erthe here,
ȝet wil we not that thei occupied shul bee
With swiche-maner offyce as to humanyte   1062   is to baptize Katharine.
longeth, and shal longen, as for moost ryght.
Goo now and baptise that noble whight!"   1064

Than spak oure lady, to swage hir heuynesse: 1065
"Beeth not discounforted in no-maner weye   The Virgin comforts her.
With my sones woordis! for, in sekernesse,
Yee muste doo his byddyng, ful buxomly obeye.
It is a goodly vsage, soothly to seye: 1069
ho shal be wedded on-to duke or kyng,   As all Brides are bathed
Be-forn her weddyng to haue a bathyng,   1071   before wedding,

"ffor to make hir swete, for to make hir clene—   1072
hellis myght she renne in ful grete offens.
Be this exaumple on-to you I mene,   so Katharine must be.
Doo ye youre dever, doo your diligens
ffor to plese youre lord! a-noon goo we hens   1076
In to ȝone chapel to youre baptistery;
After youre washyng ye shal ben ful mery."   1078

Ca.^{m.} 22^{m.}

*Bk.III.Ch.*22.

Thus arn thei walked, the mayden and the queene,   1079   She and the Virgin go into
    In to the chapel on-to the mynstre syde.   the Heavenly Minster.
There founde thei redy a font, as I weene,
With water, and with crysme in a vessel wyde.
Adryan is called fro the puple a-syde,   1083

ffor he must do all þis holy seruyse,
lycħ as our' lady þe maner' schall deuyse.   1085

Thus seyd sche to hym: "go do now þis dede,   1086
It longyth to þin ordre cristen folk to make;
A-ray þe a-none in swecħ-maner' wede
Whecħ I my-self her' þe now take;
þis mayde schal be bathyd for hyr loues sake   1090
In þis cold watyr, & crysten schal sche be,
My lord my son þus comaundyth he.   1092

"I my-selfe schal of hyr clothes strepe   1093
And make hyr all naked, redy to þis þing.
hyr name Kateryne styll schal þou clepe,
Ryght for þis cause & for þis tokenyng
þat þei whecħ knew hyr', eþir eld or ȝyng,   1097
Schul hafe an euydens sche is styll þe same
Whecħ sche was be-for—þer-for styll hyr name   1099

"Schal sche thus kepe, in confirmacyon   1100
þat all þing is trewe whech we do here,
No wyles wrowte ar' ne no collusyon—
We wyll noght suffyr þat in no maner'."
Tho was Kateryn spoyled—but blynd was þe frere, 1104
Bothe in hyr spoylyng & in hyr bapteme.
Of þat solempne fest þis was þe theme: 1106

"I baptiȝe þe her' in þe blessed name   1107
Of þe fadyr & þe sone & þe holygost,
In presens & wytenes of our' reuerent dame
Modyr vn-to cryst, of all women moste,
Godmodyr on-to þe—& þat may þou boost.   1111
lok þou be-leue, dowtyr, as I seyd to þe:
þat oo god þer is & persones thre;   1113

"Beleue eke in bapteme, & in holy kyrk,   1114
Be-leue in þe passyon of our' lord ihesu,
Be-leue þat þe miracles whecħ he dede werk

ffor he muste doon al this hooly seruyse,
lich as oure lady the maner gan deuyse. 1085

Thus seyde she to hym: "goo doo now þis dede, 1086 *Adrian is to baptize Katharine.*
It longeth to thyn ordere crysten foolk to make;
Aray the a-noon in swiche-maner wede
Whiche I my-self here the now take;
This mayde shal ben bathed for hir loues sake 1090
In this coolde water, and cristen shal she bee;
My lord my sone thus commaundeth hee. 1092

"I my-self shal of hir clothis strepe 1093 *The Virgin will strip her naked.*
And make hir al naked, redy to þis thyng.
hir name Kataryne stille shal þou clepe,
Right for this cause and this tookenyng
That thei whiche knewe hir, eyther old or ying, 1097
Shul haue an euydens she is stylle the same
Whiche she was be-fore—therfore stille hir name 1099

"Shal she thus kepe, in confirmacyon 1100
That al thyng is trewe whiche we doon here,
No wyles wrought are ne no collusyon—
We wil not suffre that in noo manere."
Tho was Katarine spoyled—but blynd was þe frere 1104 *Katharine is stript; but Adrian is blind.*
Bothe in hir spoylenge and in hir bapteme.
Of that solenne feste þis was the theme: 1106

"I baptise the here in the blyssed name 1107 *He baptizes her.*
Of the fadir and the sone and the holy goost,
In presens and wittenesse of oure holy dame,
Modir on-to crist, of alle women moost,
Godmodir on-to the—and that may þou boost. 1111 *The Virgin is her God-mother.*
looke þou beleue, doughter, as I sey to the:
That oo god there is and persones thre; 1113

"Beleue eke in baptem, and in holy kerke,[1] 1114 *Adrian bids her believe the Articles of the Christian Faith.*
Beleue in the passyon of oure lord Iesu, [1] or. kyrke
Beleue that the myracles whiche þat he dede werke

Wer' wyth-oute deceyte, stable & trewe,
Be-leue þat of a uirgyne hys manhode grew, 1118
And sche ondefouled—for sche is present,
Sche can ber' wyttenesse of þis testament." 1120

Kateryne answeryd on-to þese articles alle: 1121
"I be-leue hem, ser', as ȝe rehers be-dene;
þer-for on knes¹ as I now down falle,   ¹ MS. kneis?
In þis same funte whech ȝe may not sene,
Baptiȝe me parcharite & make me clene! 1125
ffor þis is þe wyll of þe soueren lorde a-boue,
And my wyll is it eke, ryght for hys loue." 1127

Thus was sche baptiȝed, & in þis maner' 1128
Confermed eke & renuede¹ hyr name.   ¹ renewed on the margin.
Our' lady hyr-selfe seruaunte was her',
Sche dede of þe clothes of þis swete dame.
All þis ilk tyme þer was a hame 1132
Of blyndenes be-for' þis ermytes yȝe,
ffor of all þis werk no-þing he syȝe. 1134

But sone aftyr þis sacrament is doo, 1135
hys lyght receyuyd he newly a-geyn.
þe myrth, þe ioye þat þe man made þoo,
We can not esyly expresse now ne seyn!
fful sekyrly wende he neuyr eft a seyn: 1139
Now thanketh he godd of hys hye grace
þat euyr he came in to þat holy place. 1141

Our' lady comaunded to daun Adryan 1142
þat all þis þing whech he herd & sey doo,
Wyth all hys besinesse, ryght so as he can,
To wryght it pleynly whan he may tend þer-too.
And as sche bad, full sekyrly he dyd soo, 1146
þis noble ermyte—for on-to our' ere
Who schuld it come ellys? who schuld we it lere? 1148

Were with-outen deceyte, stable and trew,
Beleue þat of a virgyn his manhood grew, 1118
And she ondefowled—for she is present,
She can bere wittenesse of this testament." 1120

Kataryne answerde on-to these articules alle: 1121 *Katharine does believe the Articles.*
"I be-leue hem, sir, as ye reherce be-deene;
Therfore on knes I am now doun falle
In this same font whiche ye may not seene,
Baptise me pur charyte and make me clene! 1125
ffor this is þe wil of the souereyn lord a-boue,
And my wil is it eke, right for his loue." 1127

Thus was she baptised, and in this manere 1128 *Her baptism is complete.*
Confermed eke and renewed hir name.
Oure lady hir-self seruaunt was heere,
She dede of the clothis of this swete dame.
Al this ilke tyme there was an hame 1132
Of blyndenesse be-forn the ermytis yȝe,
ffor of al this werk noo-thyng he syȝe. 1134

But soone after þis sacrament is doo, 1135 *The blind Adrian receives his sight.*
his light receyued he newly ageyn.
The myrthe, the ioye that the man made tho,
We can not esyly expresse now ne seyn!
fful sekerly wende he his syght a leyn (!): 1139
Now thanketh he god of this hye grace
That euere he come in to that holy place. 1141

Oure lady commaunded to daun Adryan 1142
That al þis thyng whiche he herde and sey doo, *The Virgin bids Adrian write down the Miracle.*
With al his besynesse, ryght soo as he can,
To write it pleynly whan he may tende þer-too.
And as she bad, ful sekyrly he dede soo, 1146
This noble ermyte—for on-to oure eere
how shuld it come elles? how shuld we it leere? 1148

Cam. 24m.

Now is our' lady forth wyth þis mayde 1149
In to þe temple entred a-gayn).
ȝet in hyr going þus swetly sche sayde:
"Dowtyr myn), Kateryne, loke ȝe be glad & fayn)!
ffor ȝour' desyr' schul ȝe haue, certayn), 1153
Ere ȝe goo hens; be-leue þis sykyrly!"
Swech wordes talked þei walkyng sobyrly. 1155

Now be þei come euene be-for' þe trone 1156
Of our' lord god, þe mayde[n] & þe qwene.
Our' lady had þe wordes hyr-self a-lone;
Swech was þe ordre of hyr tale, I weene:
"O kyng of kynges, blyssed mote þou been)! 1160
I haue browte her' þe[1] þe doghtyr of clennesse,   [1] r. þe her
Prayng þe, lorde, wyth alle humbylnesse 1162

"That þou schew now þe blysse of þi face 1163
On-to þi spouse, on-to þi creature;
Euene as þou grauntyd [hyr][1] þat grete grace   [1] om.
To kepe hyr virginite in clenly trappure,
So graunte hyr now þat hye portrature 1167
Of þi blyssyd ymage to se & be-holde!
ffor þan ar' sche & I mech to þe beholde." 1169

Our' lorde answerde on-to hys modyr ful fayr': 1170
"What-so-euyr ȝe wyll, modyr, it must be doo;
All heuen) & herde to ȝow must repayre
ffor help whan hem nedyth, to refresch her woo.
I graunte ȝour petycyon), I wyll it be soo." 1174
Þan fell þat qween) down) plat to þe grounde,
hyr corown) sche toke of þat was ful rownde, 1176

Sche leyd it be-for hym & þus sche spake: 1177
"lord of all creatures þat be lyuande,
No-þing þat I aske of þi grace I lake,
Euyr be þou honowred in heuyn & in lande!
I my-selfe am werk of þi hande; 1181

Caᵐ· 23ᵐ·

NOw is oure lady foorth with þis mayde 1149 *The Virgin*
In to the temple entred agayn).
Yeet in hir gooenge thus sweetly she sayde :
"Doughter myn), Kataryne, looke ye be glad and fayn) !
ffor yo*ur* desyre shul ye haue, certayn), 1153
Er ye goo hens; beleue this, certeynly !"
Swiche woordys talked thei walkyng forby. 1155

Now be thei come euene be-fore the throne 1156 *takes Katharine to Christ on His throne.*
Of oure lor[d] god, the mayden and the queene.
Oure lady had the woordys hir-self allone;
Swiche were the woordis of hir tale, I wene :
"O kyng of kyngys, blyssed mote þou bene! 1160
I haue brought here the dought*er* of clennesse,
Prayng the, lord, w*y*th alle humblenesse 1162

"That þou shewe now the blisse of thi face 1163 *The Virgin asks Christ to show Katharine His face.*
On-to thi spouse, on-to thi creature;
Euene as þou graunted þ*a*t gret grace
To kepe hir virginyte in clenly trappure,
So graunte hir now þ*a*t hye portrature 1167
Of thi blissed ymage to see and be-holde!
ffo[r] than) arn) she and I bounde to the many-foldt." 1169

Oure lord answerde on-to his moder fulfayre : 1170
"What-so-euere 3e wil, moder, it must be doo;
Al heuene and erthe to you muste repayre
ffor helpe whan hem nedeth, to refresh her woo.
I graunte youre petycion), I wil it be soo." 1174
Than) fel that queen) doun) plat to the grounde, *She lays her*
hir coroun) she took of, that was ful rounde, 1176

She leyde it be-forn hym and thus she spak : 1177 *Crown before Christ,*
"lord of alle creatur*is* that be leuande,
No-thyng þ*a*t I aske of thi grace I lak,
Eu*er*e be þou honowred in heuene and in lande !
I my-self am werk of thyn) hande; 1181
KATHARINE. R
i 9

Bk.III.Ch.21. Thow I þi modyr be, þi seruaunt am I:
þi grace I thank, for þi mercy I crye." 1183

Our' lord bad hyr' ryse, & sche rose sone. 1184
Sche was corowned a-geyn, or þei wer' ware—
Tho men myght see what is to done
Of ony creature whan þei come þare.
þis same exaumple sat þoo full sare 1188
On Kateryns hert; sche fell down a-noone
Plat on-[to] þe grounde, styll as þe stoone, 1190

Thus seyd sche in schort, for to tell pleyn: 1191
"I se wele, lorde, þat of all-maner þing
þou art maker', of erde, eyr' & þe reyn,
All be obedyent to þi comandyng:
Mercy I craue, lord, at my be-gynnyng; 1195
haue I þi mercy, I desyr' not ellys,
ffor I haue lernyd of mercy her' þe welle is." 1197

Sche was lyft vp be our' lorde hym-selfe; 1198
þus seyd he to hyr': "wolcom, doutyr', to me!"
Aboute hyr stode virgynes ten or twelue,
Wondyrly arayed & full of bewte—
Our' lady had called hem on-to þat deute 1202
To comfort þis mayde & do hyr seruyse.
Tho spak þis lorde, þis hye iustyse: 1204

"Ask what ȝe wyll, Kateryne, ȝe schul it haue 1205
Of me at þis tyme to ȝour wolcomyng;
Syth ȝe for-sake boþe castell & caue
ffor loue of me & for my byddyng,
I will graunte ȝow ȝour' hertis desyryng, 1209
ffor I am þat same whom ȝe in parlement
A-geyn all ȝour' lordes & comon[s][1] consent [1] MS. comon

"Chosen[1] on-to spowse. who leke ȝe now? [1] MS. Choson?
Wyll ȝe now haue me for euyr-more?" 1213
Wyth þese[1] swete wordes sche fel in swow [1] MS. þeses

Thou I thi moder be, thi seruaunt am I :
Thi grace I thanke, for thi mercy I cry."   1183   *Bk. III. Ch. 23. and acknowledges herself His servant.*

Oure lord bad hir ryse, and she ros sone.   1184
She was corouned ageyn, her thei wer ware—   *Her Crown is put on again.*
Tho men myght see what is to done
Of ony creature, whan thei come thare.
This same exaumple sat tho ful sare   1188
On Kataryne-is herte ; she fel doun anoon
Plat on-to the ground stille as þe stood,   1190

Thus seyde she in short, for to telle pleyn :   1191
"I see weel, lord, that of al-maner thyng   *Katharine begs for*
Thou art makere, of erthe, eyr and þe reyn,
Alle been obedyent to thy commaundyng :
Mercy I craue, lord, at my begynnyng ;   1195
haue I thy mercy, I desyre not ellys,   *Christ's mercy.*
ffor I haue lerned of mercy heere þe welle is."   1197

She was lift vp be oure lord hym-selue ;   1198
Thus seyde he to hir : "welcome, doughter, to me !"   *Christ welcomes St. Katharine.*
Abowte hir stood virgynes ten or twelue,
Wonderly arayed and ful of beauute—
Oure lady had called hem on-to þat dewte   1202
To comforte this mayde and doo hir seruyse.
Tho spak this lord, this hye Iustyse :   1204

"Aske what ye wil, Kataryne, ye shul it haue   1205   *He will grant her all she wishes.*
Of me at this tyme to youre wolcomynge ;
Sith ye for-sake bothe castell and caue
ffor loue of me and for my byddynge,
I wil graunte you your hertys desyrynge,   1209
ffor I am that same whom ye in parlement
Ageyn alle youre lordys and comouns consent   1211

"Chosen on-to spouse. how lyke ye now ?   1212   *Will she be His Bride?*
Wil ye now haue me for euere-more ?"
With these swete woordis she fel in swow

Plat on-to þe grounde þe good lorde be-for'.
But whan he hyr wyttes a-geyn gan restore, 1216
Thus spake sche þan on-to þat kyng:
"O soueren maker' of all-maner' þing, 1218
"Of angell, of man, of best & of tre, 1219
If I wer' worthy on-to ȝour hye presence
ffor to be couplede wyth solemnyte,
þan wold I desyr' of ȝour excellens
þat ȝe for-gefe me all-maner' offens; 1223
Make me ȝour seruaunt, & not ȝour' wyffe!
I am not worthy to so hye a lyffe." 1225

"Ȝys," seyd our lorde, "my modyr wyll here 1226
þat I schall wed ȝow; so wyll I saunfayle;
þerfor I ask ȝow ȝour' wyll for to lere,
If ȝe consent on-to þis spousayle.
Wyth many ioyes I wyl ȝow newly rayle: 1230
Consent ȝe, Kateryne? what sey ȝe nowe?"
"Lord," sche seyd þoo, "I wyll as þow.[1] [1] MS. ȝow; r. as wilt þow.

"I forsake here, lorde, for þi loue 1233
Crown & londe, castell & town,
Gold & syluyr, bothe hows & rofe,
Brochys & ryngys, mantell & gown;
Suffyr me no mor', lord, for to fall down 1237
In delectacyon of wordly þingys,
Kepe me þi-selfe,[1] lorde, kyng of all kyngys! [1] r. to þi-selfe

"All þat euyr I hafe, þat wote I wele 1240
I hafe it of þe, lord—of whom hafe I elles
My spech, my þowt, my mende euery dele,
My bones, my body, my flesch & my felles?
Now, as in þe of plente be þe welles, 1244
Suffyr me neuyr for to part þe froo;
ffor fro þi presens kepe I neuyr to goo." 1246

Than spak our' lorde ryght on þis wyse: 1247
"long was it ordeynde be-for þis tyme
þat ȝe schuld come on-to our' seruyse.

Plat on-to the grounde the goode lord be-fore.
But whan he hir wittes ageyn gan restore, 1216
Thus spak she thanne on-to that kyng :
"O souereyn makere of alle-maner thyng, 1218 *Katharine says*

"Of aungell, of man, of beeste and of tree, 1219
If I were wurthi on-to your hy presens
ffor to be coupled with solennyte,
Thanne wulde I desire of your exellens
That ye forgeue me al-maner offens ; 1223
Make me your seruaunt, and not your wyff! *she would rather be*
I am not worthi to so hye a lyf." 1225 *His servant.*

Yet seyde oure lord : "my moder wil heere 1226
That I shal wedde you ; soo wil I saunsfayle ;
Therfore I aske your wil, for to lere *Christ asks St. Katharine to wed Him.*
If ye consente on-to this spousayle.
With many Ioyes I wil you newely rayle : 1230
Consente ye, Kataryne? what sey ye now?"
"Lord," she seyde tho, "I wil as wilt thou. 1232 *She consents;*

"I forsake heere, lord, for thi loue 1233
Crowne and lond, castell[1] and towne,   [1] r. castell*is*?
Gold and siluer, bothe hous and roue,
Broches and ryngis, mantell and gowne ;
Suffre me, lord, no more for to falle downe 1237
In to delectacyun of werdly thynges,
Keepe me thi-self, lord, kyng of all kynges! 1239

"Alle þat euere I haue, that wot I weel 1240
I haue it of the, lord—of whom haue I it elles?—
My speche, my thought, my mynde euery deel,
My boones, my body, my flesh and my felles.
Now, as in the of plente been the welles, 1244
Suffre me neuere for to parten the froo ; *and prays that she may*
ffor fro thi presens kepe I neuere goo." 1246 *never leave Him.*

Than spak oure lord ryght on this wise : 1247
"longe was it ordeyned beforn this tyme
That ye shuld come on-to oure seruyse.

Bk.III.Ch.24. A-boue all oþir I wyll þat ȝe clyme,
Saue only my modyr, schortly to ryme ; 1251
Ȝe schal be next ioyned to my presence,
Ryght for ȝour chastyte & ȝour' obediens. 1253
" ffor þowȝ all þoo maydenes þat kepe hem clene 1254
ffor my sake & for my plesaunce,
Be wynes vn-to me, all be-dene,
Ȝet is þer' to ȝow schape a hyer' chaunce,
Be-for hem all schal ȝe go in þe daunce, 1258
Next my modyr, ryght for þis cause
ffor ȝe for-soke, to sey schortly in clause, 1260
" Emperour', kyng & duke, for my sake. 1261
I receyue ȝow þerfor' be a specyalte,
My wyffe for euyr her' I ȝow make,
Be-cause of ȝour constans in virginite.
And a new conflycte in schort tyme schul ȝe 1265
Be-gyne for my sake—but drede ȝow noght !
Who-so offend ȝow, ful der' it schal be bowte ! " 1267
Tho spak our' lady ryght in þis maner' : 1268
" Syth þat þis spousalye mote nedys be doo,
þis same mayde, lord, geue I þe here—
A mayde ȝeueth a mayde, þou seruyd me soo
Whan þou commendyd Ihon me vn-too 1272
Wher' þat þou hyng on þe blody tre.
her' is þe ryng, lord, & her' is sche." 1274
Our' lord tok þat ryng in hys honde, 1275
he put it on þe fynger' of þis clene[1] virgyne ; [1 to be om.
" þis is a tokne," he seyd, " of þat bonde
Whech[1] ȝe ȝour'-selfe as on of myne   [1 r. Be whech ?
lyst now ȝour' wyll to my wyl enclyne ; 1279
þis tokne eke beryth wytnesse full ryffe
þat her' I tak ȝow for my weddyd wyffe." 1281
Certeyn) men þat had seyn) þis ryng, 1282
As myn auctour' seyth, þei told it pleyn) ;
þei seyde þat it is a fayr' grauyn þing

[MS. Arundel.] *Christ weds St. Katharine.* 247

A-boue alle other I wil that ye clyme,
Saue oonly my moder, shortly to ryme ; 1251   *Christ says she shall be next His Mother.*
Ye shal ben next Ioyned to my presens,
Right for youre chastite and youre obedyens. 1253

" ffor though alle tho maydenes þat keepe hem clene
ffor my sake and for my plesauns,
Been wyues on-to me, alle be-deene,
ȝet is there to you shapeꝺ an hyere chauns,
Be-fore hem alle shul ye goo in the dauns, 1258
Next my moder, ryght for this cause
ffor ye forsook, to seyn shortly in clause, 1260

" Emperour, kyng and duke, for my sake. 1261
I receyue you therefor be a specyalyte,   *Christ makes St. Katharine His wife,*
My wyf for euere heere I yow make,
Be-cause of your constauns in virgynite.
And a newe conflicte in short tyme shul ye 1265
Be-gynne for my sake—but dreede yow nought !
hoo-soo offende yow, ful deere it shal be bought." 1267

Tho spak oure lady ryght in this manere : 1268
" Sith that þis spousayle muste nede be doo,
This same mayde, lord, geue I the heere—
A mayde ȝeueth a mayde, þou serued me soo
Whan þou commended Ioꝺ me oꝺ-too 1272
Where that þou heyng on the blody tree.
heere is the ryng, loord, and heere is shee."   *1273-4 transp. in the MS.*

Oure lord took that ryng in his hond, 1275   *and puts on her finger a ring*
he putte in on the fynger of this virgyne ;
" This is a tookne," he seyde, " of that boond
Whiche ye your-self as ooꝺ of myne
lyste now youre wil to my wil enclyne ; 1279
This tokeꝺ eke bereth wittenesse ful ryf
That heer I take ȝow for my wedded wyf." 1281

Certeyꝺ meꝺ that hadde seeꝺ this ryng, 1282
As myꝺ auctour seyth, the¹ tolde it pleyꝺ ;
They seyde þat it is a fayr graueꝺ thyng

Oute of a ston whech, as þei eke seyn),
It is clepyd a calcedony, lych a clowde of reyn) 1286
Or ellys lych þe watyr, swech his colour is.
hys uertues ar' touchyd¹ many, I-wys : ¹ r. if touchyd? 1288

The auctoures sey þat he is gracyous 1289
To þe berer of hym ; if þat he wyll trete
Of ony materes whech þat be perlyous,
he schall haue fortune down for to bete
All þe bate & stryffe in toun or in strete ; 1293
he is vertuous eke to ȝeue men a tast'
ffor to kepe her' body boþe clene & chast. 1295

Tho be-gan a song in heuen all a-bowte, 1296
þe [most]¹ wondyrfull notes þat euyr man myght her' ;
Wordes sounded þei to þe notes full deuoute,   ¹ om.
ffull well acordyng to her' song þer'.
þe song þat þei sungyn, if ȝe wyll [it] ler', 1300
Was þis same : Sponsus amat sponsam) ;
þe ouert þer'-too : Saluator uisitat illam. 1302

So semeth it well þis song in heuen be-gan, 1303
A-monge aungelles & seyntys in blysse.
Well may it þan be sunge of mane
her' in þis vale of wrecchydenesse ;
þis chyrch must folow, for sothe I gesse, 1307
þe chyrch a-boue in all þat it may.
þus endeth þe weddyng of þis may. 1309

Cam. 25m.

Tho lest our' lorde hys leue to take 1310
Of hys new spouse as for a space ;
þat same hand whech all þing dede make
he lyfte on hye, & of hys goode grace
he blessed þis swete boþe hede & face, 1314
" ffarwell," he seyth, " my wyffe ful der' !
lete no dyscoumfort' ȝow noy ne der' ! 1316

MS. Arundel.] *Christ comforts St. Katharine.* 249

Oute of a stoonꝺ, whiche thei eke seynꝺ   *Bk.III. Ch.23.*
It is cleped a Calcedony, liche a cloude of reynꝺ   1286   with a stone of Chalcedony in it.
Or ellis liche the water, swiche his colour is.
his vertues arnꝺ touched many, I-wis :   1288

    The auctoures seynꝺ þat he is gracyous   1289
To the berere of hym ; if þat he wil trete
Of ony materis whiche þat be perilous,   (The virtues of Chalcedony.)
he shal haue fortune dounꝺ for to bete
Alle debate and stryf, in tounꝺ or in strete ;   1293
he is virtuous eke to yeue menꝺ a tast
ffor to kepe her body bothe clene and chast.   1295

    Tho be-ganꝺ a song in heuene al a-boute,   1296   A Bridal Song is sung in Heaven,
The [most] wonderful notes þat euere men myght here ;
Woordes souned thei to the notes ful deuoute,
fful weel a-cordyng to her song theere.
The soung þat thei soungenꝺ, if ye wil lere,   1300
Was this same : Sponsus amat sponsam ;
The ouert ther-too : Saluator visitat illam.   1302

    Soo semeth it weel this song in heuene be-ganꝺ,   1303
Amongis aungellis and seyntys in blesse.
Weel may it thanne be sungenꝺ of manꝺ
heere in this vale of wretchednesse ;
This chirche muste folwe, forsothe I gesse,   1307
The chirche a-boue in al that it may.   and the Wedding
Thus endeth this weddyng of this may.   1309   is over.

Ca^m. 24^m.   *Bk.III. Ch.24.*

Tho liste oure lord his leue to take   1310
    Of his newe spouse as for a space ;
The same hand whiche alle thyng dede make
he lifte vp on hye, and of his good grace
he blissed that swete bothe heed and face,   1314   Christ blesses His new Wife, St. Katharine,
"ffar weel," he seyth, " my wyf ful deere !
lete no discomforte you noye ne feere !   1316

"Thow þat ȝe lese ȝour londe, ȝour weltli, 1317
Thynk it is bettyr þat I ȝow ȝeue;
Thow sekenes come in stede of helth,
Kep ȝe ȝour counstans in trewe be-leue!
And þe, adryane, make I my refe, 1321
As in þis mater, þou schall hyr tech
Of myn incarnacyon þe maner spech; 1323

"Tech hyr þe feyth eke of þe trinite, 1324
þe ffadyr, [&] þe sune, & þe holy gost,
Tech hyr of þe godhede þe vnyte,
Truly tech hyr, wyth-outen boste!
Of all þis cuntre I trost þe now moste: 1328
þerfor do truly my comaundement!
But if þou do, þou may sone be schent. 1330

"Thys werk, þis lesson truly to performe, 1331
Eyt dayes wyll I sche dwell wyth þe.
My modyr schall I sende hyr to enforme
Aftyr þat tyme wyth solemnyte
Of many other þinges towchyng hyr & me. 1335
But, Kateryne wyffe, þis schall I ȝow ȝeue
A-boue all women þat now erdely leue: 1337

"Myn aungellis schul honour ȝow wyth a seruyse— 1338
In tokne þat we be wedded in-fere—
þer was neuer sey ȝet swech funeral offyse
Of no seynt þat in erde deyed here.
þis schal I do for ȝour loue, dere. 1342
ffar-wel now, & þink not longe!"
Thus pased our lorde, wyth myrthe & song. 1344

And all þoo creatures fayre & bryght, 1345
Alle are I-passed, þe temple eke is goo,
So is þat chapell, þat funt & þat lyght.
Of all þis þing þei se now no moo
But Adryanes selle, wher þat þei too 1349
Ar left a-lone a-mong trees olde.
But þan was it ruthe for to be-holde, 1351

"Though that ye lese youre loud and your welthe,
Thynke þat it is better that I yow ȝeue; 1318
Though seeknesse come in stede of helthe,
Keepe ye your constans in trewe beleue!
And the, Adryan, make I my reue, 1321 *and makes Adrian her teacher.*
As in the matir, þou shalt hir teeche
Of my incarnacyon the maner speche; 1323 *Christ bids Adrian teach St. Katharine the Christian Faith.*

"Teche hir þe feyth of the trynyte,[1] [1] on erasure. 1324
The fadir, the sone, the hooly goost,
Teche hir of the godhed the vnyte,
Trewely teche hir, with-outen boost!
Of alle this contre I troste the now moost: 1328
Therfore do truly my commaundement!
But if þou doo, thou mayst soone be shent. 1330

"This werk, this lesson truly to performe, 1331
Eyte dayes wil I she dwelle wyth the. *She'll stay with him 8 days. After 8 days Christ will send His Mother to her.*
My modir shal I sende hir to enfoorme
After that tyme with solennyte
Of many other thyngis touchynge hir and me. 1335
But, Kataryne wyf, this shal I ȝow yeue
A-boue alle women that now erthely leue: 1337

"Myn aungellis shuln honowre yow with a seruyse— *At her death she shall be buried with angels.*
In tokene that we been wedded in-feere— 1339
There was neuere yet seyn swyche funeral offyse
Of no seynte that in erthe deyed heere.
This shal I doo for youre loue, deere. 1342
ffarweel now, and thynke not loonge!"
Thus passeth oure lord, with merthe and soonge. 1344 *Christ goes;*

And alle tho creatures fayre and bryght, 1345 *the Angels and Temple vanish.*
Alle arn I-passed, the temple eke is goo,
Soo is þat chapel, that font and that lyght.
Of al this thyng thei seen now no moo
But Adrian-is celle, where þat thei too 1349 *St. Katharine is in Adrian's cell.*
Arn left allone a-mongis trees oolde.
But than was reuthe for to be-hoolde, 1351

To se þis swete, who sche þan felle 1352
Down in a swow; as ded þoo sche lay.
Adrianne now is runne to hys welle,
Wyth watyr he comyth & grete a-fray,
"A-wake, madame!" he gan þoo to say, 1356
"Allas þat euyr ȝe come in [to] þis place!"
he rubbyd hyr chekys, þe nose & þe face, 1358
he wept, he prayed, he cryed ful sore, 1359
To sche a-woke, sat' vp & spake.
Adryane sayde to hyr: "lady, dey no mor'!
ffor, & ȝe do, hens schal I me pak;
Alle-maner' coumfort her' we do lak 1363
þat schuld ȝow rere: þer-for' I charge ȝow,
ffall no more in swech-maner' swow! 1365

"Thynkyth, thow ȝour loue as for a tyme 1366
hath left ȝow her', ȝet hath he nowth
ffor-sak ȝow, lady, but as a pylgryme
he wyl ȝe be, in dede & in thowte.
I wote full wele ȝe neuyr mech rowth 1370
Of no wordly ne erdely plesauns;
It may ȝow no-þing so hyly avauns 1372

"As may þat lorde to whom þat ȝe be 1373
Wedded now newly. for goddys sake,
Comfort ȝour-selue & þink who þat ȝe
þis same blesse sumetyme schul I-take
In swech-maner' sewyrnesse þat schal neuer slake. 1377
þerfor' beth glade, & loke on ȝour ryng!
It wyll remembyr' ȝow ȝour' gloryous weddyng. 1379

Caᵐ. 26ᵐ.

"Bvt now must ȝe, myn own lady der', 1380
ȝour' beleue vndyrstand ful sykyr & playn:
ȝour' swete spouse bad I schuld it ȝow lere,
Whom ȝe in flesch now full late sayn,
In whech he soked & also was slayn; 1384

To see this swete, hough she þan felle	1352	*Bk.III.Ch.*24.
Doun in swon; as deed tho she lay.		St. Katharine swoons.
Adrian is ronne now to his welle,		Adrian
With water he cometh and grete affray,		
"A-wake, madame!" he gan tho to say,	1356	
"Allas that euere ye come in [to] þis place!"		
he rubbed hir cheekys, the nose and þe face,	1358	
he wepte, he preyed, he cryed ful sore,	1359	revives her,
Tho[1] she a-wook, satte vp and spak. [1] r. to = till		
Adryan seyde to hir, "lady, deye no more!		
ffor, and ye doo, hens shal I me pak;		
Alle-maner comforte here doo we lak	1363	
That shuld ʒow rere: therfore I charge yow,		
ffal no more in swiche-maner swow!	1365	
"Thenketh, though your loue as for a tyme	1366	
hath lefte yow here, yet hath he nought		and tells her that Christ has not for- saken her, and that she will soon be with Him for ever.
ffor-sake yow, lady, but as a pilgryme		
he wil ʒe been, in dede and in thought.		
I wot ful weel ye neuere moche rought	1370	
Of no worly ner erthely plesavns;		
It may you no-thyng soo hyly avauns	1372	
"As may that lord to whom þat ye bee	1373	
Wedded now newly. ffor goddys sake,		
Comforte your-self and thenke how þat yee		
This same blysse shal ye take		
In swiche-maner suernesse þat shal neuere slake.	1377	
Therfore be glad, and look on your ryng!		
It wil remembre yow youre gloryous weddyng.	1379	

Ca^m. 25^m.

*Bk.III.Ch.*25.

"Bvt now must ye, myn owen lady deere,	1380	
Youre beleue vndirstonde ful seker and playn:		He teaches her the Chris- tian Faith.
Your swete spouse bad I shuld it ʒow leere,		
Whom ye in flessh now ful lat sayn,		
In whiche he souked and also was slayn.	1384	

But of hys goddehed, whech is grownd of all,
ffeythfully þe treuth tell now I schall. 1386

"Thys must ȝe be-leue, as I told ȝow ere 1387
Whan ȝe wer' baptiȝed, if ȝe hafe mynde—
Sette ȝour hert þer-to & bysyly it lere :
Our' lord godd is of swech a kynde
þat sykyrly, as I of hym wretyn fynde, 1391
he is on in substauns & in nature,
Thre eke in persones, I ȝow ensure; 1393

"O god, o lorde, o maker, o mageste, 1394
þe fadyr & þe sune & þe holygoost,
Thre persones in o godhede—þus be-leue ȝe—
Off whech non is smaller' ne non is most,
All ar' of euene power' in euery cost; 1398
ffor þe pluralyte of persones is no preiudyse
On-to þe vnyte of godhed, in no-maner' wyse. 1400

"And ȝet he þat is þe fadyr, is not þe sone, 1401
Ne þe sone þe gost, wyth-outen fayle ;
O wyll hafe þei in all þat is don,
O myght, o power', o lyght, o counsayle—
þis lesson must ȝe hyde in ȝour entrayle 1405
fful sadly, madame, for it is our' grounde,
On whech to beleue ful sor' are we bounde. 1407

"Dystynccyon in persones, in natur' vnite, 1408
þis is our' scole, it must be our' besynesse.
þe fader' ȝeueth to þe sune, þus be-leue we,
All substauns of deite, & he hath neuyr þe lesse ;
þe fadyr begetyth þe holy sune in blesse, 1412
þe sune is be-gotyn, þe goost fro hem too
Procedyth, þe thryd persone, þus be-lefe we, loo ! 1414

" To þe fadyr longyth myght, to þe sune cunnyng, 1415
Godeness to þe goost—þus couplede be þei, I gesse ;
And ȝet must we sey, for ony-maner' þing,

[¹But of hys goddehed, wheeh is grownd of all,
ffeythfully þe treuth tell now I schall.¹] ¹⁻¹ om. in MS. 1386

"This must ye beleue, as I toolde yow eere 1387
Whan ye were baptised, if ʒe haue mynde—
Sette youre herte ther-too and besely it leere :
Oure lord god is of swiche a kynde
That sekerly, as I of hym wreten) fynde, 1391
he is on in substauns and in nature,
Thre eke in persones, I ʒow ensure ; 1393

"Oo god, oo lord, oo makere, oo maieste, 1394
The fadir and the sone and the hooly goost,
Thre persones in oo godhed—thus beleue yee !—
Of whiche noon is smalhere ne noon is most,
Alle arn) of euene powere in euery coost ; 1398
ffor the pluralite of persones is noo preiudise
On-to the vnyte of godhed, in no-maner wyse. 1400

"And yet he þat is the fadir, is not the sone, 1401
Ne the sone the goost, withouten fayle ;
Oo wil haue thei in þat is doone,
Oo myght, oo power, oo light, oo consayle—
This lessoun muste ye hyde in your entrayle 1405
fful sadly, madame, for it is oure grovnde,
On whiche to beleue ful sore are we bovnde. 1407

"Distinccyon in personis, in nature vnite, 1408
This is oure scole, it muste ben oure besynesse.
The fadir yeueth to the sone, thus beleue we,
All substaunce of deyte, and he hath neuere the lesse ;
The fadir begeteth the hooly sone in blesse, 1412
The sone is begoten, the goost fro hem too
Procedeth, the thredde persone, thus beleue we, loo ! 1414

"To þe fadir longeth myght, to the sone kunnynge, 1415
Goodnesse to the goost—þus coupled be thei, I gesse ;
And ʒet muste we sey, for ony-maner thynge,

256 *The Virgin Mary visits St. Katharine.* [MS. Rawlinson.

Bk.III.Ch.26.
O myght, o cunnyng, & eke oo goodenesse. [1 so all MSS.; r. þow]
þat¹ þe fadyr is all-myghty, þe sune hath neuer þe lesse ;
Thow þe sune haue cunnyng, þe goost hath þe same ;
Goodenesse haue þei alle, wete ȝe wel, madame." 1421

Swech-maner' dalyauns had þese folk¹ þan), [1 r. folkis] 1422
All þoo eyte dayes, in hye communicacyon).
Mech mor' þing was seyd þan, mor' þan I can
Reherse at þis tyme—suffyseth ȝow þis lesson) ;
ffor all þoo holy wordes of swech exortacyon) 1426
May bettyr be þowth þan þei may be spoke ;
Swech langage in synfull tunge is but brok[e]. 1428

Bk.III.Ch.27.

Caᵐ. 27ᵐ.

AT þe eyte dayes ende, as was promission), 1429
Comth our' lady wyth lyght down) fro heuen) ;
Chaunged sodenly is þoo þat mansyon),
ffor it semyth now bryter' þan þe leuene.
Angellys wer' þer', mo þan sex or seuyn)— 1433
It longeth on-to hem) to do hyr' dew seruyse,
To þe emperesse of heuyn, modyr to þe hye iustyse. 1435

Many other' ladyes come þoo wyth þe qwene, 1436
Wyth mary I mene ; so ded Ihon) baptyst ;
þer' wer' eke virgines full fele, as I ween) ,
he was þer' eke Ihon) þe euangelyst.
Who had be þer', of ioye he myght a wyst ! 1440
Our' lady hyr-selfe on-to þis blyssed mayde
Swech-maner' wordes at þat tyme sayde : 1442

"Dowtyr to me, wyffe on-to my sone, 1443
My sone gretyth ȝow wyth hys good blessyng.
As he behestyd ȝow, now am I come,
To tell ȝow þe maner' of ȝoure endyng.
A tyraunt, a wers was neuyr leuyng, 1447
Schal distroye ȝour' regne, & ȝour body sle.
We wyll not ȝe repent ȝow, we wyll not ȝe fle, 1449

O myght, o konnynge, and eke o goodnesse. 1418 *Bk.III.Ch.25.*
That the fadir is almyghty, the sone hath neuer þe lesse; *Each Person of the Trinity has the others' qualities.*
Though þe sone hath connynge, the goost hath þe same;
Goodnesse haue thei alle, wete ye weel, madame!" 1421

Swiche-maner daliauns hadde þese folkis than 1422 *Adrian's teaching lasts 8 days.*
Alle the eyte dayes in hye communycacyon.
Moche more þing was seyde than, more than I kan
Reherse at this tyme—suffyseth yow this lesson;
ffor alle the hooly wordys of swiche exortacyon 1426
May better be thought thanne thei may be spoke;
Swiche langage in synful tonge is but broke. 1428

Ca^m. 26^m. *Bk.III.Ch.26.*

AT this eyte dayes ende, as was promyssion, 1429 *The 8 days ended, the Virgin Mary comes,*
Cometh oure lady wyth lyght doun from [he]uene;
Chaunged sodeynly is tho that mansyon,
ffor it semeth now bryghtere than þe leuene.
Aungellis were there, mo þan sexe or seuene— 1433
It longeth on-to hem to doo hyr dew seruyse,
To the empres of heuene, modir to the hooly Iustise. 1435

Many other ladyes come tho with þe queene, 1436
With mary I mene; so dede Iohn̄ þe baptist; *with John the Baptist, St. John, and others,*
There were eke virgynes ful fele, as I wene,
he was there eke Iohn̄ þe euaungelyst.
hoo had be there, of Ioye he myght a wyst! 1440
Oure lady hir-selue on-to this blissed mayde
Swiche-maner wordis at þat tyme sayde: 1442

"Doughter to me, wif on-to my sone, 1443 *to tell St. Katharine how she shall die.*
My sone gretheth yow now wyth his good blyssyng.
As he behested yow, now am I come,
To telle yow the maner of youre endyng.
A tyrant, wers was neuere leuyng, 1447
Shal destroye youre reigne, and your body slee.
We wil not ye repente, we wil not ye flee, 1449

KATHARINE. S

"Abydyth styll ryght in ʒour owyn place, 1450
Boldly stryue a-geyn hys tyrannye!
My sone wyll endew ʒow wyth swech grace,
Was neuyr no woman honoured so hye.
But fyrst mote ʒe sofyr schame & vylonye, 1454
losse of ʒour godys, in ʒour body passyon,
Deth at þe last, þis is þe conclusyon. 1456

"I must goo now on-to my sone a-geyn, 1457
ʒe to ʒour owne courte schall repaire.
All þis tyme þei mysse ʒow not, dar' I seyn.
ffare-wele, my dowty[r], farewel ye[1] fayre! [1] MS. þe
Whyl ʒe wyth my sone wer' in þe ayre, 1461
A qween leche to ʒow all þat tyme kept
ʒour grete a-state, sche ete & slept, 1463

"Spake & comaunded, bothe dempt & wrote— 1464
All þis dyde sche ryght in ʒour stede,
þer was no man wyth-inne þat mote[1] [1] = palace, court
þat cowde a-spye in hyr' womanhede
Ony-maner' differens, sate sche or ʒede— 1468
My sone ordeyned þis for ʒour' sake.
Whan ʒe ar' ded & ʒour corown take, 1470

"Than schall ʒe know swech preuy þingys,[1] [1] r. þing 1471
Who þei ar doo & in what maner'.
ʒet of an other' matere I ʒeue ʒow warnyngys:[1] [1] r. warnyng
þe qween ʒour modyr, þe qwych dyd ʒow bere,
Is I-pasyd & ded, leyd low on bere. 1475
But beth not dyscoumfortyd! now wyll I be
Modyr on-to ʒow, my sones wyffe, parde. 1477

"Too ʒer' in ʒour place & sumwhat more 1478
Schull ʒe dwell, or þis maxencius
Come for to spoyle ʒour tresore—
Of þat same rychesse be ʒe not desyrous.
Kepyth ʒour chambyr' wyth leuyng uertuous, 1482
Wyth prayr', fastyng, & allmes-dede,
ʒeue to þe por' folk bothe mete & wede. 1484

"Abydeth stille ryght in ȝoure owen place, 1450
Boldely stryue ageyn hys tyrannye!
Mi sone wil endewe yow wyth swiche grace,
Was neuere woman honowred soo hye.
But first mote ye suffre shame and vylonye, 1454
losse of youre good*is*, in yo*ur* body passyon),
Deth at þe laste, this is the conclusyon). 1456

Bk. III Ch.26.

The Tyrant Maxentius shall kill Katharine.

"I must goo now on-to my sone ageyn), 1457
Ye to youre owne court shal repayre.
Al this tyme thei mysse yow not, dar I seyn).
ffarweel, my dowter, farweel, ye fayre!
Qwille[1] ȝe with my sone were in the ayre,
A queen liche to yow al þis tyme kepte
Youre grete astate; she ete and slepte, 1463

[1] MS. *I wille* on er.

She is now to go back to her Court,

where her Double has personated her.

"Spak and co*m*maunded, bothe dempte and wrot—
Al this dede she ryght in youre stede, 1465
There was no man w*yth*-Inne that mote
That coude aspie in hir womanhede
Ony-man*er* differens, sat she or yede— 1468
My sone ordeyned þis for ȝoure sake.
Whan ye arn) ded an[d] yo*ur* crowne take, 1470

"Thanne shal ye knowe swiche preuy thyng*is*, 1471
how thei arn) doo and in what manere.
ȝet of a-nother mater I yeue yov warnyng*is*:
The queen) youre modir, whiche bare yow here,
Is I-passed and ded, leyd lowe on bere. 1475
But beth not discomforted, now wil I bee
Moder on-to yow—my sones wyf ar yee. 1477

The Queen, her Mother, is dead.

"Too yeer in yowre place and somwhat more 1478
Shal ye dwelle, er this Maxencyous
Come for to destroye youre tresore—
Of þ*a*t same rychesse be ye not desyrous.
Keepeth ȝoure chaumbre w*yth* leuyng virtuous, 1482
With preyng, fastynge, and elmesse-dede,
Yeue to the pore folkys bothe mete and wede. 1484

The Virgin Mary

"Aftyr þis tyme be pased & I-goo, 1485
þan shall þis tyraunt mak sone a hende
Of ȝow, doutyr, & of many moo.
þis lesson I wyll þat ȝe emprende,
Now & euyr set it in ȝour mende. 1489
ffar-wel now! fyrst I wyll ȝow kysse.
I go to my sone, to euerlestyng blysse." 1491

Thus is oure lady sodenly I-goo 1492
As now fro þis qweeṅ; sche is home eke
Vn-to Alysaundyr, myṅ auctor seyth soo—
þei þat wyll rede hyṁ, þei may it seke.
Wheyther sche cam þedyr in day or in weke, 1496
I wote noght now, but þer now sche is.
Was non all þat tyme þat dede hyr mys, 1498

ffor þat tyme whech sche was oute; 1499
þus was it ordeynyd be our soueren lorde.
þis same book whech we hafe be long a-boute,
We wyll now ende, if ȝe þer-to acorde.
God send vs alle of vnite acorde, 1503
To plese hym oonly a-boue all menne—
þer-to sey we alle wyth oo voys, AmEN. 1505

[*For the last Books, the Rawlinson MS. has been collated only.*]

MS. Arundel.] *St. Katharine is to die in two years.* 261

"After þis tyme be passed and I-goo, 1485 *Bk.III. Ch 26.*
Than shal þis tyraunt make soone an ende   *foretells St.*
Of you, doughter, and of many moo.   *Katharine's martyrdom in 2 years.*
This lessoñ I wil þat ye emprende,
Now and euere sette it in yo*ur* mende. 1489
ffarwel now ! first I wil yow kysse.
I goo to my sone, to eu*ere*-lastyng blisse." 1491

Thus is oure lady sodey[n]ly I-goo 1492
As now fro this queeñ ; she is hom eke
Vn-to Alisaundre, my auctour seyth soo—   *St. Katharine goes home to Alexandria.*
Thei that wil rede hym, þei may hym seeke.
Whether she cam theder in day or in weke, 1496
I wot not now, but there now she is.
Was nooñ al that tyme þat dede hir mys, 1498

ffor þ*a*t tyme whiche she was oute ; 1499
Thus was it ordeyned be oure sou*er*eyn lord.
This same book whiche we haue be long aboute,
We wil now ende, if ye ther-to acord̃.
God sende vs alle, of vnyte þe hord̃, 1503
To plese hym oonly a-boueñ alle meñ ;
Ther-too sey we alle w*yth* oo voys ameñ. 1505

[Liber iiij.] **Prologus.** *Bk. IV. Prol.*

These erthely dweller*is* whiche lyue now here, 1   *Folk are like bees:*
And lykened to bees whiche dwellyñ in hyue,
Or ell*is* to dranes, if that ye list to leere.
It fareth with men ryght thus in her lyue :
Some wil laboure, and some wil neu*er*e thryue, 5   *some work, some don't.*
Dyuers conceytes there bee, and eke dyuers[1] degrees.
The goode labourer*is* ar*n* lykened to the bees,   [1] *al.* dyuers ek

MS. Rawl. : 1 erdely dwellers 2 are . dwell 4 faryth 5 Sume .
neuyr 6 diu*er*se eke 7 laboures are

20 *

262 *Folk are like Bees: Workers and Drones.* [MS. Arundel.

Bk. IV. Prol.
The Workers suck good out of God's Law.

Specialy þei that oute of godd*is* lawe 8
Of dyuers parties sittynge on the floures
Leerne and teche bothe to¹ soke and drawe   ¹ *al.* om.
Of good exaumples of hooly p*r*edecessoures
Swete conceytes, weel famed sauoures— 12
Alle these ben bees, whiche to þe houshold brynge
Alle her stuf and al her gaderynge. 14

The Drones only eat, waste,

Other there be whiche ar*n* not profitable; 15
Thei ete and drynke, deuoure eke and waaste,
Thei laboure not but it be at the table—
ffor on-to werk haue þei noo grete haaste—
ffille weel her bely and yeue hem good repaaste, 19

and sleep,

Thanne wil thei slepe*n* seker with þe beste;
We sey not of hem but "dranes loue weel reste." 21

Yet to goostly laboure the dranes wil not drawe, 22

delighting not in God's Law.

ffor that in her thought*is* thei haue noo*n* delectacyo*n*,¹
In the heerynge yet of goddis lawe   ¹ This v. corrupt?
Thei not encrece ne promote her stacyo*n*;
ffor thei hem-selue to goostly occupacyo*n* 26
Wil not drawe at no mannys requeste,
Suffiseth hem her [full] bely and reste. 28

Thus semeth it to me that holy scripture is 29
In mane*r* of a feelde, with floures faire arayed;

Holy Church is the Hive,

And hooly kirke benethe, I-wys,¹   ¹ on erasure; r. þat is b. I.
She is the hyue with many stormys afrayed;

in which the good Bees store Honey.

The virtuous bees in þis hyve haue portrayed 33
her diuers cellis of hony and of wax.
What al this meneth, if 3e listen to ax, 35

Ye may it lerne: I sey the grete laboure 36
That good men haue to rede exaumples olde,
It is to hem of solace newe socour

10 to om.   13 be . wheche . housolde   15 are   17 but if it . the om.   20 slepe   21 lofe   22 the om.   23 ffor þat þei here thowte . noon om.   25 encresse   28 here full bely   31 is be-nethe   35 lyst

Katharine gathers the Honey of Faith and Love.

Bk. IV. Prol.

her virtuous lyuynge stabily to be-holde
And eke to fighte with corage fresh and bolde   40
Ageyns wordly[1] disceyuable affluens,   [1] r. þis worldys?
A-geyns the flesshly slughed[1] neȝlygens.   or. slugged   42

Oon of these bees was this same queen,   43   *Katharine is a Working Bee,*
This mayde Kataryne, whiche with besynesse
Of euery floure whiche was fayre to seen
Souked oute the hony of grete holynesse,   *being the honey of Holiness to the Hive.*
bare[1] it to the hyue, and þer she gan it dresse—   47
ffor it wil doo seruyse bothe to god and man,   [1] MS. And bare
That same likour whiche she gadered than.   49

This hony gadered she fer and wonder wyde :   50
In the lawe of nature laboured she first and[1] formest,
Where she the vyces lerned to ley a-syde,   [1] first and *al.* om.
And vertues to chese as a clenly nest,
To doo to no man, dwelled he Est or West,   54
Werre than she[1] wolde he shulde on-to hir[2] doo—   [1] or. he, [2] or. hym
This lady gadered in this feeld right soo.   56

In the wreten lawe she gadered eke moche thynge :   57   *She gathers*
The x commaundementis to kepe truly in meende ;
There lerned she the merueylous begynnynge
Bothe of the world and eke of mankeende ;
There lerned she the lame and eke þe bleende   61
To foster, and to clothe bothe oold and ȝyng—
This was hir labour, this was hir gaderyng.   63

In the lawe of grace souked she swetter mete   64
Of rippere flowris : feyth, hope, and charyte ;   *Faith, Hope, and Charity.*
She bar hem, and there she gan hem lete,
In to þis hyue to hooly cherches secree—
There ly thei yet as tresour, trust þou me ;   68

39 leuyng   41 þis werdly dec.   42 ageyne . slulkyd   44 wheche
46 the om.   47 And om.   the om.   51 first and om.   52 o syde
54 dwelle   55 he w. . hym   57 meche   58 mynde   60 mankynde
61 blynde   62 & clothe . helde   65 ryper   67 chyrches   68 trust

Bk. IV. Prol.	ho that wil labouren, may fro that swetnesse wrynge,	
	Moche beter than ony galeye can brynge.	70
	And foorth in this swetnesse wil we now procede,	71
	Whiche þat she gadered, this lady, here lyuande.	
May we go to Heaven,	God sende vs part, ryght as we haue neede,	
	In vertuous leuynge stabely to stande,	
	And for to come[1] to þat heuenly lande [1] r. comen	75
where Katharine now is!	Where she is now. for foorth to oure processe	
	Vndir hir socoure streit I wil me dresse.	77

Bk. IV. Ch. 1.

liber iiij$^{us.}$

Ca$^{m.}$ primu$m$.

Rome has 3 Emperors :	IN the tyme of Costus, as oure bookys telle,	78
	Were thre Emperour*is* in rome Citee :	
I. Maximinus Galerius,	The firste was a man of herte ful felle,	
	Maximin*us* galerius, right soo hight he ;	
II. Maximian,	The secunde hight Maximian ; the threde, [parde],[1]	82
III. Diocletian.	Was named at that tyme dioclyciane— [1] MS. lerne ye	
	he was many a cristen mannys bane.	84
No. I. stops at home ;	The firste emp*er*our, Maximin*us* galerie,	85
	Dwelled stille at rome, and kepte there þe pees,	
	The domes, the sacryfises dede he tho gye.	
nos. II. and III. sent out to fight,	The other too men with-outen ony lees	
	Were sent oute with ful grete prees,	89
	To brenne and slee, to take and to saue—	
	This was office bothe to knyght and knaue.	91
	But these same too for very werynesse	92
resign to no. I.	leften here hono*ur* and resigned her right ;	
	fful gret excuse had thei, in sekernesse :	
	Thei seyde her grete labo*ur* and her fight	
	A-vayle hem right nought now it myght,	96
	ffor the more thei dede þe more þei had to doo.	
	Wherfore, in sekernesse, thus thei too	98

69 laboure   74 lyuyng stably   76 to hyre pr.   82 parde   83 dyocleciane   86 dwelt   87 sac*ri*fyces . dyd   88 any   93 left

MS. Arundel.] *Maxentius is made Emperor of Rome.*

Resigned her right on-to this same[1] man ; [1] r. s. first? 99
And he vndir hym made thre Emperouris,
To helpe his empere al þat thei may and can,
In alle batailłis, in alle sharpe shouris,
To wynne Citees, Castellis, tounes and towris. 103
The first hight Maximinus, as seyth the gest—
he was assigned to gouerne al the Est ; 105

[To] the seconde, whiche hight tho seuere, 106
Was eke assigned the kepynge of lumbardye,
Of almayn, Tussy—the story seyth soo heere—
And many other contrees in that partye
Vndir his power were trybutarye. 110
Eke of brytayn, the lond in whiche we dwelle,
Was Constantyne made lord, the sothe to telle. 112

The first Emperour, Maximinus galerius, 113
ffor pryde and sorwe and synful lyf
Was killed in a batayll—the story seith thus ;
he had defouled many a mayde and wif,
And therfore, er he deyed oute of this stryf, 117
he stank on erthe as euere dede carayn—
lete hym goo walke on sarysbury playn. 119

Tho took þe romaynis the ʒonge maxens, 120
Sone on-to the[1] Maximine þat was in þe[1] Est ; [1] al. om.
Thei corouned hym rially with gret expens,
With moche solennyte and ful grete fest.
The fame wente oute to more and to lest 124
Tha[t][1] he was emperour, and his fadir forsake. [1] MS. Thanne
This made his fadir, short tale to make, 126

To leue his conquest and come to rome there. 127
But er he cam there, his pride was I-cast :
In Cecile he deyede—right soo dede I lere
Of cronycles whiche [þat] I saugħ last—

Bk IV. Ch. 1.
The Emperor, Maximinus Galerius,

makes Maximinus ruler of the East;

Severus, ruler of Lombardy, &c.;

and Constantine lord of Britain.

On Galerius's death,

Maxentius is made Emperor of Rome.

His father, Maximinus, dies in Sicily.

101 empyre . or can 102 batayles . schowres 103 wyne . town
106 And to 111 weche 112 the om. 113 þis 117 or 118 erde
119 in salysbury 121 the om. þe om. 122 realy 123 myche
125 þat 128 or 129 cycile . deyd 130 wheche þat . sey

Bk. IV. Ch. 1.	There blew he oute his endyng blast;	131
	And there leyth[1] he to abyden his chauns, [1] r. lyght = lyth	
	Whet[h]er it be to weepyng or to dauns.	133
Severus raises an army	This seuerus eke þat dwelled in lumbardie,	134
	Gadered vp almayn and al his myght,	
	ffor with þis eleccíon had he grete enuye;	
	Therfore bothe be day and eke be nyght	
	he laboured be wrong and [eke] with right	138
against Maxentius,	To destroye this Maxence, sooth for to sayn,	
	That he myght reigne whan he were slayn.	140
	But er he cam fully at this same rome,	141
but is slain by his own men.	he was slayn of his sowdyouris be the weye.	
	Than was there no more for to doone,	
	But maxence regneth, the sooth for to seye,	
	As now allone—euery man must obeye	145
	If he wil keepen his lyf on lofte;	
	But if he doo soo, he slepeth not ellis softe.	147
Maxentius turns tyrant in Rome.	Thus regned this Maxence in rome al allone;	148
	No man spak to hym what-euere he wil doo;	
	There was noo mayde, noo wif ne noon matrone,	
	But whan he sente, þei muste come hym too	
	To suffre his lust, to suffre what he wil doo;	152
	What husbond letted it he shuld a-noon be deed,	
	Vp-on his ȝate thei shulde setten his heed.	154
	he turned the lawe, al wente than be powere;	155
The people curse the womb that bore him.	The puple curs l the wombe þat hym had born.	
	Was noo man durste[1] in open langage there [1] MS. that d.	
	Ones sey to hym "lord, youre lawe is lorn!"	
	Of al the senate sette he but a scorn;	159
	Pride and power hadden enhaunced hym soo,	
	Al þat he coueyted he wolde haue it doo.	161

132 lyghte . abyde   133 wheythyr . or ellys   134 dwelt   138 laboureth . & eke   139 sothe   141 or   144 the om.   146 kepe . o lofte   147 slepe   149 speke   150 ne no   153 lett   154 sett   156 pepyll   157 that om.   160 had enhaunsed   161 coueyte . haf

Ca^m. 2^m.

Tho the romaynis,[1] with a comoun consente,	162	The Romans appeal to Constantine
letteris preuyly of grete sentens ded wryte		
And in to bretayn to Constantyn hem sente,		
In whiche þei preyed hym, as he was knyte,	[1 MS. tyrannyte]	
That he com helpe hem ageyn this tyra[unt to fyght][1];		
Thei wolde be-traye hym, thei seyde, he[2] shuld not spede;		
This was her ende: "come helpe vs at oure nede!"	[2 MS. þat he]	to help them.

A-noon þis man dede gadere a grete strengthe	169	He raises a great army,
Bothe of þis lond and of fraunce there-too;		
Euere gan his ost encrece in brede and lengthe		
Be euery contree in whiche he gan goo;		
In Ytayle reysed he up puple many moo	173	
Thanne euere dede seuere, right for þis tyrannye		
Of this fals Maxence and for his lecherye.	175	

he is at rome; the oostis to-gedir mete.	176	and reaches Rome.
But maxcence trusteth[1] oonly in the Citee there;		
he is deceyued, allone thei hym lete	[1 MS. trursteth]	
With his hushold, in moche care and fere.		
Be this exaumple wyse men may weel leere	180	
To truste on the puple; for thei wil faile at nede.		
Soo dede thei here; for streite fro hym thei yeede	182	

To constantyn, that now cam fro bretayn.	183	
Thus [is] he fledde, the same Maxcencius,		Maxentius
Deceyued rigtfully thus be her trayn—		
Right for his leuyng, that was soo vicyous.		
he fledde to perse, and there as man victorious	187	flees to Persia, where he fights well,
Dede grete thyngis, and many strengthes wan;		
Soo as for lord, and for he was a man,	189	

Thei crowned hym there and called hym kyng of pers.		and is made King.
Thus hath constantyn wonne the feeld this day,	191	

163 wryght   165 preyd. a knyte   166 tyraunt to fyght   167 þat om.   169 strenght   171 lenght   176 hostys. mette   177 trostyth. on   178 lette   179 howsholde. meche   180 ensaumple   181 in   182 so streyt   184 is he   186 lyuyng   187 vyctorous   188—263 om., as a leaf is torn out.

268 Maxentius orders Christians to be persecuted. [MS. Arundel.

Bk. IV. Ch. 2.

The other tyrant is put al to the wers.
Al this is told to this ende, sooth to say,
To knowe how Maxcens with soo grete aray   194
Cam to Alysaundre swiche maystries for to make,
Whan he this lady dede arreste and take.   196

ffor whan he was thus exalted in pers,   197
Thus set in astate and in his faderis office,

Maxentius grows wickeder in Persia,

Tho wex he in condiciouns euere wers and wers,
And more enclyned to synne and to vice.
he sente oute letteris on-to euery Iustice   201

and orders Christians to be hung.

To serche the cristene, to hange hem and to-drawe;
ffor truly, he seyth, he wil destroye that lawe. 203

These letteris come to surry al aboute,   204

He goes to Syria,

And he hym-self folwed after hem sone.
The Copy of hem I wil with-outen dowte
Write here in english, me thenketh it is to doone.
"The lord of lordis that dwelleth[1] vnder the moone, 208
Maxcens, the emperour of pers with-outen peere,   [1] *al.* dwel
Greteth weel oure lyges thurgh-oute oure empere. 210

"We wil ye wete, oure faderis here-be-forn), 211
That wurshiped goddis with her dew seruyse,
Were neuere in bataill neyther conuycte ne lorn):
Sweche was the keepynge of goddis tho[1] ben wise [1] r. þat

bids his folk turn from Christ's law,

Ouere her puple. therfore we, as Iustise   215
And as a preest in religyon of saturne,
Wil that ȝe alle fro alle veyn lawes turne;   217

"Moost specyal fro cryst whiche heyng on tree; 218
That noo man be soo hardy hym for to name!
What-maner god[1] shuld he now be   [1] r. of god?
That was I-brought in to swiche fame
To be hanged on a tree with so moche shame?   222
Therfore noo man dwellynge now in oure lond
Shal be so hardy, neyther free ne bond,   224

and not even name Him.

"To name hym oones, or for to sette   225
his merke in þe forhed, as is the vsage

Of alle these cristen! we wil hem lette
Of alle her cerymonyes and her pylgrimage;
If that thei forfete,[1] thei shul haue wage   [1] MS. forȝete   229
Swiche as thei deserue[1] for to haue;   [1] r. deseruen
lordshipe ne richesse shal hem noon[1] saue.   [1] al. not   231

"Therfore, what man oony godd*is* honoure   232
Other than we doo now in oure sette,
We wil þat thei be take w*yth* officeris oure
And led to preson with-outen ony lette;
We wil ordeyn for hem swiche a gette   236
Thei shul neuere eft swiche maystries make
In all her lyue, and that we vnder-take."   238

This is the sentens of the letteris longe   239
Whiche he sente oute on-to al the Est;
Commaundynge lord*is* and knyghtes stronge
That thei come in hast, bothe more and leest,
And in most specyal on-to that grete feest   243
Whiche he wil make w*yth* ful grete store
That ilke same day whiche he was boore.   245

The massanger*is* arn goon bothe fer and wyde   246
To bere these copyes in to diuers londe.
The emperour hym-self, he wil abyde
On-to that tyme, as I vndirstonde,
In grete Alisaundre with ful myghty honde;   250
In whiche Citee eke this noble queen soo dere
W*yth* a preuy mene leued al in preyere.   252

To this Citee cam kyng, and soo ded queen,   253
Theder cam lord*is*, mo than I can telle;
The Innes arn ful as hyues of been;
There is now not elles but bye and selle,
In specyal mete and drynk—for there was neuere welle   257
More plenteuous of watir than was the cytee of mete,
Soo were thei stored there, the marchaunt*is* grete.   259

Whanne alle were come whiche shuld be there,   260
The Emperour thre poynt*is* dede tho declare,

270   *Maxentius's Edict against Christians.*   **[MS. Arundel.**

Bk IV. Ch. 2.   Whiche poynt*is*, he seyde, with-oute*n* dwere,
                   Euene as thei in sentens stood plat and bare,

Maxentius commands   he wulde euery man, what-soo-eue*r*e he ware,   264
                        Or in what parti he dwelled of his domynacyo*n*),
                        Shulde keepe hem, in peyne of damnacyo*n*).   266

Bk. IV. Ch. 3.   Ca*m*. 3*m*.

Christians to give up their Faith,   The firste poynt was that Criste*n* alle and sum   267
                                        Muste leue her feyth and that grete honour
                                        Whiche that thei doo to crist, godd*is* so*n*),
                                        Whom eke thei clepe[1] now her salua*t*our ;   [1] r. clepen
                                        " his disciples in to ful grete errour   271
                                        haue brougĥt alle me*n*) þ*a*t wil tende hem too,
                                        Right w*yth* the feyned myracles that thei doo.   273

                                        " Therfore wil we that thei come now alle   274
                                        To oure p*r*esens, for to see and here

and take up   What-man*er* decree þ*a*t we yeue shalle
                On-to swiche witches, bothe ferre and nere ;
                We thenke for to make oure lawe ful clere,   278
                And whanne alle ar*n*) looked, to chese þe beste ;

his Religion.   This is the religio*n*) that we haue keste."   280

                   The seconde poynt whiche he shewed tho,   281
                   Was this : he seyde " thei had remembrauns

He was deprived of Rome   how that of rome no*t* longe a-goo
                              he helde the honour and al the goue*r*nauns ;   284
                              But be-trayed he was with hem of Bretay*n*) and frans,[1]

by Constantine,   Whiche oo*n*) Constantyne had brought in-feere,   [1] MS. of frans
                     A grete puple and a statly powere.   287

                    " Thus had this traytour," he seyde, " this constanty*n*),
                    As a fals intrusore entred in to his lande,   289

who had won his city.   Wonne his Citee with gonnes and w*yth* my*n*),
                           There myght no wal ne noo tour tho stande "—
                           Thus bar Maxcens the lord*is* on hande   292

264 wold   265 dwelt   269 sunne   274 come om.   277 wycchys .
fere   279 are   280 hafe   282 remembrauns   283 who   285 of 2
om.   287 stately   290 gu*n*nes

Whiche were w*yth* hym at Alisaundre that tyde;
"Wherfore sekyrly," he seyth, "he wil ryde   294
   "Euene to rome, his right to conquere,   295
To venge hym on this tyraunt, on þis Constantyn;"
Wherfore he preyed the lord*is* that ben there
That "thei shal be redy w*yth* bowes and engyn;
ffor he wil rewarde hem with yeftes good and fyn,   299
With rentes, londes, castell*is* and toures eke;
If thei wynne rome, rychesse nede hem not seeke."   301

   The thredde poynt whiche þ*at* he purposed there,   302
Sittynge hym-selue right in the p*ar*lemente:
he seyde " he wolde renewe with-oute[n] dwere
Alle tho seruyseȝ and al that dew rente
Whiche to the goddis was ordeyned be comon assent; 306
The godd*is*," he seyde, " shul[d] be more p*ro*picyous,
If þ*at* here ceremonyes were renewed thus."   308

   A bysshop stood vp tho with myter and w*yth* croos, 309
Swiche as þei vsed tho in her lawe.
There was cryed " eu*er*y man keepe cloos
his mouth and his tunge, and [h]erkene to this sawe!"
Whan he had his breth a litel while I-drawe,   313
Thus spak he thanne in man*er* of sermonyng: [1] he s. to be om.
" I wil ȝe weten," he seyth,[1] " þ*at* Iubiter, þ*at* hey kyng,

   " hath turned awey his good conseruacye[1]   [1] MS. conseruatye
ffrom al oure nacyon, I telle ȝow shortly why: 317
We haue forsaken hym and falle in maumentrye—
Many of vs heere, I drede me, ar gylty
In this same mater. wherefor Iubyt*er* almyghty,   320
And saturne, his fadir, be preuy op*er*acion[1]   [1] *al.* apparicyon
In sleep yone warnynge be very reuelacion: 322

   " Thei bode we shulde þe puple teche to renewe   323
The olde Cerymonyes and the old rightes[1]   [1] r. rites

Side notes:
Bk. IV. C). 3.
Maxentius will attack Constantine in Rome.
He will revive the dues of the heathen Gods.
A heathen Bishop
reproaches the Alexandrians, &c., with having forsaken Jupiter.
They must renew his worship.

297 be   302 thyrd   304 w*yth*-outen   306 ordeynd   309 crose
310 vsed om.   312 herken to hys   315 wetyne . iupit*er*. hye   316 conseruacye   318 forsak . fall   321 apparicyon   324 held . elde rytes

Bk. IV. Ch. 3.
A heathen Bishop

Whiche oure faderis vsed or we ony thyng knewe,
And soo vsed many lordes and many knyghtes.
ho ȝeueth¹ us helpe in pees or in fyghtes ¹ MS. he ȝoueu 327
But Iubyter allone? helth euere up-on hym,
honcure and seruyse to hym and [to] his kyn. 329

exalts the great God Jupiter,

" Noman may maken so grete maystrye 330
As Iubiter dooth whan he wyth anger quaketh;
The grete thunder whyche he maketh flye, ¹ MS. horrrible
The horrible¹ lightnyngis whiche he maketh,
Alle these shewe² to vs þat what man hym forsaketh, 334
he is ful likly wyth vengeauns to be brent. ² MS. shewed
Turne to hym ageyn therfore, lest ȝe be not¹ shent! 336
  ¹ corr. to nov

denounces Christ,

" Leueth alle these newe thyngis, keepe stille your olde!
What shal crist a-mongis goddis? put hym in place! 338
The shepherdis and ploughmen in feeld and in foolde,
Thei wote weel it stant not in mannys grace
On-to al the world saluacyon to purchace, 341
As seyn these cristen, for crist, as seyth her book,
With his blood fro the world alle synnes took. 343

" he muste ben eterne that shal swiche thyngis doo 344
That yeue encrece to ilke generacyon—
ffor to a god of ryght this it longeth, loo,
To haue in his nature euerelestynge duracyon.

and bids the people withstand Him.

Repelleth fro ȝoure counseyl this cristen nacyon, 348
This charge I ȝow in [þe] goddis name;
Saue your soules and your bodyes fro blame!" 350

This was the sentens of this grete sermoun 351
Whiche þat the bisshop at þat tyme spak;
And this was eke his determynacion
That no man in that lond, but he wil to þe rak
And on the same ly with a broken bak, 355

326 knytes 327 who ȝeueth . fytys 329 & to 330 make 331 hangyr 333 lytenynge eke 334 schew 336 not 337 leue . þis 338 among 339 scheperdys . plowmen 340 full well 341 On 342 sey þis 344 be 345 þat schall ȝeue 348 counsell 349 þe g. 354 in to þe rak 355 þat

MS. Arundel.] *Maxentius in the heathen Temple.*

Be so hardy in [no]¹ maner of wise   ¹ corr. to ony   *Bk. IV. Ch. 3.*
Speke ageyn þe goddis or her seruyse.   357

Ca^{m.} quartum.   *Bk. IV. Ch. 4.*

The Citee of Alisaundre, whiche his ful large,   358   Alexandria is cram-full.
It his now replesshid wyth-oute and wyth-Inne
With lordes and ladyes¹—there was many a barge
At the princypal poort, for thei lay not thynne.   ¹ MS. with l.
Weel his he at ease [þat may cacch an Inne],¹   ¹ MS. in to the toun) may wynne
The puple was so gret, the prees was so strong.
There is [now] not ellis but trumpynge and soong: 364

ffor [þe] nyght was come of that feestful day   365   On the eve of Maxentius's birthday,
In whiche Maxcens was bore; therfor he ded crye
That euery man there shal in his best aray
Sercle the Citee with noyse and menstralsye.
he þat shal sleepe this nyght, must be ful slye   369
That he be not perceyued, for indignacyon
Whiche he shal haue for he went not his stacyon!   371

There was noyse of trompes and noyse of men,   372
Moche more of beestes that deyed in her blood—   many beasts are kild.
ffor al þat nyght sekirly, ye may ful weel ken,
The bocheres laboureden as thei had be wod;   ¹ al. don)
The wasshynge of the carkeys doun¹ in the flood   376
Shewed the gret moordre of the bestes slayn:
The water was al blody, sauely dar I sayn.   378

To the temple thei goo the nexte day be-tyme.   379   Next morning, in the Temple,
The bisshopes haue arayed hem to do the seruyse—
There was noo matynes seyd, [seruyse]¹ ne pryme,   ¹ MS. houres, on eras.
Thei had another [vsage]¹ than I can deuyse.   ¹ MS. seruyse
Thus moche can I sey, the emperour as Iustise   383   Maxentius is set on high.
Was set vp-on hy, that he myght al see
how the puple honoured that solennyte.   385

356 no manere wyse   358 is   360 with₂ om.   361 no th.   362 ese þat may cacche an Inne   364 now . song   365 þe nyte   372 trumpys   375 laboured   376 carcays done   378 as . sauerly   379 tempille   381 matens . seruyse   382 anodyr vsage   385 who . solempnite

KATHARINE.   T

2 1

274 Heathen Services on Maxentius's Birthday. [MS. Arundel.

Bk. IV. Ch. 4.

Thei kneled and thei cried w*yth* marred deuocyon)—

Maxentius's Gods are
Al this be-held the emp*er*our with sad y3e,
ffor euere-more hath he a fals suspecyon)
That some arn) there whiche wil not sacrifye.
The firste god of alle, whiche stood moost hye, 390

1. the Sun,
Was the bryght sonne with his hors and cart,
Whiche was I-graue of ful sotil art ; 392

2. the Moon,
Next was the mone whiche we clepe dyane, 393
With hir wellis nyne and the maydenes eke ;

3. Saturn,
Next hir was saturne with his bitter bane
And his sekel in hande—[many me*n* hym) seke],[1]
ffor noon) other cause but whan) þei are seeke, 397
Thei wene tha[n][1] it were of his vengeauns— [1 MS. that]
Soo cruel is his planete in his goue*r*naun*s* ! 399

[1 MS. as men) seyn in greke, on erus.]

The auter next hym was ful weel arayed, 400
4. Jupiter, On whiche that Iubiter stood al on hy,
with Juno, With his wyf Iuno, ful weel I-portrayed ;
Venus, Venus the fayre, she stood next by,
Cupid, With hir blynde sone, Cupyde,—soo wene I, 404
Thei calle hym soo þ*a*t owe hym seruyse,
I owe hym noon), for mawmentrie I despise. 406

and others. Moche more thyng was there, not to purpos now ; 407
But thus moche I telle : there were grete offrynges,
Sacrifices are made, Thei spared neyther hors, oxe, beer ne kow,
But " slee and slee," these were her crienges.
rites and songs performd. The bysshoppys and the prestes, thei doo her þinges ; 411
The menstrall*is* faile not, for thei shal haue wage ;
Euery man maketh noyse after his age. 413

The olde seyde they seyn neue*r*e in her dayes 414
Swiche a-nother sacryfise as this emp*er*our
hath renewed in her temple, in many-mane*r* layes,[1]
" The grete godd*is* alle thei sende hym honour,
long lif and stable, make hym a conquerour." 418

[1 on erasure, al. wayes.]

389 some om. are   391 bryth*e* su*n*ne   396 many me*n* hym*e* seke
398 þan . veniaunce   402 I-porterayed   408 offeryngis   410 cryingis
412 mynstrelles . shul   414 elde . sey   416 wayes (corr. fr. dayes)

MS. Arundel.] *Katharine hears the Alexandrians' revel.* 275

The ȝong men daunced Iolyly on þe¹ grounde ;	¹ MS. þat	Bk. IV. Ch. 4.
There was reuel a-mongis hem, lightly and rounde	420	
Traced thei þat tyme at that solennyte.	421	
The noyse is herd a-bowte a myle on euery syde.		
Thus leue I hem in myrthe, [þese seres stoute],	¹ ¹ MS. withoute ennyte	
Thus arn thei occupyed in ful moche² pryde.	² r. in mechil	
The emperour hym-self looketh [on euery syde],³		Maxentius closely
ho dooth moost reuerens to his goddis there.	³ MS. tho ful wyde, on erasure.	watches everything.
This made the cristen to haue ful grete fere.	427	

          Cam. **qui**n**tum.**   Bk. IV. Ch. 5.

Owre noble mayde, oure hooly devoute queene	428	
To whom this story loongeth as now oonly,		
This hooly virgyn Kataryn, hir I¹ meene,	¹ MS. I hir	Katharine, in her study,
Was tho in silens syttynge in hir stody		
Al contemplatyf, spered fro hir meny ;	432	
The wordly welthes arn now fro hir shake,		
After the tyme that cryst hath hir thus take	434	
To wyf or spouse—reede lyke as ȝe lyst.	435	
This mayden was there and herd tho þis cry.		hears the noise,
"O ihesu," seyde she, "I wolde now þat I wist		
What that it meneth, the noyse that is so hy."		
Knyghtis were walkynge thre or foure faste-by,	439	
Waytynge vp-on hir ; thus to hem seyde she :		
"This grete noyse, seres, what may it bee ?"	441	
"I-wis, madame," tho seyde an olde seruaunt,	442	and is told that it is for Maxentius's birthday.
"The emperour Maxcens, this day was he bore,		
he hath commaunded to olde man¹ and [to] faunt²	¹ MS. men ² MS. infaunt	
The olde rightis, the³ seruycis to restore	³ MS. and the, and overl.	
Whiche to⁴ the goddis longe⁵ and [haue] doo yoore.	446	
This is the cri, if ȝe wil wete al-gate.	⁴ MS. haue to ⁵ longet, orig. longeth	
No man on lyue, pouere ne of astate,	448	

    419 ioylyly . þe   420 amonge   423 þese seres stoute   424 ar .
ful om. mechil   425 lokyth on euery syde   426 who do   430 hire
I m.   432 sperdo   433 are   435 ryth inst. of lyke   436 mayd   442
a elde   444 eld . & to faunt   445 elde rythes . and om. seruises
446 haue om. long . haue do   448 of l. . pore

                                                                                      T 2

Bk. IV. Ch. 5.

"Is [not]¹ so hardy this mater to disobeye; 449
Thei shal be ded that ageyns it speke. ¹ so all other MSS.

Katharine is told to keep in her closet,
Keepe stille youre closet, there is no more to seye—
It is¹ not oure power his wil [for]² to breke; ¹ overlined. ² so all other MSS.
lete hem¹ calle, lady, lete hem¹ crye and creke, ¹ MS. hym 453
suffyseth¹ you if ye may leue in pees. ¹ MS. it s.
The man is comerous, with-oute[n] ony lees: 455

as Maxentius
"ffor he hath made, if ȝe wil leue me, 456
A strong decree, whiche he wil we keepe:

has orderd that all shall adopt his religion,
That alle sectys of his secte now shul bee,
The child, anoon as he gynneth to krepe,
Shal be taught vp-on the goddis to cleepe, 460
In peyne of deth the faderis shal hem teeche—
This herde I this day the grete bysshop preeche. 462

"Wherfore, madame, now is come that hour 463
That was dred tho¹ of youre freendes alle ¹ al. tho dred
Whan that ye wolde receyue no counseillour,
ffor no thyng that men myght on-to¹ [you] calle. ¹ al. on, vppon
I amful soory, for now are² lykly to falle ² MS. are ȝe ³ MS. And all 467
aH³ tho myshappes whiche that'⁴ were seyde before. ⁴ al. om.
Avyse ȝow weel what ye wil doo [þerfore]⁵!" ⁵ MS. now more, on erasure.

She remembers
Whan the mayden had herd these wordis alle, 470
She gan remembre hough oure lady sayde,
Whan she passed fro hir, what shuld be-falle—
She spak thus: "to you I telle, my mayde,

the Virgin Mary's warning.
Yee shal heer-after been ful soore afrayde 474
Off an enmye bothe to my sone and to¹ me"— ¹ al. om.
At hir leue-takyng swiche woordis seyde she, 476

Oure blyssed lady mary, to this queen. 477
Therfore the queen thought: "now is the hour

. 449 Is not   452 forto   453 hem . hem   454 It om. Suffisith .
lyue   455 comorows . wyth-outen   456 haue   458 settis   461 shul
464 þoo drede   465 concelloure   466 on yow   467 ȝe om.   468 And
om.   that om.   469 þerfore   470 þis mayd . þeis   471 how   474
be   475 a . & me   478 þis

Whiche she behested, now is it weel I-seen)
Right be þe booldnesse of this emperour
Whiche ageyn) oure makere and creatour   481
Thus boldely ryseth in destruccion) of his name,
Whoos wyf I am and seruaunt to his dame."   483

Tho she remembred what conuenaunt [þat] she made
Right in hir baptem whan she washed was,   485
Eke in hir weddynge, with beheestes ful sade:
That she shulde neuere, for more ne for las,
Though she were throwe in hote cawdron) of bras, 489
fforsake hir loue whyche she hadde oonly chose.
Tho wex she ruddy and fayre as the rose,   490

Right in remembrauns of þat swete spousayle 491
Whiche þat she caught be leedynge of Adryane;
It is so emprended with-inne hir entrayle,
Of werdly lustes there shal no fekyl fane
Blowe it awey; neyther Iuno, Venus ne Dyane, 495
ffrom) hir herte this loue thei shul not race.
Thus walked she foorth softly than) a-pace, 497

fful sore astoyned what hir is beste for to doo. 498
If she holde silens, þan) is she not truwe
Of hir beheestes—right soo thought she, loo.
The fair ryng whiche was somwhat blewe,[1]   [1] MS. blowe?
Whiche was eke youe hir at hir weddynge newe, 502
She tho beheld, and seyde thus be hir oone:
"ffy on) the world, fy on) crowne and trone!   504

"I shal keepe that truthe whiche þat I [made][1]   505
On-to myn) husbond, though I shulde be ded—   [1] MS. dede make
I shal the sonnere come to hym) that [me made][2];
ffor in this world is nought but sleep and dreed. 508
Allas, that euere ony lord or hed   [2] MS. deyed for my sake, on eras.

484 cōnaunt þat   485 baptim   490 a rose   496 ffro in   498 for om.   499 trewe   501 blewe   505 made   506 my   507 soner. me made   508 brede

278 Katharine goes to the Heathen Temple. [MS. Arundel.

Bk. IV. Ch. 5.

Shulde thus bodyly¹ men dragge and drawe ¹ r. boldly
Ageyns all truthe, ageyns a ryghtful lawe ! 511

Why does Christ let the Heathen rage?

"Why sufferyth my spouse now swiche cursed men 512
To breke his cherches, his seruauntes for to kylle?
Oo cause there is oonly, þat weel I ken :
his seruauntes here shul not haue her wylle—
hoo-so loue this woord,¹ þat loue [will]² hym spylle ; 516

His servants must suffer tribulation here.

Tribulacion is ordeyned for his seruauntys here, ¹ on eras. ² MS. shal
Whiche to heuene shul, streyt fro the beere." 518

Bk. IV. Ch. 6.

Caᵐ· sextuₘ.

Katharine walks out,

Thus walketh she foorth soberly a-paas 519
  Thurgh hir paleys, she hath forgete al thyng.
Thei folwe hir eke, the seruauntis of þat plas,
Not many, but some, for thei goo to the kyng ;
Thei wot not eke what she in hir goyng 523
Purposeth to doo—for be-twix loue and fere
Staker the seruauntis alle tho¹ she hath there. ¹ al. that 525

The temple-gatis soo ful of puple now bee, 526
Soo ful repleshed no man may entre there ;
And euere on-to the porteres thus seyde shee :

and asks entrance at the Temple gates.

"lete us entre, lete vs oure erande bere
On-to the emperour ! for and he wist what we were, 530
he wolde not suffre vs no while stonde with-oute.
We wil hym lerne soone wyth-outen dowte 532

"These solennytes better for to make, 533
Not to no vanyte, to¹ noon presumpsion, ¹ MS. ne to
But to his wurshipe that al thyng dede [make]."¹ ¹ MS. shape
This was at þat tyme hir peroracyon.

Foreign Lords meet her.

Tho mette she lordis of ful straunge nacyon, 537
Whiche had parfoormed her offryngis and I-doo,
fforth to her Innes thei dresse[d] hem to goo ; 539

510 boldly 511 treughth 512 sufferth 513 chirchis 516 who
loueth . world . will hem 520 pales . forgote 525 alle þat 529 late
533 Theis 534 ne om. no 535 wirchip . make 539 dressyd

The emp*er*our*is* son*e* cam with these lord*is* in-feere. 540   *Bk. IV. Ch. 6.*
But wha*n* thei sey*n* this lady soo bryght and shene,   Maxentius's son and his lords
Thei turned her Iornay, and with ful mery chere
Thus spoke*n* thei alle ful goodly to the queene :
" Madame," thei seyde*n*, " the grete puple that ʒe seene
Ar*n* come fro ferre with grete deuocyo*n* ;
Blame hem nought though þei wolde haue doo*n* !   546

" But we shal, lady, right for youre reuerens   547
Turne with yow on-to the temple ageyn ;
We shal make space with strengthe and resistens,   clear Kátharine's
That ʒe shal entre, shortly for to sey*n*."
With mace and manace thei made bare the pley*n*,   551
Til she was entred right to the[1] hye autere.   [1] MS. that   way to the high Altar.
Tha*n* seyde she suche woordes, liche as ye shal heere ;

Thus she be-ga*n* and thus she spak to hym :   554
" Bothe keende and curtesye wolde teche us this   She reproaches
To honoure thi crowne, be-cause of thi ky*n*,
And ʒet for thi degree moche more, I-wys ;
Alle this shulde excite vs the for to blis   558
And for to loute with reue*r*ens, ne were oon thyng
Whiche þou hast doo ageyns the grete[s]t[1] kyng,   [1] MS. gretet, *al.* grete

" Lord of alle lordys, ihesu crist I mene :   561   the Emperor for paying to Idols the honour due to Christ,
Thou takest here fro hym his hy honour,
And yeuest it to maumentys, as is weel seene,
Whiche may neyther helpe the ne eke socour
In noon of thi causes, in no-man*er* dolour.   565
But if þou woldest[1] leue this cursed ydolatrie   [1] r. wold
And knowe thy god that sitte a-boue ful hye,   567

" Whiche made the sonne, þe sterr*is* and the mone,   568   who made the Heavens.
Thanne wolde we honoure the w*yth* dew seruyse,
Knele dou*n* on-to the and oure homage ful soone
ffor to brynge on-to the as oure Iustise.
But be-cause ageyn crist þou makyst men ryse   572

541 sey 543 spake 544 seyde 545 Ar*e* 547 right om. 552 þe 553 shull*e* 558 þes*e* 559 o 560 grete 566 wold 567 sitt 568 þe om. 572 to ryse

Bk. IV. Ch. 6. And worshepe swiche deueles as ben in helle,
Katharine refuses to honour Maxentius, Therfore shortly, syr, I wil the telle : 574

"Oure seruyse wil we for a tyme wyth-drawe 575
Right fro thi persone, til þou þe amende.
unless he turn from Idolatry; Turne fro this cursednesse, fro this wikked lawe,
Knowe now thi makere that all þing can sende,
On-to his byddynge looke þou condescende! 579
Than shal þou haue[1] more prosperyte [1] r. hauen?
Than euere þou hadde yet, truste vp-on me! 581

"These cristen men[1] here whiche are I-drawe [1] r. folkis?
To offere to þin ydoles magre[1] her hed, [1] MS. m. in
A-geyns all reson, ageyn al the lawe
Thou thretest hem with turment and wyth ded,
With bath of pich and beuerych of leed. 586
I sorwe for her sake, thei dar non other doo;
If thei were stable, þei shulde not werke soo. 588

his Gods are Devils, "Thi goddis arn deuellis, and thi preestis eke 589
Disceyuouris of þe puple, right for couetyse;
Thei wote as weel as I, though men hem seke,
senseless Idols. These maumentis I mene, þei can not sitte ne ryse;
Thei ete not, [þei][1] drynke not in no maner of wise; 593
Mouth wyth-oute speche, foot that may not goo, [1] MS. ne
handes eke haue thei and may noo werk doo. 595

He must give them up, "Wherfore turne thyn herte fro thys illusyon, 596
Knowe thy god that made þe and alle þing for the,
Be not vnkeende in thi condicyon
Ageyn thi makere, ageyn the trynyte!
But if þou be amended, thou shalt leue me 600
or be punisht everlastingly. Grete peynes god shal the sende,
Whiche peynes shul neuere haue [an] eende." 602

573 þat be   574 sothly   580 þou . nore   582 þeis   583 in om.
584 agens . ageyns   589 are   593 þei drynke . of om.   599 Ageyns
602 a ende

Ca^m. 7^m.

The emperour be-held hir woord*is* and hir chere, 603 *The Emperor Maxentius*
Wonderynge sore hough she durste be soo boolde
Be-fore swiche puple right in his presens there,
And not considerynge the feste whiche he had holde—
ffor that same tale whiche she hath now toolde 607
Durste noo man telle, but if he wolde be deed,
hir fair colour be-twixe[1] whight and reed, [1] r. betwixen?

Whiche shone ful bryght, he gan to be-hoolde, 610
Astoyned with [hir] bewte, *pa*rty w*yth* hir plesauns.
fful sobyrly his armes thoo gan he foolde,
And thus he seyde w*yth* angri contenauns:
" Be war, good woman, of þat gret grevauns 614 *rebukes Katharine,*
Whiche oure godd*is* on her enmyes take !
Many a prowde man ful lowe haue þei shake. 616

" ffor but [her] m*er*cy were more than her Iustise, 617
ȝe shulde soone falle in that sory trappe
Whiche þei haue ordeyned to tho that hem despise—
A wooful chauns haue thei and a soory happe. 620
Beth war, suster, that þei yow not clappe [1] *MS. of thoundir and leuene, on erasure.* *and warns her of the vengeance of his Gods.*
With her vengeauns right [for ȝou*r* blaspheme][1] !
Yee speke of helle, ȝe speke also of heuene : 623

" And thei may graunte yow bothe to ȝo*ur* wage. 624
Keepe ȝo*ur* tonge clos, kepe yo*ur* lyf on lofte !
Ne were the reu*er*ens of youre gret lynage,
Yee shulde not this nyght slepe, I trowe, ryght softe !
ȝe were [wel] worthi to [be lyft on lofte][1] 628 *She ought to be haugd.*
Ryght on a gebet, for yo*ur* bitter speche [1] *MS. suffre grete peynis ofte*
Whith the whiche ȝe now ageyn oure godd*is* preche." 630

Ca^m. 8^m.

Tho seyde the mayden w*yth* ful sad visage : 631
" how be thei godd*is*, these mawmentis þat we see ?

604 who 609 qwite 611 her*e* b. 612 harmes 614 ve*n*iauns
615 hath take 617 her*e* m*er*cy 620 hafe 621 Be . systr*e* 622
for ȝour*e* blaspheme 628 wel . be lyft on lofte 629 gybbet 630
the om. 631 mayde 632 who

Reede in youre book,¹ loke in her lynage,   ¹ r. bookis
Than shal þou knowe that erthely as we be   ² MS. weete weel ȝe
Were thei somtyme. for ȝoure saturne, [parde],²   635
Was somtyme kyng, as bookys telle, of crete,
And so was Iubiter—thus seyth youre poete.   637

" Be-cause thei myght not bothe in þat lond acoord, 638
Iubiter the sone made saturne, his fadir, to fle
Right in to Ytaile, youre bookis wil it recoord;
In wiche¹ tyme there tho regned hee,   ¹ MS. swiche
Ianus ȝe calle, with double face [parde],²   ² MS. as rede we   642
Be-cause he looketh to the olde ȝeer and the newe.
Thanne is this sooth, thanne is this tale trewe   644

" That men thei were, and arn not eterne—   645
hough shuld thei be goddis¹ whan thei were made?
It longeth to a god for to be sempiterne.   ¹ MS. gooddis
fful falsly the puple ȝe disceyue and glade.
he is a god that may neuere fayle ne fade,   649
he is a god þat made al thyng of nought,
he is a god of whom ȝoure goddis were wrought."   651

Caᵐ. 9ᵐ.

The emperour thought tho besyly in his meende,   652
    In worshipe and strengthe of his beleue
Bothe with exaumples of craft and of keende
his secte wil he true and stable preue;
" Mayde," he seyth, " I trowe I shal ȝou meue   656
ffro þat ground that ye haue newly take.
lete ȝoure wordis [as] for a while now slake.   658

" ffor I wil preue now openly fyrst of alle   659
That your secte, whiche ȝe crysten clepe,
May not stande, for it muste ned[is]¹ falle,   ¹ MS. nede
Right for þe impossibles whiche þer-inne ȝe hepe.
Al þat I sey now, looke þat ȝe sadly repe!   663

635 parde   636 telles   639 sun   640 ytale   641 wheche   642
parde   643 elde   645 are noght   646 who   647 for om.   648
deceyue   652 mynde   654 ensamples . kynde   655 strenght   658
as for   661 mut nedis

how shulde a mayde in hir wombe bere ⹀
A childe, and she mayden as she was eere? 665
"This þing is contrarye, ye may see, to nature, 666
This þing is impossible on-to scoles alle.
Remeueth ȝour herte; for I you ensure,
In swiche errour ȝe may soo deepe douɳ falle
That, though ye after mercy crye and calle, 670
We may not graunte yow, be-cause þat oure lawe
Wil condemne ȝow to ben hange and drawe. 672

"Therfore chaunge ȝoure feyth, I reede, [&]¹ forsake 673
Swiche-maner oppynyons that ilke maɳ on lyue
As for heresies euere-more hath take.²
ȝe³ sey a childes blood with woundes fyue
Shuld washe fro euery maɳ and euery wyue, 677
ffrom euery chyld, her synnes iche ooɳ:
These fonned conseytes, resoɳ haue thei nooɳ." 679

Bk. IV. Ch. 9.
How can a Mother be a Maid?
It's impossible.

¹ MS. ȝow on erasure.
² MS. be take.
³ MS. ffor ȝe
How can a Child's blood cleanse folk from sin?

Cam. 10m.

ON-to these woordis, whiche sempte soo wyse, 680
Answerde the queeɳ with ful gret constauns:
"Sir emperour," she seyde, "I wolde now¹ deuyse
To proue on-to ȝow with grete circumstauns—
But that the tyme letteth us of swiche daliauns— 684
That ȝoure groundes arɳ noo-thyng true
Off ȝoure beleue, neyther the olde ne the newe. 686

"Ye takeɳ the bark whiche is open to þe ye, 687
Ther-on ye fede yow ryght in ȝour dotage;
The swete frute whiche with-Inne dooth lye,
ȝe desire it not—loo, swhiche is the wood rage
Of ȝoure customes in al ȝoure age, 691
The leues ye take, the frute leue ye stille.
More openly my sentens declare now I wille. 693

Bk. IV. Ch. 10.

Katharine tells the Emperor that

¹ MS. you now, on erasure.

he takes the outside bark,

and leaves the inside fruit.

---

664 who 665 mayde 672 be 673 & inst. of ȝow 674 opiniones.
olyue 675 be om. 676 ffor om. 678 eche 679 þeis. thei om.
682 sere. you now om. 685 arc. trewe 686 neþir. elde 687 take
690 nought 693 now om.

Bk.IV. Ch.10.

God is not visible on earth.

"Who seketh roses there noo rose[s] growe? 694
Who seketh grapes oute of the brere?
The hye very god, this may ʒe weel knowe,
Is not now visible a-mongɪs vs here;
he is feer above, wyth-outen ony dwere, 698
Dwellynge in blis with his seruauntes alle.
Therfore I seye ʒou : though ye crye and calle 700

"Vp-on these stookes to sende¹ you good grace, 701
To sende ʒou of myschef relef and socour, ¹ r. senden?

Stocks cannot give help.

leueth [þis]¹ weel, ye shal it neuere purchase, ¹ MS. it
Be-cause ye forsake youre creatour,
Wurshipe creaturɪs and geue hem honour 705
To whom ʒe shulde noon swiche honour ʒeue.
Be this exaumple I may than weel preve 707

"The roten bark of thyngɪs visible heere 708
Whiche ʒe [se] outeward, this byte [ʒe] and gnawe,
The swete frute, the solace eke soo deere
Whiche shulde be [þe] parfytnesse of youre lawe,

The heathen are obstinate,

ffro þat swetnesse ye your-self withdrawe 712
With ful grete herte of cursed obstynacye,
Whiche hath you brought in ful grete heeresye. 714

"And as longe as ʒe thus dulled bee 715
In this same rudenesse of oppynyon,

and will never gain Truth till they repent.

Shul ye neuere, sekyrly, leue now me,
Of very truthe haue the possessyon.
Therefor repente ʒow of youre transgressyon, 719
Than are ye able to receyue the feyth.
This is the truthe, what-euere ony man seyth." 721

Bk.IV. Ch.11.

Caᵐ· 11ᵐ·

Tho[u]¹ myght a seyn at this tales ende ¹ u erased 722
Many man there [al] other-wyse [I]-chered

694 no rose   696 will k.   697 amonge   698 abouen . wythout any   701 stokkes   703 þis wele   706 no   709 ʒe se . byte ʒe . knawe   711 þe parfytnes   722 Thou   723 al oþir . I-cheryde

MS. Arundel.] *The Emperor bids Katharine wait a while.* 285

Than thei were ere; some her browes gonne bende — *Bk.IV. Ch.11.*
Right on tho ydoles whiche he had rered. — Many of the bystanders
ffor peyne of deth had hem soo I-fered 726
Be-fore this tyme, that in al her obseruauns
On-to the godd*is* thei made but feyned plesauns; 728

But now this lady with hir woord*is* swete 729
A newe light of grace on-to her hert*is* alle,
Whiche be-fore her feyth thus had leete,
hath brought in. for now thei gonne to calle :
" Mercy, ihe*s*u, graunte us noo more to falle 733 — cry to Christ for mercy.
In to swiche errour, to swhiche apostacye ! "
This was her noyse and thus thei gonne to crye. 735

This sey the emp*er*our and wyth ful heuy chere 736 — The Emperor sees his mistake in letting Katharine speak.
he gan to chaunge his colour and his face;
" In euele tyme," he thought, " I graunted heere
On-to þis mayde, whanŋ she camŋ to this place,
To sey this sermonŋ with a sory grace ! 740
Myn owenŋ menŋ, me thenketh, thei gynne despise
Alle my godd*is* and alle my sacryfise; 742

" The other syde whiche thei cristen calle, 743
Thei han caught boldnesse, and that me*r*ueilously,
ffor in my p*re*sens þei haue now late doun falle
Alle her offerynges, and that sodeynly."
Thus thought this manŋ; and eke ful besyly 747
he thanne be-heelde the beaute of þis mayde,
And thanne right thus on-to hir he sayde : 749

" Mayden," he seyth, " heere haue we newly gonne 750
A blessed sacrifise on-to oure goddis to make,
And ʒe ful onreuerently ageyn oure god, the sonne,
Whiche eue*r*y man for a god hath take,
Spende ʒoure speche. but now I rede ʒe slake, 754 — He bids her wait till his sacrifice to the Sun is ended.
Til that oure seruyse eended be this tyde,
That tyme we wyl ye drawe you asyde. 756

724 þan þer were here. su*m*me. gun*e* 726 & deth 732 gun 735 gune þei 741 gyne 743 seyde 744 hane 745 now om. 750 mayde. gune 751 *n*ake 752 ʒe om. . sunne

Bk.IV. Ch.11.	" Appollo graunte that ye no vengeauns haue	757
May Apollo not take vengeance on her!	ffor ȝour blaspheme, newe[ly] heere¹ I-sowe ! ¹ MS. heere newe he may yow damne and eke he may ȝow saue, Ye ȝoure-selue, I wote weel, this ye knowe.	
	Right for your beaute aughte ȝe stoupe ful lowe	761
	To thanke hym ther-of, though there were not ellis ;	
	Now are ȝe most, I trowe, of his rebellis."	763

Bk.IV. Ch.12.   Ca^{m.} 12^{m.}

Katharine says the Sun	" Whi shulde appollo bere ony deyte,"	764
	Seyde the mayde, that alle men myght here,	
	" And is but seruaunt to goddes mageste,	
	With his bemes shynynge fayre and clere ?	
moves only as God orders it.	he walketh noo cours, neither ferre ne nere,	768
	But at the byddyng of his makere aboue,	
	Whom we arn bounde oonly to drede and loue.	770
	" But traytoures arn we [þe] most part, dar I seyn.	771
He suspends His vengeance on men.	And ȝet he suspendeth his grete vengeauns. An open exaumple be-fore yow wil I leyn : Ye ben a lord of ful grete puissauns,	
	There is noon swiche be-twyxe this and frauns—	775
	ffor, as I haue lerned of al the orient,	
	Youre meny calle yow kyng omnypotent.	777
If subjects were traitors to the Emperor,	" I sette caas now, þat ageyn ȝour regalye	778
	Certeyn of youre men wyth treson wolde ryse,	
	Despyse ȝour degree, youre persone defye :	
	Shulde ȝe not thanne as [a] true Iustise	
	ȝoure grete power fully excersyse,	782
he'd kill them.	To kille tho traitoures, that thei leue no more ?	
	But ye dede thus, ȝe shulde repente it soore !	784
	" Right thus it semeth be oure creatour,	785
	God of heuene, that al made of nought :	
	Ye take awey fro hym that dewe honour	

757 veniauns   758 newly here   764 any   768 cors . farre   77
are   771 þe most   773 A   774 be . pusaunce   775 no   781 as a

That he shulde haue, whiche he ful deere bought   *Bk.IV. Ch.12.*
Whanne that in erthe oure helthe besyly[1] he sought ; 789
This same honou*r* ʒeue ye to deueli*s* ymages,   [1] *al.* besyly oure helth
Whiche ye haue sette heere solemnely on stages.   791

" Looke now ʒou*r*-self in what ye are falle :   792
Traitoures are ʒe, and as traitoures shul[d] ʒe brenne—   The Emperor is a traitor to God.
ffor other name wil I ʒow non calle
On-to the tyme þat ʒe youre lord kenne.
lete alle these vanytes fro youre breestes renne,   796
Good sir empe*r*our, and turne to yo*u*r loord !   He should turn to Him.
Than) shul ye and I ful sone acoordk."[1]   [1] MS. be ac.   798

Ca^{m.} 13^{m.}   *Bk.IV. Ch.13.*

Now is the empe*r*our [stoyned][1] more and more ; 799
Al her seruyse as for that day is doone—
This tormenteth hym in his herte ful sore,   [1] MS. tormented
ffor neither to sonne, to venus, ne to moone
Wil no man lowte now, and passed is the noone.   803
Therfore he þenketh right thus in his herte :   The Emperor
" Though that I puneshe þis lady wyth peynes smerte, 805

" Though þat I sle hir, strangel or elli*s* brenne,   806
Yet shal hir doctryne therby no-thing[1] cees.   [1] *al.* no-thing therby
Wherfore I thenke a slyere weye to renne,
That hir purpos shal not thus encrees.
Ageyn) oure goddi*s* is she, and ageyn) oure pees ;   810
Therfore with resons wil we hir oppresse—
This holde I beste ageyn) hir sotilnesse."   812

Therfore hath he now, and that in grete hast,   813
Cleped his counseil in to a preuy place.   asks his Council
With ful grete sadnesse tho gan) he tast[1]   [1] MS. cast ?
how þat he may fro this lady race   how to convict
hir newe oppynyon) ; whether wyth solace   817   Katharine.

789 bysyly oure helth*e*   793 shuld   795 þat tyme   796 brest
797 ser*e*   798 be om.   799 stoyned   800 hir   805 ponysh   806 strangill*e*   807 no-þing herby   814 cou*n*sell*e*   815 tast   816 who

Bk.IV. Ch.13. Or ell*is* w*yth* peyne be beste to procede.

his counseℓℓ seyde thus right[1] in þat stede   [1] *al.* right thus   819

The Council advise the Emperor to send for great Clerks.

That he shal sende after grete clerkis,   820
lerned in gramer, rethorik and philosophie,
wiche[1] haue in sciens soo sekyr merkes   [1] MS. Swiche
That no ma*n* ageyn hem [may][2] replye;   [2] MS. can, overlined
Thei shal sonnest destroyen this heresye   824
Of this same lady—thus seyde thei alle.
A-noon the emp*er*our dede foorth I-calle   826

He does so, from Cyprus and Syria,

Many massanger*is*, for letter*is* wil he sende   827
Thurgh-oute the londe of Cipre and surre:
Alle tho clerkys tho[1] wil her lyfloode amende   [1] *al.* that
Thei must come now to this palustre,
On-to this place where þis conflicte shal bee.   831
The letter*is* arn wrete now, and seeled iche oon;
The massanger*is* in haste for these men arn goon.   833

by letters seald with his ring.

The emp*er*our hym-self as of a spec*y*alte   834
Seeled these letter*is* w*yth* a p*r*ecyous ryng,
Whiche was I-graue with ful grete sotylte.
The sentens of these letter*is* whiche þat this kyng
Wrote at þat tyme, if youre desiryng   838
Bee for to liste it, ʒe may heere it soone:

How the letters run.

"Maxcens the lord, saue sonne and moone   840
" Moost grettest in erthe, whiche hath I-bee   841
Thre tymes Consul in rome, that Citee hy,
ffader of the puple, and on-to the deite
Of Iubiter the kyng of kynrede ful ny,
Sendeth loue and helthe to al [þe] clergy   845
Of surre and Cipre and other prouynces alle
Whiche to his lordshepe newly arn falle.   847

"We wil ʒe wete, we sende at this tyme   848
On-to ʒoure prouydens counseℓℓ to haue;

819 rith þus   822 whech*e*   823 may   824 sonest destroy   827 massageris   829 þat will . lyuelode   832 ar*e* wryte . sealed . ych*e* 833 ar*e*   837 of þe   843 on om.   844 kynrode   845 all*e* þe clargye 847 ar*e*   848 wyte

[MS. Arundel.] *The Emperor offers to wed Katharine.*

We axe [not] of you neyther taske ne dyme,
But oonly youre feyth and oure secte to saue.
ffor these cristen folke[1] make oure puple to raue 852
With sotil suasyons whiche that thei vse,   [1] r. folkis
On whiche sotiltees we oure-selue muse. 854
  "But moost specyaly a lady haue we newe [I]-caught,
Enforced with eloquens merueilously; 856
Mekel of oure puple soo hath she taught
That fro oure feith flee they sodeynly;
Thus party with witte, party wyth nygramauncy 859
She peruerteth oure lond in wonder wise.
Therfore we bydde, ye that are wyse, 861
  "Ye haste you now[1] to Alysaundre for this same cause,
To looke if ȝe may this womand oppresse. [1] MS. you now, you overl.
ffor this I telle you shortly in clause, 864
But she be ouercome with ȝoure besynesse,
Alle shul be cristen, the more and the lesse. 866
And if ȝe conuycte hir, avaunced shul ȝe bee
With plente of richesse, if ye troste me." 868
  Thus and the letteris wretten and I-goo. 869
The emperour is walked foorth with the mayde
On-to the paleys, with lordes many moo,
Whiche w[as][1] at that tyme ful weel arayd. [1] MS. were
Many plesaunt woordis on-to hir he sayd, 873
And many grete behestes tho he be-hyght,
To turne hir oppynyon, if þat he myght. 875
  he hight hir: if she wolde to hym consent, 876
To haue ful power of al maner of thyng,
More than ony lord of his parlement;
ffor alle men shulde bowe on-to hyr byddyng,
She shulde be queen as he was kyng, 880
hir ymage wolde he sette in the market-place,
Whiche shulde be lyke hir in body and in face, 882

Bk. IV. Ch. 13.

The Emperor asks the learned Heathens to

come and answer Katharine,

or all his folk will turn Christians.

He takes Katharine to his palace,

and offers

to make her Queen,

850 ax not . nethir   851 oure . and om.   853 suasiones   855 haf . I-caut   857 meche   859 wyth om.   862 you om.   868 ryches   869 are   871 pales   872 was   873 on om.   874 behyte   875 mythe   876 hite   877 of om.

KATHARINE.

290　　　　　*Katharine refuses the Emperor.*　[**MS. Arundel.**

Bk. IV. Ch. 13.
and have her Image worshipt,

And alle man*er* [of] men shulde wurship yeue　　883
On-to þat ymage as on-to a goddesse ;
Thei shal not chese if that þei wil leue,
Wurship shul thei hir bothe more and lesse.
That was his p*r*omys that with swiche worthinesse　　887

if she'll forsake the Christian faith.

he wil hir auaunce, oonly if she wil forsake
hir cristen feyth and his feith now take.　　889

She refuses.

But alle these promyses set she at nought,　　890
This blyssed lady, ryght for crystes sake ;
This same vers was tho in hir thought
Whiche oure lady hir-self gan make :
" Thei that are proude, god wil hem forsake ;　　894
Meeke he wil lifte vp right for her meekenesse."
Thanne seyde she to the emp*er*our w*yth* sadnesse :　　896

She has given up this world for Christ's love.

" Al this world haue I for my lord*is* loue,　　897
Ih*es*u I mene, forsaken for eu*er*e-more ;
There shal no mene of dreed ne of [loue][1]
putte myn herte fro that grete tresore ;　[1] MS. other be-houe, on eras.
It shal ly ful stille there as a good store,　　901
Til þat I deye and yelde up my goost
On-to þat lord whom I loue moost.　　903

" But sith that thyne[1] godd*is* of swiche myght*is* bee
As þou hast p*r*onunced heere in this place,　[1] r. þi　905

Let the Heathen Gods take vengeance on her if they can.

lete hem take vengeavnce now vp-on me,
If that thei may ; lete hem my body race !
her myght is right nought, ne nought is her grace.　　908
Therfore I despise hem as thei stonde on rowe,
ffor feendes arn thei, ful weel þat I knowe.　　910

" And, sir, to ȝow I wil touche another thyng—　　911
I wil ȝe shul enclyne al youre entent
To herken my woord*is* and myn talkyng :

883 of me*n*. shull*e*　890 promissis　895 vp right om.　898 forsake
899 other om. loue　904 þi . myth*e*　905 p*r*onounced　906 late
907 that om.　908 right om.　909 stand a-rowe　910 ar　911 ser*e*
912 wole　913 my

It is not onknowen) to al the orient
That bothe be descens and be testament 915 *Katharine says Alexandria is hers;*
This citee is myn), as for myn) erytage,
To whiche ye haue maad now this pilgrymage. 917

"Sith ȝe arn kyng, and rightwisnesse shulde keepe, 918
Whi make ye swiche maystries in other mennes londe,
Compelle my tenauntes, though þei soore wepe, *the Emperor wrongly oppresses her tenants.*
To goo with her offeryng*is* ryght in her honde,
With trompes and tabour*is* be-forn) you to stonde, 922
With-oute my leue, w*yth*-oute[1] my licens? [1] r. wyth-outen
This is wrong to me, and to god offens. 924

"If youre godd*is* teche ȝow to do this synne, 925
Thanne are thei onrightful in her co*m*maundement;
If ȝe ageyn) her bydyng thus wil be-gynne,
Thanne doo ye wrong ageyn)[1] her entent. [1] r. ageynis?
On what-maner wise ȝe make yo*ur* weent,— 929
I wil not tarie ȝow w*yth* no tales longe,
But thus I conclude, that ye doo me wronge." 931

Tho was the emp*er*our so ful of malencolye 932 *The Emperor*
he myght no lengere suffre hir in his presens;
To a knyght he co*m*mavnded þat stood faste bye,
he shal taken this lady and leede hir thens, *orders Katharine*
Put hir in preson) for hir grete offens; 936 *to prison,*
"look ye keepe hir soo she[1] goo not aweye; [1] MS. that she
ffor if þat she doo, ful horrybyly shal ye deye." 938

Gladly and iocundely with the knyght she gooth 939 *and she goes gladly.*
As a spouse to chaumbre, for hir lord*is* loue;
No-thyng dismayde, no-thing is she wrooth—
Thus can) oure lord the pacyens proue
Of hem þat arn) chosen) to dwelle al aboue 943
In heuene in his presens. but thus I lete hir ly,
And foorth I shal telle of this story. 945

916 myn 2 om. 918 are 919 mastries . otheris menis 921 hond*is* 922 taburs . befor 925 for to 926 hyr 928 Intent 929 went 932 so om. 935 take 936 grete om. 937 he . that om. 938 shall he 939 goo 943 are

Cam. 14m.

The Emperor

Whil Katarine is in presoṅ thus I-closed, 946
 The empe*r*our is rydeṅ in to the lond,
ffor certeyṅ causes—but as it is supposed,
It was for brekyn[g of][1] a certeyṅ bond   [1] MS. corr.: for to brekyṅ; of erased.
Be-twyxe too citees, as I vndirstond :   [3] MS. corr.: beg. there 950

makes peace between 2 cities,

he rood to cece[2] the sysme that was [new] begonne[3]— [2] or. cesso
Eche of hem on[4] other had spent many a [gonne].[5] 952
      [4] MS. corr.: vpon   [5] corr.: speere.
But he hath maad pees, and his iornay is sped, 953

and returns to Alexandria.

he is come hom now to Alisaundre ageyṅ.
The massange*r*is that he sent, eke thei haue led
Alle these clerkys to Alisaundre, certeyṅ.
Thus be thei come bothe, shortly to seyṅ,   [1] MS. arṅ) 957
The empe*r*our and the clerk*is*, [þus][1] mette in-feere.
A counseH is set now of lord*is* þat were there. 959

The Philosophers he has sent for

The philysophres arṅ entred in to the same counsayH,
To wete whi the empe*r*our hath for hem[1] sent. [1] al. for hem hath
There was a faire sight, withouteṅ ony fayH :
ffor oute of the coostes of al the oryent
Are these mayster*is* chose, right for this entent 964

to argue with Katharine,

To conquere this lady be philosophie.
The noumbre of hem, if I shal not lye, 966

are 50 very learned men.

Myn auctour seith, was fyfty euene, 967
lerned meṅ in art and in arsmetrik,
In retorik, gramer, in alle þe scyens seuene,
In al this world were hem nooṅ[1] like,   [1] al. noon hem
Thei had stodied the groundes of alle musike. 971

The Emperor tells them why he sent for them:

The empe*r*our is ful glad now of her comynge ;
Thus seide he to hem at her enteryng : 973
" Maister*is*, we sente for yow for this matere : 974
We haue heere a mayde whiche with obstinacye

948 but om.   949 for brekyng of . certen   951 sesse . new begun ; there om.   952 Iche of them of o. . gonne   953 pece   954 cum   955 massengers . hafe   956 eke certeyn   957 cum   958 arṅ om. thus mete.   960 philosofer*is* are . cownselle   961 for hem hath   966 shuld   969 and alle   970 the . non them   971 grownde   972 hyr cummyng   973 hyr   975 hafe

Ren[e]yeth oure lawes, swiche as we vsen heere,		Bk. IV. Ch. 14.
ffor she is fallen in to[1] that cursed heresie [1] om. to		Katharine has turned Christian;
Whiche the[1] cristen clepe, ful of ypocris[i]e; [1] r. thei	978	
She eke so deepe in to this errour is falle		
That alle oure goddis "deueles" doth she calle.	980	
"And I suppose verily 3e teeche but truthe,	981	
Be-cause that 3e been soo grete lerned men.		
To sle so yonge a lady me thenketh ruthe;		
Therfore the right weye I wil 3e hir ken,		she must be converted to Heathenism.
To conuerte hir to oure lawe—ellis I must hir bren.	985	
This is þe cause whi I sent for 3ow.		
Goo cast your wittis in the best maner now	987	
"how ye wil procede, for she shal come anoon;	988	
hir answeris and sly, grete is hir lernyng.		
I make yow seker 3e shal not hens goon		
On-to the tyme that 3e hir bryng		
In to the same feith whiche hir fadir þe kyng	992	
leued al his lyue, and hir modir also.		
This is the matere whiche I wil haue doo."	994	
Oon answerde for alle, and thus spak he:	995	
"We weene heere is gadered swyche a companye,		The Philosophers are the wisest in the world.
In al this world shulde not a man fynde thre		
So[1] wise, so stodyous in philosophie. [1] MS. Sho		
But ouere alle these Maister Arioth is moost worthye;	999	
he nedeth not his labour on a woman spende,		
he shal on-to hir but his discipulis sende.	1001	
"And if she conclude hem be auctoryte	1002	If Katharine poses them, she is a Goddess.
Or ellis be reson,[1] leue me ful weel, [1] MS. resons		
I wil sey thanne that a goddesse is she,		
And moost worthi to be sette on the wheel		
Of natural sciens, but I can not feel	1006	

976 reneyhithe. whyche; as om. vse   977 falle   978 clepeth
979 is In-to   980 goodis   982 be   987 To cast   988 who. cum
989 are   991 that t.   993 lyued. lyfe   994 hafe   996 cumpenye
999 maysteres. Arioth   1001 vnto. disciples   1003 reson   1004 goddes   1006 kannot

Bk. IV. Ch. 14.	In no maner that a woman shul[d] come þer-too,
	I haue not herd speke that ony woman dede soo." 1008
	After this sermonynge on-til the nexte day 1009
The Philosophers are housd.	The emperour commaunded knyghtis hem to cheere,
	To leede hem to her Innes with ful good aray
	In sencyaH[1] of bookis and swiche other gere [1] al. specyall
	As longeth on-to men that swiche sciens lere. 1013
	Thus leue I hem stille in thoughtful besynesse, [1] MS. and in
Katharine is in prison.	And Katarine, oure mayden, in presun and[1] distresse.

Bk. IV. Ch. 15.   Ca^m. 15^m.

The Emperor in Council,

The other day is come. but the emperour thought 1016
To asaye hym-selue with his preuy counsayH
ffor to conquere hir—but it avayleth nought;
ffor whan moost nede is, his resons wil quayH—
Soo weel can oure mayden hir proporsyons rayH. 1020
lordes were there many tho in presens,
Statly, manful and of grete expens : 1022

and the Kings of Armenia,

The kyng of Armenye was tho in þat place 1023
Where she was apposed of hir beleue ;
Soo was þe kyng of Mede, a faire man of face ;

Macedon, &c.,

The kyng eke of Macedoyne, whiche made many a preue
Ageyns this lady, but he coude hir not meue ; 1027
The prouost of perse was there also,
Wyth bishopes and lordes many mo. 1029

argue with Katharine in vain.

Thei made her resons, but þei avayled nought. 1030
ffirst[1] seyde þe emperour right thus to þe may :
" Myn owne suster,[2] hedir I haue yow brought [1] MS. ffyrst tho
Be-forn my special frendes this day, [2] MS. o. s. on erasure.
To see whether ye wil stille in your olde lay 1034
helde ȝoure perseuerauns or ellis consente[1] to vs
And ren[e]ye for euere that traytour Iesus, [1] MS. ye wille 1036

1007 shuld cum   1008 hafe . hard . dyde   1012 In specyalle
1016 cum   1017 coūncele   1018 it om.   1019 resonys . whayle
1020 mayde   1023 Ermenye   1024 opposed   1026 macedon   1027
A-geyn . mend   1030 hyr   1031 tho om.   thys may   1032 syster .
hafe   1033 Befor   1034 whedyr . eld   1035 ȝe wil om.   1036 rency

"To turne to appollo, venus and mynerue— 1037 *Bk. IV. Ch. 15.*
ffor ȝoure presonꝺ shulde cause yow, I suppose, *The Emperor urges Katha-*
To chaunge ȝour lyf, lest þat ye sterue. *rine to change her Faith.*
ffor of alle maydenes ye be the rose,
And to maydenes it longeth to be led wyth glose. 1041
lete see now, telle how ȝe avysed bee!"
On-to these woordis thus answerde shee: 1043

"A loue haue I, sere, whiche liketh me soo 1044 *She declares*
That woordly[1] delite to me is but peyne
And wordly[1] Ioye to me is but woo, [1] *al.* all worldly
If I very truthe to yow shulde now seyne.
Therfore knoweth this for a certeyne: 1048
I wil neuere chaunge, whil I haue lyf, *she never will.*
I shal been euere to hymꝺ truwe spouse and wyf." 1050

Tho seyde the emperour: "th[an][1] is al nought [1] MS. this
That we with oure wittis haue laboured ȝow to saue!
Turne ȝoure woordis, turne eke ȝour thought, 1053
Or ellis swiche ende muste ye now haue
As longeth to traitouris that wil thus[1] raue. [1] *al.* thus wil
Avise ȝow of too thyngis whiche ye wil take: *He says she must, or die.*
Eyther shal ȝe deye, or youre lawe forsake." 1057

And eke the grete kyng of Armenye, 1058
Eem on-to Kataryne he was, as I wene, *Her Uncle, the King of Armenia, tries to per-*
"Cosyn," he seyde, "leueth this heresye, *suade her.*
Thenke on ȝoure kenerede, bothe kyng and queene,
Was noon[1] of hem swiche thyng wolde sustene. 1062
Allas, womanꝺ, why despise ȝe saturne? [1] *al.* neuer noon
he may, and he wil, in to a ston ȝou turne." 1064

The kyng of Mede, whiche sat tho be-syde, 1065
In oure lord ihesu he ganꝺ putte swiche blame:

1042 lat. who 1044 hafe. syr 1045 alle worldly 1046 alle w.
1047 now om.. sayn 1048 know. a certen 1049 hafe 1050 be.
trewe 1051 thaɴ is 1052 hafe. safe 1054 hafe 1055 thus wyll
raffe 1057 Ethyr. dye 1058 Armonye 1059 on om. 1060 leve
1061 Thynk of. kynrede 1062 was neuer non of them. susteyn
1066 gan om. put

Bk.IV.Ch.15.	"ȝoure god crist," he seyde, "is knowe ful wyde	
	That he was a whitche, and soo was his dame,	
The King of Media says Christ was a witch.	And grettest in whitchecraft, as is the fame.	1069
	ffy on swiche wisdam, fy on swiche feyth!	
	This same recorde al the world seyth."	1071
Another king says no one shares her belief.	An other kyng was there, and thus he hir repreued:	
	She stood in this mater, he seyde, but allone,	
	There is noon but she þat in crist leued;	
	"looke now," he seyde, "whether oon persone	
	Is more wurthi to be leued þan we iche oone;	1076
	Reson wil conclude þat where multitude is,	[1] r. not but?
	There is the truthe, a man may not[1] mys."	1078
King Caspanus says	The kyng of Macedoyne, sir caspanus,	1079
	On-to þe lady ful sobirly thus seyde:	
	"Youre god, youre lord whiche ye calle Iesus,	
	As ȝe sey, he was bore of a mayde;	
that no King would let his subjects treat him as Jesus was treated.	But why suffred he to be soo arayde	1083
	Of his owne seruauntis, soo as he was?	
	And a wyse lord had stonde in that cas,	1085
	"he wolde haue hangen hem of very Iustise."	1086
	Thus seyde the bishopes, þus seyde thei alle	
	On-to this lady in her best wyse,	1088
	And with besynesse soore on hir [they][1] calle,	[1] MS. to
	That she fro this vanyte must nedes[1] falle	[1] al. nedes must
	And make of hir enmyes hir freendes deere.	
	Than spak this lady right as ȝe shal heere:	1092
Bk.IV.Ch.16.	Ca^m. 16^m.	
Katharine answers her objectors.	"Sir emperour," seyde she, "I haue or this	1093
	On-to youre reuerens declared ful weel	
	Whi my lord Ihesu of seruauntis his	
	Wolde suffre al this peyne[1] euery deel;	[1] r. peynes?
	But of my feyth no-þing ye feel,	1097

1068 wyche   1069 the gr.   1072 Anoder thyng. he hir thus
1075 wheder o   1078 but om.   1082 sayd   1083 soo om.   1086 hanged   1088 hyr   1089 they c.   1090 And she. nedis muste
1091 her enmes   1093 hafe   1096 peyn

Soo ar ʒe harded with obstinacye.
Therfore hold I now [but] a grete folye   1099

"Youre demonstracyons for to declare.   1100   *Katharine says that Mahound will not save them from Hell.*
But thus moche I seye on-to you euerychon:
ʒoure mahound of whom ye make swiche fare,
Shal not saue yow whan ye shul goon
Doun in to peynis, heuy as a stoon;   1104
he may not delyuere hym-self fro þat peyne,
Where he is bounde with many a cheyne.   1106

"But witche was he neuere, Ihesu, my lord,   1107   *Christ and Mary are not witches.*
Ne his blysse[d] modir mary, þat may;
he was god and man, as bookis record,
And alle tho myracles were put in asay
Be his mortal enmyes with ful grete afray   1111
And euere were thei founde truwe and stedfast.
Therfore ley doun that horrible blast   1113

"Of youre cursed tounges, ʒe lordes, I ʒou pray;   1114   *Let the Kings stop their barking!*
Berke now no more ageyn that hooly name,
ffor ye shal somtyme see that day
Ye shal for þis berkyng be put on-to blame.
Alas, þat euere ony wretchis shulde defame   1118
Soo hy a lord, soo grete of dygnyte,
To whom mote nedes bowe[1] euery kne!"   [1] r. bowen   1120

Than spak the prouost of perse ful sone: 1121   *The Provost of Persia calls for the Philosophers.*
"Sende after these cle[r]kys, sir, and lete hem seye;
Thei can oure feith, thei wote what is to done.
lete hir beleue hem or ellis shal she deye,
She shal chese oon, there is noon other weye.   1125
With this longe claterynge, tyme lese we heere;
Thei wil appose hir in an other manere."   1127

1098 abstinacye   1099 but a   1101 myche . on om.   1102 of whyche   1103 shall   1104 a om.   1105 deleuer . from   1107 Ihesu om.   1108 Be . blyssed   1110 myrakyls   1111 mortaylle enmes   1112 trew   1113 orible   1114 tungis   1117 barkyng   1118 euere om.   1119 hyghe . grete a d.   1120 nede   1122 them   1124 lat   1125 chese om.   1127 oppose . an om.

Cam. 17m.

The Emperor appeals to the Philosophers to answer Katharine.

The philosophres arn�; entred to the counsayH.　1128
　　The emper̃our seyde : "siris, this is the houre
In whiche we shal see if connynge wil avayle.
Therfore, maistres, dooth now ȝoure laboure,
ffor ye muste defende vs fro this sharpe shoure　　1132
With the whiche we arn̄ heyled now on euery syde ;
But if ye spede, oure feyth wil sone slyde."　　1134

Thei answerde ageyn, thei seyde thei had scorn　1135
That soo many[1] ageyn̄ a mayden ȝyng　　[1] al. many men
Shulde now dispute ; for he is not born̄
In erthe as yet that durste stere ony thyng
Ageyn her conclusyons, neither duke ne kyng—　1139
Swhiche grete roos was made þan[1] in þat place.　[1] al. þo
"lete hir come," thei seyde, "lete vs see hir face !"　1141

But whil thei were carpynge in this matere,　1142

A knight warns her in prison of her coming trial.

A knyght is goo to hir in preson̄ in hast,
Warnynge hir as a genteH officere
In what maner the emper̃our wil hir a-taast.
What nedeth now mo woordis for to waast?　1146
The lady seyde that it was glad tydyng,
There coude no man̄ gladdere to hir bryng.　1148

Tho fel she doun̄ plat al in a traunce,　　1149
Commendynge hir cause right on-to god allone,

She prays to God for help.

"Graunte me, lord," she seyde, "perseueraunce,
To serue thi godhed whiche sitteth in trone ;
Of whiche godhed thi sone, the secunde persone,　1153
Deyed in erthe for synne of al man-kynde,[1]　[1] corr.: keende
Whiche on-to hym ful ofte [he fynt onkynde].[1]　　1155
　　　　　　　　　　　[1] MS. corr.: onstable is in meende.
"Thou graunte me, lord, this day eloquens,　1156
To saue thi feith, right as þou best can̄) ;

1128 are . councelle　1130 conyng　1131 do　1132 from　1133
the om.　are haylyd　1136 many men　1138 erde　1139 hyr .
neþer　1140 rowse . þo　1141 cum　1143 gon . in preson om.
1145 a-taste　1151 sche sayde lord　1153 sune　1154 kynde　1155
he fynt onkynde

Katharine's Prayer for Help.

Suffre not these clerk*is* to make resistens
Ageyn þat doctrine whiche þou, god and man,
here in this world with woundes blewe and wan 1160
Confermed thus; geue me, lord, that goost
Whiche can put doun soone al wordly boost! 1162

Katharine prays for the Spirit

"And as þou graunted to thyne Aposteles heere, 1163
Whan thei shulde stonde be-fore prynce or kyng,
Thou seyde to hem thei shulde not be in dwere
What thei shulde speke, neither to olde ne ȝyng,
ffor thou shulde graunte hem witte in answeryng, 1167
Ageyn whiche there shulde noo man replie,
Neither of the secte of hethen ne of heresye: 1169

"Right soo graunte now to me, þi seruaunt, heere, 1170
That I haue strengthe thi cause [for] to defende,
That I may proue be resons sharpe and clere
Thi cherches feyth, for whiche þou gan descende
Euene fro heuene oure maner*is* to a-mende. 1174
This prey I the, put this in my breest,
As þou art god and man, bothe kyng and preest. 1176

to defend Christ's cause.

"Thou art my connynge, þou art myn hardynesse, 1177
Thou art al in whom oonly I trust;
There cometh noo vertu but of thi worthinesse:
Lete not thi power at this day be loost!
Thou makest al thyng, bothe þe hete and the frost; 1181
Wherfore I prey, lord,[1] thoug I a woman be, [1] MS. the, lord
Yet for thi wurshipe ȝet soo enforce me 1183

In Him only does she trust.

"That I may speke word*is* to thi plesauns. 1184
As þou graunted hester to plese hir assuere,
To leue his stately solenne countenauns
And speke to hir word*is* of goodly cheere:
Soo graunte me now, lord, thi seruaunt heere, 1188

May He strengthen her to speak aright!

1158 suffyr 1164 stande 1166 elde 1171 hafe . forto 1172 preue 1173 chyrches . kan 1174 maners 1177 conyng . my 1179 comth . verteve 1180 as þis d. 1182 the om. . thow 1185 ester

300 The Arch-Angel Michael comforts Katharine. [MS. Arundel.

Bk. IV. Ch. 17.   That I may plese and plete in thi cause.
  This is the sentens that I prey in clause."   1190

Bk. IV. Ch. 18.   Ca^{m.} 18^{m.}

An Angel comes from Heaven,

Whan that this lady had made hir orysoun,   1191
Ther cam an aungel glidyng doun from heuene;
With meruey̆lous noyse cam he þat tyme doun,
As bright he semed as it were the leuene.
Alle th[e][1] preson whiche had vowtes seuene,   1195
Was light that tyme right of his presens;   [1] MS. tho in
The derke corneres cowde make no resistens.   1197

And she myght not susteyn that vysyon,   1198
Soo was she rauyshed with th[at][1] newe light;   [1] MS. the
Right with his comynge she fel soone doun.

and comforts Katharine in prison.

The aungel comforted hir and bad hir be [l]yght;[1]   [1] MS. wyght
"Drede not," he seyth, "though þat I be bryght!   1202
I am a seruaunt bothe on-to god and yow,
And for ȝoure comfort fro heuene cam I now.   1204

Christ greets her,

"My lord youre spouse be me greteth ȝow weel;   1205
ffor very loue this massage now he sent:

and bids her not fear.

he commaunded ȝou to drede neuere a deel,
Of these clerkis ȝe shal not be circumuent;
Ye shal conceyue ful clerkly[1] her entent,   [1] *al.* clerely   1209
And ȝet moreouere thei shul haue noo powere
ffor to conclude ȝou now in noo manere.   1211

"But ȝoure power shal be ouere hem more large,   1212

She shall convert her opponents,

ffor ȝe shal conuicte hem with gret auctorite;
Ye shal leden hem on-to peteres barge,
Whiche fygureth oure feyth, as seyth dyuynite.
And not oonly thus, but soo deuoute shul þei bee   1216

and they shall die for Christ.

That as martirs for crist thei shul deye—
This same prophecye whiche I to ȝou seye   1218

1192 fro   1194 bryth   1195 alle þe preson   1199 þat   1201 lyght
1202 noght . bryto   1203 & to   1206 lofe . message   1208 þeyse
1209 clerly   1210 hafe   1214 leden om. þe peteres b.   1217 martyres

The Arch-Angel Michael comforts Katharine. 301

"Is determyned a-boue be godd*is* prouydens. 1219 *Bk. IV. Ch.* 18.
These clerkes shul than)[1] despise her book*is* alle   [1] *al.* now   The Philosophers shall despise their heathen books.
In whiche thei haue had a ful grete confidens;
Al her gret trost now shal fro hem falle
With þe whiche thei haunted her godd*is* for to calle. 1223
This shal oure lord doo, lady, be ȝoure labour:
Rise vp now and thanke yo*ur* sauyour! 1225

"And ȝe youre-self, after that thei be dede, 1226
Shul suffre for hym moche more thyng
Than I haue leyser to telle now in this stede.
But of thus moche I geue you ful warnyng:
ȝe shal make the queen) for to forsake hir kyng 1230   Katharine shall make the Queen forsake her King.
ffor crist*is* loue, and deye soo in hir blood;
ȝe shul be cause, lady, of alle these werk*is* good. 1232

"Yeue credens to me as to a truwe massagere, 1233
And as noo feyned spyrite with doubilnesse;
My name is mychael, if ȝe wil it heere,
Archaungel of heuene, whiche hath þat besynesse   The Archangel Michael tells her this.
That alle soules, the more and eke þe lesse, 1237
That shal to blisse, I peyse hem alle be wyte
Whether in goodnesse thei ben) heuy or lyghte. 1239

"This is myn) office, leue me, lady, weel! 1240
There is a sete ordeyned in heuene aboue   She shall sit in Heaven after her martyrdom.
ffor yow, lady, after youre sharpe wheel
Whiche ȝe shal suffre for youre spouses loue;
Was neue*r*e no mayde to swiche sete myght proue 1244
Saue Mary allone, cristes moder deere.
ffarweel now, lady, and beth of ryght good cheere!" 1246

Thus was she comforthed, and left al þ*a*t nyght 1247   Katharine is comforted.
In p*r*eson stille, in swete orison) allone;
The sauo*ur* abode and somwhat of þe light
After the tyme þ*a*t the Aungel was goone.
he hath made hir hardy and stable as þe stoone, 1251

1219 determyñde 1220 now inst. of than 1221 hafe 1223 þe om.
1227 mech 1229 myche. you om. 1233 trew mess. 1234 not f.
1238 hem om. . wyght 1239 wheythyre . he 1247 coun*n*forted

302 *The Emperor encourages the Philosophers.* [MS. Arundel.

Bk. IV. Ch. 18. There shal noo peyne hir herte now remeue
ffro the feyth ne fro hir beleue.   1253

Bk. IV. Ch. 19.   Ca^m. 19^m.

All Alexandria gathers to hear the Discussion.
Now is the Citee, for to see this mayde,   1254
Gadered in-feere with noyse and rumo[u]r;
Euery man there after his connynge sayde:
"Now is come the day and eke the hour
In whiche there shal falle ful grete honour   1258
On som party, or elles ful grete shame."
And be-cause this lady was of soo grete fame,   1260

Euery man is besy to stoonde that tyme ny,   1261
That he myght heere and see al þat was doo.
The Emperor The emperour is sette, the lordes sitte faste by,
The cle[r]kis eke were sette be too and too;
The may is sette in a sete also   1265
Right be hir-self, for she is lefte allone.
The emperour, sittyng al hy[1] in his trone,   [1] MS. on hy   1267

exhorts the Philosophers
Thus exorted[1] these noble clerkis alle: [1] MS. ex. he, he overl.
"Maistres," he seyth, "heere is the concionatrix,   1269
heere is the mayde on whom we dede soo calle,
heere is the newe dyuynour, heere is þe newe Vlix,
heere is she whos errour is soo fyx   1272
And soo sore glewed she wil not fro it remeue;   [1] al. schaftes
to prove their skill on Katharine.
Therefor ʒoure craftes[1] on hir now must ʒe preue."   1274

Than made the mayde on-to the emperour   1275
A ful strong[1] chalange, seyenge on this wyse: [1] al. strange
She asks him
"On-to these clerkys, whiche are heere in this hour
Gaddered to-gedir be-fore you as Iustise,
ʒe haue graunted a guerdon of grete apryse   1279
If that thei conuicte me; to me graunte ye noon):
Wherfore me thenketh al wrong haue ʒe goon).   1281

1256 cunnyng   1261 stand   1267 on om.   1268 he om.   1269 þis c.   1273 glewyd   1274 schaftys   1276 straunge   1277 in om.   1279 hafe   1280 ʒe inst. of thei   1281 hafe

MS. Arundel.] *The Debate with Katharine is opend.*

"But wolde ȝe graunte[1] now to my guerdoñ) [1] r. graunten *Bk. IV. Ch.19.*
That, if I spede and conuicte hem alle on rowe, 1283 whether, if she wins,
That ȝe shul leue ȝowre maumentrye ful soon,
And my lord Ihesu as for ȝoure god knowe, he'll take Jesus as his
Thañ) wolde I seye with woordis meke and lowe 1286 God.
That ye were iuge, iuste mañ) and[1] truwe." [1] Ar. 20 *tr.* and man
With these woordis the emperour chaunged hewe. 1288

he seyde on-to hir wyth ful stoute countenaunce: 1289
"What hast þou to doo of oure reward now? The Emperor bids her
Defende thi feith with al the circumstaunce defend her Faith.
That þou can thenke, it shal be litel [enow].[1] [1] MS. corr.: to litel to ȝow.
lete be, damysele, make it not soo tough! 1293
Entermete[1] the where thou hast too doone; [1] MS. Entermente
If þou haue witte it [wil][2] be seene [ful] soone." [2] MS. shal

Tho spak the mayde on-to the clerkes alle: 1296
"Sith ȝe be gadered now in to this place Katharine calls on the
Vp-on me oonly for to crye and calle, Philosophers
With ȝoure argumentis to loke if ye may chace
My witte, my meende fro that newe purchace 1300
Whiche I haue wonne, I mene fro cristen feyth,
lete see what ony of yow to me seyth!" 1302 to begin.

Tho spak a philosophre of ful grete age, 1303
An honourable mañ), Amphos of Athene:
"We are come," he seith, "at the emperouris wage Amphos says
ffor a mayden, he wrote, of yeeris eytene:
That same is ȝe, pleynly as I wene. 1307
But wherfore we come, as yet we knowe[1] not' now;
Of that mater the answere lith in ȝow. [1] *al.* know we 1309

"Sith ye be causere thanne of this affray, 1310
Sey ye ȝoure groundes, and we shul puruay she must state her case.
Answeris ther-too. or we goo [hens] this day,
We caste us sekyr newely you to conuay

1283 o rowe   1284 schall   1285 to know   1287 trewe   1289
vn-to   1292 to om. lytyll enow   1293 towe   1294 Entermet   1295
hafe . wilbe . ful sone   1300 mynde   1301 hafe wunne   1306
mayde   1308 know we   1311 purueye   1312 goo hens   1313 conueye

304 *Katharine's heathen Books given up.* [MS. Arundel.

Bk.IV.Ch.19.
On-to that feyth whiche ȝe dede reneye 1314
Be wykked counsail. therfore first shal yee
Speke in this mater, and than answere wee." 1316

Bk.IV.Ch.20. Ca^{m.} 20^{m.}

Katharine crosses herself,
The mayde stood up, and wyth ful good chere 1317
She crossed hir hed, hir mowth and hir brest ;
Thanne spak she to hem right as ȝe shal here :

and speaks.
" In me it lith at the begynnyng of this fest
To pronunce first, though þat I be lest 1321
And moost onwurthy, but oure lord Ihesu,
Blissed be he syth tyme that I hym knew. 1323

She has got rid of her heathen books,
" I haue lefte alle myn̄ auctouris olde, 1324
I fond noo frute in hem but eloquens ;
My bookis ben goo, ȝouen̄ or ellis solde.

Aristotle,
ffarweel, Aristotil ! for ful grete expens
Made my fadyr and had ful grete diligens 1328
To lerne[1] me thi[2] sotyl bookys alle   [1] r. lernen ? [2] MS. the
Of dyuers names as thou dede hem calle. 1330

Homer,
" Of omere eke haue I take my leue, 1331
With his faire termes in vers and eke in prose—
fful erly sat I and eke ful late at eue
To lerne the texte and to lerne the glose ;
I haue chose better, truly, I not suppose 1335

Ovid,
But wote ful weel. farweel eke, ouyde !
Thou loued ful weel blynde Venus and Cupide. 1337

Æsculapius,
" I haue take leue of esculape and Galiene 1338
And of alle her preuy sergyng of nature—
I haue a lesson̄ moche truere to sustene
And more directe to knowe[1] creature.   [1] r. knowen

Plato, &c.
Ȝe plato bookis eke, I you ensure, 1342
We haue doo now, we shal neuere more meete ;
Ne hym philistion, bothe philosophre and poete. 1344

1318 breeste 1320 lyghte 1321 pronownns . leest 1324 hafe .
my 1326 be 1329 þi 1340 meche trewere . susteyne

MS. Arundel.] *Katharine declares her Belief in Christ.* 305

"Be-helde ye, maistres, alle these mennes werkes 1345   *Bk. IV. Ch 20.*
haue I stodyed and lerned ful besyly;   These Pagans'
Thei were red me of ful sotil clerkes,   works
There lyue noon better at this day, hardyly :
And in these bookes noon other thyng fond I   1349
But vanyte or thyng that shal not leste,   were vanity.
And euere me thoughte that swiche lernyng was beste 1351

"That treeteth of thyng whiche shal euere[1] endure. 1352   Christ is eternal,
Swiche thyng lerne I now, turned to crist Ihesu ;
I lerne how god is lord of creature,   [1] *al.* euer shal   Lord of all creation,
I leerne hough he the heuene white and blew,
The water, the feyr, the erthe, eer þat it grew, 1356
Made al of nought—this is now my lernyng.
I lerne also that he a childe ful ying 1358

"Was bore in erthe of Mary, and she a mayde, 1359   born on earth of Mary,
Grew to[1] manhod, to thretty wynter and thre,   [1] *al.* on to
And thanne wilfully, as the prophetes sayde,
ffor synne of man heyng[1] vp-on a tree ;   [1] *al.* hyng   hangd on a tree.
Many myracles in erthe tho dede hee 1363
Whil he wente here—this I ȝow ensure.
Be dyuers werkys knowe was sondry nature : 1365

"That he was god, he shewed be werkes grete, 1366   He is God
ffor alle the clementis obeyed his commaundement;
That he was man, ful esy is to trete :   and man.
Thei sey and felte hym that with hym were present.
I telle you pleynly [now] al my[n] entent, 1370
This is my scole, þis is my philosophie,
This is þe scyens I hope shal neuere lye ; 1372

"This is my feyth, this is my victorie. 1373   This is Katharine's Faith.
What-euere men sey, a god muste we haue,
Aboue alle men that euere regned erthely
Most souereyn lord, whos power may al saue.

   1348 noo   1349 no   1352 euyr schall   1354 who   1355 who .
whyght   1356 fyyre . erde or   1360 on-to m.   1362 hyng   1363 dyd
1366 obeyd   1370 now all myne   1374 hafe   1375 reygned erdely
1376 sofrene . safe
   KATHARINE.   X

Bk.IV.Ch.20.	looke on your goddis how þei toumble and waue	1377
	Right whan men swepe hem—so litil is her myght!	[1] al. ye
	Wype awey[1] þat blyndenesse whiche hath hilled ȝour sight!	
Christ said that those who see shall be blind.	"ffor crist seyde soo, whan he the gospel sew:	1380
	'Thei that see,' he seyth, 'shul be ful blynde,	
	And thei þat neuere of my vertu knew,	
	fful truly wil thei ha me[1] in her mynde.'	[1] MS. haue
	But pulle we the frute oute of the rynde,	1384
	To telle ȝou platly what þis sentens is:	
	The seeynge men be-tokene ȝow, I-wis,	1386
	"ffor ȝe can see alle thyng þat to nature	1387
	Perteyneth, be craft whiche ye of bookis haue:	
And blind the Philosophers are to their Salvation.	But ȝoure saluacion, that I you ensure,	
	Considere ȝe nought, ne how ȝe may be saue.	
	Yowre blasyng sciens maket[h][1] you soo to raue	1391
	That endeles truthe can ȝe neuere-more fynde;	[1] r. make? Ar. 168 make
	This same errour is þat maketh yow blynde.	Ar. 20 makis
	"But in his name whom I now rehers,	1394
They can never overcome Katharine.	I shal be strong alle materis to conclude;	
	There shal no man haue myght me to reuers,	
	Though ȝe brynge a grettere multitude.	[1] MS. gyse, on eras.
	he can make wittis that been ful dul and rude,	1398
	To shyne wyth scyens on the freshest [w]yse,[1]	
	My lord ihesu, and fooles ofte maketh he wyse."	1400

Bk.IV.Ch.21.   Ca^m. 21^m.

	Whan this mayde[1] of this fair processe	[1] r. mayden
	had made an ende, there stod vp tho a man	
	Of fers corage, though[1] it were wodnesse—	[1] Ar. 20 os þowe
Master Astenes	Maister astenes, soo thei called hym than;	
	ffor very anger of colour was he wan;	1405
speaks angrily:	with cryenge voys he filled tho the place,	
	Thus spak he than: "allas, what is oure grace?	1407

1377 who . tu*m*byll . wafe   1379 ȝe inst. of awey . hyllyd   1380 seew   1381 schall. ful om.   1383 hafe me   1388 hafe   1389 sauacyon   1390 who . safe   1391 make . rafe   1398 be   1399 wyse   1400 he make   1402 a hende

Astenes denounces Christ and Katharine.

"Ye of rome, lordes and cites[e]ines alle, 1408 *Bk. IV. Ch. 21.*
ȝe blood ryal, ye men of nobelnesse,   *"Men of royal blood,*
What cause shul men haue, you to calle
Wysemen endued with sobyrnesse ?
If wysdam were wyth ȝow, than wolde I gesse 1412
ȝe shulde not suffren þis cristen foolk[1] here   [1] r. folkis *why do you let Christians*
Repreue oure goddis with swiche veniable manere. 1414 *abuse your Gods?*

"ffor we were called be oure emperour, 1415
ffader and kepere ful gracyous of this lond,
To conuicte, he seyde, here a newe errour.
Whiche is not newe, ȝe may weel vndirstond;
Many of hem haue I brent with brond 1419 *I have burnt many of these Christians.*
Of these cristen, right for this entent,
That thei calle feith, we calle delirament. 1421

"Oure goddis may seyn that we been on-keende, 1422
ffor alle the benefetes that thei to vs sende
We to suffre the ȝongthe[1] of woman-[k]eende[2] [1] Ar. ȝynkith [2] corr.: leende
Thus openly crist for to commende
And al his treson with colouris to defende, 1426
Oure goddis eke deueles for to calle—
This suffre we, and that is werst of alle. 1428

"Wherfore, sir kyng, be war of hir offens, 1429
Suffre no[w][1] this lady [no] lengere [for] to speke; [1] MS. noȝt *Stop this Katharine,*
These lewde foolkis that listen with grete silens,
With apparent resons she shal soone I-cheke,
That fro her feith she shal soone hem breke— 1433 *or she'll pervert our folk*
Thei come neuere hom, though we wolde hem drawe.
To suffre swiche prechouris it is agayn oure lawe. 1435

"We cam now heder to heere som nouelte, 1436
And she be-gynneth with Ihesu of Naȝareth! *with her Jesus of Nazareth.*
Cryst thei calle hym, and prophete of galyle,
She calleth hym lord of wynd and of breth,
Of erthe, of watyr, of lond[e] and of heth. 1440

1408 ceteseyns   1411 endewyd   1413 suffyre þese   1422 sey . be · onkynde   1424 ȝyngth . woman-kynde   1430 now . no lengere for to   1431 lewyd folk   1435 suffyre   1437 of om.   1440 erde . londe

Bk.IV.Ch.21.	This olde errour knowe we weel I-nough,[1]	[1] r. enow
	I haue my-selue conuicted many of yow,	1442
How could Christ's mother be a maid?	"Of [ȝ]oure secte I mene. how may ȝe for shame	1443
	Reherse of Ihesu that grete doubelnesse?	
	Some men seyn that he had a dame	
	Whiche was a mayde, in very soothfastnesse,	
	After the tyme that she had suffred distresse	1447
It is a lie.	Of childe-birthe—this knowe alle men a lye,	
	This leude doctryne is noȝt wurth a flye.	1449
	"Ye magnyfie hym for this cause also:	1450
As to His rising from death,	Ȝe seye he roos fro deeth to lyue ageyn.	
	But of his discyples in sekernesse weere there too	
	Whiche wente to the graue, as I herde Iues seyn:	
2 of His disciples only stole His body."	Thei stoole the body ful preuyly in a reyn,	1454
	And thanne seyde thei, her maister was I-goo	
	Be very myracle, and thus seyde many moo."	1456

Bk.IV.Ch.22.	Ca.m 22.m	
	ON-to these wordes, on-to this blaspheme	[1] al. om. 1457
Katharine says	She[1] answerde, þe mayde, with moost goodly chere,	
	She seyde thus: "at my lord of heuene	1459
	Tooke I be-gynnynge[1] of myn conflicte heere:	[1] MS. my beg.
	A makere is there withouten ony dwere	[2] overlined; r. or
	Ouere al thys world, whiche was er[2] it be-gan.	
Jupiter	ffor, as I haue proued, Iubiter was but a man,	1463
and Saturn were but men.	"No more was saturne, whiche was fadir his.[1]	1464
	Thanne sith thei were men and took her begynnynge,	
	Than muste we ferther procede, I-wis,	[1] al. his fadir is
	To seeke hym whiche be-forn this þinge	1467
	Was euere in heuene eternal[1] regnynge.	[1] r. eternally? al. eterne
	This same is god of whom now I preche,	
	Ageyn alle synnes moost souereyn noted leche;	1470

1441 elde . enow   1442 conuicte   1443 ȝour . who   1449 lewyd .
not worth   1451 lyffe   1453 iewys   1458 She om.   1460 my om.
my   1462 or   1464 hys fadyr is   1466 procede now   1467 befor
1468 eterne

"Spryng of aH þinge þat euere be-gynnyng hadde 1471
Soo is he called ; in whom alle þing is eke,
Of whom aH good þing, and no thyng hadde,
Procedeth, truly,¹ bothe be day and be weke,   ¹ *al.* newly
Be whom alle creaturis, be þei wylde or meke, 1475
Are conserued—at hym thus I began);
But if I dede, I were no wys woman). 1477

"Make no comparyson be-twyx ȝour god and myn)!
ffor my god hath made¹ al þing of nought,   ¹ h. m. on eras.
Eke your goddis arn) not soo goode as swyn)— 1480
Thei can) noȝt grunten) whan) hem eyleth ought.
As fer as ye in this mater haue I sought, 1482
I fond noo truthe : therfore fro ȝou I fledde ;
In truere weyes ful seker am I ledde." 1484

This man) was tho of these resons grete 1485
Soo troubled, he qwok be-twyxe ire and drede.
lete other men) now in this mater trete,
ffor he hath doon), he hath sowe his seede—
A seker help whan) ther cometh grete neede ! 1489
But god wulde haue hym) turned in this manere—
his merueilous menes shul we neuere lere. 1491

Cam. 23m.

Another clerk stood vp tho in haste, 1492
On-to the mayden) he made swiche euidens :
"Alle yowre wordis haue ye not spent in waste,
I vndirstonde ful weel ȝowre grete eloquens.
Ageyn oure goddis ȝe maken) this defens : 1496
Ye sey, her ymages whiche we worship heere
May noȝt feele ne haue noon) poweere. 1498

"This wote I weel, thei ben) but figures, 1499
Representynge other-maner thyng,
Liche to these fayre riche sepultures

1474 newly   1479 nowte   1480 are   1481 not gruntyn . ayleth
owte   1482 sowte   1483 flede   1484 trewer . lede   1485 resones
1493 mayde   1495 undyrstand   1496 make   1498 not . hafe . no
1499 be

2 3 ✱

310   *Katharine abuses Saturn and Jupiter.*   [MS. Arundel.

Bk.IV.Ch.23. Whiche be-tokene in her representyng
           That there is beryed duke or ell*is* kyng—   1503
the Gods   Soo arn these [ymages]¹ tooknes of godd*is* oure. ¹ MS. thyng*is*
themselves,
           To whom we ȝeue with herte grete honore,   1505
           " Not for her cause, but for signifycacio*n*)   1506
           Of the worthy whom thei represent.
           Therfore I answere to ȝoure replicacio*n*),
           Seruynge somwhat now ȝoure entent :
and are but Thei þat made hem, neu*ere* otherwyse ment   1510
set up to
stir men to To sette hem up, but for this cause o*n*nly,
devotion.
           That to hyere deuocio*n*) men shuld goo therby."   1512

Bk.IV.Ch.24.   Ca$^m.$ 24$^m.$

Katharine   Thanne seyde the mayde*n*) : " I wold ȝe shulde now shewe
denounces   of alle these godd*is* whiche þat wurthiest bee. 1514
           ffor as thei stonde in ȝoure temple on rewe,
           I can p*er*ceyue*n*) in hem noo dyuynyte   1516
Saturn as a More in oo*n*) than other.¹ for ȝo*ur* saturne, [parde],²
man-killer,   ¹ MS. in an other.
           Whil that he leued was a fals traytour, ² corr. : hardile
           homycide cruel, debater and robbour.   1519

his wife as " his wyf was woma*n*) ny of the same vice,   1520
a chider;
           Vengeable, dispitous, a¹ chidere eu*er*y tyde,   ¹ *al.* om.
           Of hir condicio*n*) onstable, and ful nyce—
           There myght no ma*n*) w*yth* hir no while abyde ;
           hir owne childre*n*) kylled she be hir syde.   1524
Jupiter as Iubiter was gelt of his fadir saturne eke,
           Banyshed his lond, his herberghe gan he seke.   1526
incestuous, " his owne suster Iubiter defouled tho,   1527
and a
banisher of his fadir after banyshed he oute of londe—
his Father.
           These ar*n*) the dedes of youre godd*is*, loo !
           how may ȝoure lawe eternally thus stonde
           Wha*n*) it is biled on soo brethel bonde ?   1531

        1503 byryed   1504 ar*e* . ymages   1513 no new chapt. mayde
        1515 stande . o rewe 1516 p*er*ceyue 1517 in an om. parde 1518
        lyued   1520 a woma*n* . þat   1521 a om.   1526 Banyschide . her-
        borow   1527 syster*e*   1529 ar*e*   1530 who   1531 bylyd . brythyll

Pluto was rauyshere of maydenes ful violent,   *Bk. IV. Ch. 24.*
Venus was lecherous and also vynolent,   1533   Pluto, Venus,

"Vulcane was cruel and ȝet was he cokhold—   1534   Vulcan,
how shulde swiche personys to ony godhed proue?
Some arn̄ ȝonge, some of hem arn̄ old.
Cupyde encreseth in men that onclene loue—   Cupid,
These grete velanyes can̄ ȝe neuere shoue.[1]   [1] *al.* fro hem shoue.
Of wytchecraft noted was ȝoure god Mercurie,   Mercury,
Maister of charmes and of swiche so[r]cerye.   1540

"Youre god appollo, whan he was drunken of wyn̄,   Apollo,
Thanne wulde he iangel in maner of prophecie,
fful sotil lesyngis wolde he tho dyuyne
To hem that knewe not his tretcherye,
Somtyme soothsawed, somtyme dede he lye.   1545
These are ȝoure goddys wiche þat ye honoure!   heathen Gods,
Alle to vices set was her laboure.   1547   were all vicious.

"ȝoure offerynges eke, thei be abhomynable: 1548   Offerings to them
To some goddes offre ȝe swynnes dunge;   abominable.
There cometh no mete be-fore you at the table
Til ȝour god hath awey the tunge.
If al ȝoure harlotrye thus openly were I-runge,   1552
It wolde shame ȝow. therefore ȝe þat ben̄ wyse,
ffle this foly, drede the hye Iustise!"   1554

Tho stood the man afrayed as oute of mynde,   1555   The second Philosopher
he coude noȝt speke to hir oon woord moo.   is silenst, and con-
Oure blissed lord his herte gan tho bynde   verted.
On-to his seruyse—therfore lete hym goo,
Sitte and reste as for that tyme with wo!   1559
Thus shul thei stynte whan god wil sey pees;
Of alle wysdam he can[1] soone relees.[2]   [1] MS. gan   [2] *al.* make relees.

1534 Wulcane 1535 who 1536 are 1538 vylonyes . neuyr fro hem 1541 drunk 1542 wold . iangyll 1544 tresceyre 1549 offyr . swynys 1550 comth 1553 be 1556 o 1561 can . make relees

Ca^{m.} 25^{m.1}

<small>A third Philosopher explains</small>

Another clerk thought deppere to procede,   1562
he stood vp tho, and this was his sentens :
"Of oure godd*is* ȝe shewe the shameful dede,
No-thyng speke ȝe of her good prouydens.
We haue in this mater ful mysty intelligens,   1566
Whiche may noȝt be comon to euery man;

<small>to Katharine</small> But to you, lady, soo now as I can,   1568

"Wil I *þat* comon, right for this entent,   1569
Be-cause youre-selue of wit sotil bee,
And for these lordes eke *þat* be present—
These same motiues at this tyme meue[1] me.   [1] MS. meueth
ffor I wil telle now the moste preuy secree   1573
Whiche *þat* we haue in oure philosophie
Touchynge the godd*is* and her p*ro*genye.   1575

<small>that Saturn is Time,</small>
"Saturne, þe firste whom ye soo dispreue,   1576
hym take we for tyme, be-cause he is oold,
And tyme, [parde][1], after oure beleue   [1] MS. weteth weel ȝe
As for a god among*is* us is hoolde.

<small>Jupiter, Fire,</small> Iubiter the kyng, as the truthe is toolde,   1580
he is take for fyre,[1] and [Iuno] eke, his wyf,   [1] MS. the f.
<small>Juno, Air.</small> She is take for eyr that vs ȝeueth lyf.   1582

<small>These Gods are an Allegory</small>
"Thus are oure godd*is* in man*er* of Allegorye,   1583
Resemble to natures whiche that be eterne.
Than is oure feyth grounded on noo lye,

<small>of things eternal.</small>
But on swhiche thyng whiche is sempiterne.
Myn owne lady, ye soughte noȝt weel this herne,   1587
Whan ȝe blasphemed oure godd*is* alle on rowe.
I telle you this ; I wolde alle men it knowe."   1589

Ca^{m.} 26^{m.}

<small>Katharine says</small>
The lady answerde with sad avisement,   1590
She seyde she knewe his circu*m*locucyon,

<small>1562 þouth   1566 hafe   1567 not . comyn*e*   1569 comown*e*   1572 meue   1578 parde   1579 now is   1581 the om. and Iuno . wyffe   1582 lyffe   1587 sowt not   1588 o rowe   1590 no new chapt.</small>

MS. Arundel.] *Katharine ridicules the Planets being Men.* 313

The kyng of Thebes a book had[1] hir sent		[1] MS. hir had *Bk. IV. Ch. 26.*
In whiche she fonde swiche exposicioun;		she has seen this explana-
But she halt it now but for abvsyoun.	1594	tion before.
Yet these resons whiche the man had shewed,		
Be very resoun she wil proue hem lewed.	1596	
ffor at this tale whiche this man had tolde	1597	
Gladdyng[1] the emperour, tremelyng euene for ioye,		The Emperor
To speke than was he waxe ful bolde; [1] *al.* Gladed		
"Clerke," he seyde, "saturne keepe the fro noye!		
I troste this lady wil now bere hir[1] more coye.	1601	
What sey 3e, mayde? where is 3oure answere?		challenges Katharine
If 3e can ought, lete us now it lere!" [1] *al.* bere hir now	1603	to answer.
The mayde seyde tho on-to that maister soone:	1604	
"3oure shameful doctryne wolde 3e ful fayn hyde		
With figures and colouris, as 3e are wont to doone;		
But 3e muste leyn these exposicions asyde.		
Arn not these planetes knowen wonder wyde?	1608	She asks, How can the
May we[1] not seen hem whan thei shyne soo clere? [1] MS. 3e		Planets,
The sonne, the mone, whiche shyne[1] on vs here, [1] r. shynen		Sun and Moon,
"This wote we weel that these been noo men.	1611	be men?
Why arn thei grauen thus of stoon and of tree?		
This errour is ful esy for to ken		
That men arn thei no3t, ne neuere-[more] shal bee.		They are not.
In these fyguris thanne ful foule erre 3ee;	1615	Their images are shams.
Ye wurshep the shadwe and leue the substauns,		
here is in 3ow a ful grete varyauns.	1617	
"Eke the planetes whiche shyne thus aboue,	1618	The Planets can't be proved eternal.
Though thei shul stonden euere and be eterne,		
Yet can 3e not with 3oure bookys proue		
That þei haue euere be-fore be sempiterne.		
If philosophie were looked in his preuy herne,	1622	

1592 had hir   1595 resones   1598 gladed   1601 bere hyre now . koye   1604 tho om. þe   1606 fygure . coloure . wone   1607 ley 1608 Arc . knowyne   1609 we . se   1610 sune . on-to   1611 þei be 1612 are . graue   1613 ken   1614 are . neuer more   1616 schadow 1619 schuld stand   1621 hafe   1622 phylophye

314 *A Philosopher is convinst by Katharine.* [MS. Arundel.

Bk.IV. Ch.26.
The Planets

Ye shulde fynde þere þat planet*is* alle ben made.
What wil ȝe ferthere in this mater wade? 1624

are made by their Creator, God.

"If thei be made, than aru þei creatures, 1625
And he that made hem, [he] is god allone.
ley hem in wat*er*, alle youre mysty figures,
ffor noȝt aru thei, neither þe stok ne the stoone.

Pray to Him!

On-to that hye god loke ȝe make yo*ur* moone, 1629
Prey hym to sende ȝou of errour repentauns!
Thanne haue ȝe of treuthe the very assurauns." 1631

Bk. IV. Ch.27.

Ca^m. 27^m.1   ¹ = Rawl. 25^m.

The Philosophers marvel at Katharine.

The philosophres merueyled of this answere, 1632
Of hir wit and of hir eloquens;
Thei that now in presens aru there
herde neu*er*e be-fore swiche-man*er* sentens.
She can alle thyng of very exp*er*iens. 1636

One Master

A maister stod vp and spak tho to hem alle:
"I wolde a supposed," he seyd, "þat the heuene shuld falle,

exhorts the others to

"Rather than woman swiche sciens shulde attame. 1639
lete vs leue, felawes, now oure olde scole,
Yeue attendauns at þis tyme to this dame!
ffor in þis word¹ in cunnynge stant she soole.   ¹ = world
Alle oure lernynge wil turne vs to doole 1643
But if we folwe, as meche as we may,

learn the Truth from Katharine.

To lerne the trewthe whiche shal lasten ay. 1645

"Therfore lete vs lerne now of þis mayde 1646
What þat god is whiche made thus alle þing.
With this mater haue I ben ofte dismayde,
ffor I coude neu*er*e with natu[r]al arguyng
Diuyne so ferre, and eu*er*e oure stodyeng 1650
hath ben therto ful directe, as me semeth.

He believes her doctrine.

I wil beleue now as þis lady demeth." 1652

1623 be   1625 are   1626 he is   1628 nowt are . the om.   1631
hafe   1634 are   1640 elde   1641 entendauns   1642 worlde . stand
1645 lestyne   1648 hafe . be   1650 stodyyng   1651 be

MS. Arundel.] *Katharine expounds Trinity in Unity.* 315

Thus is consented now alle þe companye; 1653 *Bk. IV. Ch. 27.*
Thei wil lere of hir, þei sey plat and pleyn,
ffor it is aboue al her phylosophie,
What lord he is þat made the wynd and reyn.
That there is swiche on, can thei weel [I]-seyn, 1657
But what he is, or what is his name,
This desire thei to lerne now of this dame. 1659

All the Philosophers ask Katharine to teach them about God.

The mayde eke was as glad as thei, 1660
To enforme hem in this same matere;
On-to these men ful sadly gan she sey:
"Sith that ȝe take the foorme now of scolere,
Ye arn the rediere these mysteries for to lere. 1664
But we wil leue this godhed for a tyme,
And of the manhod a while wil we[1] ryme. [1] MS. we wil 1666

She says

" Ye shal knowe first, þat oo god is in heuene, 1667
Distynct in persones, as we beleue,[1] thre, [1] r. beleuen
ffadir and sone and holygoost ful euene:
These same persones oonly oo god [be].[1] [1] MS. arn hee.
Oure auctouris seyn that if god had bee 1671
Oonly oo persone, than shulde not his hooly blys
Be comound to other soo parfytly as it is, 1673

One God is in 3 persons.

" ffor creature noon myght receyue [no][1] swiche; 1674
Therfore he ordeyned be his eterne counsayle [1] MS. corr.: ony
That thre persones in myght and nature lich
In oo godhed—to vs ful gret meruayle— [1] MS. considered
Shuld be con[fe]dered[1] to mannes grete avayle, 1678
And iche of other his substauns shulde thus take,
Noon lesse, noon more—thus oure feith we make 1680

These 3 form 1 Godhead.

" Of [þe] thre persones the secunde, whiche is the sone,
Cam doun to erthe, here he took [mankynde],[1]
ffor man had lost al þat euere was done [1] MS. corr.: mannes keende
Whan he [to][2] god was falle [so vnkynde][3] [2] MS. fro [3] MS. to the feende

The Second took man's nature, to redeem man.

1657 I-seyne 1664 are 1666 wy!l we 1670 be 1671 sey 1674 no sweche 1678 confederyd 1679 eche 1681 þe thro . qweche . sune 1682 crde . mankynde 1684 to god . fall so vnkynde

316 How can one Being be God and Man? [MS. Arundel.

Bk. IV. Ch 28.

Christ came to unite God and man.

He was born of a Virgin, and died for us.

he brak þe precepte with whiche he gaue hem b[y]nde[1]
A-mongis the trees in the place of delice, [1] MS. beende
Whiche þat we clepe in bookis paradice. 1687
" And for there was no man able in erthe ther-too 1688
To make vnyte be-twix god and man,
This was the cause that þat lord dede soo.
he light to erthe and in a ʒong woman,
A clene mayde[n], flesh and blood he nam; 1692
There-in he deyed to slee oure synnes alle.
This is the god on whom we cristen calle." 1694

Bk. IV. Ch.28.   Ca[m]. 28[m.1]   [1] = Rawl. 26[m].

The chief Philosopher

asks how the

natures of God and Man can join in 1 person.

God is eternal, man is mortal.

The maister princypal, whiche the woordys hadde 1695
   ffor hem alle at that same day and tyme,
Of hir doctryne was ful Ioyeful and gladde ;
ffor god had poynted in hym a newe pryme,
Oure lord ihesu had purged hym of his cryme, 1699
Made hym disposed to his conuersion.
But he merueyleth soore of this informacion. 1701
he seyde to the lady in ful faire manere : 1702
" Oo thyng there is heere in youre techyng
Whiche I can noʒt conceyue it ʒet ful clere :
ffor god and man in her coupelyng
Been ful diuers, and ʒet sey ʒe this thyng 1706
That bothe natures ben ioyned in oo persone ;
There was neuere swiche but if it be he allone. 1708
" ffor if he be god, than muste he be eterne ; 1709
If he be man, þan is he corruptible.
[A][1] nature [or][2] persone whiche is sempiterne,
To sey of it that it is passyble,   [1] MS. corr.: Of [2] MS. a
Semeth to me a ful gret insolible. 1713
This is the mocyon, lady, ʒe muste declare,
ffor in þis mater oure wittis been ful bare." 1715

1685 bynde   1692 maydyne . of flesche   1693 deyd   1698 hath
1701 mcruelyth   1706 Be   1707 be   1711 A n. or p.   1715 be . but

Ca^m. 29^m.

Thus to this mocyon answerde tho þe mayde: 1716
"Ye muste conceyue," she seyde, "in ȝoure mynde
That these too natures in oure lord ihesu were layde
And coupled to-geder ageyn vsed kynde.
Thus we of hym in solenne book*is* fynde; 1720
But the very proue of his werk*is* grete
Is right I-now this mater for to trete. 1722

"ffor he þat reysed laȝarus fro the graue 1723
Where he had loyn foure dayes euene,
he that petir in the see dede saue
And walked there as men doon on a grene,
he þat commaunded the wynd þat was soo kene 1727
That it shulde cese and blowe noo more þat tyde,
he þat so merueylously on-to heuene gan glyde 1729

"Body and al: he was more þan man, 1730
ffor be his godhed wrought he this meruayles.
Moche more þing now reherce I can,
But I passe ouere, ȝeuynge to ȝour assayles
Tyme and space. I prey god þat ȝour entrayles 1734
he endewe with grace, that ȝe may knowe the truthe—
Of ȝour damnacyon haue I ful grete ruthe. 1736

"But alle these werkes whiche were soo grete 1737
Shewe be reson that more than man was hee.
Whan he the Iewes mette right in þe streete,
There shewed he thanne his diuynyte:
Thei durste noȝt looke, but fel doun at his kne. 1741
There myghte noo creature be reson doo these werkys,
But he were god—thus proue oure clerkys. 1743

"And that he ete his mete, slepe and wente, 1744
Spak and drank, rested, and wery was eke,
This serueth ful pleynly to youre argument

Margin notes: Katharine says that Christ's raising Lazarus, making Peter walk on the sea, and His bodily ascension into heaven, prove His Godhead: that He was more than man, though also man.

1716 no new chapter 1722 enow 1723 laȝare 1724 loy fourti (!)
1726 do 1728 he 1730 a man 1731 wrowt . þese 1732 meche
1734 pase 1735 treuth 1736 reuth 1741 not

Bk. IV. Ch. 29.

Christ's 2 natures workt diversely here.

In whiche ȝe gaɴ ful sotylly for to seeke.
ȝowre answere haue ȝe, if it may ȝow leke : 1748
That these too natures whiche in hym were,
Diuers werkyng*is* had, whil he was heere. 1750

Even the heathen Sybil said that God should be hangd like a thief;

" Yet of [ȝ]oure aucto*ris* may we take witnesse. 1751
Sibille seyde me*r*ueylously in þis matere :
That holy god, she seyde, eu*er*e be in blesse
Whiche shal¹ be hanged liche a thef heere ¹ MS. shulde
Right on a tree, and after leyd on beere. 1755
What wil ȝe more? what shulde I to ȝou say?
On-to this auctrix ȝe may neu*er*e seye nay. 1757

and her authority is unquestionable.

" ffor as an auctour a[d]mitted in ȝoure lawe 1758
Is she receyued, and pleynly to oure feyth
Bereth she wytnesse in hir mysty sawe,
ffor these too natures in oure lord she leyth :
God, he his fulblyssed, as she seyth, 1762
And manhod¹ it is that heyng vp-on the tree. ¹ MS. mandhode
Oute of ȝowre lawe cometh this auctoryte." 1764

Bk. IV. Ch. 30.

Ca*m*. 30*m*. ¹ ¹ = Rawl. 27*m*.

Another Philosopher

Another maister, euene ful of eloquens, 1765
Of curtesye eke, and a ful seemly maɴ,
Spak to this lady with ful grete reuerens ;
he seyde hir [wytt]¹ be-fore her wyttys raɴ) ¹ MS. woordis
Soo grete a paas it caɴ not be ou*er*-taɴ ; 1769

asks Katharine

But ȝet he preyed hir that he myght seye, ¹ r. hir? ² r. sche?
In his¹ arguyng ful naturally he² took the weye. 1771

to prove her doctrine by Nature.

" ffor nature," he seyde, " be swiche influens 1772
Was soo confermed that it myght not faile ;
Euery thyng therfore that maketh resistens
Ageyɴ nature, ful soone wil it quayle ;
With-oute nature may no thyng avayle." 1776

1751 ȝo*ur* 1754 schallbe hankyd lech*e* 1758 admittede 1762 is . byssyd 1763 hyng 1768 wytt inst. of woord*is* 1776 wyth-outyn

Christ's 2 Natures like Man's Body & Soul.

Wherfore he wolde, swhiche thyng as she shal preche,
Be natural resons hir thyng*is* shulde she teche. 1778

"ffor hard it is to constreyne a mannes wil 1779
To trowe a þing whiche he can not proue.
hoo shal beleue good thyng*is* or ell*is* il,[1]   [1] orig. ille
That same beleue muste come of very loue 1782
And very trost whiche is on-to his be-houe."[1]   [1] *at.* houe
Therfore this man desyreth that naturally
hir conclusyons she proue now openly. 1785

Prove Christ's two natures, naturally.

Ca^m. 31^m.

She seyde, she wolde with good entent 1786
Soo as hir wit[1] wolde serue hir for þis tyme, [1] MS. with
And soo as god of his grace hath sent
On-to hir knowleche at þat day to dyuyne,
fful fayn wulde she this mayster to enclyne— 1790
ffor she to crist cast hir hym to drawe,
he shal no more troste now on is lawe. 1792

Katharine quotes the

This same exaumple putte she to hym tho, 1793
Of body and soule whiche we bere aboute,
how thei arn[1] Ioyned in on þus, these too, [1] MS. arn thei
And oon is hyd, the other is seen with-oute.
She seyde, "to alle men it is ful grete dowte 1797
how þat the soule whiche þat [m]euere is
Cam to the body, whan he cam fro blys; 1799

analogy of man's body and soul.

How does the Soul come to the Body?

"What weye he cam, or ell*is* in what hour 1800
Whan to the body he cam it for to queke;
It is but foly to spende ony labour
Swiche preuy thyng*is* for to serge and seeke.
Ʒe may leue these thyng*is*,[1] if ye leeke, [1] r. this thyng 1804
That soule and body arn ioyned now in-feere
In what persone þat Ʒe see walken heere; 1806

It's folly to search into such hidden things.

1778 resonis   1781 þing   1783 houe inst. of behoue   1786 no new chapt.   1787 wit   1790 wold she now. to om.   1792 his 1794 abouthe   1795 who . are   1796 his hyd . wyth-outhe   1797 douthe   1798 who . meuere   1802 oure l.   1804 þis þinge . like 1805 are   1806 walke

Lk. IV. Ch. 31.	" And if ye liste not to be-leue this thyng,	1807
If then men know nothing	Ye may leue—but ȝe shal it neuere I-knowe,	
	The maner or¹ tyme of [þis] preuy werkyng,	¹ MS. of
	Youre scole therto is ȝet ouer-lowe.	
	Ye may weel booste of ȝour connynge and blowe,	1811
	But ȝe shal faile whanne ȝe come to the poynt ;	
	Oure lord [god] hath hyd fro yow that ioynt.	1813
of their own souls and bodies,	" Thanne, sith ȝe may be no natural weye	1814
	haue the knowleche of these creatures heere,	
	how shulde we of ȝow now þan seye	
	That ȝe shulde knowe þing aboue ful clere ?	1817
how can they know about Christ's being ?	how shulde ȝe knowe þe¹ lord þat hath powere	¹ al. þat
	Ouere alle thyng ? how shulde ye to hym gesse,	
	Whanne þat ȝe may not knowe moche þing lesse ? "	1820

Bk. IV. Ch. 32.   **Caᵐ. 32ᵐ.¹**   ¹ = Rawl. 28ᵐ.

	Whanne this answere was youe thus to þis man,	1821
	Eche man be-syde þat stood tho aboute	
	fful merueylously chaunge¹ thei be-gan.	¹ r. chaungen
The Christians who've bowd to idols,	ffor thei þat cristen were, with-oute[n] doute,	
	Whiche to the maumentis before-tyme dede loute,	1825
repent and lament	Now wayle þei soore with ful grete repentauns,	
	Demyng hem-self ful worthi grete penauns ;	1827
	Thei haue remembred her god moost of myght,	¹ MS. hem
at Katharine's last answer.	And where that a woman precheth him¹ constantly,	1829
	There thei forsake hym ; " this thyng gooth not right,	
	That [þe] frelere kynde shal soo stab[y]ly	1831
	Confesse oure feyth, where þat¹ more myghty	¹ r. þat þo
	helde her pees and dar speke ryght nought "—	
	Of the cristen this was bothe cry and thought.	1834
The Pagans see their Philosophers silenst.	The other syde, tho that paynemes were,	1835
	Thei sey hir resons and hir grete euydens	
	Whiche stoyned the clerkis alle tho¹ ben there ;	¹ r. that

1809 or tyme of þ·s   1813 lord god   1816 who   1817 ful om.
1818 þat   1819 who   1820 meche   1821 Whan þat þis   1824 with-
outen   1826 ful om.   1828 hir . myth   1829 hem om.   1830 no
ryth   1831 þe freler . stabyly   1832 myty   1837 that be

MS. Arundel.] *Appollymas questions Katharine.* 321

This putte þe puple in conceytes [ful] suspens.   *Bk. IV. Ch. 32.*
ffor al her labour and al her grete expens   1839
ffor thys þing her reward shal be woo.
Grete murmur was there, and some be-gunne to goo. 1841

Ouer al this þe emperour he his now wood,   1842   The Emperor
On-to the clerkis with ful angry face
he cried, " be armes, bones, and be blood,   abuses the Philosophers
It was a shame and a soory grace
That soo fele clerkis gadered in a place   1846
Shulde be astoyned sodeynly of a mayde ;"   [1] MS. cowardis   for being put down by
" Coward[1] churles!" right thus to hem he seyde, 1848   Katharine.

" Pluk vp 30ure hertis, lete no3t oure lawe thus falle,
lete not oure goddys suffre thus this wrong!   1850
But if 3e doo, the moost part of yow shalle   Unless they answer her,
Er longe tyme be the nekke shul be hong.   he'll hang 'em.
Speke, men, for shame! the tyme is not long, 1853
It paseth faste and we doo no note ;
Me thenketh ye stoonde euene as men that dote." 1855

Ca^{m.} 33^{m.1}   [1] MS. 32^{m.} = Rawl. 29^{m.}   *Bk. IV. Ch. 33.*

Tho stood up with a newe motyf   1856
   A fressh clerk, mayster appollymas—   Appollymas
Soo aferd was he neuere in al his lyf
Of no mater ne of no diuers cas
Soo as of this mater now he fesed was ;   1860
But thus seyde he þan softly to the mayde :   objects that Katharine
" In 3oure declaryng, lady, me thought 3e sayde 1862

" Too sundry thyngis, if we considere weel ; 1863
Contradiccyon ful soone in hem shal be founde.
Youre lord ihesu, whiche is knowe ful weel,   said Jesus made the World,
As 3e sey he made this world soo rounde,
Adam and Eue he foormed fro the grounde,   1867   Adam and Eve, &c.
And al other thyng whyche that hath substauns
It was made, 3e sey, be his ordynauns.   1869

   1838 ful suspens   1846 soo om.   1848 coward   1849 not   1854 passith   1855 stand   1857 apollinas   1868 haue

Bk. IV. Ch. 33.

Whereas Jesus was, in fact, born

not 300 years ago.

How could He then have made the world?

Let Katharine answer plainly.

"Ageyn ȝou now thus I wil replie,   1870
Prouynge on-treuthe in youre marred feyth.
I haue made rek[e]nynge, whiche may not lye,
A-mongis oure storyes, what[1] ony man seyth :   [1] r. what so?
The berthe of ihesu ful truly oure book leyth,   1874
ffor he was bore[1] vndir octauyane   [1] r. boren
At lytel bethleem in a l[ewde][1] lane ;   [1] MS. lowe   1876
"It is not ȝet fully[1] thre hundret ȝeere   [1] al. not fully ȝet
Sith þat ȝoure ihesu of his modyr was[2] bore.   1878
how dar ȝe thanne in swhiche presens here
Afferme of thyng þat was soo longe before,   [2] al. was of his modyr
That he this [worlde] shulde make or restore ?   1881
how myghte he make thyng whyche thowsendis fyue
had her duracyoon er than[1] he took lyue ?   [1] al. that   1883
"This is my motyf, an[1] answere I desyre   [1] MS. and   1884
In pleyn langage with-oute distynctyon.
This symple puple haue ȝe set on fyre
Wyth youre crafty circumlocucyon.
Answere in short to this conclusyon,   1888
Than shal I sey that ȝe be þat mayde
Swiche another no man hath assayde."   1890

Bk. IV. Ch. 34.

She says Appollymas

has thought only of Christ's temporal birth, not His eternal.

Ca**m. 34**m.[1]   [1] MS. 33m.

Thus spak the lady on-to the clerk ageyn :   1891
  "Alle ȝoure groundes, sere, in youre arguyng
haue take oo partye and, shortly for to seyn,
lefte the other ; wherfore the concludyng
ffayleth ful foule now in ȝour rekkenyng.   1895
his manhod counte ȝe, and his birthe temporall,
And not that birthe whiche is eternall.   1897
  "ffor this temporal birthe, as ȝe seyde late,   1898
Was now before us not many ȝeeres goo—

1871 marrethe   1873 stores   1875 borne   1876 bethlem . lewde lane   1877 fully ȝete   1878 was of his m.   1879 who   1881 þis worlde   1882 who . thousandis   1883 er þat   1884 an   1888 a folio is missing in the MS. to v. 1963.

As to compa*r*iso*n* of the largere date
It may be counted but for a ȝeer or too.
But of this mater the mistery wil I on-doo, — 1902 — Katharine explains
ffor of this same haue ȝe grete m*er*uayll,
As me semeth right be ȝoure assayll. — 1904

"At the gynnynge first shul ȝe vndirstande, — 1905 — that Jesus was God from eternity,
That god eternally hath eu*er*e oure ihe*s*u bee ;
Makere and shapere of all thyng þat is leuande,
Thus is he called, and thus beleue we.
But now in[1] late dayes of his charite — [1] *al.* of — 1909 — but lately took man's nature, to redeem him.
he took oure keende to oure redempcyo*n*),
In whyche keende he suffred his[1] passyo*n*). — [1] *al.* om. — 1911

"ffor the manhod was not able to doo this thyng, — 1912
And the godhed myght not suffre swiche disese ;
Wherfore of these too he made a coupelyng, — He coupled His Divine Nature with human.
The faderes offens thus for to plese,[1] — [1] r. pese ?
The deueles power thus for to fese. — 1916
In godhed and manhed he took this batayll,
ffor manhed allone myght not avayll. — 1918

"Thus, for his godhed hath be eternally, — 1919
Therfore sey we that he made al thynge
Thurgh power of the same, and eke þat body
Whiche was conceyued of a mayde[n] yinge ;
That same body on the crosse hyng, — 1923 — The body born at Bethlehem hung on the cross.
That same body at bethleem was bore—
ffor the godhed hath be eternally before." — 1925 — The Godhead was eternal.

Wha*n*) she had sayde this glorious vers, — 1926
The ma*n*) stood stoyned and marred in meende ;
Noon of hir woordes coude he reuers,
Thei passed of his lernyng al the keende ;
Resons ageyn) hir coude he noon fynde, — 1930
But thus seyde he tho openly with cry : — Her opponent believes in Christ.
"As ȝe beleue, lady, soo beleue I." — 1932

Ca. 35.[1]   [1 MS. 34m.]

Another Philosopher asks why

Another mayster made hir thys motyf: 1933
"ȝe preche of crist," he seith, "and of his dede,
how he for man thus freely lost his lyf
ffor to brynge hym to þat heuenely mede;
his deth, ȝe sey, awey tho gan lede 1937
Alle-maner synne, the power eke of helle
With his deth that lord gan than felle. 1939

Christ didn't send an Angel to fight the Devil,

"Might not þat lord with his real power 1940
A maistred the deuel and putte hym soo to flyght?
Might he not a sente an aungel or a massager?

instead of doing it Himself?

What was the cause that he hym-self wolde fight,
Suffre swiche passyon and lese soo his right? 1944
If he was myghty, whi suffred he that wrong?
Answere my tale, for it is noȝt long. 1946

"If he hym-selue myght not redresse þis thyng, 1947
Than was it foly to take[n] it on hande;
And if he were, as ȝe seye, soo myghty a kyng,
There myght no powere þan ageyn hym stande.
Yowre prophete seyde that he with yrn wande 1951
Alle his enemyes shulde bothe bete and bynde.
In swiche sufferaunce me thenketh he was blynde." 1953

Ca. 36.[1]   [1 MS. 35m.]

Katharine answers,

"Youre motyf, sir," seyde the noble queen, 1954
"hath grete colour, but ȝet I voyde it thus,
A[s][1] I haue lerned in bookes that I haue seen. [1 MS. And]
Oure lord crist, oure sauyour Iesus,
list for to feyten with the deuel for vs 1958
And ouere-come hym in swiche keende as he took,

"because Adam's sin had to be redrest by man."

ffor the synne of Adam, if we wil look, 1960

"Muste been redressed oonly be mankeende; 1961
And be-cause ther were a-mongis men non able—
ffor in al erthe myght he than noon fynde

Man soo clene, soo parfight, soo profytable
As Adam was whyl that he was stable 1965 *As Adam*
In blissed paradys er he dede offens,
Therfore oure lord with his fleshly presens 1967

" Took þis iornay and deyed on [a] tree, 1968
That, euene as synne in the tree was doo, *sind by a tree,*
Right soo on the tree deth suffred hee. *so Christ died on a tree.*
It was conuenyent he shulde feyte soo :
In tree[1] was ioye bore, and in the tree woo ; [1] *al.* þe tre 1972
Woo be sathan, Ioye be oure lord Ihesu ;
Oute of the tree a blissed frute grew." 1974

Ca^{m.} 37^{m.1} [1] MS. 36^{m.} = Rawl. 31^{m.} *Bk. IV. Ch. 37.*

There stood vp thanne with a [full] boold face 1975
A grete clerk, thei called Alfragan ; *Alfragan objects*
he thoughte to haue worship in þat place,
his apposayle right thus he be-gan :
" Youre ihesu crist, he is bothe god and man, 1979
As ȝe seye, lady. but ley that a-syde,
As for a space lete that mater abyde ! 1981

" Ye cristen putte euere in ȝoure posycion 1982 *that though there is but one Christian God,*
That there be noo moo goddis but oon ;
But if youre owne booke come to reuolucion,
I trowe oo god shal not be founde there allon.
I rede in a cristen prophete not longe a-gon— 1986 *a Prophet says,*
I wot not ȝet veryly[1] what ȝe hym calle— [1] *al.* not veryly ȝet
Thus speketh he that ȝe be goddis alle. 1988 *"Ye are all Gods."*

" Whom mente he heere in this pluralite 1989
But god, whiche ȝe syngulere confesse ?
Be-twyxe these too is noon n[eut]ralite.[1] [1] MS. naturalite *How can this be ?*
But, be thei more goddis or be thei lesse,
Youre owne bookis of hem bere wetenesse 1993

1964 parfyth . profithable 1966 or . 1968 on a . 1971 fyte
1972 þe tre . in 2 om. 1974 þat tre . 1975 wyth full bold 1980 o syde 1987 ueryly ȝit 1991 no neutralite 1993 witnesse

Bk. IV. Ch.37. That many be there and moo than oon).
lete see what weye that ȝe wil now goon) ! 1995

Christians say there is one God, with a son Jesus;
" Ye putte to vs here a grete god of heuene 1996
Whiche hath a sone, ȝe sey hight Ihesu :
And in ȝowre book*is* fynde we ful euene
Of a-nother god, bothe iuste and true,

yet their books speak of the god Baal.
Thei calle hym) baal—I trowe ȝe hym knewe ; 2000
Thre hundret prophetes on-to his seruyse
Were endued there, ful sad men and wise. 2002

" How may ȝe sey thanne þat god is but on) ? 2003
hough may ȝe for-barre oure oppynyon) ?
If þat ȝoure god be regnande thus allon),

This is contradictory.
Why speke ȝoure book*is* of swiche dyuysyon) ?
Why may not Iubiter make his coniunccyon) 2007
With Iuno, his wif, syth there been) godd*is* fele ?
Youre resons, lady, avayle not a rake-stele." 2009

Bk. IV. Ch.38. Ca^m. 38^{m.1} [1] MS. 37^m.

Katharine says the Scriptures use figurative language.
" YE muste conceyue, sir," seyde the mayde, 2010
" That oure scripture in his mysti speche
hath many fygures if thei ben) asayde :
Oure lord god is somtyme called a leche,
Somtyme a Iustyse and ful of wreche, 2014
Somtyme a fadir al ful of loue ;
Swhiche sondry predicates in hym wil[1] proue [1] MS. wil I

"The sondry effectes that in hym bee. 2017
Wherfore I telle you, sir, if ȝe wil here,—
Of oure feyth a ful grete verite
Ye may consydere now, and ȝe wil lere :
Godd*is* are there noon), ne [neuer]-more were, 2021

But there is only One God, the Creator of all things.
But on) allone whiche made erthe and heuene,
hayl, reyn, wynd, thounder and leuene, 2023

1997 sun . hith   2002 endewid   2003 who   2004 who   2008 be
2010 no new chapt. ser*e* 2012 be   2016 sundry . I om.   2018 ser
2021 ne neu*er* more   2022 erde   2023 þundir

Of God's Sons by birth and by adoption.

"And be nature he is god regnyng thus allone ; 2024 *Bk. IV. Ch. 38.*
But yet of his goodnesse he hath to hym chose   *This One God has chosen*
Certeyn persones to dwelle in his woone :   *folk to dwell with Him.*
Tho calleth he goddis, as I suppose.
This þat I seye now, is noo fals glose,   2028
But folweth of the texte, if ȝe take hed ;   *These, tho Scripture*
ffor there that ye now on this wyse gaþ red   2030 *calls Gods,*

" ' I sey ȝe be goddis,' there folweth[1] thus   [1] r. it f. 2031
' And sones of hym that sytteth hyest.'   *and Sons of God.*
This is a gret distynccyoþ, sir, amongis vs   *We distinguish*
Of nature and adopcyoþ, whiche is the best.   *between nature and*
Adopcyoþ, we seye, is but as a gest,   2035 *adoption.*
ffor he is chosen in right be fre wiH ;
B[ut] natural regnynge hath an hyer skiH.[1]   [1] MS. Be 2037

" ffor who-so regneth naturally in ony place,   2038
he may not be putte oute but he haue wrong ;
And he þat chosen is, he cometh in be grace.   [1] MS. brynge
Myn answere wil I br[egge][1] and make not longe ; 2041
ffor[2] catche now this conceyte and in ȝour wit it fonge
That naturally god regneth al allone ;   [2] MS. ffor to
Whiche of his goodnesse hath called to his trone 2044

" Certeyþ folkys right of his good grace,   2045 *The folk thus cald Gods*
Whiche goddis we calle be-cause thei haue blis.   *are with God, see His face,*
Thus are thei with hym euere and see his face,   *and are Sons by adoption.*
Regne there in Ioye whiche may neuere mys ;
There arþ thei treeted ryght as childreþ his.   2049
This is the entent of that auctoryte.—
A-nother thyng efte allegge yee   2051
                                                 [1] MS. the god prophete
" Of baal the god[1] and of his seruauntes alle ; 2052 *As to Baal, the Scripture*
But noo-thyng to purpos is[1] that ȝe conclude. [1] MS. if *only says that false prophets*
Oure scripture reherseth thei dede hym soo calle,   *cald him God,*
Tho same prophetes, of his simylitude.

2024 is he 2029 folowith 2036 chose in, rith 2037 But . a
2040 chosyn . comth 2041 bregge 2042 to om. 2049 are 2052
þat god ; prophete om. 2053 is

328 *The Pagan Philosophers are all converted.* [**MS. Arundel.**

Bk. IV. Ch. 38.
and that they were damd for it.

Reede better þat book of tho dyuyno*ur*s rude, 2056
ffor there shal ȝe fynde that thei damned were
ffor heer fals beleue, alle þat were there." 2058

Bk. IV. Ch. 39.

Ca^m. 39^m.1   [1] MS. 38^m. = Rawl. 32^m.

Alfragan confesses that Katharine

The maister avysed hym and than cryed loude: 2059
 "Thys mayde wil oue*re*-leede us, sirs, we are caught
In oure artes, be we neuere so proude;
A newe maistresse sekerly haue we laught,

has beaten him.
He gives up.

Alle oure lernynge as now avayleth naught. 2063
Therfore I sey, as for me, I ȝeue it vp,
This lady hath drunken of an hyer cup, 2065

"Of preuyere secret*is*[1] þan euere we coude fynde; 2066
She passeth plato, she passeth philosophie,   [1] r. secres
She speketh of hym þat auctour is of kynde.
That she seyth, I wote weel is noo lye.
Wherfore of herte entierly thus I crye: 2070

He turns to her Faith,

I can noo more, I wil turne to hyr feyth
And leue myn olde, what[1] ony man seyth.   [1] Ar. 20 what so

"Ye shul doo soo eke be myn consent. 2073

and acknow-ledges One God, and Him alone.

ffor oo god I knowleche and noon but hym allone—
Though I seyde nowht, eue*re* haue I soo ment.
lete vs submytte vs therfore to hys trone!
I am conue*r*ted, I sey, for my p*er*sone, 2077
I shal neue*re* berke ageyn that deyte.
In this mater, sirs, what sey ȝee?" 2079

All the others do so too.

Thei cryed alle concoursly[1] with oo voys   [1] MS. comoursly
That thei consenten to his conclusyon,
Oo god confesse thei whiche þei calle noys;
What he co*m*maundeth, of nede it muste be doon.
But ȝet her conseyt*is* wil thei vtter soon 2084
Of other thyng*is* longynge to this crede.—
To telle the rumour, I trowe it is noo nede, 2086

2056 dyuynouris 2060 seris . caut 2062 laut 2063 naut 2065 drunke . a . cupp 2066 secres 2068 autor 2070 enterly 2072 elde 2073 my 2079 seres 2081 consent 2084 uttyr sounc

Whiche in the puple is encresed this tyde.	2087	
"Allas!" þei sey, "what lif haue þei ledde,		The people rail at the Philosophers.
Oure grete clerk*is* whiche arn) knowe soo wyde?		
It were as good thei had loyn)[1] in bedde, [1] *al.* loy		
Whan) thei teche thyng whiche must be fledde,	2091	
Whiche thyng is holde but for vanyte."		
The lordes eke there after her degree	2093	The Lords
Disputed þis mater, and bete it up and doune;	2094	
"Noo god but oon)?" þei seyde, "thanne what is[1] saturne?"		
Eche to other ful preuely thus dede rowne: [1] *al.* what is thanne		
"ffro these maument*is* good is that we turne;		
lete vs despyse hem and with oure feet hem spurne,	2098	propose to spurn their idols.
ffor this falshed haue we folwed to longe"— [1] *al.* thanne there		
This was the noyse there thanne[1] hem amonge.	2100	
The emp*er*our looketh, but I trowe he is wrooth;	2101	The Emperor is angry
"ffy on feynte harlott*is* that thus ren[e]yeth oure lawe!"		
Thus seyde he þanne, he thought his lyf ful looth;		
That ony mayden) clerk*is* shulde thus drawe,		that a Maiden beats his wise men.
That she shuld be wysehere[1] in hir saughe, [1] = wysère	2105	
This greueth hym sore. but ȝet in his greuauns		
Stood vp a clerk whiche with his dalyauns	2107	
Seyde he wolde proue be reson) naturall	2108	One Philosopher undertakes to prove Katharine's doctrine false.
That moche thyng touched was ful ontrewe;		
Oo p*er*sone eterne an[d] eke mortall, [1] MS. is		
This doctryne, he seyde, [was][1] come on [þe][2] newe.		
But the same resons that other dede sewe [2] MS. on-to vs, on eras.		
Reherseth my[n] auctour, as he dooth ful ofte.		I leave that out,
I suffer tho leuys to ly[e]n) stille ful softe,	2114	
lete other men here hem that loue nugacyon);	2115	
ffor other many mater*is* must come on hande.		
I wil reherse first the grete disputacyon)		and pass over to Ariot's dispute.
In whiche that þis lady feythfully gan) stande		

2088 hafe 2089 are 2090 loy 2092 for a 2094 beet 2095 what is þa*n* 2100 þa*n* þere 2102 reneyth 2104 schul 2105 wysere. sawe 2108 naturale 2109 mych 2110 & . mortale 2111 was come on þe newe 2112 resones 2113 my*n* 2114 lye 2116 most

Bk.IV.Ch.39.	With maister Aryot, thorgh-oute that lande	2119
	Most famous man) noysed in þat tyme;	
	Of þis mater wil we now ryme.	2121

Bk.IV.Ch.40.   Ca^{m.} 40^{m.1}   [1] MS. 39m. = Rawl. 33m.

Aryot disputes with Katharine.	This Aryot was chose be comon) assent	2122
	To dispute with hir, to looke if þat he may	
	Destroyen) hir feith and alle hir fundament;	
	On hym haue thei put now al this affray.	
	Now shal be seene hoo shal haue the day;	2126
	If he be conuycte, thei wil ȝelde hem alle,	
	If he be victour, than) wil the reuers falle—	2128
	ffor victour*is* be thei thanne be his conquest.	2129
	he stood vp ful solemnely with ful sober chere,	
	Commendynge the lady as he though[t] best;	
	Thanne seyde he to hir in this manere:	
	"Many thyng*is* haue ben) rehersed heere,	2133
	I herd aH, and ȝet I helde me in[1] pees.	[1] al. my
	But now is the mater soo sette, dovteles,	2135
	"It is put in vs too al þis thyng to treete.	2136
	Oure lord god sende us good speede!	
If he converts her,	If it soo be-falle þat I, with argument*is* grete	
	Or ell*is* with auctoryte, þat I may ȝow leede	
	ffrom alle ȝoure feyth and fro ȝoure fekel creede,	2140
he wins.	Than) haue we wonne; and if that ȝe lede me,	
	Thanne haue we doo, for victour[1] are ȝe."	[1] r. v. þan 2142
He first objects to Christ's two natures.	His first question), as I vndirstande,	2143
	Was of too natures whiche we in cryst reede;	
But this we've before treated.	Whiche mater be-forn) hath ben) in hande,	[1] MS. it is; it overl.
	And for that cause me thenketh it[1] noo neede	
	With swiche prolixite oure book ferthere to leede.	2147
	Turne, and rede ȝe that [wyll][1] it renewe.	[1] MS. and
	An other mater this philosophre gan) pursue,	2149

2124 dystroy 2125 hafe 2126 who 2130 ful 2 om. 2131 hym
thowt 2133 hafe be 2134 my pees 2135 þis. m. þus 2138 it om.
2141 wnne 2142 uictoure þoo 2145 before haue be 2146 is om.
2148 þat wyll it r. 2149 pursewe

Of crist*is* incarnacion), hough that it myght be, 2150 *Bk.IV.Ch.40.*
And hough he in bethleem thus born) was. *Aryot then doubts Christ's Incarnation.*
Eke al this mater, as thenketh me,
A-forn) in his werk þis man dede it tras;
Wherfore fro alle these þus shortly I pas, 2154 *This too we've dealt with before.*
Supposynge that þis same prolyxite
Wulde make men) wery of reedynge to be. 2156

Yet a-nother mater touched he to the mayde: 2157
Of oure ladyes clennesse in hir concepcion) *He also objects to Mary's purity,*
he had ful grete m*er*uayle, as he sayde;
Sith the synne of Adam in his progressyon)
Was ʒoue to mannys flessh as possessyon), 2161
hough myght she haue clennesse [&]¹ maydenhed ¹ MS. in *as she was of Adam's*
Whan she cam of that corrupte seed? 2163 *corruption.*

Ca^{m.} 41^{m.1} ¹ MS. 40^{m.} *Bk.IV.Ch.41.*

The mayde answerde right thus to his tale: 2164 *Katharine*
" Thyng that is foule, oure lord may make clene,
he is very medicyn) ageyn) al oure bale.
his wondyrful werk*is* are harde for to seene,
But be exaumples we may proue, I wene, 2168
That this coniunccyon) of mayden) and of man)
With-outen ony synne þis lord thus be-gan). 2170

" ffro the seed first of al mankende, 2171 *says that God preservd Mary from hereditary corruption.*
That was soo corrupte, he preserued this mayde—
It had ell*is* ful moche been) ageyn kynde,
But if hir soule had ben) arayde
With vertues grete and no-thyng afrayde 2175
With no vice of synne or vyllonye—
Thus dede this lord þat sitteth soo hye. 2177

" ffferthermore, whan) he cam to þat herburgage, 2178
his comynge was liche the sonne shynynge bryght;

2150 who   2154 for   2156 wolde   2162 whoo . & m.   2164 no new chapt.   2168 ensau*m*ples   2169 mayde   2170 with-oute   2171 man-kynde   2173 be   2174 be   2176 velenye   2177 þus hye   2179 sune . bryth*e*

332 *Objections to Christ's union of God with Man.* [**MS. Arundel.**]

Bk.IV.Ch.41.
Mary's womb was like glass,
and God past through it like light.

She was pure in Christ's incarnation.

lyche to þe glas I lykne that maydenes kage,
The sonne shyneth ther-on with bemes lyght
And thurght it gooth, as we see in sight,   2182
Yet is the glas pe*r*sed in noo manere—
Soo ferde that lord, whan he cam doun heere.   2184
" Thus was she clene in hir concepcyon,   2185
Thus hath she receyued the godhed of blis,
Yet was she clennere in his incarnacyon[1]—   [1] *al.* carnacion
Of whiche clennesse shal she not[1] mys.   [1] *al.* neuer
This muste 3e beleue, sir, if 3e wil ben his,   2189
Than shul 3e knowe þat 3e neuere knewe—
In my behestes 3e found me neuere ontrue."   2191

Bk.IV.Ch.42.   Ca*m.* 42*m.*1   [1] = Rawl. 34.

Another questyon meued this man that tyme,   2192
Replyenge sore ageyn hir declaracyon.
It is ful hard swiche þing*is* for to ryme,
To vtter pleynly in langage of oure nacyon
Swhiche straunge doutes þ*at* longe to the incarnacion,   2196
But that myn aucto*ur* took swiche þing on hande,
And yet his langage vnnethe I vndirstande ;   2198

    Wherfore with other auctou*ris* I enforce hym thus,   2199
Whiche spoke more pregnauntly as in this matere.

Aryot objects

ffor ageyn the birthe of oure lord Ih*esus*
And his concepcyon argued tho this sere.
" 3oure oppynyon set 3e alle in mere,"   2203
This[1] seyde this man on-to this lady mylde,   [1] *al.* Thus
" ffor ye rehers hough that god and chylde,   2205

that Christ's union of God with Man

" Bothe to-gedyr coupled in oon p*er*sone,   2206
Was 3oure ihesu, and eke 3e thus confesse
That this myracle dede he not allone,
But it was doo be alle thre, I gesse—
This is 3oure feyth, to this 3e you professe—   2210

    2182 thorow   2187 carnacion   2189 ser*e* . be   2191 vntrewe
    2193 Replyinge   2204 Thus   2205 who   2206 oo

That be the fadir, the goost, and eke þe sone
Wrought was thus this incarnacyone.　　　　2212
Whi shal we not thanne of ȝoure woord*is* conclude 2213
That fadir, and sone, and hoolygoost in-feere,
Sith that thei been) alle of oo symilitude,
That eche of hem flesh and blood took heere?
Thre sundry men) þan) arn) thei, with-oute[n] dwere, 2217
And eke oo god—hough acordeth this tale?
Al a wrong, me thenketh, wriheth the male.　　2219

"ffor ȝe sey eke þat but oon) was incarnat,　2220
Oon and no mo, and that was ih*e*su, ȝo*ur* lord;
Therto the fadir put ȝe in that astat
That he dede this—hough may this accord?
Sith that he wrought this of ȝoure owne record, 2224
Thanne was he Ioyned on-to that same werk—
That it[1] thus folweth, perceyu[eth][2] eu*er*y clerk." 2226
　　　[1] MS. it is　　[2] MS. p*er*ceyuynge

Ca. m. 43 m.1　　　　　　　[1] MS. 42 m.

This motyf preysed the queen) wit[h] the beste,　2227
　　She seyde on-to hym: "sir, ȝe lakke no þing
That longeth of vertu to ȝoure soules reste
But feyth alone; I prey that heuenly kyng
That he may touche yow with som pr*eu*y m*er*kyng, 2231
That ye may knowe whiche is the very truthe;
But if ye dede, it were ell*is* grete ruthe.　　　2233

"As moche as nature may, she hath ȝou taught, 2234
She coude noo ferthere in hir weye procede;
But the wisdam of god, þ*at*[1] may naught　　[1] r. yt?
Be caught be nature, leue this as youre creede.
Yet as I can, I wil ȝow mekely leede　　　　2238
On-to oure scole, and telle of this matere
The exposycion), if ȝe wil it leere.　　　　　　2240

Side notes: Bk.IV.Ch.42. was wrought by all three Persons of the Trinity. So they all took flesh, and were 3 distinct men, yet 1 God. How can this be? Bk.IV.Ch.43. Katharine praises Aryot for his skill; but he lacks God's wisdom.

2211 sune　2215 be　2217 are. wyt*h*-outen　2218 whoo　2219 wryhith　2223 did. whoo　2225 to om.　2226 þat it þus folowyth p*er*ceyueth eu*er*y clerke.　2227 no new chapt. wyt*h*　2228 sere 2230 heuyn　2232 he　2235 coude om. fard*er*　2237 Be cause of n. lerne

Bk.IV.Ch.43.	" Thus seyn) oure book*is* : on-to the fader*is* astat 2241
God the Father has power; the Son, wisdom ;	Longeth powere, with whom)¹ he gouerne² may alle, And to the sone longeth this appropriat ¹ Ar. whech ² om. in Ar. Whiche we calle wysdam)—the world, round as a balle, And heuene eke, whiche may not falle, 2245
the Holy Ghost, goodness.	Were made in hym ; to the goost longeth goodnesse— This is oure scole, wyth-oute[n] more or lesse. 2247
	" Thanne folweth thus that, sith the fadir alle thyng 2248 Made in this wysdam, it was ful conuenyent That be that same [þ*a*t]¹ grete refoormyng ¹ erased, or þe ? Of al mankende, whiche with synne was shent, Shuld be redressed. loo, this is her entent 2252
To the Son the Incarnation was due;	That proue¹ be feyth and demonstracion) ¹ MS. pr. we, we overl. That mooste to the sone p*er*teyneth þis incarnacion), 2254
the message and providence, to the Trinity in one God.	" As in praktyk ; but the soonde and the prouydens, As the menes of mercy whiche were tho I-doo, Tho longe to the trynyte, oo god in existens, Thre p*er*sones,¹ oure god we descryue hym) soo. ¹ *al*. in p. Exaumple, sir, may we putte ther-too, 2259 As putte oure clerk*is* in her book*is* wyse, Whiche write there in this man*er* of [w]yse¹ : ¹ MS. gyse
	" ' Dauid,' thei seyn), ' whanne he thristed sore, [On the margin : he desyred to drynke of that fresh welle þe secunde book of Whiche stood in bethleem where he was bore : kyng*is*, 23 chapetre]
3 Princes fetcht David water from Bethlehem,	he sente thre pryncys, the sothe for to telle, Thurgh al the oost of philestees¹ soo felle, ¹ MS. þe ph. 2266 Thei brought this watir w*yth* perell on-to þe kyng, On of hem in a basenet bar this þing.' 2268
	" Alle had thei labour egal, as I wene, 2269
but only one bare it.	And yet oon) bar the vessell, and noo mo.

2241 on om.   2242 powere wheche we beleuyn) alle   2243 þus a parte   2244 callen wisdom   2245 eke also   2247 w*yth*-outen   2248 sith om.   2249 his w.   2250 þat om.   2251 mankynde   2253 prouyth be f. & be   2254 þe inc.   2256 þ*er* doo   2257 longen   2258 i*n* p. . oure god om. hem   2260 putten . wysse   2261 Wheche were wretyn w*yth* ful good avysse   2262 he seyd   2263 desyred sor*e*. fresh om.   2265 the om.   2266 hoost. þe om.   2267 philestis   parelle.   on om.   2268 basnet   2270 vesselle

This same figure oure clerk*is* thus remene,[1] [1 = interpret (Wycliffe).] *Bk. IV. Ch. 43.*
That, though the fadyr and the goost bothe-too *The Father and Holy*
Wrought this thyng and ordeyned it shulde be soo, 2273 *Ghost pland the Incarnation,*
Yet was the byrdene on oure lord allone, *Jesus carried it out.*
Ih*e*su I mene, the sone, the secunde *per*sone. 2275

Ca^m. 44^{m. 1}   [1 = Rawl. 35.]   *Bk. IV. Ch. 44.*

After this had thei ful grete comm*u*nycacyo*n* 2276 *Katharine and Aryot discuss Adam's sin;*
Of the synne of Adam and of the serpent,
Enterfered with speches; but this dilatacyo*n*,
As me thynketh, longeth not to this lyf present, *but that I'll leave out.*
It occupieth ny al the newe testament, 2280
That men myght plod in her,[1] if þ*a*t hem lyst. [1 MS. hir]
Wherfore myn entent I wolde that ȝe wyst: 2282

I loue no longe tale, euere hangynge in oon. 2283 *I don't like a long tale!*
Wherfore as of this book I wil make an ende
Right in this Chapetre—me thenketh it longe a-goon *I'll end this 4th Book.*
Sith that I be-gan this book for to bende
Oon-to youre eres and on-to youre mende. 2287
Knoweth thys first, þ*a*t þis noble queen
hath concluded these mayster*is* thus be-dene, 2289

And in especyal Aryot; for al that he cowde replye
Avayleth as nought, his witte is but boost, *Aryot is at his wits' end.*
he stant al[1] mased, no-thyng now hardye [1 orig. as]
To speken oon woord. thus can[1] the goode goost [1 = gan]
Gadere to hym alle thys wyse oost 2294
And make[n] hem to trowe as the mayde[n] taught;
ffor al her philosophie thus arn thei caught. 2296 *He is caught.*

ffor after thei had spoken of the filiacion 2297
of crist, oure lord, whether there be too or oon,
And eke of the hooly goost and his p*r*ocession—

2273 ordeyn 2274 bordeyn i*n* 2278 this om. delectacion 2276 this om. 2281 þ*a*t myth it here if. 2285 this om. 2286 Sithen I 2288 weel inst. of thys 2290 speciall al om. 2291 It av. 2292 standith a-masid, & noþing. now om. 2293 spekyn o 2294 hoost 2295 makyn . mayden 2296 are 2297 spokyn 2298 þ*er* were 2299 of om. w*y*tℎ inst. of and

336 *Aryot and his fellows believe in Christ.* [MS. Arundel.

Bk. IV. Ch. 44.
Aryot confesses

Where that this lady fayled answere¹ noon), ¹ MS. answered
This same Aryot stood stille as ony ston); 2301
ffor the hooly trynyte she proued hym be kynde,
he cowde¹ fro the resons no weye fynde. ¹ Ar. 168 c. not. 2303
  On-to his felawes thus ful loude he sayde : 2304

that he and his fellows are wrong;
" We haue gon) wrong euere on)-to this day ;
Blissed be god and this holy mayde
That to us hath taught a truere way !
Sey ȝe as ye like, I can) noȝt sey nay ; 2308

he now believes in God the Father, Son, and
ffor on oo god I beleue whiche is in blis,
I beleue on) Ihesu eke whiche is sone his,¹ ¹ at. his s. is 2310

Holy Ghost,
" I leue in the goost, knettere of hem too ; 2311
I leue that þis Ihesu deyed for my sake,
Thus were oure synnes be hym clensed soo.

and commits his soul to Christ.
On-to his handis my soule I be-take,
Prey^eng hym hertely that fro þe feendis blake 2315
he now defende me, þat I noȝt damned bee.
This is my crede ; felawes, what sey ȝee ? " 2317

His fellows do so too,
Thei answerden) alle þat thei had now founde 2318
Thyng þat thei [had] sought¹ alle her lif-dayes ;
This wil thei kepen now as a true grounde, ¹ MS. soughten
ffor thei haue walked many perillous wayes,
With veyne argumentis iangelynge [euer] as Iayes ; 2322

and turn to Christ.
Now wil thei leue it and to crist hem turne,
With Aristotil or plato wil thei no more soiurne, 2324
But put hem in the mercy of oure lord Ihesu, 2325
Preyenge this mayde that she be her¹ mene ¹ MS. hir
To purchace hem pardon) of her feith ontrew,
That thei so longe shulde it sustene ;
Thei felle on knees, the[se] clerkis alle be-dene, 2329

  2300 lady om. answere was non. 2301 a stone. 2305 into
2307 haue . trew 2308 leke 2309 on om. 2310 I leue . his sone is
2311 And I l. on . knyte 2315 prayng . hertily 2318 answerd
2319 þat om. had south 2320 kepyn. now om. 2321 had . per-
lous 2322 euer as Iayȝes 2323 leuyn. hem om. 2324 Ar. nen
Ovide 2326 her om. 2327 hem om. 2328 susteyne 2329 fellen .
þese

Cryenge loude with grete deuocyon) : *Bk. IV. Ch. 44.*
"O[1] Ihesu cryst, for thy swete passyon)   [1] MS. On   2331   The converted pagan Philosophers pray for Christ's forgiveness.
"Haue mercy up-on us, forgeue vs oure trespas!   2332
Demene vs [not],[1] lord, after oure mysdede!   [1] MS. Deme no vs, on eras.
As þou art pytous,[2] soo þou graunte us gras,   [2] MS. pytousful
Of thi protectyon) haue we ful grete neede.   2335
We wil do oure diligens for to lerne [our][1] crede,   [1] corr.: this
To meynten) it and susteyn) with al oure myght;
There shal neuere man) brynge us in other plight."   2338   [[1] vv. 2339—2345 follow in MS. Ar. 20 after V, 329.]

[1]Thus are thei conuerted; this conflicte is I-doo;   2339
Oure book is at an ende, a newe we wil be-gynne—   Book IV is finisht.
It is ful conuenient that we shul[d] do soo.
God and seynt Kataryne kepe us oute of synne,   We'll start Book V.
Sende us the weyes heuene-blisse to wynne,   2343
Where we may dwelle and looke[n] on his face,   [1] al. men
Whiche gladeth alle creaturis[1] that been) in þat place! 2345

Liber quintus
Prologus.

Bk. V. Prol.
[vv. 1—63 are wanting in Ar. 20.]

NOw is it come, oure leyser and oure space,   1   Now we'll turn
In whiche we may, after oure grete labour
Of other maters, now, whil we haue grace,
Turne ageyn) and taaste the swete sauour   to the sweet savour of the pure Virgin Katharine.
Of this clene virgyne, of this weel sauoured flour,   5
Whiche with fyue braunches grew thus here in erthe.
The firste, the secounde, the thredde, and[1] the feerde   7
     [1] Ar. & eke
haue 3e perceyued, if 3e haue red alle;   8
Now shal the fyfte be shewed on-to 3oure sight.
ffor now we[1] lyste this lady a rose to calle,   [1] al. me
Of fyue braunches ful precyously I-dyght.
The rede colour, that shon in hir so bryght,   12

2330 Cryinge long . ful grete   2331 O   2333 Deme us not   2334 petous (ful om.) soo þou om. of þi g.   2336 don . 3oure c.   2338 bryngen   2339 counselle   2341 shuld   2343 And send . þe hey weyes   2344 dwellyn . lokyn . þat face   2345 alle men   1 it om. 3 materis . whil om.   6 erde   7 thrid . ferde   9 vnto   10 me lyst

338 Book V will tell of Katharine's Martyrdom. [MS. Arundel.

Bk. V. Prol.

We shall now tell of Katharine's martyrdom.

Martyrdom is the greatest of all virtues.

Our first 2 Books

spoke of Katharine's heathen life.

That was hir martirdam; the fyue leues grene
Be-tokne hir lyf, thus distincte, I wene, 14
In diuers book*is*, liche as we haue dyuysed 15
Be-fore this tyme, and now this is the last.
These fyue leues, right thus are þei sysed
That on the stalk thei cleue[n] wonder fast,
The reed flowres kepe thei fro the blast 19
Er thei hem-selue dilate[1] thus a-brood,   [1] r. dilaten
And after that thei make than her a-bood 21

Euene vndir tho same swete reed floures ; 22
Be-tokenynge that al hir lyf was spred
With martirdam and wyth tho sharp shoures
Whiche she for crist bothe suffred and ded.
ffor in diuers book*is* as I ofte haue red, 26
Martirdam hath a sou*er*eyn dygnyte,
A-boue alle vertues whyche that goostly bee. 28

Thus grew this rose oute of the thorny brere 29
Whan that this martir of hethen folk was bore.
I wil declare ȝet ferthere, if ye wil here,
Whi that these leues that cleue so sore,
Thre of hem arn berded, and no more, 33
And too stande naked with-oute[n] dagge or berd—
Thus arn thei wonet[1] to growe[n] in oure ȝerd. [1] r. wone 35

These fyue leues, as I seyde wol late, 36
Be-tokne these book*is* whyche we haue in hande ;
Too of hem expresse the tyme and the date
In whiche this lady, as I vndirstande,
leued as hethen, as dede tho al hir lande— 40
Therfore are thei naked in her kynde,
Expressynge thus this ladyes leuyng blynde. 42

15 like   16 Beforn*e*   18 cleue*n*   20 Or . þus lateth hem   21 her*e* þan abode   22 þe. reed om.   23 Betokynyth. al om.   24 tho om. 25 she om. . suffered   26 haue oftyn   27 suffereyn   30 folk om. 31 ferthere om.   32 þeis. that om. cleuyn   33 ar*e*   34 w*yth*-outen 35 ar*e* . wont . grow*e*n   36 wolate   37 Betokenes . hau*e*n   40 and so dede al

Blynd I calle hir whil she was in that lyf, 43 *Bk. V. Prol.*
Knewe not crist, baptem had noon I-take,
Of heuenly thyng*is* litel inquisityf
hir olde oppynyons had she no3t forsake.
ffro this blyndenesse cryst made hir a-wake, 47
In oure thredde book ryght as we seyde before— Our last 3 Books deal
It nedeth not as now reherce it no more. 49

The other thre with berd*is* are soo I-growe 50
That leues of vertu we may hem alle calle;
To al the world openly thus is it knowe with Katharine's Christian graces.
That she hath graces whiche may not falle.
Soo are her leues endewed, and eue*r* shalle, 54
Euere arn thei grene, and eue*re*-more wil bee,
Regnynge with crist in very felicyte. 56

And in hir honour now I wil procede 57
To my fyfte book, in whiche I wil speke The 5th and last
Of hir martirdam, so as the story wil lede;
hough god the wheles for hir cause gan breke
And on the puple tho took[1] ful grete wreke : [1] Ar. toke þo 61
This shal be translated now newe fro latyn, I'll now english from Latin.
To the wurshyp of god and of seyn Kataryn. 63

Ca^{m.} 1^{m.} *Bk. V. Ch.* 1.

Whanne the clerk*is* had mad thus her compleynt 64
Of alle her errour and wrong credulite,
The emp*er*our*is* herte for sorwe gan feynt. The Emperor
ffor now is noon that dar spekyn but he—
In al this mater conuicte is this mene. 68
Wherfore with cheer ful angry and dispytous looks angry.
Thus seyde he to hem as he stood in the hous: 70

44 baptem ne had non. I om. 46 her elde 49 it rehers 51 me*n* may . alle om. 52 it is 53 grace 55 are . shall*e* bee 58 myn 60 quelys . his c. dede 61 puple to full 62 Thus sh. it be translate. lateyn*e* 64 þeis c. 65 crudelyte 66 to feynt 67 speke 68 þeis materis 69 ffor w*yth* angry cher*e* & word*ys* full dispitous 70 in þat

340 The Emperor reproaches his Philosophers. [MS. Arundel.

Bk. V. Ch. 1.
The Emperor says his converted Philosophers have deprived him of all bliss.

"ffy on youre scoole! we had a ful gret trost 71
ȝe shuld a made weel al þat went amys:
Alle oure expens,[1] al oure counsel is lost,   [1] MS. expensens
ȝe haue reued me of al this wordly blis,—
Not wordli, but goostly—for I seyde amys, 75
It is goostly ioye that longeth on-to oure feyth.
heere ȝe noȝt now what the puple seyth? 77

"Thei seyn, a mayde hath conuicte in this place 78
ffifty clerkis, in this world noon liche;

His folk will turn Christians.

Thei sey thei wil the same feyth purchace;
Thus sey thei alle, bothe þe pore and þe ryche.
God wolde[1] ye hadde be beryed in a dyche [1] r. Wold god 82
Whanne ȝe cam heder! for now al is lost,
Labour and connynge, rydyng and mekel cost. 84

Let them take heart again,

"[Lete][1] now ȝoure prudens make you a newe corage,
That ȝe lese not youre konnynge & ȝour fame! [1] MS. ffette
þenke what I hight ȝou, wurshype & eke wage!
Beth noȝt a-ferde, for þanne ȝe lese your name,
Left vp youre hertis, men, for very shame! 89

and argue down Katharine.

Speke to þis woman, wyth reson bere hir doun!
Thanne are ye worthi in sciens to [b]ere[1] þe croun. 91
                                        [1] MS. were

"Ȝe stonde as herteles! where is ȝour connynge goo, 92
That ben astoyned with nature femynyne?
Be hooly saturne, I wolde a supposed soo

One of them ought to be worth 9 women.

That oon of ȝou, myghty had be for nyne!
Ye fare[n] as though ȝe were bounde with lyne; 96
What answere wil ȝe yeue of youre connynge,
Whan that at nede it avayleth no-thynge?" 98

---

71 a om.   72 was amysse   73 expens . consayle   74 al om.   75 noth   76 & longith to   77 what þat þe   78 maydyn   80 wollyne   81 bothe om.   82 Wold god . byryed   84 coost   85 Lete   87 hyth. eke om.   88 & 89 transposed   88 lesen   89 Lyft   91 bere   92 stand alle h.   95 myth a ben for sweche n.   96 faren. though om.   97 ȝeuyn   98 Whech (corr. from what). it om.

Ca^m secundum.

The grettest of hem, maister and ledere eke, 99   Aryot tells the Emperor
This same Ariot of whiche I spak before,
To the empervur thus he gan to speke:
"On-to thi court come we, lesse and more,
Thi goddis scruyse to renewe and restore; 103
And as I wene, of alle the est-syde
Of al this world, to seke ferre and wyde, 105

"Shulde þou not fynde soo pyked a company 106   that tho' the Philosophers knew Arts,
In gramer, rethorike, and tho artes alle;
But specially in natural philosophi
Are we endewed. but to þe[1] sciens whiche þei calle   [1] *al.* om.
Theologye, [to þat] cowde we noȝt falle, 110   they didn't know Theology till Katharine taught 'em it.
Tyl that þis lady made vs an Introduccyon—
Euere blessed be she for hir instruccyon! 112

"What-maner man þat wolde er this tyme 113
Dispute with vs be reson or be auctoryte,
his demonstracyons coude vs not trappe ne lyme,
But he w[as][1] caughte for al his sotilte;   [1] MS. were
he passed not from vs wyth-oute a vylone— 117
This was oure vsage[1] right thanne for victorye,   [1] *al.* wage
Soo loued we tho this wordlys veynglorye. 119

"Now it is turned, oure fortune & oure chauns, 120
Oure appetite eke, I not hough it is went;
This mayde[n] maketh that we falle in trauns,
Oure connyng now it semeth þat it is spent;
She speketh of god whiche was hangen & rent, 124   She speaks of God on the Cross.
A goostly speche hath she brought to place,   [1] MS. in maner
Natural scyens hath in [þis] ma[t]er[1] noo space. 126

---

99 maister om.   101 On-to   103 ȝefe inst. of renewe   106
Shuldist, þou om.   sweche a pykyd   108 speciall   109 þe om.   110
Th. to þat coud we.   111 bryngyth us to induction   112 hir good
113 or   114 & auctorite   115 neythere t.   116 was caute . sotelte
117 pased . fro . velanye   119 tho om.   þese wordes of v.   121 wote
neuer how   122 mayden   124 wheche þat   125 And inst. of A   126
in þis matere

Bk. V. Ch. 2.	"Therfore can we as in this soleynte	127
Aryot	Speke right nought; but resons maketh she grete,	
	hir prechyng passeth al oure carnalite;	
	ffor whan) I firste thus mystyly herde hir trete,	
	In my body myne bowayles[1] sore gonne bete,	131
	ffor very rebuke that I hir langage [1] *al.* my bowels	
	Coude not conceyue. wherfore, sir, al ȝour wage	133
refuses the Emperor's fees,	"And youre reward*is* whiche ye p*r*ofered vs,	134
	We refuse it; ȝour godd*is* and your lawe	
renounces his faith,	We renunce, for the loue of oure lord Ih*esus*.	
	Shewe ȝe som) reson) openly that we may knawe	
	If þat ȝoure godd*is* wyth the[1] rough pauwe [1] *al.* her	138
	haue other euydens þan) we[1] can) proue þis tyde! [1] *al.* ȝe	
	ffor in this errour we wil noo lengere a-byde.	140
and confesses Christ.	"Cryst, godd*is* sone, that with his passion)	141
	Boughte al mankende, heere we now confesse;	
	On-to his m*er*cy with good deuocyon)	
	We now com*m*ende vs, the more and eke the lesse.	
	Slee and flee, brenne & put in distresse:	145
	Other feyth shalt þou neuere-more plante	
	In to oure hert*is*; for noo thyng now we wante	147
	"But of baptem) the hooly sac*r*ament.	148
	God, as he boute vs, on vs haue mercy!"	
	Thus seyde his felawes alle w*yth* oon entent:	
	"There is noo god but he þat sit on hy;	
	On alle these maument*is* eue*r*e sey we fy!	152
All the philosophers will die rather than give up the Christian faith.	We wil deye rathere þan) we shulde forsake	
	The cristen feyth whiche we haue now take."	154
Bk. V. Ch. 3.	Ca^m. 3^m.	

[1] overl.; om. in Ar.

NOw was the emp*er*our ny wod and[1] oute of mynde,
his eyne rolled as thei wolde falle oute. 156

127 solennyte 128 make 130 mystly 131 my bowelles . gunc
134 Alle 135 refusen. it om. 137 pleynly 138 here rowe pawe
139 þ*a*t inst. of þan . ȝe . preue 141 hys blyssyd p. 142 kynde
143 ryght w*yth* 146 schall . neu*er in* oure hert plant(!) 147 hert
150 seyden 151 syttyth 153 schuld dey 155 wax

MS. Arundel.] *The Emperor orders the Converts to be burnt.* 343

"ffy on you," he seyde, " cherles kynde,
Now is oure feyth for ȝou in more¹ doute
Than euere it was." and to hem that stood aboute 159
he tho commaunded in ful hasty wyse:
"I wil," he seith, " her deth ȝe thus deuyse : 161

"A fyre I wil þat ȝe now hastily make 162
Right in the myddes of this grete Cytee ;
Spare no wode, for hooly saturnes sake,
Spede you faste, these renegates þat we may see
ffrye in her grees ! for be þat deyte 166
Of swete appollo, I shal not ete ne drynke
Til that I se hem bothe brenne and stynke. 168

"Put in roseyn, pych and other gere, 169
Spare noo cost, for in this doo ye seruyse
On-to oure goddis with-outen ony feere.
Thus shal thei deyen that oure goddis despise ;
I shal be there my-self as very¹ Iustise
And see this Iugement be¹ doon in dede. 173
Whan ȝe haue ended,² ye shul haue ȝour mede. 175

"I wil ȝe bynde hem bothe in foote and hande, 176
Drawe hem foorth as doggis on-to the place,
Looke youre ropys be myghty, and ȝour bande,
Spare neyther bodyes, heedis ne her face !
God geue hem¹ alle swiche a sory velenous grace, 180
That thus forsake oure goddis þat ben eterne !
Looke noon of hem scape¹ ȝou in noon herne ! 182

"Thei shal be dede right as I haue sayde, 183
Brent in to asshes—they gete noo remedye.
lete hem crye now on-to¹ this wilful mayde
Whiche hath brought hem in to this heresie.

¹ *al.* more in — The Emperor orders
a fire to be made in the city,
to burn the Christian converts.
¹ *al.* om.
¹ Ar. Iewesse that it be
² *al.* don
¹ om. in Ar.
¹ r. ascap ?
¹ *al.* on — Let them cry to Katharine!

157 charles vnkynde 158 more in 159 and om. stonden 161
he seith om. her d. þat ȝe þus. 162 now om. hastely 163 of þe
164 saturne 165 þat renegatys þat ȝe see 166 ffrye hem . grece 169
rosyn¹ 172 schul . dey 173 very om. 174 se þese Iwes don 175
haue done . schall h. . ryght goode m. 176 in om. 178 ȝoure ropes
loke þei 179 body . nyne (inst. of ne) 180 ȝefe. velenous om. 181
be 182 hyrne 183 be brent d. 184 askes 185 to om. 186 þat h.

344 *The Christians rejoice in their Death-sentence.* [**MS. Arundel.**

Bk. V. Ch. 3. I wil no woord*is* as now more[1] multiplye,   [1] *al.* om.   187
Goo now foorth in hast and doo yo*ur* dede!
Whan) it is doon), ȝe shul haue ȝoure mede."   189

Bk. V. Ch. 4.   Ca^{m.} 4^{m.}

The Christians do not contest their doom.

Thus are thei drawe[1] with grete velonye   [1] r. drawen?   190
    On-to her doom); thei wrestlen nought ageyn).
Men myght see theere many a wepyng yȝe,
But for feer no man) now dar[1] seyn);   [1] r. dar noȝt?
Glad are these meny alle of her peyn).   194
The mayster of hem, thus he cryed at þ*a*t tyme:
"God be thanked, that for noo synne ne cryme   196
"Be we appeched, but oonly for trewe feyth!   197
Therfore, felawes in crist, ȝo*ur*-selue confort;
What-eue*re* þis tyraunt or ony of his seyth,

They thank God that they are going to Bliss.

Thanke oure lord, for we are in the port
Whiche þat ledeth to þe[1] blessed counfort   [1] *al.* þ*a*t   201
Where alle seynt*is* arn) gadered right be grace,
In an heuenly Ioyeful blissed place.   203

"Oure lord hath called vs fro oure olde errour   204
On-to þis ende; thanke we hym therfore,
Whiche to the beute of his fayre merrour
Wolde of hys goodnesse newely us restore.

They desire only to be baptised.

In this world, as for me, I wil no more,   208
But that we shulde be baptised or we deye:
Than) were we redy to walke th[at][1] goodly weye.   [1] MS. the

"ffor þ*a*t same baptem) is an hooly werke,   211
It causeth grace, feyth eke it endeweth;
Be-twixe god and man it is a very me*r*ke,
That who-soo-eue*re* crist*is* steppis seweth,
Al his lyuynge soothly he reneweth   215

187 more om.   189 treuly schall ȝe   190 vylony   191 wrestyll not   192 eye   193 dar*e* now   194 þeis meny. of very p.   195 at om.   196 To god be it þ*a*t   199 tyraunt dothe or seyth   200 hys port   201 l. vs to þ*a*t   202 are gadered to-gedyr be g.   206 on-to. fayre om.   208 werde   209 ben   210 forto. þ*a*t goode   212 gr. & feyth & eke. it om.   213 Be-twys   214 crysten   215 leuyng

The Converts ask for Baptism.

Whan that he wasshet[h] in this water his synne.
Oure lord hym-selue, he was wasshe ther-Inne, 217

"Right for this cause þat noo man shulde dysdeyne 218
To vse the same whiche þat this lord vsed.
Of my conseyte I wil noo more now feyne,
ffor in this mater ofte-tyme haue I mused;
Many a ȝeer this sacrament I refused: 222
That I repente now, and euere I shal it rue
That I soo longe lyued a lyf on-true. 224

"Wherefor my care now is this oonly, 225
That sith we shal and nedes muste we deye,
Off alle oure synnes mercy for to cry,
Alle oure defautes vndir foote for[1] to leye,   [1] *al.* om.
To trede hem doun; thanne sauely may we seye 229
Th[at][1] we arn purged and of hem alle made clene.
Thus muste ȝe trowe, felawes, alle be-dene."   [1] MS. Thus

[Rawl. Ca^m. 5^m]
And to the mayde he turned hym with his voys: 232
"lady," he seyde, "for god that sitteth aboue,
And for the passion that cryst had on the croys,
Prey for vs to hym—he[1] is thi loue!   [1] *al.* þat
Thou seest ful weel we may no lengere shoue 236
Oure leuynge dayes, for thei arn at an ende:
Prey that lord he wil his merci sende 238

"On-to his seruauntis and spare vs at þis tyme, 239
Suffre vs eke that we may washed bee
With hooly baptem, that we may better clyme
On-to that place of grete felicite.
And if this preyere plese not hym, but he 243
Wil algates that we shal wante þis thyng,
We wold desire thanne of þat blyssed kyng 245

Marginalia:
Bk. V. Ch. 4.
Aryot has long refused Baptism,
now he desires it.
He appeals to Katharine
to baptise him and his fellows.

217 he om. wasched 222 a om. 223 rewe 224 leued. vntrewe
226 we 2 om. 228 And all. for om. 229 treden) 230 þat. are
hem om. 231 we beleuen) 232 onto. maydene 234 on crosse 235
þat is 236 seyst 237 lyuyng. are nye at ende 238 lord om. 239
hem inst. of vs 240 Suffryng eke 241 þe bettyre 242 On om.
245 of þis

346 *Martyrdom is a substitute for Baptism.* [MS. Arundel.

Bk. V. Ch. 4.

But if God will dispense with their Baptism,

"he wolde with us make dispensacyon)— 246
ffor al[1] may he, he is omnypotent,   [1] *al.* al þis
he loueth alle men), he loueth iche nacyon)
Egaly, ȝe sey—this is oure fundament.
If he dispense with vs of this sacrament, 250
That for the wantyng we may bere no blame,

they'll die gladly.

Than shal oure deth ben) to us but game." 252

Bk. V. Ch. 5.   Ca^m. 5^m.

Katharine says

Thanne seyde the mayde [on]-to hem alle in-fere : 253
"ffere you[1] right nought though ȝe wante þis thyng!
Soo as I can) now wil I ȝow lere.   [1] *al.* ȝe

that those who die for Christ are borne to Bliss by Angels.

Tho men) that deye for loue of cryst, oure kyng,
Whiche wante [of] baptem) þat hooly washyng, 257
Thei shul to blysse, for Aungell*is* shul hem cary ;
The feendes power noo-þing may hem tary. 259

"In stede of baptem) serueth her passyon), 260
Not oonly blood whiche thei for hym) blede,
But al other deth whyche with deuocyon)
Thus thei suffre on-to her grete mede.
leue this doctryne hardyly as ȝoure crede! 264

Their suffering is reckond as Baptism.

The grete peyne whiche þat is dempt to ȝou,
In stede of baptem) shal it be as now. 266

"God may with feer[1] purge[n] mannes synne, 267
With water eke, right as hym lest demene ;   [1] *al.* fyer (2 syll.)
Somme men) arn) baptised heuene for to wynne
With that water whiche in þe fount is seene,

They are purgd by their blood.

Somme arn) purged in her blood, I wene, 271
Thei deye as martirs, this is oure decree ;
Somme men) arn) baptised eke, as leue[1] wee, [1] r. leuen 273

247 all þis 248 eu*er*y n. 251 þan for wantyng may we 252 be tyl 253 no new chapt. vntyll 254 ȝe 256 deye om. 257 wante of 258 schall 260 hys p. 262 wheche þat he for hem dyd blede 263 suffred . hem 264 leue ȝe wel þ. d. trostly 265 þe wheche is 266 it om. 267 fyrc purgen) 268 right om. lyst 269 are 270 fonte 271 wyth 272 deyn . marteres 273 men om. . are

"Right in her feyth, that stedfastly trost 274
In goddis mercy and deyn̄ oute of synne—
This calle oure cle[r]k*is* baptem̄ of the goost.
Therfore, ȝe knyght*is* of crist, now be-gynne
To cleyme ȝoure herytage, þat ȝe were ther-Inne; 278
Beth not a-feerde, but suffre the peyne mekely,
Than̄ are ȝe baptised, troste me now, truly!" 280

marginal: Martyrdom is spiritual Baptism.

Ca^{m.} 6^{m.}

Whanne that thei were of this hooly mayde 281
Thus recomforted, the officer*is* come anoon̄;
Thei bynde her hand*is*, right euene as I sayde,
Thei lede hem foorth, as fast as thei may goon̄,
On-to a strete whiche was pathed with stoon̄. 285
Weel is hym that may a fagot bere
To brenne the clerk*is*! the em*per*our tho was there, 287

Sette in a stage, for he wolde see the eende. 288
The fyre is made, blokk*is* arn̄ leyde on hepe,
ffagott*is* gonne they among*is* the clogg*is* bende,
There is not ellis but fette,[1] renne and lepe,   [1] *al.* feche
Blowe now faste, the fower*is* shal not slepe. 292
Thei bynde her feet and through[1] hem in the fere.
But thei arn̄ glad, ful mery eke of chere,   [1] *al.* throw 294

Thankynge god that al thynge made of nought, 295
That thei may deye for swiche a lord*is* sake;
Thei prey to hym̄, right as he hem bought
her soules now fro hem þat he wil take.
What shulde I now lengere this tale make? 299
Thus are thei dede, her soules gon̄ to blis.
Eke to her bodyes oure blessed lord graunted this: 301

Skyn̄ ne flessh was noon̄ of hem brent, 302
Ne hood ne cloth, ne her on̄ berd ne heed;

274-7 out of order (b c a d)   277 begune   281 weren   282 comforted . offycers comene   283 bondyn̄. euene om.   284 leden. as om.
287 tho om.   289 are   290 gan . amonge   291 feche   292 shuld
293 and om. þei throw   294 are . & full. eke om.   298 tyll hy*m*
now þat he wold   300 on inst. of gon   301 tyll   303 of berde ne of

348 *Their corpses are not chard, but fresh-coloured.* [MS. Arundel.

Bk. V. Ch. 6.
Yet the fire only kills them, doesn't discolour them.

Thei lay there ded with browes fayre I-bent,
With fayre faces coloured white and reed.
ffor right as fyre maketh þe rusty leed 306
Bryght and shene, so made the fyre these men[1]; [1] MS. hen
hoo knewe hem be-forn, yet he myght hem[1] ken. 308

In her peynes men seyde thei cryed thus: 309
"Blissed be god, þat we neuere knewe ere,
Blissed be crist, honoured be oure lord Ihesus!
ffor of [þis] torment haue we now noo fere."
This was a scole merueylous to[1] lere, [1] *al.* meruelous forto 313
That thei in torment merthe and Ioye shulde make!
On-to god oonly her soules gunne thei take. 315

They are martyrd on Nov. 13, and lie as if alive.

Thus deyed these men in Nouembre þe xiij. day. 316
After her deth, semynge not to be ded,
As slepyng men in fayre coloure thei lay,
In handes, bodyes,[1] legges eke and hed [1] *al.* body
With colour fressh, lyuely and also red. 320
This[1] þe puple sey[2] and merueyled wonder sore; [1] MS. Thus
God thei preysed for now and euere-more. [2] *al.* sey þe p. 322

Many are converted by this miracle.

ffor be this myracle conuerted was that day 323
Meche folkis[1] to cryst, and for deuocyon [1] *al.* folke
Bothe of the clerkis and eke of the may

[[1] Here follows in MS. Ar. 20 the last stanza of Book IV, and ends Book IV. V. 330-420 are wanting.]

Thei took the bodyes with solenne oryson,
Beried hem there in dyuers mansion, 327
Trostynge to spede the betere for her cause.
Thus endeth her martirdam right in this clause.[1] 329

Bk. V. Ch. 7.   Ca[m]. 7[m].

Tho sey the emperour there is non other spede 330
On-to this mayden whiche is soo stedfast,

---

304 I om. 305 face . bothe whyght   306 ffor lyk as þe f.   307 makyth . þis mene   308 who so . before.   yet om.   myth ken hem & see   312 of þis t.   313 for to   314 myrth   315 gan   316 þis mene   317 þei semed not to a be dede   319 body   320 louely   321 þis see þe puple   322 for þan   324 miche folke   326 token   327 And biried þem   328 the om.   330 oþir botte

But fayre wordes, whiche drawe womanhede
And maketh hem often other thyng to tast
Thanne thei shulde doo if thei wolde be chast.   334
Therfore this mayde[n] right thus tho he gloseth:
"Kataryn," he seyth, "ther is no man supposeth,   336

"Not 3e 3oure-selue, þat I wolde but good   337
On-to 3oure persone; but this grete distresse
To whiche I putte 3ou, spillynge as 3et noo blood,
Was for to chace you fro þat fykelnesse
Whiche 3e haue caught of fonned hoolynesse   341
And lefte þe ryghtes þat oure¹ olderis be-fore   ¹ orig. 3oure
Receyued and honoured as for souereyn lore.   343

"This was the cause whi I distressed 3ow soo;   344
But loue haue I on-to 3ow, sekirly,
As to best of alle saue oon and no moo.
[&] whi I doo soo if 3e wil wete why:
Yowre beute it causeth, 3oure connyng eke, þat I   348
loue 3ow so weel that, if 3e wil consent
And thuryfye to Iubiter omnypotent,   350

"3e shul haue honoure, no woman shal be lich.   351
O swete virgyne, enclyne 3our wil to me!
O fayre visage of beute now most rich,
O woman wurthi to Imperial degree,
O very merour of parfighte felicite,   355
Wolde god 3e knewe what care I haue for yow,
And what behestes I made in myn avow!   357

"Whi wolde 3e despise oure goddis immortal?   358
Whi wolde 3e calle hem soo villenous a name?
Why seyde 3e thei were feendes infernal?
Whi slaundre 3e soo her hooly endued fame?

332 womanhoode 333 thingis 335 mayden 337 nothe 339 putte 3ou om. spellyng 3et as 340 chast. sekenes 341 Wheche þat 342 riches. elderes 344 whi þat 346 þe best 347 And why 348 & inst. of þat 349 lyke to consent 350 Iupiter þat is 351 shalle. 3ou liche 352 youre loue 354 most worthy of 355 merueyle 356 knewen 357 beheest I haue made 359 uenemous 360 þat þei are deueles. 361 hooly om.

350 *The Emperor tempts Katharine to be Pagan.* [MS. Arundel.

Bk. V. Ch. 7.

ffor this blaspheme, I-wys, ȝe be to blame— 362
Disceyuours thei be of puple, as ȝe sayde.
Chaunge ȝoure langage, o noble goodly mayde, 364

The Emperor urges Katharine to propitiate his Gods.

" Chaunge be-tyme! for though thei suffre longe, 365
At the last thei smyght and [taken hy veniaunce][1]
Tender ȝoure thought, speke hem no more wronge:
Thus shal ȝe best her grete Ire aswage.   [1] MS. corr.: pay ful hard wage
Take ȝoure offerynge ȝet, in short langage, 369
And plese hem soo, thei may ben ȝour freendes!
[&] sey neuere more that thei been feendes! 371

" If ȝe wil doo as I ȝow now counsayle, 372

She shall be next his Queen,

This shal ȝe haue: next after the queen
Shal ȝe be to us, with-outen faile;
To ȝoure commaundement alle [men] shul been

her friends shall be his,

Obeyᵉnge for euere; whom ȝe wil susteen, 376
he shal be fauoured with al myght & mayne,

her unfriends his foes.

And whom ȝe hate, compendiously to sayne, 378

" That man shal lyue[n] in ful grete distresse. 379
Comforte ȝoure-self, despise not good counsayle,
Make not ȝoure freendis to lyue in heuynesse;
Lete my woordis synke in ȝoure entrayle,
fflee swiche thyng[1] that may not avayle!   [1] r. thyngis? 383
With-inne my kyngdam may ȝe haue this right:
What þat ye wil, shal be fulfilled as tight. 385

" If that ȝe wil exile[n] oony man, 386
That man shal goo, þer shal no good hym saue;

In all, her will shall be done.

More plesauns to ȝow noon graunte I can
But suffre youre wil, al þat ȝe wil haue.
ffro this decree shal I neuere-more waue. 390

---

362 are   363 deceyvoures . thei be om.   of þe p.   364 ȝe noble
366 smyten & taken hey veniaunce   367 hem om.   368 grete om.
swage   370 plesith . be   371 And sey . be   372 don   375 alle men
shalle   376 Obeynge but whom þat . susteyne   378 whom þat   379
leuyn   380 Coumforthe   381 makith . leuyn   382 myn . sinken
383 thyng om.   385 tythe   386 exilen   388 noon om.   I ne   390 ffor

hom þat ȝe liste of grace to avaunce,		
In ioyeful dayes that same man may daunce.	392	
" Be-twixe the queen and you shal be no distaunce	393	The Emperor promises Katharine
But oonly this, be-cause of oure spousayle:		
She must of me haue more dewe plesaunce;		
The loue be-twixe vs, I trowe, shal neuere fayle.		
But to ȝou shal longe bothe lawe and counsayle	397	
Thurgh al oure reem, to gouerne at ȝoure wille;		absolute power,
Right as ȝe bydde alle men shul fulfille.	399	
"Yet shal I make right in the market-place	400	
A solenne ymage like an emperesse;		and the setting-up of her image
As liche as craft wil countirfete ȝour face		
It shal be made: ilke man, more and lesse,		
Shal honoure þat[1] with ful grete besynesse, [1] r. yt?	404	
Whan thei come forby shul falle on kne anoon.		
This ymage shal not oonly be made of stoon,	406	to be worshipt,
"But of clene metal, gilt ful bryght & shene.	407	
Who-so come forby, be sufficient euydens		
Shal knowe ful weel þat she was a queen		
Whos ymage stant there, and in grete offens		
Shal he falle that dooth noo reuerens	411	
To þat same ymage, and ho-soo flee ther-too,		
What-maner offens that he hath doo	413	
" Shal be forȝoue, for reuerens of yow, mayde.	414	
Thus may ȝe ben deifyed, if ȝe wil it take."		if she will turn Heathen.
Swiche-maner woordis on-to hir he sayde,		
he wolde a temple al of marbil make		
Of ful grete cost, right for hir sake,	418	
Wenynge euere with swyche feyned plesauns		
To brynge this mayde fro hir perseuerauns.	420	

391 whom . forto   393 non   394 youre   399 shall   400 right om.   401 solempne . liche a   402 As man of craft   405 comen . fallen . knes   408 comyth . wyth   409 knowen   410 & þat   412 same om.   800 om.   413 þat ouer   414 forȝoue at þo r.   415 be 416 vntill   417 marbelle   420 oute of hir good p.

Ca^m. 8^m.

Katharine is amused at the Emperor's offer

She low a lityl whan she herde al this, 421
And thanne she spak with mery countenaunce:
"fful happy am I," she seyde, "on-to blys
Whanne þat the emperour wil me thus avaunce

to set up her Statue
To rere an ymage of soo grete plesaunce 425
In wurshep of me, and of so grete prys!
Somme men wolde sey þat I were ful nys 427

of gold or silver,
"If I refused it, for of goold it shal bee 428
If I commaunde, but ȝet at the lest
Of siluer he wil it make, and of swiche quantite,
The chaungeouris shul stryue and be in on-rest
To brynge so moche tresour out of the nest 432
To make a memoryal to Kataryn the mayde"—
[S]whiche-maner woordis at that tyme she sayde. 434

"And though this ymage be made of marbil grey, 435
Suffiseth it that to my laude eterne
Euery man that shal come be that wey
Where þat it shal be sette in an herne,

to be knelt to.
On bothe knees he muste falle ȝerne 439
An[d] doo his homage, ellis muste he deye.
What-maner woordis hope ȝe thei shal seye?: 441

"'heyl ymage, made right in memorial 442
Of a lady ful wys and ful prudent,
heyl statue that art now as eternal,
heyl signe made right to þis entent,
The grete beute of Kataryn to present.' 446
Wil not þis noyse ben ful grete plesauns
To hem þat loue this wordly lusti dauns? 448

She asks what her legs are to be made of.
"But this wolde I knowe[n], er we þis thing make,
Of what mater shal my leggis bee?

421 had hard 423 vn-to 425 reren a 427 seyne. ful om. 429 last 431 chaungours . in no rest 432 bregyne 433 of 434 Sweche 437 that om. be þe 438 a 439 hym muste 440 omage . must hym 447 noyse om. be 448 Tyl . louen) . worldly 449 knowyne . or

What-man*er* werkmaȝ is he that dar vndirtake
To make hem meve and walke in her degree?
Myȝ hand*is* eke I wolde wete hough that hee 453
Shul[d] make to fele,¹ and of what matere? ¹ r. felen
Er we goo ferthere, this thyng wolde I lere. 455

"The eyne eke whiche þis ymage shal haue, 456
If it¹ shul looke right as I doo in dede, ¹ *al.* þei
Where is that werkmaȝ that swiche þing*is* caȝ graue?
he were ful worthy to haue ful grete mede!
I leue neuere þ*a*t this werke shal spede; 460
This cristallyȝ matere thus sotilly to congelle
There is no werkmaȝ in erthe that caȝ it welle. 462

"A tounge eke, if he shul[d] to it make, 463
On-to th[is]¹ ymage to² speke and for to crye, ¹ MS. the ² MS. for to
Where is he that dar this vndirtake?
If he doo thus, he werketh a grete maystrye!
But for this cause that there is noo maȝ so slye, 467
Therfore I conclude thus in short sentens:
Whan ye haue wared ȝoure wyt and [your] expens 469

"To make this ymage, it shal be insensible, 470
Stonde liche a stoȝ, and byrdes flye rounde aboute,¹
As I suppose it shal be right possible ¹ *al.* þat flye ab.
That þei shal come somtyme a ful grete route,
her on-clene dunge shul thei there putte oute 474
And lete it falle right on the ymag*is* face.
loo whiche a reward¹ I may now purchace, ¹ *al.* sw. a gwerdon)

"That meȝ shul[d] drede and birdes shulde defyle; 477
But whaȝ deth hath shake on vs his blast
And þat oure mynde is passed a litel whyle,
I am a-ferd this werk shal not last.
Wherfore to make it me thenketh but [a] wast; 481

451 is he om. 452 to meue 453 my. who 454 shuld 455 Or. thyng om. 457 þei schul 459 wel w. 460 shuld wel sp. 461 cristallyne om. 462 it fulfylle 463 shuld it 464 þis . for om. (twice) 468 in a 469 & ȝoure 470 vnsensible 471 lyke . þat flyes ther abowthe 473 That om. comyne . rowthe 474 shall 475 ymage 476 sweche a gwerdon⁾ 477 shuld dredyn⁾ . foules 479 be p. 481 a wast

Bk. V. Ch. 8.	To truste in fame and fonned veynglorye,	
	It is but feyned[1] and fykel flaterye. [1] Ar. feynyng	483
Katharine says dogs 'ud defile her Statue.	"And though thei make it as fayre as þei can),	484
	ʒet shul dogges defyle it eueri day;	
	ffor þough it be honoured of euery man),	
	The smale childern) þat come be þe way	
	Shul somtyme make there [ful] foule aray.	488
	Shal I for this leue my god for euere	
	And fro his frenshipe my soule now disseuere,	490
	"To wurshipe deueles þat stande in temple here	491
	Kepte as beres? do wey, it shal not bee,	
She will never leave her Lord Jesus.	There shal noo Ioye ne peyne me [n]euere[1] stere [1] corr.: euere; al. neuer.	
	To leue my lord, to leue my felicyte,	494
	To renne in Apostasie, fy! [it will not be].[1] [1] MS. ʒe shal it neuere see, on erasure.	
	Lete be ʒoure labour, sir, lete be ʒoure promysse!	
	Thei shal not make me [n]euere[1] to doo amysse. [1] al. neuer	497
What would be the good of a Statue to her soul?	"What, shuld my lyf better ben) in ese	498
	ffor swiche a statue? what shulde it profyte	
	On-to my soule? me thenketh, it coude not plese	
	No good man); for though it were to the sight	
	fful delectable, with colouris shynynge bryght,	502
	On-to oure dayes it shulde ʒeue noon) encrees,	
	On-to oure siknesse it shulde be no reles,	504
How could it comfort her at death?	"On-to oure lyf it shulde be noo myrthe,	505
	On-to oure deth it shulde noo comforte bee,	
	N[o]n[1] avayle to ende ne to birthe. [1] MS. Ne	
	To what parte longeth it of felicyte?	
	If it myght kepe my flesh in swiche degree	509
	It shulde not rote, I wolde it neuere weyue, [1] on eras., al. om.	
	But as profytable thyng[1] I wolde [it] thanne receyue.	511

482 trosten . & in . fonned om.   483 feynyng a fekyl   485 shalle .
defylen   486 honoured be   487 childeryn   488 a ful fowle   490
frenchip . deseuyr   491 standen   493 neuer   495 fye it wille not be
496 sere   497 maken . neuer   499 profythe   501 sythe   502 brythe
503 ʒeue om.   504 be om.   non   506 non coumforthe   507 None
avayle   509 mowte   510 I shuld . weyuen   511 thyng om. it þan
reseyuen

"I haue a promys, made of a grettere lord, 512
Of a[1] grettere fame þan) I wil now expresse,   [1] om. in Ar. 20.
And made a-fore pe*r*sones of record,
In whiche is graunted, truly, w*yth*-oute[n] gesse,
A memoryal of parfight stabilnesse, 516
As ȝe shal knowe, many that here bee.
Leueth ȝoure besynesse as now on-to me! 518

"Laboure no more to wynne me to ȝo*ur* part, 519
It shal not be, I wil be as I am;
It wil noȝt avayle, ȝoure sotilte ne yo*ur* art.
he is my spouse whiche is bothe god & man),
I am his mayde, and wil doo that I can) 523
To haue his loue; he is al my swetnesse,
he is my Ioye, he is my gentilnesse." 525

Ca[m]. 9[m].

Tho chaunged the empe*r*our bothe word and chere, 526
And on-to the mayde he seyde as I rehers:
"The more benyngnely that we trete ȝow heere,
As me semeth, þe more ȝe reuers.
This shul ȝe haue, shortly in a vers: 530
Deth or Ioye; chese now whiche you[1] lest!   [1] Ar. ȝe
If ye wil lyue in solace and in rest, 532

"Thanne shul ye now w*yth* hy deuocyon) 533
Thuryfie on-to that mageste
Of grete appollo—his exaltac*ion*),
As ȝe knowe weel, for it is noo secree,
Redresseth þis world with hete whiche þat hee 537
Spredeth vp-on it. mayde, obeye her[1]-too!   [1] MS. hir
There is noo choys, this thyng muste nedes be doo. 539

"ffayre speche avayleth not [to] ȝou in noo wyse— 540
I wolde with solace a led ȝoure gentilnesse,

513 a om.   514 aforne   516 (stabyl p*a*rfytnesse expunged)   523 I inst. of and   524 hauen . al om.   527 on om. mayden   528 The benyⁿnglyer . treten   530 shalle   531 chese now om. leuest   532 leue   533 shal . hey   534 on om.   537 werd   538 upon iche . þer-too   540 to ȝou . wysse   541 wold wele . salas

Bk. V. Ch. 9.

The Emperor threatens Katharine with Death by Fire,

But alle[1] my promyses ye sette at[2] lytel pryse;   [1] *al.* at   [2] *al.* om.
Ye shul repente it sothly, as I gesse.
There is the fire; dispose you to hoolynesse,   544
Doo it with good wyl: ye shal the sonnere purchace[1]
Pardon) of synne[2] and encrece of grace.   [1] This v. on erasure. [2] r. synnes?   546

"If ȝe doo not, in short tyme ȝe shul be ded,   547

as an exaumple to deter others.

Right in exaumple of [þe] puple that is heere.
here hertes arn) hangynge heuy as the leed;
A[1] man) may perceyue right be her cheere   [1] all MS. A, r. As?
It may noȝt passe[n] lyghtly, swiche matere,   551
It muste be punysshed right for fer of other;
he shulde ben) ded th[o]ugh he were my brother."   553

Bk. V. Ch. 10.

Caᵐ⋅ **10**ᵐ⋅

Katharine welcomes Death.

"Peyne is weelcome to me," seyde she thanne,   554
"And deth eke, I wil it noȝt forsake;
ffor þough ȝe smyghte, sle, curse and banne,
It skilleth me nought for my [lordis sake][1]   [1] MS. souereyn) make, on erasure.
Swiche myschefis for his loue to take;   558
he tooke for me meche more wretchednesse,
Whil he leued here in this wyldernesse.   560

As Christ sufferd for her,

"Pouerte he suffred, that lord, ful buxomly,   561
Whanne that he myghte haue had richesse at his wylle—
This same myschef ȝet suffred neuere I,

so will she suffer for Him.

But if it come, I wil obeye þer-tille.
Ageyn) bla[s]phemours stood [þat lord][1] ful stille,   565
Yeuyng exaumple to us of pacyens—   [1] MS. he stood, he overl.
Why shulde his seruauntis make ony resistens   567
"Whanne þat the wykked purpos[1] to doo hem wrong?
ffor his cause, his feyth, or his loue   [1] MS. purpos ⁱˢ⋅ Ar. purpos

542 But at my promysse. at om. prysse 543 shalle 545 ȝe schon(!)
547 in syght inst. of in short tyme. shal 548 of þe 549 arne. the
om. 550 perseyuen 551 passen 552 ponched 553 be. thou 556
smyth fle sle or banne 557 rithe nothe. my lordis sake 558 myscheuys 559 myche 560 lyued. þis werldly wyldernes 561 þan
inst. of that lord 562 an had riches 563 þe 565 he om.; stod
þat lord 566 til 567 shulden. maken 568 þat om. purposyd.
don hym

Am I now redy, be it short or long,
To suffre despyte, peyne¹ or² reproue.   ¹ r. peynes   ² al. &
I wote ful weel it wil¹ falle to my behoue   ¹ MS. wel   572
Whan I am gon); the more we suffre heere,
The more Ioye [shal we hauen]¹ ellis-where.   ¹ MS. haue we   574

"he offred hym-selue on-to the fadyr of blis   575
An oste ful clene, ondefiled with synne;
And I wil offre my body, for it is his,
On-to his plesauns whiche I wolde wynne.

As Christ offerd Himself as a sacrifice, so will Katharine offer herself.

looke ȝe ȝoure-self whan ȝe wil be-gynne,   579
flor I am redy, in body and in goost;
Slee or fle, frye or ellis roost!   581

"There shal come tyme¹ þou shalt repente ful sore   582
Of cruel domes whiche þou vsest heere;   ¹ MS. the t., the overl.
Of thi powere settest þou ful grete store,
Whiche shal rewe the ful soone after þi beere;
Cristis seruauntis hast thou brente in-feere,   586
In tyme comynge therfore þou shalt be shent,
Whan þat with feendis in helle þou shalt be brent.   588

But the Emperor shall burn in Hell.

"The more þou thretest, the more glad am I;   589
The moo peynes þou aplyest to me,
The more my Ioye encresseth, sekyrly!
I go not alone whan þat I parte fro the,
ffor whan I deye, many of thi mene,   593
Of thyn housholde shul folwe me ful soone;
Of crist my lord haue I asked þat boone   595

Her death will turn many of his men to Christ.

"That of thy mene right a ful grete part   596
Shul trowe in hym & leue her ydolatrye—
Wayte a-boute with al thi sotil art,
Thou shalt fynde[n] that I make noo lye.
her soules fro peyne frely shul thus flye   600

570 I am   571 & r.   572 ful om. wille. myn   573 I suffyr   574 shal I hauen   575 on om.   576 And host   582 the om.   583 domus   585 sore   587 shalbe   588 þat þou wyth . shalbe   591 Ioyes encres   594 shal folow   596 meny   597 leuyne hire   598 þin   599 shalle fynd   600 þus shal

Bk. V. Ch. 10. Streyte to heuene, & þou shalt brenne in helle.
This thyng is sooth that I now the telle." 602

Bk. V. Ch. 11. Ca^m. XI^m.

The Emperor orders men

Thanne was þe emperour ny wood for Ire ; [1 r. stoden] 603
he commaunded his men þat stood[1] there aboute,
To gete[n] ȝerdes of ful sotiłł wyre ; [2 MS. þat were eke]
he chase men eke[2] þat were of body ful stoute,
To hem he seyde right thus, with-outen doute : 607

to strip Katharine naked,

" Take this mayden and strype hir modir-naked—
I trowe, she shal soone of [hir] sleep be waked. 609

" Bete hir weel, right for hir blaspheme, 610
To fese hem alle that troste in hir doctryne !
lete hir no more speken of that bethleeme,
Ne of that galyle shal she no more dyuyne.
I trowe that peyne shal hir rathere enclyne 614
On-to oure wil, than may besy plesauns :

and flog her. Doo ȝe ȝoure dedis, though that she falle in trauns." 616

The tormentouris haue take hir now a-syde, 617
Made hir naked, bak and armes ther-too,

They do so till her blood flows.

With yern roddes as faste as thei myght[1] glyde [1 al. may]
Thei beten hir body, the blood gan oute goo.
Whanne thei were wery, than cam fresh [men] moo. 621
Thus is she beten for hir spouses loue,
She trosteth on comforte þat cometh fro aboue. 623

She prays to God.

These were hir woordis : " lord, sende me pacyens, 624
Make me strong to suffre þis penauns ;
If þat I haue ronne in thyn offens,
lete it be purget be this same grevauns !
Thankynge be euere on-to thi puruesauns, 628

---

602 trew . þe now   604 comaund. stodyn hem a.   605 To fecchen
606 eke om. stouthe   607 Tille . hei . wythout douthe   609 hire slepe
610 feryne . alle om. trostyne.   612 lere . spekyn   613 that om.   614
rether   615 þat may be oure pl.   616 deuer   617 taken . now om.
on syde   619 Wyth eyrend wandes . may   620 cam fast hir froo
621 fresh men   622 betyn   624 þeis weren   626 þi   627 purged
628 vnto . puruyauns

Eternal lord, makere of man and beeste;
Of thy seruauntis I that am the leeste, 630

"Thanke the more for this same betynge 631
Than for the welthes þat þou sent me before;
ffor weel wot I that this tormentynge
It is to me [as] a gret[1] tresore. [1] or. grete
ffarweel the world now for eueremore! 635
Stele and robbe the[1] goodes that I haue, [1] MS. tho
I care not now neyther for tour ne caue." 637

The tyraunt asked a-mongis this bitter peyne, 638
Whan al was blood, and [þe] beteris wery alle:
"What sey ye, mayde[n], wil ȝe yet susteyne
Youre olde heresye in whiche þat ȝe be falle?
If ye wyl mercy of oure goddis calle, 642
Ye shul it haue; and ellis alle-newe game.
Er þat ye goo, I trowe ȝe shal be tame." 644

She answerde thus:[1] "sir, knowe þis weel, 645
That I am strengere in body & in goost   [1] Ar. 20 þus ageyn
Than [euer] I was, to suffren euery deel,
Al-maner torment, wheder þou frye or roost.
But þou myssha[m]ful[1] dogge ful of boost,   [1] Ar. 168 shameful
Doo what þou wilt, for I shal strengere bee   Ar. 20 vnshamfull; r. mysshapful?
In my sufferauns than þou in thi cruelte. 651

"Be-thenke þe weel on ylke-maner syde 652
how þou may slee and brynge[1] now of dawe   [1] r. bryngen
The crysten puple that knowen is so wyde,
Whiche doo no wrong but kepen a ful true lawe:
I shal deyn and passe this wordly wawe, 656
ffolwen my lord and dwelle with hym in blys,
Where noo thyng is thought ne doo amys. 658

632 sett 634 as a 635 werd 636 þe 638 amonge 639 þe beters wery were a. 640 mayden 641 elle . þat om. 643 shalle . alle om. 644 Or 645 sere 647 euer . sufferne 648 wheyther þou wolt fry 649 myschamful 653 Whom . or . now om . on d. 655 kepyn 656 dey . passene . wordes 657 folow 658 wher þat

Bk. V. Ch. 11.

Katharine tells the Emperor he shall be in Hell,

"There shal I dwelle in Ioye and al solace, 659
Whan̄ þou thi-self shal be in horry[b]le peyne.
Thou shalt desyre, but þou shalt haue noo grace,
Thou shalt be bounde[n] with þat wooful cheyne
Of obstynacye; þou shalt repente, and seyne 663
'Allas þat euere I wrought swiche torment
On-to ȝon heuenely blessed heygh couent!' 665

while she is in bliss in Heaven.

"Thus shalt þou wayle whan̄ þou seest us[1] in blis, 666
And þou in sorwe with-oute[n] remedie, [1] Ar. 20 wo are
Lyenge in peynes whiche shul neuere mys—
This shalt þou knowe vp hap ful hastylie.
· Therfore fulfille now of ire al thi malencolye, 670
And I shal suffren̄ for the loue of heuene."
Thus seyde this lady with [a] ful boold steuene. 672

Bk. V. Ch. 12.

Cap^{m.} 12^{m.}

The Emperor orders Katharine to be put in prison,

The emperour commaunded on-to his seruauntis an-noon̄
They[1] take this mayden̄ and to preson̄ lede. [1] so Ar. 168; Ar. 20 þat þei
he wil thei putten̄ hir in the depe caue of stoon̄,
Noo man̄ soo hardy hir for to feede.
"I wil," he seyth, "ȝe fulfylle this in dede; 677

and left 12 days without food,

Alle these twelue[1] dayes whiche I shal ryde. [1] so Ar. 168 and 20.
Lete hir no mete haue, to slake hir pryde, 679

drink, or light.

"Geue hir noo drynke, ne lete hir noo light haue! 680
ho-soo-euere trespace a-geyn̄ my commaundement,
Soo hooly Iubiter mote my soule saue,
Whan I come hom, he shal be brent!
I wyl [þat] ȝe fulfille al myn̄ entent 684
Euene streytly, with-outen̄ dispensacion̄,
Noo man̄ soo hardy of noo-maner nacion̄ 686

---

659 & in s. 660 schalt. orybylle 661 schalt þan d. 662 bounden 665 ȝoure. heygh om. 666 qwan 667 wyth-outen 669 ful om. 670 al om. 671 suffyr. of god of h. 672 þe. a ful bold 673 comaunde. anon 674 ȝe take. mayd. into p. hire 675 I wille ȝe put 676 in no maner hire to f. 677 þat þis be done in d. 678 þeis fourty. wheche þat 679 slake þerwithe h. p. 680 ȝeue. drynke inst. of light 681 Who so operwyse do a. m. c. 683 sone shalle he be b. 684 þat ȝe 685 wyth-oute delacione

"Bere[1] hir mete or drynk or ony lyght." [1] r. To b. 687

This cruel maundement and this same decree
Made the emperour thus ageyn lawe & right,
And he is ryden foorth with his mene
Vp in to the lond, for causes whiche that hee   691
had for to doo, as potestates haue.
Thus is this mayde allone in the caue,   693

With-outen comforte, with-outen solace.   694
But crist hath not for-geten his wyf
Alle these xij. dayes of his good grace,
he wold not leue[n] hir liche a caytyf,
he sente doun seruauntis fro the hous of lyf,   698
his Aungellis I mene, to counforte this mayde.
Swiche maner of woordis thei to hir sayde: 700

"Oure lord commaunded[1] that ȝe shuld be glad,   701
Suffre this disese with sobre pacyens;   [1] r. commaundeth
Mete shul ȝe haue ȝe neuere swhiche had,
light hath he sent now with oure presens.
The emperour for youre cause renneth in offens,   705
Whiche he shal somtyme ful soore repent."
Thus was she comforted in hir torment   707

With light of heuene and with heuenly mete,   708
With presens of Aungellis—for thei þat hir keepe,
Thei myght heere[1] noyse hough thei hir trete,   [1] r. heere her?
Thei myght see light[2] as it gan creepe   [2] r. þe l.
Thurgh-oute the scarres; thei myght not sleepe,   712
Soo haue thei meruayle of al this thyng.
But ryght nowght tolde thei on-to þe kyng.   714

But to other foolk in the court there   715
Sprang this woord soore hough that þis mayde
Was kepte fro light, in ful grete fere,

Bk. V. Ch. 12.

The Emperor rides into the country.

But Christ sends his Angels to comfort Katharine in prison

with heavenly light and food.

This becomes known.

689 þe law of r. 690 he om. redyn 691 cause 692 don 693
And þus . left alone in caue 694 ony comforthe or ony s. 696 fourty
697 leuyn . like 698 his s. 700 of om. þoo til hir þei 701 comaund
703 shalle . sweche 704 lithe . ȝow inst. of now 707 tornament
709 kepte 710 þe n. 711 sene . strepe 712 oute om. skarrys
714 nothe 716 spronge . þer inst. of soore . how.

362 *The Queen pities Katharine in prison.* [MS. Arundel.

Bk. V. Ch. 12.
Katharine's miraculous help gets known.

And fro mete eke, right as I sayde,
And hough the gaylerɩs were sore afrayde   719
Of certeyn) light at the dongeon)-doore—
This woord in the court abouten) gooth soore.   721

Bk. V. Ch. 13.   Cap^{m.} 13^{m.}

The Queen hears of her cruel sentence,

The tydyngɩs are come to the queenes eere[1]   [1] or. heere 722
   Of the cruel sentens, of the light eke,
hough that the mayden) with-outen) ony feere
had answered the clerkɩs this other weke,
hough þat the mayde[n] with woordɩs meke   726
had turned hem) to crist and hough thei were brent,
And she for that cause in preson) was ny shent.   728

     The emperour was absent, as I seyde be-fore,   729
ffoorth in to þe lond ryden in haste.
Thei toold the queen) that he commaunded soore
That she neither mete ne drynk shul[d] taste,
But for pure hunger she muste deye & waste,   733
"These laste woordɩs seyde he[1] on the heth   [1] MS. he seyde
No man) ȝeue hir mete in peyne of deth!"   735

and pities her.

     This meued the queen) of very womanly pete   736
To haue compassyon) of these peynes alle
Whiche þat this lady be very cruelte
Of the kyng had suffred; thus is she falle,

The Queen

The queen), al in stody, walkyng in the halle,   740
Thenkynge besyly euere on this mayde;
On-to[1] hir-selue ful preuyly thus she sayde: [1] al. And to 742

says the Christians do no man wrong.

"These cristen foolkɩs,[1] thei doo noo man) wrong;   743
Alle that thei beye, truly therfore they pay,   [1] al. folke
On-to her god thei synge ful good[ly] song,

---

718 right om. as I ere   719 iayloures. so   720 dongon   721 gothe aboute   722 tydens. onto   723 & of   724 wyth-out   725 in þat tothir   726 And how þat þe mayden)   728 is   730 redyne   732 shuld   734 þeis. seyd he   735 ȝefe. mete ne drynke ne lyght   741 euere om. vpon   742 And til. ful om.   743 Theis. folke   744 bye   745 syngyne. goodly

Newe and newe as men seyn euery day ;
Wastful are thei nought in [no]¹ maner of aray,   ¹ MS. ony 747
Glotones ne drunkelewe wil thei neuere bee—
This same lyf, ful weel it pleseth mee.   749

Bk. V. Ch. 13.

  "And oon of hem had I be or now,   750
had not oure lawe [for]fended¹ us that scoole ; ¹ MS. defended
If it were seyn that I to hem drow,
Men shuld seyn that I were a foole ;
It myght turne me eke to mekel doole,   754
If that my lord myght this chaungynge knowe.
But in myn herte euere there gynneth growe   756

The Queen says she would have been a Christian but for the Pagan law.

  "A grete desyre for to see this mayde.   757
Allas, hough shal I fu[l]fille myn entent?"
Thus be hir-selue this lady thought & sayde.
But in this stody ryght euene as she went,
happed to come, as though god hym had¹ sent,   761
A noble knyght, a wyse man in al thyng,   ¹ al. had hym
preuy in counsayl, right specyal with the kyng,   763

She wants to see Katharine.

A wise knight,

  Gouernour of knyghtis, ledere to hem alle,   764
A very fadir to 3ynge folkis¹ that shulde lere— ¹ al. folke
Porphirye, the storyes right thus thei hym calle ;
On-to the queen he kneled with ful sad cheere.
"I am glad, porphiry," she seyde,¹ " þat 3e been here ; 768
Ye ben a man that may meche avayle : ¹ al. she seyde, porphiry.
To 3ou I wil telle now my preuy counsayle.   770

Porphyry, comes to her.

  "I am so troubled newly with the¹ cristen lawe,   771
I can not slepe, I may not ete ne drynke ;   ¹ al. om.
Euery day, er it be-gynneth to dawe,
And eke al nyght on þis mater I thynke ;
I trowe I am ful ny my lyues brynke,   775

She tells him how troubled she is about Christianity.

747 in no . ray   748 In gloteny ne drunkchip   750 ben   751 forfend   752 sene   756 But 3ete . my . euere om. begynnythe to 757 An . sene   759 þe   760 ryght om.   761 hym om. had hir 763 pryuy of   764 leder of   765 3onge folke   766 porphery   768 she seyd porphery . be   769 myche   770 now I wille tellen   771 trobilled . the om.   772 neythir ete   773 or

Bk. V. Ch. 13.	But I haue comfort"—right thus tho she sayde;	
The Queen begs Porphyry to let	"Goode porphirye, I muste nede see ȝone mayde.	777
	"Ordeyne ye the mene ryght as ȝe can),	778
	Geue the gayler*is* golde and sylner I-nough,	
her, with him,	Ordeyne soo þat I and ye, my man),	
	May speke this lady. to god I make a vough,	
	Looke my lord neue*re* soo wroth ne row,	782
speak to Katharine.	I muste nedes speke hir, or I shal be ded;	
	ffor in this mater myn) herte is [h]euy as led."	784
	Porphirye seyde, "madame, it shal be doo,	785
	I shal parfoorme this thynge, trost in me!	
	In swyche degree the doores shul be [on-doo],[1]	[1] MS. be ordeyned for soo
	There shal noo man) be preuy but we thre,	
	That is to sey the gayler, I, and ȝe.	789
He promises he will manage it.	Drede ȝow nought, ȝe shul haue yo*ur* entent.	
	With this mater haue I ben) sore torment;	791
Katharine has sufferd great wrong.	"Me thenketh, grete wrong this lady suffreth heere,	792
	Soo horrybely bete[n], kepte fro mete and drynk,	
	And she noon) harm) dooth in noo manere!	
	fful ofte[n]-tyme she made me on hir thynk,	
	Sith that I herde hir the noble argument*is* clynk	796
	With the clerk*is*, whan) she conuycte hem alle.	
	Therfore, madame, falle what may be-falle,	798
The Queen and he will see her this night.	"We wil see hir, and that with good leyser,	799
	And speke wy*th* hir this same nyght fol[o]wyng.	
	Grete ȝeftes wil I ȝeue on-to the gaylere	
	To holde his pees and speke of this noo-thyng.	
	Go ȝe to chaunbre, & whane I ȝeue you[1] warnyng,	803
	Come foorthe alone, lete yo*ur* women slepe;	[1] *al.* om.
	Looke ye be redy whan) I shal yow cleepe."	805

777 me muste nedes 779 ȝefe . gaylere . enowe 780 ȝe & I may than 781 May om. vowe 782 & rowe 784 heuy 785 seyde om. 787 þe dorys shalbe ondoo 788 pryuey 789 seyne 790 schal 791 sore be 792 þat þis l. 793 horribily . beten) 794 no 795 oftene . to thynke 796 Sithin, that om. hir herde 798 what so ; may om. 799 that om. 800 nyte 801 shalle . on om. 802 To kepe counsayle & 803 you om. 804 Comyth . & lete

Cap^{m.} 14^{m.}

Thus be consent the queen) and porphirye, 806
whanne alle men) slepte, to preson) are thei goo
Al alone, right soo seyth oure storie.
Whanne thei too come there[1] and no moo,
So grete light in preson) sey[2] thei thoo 810
That thei falle [doun] with-oute[n] speche or breth—
Thei supposed neuere to[1] haue be so ny her deth.

ffor that brightnesse was lyke a lyghtenynge 813
Whiche thei seyn) thanne, soo wonderful & soo bright
her witte is goo and doun) in stamerynge
Are thei falle now for feer of that sight.
There was a sauour also with that light, 817
Thei felten neuere swiche, the story seyth, certeyn),
ffor with that sauour her comfort cam) ageyn). 819

Tho spak the mayde swiche woordis on-to hem) : 820
" Ryse up, sister, ryse up, brother, in-feere !
Crist that was bore in þe Citee of bethleem,
he hath called you to his seruyse here.
Beth glad and mery, be of right good chere, 824
Oure lord hath chosen 3ou newely of his grace ;
ffor that cause he sente 3ou to this place." 826

Thei behelde the mayden) at that tyde 827
how þat she satte on knees ful mekely,
Many Aungellis seyn) thei on euery syde
With swete gummes anoy[n]tyng hir softely ;
Euere as thei touched with handis, by & by 831
The flesh was heeled, þe skyn) closed ageyn),
Wyth meche more beute, soothly for to seyn), 833

Than) euere it was whil [þat] it was hole. 834
Thus can oure lord redresse[1] al doloure   [1] r. redressen

Margin notes:
- The Queen and Porphyry go to Katharine's prison,
- and see so bright a light that they fall down.
- Katharine welcomes them
- as chosen by Christ.
- Angels anoint Katharine's wounds,
- and heal them.

[1] Ar. 1C8 þei come þer, þei too
[2] Ar. 1C8 so
[1] om. in Ar.

807 slepyne   808 soo om.   809 too om.   comen þer þei too &.   810 lithe.   sow   811 fallene downe.   wyth-outene   812 hopyd.   a ben.   hir   813 brytnes.   lyche   814 sey.   soo 2 om.   816 fallen.   nowom.   817 þe l.   818 felt   820 maydene.   on om.   823 onto   824 Be   825 chose.   to   827 beheldene.   mayde   828 sate   829 sey   834 whyle þat

366 *The Queen's visit to Katharine in Prison.* [**MS. Arundel.**

Bk. V. Ch. 14. Whiche men) suffre, be it in heed or sole,
he can) in lesse tyme than an houre
hele oure soores, comforte oure labour. 838
These folke, I trowe, thei had a blessed sight,
fful of comforte, ful of heuenly delight. 840

Nine or ten old men also comfort Katharine.
There sat be-syde eke sundry olde men), 841
Yeuynge comforte on-to hir heuynesse—
Were thei nyne or ellys were they ten),
Of her nombre haue I no sekernesse;
Thei were sente thedyr, soothly, as I gesse, 845
Be-cause this woman) was with-oute solace,
hir to comforte with som heuenly grace. 847

From one she takes a 5-brancht crown,
On of hem held in his hand a crowne, 848
ffayre[1] and ryal, we can) it no3t discryue; [1] r. So f.?
Right fro his hand Kataryn) tooke it doune,
To the queen) thus she seyde belyue:

and says the Queen shall wear it after death.
"This croune, suster, with his braunches fyue 852
Shul 3e haue and were it on youre heed,
As for assay, but after that 3e ben) deed, 854
"Thanne shul ye haue it for a[1] reward eue*r*elastyng."
On-to the olde men) tho turned the mayde [1] *al.* om. 856
Whil she helde the croune, in þe settynge,
Thus to hem with meke voys she sayde:
"ffor these p*er*sones to my lord I prayde, 859
Thei shul be wreten) in the book of lyf:
Therfore, sirs, as I am crist*is* wyf 861

The names of her and Porphyry are in the Book of Life.
"Graunted be patent, soo wil I that 3e wryte 862
These too names in þat book for eue*r*e,
Clense her synnes, make þat heuy wighte
ffro my lord no more hem disseuere.

837 in halfe a houre   839 þeis. I trowe om.   þe*r*e hadden. blysfull
840 delyte   841 s. ful elde   842 on-tyll   843 þe*r*e were i*n* cumpanye
no mo þa*n* nyne or tene   844 hyr nowmb*r*e   849 reall. not   851
Onto   852 syst*er*. þeis   853 shall*e*. hauene. weryne. it om. up-on
854 aft*er* whan. be   855 shall*e*. a om.   856 þat mayde   857 Wille.
elde   858 tyl   859 þeis   861 seres. am om.   862 wryth*e*   863
Theis   864 make so. with*e*   865 deseuyr*e*

I pray to god that now falle thei neuere 866
After þat tyme that thei receyued the feyth."
Oon) of the olderes ageyn) on-to hir seyth : 868

"O precyous spouse of god that sitteth aboue, 869
O gemme ryal shynynge in chastyte !
What-soo-euere þou aske of cryst þat is thi loue,
Thou can) not fayle it, soo propicyous is hee
On-to thi persone. therfore, trost þou me, 873
This lady shal proue to grete perfeccion);
The knyght shal haue eke swiche progressyon) 875

"In vertuous lyf, þat thurgh his good counsayle 876
Too hundred and mo fro her fals beleue
Shul turne to cryst, and ful soore wayle
her false feyth whiche thei can) not preue."
Thus haue this folkis at Kataryn) taken) her leue, 880
Walkyng to chaunbre with hertes ful suspens;
keepyng this mater al clos in sylens. 882

Cap^{m.} 15^{m.}

The mayde is kepte in preson) euere stille, 883
with swiche comfort as 3e herde[n] heere;
Of mannes comfort hath she neyther letter ne bille,
Noo man) dar doo it, swiche is now her feere;
Twelue dayes ful thus was she keepte there, 887
With-oute[n] mete, but be alle these dayes
Of heuenly mete had she swete asayes. 889

ffor he þat fedde Danyel in the lake, 890
And caryed Abacuc soo fer oute of Iude
To brynge hym) vytayll, that same lord myght make
That in preson) this mayde soo feed shuld bee.
In storyes redde I deuers too or thre, 894

Bk. V. Ch. 14.

An Elder

assures
Katharine
that

the Queen
shall reach
perfection,

and that
Porphyry
shall turn
200 Pagans
to Christ.

Bk. V. Ch. 15.

Katharine

is fed for
12 days in
prison with
heavenly
food.

---

866 now mote þei falle 867 þe . reseyuyne 868 eldest 870 realle .
shynyst 871 soo om. 872 It can not fayle so precious to 3ou is he
873 to me 874 preue onto 875 þis knyte 878 shalle . & ful sore
for here synne wayle 880 þeis folke of . take 881 ful om. 883
This maydene 884 haue herdyne 887 ffourty . kepyd 888 wyth-
outene . in . þeis 889 metis 890 D. þe prophete 891 abouthe (!)
893 maydene . þat þus inst. of soo feed 894 þat I rede in dyuers

368   *Christ visits Katharine in Prison.*   [**MS. Arundel.**

Bk. V. Ch. 15. A fayre dowe fro heuene brought hir mete— [1] overlined.
A Dove brings Katharine food from Heaven.
Whether bodyly or goostly it[1] is hard for to trete, 896
ffor as Austyn̄ seith, þat same seed 897
Whiche oure faderis receyued in wyldernesse,
Whiche serued hem thanne in stede of bred,
This doctour seyth in very soothfastnesse
That possyble it is swiche seedes mo and lesse 901
Shul[d] be noryshed in the eyr, be supposicyon̄
In the lowere part whiche hath disposycyon̄ 903
    Somwhat to erthe acordynge in nature— 904
This is his sentens, hoo-[so] wil it reede,
In his book whiche treteth þe merueile of scripture.
I trowe this same was doo heere in dede :

The Holy Ghost feeds her with heavenly food.
The holy goost this goodly mayde gan̄ feede 908
With heuenly thyng whiche had erthely kynde—
Thus wene I, [but] I wil no man̄ bynde 910

But if he[1] wil, for to leue my tale. [1] MS. 30 911
She was fed—that haue we of treuthe ;
If god had lefte hir in soo bitter bale
With-outen comfort, it had ben̄ grete reuthe.
In that preson̄ thus leued she with-outen̄ slewthe 915

On the 12th day
Alle these xij dayes. but in the last of alle,
As she in preyer ful besyly gan̄ calle 917

    On-to crist, she saugh an heuenly syght : 918
Christ comes to her in prison,
Oure lord hym̄-selue to preson̄ is come doun̄,
With many Aungellis shynynge wonder bryght,
With many maydenes, noon̄ swyche in this toun̄.
ffor very Ioye kataryn̄ is falle in swoun̄ ; 922
and comforts her.
Oure lord comforted hir with goodly cheere,
"Doughter," he seyth, "look up whom ȝe see heere ! 924

896 wheythir   897 Austene   899 hyme   900 þis very doctir . very om.   901 more or   902 shuld . eyȝere   904 to þe erde   905 who so   906 þe merueile om. . in sc.   907 don   908 mayden   909 erdly   910 but I wil   911 he . leuyn͛   915 prysone . thus om. she lyued . sleuth   916 these om. fourty   918 saw   921 maydenes of ful grete renowne   922 felle (is om.)   923 coumforth . ful goodly   924 he seyth om. lokyth

"Knowe youre makere, for whom al þis disese	925	*Christ bids Katharine know Him.*
ȝe haue suffred. take it in paciens!		
The more ȝe suffre, the more ȝe me plese;		
keepe ȝoure constauns, drede noo wordly offens,		
Thenke not longe, lyue not with herte suspens!	929	
I am with ȝow, I shal you neuere forsake.		*He will never forsake her.*
Many an herte ful redy shul ye make	931	

"On-to my seruyse, er ȝe departe[1] fro this lyf;	932	*She shall turn many folk to Him.*
Grete noumbre of puple shul ȝe tourne, [1] *al.* part		
Many an husbonde, mayde, wydewe and wyf		
ff[ro][1] here maumetrye shal ȝe [hem tourne][2] [1] MS. corr.: ffor		
And to my feyth lede hem to soiourne." [2] corr.: make mourne; Ar. 168 returne.		
Whan this was seyde, oure lord is up to heuene,		*He goes up to Heaven.*
With grete brightnesse, as it were a leuene.	938	

Shee looked[1] after til she seeth no more, [1] Ar. 168 lokith	939	
Returned[2] to prayere, as tho was hir vsage; [2] returneth		*She prays.*
It was to hir a ful grete tresore		
That ihesu lest to make þat pilgrimage		
hir hertly sorwe soo goodly for to swage	943	
With his presens—blessed euere he bee!		
And be this mayden, commended to hym be we!	945	

Ca^{m.} 16^{m.}

Bk. V. Ch. 16.

[1] *al.* his		
Whanne these[1] causes arn brought fully to ende	946	*When the Emperor Maxentius comes home, he sends 6 knights for Katharine.*
whiche that he rood fore, Maxens now I mene,		
he is come hom. a-noon he gan to sende		
ffor þis mayde be sexe knyghtis, I wene;		
If thei ben fals, soone it shal be seene,	950	
Thei þat kepte hir, thei shul it ouere-thynke [1] MS. eyther mete		
If it be proued thei ȝoue hir mete[1] or drynke.	952	

926 t. it euer   928 worldly   931 hart   932 or ȝe part   933 shalle ȝe returne   934 a . wedow   935 & 6 transp.   935 ffro hire m. shalle ȝe hem returne   936 Onto . ledyne   937 do . went up   939 sey   940 Returnyth . as euer was   942 lyst   943 goodly om.   945 comend 946 his c. arne . to þe e.   947 Wyth þat . forthe   948 comyne   949 ffor hir . rithe as I w.   950 be   951 it shalle hem o.   952 ȝouen . eyther om.

370 *The Emperor is wroth to see Katharine better.* [**MS. Arundel.**

Bk. V. Ch. 16.

Al the Citee is gadered to see þis sighte, 953
A grete puple, some for cruelnesse,
Som*e* arn) there that han) ful grete despite
The Emperor On-to the emper*o*ur for his wykkydnesse,
Thei thenke this lady is put to grete distresse 957
ffor noo cause oonly but for good.
The emper*o*ur seyde with ful sturdy mood : 959

orders Katharine to be brought forth.
"Brynge foorth this woman), brynge þis concyonatrix,
Brynge that wytche ! noo man may turne hir herte ; 961
In hir errour is she made soo fix
That fro it noo man) may make hir to sterte.
But if she doo, ful soore shal she smerte !" 964
Thus is she brought be-fore[1] his presens. [1] r. beforen
he supposed veryly that for[1] abstynens [1] *al*. for hir 966

She had be peyned euene to the detħ : 967
Now looketh she fresh, [wyth] white and rody colour.
He is furious to find her fairer than ever,
Very anger his herte now ny sletħ,
ffor she is fayrere than) she was that hour
Whiche he com*m*aunded to lede hir to the tour. 971
"Tretoures," he sayde, "ȝe shul deye ilke oon),
But if ye telle me in this place anoon) 973
" hoo hath fedde, a-geyn) oure com*m*aundement, 974
This froward caytif that no man) may ou*er*lede.
and swears he'll find out who has fed her.
I swere be Iubiter, whiche is omnypotent,
It shal be wist hoo þ*a*t dede this dede !
There shulde[1] noo man) for noo-man*er* nede [1] *al.* shal 978
Doo this thyng whiche we [for]fende[2] soo." [2] Ar. forfended
he dede hem byndyn) wit Iern) be too and too. 980

Thanne the mayde[n], to excuse hem alle, 981
Seyde to the kyng swhyche-[maner] woord*is*, certeyn) :

953 sene . sythe   955 ar*e* . despythe   956 At the   959 stordy   960
2 bryn*g* forthe   961 Br. forth*e* ; that wytche om.   966 for hi*r*e   967
pynyd . the om.   968 freshe w*yth* coloure (white and rody om.)
969 ffor very a.   now om.   ny it.   971 Whan . comaunde . ledyn*e* .
þat   972 Traytoures . shal   973 if om.   978 shall*e* . mede   979
forfend   980 bynd w*yth* eyryne   981 maydene . excusen   982 swcche
maner

MS. Arundel.] *Katharine says her Jailers are innocent.*

" Thou art a lord, an emperour men) the calle,		*Bk. V. Ch. 16.*
Thou art ordeyned al treuthe to susteyn) ;		Katharine begs the
Thei that doo ageyn) the lawe or seyn),	985	Emperor
hem shuldest[1] þou punyssħ ; but innocentis noone ;	[1] r. shuld	not to punish
If thou doo, þou doost ageyn) thi trone.	987	
" ffor these men) whiche had keepynge of me,	988	the jailers, for they didn't feed her.
Brought me no mete ne drynke, þou vndirstande ;		
I was susteyned al in other degree :		
Be my lord whiche is al-weeldande ;		Christ fed her
ffor be his massageris sente he me to hande	992	
Al my sustenauns—no dore myght hem lette		
To spere hem) oute—sir, þou can) noo iette.	994	
" Therfore these Innocentes, do hem no torment,	995	
Thei be not worthi, sir kyng, I sey the why :		
Be hooly Aungellis my lord this mete sent,		by His Angels.
Noon) erthely creature was ther-to preuy ;		
ffor hunger he wolde not suffre me to dy.	999	
he is my loue, I am his for euere,		He is her Love.
Ioye ne sorwe shal us not disseuere."	1001	
Ca^{m.} 17^{m.}		*Bk. V. Ch. 17.*
To these woordis the tyraunt with doubelnesse	1002	The Emperor answers her with fair-seeming words at first.
Answerede ful faire, that thei whiche stood aboute		
Shulde not suppose in hym) suche cruelnesse ;		
The sturdy herte in hym whiche was soo stoute,		
Was hid with langage as venym) in a cloute ;	1006	
fful fayre woordis at that tyme he sayde :		
" I am for you ful sory, most goodly mayde,	1008	
" Ye born) of kyngis, douter to kyng and queen),	1009	
Cosyn) to lordis many þat serue[n] me,		
The [best] bore woman) of this contre ȝe been)—		

985 done . þi 986 shuld . ponyshe 987 dost 988 þeis 989 neythire m. 990 a-nothir 992 massangeres 994 sir om. canst not gette 996 sere 997 me mete 999 dey 1002 Tho þeis . dobylnesse 1003 þei þat stodyne abouthe 1005 stouthe 1006 hid om. venyne . c'outhe 1009 a kynges dowter of k. & of 1010 seruyne 1011 The best borne

B B 2

Bk. V. Ch. 17.

The Emperor tells Katharine

Thus arn) ye named : and al þis with sotylte
Of certeyn) witches—cursed euere thei bee!— 1013
Is turned and lost ; for other Ioye haue ye noon)
But Ihesu crist, mary, petir & Ion), 1015

"Whiche arn) tretoures proued be þe senat, 1016
And damned to deth for treson) & heresye.
Why wil ȝe lese thus youre honourable astat

she has turnd to witchcraft and lying.

And yeue attendauns to wytchecrafte & to lye ?
It had ben) beter to haue kepte the same sophie 1020
Whiche þat youre maysteris lerned you first in scole !
This-maner lernynge wil proue¹ you a foole. ¹ r. prouen? 1022

"Eke ageyn) oure holy goddis seruyse 1023
Ye speke & crie, and that soo malycyously,
With woordis¹ and cheer on)-goodly hen) despise : ¹ al. worde
This causeth me, I sey you suerly, ² or. not-wythstand (so Ar. 168).
That, not-wythstandyng,² so mote I haue mercy, 1027

He must punish her, to protect his people.

That I wolde saue you, I muste¹ nedes punysshe þis pride,
Right for my puple þat standeth heere be-syde. ¹ al. mut 1029

She must die,

"Therfore chese now whether þat ye wil deye 1030
Whith suche deth as lawe wil damne you too,

or deny Christ.

Or ellis youre feith if ye wil reneye ;
Thanne shal ye haue mercy & worship eke alsoo.
Come of a-noon), lete see what ye wil doo, 1034
Offre to Iubiter, ȝoure god omnypotent ;
Youre tendre body with yern) shal ellis be brent." 1036

Bk. V. Ch. 18.

Cam. 18m.

Katharine says she

The mayde answerde to the emperour agayn) : 1037
"Though that my lyf bee ful swete to me,

will die rather than offend Christ.

Yet had I leuere with a swerd be slayn)
Than) that my lyf in ony-maner degree
Shulde offende the blessed mageste 1041

1012 are 1014 is þer none 1016 are 1017 to þe 1018 lesse
1019 ȝeuyne . to 2 om. 1020 to a k. 1021 youre maysteris om.; ȝe
lerned fyrst 1022 I wille preue 1025 word 1026 sewirly 1027
not wyth-stand 1028 mut nede 1029 stand 1030 wheyder 1031
sweche 1036 yrne 1038 Thou

Of my lord god. I sey the, cryst is my lyf,
And grete encres, though I deye on¹ knyf,   1043
"Soo that I deye in charyte and for his sake.   1044
Therfore, thou deth come to me this hour,
ffor his loue ful mekely I wil it take,
I shal neuere with myght ne with labour
Grutche ageyn my lord, my saueour;   1048
Deeth shal avaunce me with grete emolume[n]t,
Deeth is a chaungeour—fro this lyf present   1050
"To beter he leedeth us, this is oure beleue;   1051
Oure dedly bodyes whiche arn corruptible,
Whan that he cometh he bryngeth hem to þis preue
That thei shal reste and rote, as seith oure bible;
After þat restynge, yet it is possible   1055
On-to oure lord tho bodyes to rere ageyn,
In fayrere foorme than euere thei were seyn.   1057

"Therfore, þou tyraunt with thi feyned langage,   1058
Doo what þou wilt, put me to torment,
Brenne me with brondes thyn Ire for to swage!
I wolde offre to cryst, whiche is omnipotent,
Som plesaunt offrynge, som delectable present;   1062
Keen and caluern or sheep I al forsake,
Myn owen body to offerynge wil I take.   1064

"But for I may not leeffully do it my-selue,   1065
As make this offerynge, therfore thi cruelte
Shal bydde thi seruauntes other ten or twelue
With vengeable herte to make an ende of me.
To hym that was offred in caluerye on a tree,   1069
To hym I offre my flesh, my blood & felle.
But for thi cruelnesse yet efte I the telle,   1071

"Thou shalt ful soore heer-after this thyng repent,   1072
Nought oonly in helle whiche þou shalt be Inne,

¹ al. on a

Side notes: Bk V. Ch. 18. / Katharine welcomes death for Christ's sake. / Death will lead her to a better Life. / Her body will rise again. / "So, Tyrant, burn me! / I offer up my body, / to Him that died on Calvary. / But you shall not only go to Hell here-after;

1043 one a k. 1046 lufe 1051 ledyth 1052 are coruptible 1057 fayrrer 1058 teraunt 1063 kyin . calueryne 1064 owe 1065 lefully 1067 eythere 1068 a hende 1070 & my felle 1073 Not. shalbe

374 *Katharine foretells disasters to the Emperor.* [MS. Arundel.

Bk. V. Ch. 18.
on earth you shall lose your land,

But here in erthe shalt thou fayle thyn e[n]tent;
ffor thyne[1] deedes, whiche arn) ful of synne,   [1] r. thi
God shal rere a lord whiche[2] shal wynne   [2] r. þe whech?   1076
Alle thi londes fro þe, and make the pore,
Take awey thi worshipe and thi tresore;   1078

and your wicked head.

"Yet shal he sleyn) the, as þou art wurthi,   1079
Thi wykked heed he shal make of smyte,
Thi blood shal ben) offred thanne ful solemnely
On-to thi goddis right for despyte.
Looke my woordis that þou note & write!   1083
This man) that shal brynge the thus of[1] dawe,   [1] *al.* a d.
Shal be a lord of the cristen lawe.   1085

Still, you may escape if you'll repent.

"Yet may þou skape[1] al this grete myschauns,   1086
If þou wilt turne the and aske god mercy,   [1] r. skapen?
Of thi wikkednesse if þou haue repentauns
And forsake these maumentis whiche stande on hy."
These were the woordis whiche that þis lady   1090
Seyde at that tyme this man) to conuerte;
But alle hir woordis sette he not at herte.   1092

Katharine is thus made a Prophetess;

So semeth it weel, this lady for hoolynesse   1093
Was soo avaunced, whil she was lyuande,
That god made hir as a prophetesse
To telle þinges þat were after comande.

for the ill end she foretold

ffor this same deeth, as I vndirstande,   1097
had this same Maxcens as she seyde, truly :
ffor in storyes [I] am weel avysed that I   1099
haue red of hym), that he wente to rome   1100
To feyghte with oon) whiche had gouernaunce

befell Maxentius.

Of alle þat Citee and oonly to[1] his dome   [1] *al.* on-to
Stood al þat contre with al here puissaunce,
Bothe Ytalie and almayn), engelond, spayne & fraunce—

1074 erde . schal   1075 þi . are   1076 þe wheche   1078 tresoore
1079 slee   1081 be . solennyly   1083 noote   1084 a dawe   1087 wyll   1089 þe m.   1090 are   1093 Tho   1094 lyuaunde   1096 comaunde   1099 I am   1101 fyght   1102 on-to   1103 pusauns
1104 ytayle . ynglond

MS. Arundel.] *The Emperor orders Katharine's death.* 375

Constantyn̄ he hyght, whiche tho baptised was   *Bk. V. Ch. 18.*
Of seynt syluestre be a ful specyal gras.   1106   The Christian Constantine
This same constantyn̄ discoum̃fyted in batayle   1107   conquerd Maxentius.
This forseyde maxcens, for al his pompe & pride,
As this lady in prophecye, whyche myght not fayle,
had seyde be-fore. the fame was bore ful wyde,
And merked ful weel the day & eke the tyde   1111
Of sundry men̄, whiche afterward ful weel knewe
Al þat she seyde was ful stable and true.   1113

        Ca^m. 19^m.   *Bk. V. Ch.* 19.

Bvt whanne the[s] woordes were seyde of þis mayde,
    he cryed loude to the puple a-boute—   1115   The Emperor
Soo was he with hir woordis now afrayde,
What he shal doo now is he fallen̄ in doute—
Swiche was his cry : " fy on swiche a route,   1118   calls on his men
That shal suffre here a woman̄ þus defame
Oure hye goddes, her seruyse and her name !   1120

"hough longe shal we this witche thus susteyne?   1121
hough longe shal we suffre this cursednesse?
To alle goode leueres it shul[d] be very peyne
To here a woman̄ with suche sturdynesse   [1] MS. he cryed, he overl.; Ar. 20 cryed he.
A-geyn̄ alle men̄, the more and eke the lesse,   1125
Thus euere-more crye[1]. ley on handes, for shame !   to seize
Ye stande as men̄, me thenketh, þat were lame ! "   1127

Thus cryed this tyraunt with ful loude voys,   1128
Thus berked this dogge ageyn̄ th[at][1] heuenly name,   [1] MS. the
Ageyn̄ ihesu that was hanged on a croys ;
his men̄ a-boute hym̄ thus he gan̄ to blame ;
" Come foorth a-noon̄, looke ye take þis dame,   1132
Bete hir and reende hir with Iern̄ and plummes of leed !   and send Katharine
leue not youre labour til that she be deed ! "   1134   to death.

   1107 discoum̃fetyd   1114 þese   1116 now om.   1117 fall   1119 þus suffyr a w. here d.   1121 who . whyche   1123 schuld   1126 he om. ; crye . hondys   1127 þat om.   1129 bergyd. þat h.   1130 a om.   1131 gan he   1132 Comforthe   1133 yrne . plum̃bys

Bk. V. Ch. 19.
Katharine is cruelly beaten,

She was beten) newe [þan] be-forn) his face, 1135
Soo dispitously that shame it was to see.
ffor many man) that stood tho in þat place,
Might not looke on hir for reuthe & pytee.
The tyraunt wolde neuere seyn) "now leue yee," 1139
But euere he cryed : " of hir make an eende !
ffor if she lyue, oure puple wil she shende." 1141

Bk. V. Ch. 20.

Cap^m. 20^m.

[1] on eras.; Ar. to, into

and led into the town.

Thus is she bounde & ledde foorth in[1] the toun). 1142
   The puple that folwed, on hir thus gunne thei crye :
" O noble mayde, whi wil ye not falle doun)
On-to the emperour and of hym aske mercye ?

The people sorrow for her,

We are ful sory þat youre fayre bodye 1146
It is soo reent, ȝoure skyn) is al to-tore ;
But ye asken) mercy, ye arn) lost for eueremore. 1148

" What woman) are ye that soo despyse youre age, 1149
Youre body, youre beute þat ye sette at nought ?
Ye may haue wurship, ye may be sette in stage
Ryght as a goddesse—where-on is your thought ?
And al the world for beute shulde be bought, 1153
here myght thei fynde yt,[1] thei nede no ferthere seeke.
Sith ye be wys, sith ye be hoolde soo meke, [1] MS. þt, *al.* it 1155

" Whi wil ye not obeye on-to the kyng ? 1156

and urge her to give way to the Emperor.

Beter it is to bowe, than) velenously[1] to be dede. [1] *al.* vylensly
In youre bok*is*, I trowe, ye lerned this thyng :
The grete dignyte may ye not doun) trede,
It longeth to you to obeye on-to youre hede. 1160
Sith it is right, [why] wil ye not it doo ?
We wolde doo thus, if ye counseilden) us soo. 1162

" Ye lese the flour of youre virginyte, 1163
Ye lesen þat god plenteuously in you sette,

    1135 bete new þan befor   1137 many a   1139 sey   1140 an hende
1143 thei om.   1147 It om.   1148 aske . are   1153 werde   1154
it inst. of þat   1157 vylensly   1161 why wyll   1162 councelled
1164 lese

MS. Arundel.] *Katharine rejects the People's craven counsel.*

Ye lese youre herytage, ye lesen) yo*ur* degree,   *Bk. V. Ch.* 20.
Al for on) woord whiche that is youre dette.   [1] MS. knette   The Alexandrians
Ouere-soleynly thenke we that youre herte is [s]ette[1]   1167
Whan) that [no] counseiH may you reden)[2] ne rayle,
Most specyaly whan) it is youre avayle—"   [2] *al.* lede   1169

    Swiche word*is* spak the puple there-aboute.   1170
"Remembre yow, mayde, what ye shal now lese,   still urge Katharine
Al for youre herte, for it is soo stoute.   to feign compliance,
ffeyneth som plesauns, sith ye may not chese!
Bothe body and bones with betynge [wyll ʒe lese];[1]   1174
Oones mercy may avoyde al this—   [1] MS. he wil you fese
This is oure counseyl, it may ʒou brynge to blis.   1176

    "Youre white skyn) þat shyneth as the svnne,[1]   1177   and save her skin.
Ye wil shende it, and make it pale and wan),   [1] corr.: sonne
ffor very betyng it wil ben) al dvnne;[2]   [2] corr.: donne
Youre blood ryal, whiche now þat[3] no man)   [3] Ar. 20 wh. þat now
In these dayes remembre noon) hyere can),   1181
This wil ʒe spylle right vp-on [þe] grounde.
Youre counseyH in this is neyther saue ne sounde."   1183

       Ca^m. **21**^m.   *Bk. V. Ch.* 21.

"O wycked counsel!" seyde the mayde ageyn),   1184   She reproaches them.
   "Go to youre werk*is*, and thenke no more on me!
ffy on beute, that wil with wynde and reyn)   Her beauty will fade;
Be steyned ful sone! my fayrenesse whiche þat ʒe
Compleyne soo sore, though [þat] I lyue [parde][1]   1188
And falle in age, yet wil it [þan] apeyre;   [1] MS. so longe as it may be
Thanne for my flesh falle ye not in dyspeyre!   1190

    "But troste ye this as for a sekernesse: 1191
Alle oure bodyes, be thei neue*r*e so bryght,   her body will die and rot.
Shal deye and rote[1] in her wretchednesse—   [1] r. roten
ffor this same deth longeth on-to vs be[2] right,   [2] *al.* of

1165 lese   1166 a w.   1167 solenly. sette   1168 no c. . lede ne
1174 he om. wyll ʒe lese   1176 consell   1177 whyght. sune   1179 wylbe. dunne   1180 reall   1181 no   1182 þe gr.   1183 counsell
1188 þowʒ þat I lyue parde   1189 it þan   1194 of ryght

378 *Katharine is assured of future Bliss.* [MS. Arundel.

Bk. V. Ch. 21.
Katharine says that

Condemned for synne be the prouydens & the sight 1195
Of god oure lord. what shal we thanne soo wayle
ffor fykel beute that soo sone wyl quayle ? 1197

every man must rot,

"Euery man muste thus, as of necessyte, 1198
Deye and rote, but if that specyal grace
Be graunted to some of that deite— [1 MS. byen]

save those pure folk

ffor somme with clennesse ben[1] there þat purchace
Swiche dispensacyon þat in what-maner place 1202
Thei be leyde, thei shal neuere rote,
fflessh ne senewe[s], veynes, sheete ne cote. 1204

to whom exemption is granted.

"This specyalte is to hem graunted heere 1205
That keepe here bodyes fro al onclennesse
Of lust and filthe, and fro that loue on-clere
Whiche þei calle letcherie—it is no loue, I gesse,
I calle it rathere a wylde rage of wodenesse. 1209
But now to purpos: thei þat keepe hem clene,
Thei haue this pardon graunted, as I wene ; 1211

"And if my lord my loue wil graunte it me 1212
That after my deeth my flesh shal not rote,
Thanne am I more bounde on-to his deyte
Thanne euere I was, &[1] this I hym be-hote, [1 MS. in]
There shal neuere man make me soo to doote 1216
That I shal leue his loue or his plesauns.

The people

Therfore ye puple, leue this obseruauns, 1218

are to wail for themselves, not for her.

"ffolweth noo lengere, gooth hom to your werke, 1219
Weepe not for me, but for your-self ye wayle !
I shal deye bodyly, but be-cause I haue the merke
Of crystes baptem, I shal skape that grete asayle

She will escape the Devil,

Of alle the feendes whiche with grete trauayle 1223
Are ful besy oure soules for to gete
On-to her preson where thei shal hem bete. 1225

and rise fairer than euer.

"This shal I escape, and efte[1] ryse ageyn, 1226
In fayrere foorme than euere ye seyn in me— [1 Ar. 20 after]

1197 fckylle   1199 but of   1201 be   1204 senowis   1208 it is om.   1215 & þis   1225 persone   1227 sey

Cursates's Engine of Torture for Katharine.

I beleue and troste this thyng as for certeyn).
Therfore, seres, for youre-selue weepe yee,
ffor youre errour that ye in derkenesse bee! 1230
ffor if ye deye[n] in this same errour, [1] Ar. rysyng
Youre rerynge[1] ageyn) shal cause you grete dolour." 1232

Bk. V. Ch. 21.

Many of hem þat herde[n] hir thus speke, 1233
Were conuerted to crist, oure saueour;
fful preuyly her maumentis dede thei broke
Whiche þat thei hadde in ful grete honour;
With-drowe hem fro synne and wayled her errour, 1237
Al preuyly, soole, heuy as oony leed,
ffor natural fer, that thei shulde not be deed. 1239

Many who hear Katharine, turn to Christ.

Cap. 22ᵐ·

Bk. V. Ch. 22.

There was a man) in Alisaundre at þat tyme, 1240
Meyer and leedere of alle the puple there
Vnder the emperour, punyshere of alle cryme;
Of whom the cytee had ful meche[l] fere,
Venemous in anger was he as a[1] bere, [1] al. any 1244
Dispetous, vengeable, with-oute discrecyon)—
Cursates thei called hym thurgh-oute þe toun). 1246

The Mayor of Alexandria is a bad man,

Cursates.

he sey the emperour in anger and wodnesse, 1247
And of pure malice sette hym more on feere;
"O emperour," he seyde, "thy wysdam), as I gesse,
Shulde make the ashamed of this matere heere,
That oon wenche shulde brynge the thus in dwere; 1251
Thou standest stoyned as though þou were bounde.
listen) my counseyl therfore now a stounde. 1253

He advises the Emperor

"This mayde Kataryn) sey yet noo torment 1254
Whiche shulde fese hir, to make hir afrayed;
Therfore, sir, I telle you myn) entent:
We shal make thyng soo horrybely arayed

to make a horrible engine of torture for Katharine.

1231 deye 1233 herde 1238 And pr. 1241 ledyr(!) 1242 punchere 1243 mechille 1244 venemhous . ony bere 1245 dispitous ueniabill 1249 wisdom) 1251 o 1254 Katereyne 1255 hir 2 om. 1256 ser 1257 a þing (a overlined)

380 Cursates's Wheels to tear Katharine to bits. [MS. Arundel.

Bk. V. Ch. 22.

It shal be dred or it be fully assayed ; 1258
lete hir see oonys this thyng I shal denyse,
She shal leue sone thanne, I trowe, al this gyse. 1260

The Emperor's workmen are

"Commaunde werkmen for to obeye to me, 1261
I shal be mayster, thei shal doo her werke ;
ffor I haue conceyued now a newe cruelte,
fful sekirly therof haue I take my merke.
In this mater bothe countrerollere and clerke 1265
Wil I bee, and noo man but my-selue,
Werkemen wil I haue with me ten or twelue. 1267

"Thus haue I denysed in my besy thought : 1268

to make 4 great Wheels

ffoure grete qwheles thus shul we make,
In swiche-maner wyse shal thei be wrought,
What-maner thyng that euere thei take
Anoon in pecis thei shul it reende & shake 1272
With her sharpenesse whiche þei shul haue ;
ffor alle the spokes that come fro the naue, 1274

with sharp nails on their spokes,

"Shul haue nayles sharpe as a knyf, 1275
I-fastned to the sercles rounde al-aboute.
There is no man now that bereth lyf,
Be his herte neuere soo styf and stoute,
And he be oonys In, hee cometh not oute 1279
Or he be deed and al to peces drawe—
Right be experiens þis thing shal ye knawe. 1281

and saws on their fellies, hookt,

"Sharpe sawes shul thei haue somwhat croked, 1282
Nayled on-to the wheles on þe vtter syde ;
In swiche-maner foorme thus shul þei be hooked,
Eche of hem be other fful sotilly shal glyde,

some up, some down, that will tear everything between them to bits.

Somme shul come vpward with her cours wyde, 1286
Somme shul goo dounward, & þus shal þei rende [1 MS. and]
Alle thyng be-twyx hem & thereof maken an[1] ende. 1288

"Therfore lete these wheles be made now in hast ; 1289
Sette the mayde right be-[twyx][2] hem whan þat thei goo,

[2] MS. be, Ar. 20 be-twene

1259 þat I   1265 controllere   1276 I-fasted   1279 com   1281 we
1283 qwelys   1286 shalle   1288 make   1289 qweles. now om.   1290 be

MS. Arundel.] *The Torture-Wheels are ready for Katharine.* 381

She shal beŋ afrayed, or she hem taast— *Bk. V. Ch. 22.*
There is noo maŋ lyuenge hath seeŋ swiche wheles moo.   Katharine will be afraid
This same deuyse shal plese youre lordshipe soo," 1293   of these awful Wheels.
Seyde this Cursates, " ye shulŋ cuŋ me thanke ;
Yonder wil we make hem right on the banke." 1295

The emp*er*our commaunded, & þat in hasty wyse, 1296   The Emperor orders
These wheles shul[d] be made, & þat an-nooŋ),   Cursates's Wheels.
Right as Cursates thus can[1] deuyse.   [1] = gan
Thei arŋ called foorth, bothe robyŋ and Iohŋ,
Carpenters and smyghtes, as faste as þei may gooŋ ; 1300
Thei hewe and thei blewe ful soore, leueth me !
The wheeles musteŋ be redy with-inne dayes thre. 1302

Cap^m. 23^m.   *Bk. V. Ch. 23.*

Now it is come, the same thredde day ; 1303   On the 3rd day the Wheels are ready,
The wheeles arŋ redy sette as thei shal bee ;
She is brought fortht, Kataryŋ þis same may,
Right betwyx hem sette now is she ;   [1] MS. before seyde we   and Katharine is set between them.
Too wheeles goo dounward, as [we seyd, pa*r*de],[1] 1307
And too reende vpward—there is nooŋ that it seeth
But for feer he gruggeth with his teeth. 1309

O noble mayde, hough shalt þou scape this thyng ? 1310
This Irous emp*er*our, he is noot thi frende,
The meyer is cruel in his ymagynyng,
ffor he hath stodied with al herte and meende
Thi virgynal body to destroye and shende ; 1314
There is noo comforte but fro the courte aboue—   She has no comfort but
he wil not fayle the, Ih*es*u that is thi loue. 1316   Jesus.

Thus is she sette, and likly to be reent, 1317
With al her labour the seruaunt*is* dresse her gere ;
Thei tarye somwhat [be-cause] that hir entent
Thei wene to chaunge[n] right for very fere.

1291 be . he   1292 sey   1294 shull*e*   1297 shuld . anon*e*   1298 gan   1299 ar*e*   1300 Carpenter*e*s . smythes   1302 must   1303 is it . þat s. thrid   1304 ar*e*   1307 as we seyd pa*r*de   1308 seyth*e* 1310 who shall*e*   1311 noth*e*   1312 meyhir   1318 hir   1319 be-cause þat   1320 chaunge

382 *Katharine prays God to shatter the Wheels.* [**MS. Arundel.**

Bk. V. Ch. 23.

hir eyne and handes ful mekely gan she rere 1321
Vp on-to heuene, swiche was hir oryson :   [1] *al.* om.

Katharine prays to God

"Lord god," she seyde, "that made bothe[1] sonne & mon,

"Lord that art al-myghty in mageste, 1324
Thou can alle thynge and may fulfille in dede;
Lord that neuere hydest thy grete pytee
ffro tho folke that cry[n]e on-to the at nede,
O lord of lordis, my prayere þou may spede: 1328
I prey the, lord, with ful besy entent
That þou destroye this horryble newe torment; 1330

to strike the Torture-Wheels with lightning,

"Make thi thunder descende now with the leuene, 1331
Brenne it, breke it, lord; this tyme, I praye,
Shewe thi power, open now thyn heuene,
That men may knowe þi lordshype at this daye—
It is ful esy to the to make heere swiche afraye, 1335
And to the puple it is ful merueylous.
Goode blyssed lord, þat art soo gracyous, 1337

not because she fears Death,

"This aske I not for ony fere of deeth, 1338
But for thi[1] puple that standeth[2] here-aboute;   [1] r. the? [2] *al.* stand
Me thenketh, lord, her langage myn hert sleeth,
That þei with toungis and woordis proude and stoute
Shuld blaspheme thy name, and putte in doute 1342
Thi true feyth. this is, lord, my cause,
To shryue me shortly to the in a clause, 1344

but that the folk may be converted,

"That thei shulde troste thi myght & þi powere 1345
And honoure thi name, [&] be conuerted eke,
Be turned fro maumentis whiche þei wurshipe heere,

and turn to God.

The, lord, oonly her god for to seeke.
This prey I the with herte lowe and meke; 1349
Graunte me this as thou art omnypotent,
Suffre not thi seruauntis with maumentis be circumuent!"

1321 yne   1323 bothe om.. sune   1325 & myn f.   1327 cryne
1331 þi l.   1332 lord om. I the   1333 thy   1335 to 2 om.   1339 stand   1346 & be   1348 þe lord godd only forto s.

Cap^m. 24^m.

Whanne þat this lady had ended hir orisoun, 1352 *At Katharine's prayer*
A-noon an aungel was sent doun fro heuene;
With wynde and thunder tho cam he doun,
There cam with hym eke an horryble leuene—
The houre of the day, thei sey, it was but seuene, 1356
But er eyte; he with wynd and feere
Brake alle the wheles, thei fleyn heere and there, 1358 *the Torture-Wheels fly in pieces,*
Thei spryngyn aboute be pecys in the place. 1359
Somme haue[1] harm on legges and on knes, [1] Sum man hath
Somme men[2] arn hurt on handes and on face. [2] al. om.
The feer fley [ful] wundyrly with the trees.
Meche of the puple haue take there her fees: 1363
Thei that blasphemed oure god with cruel herte, *and kill the blasphemers,*
ffro this vengeauns thei may not lightly sterte; 1365

The lady sat stille, for she felt noo grevauns, 1366
Makyng hir preyer with gret deuocyon.
Thus can oure lord for hese make purueauns,
Thus can he shape hem her sauacyon.
Thus dede he somtyme in the calde nacyon 1370
Whan that his seruauntis in the ouene were sette,
Where that þe feer of his myght was lette; 1372

ffor thei in the ouene were noo-thyng brent, 1373
But þei a-boute it, thei took the harm.
This lady is lyke hem in this myracle present:
The fyre fley aboute hir, and in hir barm
It rested ofte-tyme, but she was not warm, 1377 *though Katharine is unhurt.*
Ne hurt ne harmed in no-maner degree.
Yet was this fyre soo horryble that hee 1379

Brente the wheles and threw hem alle-aboute,[1] 1380 *4000 Pagans are burnt.*
Brent men eke, and tho were not fewe[2]— [1] This v. follows 1383 in the MS. [2] r. a fewe?

1353 a   1357 or   1358 breke . qwelys . fley   1359 spryng   1360 Sume man hathe   1361 men om.   are   1362 þere fley fere ful w.   1368 his   1375 lyche   1377 of tyme   1379 fere   1380 alle om.

Bk. V. Ch. 24.	ffoure thousand, sey[th] oure story with-oute[n] dowte,	
	Were ded with the blast, leyde alle on) rewe	
	Of hethen) caytyues, [shrew rith be shrewe],[1]	1384
	herowdes noumbred hem) for thei can) best. [1] MS. right a shrewde rowte	
Katharine sits still.	The lady sat stille in hir holy nest,	1386
	Knelande deuoutely in sobyr prayere.	1387
The Angel and Fire go back to Heaven.	The AungeH and feer bothe thei took her weye	
	To place thei can) fro—for[1] men) myght hem here [1] al. om.	
	Bothe in her comyng and goynge, thei seye.	
	Mechel fook[1] for feere were in poynt to deye,	1391
	Saue þat the comforte of this swete may [1] al. folke	
	Lefte hem) a-geyn)[2] fro þat afray. [2] Ar. 20 vp ageyn	1393
	This is the ende of al this costful werke.	1394
The Heathen are sad,	hoo arn) now woo but hethen men) there?	
	hoo arn) now mery, hoo gonne her frontes merke	
the Christians glad.	But crysten) folkys, whiche han) skaped this feere?	1397
	Somme[1] for vengeauns may not goo ne stere. [1] al. Sum men	
	Thus oon) syde is in Ioye, the other in sorwe & care.	
	Of swhiche-maner vengeauns lete euery man) be ware!	1400

Bk. V. Ch. 25.

Ca^m. 25^m.

The Emperor is wild,	Now is the emperour oute of mesure wood,	1401
	ffor alle fayleth and falleth þat now shul[d][1] stande;	
	ffor very anger he rente habyte and hood, [1] al. shuld now	
and reproaches Saturn	"Saturne," he seyde, " why take ye not on hande	
	Youre owen) cause[1]? for, as I vndirstande, [1] MS. causes	1405
	This vengeauns is repugnynge to your deyte.	
	Where is now youre myght? where is now hee,	1407
and Jupiter.	"Iubiter, youre sone, that hath the gouernauns	1408
	Ouere these ciclopes, smethes I mene,	
	Whiche with her thunder make the erthe to dauns,	
	Soo it is aferd of tho strokes keene?	

1382 seythe . wyth-outen) 1383 on rowe 1384 shrew rith be shrewe 1385 heraudes . coud 1389 for om. 1391 Meche folke 1393 lyft 1394 al om. 1395 who are n. who 1396 gune . fruntes 1397 folke . hathe 1398 Sume mene 1399 o 1402 shuld now 1405 cause 1409 smythis 1410 erde

But ye defende yow, youre offerynge wil be lene.   1412
Rise vp ye godd*is*, and suffre not þis wrong! [1 Ar. 163 wondlr]
Me thenketh, ye abyde now wondyrly[1] long."   1414

In al this care the queen, that stood aboue   1415
hy in a tour for to be-holde this sight,
Whiche on-to that tyme had bore the loue
ffuI preuyly in hir herte of god al-myght,
Now wil she pleynly [rith] be-forn hy[s s]ight[1]   1419
Vtter hir herte, falle there-of what falle;   [1 MS. hym right]
She is come doun, and hir seruaunt*is* alle,   1421

To the presens of hir lord; thus thanne she sayde: 1422
"Thou wretched husbonde, what [h]ast þou I-doo?
Whi tormentest þou soo wrongly this goodly mayde?
A-geyn the grete god whi wrestillest þou soo?
What woodenesse maketh the with care & woo   1426
To pursue godd*is* seruaunt*is* with peyne & deeth?
O cruel best, whan þou shalt yelde thi breth,   1428

"Wh[i]dir[1] wylt þou sende thi wretchede goost?   1429
Thou fyghtest ageyn the prykke, þat shalt þou fynde;
ffor whan thou art hyest and in pryde most,   [1 MS. whedir]
Oure lord god ful soore shal the bynde.
Turne thyn bestialte to mannys mynde!   1433
knowe the grete power of thi god aboue,
Whiche werketh soo wonderly for hem þat hym loue!   1435

"The grete myghty god of crysten men,   1436
See what he dede this ilke same day:
With oon thunder-clap, of thi lord*is*, ten
Smet he to deth—þou thi-self it say;
ffoure thousand of [þe] comouns in her aray   1440
Thei lyn yonder ded—hoo shal hem reyse?
If appollo doo it, I wil than hym[1] preyse.   [1 *al.* hym than]   1442

1414 now om.   1416 hey   1417 to om.   1418 hir om.   1419 ryth before his syth   1421 now come   1422 the om.   1423 hast   1425 wrestyllist   1429 whidir   1430 fytyst. shalle   1433 þi   1434 þi, grete om.   1436 myty   1438 a   1439 þe dethe   1440 þe comonys   1441 ly. who.   1442 hym þan

386 *The Emperor orders his wife to be torturd.* [MS. Arundel.

Bk. V. Ch. 25.

The Queen bids the Emperor forsake his Idols and turn to God.

"he that with oon) strook may swyche thyng make,
he is a lord : I counseyl,[1] knowe hym for thi kyng ! 1444
Thi false maumentrye I reede thou forsake,   [1] *c. al.* om.
Turne the to that lord that made al thyng !
The synnes that we dede w[h]il we were ying,   1447
he wil forgeue vs, if we mercy craue ;
Aske mercy of hym) and thou shal it haue."   1449

Whan the tiraunt herde what the queen) sayde,   1450
"Woman)," seyde he, "wote ye what ye say ?
I am ful seker ye haue spoken)[1] with the mayde [1] *al.* ȝe spoke
Whan) I was oute on the[2] other day. [2] *al.* on om.; þis   1453
A-vyse yow[3] som)-what beter [or ȝe asay][4] [3] MS. yow weel [4] MS. of this afray, on erns.

He threatens her with horrible punishments,

The horryble peynes whiche þat ye shal haue,
Youre freendes ne youre kynrede shal you not saue.   1456

"ffor be the hye mageste of oure goddis alle, [1] *al.* om.
                                                [2] MS. prouydens
And be the gracyous[1] pr[o]uydens[2] of Iubiter, oure[3] kyng,

unless she gives up the Christians.

But ȝe fro these fonnes,[4] and that in hast, falle, [3] *al.* þo
Dame, ye shal haue as foule an endyng   [4] *al.* þis fonnednes
As euere had woman), eyther old or ying,   1461
In youre dayes. therfore avyse you weel !
ffor, thou youre god hath broken) oure whel   1463

"[Be][1] wytche-craft or [be] nygromauncye, [1] MS. In   1464
Troste me in this, we shal ordeyne a mene
ffor to destroye the[1] fals tretcherye.   [1] *al.* ȝour
What, art thou [now], dame, led on that rene ?
Thi witte[1] counte I not worth a beene [1] MS. with   1468
Whan) þou forsakest þi goddis protectyon)
And as a fool takest the crysten illusyon)."   1470

Bk. V. Ch. 26.

Cp. 26m.

He orders her to be seizd.

Thus in his anger and in his grete Ire   1471
he byddeth his mynystres to take the queene,

1443 a   1444 I counseyl om.   1452 ȝe spoke   1453 on om. þis
1454 weel om.   sumwhat or þat ȝe asay   1455 shul   1456 kynrod
1457 be þat . of þe   1458 be þat. gracyous om.   prouydens . þe
kyng   1459 þis fonnednes   1460 an om.   1461 eld   1464 Be . or be
1466 ȝoure f.   1467 þou now   1468 witte. I om. w. to a   1469 þe g.

MS. Arundel.] *The Queen is frightfully torturd.* 387

With sotil launces made of Iern̄ wyre 1473   *Bk. V. Ch. 26.*
Thei shul[1] rende hir tetes right a-noon̄ be-deene ;   [1] MS. shuld   The Emperor orders his
In his presens it shal be doo,[2] for he wil it seene ;   [2] *al.* þei shal do it   Queen's teats to be torn out,
longe peyne and woo[3] he wil his wyf shal haue,   [3] *al.* Long sorow
"lete see," he seyth, "if crist shal hir now saue!" 1477

After this is doon̄, he wil thei hir take, 1478
leede hir to the feeld there tretours alle
han̄ as thei haue deserued ;[1] tey hir to a stake,
Smyte of hir hed & lete it doun̄ falle ;   [1] *al.* deserue, haue om.   and her head struck off,
lete it lyn̄ there, hungry dogg*is* shalle 1482   for dogs to eat.
Ete it and deuoure in despyte of Ih*es*u.   [1] *al.* men
As the tiraunt bad, his seruaunt*is*[1] dede pursue : 1484

Thei pulled hir tetes in ful horryble wyse 1485   His men pull her teats out.
Right fro hir brest—pitee it was to[1] see   [1] MS. te
Th[e][2] blood in the veynes with the mylke ryse ;   [2] MS. That
Al rent and ragged and[3] blody was shee.   [3] *al.* all
Yet on-to Kataryn̄ she fel doun̄ on knee, 1489   She kneels, and begs Katharine
preyng ful doolfully, and ryght thus she sayde :
"O crysten p[eler],[1] o moost holy mayde,   [1] MS. puple 1491

'Prey now for me on-to thi lord aboue, 1492   to pray that
That this peyne whiche I suffre heere
Oonly for his wurshipe, his feyth & his loue,
May ben̄ to my soule a sufficyent cheere
Whan̄ I shal come to that blis ful cleere 1496   she may go to heaven,
Whiche thou be-hight me not longe agoo.
Prey eke for me that I may kepe alsoo 1498

"The same good purpos whiche I am Inne, 1499
That this peyne horryble make me not reneye   [1] *al.* þis holy lyfe, to turne agayne to synne.   and not deny the Christian faith.
The lawe of you cristen, for more ne for mynne ;[1]
I am soore[2] a-feerde my flesh, er þat I deye,   [2] MS. ful s.
ffor very dreed the contrarie shuld seye : 1503

1473 yrun*e*   1474 shul   1475 þei shall do it   1476 longe sorow. and woo om. þat his   1479 tretoures   1480 haue. haue om. ; deserue   1482 lye . it sch:lle   1483 it om.   1484 hys men   1486 from   1487 þe   1488 all bl.   1490 euy*n* inst. of ryght   1491 peler*e*   1495 be . suffycyaunt   1501 þis holy lyffe to turne ageyne to synne   1502 ful om. . or   1503 þe c. of þis

C C 2

388 *Katharine comforts the torturd Queen.* [**MS. Arundel.**

Bk. V. Ch. 26.

Wherefor, lady,—al this lyth in the,—
prey thou to god that he may kepe me!" 1505

The mayde[1] seyde on-to the queen ageyn : [1] r. mayden 1506

Katharine assures the Queen that
"O blyssed lady, þat hast forsake al thyng,
Croune and Ioye, shortly for to seyn,

she has won Christ.
And wonne the therfore oure heuene kyng,[1] [1] al. þe lufe perfore of oure k.
Crist I mene; make now noo stakeryng 1510
As in this mater, for he shal make the strong
ffor whoos loue þow sufferest [now þis][1] wrong. [1] MS. meche

She will please Him by her suffering,
"Suffre[1] hertely al this grete disese, [1] MS. Suffre now 1513
It shal not lesten but a lytil space;
Cryst youre lord her-with shal ye plese,
Whiche hath graunted of his specyal grace

and will see His face this day.
That this same day shal ye seen his face. 1517
A meruelous chaunge, lady, shal it bee,
Whanne þat ye come be-forn the trinite: 1519
[1] MS. shal ye

"ffor temporal lond, ye shal[1] haue heuene[ly] blys; 1520
ffor erthely husbonde, y[our][1] spouse shal bee he[2] [1] MS. ye [2] MS. he bee
That may alle thyng a-mende[3] þat is a-mys, [2] al. am. all þing
A lord þat dwelleth euere in felicyte,
A lord þat hath neuere [non][1] aduersite; [1] MS. ony 1524
Thus shal ye chaunge, lady, on-to the beste.

Katharine will soon join her.
I shal not long ben absent fro þat reste."[1] [1] al. nest 1526

Thus is she comforted, this noble cristen queene,[1] 1527
Thus is she stabled myghtyly in oure feyth, [1] In the MS. v. 1527 and 9 are transposed.
Thus is she led with knyghtis, as I wene,

The Emperor bids his men make an end of the Queen.
And euere the emperour on-to his meny seyth
fful boystous woordis, strokis eke he leyth 1531
Vp-on her bakkys, that they shulde make an ende
Of this woman, for now hir tetes[1] thei reende, 1533
[1] al. hir t. now

1504 lyghte 1509 þe lufe perfore of. heuene om. 1512 lufe . now þis w. 1513 now om. 1514 lest 1517 se 1519 þat om. before 1520 ȝe shul . heuenly 1521 ȝoure sp. sha!be he 1522 amend alle þing 1524 non 1525 shul 1526 be . nest 1527-9 in their right place. 1532 a e. 1533 for hire tetys now

As I seyde her; anoow[1] after that grete payne, 1534 *Bk. V. Ch. 26.*
With a sharp swerd hir hed of thei smyte— [1] *al.* and *The Queen's head is smitten off.*
Oure lord god to suffre graunte hir myght & mayne[2]
with grete pacyens al þis same vnrighte. [2] *al.* O. l. g. strenghid hir to susteyn
Thus is[1] passed hir soule to heuene[2] lighte 1538 *Her soul goes to Heaven,*
Whiche is endeles, right as we beleue. [1] *al.* is she [2] *al.* is to þat
The thre and twenty day of nouembre right at eue, 1540 *on Nov. 23.*

And on a wedenesday was this martyrdam 1541
Thus consummat. hir body whan it[1] was dede, [1] MS. þat it *Her body is left unburied.*
Was left stille vnberyed,[2] in despite of cristendam, [2] *al.* om.
lyande ful faire coloured, both[e] white and rede,[3] [3] *al.* = Rawl. [4] *al.* it
No man soo hardy to wynden hir[4] in clooth or leed— 1545
Thus bad the emperour of his cruelte; [1] *al.* om. [2] *al.* þouȝt.
And[1] that she lay thus, moche folk had[2] pyte. 1547

Cap[m]. 27[m]. *Bk. V. Ch. 27.*

Now is the nyght come, and on-to her rest 1548 *At night,*
Is euery man goo that was abydyng there.
Porphirye thought it was most[1] honest [1] *al.* om. 1550 *Porphyry*
And eke [m]edeful[2] this body for to rere, [2] MS. nedef.
Eke[3] to the beryenge deuoutely it [to] bere : [3] MS. And eke
Therfore cleped he certeyn knyght*is* to hym, *and his knights*
And whan the wedyr was ful derk and dym, 1554
Right in the wyntyr a-boute seynt Katarynes day, 1555
he cam to the body with ful holy entent,
Euene in [hir lyuand][1] ryght as she lay ; [1] MS. the lyuene, Ar. 20 hyr lynnyn
With ful swete and costeful onyment
he baumed the body, and foorth with it he went. 1559 *embalm and bury the Queen's body.*
With preyere, wepyng and ful besy cure
Thus thei lede it on-to the sepulture. 1561

1534 ere and after . peyne 1535 a om. . smythe 1536 Oure l. g. strenghid hire to susteyne 1537 vnrythe 1538 is she . hire s. is to þat lythe 1539 wheche was 1541 wednesday 1542 þat om. 1543 vnberyed om. 1544 lyinge þer fulle white & eke fulle rede 1545 wynd it 1546 had 1547 And om. þouthe pyte 1548 nythe 1550 most om. 1551 medfulle 1552 And om. . to bere 1553 called . knythis onto 1555 kateryne 1557 in hire lyuand 1559 hire b. . he om. 1561 on om.

Bk. V. Ch. 27.

Question being raisd, who buried the Queen,

Porphyry boldly blames the Emperor for torturing Katharine and killing his wife.

He, Porphyry, buried the Queen,

to save her body from being eaten by dogs.

The nexte day after[1] is[2] grete questyon) 1562
hoo beryed the queen), hoo was soo hardy   [1] *al.* om.   [2] *al.* is þer
To fallen) in[3] sueche greuous transgressyon)   [3] MS. in to
To remeue or bere[1] this ladyes[2] body ?   [1] *al.* bery   [2] *al.* same
Oonly for[1] suspecyon) certeyn) foolk*is*[2] openly 1566
Weren arested be the offycer*is* there,   [1] *al.* of   [2] *al.* folke
And porphyrie boldly with-outen) fere 1568
Appered to the empe*r*our, and thus he sayde : 1569
" Sethen þou art lord, and Iustyse shuldest keepe,
Whi [h]ast thou tormented thus this holy mayde ?
Thi owen) wyues heed of dede þou[1] sweepe—   [1] MS. þou dede
Grete cause hauest þou soore for to weepe ! 1573
These Innocent*is* eke this is þin entent
With-outen) cause now to doo[1] torment.   [1] *al.* om. 1575
" Cece of thi Ire, cece of thi wronge, 1576
Leue thi besynesse of Inquysy[cy]on) !
I telle thee pleynly, þough þou shul[1] me hong,   [1] *al.* om.
I am that man) whiche with deuocyon)
þat beryed thi wyf—I thought it reson),[1] 1580
And[2] ful weel a-cordynge to nature,   [1] *al.* me th. it no treson,   [2] But
To brynge that body [on]-to sepulture. 1582
" Where hast þou seen) sweche cruelnesse ? 1583
Yet theues[1] and robbour*is* whan thei arn) dede,   [1] *al.* to th.
her frendes han) leue of the lawe, I gesse,
To wynde hem in clothes, in boord[1] or leede,   [1] MS. in boord in clothes
To solace her neyghbour*is* with drynk and breede. 1587
Al this is turned ageyn) discrecyon),
Ageyn) keende eke and[1] ageyn) relygyon).   [1] *al.* om. 1589
" Where lerned þou eue*r*e þat beest*is* shulde ete 1590
Bodyes of men), of alle creatur*is* best ?

1562 after om. is þer   1563 who   1564 fall*e*. to sueche om.   1565 bery þis same body   1566 of s. . folke   1567 wer*e*   1568 ful boldly   1570 Sith*e* . a lord . shuld   1571 hast. thus om.   1572 thin . of þede þou s.   1573 hast   1575 doo om.   1576 Chese . þin ire.   1577 in I.   1578 shul om.   1580 þat om. me thout it no treson)   1581 But. weel om. acordand on-to   1582 onto   1583 seyn)   1584 ȝete to . are   1585 haue   1586 in clothis in bord   1587 or br.   1589 kynd . and om.   1590 lered

Thus writen) oure Autour*is* and þus þei trete :   *Bk. V. Ch. 27.*
It is neyther wurshipful ne[1] honest   [1] *al.* ne ek
On-to mankeende to foule[1] soo his nest.   [1] Ar. defoule   1594
Sir empe*r*our, I confesse heere, þis dede haue I doo :   *Porphyry declares that he buried the Queen.*
Punysh[1] notȝ þese Innocent*is*, but lete hem goo !"   1596
                       [1] MS. Punysh þou

Cap^{m.} 28^{m.}   *Bk. V. Ch. 28.*

These woord*is* of porphirye, thei arn) a wounde   1597   *The Emperor is greatly hurt by Porphyry's words.*
On-to Maxcens-is herte : for he made a cry,
Whan) he had sor[o]wed a litel stounde,
Soo grete and soo loude, the halle, whiche was hy,
Souned with the noyse; the very malencoly   1601
Made hym soo wood he wiste not what he sayde.
But sone after suche woord*is* he up brayde :   1603

"O me most wretched of alle men) þ*a*t leue !   1604
Wherto brought nature me on-to lyf ?   *He blames Nature for killing his wife,*
Whi wolde she to me suche astate geue,
Whanne she thus wretchedly hath taken my wyf ?
had she suffered me with a sharpe knyf   1608
Be steked in my cradel, she had doo þe best !
ffor[1] now am I reued of my[2] dewe reste.   [1] *al.* om.   [2] *al.* all my

"ffor porphirie here, on whom I most trost,   1611   *and depriving him of his best friend, Porphyry,*
A,[1] porphiry now,[2] the beste frende I haue,   [1] *al.* om.   [2] *al.* here
My good[3] porphirye, my gentel[3] knyght, is[4] lost,   [3] *al.* om.   [4] *al.* þus is he
So disceyued of witchecraft þ*a*t he gynne[th][1] to[2] raue.
Euene as the spokes resten in the naue,   [1] MS. gynned   [2] om. in Ar. 168   1615
Soo in his breste stood al my comforte ;
To swiche a-nother frend can I neue*r*e resorte.   1617

"He dysceyued my wyf, but she now is ded ;   1618
he hath disceyued hym-self, that greueth me most.   *who is self-deceivd.*

    1592 þus oure a. wryth*e*   1593 ne eke h.   1594 ma*n*kynd . to folow his own) n.   1595 sere   1596 punch*e* not   1597 aren   1598 is om.   1599 sorowed   1601 sounded   1603 sweche   1604 lyue   1605 on om.   1606 gyue   1607 take   1608 a om.   1609 stykyd   1610 ffor om.   alle my   1611 of wh.   1612 A om. here   1613 good om. gentel om.   þus is he l.   1614 begynnyth raue   1615 rest in here n.   1618 deceyuyd.   now om.

392 *The Emperor threatens Porphyry with Death.* [MS. Arundel.

Bk. V. Ch. 28.

The Emperor is sad.

Myn herte is waxen[1] as[2] heuy as ony leed, [1] *al.* it waxith [2] *al.* om.
Soo am I comered with thought*is* in my goost.
Allas, my porphirye! I durste a made a boost : 1622
Though al my kyngdam had me forsake,
ffals to my croune no man shuld the make ! 1624
 "Yet, though thou hast[1] doon this grete despite, 1625
Disseyued my wyf and[2] disceyued thi-selue, [1] *al.* haue [2] *al.* but
Yet of þi treson thou shalt haue respyte ;

He will give Porphyry 12 days to forsake that elf Christ,

Ten dayes I graunte the or ell*is* twelue :
Leue þ*a*t[1] crysten company, forsake þ*a*t clue, [1] *al.* þis 1629
Ihesu of naʒareth--he dede neue*re* man good,
he is cause of spillyng of[1] mekel gentel blood. [1] overl. 1631
 "If þou wi!t leue this newe cursed scole, 1632

and so escape death.

Thou shalt haue grace þou shalt not deye.
Soo wyse a man now made a foole !
hoo caused the soo[1] sone to reneye   [1] *al.* hym þus
The holy relygion, the very[1] true weye [1] *al.* eld, olde 1636
Whiche that oure fader*is* kepten with-oute[1] mynde?
Allas man, allas ! thi reson is ful blynde." [1] Ar. out of 1638

Bk. V. Ch. 29.

Ca*m*. 29*m*.

The Emperor examines all his knights,

Right with this langage th[e][1] empe*r*our dede calle 1639
Alle the knyght*is* of the courte be oon & oon,
he examyned hym-self that tyme hem alle [1] MS. that
how that thei thoughten the[1] mater shulde goon). [1] *al.* this
fful doolfully to hem he made his moon, 1643
 "Be-holde," he seyth, "how my porphirye
Al sodeynly is fallen on-to this myserye ! 1645
 "I hope it is to you not[1] but ignorauns, [1] *al.* om. 1646

and threatens them if they side with Porphyry.

If that ye fauoure now hym[1] in his dede, [1] Ar. hym now
But ye be ware of that grete vengeauns
Whiche may falle with-outen drede

1620 My h. it waxith. as 1 om. as þe 1621 acomered 1625 haue do 1626 but inst. of and 1627 shall 1629 þis c. 1631 mech*e* 1633 shall*e* 1 1635 hym*e* thus 1636 þe eld trew 1637 kipt 1639 þe e. 1640 the 1 om. & be 1642 who . thouth*e* þis 1644 Be-holdith . who 1645 I-fall*e* 1646 not om. 1647 now om. 1648 be ʒe 1649 whech*e* þ*a*t

O[n] swiche renegates that other men leede   [1] MS. of   1650
ffro her trewe lawes. hough wil ye answere?"
Alle seyden tho[1] thus, that stoden theere: [1] al. thei   1652

"Be it knowen to the now, sir emperour,   1653
That god and lord whiche this same man
honoureth at this tyme, ihesu oure saueour,   1655
This same god we[1] with al that we may & can   [1] al. om.
hym[1] wil we[2] euere seruen, curse þou or ban,   [1] al. om. [2] al. We wil
Endyte thou or smyte þou[1] with tormentis strange;   [1] al. om.
Leue this weel, þou shalt vs neuere chaunge.   1659

"ff[e]re o[f][1] deth, or loue of lyf swete   [1] MS. ffyre or   1660
May neuere departen oure hertely loue
ffro Ihesu crist, the trueste prophete
That euere was sente fro heuene aboue;
Whan peynes arn plyed, than shalt þou proue   1664
That alle oure hertis arn sette thus[1] in oon   [1] al. om.
In th[is][1] same feyth, as stable as ony[2] stoon."   [1] MS. the [2] al. the   1666

The emperour commaunded in hasty wise   1667
Thei shulde be led on-to her passyon—
ffor of swyche renegates he wil be Iustise,
To venge the wronge whiche that was don
Vp-on the goddis, þe sonne and the mon.   1671
Thus arn thei led foorth tyl her ende;
Saue porphirye allone now thei haue noo frende.   1673

ffor he, to comforten hem with ful myghty feyth,   1674
On-to the emperour preced there[1] he stood,   [1] al. where
Swiche-maner woordis at that tyme he seyth:
"Men wil wene[1] that thou be ny wood   [1] r. wenen   1677
To sle th[is][1] puple thus[2] sodeynly in her blood   [1] MS. the [2] al. om.
And lete me scape whiche stered hem alle.
ffor perel I counsel, whiche may falle   1680

1651 who 1652 seyd þei þus 1653 knowe. ser 1656 we 1 om.
1657 hym om. euere om. serue 1658 endithe. & smythe. þou om.
1659 shalle 1660 Sere of d. 1661 depart 1664 ar applyed. shalle
1665 are. thus om. 1666 þis. as þe 1667 comaund 1672 are. to
1674 conforthe. myty 1675 where 1678 þis. thus om. 1680
perelle. wheche þat

<small>Porphyry comforts the knights,</small>

"On-to the and eke on-to thi londe,   1681
Euene with the membres take now þe heed!"
Thus seyde this man as I vndirstond,
To comforte hem þus er thei be deed;
Be-cause thei were of visage heuy as leed,   1685
he was adred ful soore þat thei shulde fayle
If thei with-oute hym had goon to [þis] batayle.   1687

Therfore after[1] his holy hert*is* desyre   1688
Is he now serued, bounden and foorth led.   [1] *al.* Wherfore euen n.
Thei were not brent as heretikes in fyre,
But in her martirdam thus were thei sped:

<small>who, 200 in number, have their heads cut off,</small>

Too hundret were there, [of] whiche not oon fled,   1692
here hedes the emp*er*our bad thei shuld of smyte.
This was her ende, shortly to endyte.   1694

<small>and their bodies are left for dogs to eat,</small>

The bodyes were lefte, þat dogg*is* shulde [hem] ete, 1695
ffor very despite right of cristen feyth.
[On] of the Auctour*is* whiche this legende trete
In very sothnesse thus writeth and seyth;
The day of her deth eke ful fayre he leyth   1699

<small>on Friday, Nov. 24.</small>

Of nouembre moneth the foure and twenty eke,
The fyfte day also of the same weke.   1701

Bk. V. Ch. 30.

Cap^m. 30^m.

<small>The Emperor has Katharine up, and says</small>

The nexte day fol[o]wynge he clepeth this mayde; 1702
Be-fore his trybunal now is she presente.
With ful sotil langage on-to hir he sayde
Alle [his] male-corage and his euele entent;

<small>she is guilty of the deaths of his wife, of Porphyry and his knights.</small>

"Though þou be gylty," he seyde, "of this torment 1706
Of porphirye and[1] my wyf & my knyght*is* alle—   [1] *al.* of
ffor fro her feith thou madest hem to falle,   1708
                   [1] *al.* modyr
"With so[r]cery and myschauns þou hast turned hem,
Thei cowde neu*er*e resorte on-to her moder*is*[1] wytte; 1710

1683 vnde*r*stand   1684 or   1687 go to þis   1688 euyn aftyr
1689 bounde . & f. eke l.   1692 of wheche   1695 shuld hem   1697 On
of   1699 aftyr inst. of of   1700 tw. day eke   1701 also om. þat s.   1705
Alle þis male   1707 of inst. of and   1708 ffer . made   1710 modyre

Thei dede more for the than for fadir or em;   [1] *al.* knottis þat ȝe   *Bk. V. Ch.* 30.
I coude neuere perceyue the knot til it were[1] knytte—   The Emperor
But deed are thei alle, [&] we repente not yitte;—   1713
Mayden, þou may leue, if þou haue grace,
Not-withstondynge thyn treson & thi trespace.   1715

"Wherfore I counseyl now on-to thi fonnednesse,   1716   offers to forgive
fforsake thy witchecraft, & wepe[1] and weyle   [1] *al.* þi magik, wepe sore   Katharine
That euere were thou[2] soo boold in fool-hardynesse   [2] *al.* thou were
To yeue the queen or porphirye swiche cuele counseyle;
ffro thi eyneȝ lete the water now be[1] thi cheekis reyle,   1720
ffle thi deeth now! for, though [þou dede] this gylte,   [1] *al.* om.
That is to seyne, thou art cause of the[1] blood þat is spilte,   the blood he says she has spilt,
   [1] *al.* om.
"Yet may thou amende it with deuocyon   1723
To make an offerynge on-to[1] hooly saturne.   [1] *al.* to þe   if she will worship Saturn.
We alle wil folwen the right in processyon,
Soo that thou wilt on[1]-to this counseyle turne.   [1] *al.* om.
Allas, woman, hough longe wilt þou soiorne   1727
In this grete cursednesse oute of al reson?
Yet wil I forgeue the alle thyn olde treson,   1729

"Thou shal haue, mayden, tho[1] behestis alle   [1] *al.* al þo   1730
Whiche I promysed the,[2] to brynge þe to astat;   [2] om. in Ar.
Tarye noo lengere, for pereH þat may be-falle,
Chese the better, or ellis sey chek mat.
But if thou offre, we too arn at debat,   1734   If not, her
ffor thou shalt deye, and that in hasty wyse,
Thi deth a-noon in this maner wyse:[1]   [1] *al.* I wil deuyse   1736

"I wil make thyn hed to smyte of with a blad   1737   head shall be cut off with a two-edgd sword.
Sharpe on bothe sydes, whiche may not faile—
he warented it, the smyth þat it mad,
That it was suer at eche-maner assayle,

1712 knottys þat ȝe knyte   1713 & we   1714 May . lyue . hafe
1715 þi   1716 counsell . fondenesse   1717 þi magyke wepe sore
1718 þou were   1720 þin eyne. be om. . rayle   1721 thow þou dede
1722 sey. the om.   1724 on om. to þe   1725 folow   1726 on om.
1727 who   1728 cursydhed   1729 elde   1730 al þoo b. alle   1731 þe om.   1732 falle (be- om.)   1734 are   1735 ful h.   1736 on þis m. I wyll deuyse   1737 make smyght of þi heed wyth   1739 waraunt
1740 sewyre . ilke

396   *Katharine is ready to die for Christ.*   [**MS. Arundel.**

Bk. V. Ch. 30. Were it flesh, were it boon), or mayle, 1741
It shulde it kerue. therfore, mayde, consente,
And of thi errour I counseyl þe to[1] repente."   [1] *al.* om 1743

Bk. V. Ch. 31.   Cap^{m.} 31^{m.}
                                                            [1] *al.* meke

Katharine declares she is ready to die for Christ.
T̄he mayde [answerde] thanne with ful mylde[1] voys :
"Euere haue I seyde þat I am redy to deye 1745
ffor his loue whiche was hanged on croys.
This[1] shal ben), shortly for to seye,   [1] *al.* þis day
A grete spectacule to the wordly[s] eye, 1748
ffor[1] to seen) a queen) forsake lond and halle,   [1] *al.* om.
Soo sodeynly on)-to deth for to falle. 1750

Her death-fall
"Som) men) wene that deth-fal were[1] myserye, 1751
Som) men) wene the fal were[2] reprouable, [1] *al.* þe fall is   [2] *al.* is
Som) wenen) we cristen), whanne we deye,
We lese þing, to us that is supportable ;

will be gain to her:
I seye we lese þing that is disseyuable, 1755
I sey we lesen a leuynge ful of stryf,
And wynne a regyon) whiche is the lond of lyf. 1757

"ffor grete sekenesse here, there shal we haue helthe,

she will change tears for joy;
ffor weepynge teeres we shal haue lawhynge Ioye ; 1759
That place abundeth euere-more in welthe,
That place in seker hath neuere [no] noye,
It is more seker than euere was the tour of troye 1762
ffro shot and treson). therfore theder I glyde ;

Christ will be her guide.
Whan) I shal deye, crist shal be my gyde. 1764

"Wherfore I wil no lengere now the drawe 1765
With veyn) termes—doo as[1] thou hast thought !   [1] MS. ast

She despises the heathen Gods and Idols.
I despyse thy goddes, thyn) offeryng' and thi lawe,
Alle thi maument*is* eke I sette at nought.
Too hym) I goo that hath me ful deere bought, 1769

1743 þin . counsell . to om.   1744 answerde . meke   1745 hafe
1746 hang   1747 þis day . be   1748 spectacle. werldylys eye   1749
ffor om. . se   1750 on om.   1751 weene we crysten whan we dey   1752
is r.   1753 Sume men weene þe fall is myserye   1754 ful s.   1756
lese a lyuyng   1757 wyne   1758 here om.   1761 neuer no   1767 þi

MS. Arundel.] *Katharine is sentenst to Death.*

Too hym I wil, I coueyte to see his face.
The Aungell*is* song whiche is in that place, 1771
"Iff thou myght heere it, þou shuldest astoyned be; 1772
Thou hast noo grace suche mysteryes to approche.
ffarweel my freendes, farweel al my mene,
ffarweel my castell*is* tho[1] stonde hy on roche!   [1] *al.* that
A newe drynke my loue wil me [a]-broche, 1776
After my blood be spilt heere on the grownde.
ffarweel thys world that is shape soo rounde! 1778

"I shal folwe the lomb that washed with his blood 1779
Oure blody synnes wretched and onkynde;
I folwe the lomb whiche is ful meke and good,
Whos steppes folwe virgynes with-oute[n] mynde.
Come of, tiraunt, slee, and doo thy kynde! 1783
I abyde not ell*is* but deth and goo to lyff*t*,[1]   [1] MS. lyff*is*
I drede noo fyre, watyr, swerd ne knyff*t*."[2]   [2] MS. knyff*is* 1785

With these woord*is* sentens was youe anoon, 1786
She shal be ded as was denysed before.
fforth his she drawen; men and women ilkon
ffolwen on faste and presse wonder soore,
Wepyng, and cryenge euere more and more: 1790
"O hooly mayde, whi wilt thou þus wretchedly
Take thi deth, [&] wyth swyche velony?" 1792

She seyde ageyn: "moder*is* and ma[i]denes alle, 1793
Weepe not for me, lette not myn passion,
leue youre woordis with whiche ye on me calle!
ffor if nature enclyne you to consolacyon,
To haue mercy on myschef and desolacion, 1797
Weepe ye thanne ryght for youre owne synne
Whiche ye haue haunted, in whiche ye be Inne, 1799

"Weepe for youre errour, whiche shal you brynge 1800
On-to brennyng fyre, where youre godd*is* dwelle!

Bk. V. Ch. 31.

Katharine

bids farewell to her friends.

She awaits Death, and goes to Life.

She is sentenst to death.

The folk follow her.

She bids them weep for their own sins, not for her.

1770 couett   1772 astoyned shuld þou   1775 castels *þat* stand
1776 abroche   1778 þe   1782 w*y*t*h*outen   1785 fere   1788 is . drawe
1789 folow . & folow on w. s.   1792 & with . velany   1793 moder-
his . maydenys   1794 my   1801 fere

398 Katharine's Prayer before her Execution. [MS. Arundel.

Bk. V. Ch. 31.

The heathen Gods are in Hell.

Though þat youre prest*is* reede to you and synge
Of þe godd*is* hoolynesse and moche thyng you telle,
I suer yow this, that thei ben in helle, 1804
And euere with-outen ende in þat place shal be;
And but if ye amende yow, eke soo shal ye." 1806

Bk. V. Ch. 32.

Ca^m. 32^m.

When at the place of execution,

After this is seyde, she is come to þat place 1807
where she shal deye. and of the man tho
Whiche shulde hir smyght, she prayed a space
ffor to haue, eer she fro this world goo,
That she may seyn woord*is* oon or too 1811
In preuy meditacion on-to god aboue,
Whiche is hir maker, hir lord and hir loue. 1813

Katharine kneels, and

The man graunted, and she kneled doun, 1814
With hand*is* and eynes[1] lift up to heuene, [1] *al.* eyne & hand*is*
In suche sentens she made hir orison:

prays God,

" O myghty god, whos name for to neuene
Is ful merueylous, makere of planetes seuene, 1818
helthe of hem alle tho[1] trosten in thi mercy, [1] *al.* that
hope of al virgynes that to thyn helpe cry; 1820

her sweetest Jesus,

" O Ihesu most swettest, whiche hast noumbred me 1821
Right in th[i][1] collage a-mong*is* thi maydenes alle: [1] MS. the
Doo with thi seruaunt after thi benyngnyte,
Spreede me in[1] thi mercy, lete me neuere falle [1] *al.* wyth
In to myn enemyes handes. lord, to the I calle, 1825
Doo me this mercy for thyn hye name

that whoever

That what-maner man, the right or the lame, 1827

thinks of her death,

" Whiche hath my passyon in rememb[e]rauns 1828
Eyther in his deth or ellis in sekenesse
Or in his persecucyon or other greuauns,

1803 meche 1804 sewir 1805 wyth-oute 1806 And om. 1809 smythe. a om. 1810 or 1811 sey 1815 eyene & handes 1816 On sweche 1819 þat trostyne 1820 þi 1822 into þi college amonge 1823 seruauntis 1824 me om. wyth þi 1825 my enmy 1826 þi hey 1828 rememberauns 1830 eythir g.

If he with deuocyon) and hertly besynesse
Aske ony reles, lord, of thi wort[h]ynesse 1832 *and asks any boon of Christ,*
Graunte hym) his bone, lord, for my sake *may have it*
As I now my deth for thi loue take. 1834 *granted for her sake.*

" And alle tho that my passion) haue in memorye, 1835
Pestilens ne deth mote hem neuere greue ;
hunger and sores and other myserye,
And alle euele eyres on morwe or on eue
Suffre hem not to haue, but rather hem yeue 1839
Abundauns in heruest, and eyr temperat ;
lete not her londes abyde desolat, 1841

" But graunte hem plente of her greynes alle— 1842
Be-cause thei loue me, thou shalt hem loue.
Beholde, lord, for thi cause I muste[1] now falle [1] *al.* mut *Katharine prays*
Doun) in to deth : take to thin behoue
Thyng that this bocher may not hale ne shoue, 1846
Take þou my soule—no man) may but þou ; *Christ to take her soul ; and*
O Ihesu crist, my soule I commende now 1848

" On-to thyn) handis, I pray the þou it take, 1849
Lete þin Aungellis whiche þat see thi face *to send His Angels*
Come doun) fro heuene for thyn maydenes sake,
Suffre hem) to come now on-to this place,
To lede my soule, lord, on-to thyn grace, 1853 *to lead her soul to Him.*
On-to that felawshepe whiche þou me behight, [1] *al.* that
A-mongis thyn seyntis tho[1] shyne with the ful bryght."

Ca^m. 33^m.

She had scars mad hir conclusyon) 1856
Of this preyere, but anoon) sodeynly *At once a Voice from*
ffro [þe] heuene thei herden tho a soun, *Heaven*
A swete voys, and thus it gan) to cry :
" Myn) owne spouse, my wyf & mayden) holy, 1860

1831 hertyly 1840 eyir temporate 1844 mote 1845 þi 1849 þi 1851 þi 1853 þi 1854 feleschepe 1855 among þi s. þat 1856 scarise 1858 þe h. . herd þoo a sownde soune 1860 mayde

A Message from Heaven to Katharine. [MS. Arundel.

Bk. V. Ch. 33.

 Come now to me, [come now] on-to thi reste!   [1] *al.* as best
 ffor in my feyth þou hast laboured at þe beste.[1]   1862

tells Katharine that her dwelling in Heaven is ready for her.

"The blissed yate of heuene is now ope,   1863
It is made redy to the, that mansyon;
ffor thy feyth, thi charyte and thi hope
Shal thou haue my specyal benyson.
There abyde the *per*sones of thy nacyon   1867
ffor to receyue the to that eternyte
Where thou shal Ioye be-forn the trynyte;   1869

"Maydenes arn redy to brynge the thi croune,   1870

Angels will bring her to it;

Aungell*is* arn ordeyned eke thi soule for to[1] lede.
As for a tyme caste of thi fleshly goune,   [1] *al.* þi s. eke to
Thou shal receyue it in an other stede.
Come forth in hast! looke þou haue no drede   1874

her petitions are granted;

Of thi peticyou*n*s, for I graunte hem alle.
What-mane*r* man that on the wil calle   1876

those who worship her

"Or wurshipe with herte thyn hooly passyon,   1877
What-mane*r* myschef whiche he be Inne

will be forgiven their sins.

I wil relesse it, and al transgressyon
Of her defautes or of her olde synne,
If thei wyl leue it and newe lyf begynne,   1881
ffor thi sake I wil foryeue hem alle,
Conferme hem eke no more after to falle."   1883

Bk. V. Ch. 34.

Cap. 34ᵐ.

Katharine lays down her neck for the Executioner.

The mayde leyde foorth hir nekke fayr & white,   1884
 And thus she seyde on-to the smytere thoo:
"I am called to feste now of god al-myghte:
Do thou thyn office! the tiraunt bad the soo;
ffulfille his co*m*maundement! and thanne may þou goo
With-oute[1] daungere, stonde eke in his grace—   [1] r. Withouten
I prey to god forgeue the thi trespace."   1890

 1861 come now on-to þi rest   1862 as best   1865 þat f.   1869
schalt . before   1871 are redy ord. þi sowle eke to   1877 þi   1879
relese   1880 eld   1884 qwyte   1886 almythe   1889 stand

The man was glad to doo the commaundement 1891
Of his lord, wherfore with besy corage
he applied hooly al his entent
Somwhat to spare this yonge tender age:
ffor with oon strook, þat was ful wood of[1] rage,   [1] al. & 1895
hir heed he parted from hir body there.
Too grete myracles a-noon men myght lere: 1897

Oon was, in tokene of vyrginal clennesse 1898
In stede of blood mylke ran at hir nekke,
Whiche of hir purite þat tyme bar wytnesse—
There myght noon other thyng renne at þat bekke
Than swiche as was be-fore in the sekke, 1902
I mene thus, to putte you oute of doute:
Swiche thyng as was in hir, swiche þing ran oute. 1904

It ran so plenteuously it wattered al the ground 1905
That lay abouten hir. O most merueylous welle!
There[1] is the heed, the mylk aboute al rounde! [1] al. here
What shuld I more of this myracle telle?
Saue mary allone, of maydenhod she bereth þe belle;
That witnesseth weel this present visyon,
Whiche may no-weye be called Illusyon. 1911

A-nother myracle eke was seyn at eye: 1912
Aungellis apperynge in ful merueylous aray,
Bodyes liche men, wenges had they to flye;
Thei cam doun ful sodeynly, auctouris say,
Thei tooken the body and sone bore it away 1916
On-to the mount where Moyses þe lawe took.
Of this myracle right thus seith oure book: 1918

The hill in whiche god yaf the wrytyn[1] lawe 1919
On-to the Iewes, ledeth to that perfeccyon   [1] MS. wrytynge
Of crystis gospell and of his vertuous sawe,
In whiche we fynde ful sweete instruccyon.
Paule in his bookis maketh swyche induccyon: 1923

1893 holly   1895 a stroke . & rage   1897 mythe   1906 aboute
1907 here   1909 she hathe   1912 yȝe   1914 bodys . wynges   1916
toke   1919 wretyn'   1922 *I* wh.   1923 Poule

402 *Of Katharine's Tomb, and its healing Oil.* [MS. Arundel.

Bk. V. Ch. 34.

he seyth it longeth to Ierusalem as in seruage,
With alle his children heere in pylgrimage. 1925

Thanne, syth this hill is as it were a gyde 1926
On-to that mount whiche þat stant in blysse,

Let us follow St. Katharine.

It is good to us þat we ful hastyly ryde
After this mayde, þat she may vs wisse
A stedefast lore for to amende oure mysse; 1930
Soo shal she been in maner of a fygure,
To brynge us to heuene after oure sepulture. 1932

Mount Sinai is in Arabia,

This mount, þei seyn, stant in arabye; 1933
It is fro Alisaundre of lond ful grete distauns;

20 days' journey from Alexandria.

In twenty dayes, if I shulde not lye,
Myn auctour seith, thou men had purueauns
And gydes goode & eke grete puissauns, 1937
fful scarsely shulde he labouren it in these dayes—
There leue[1] but fewe [þat] han made asayes. [1] MS. lenue

Katharine was martyrd on a Friday,

[1]This passyon was, as oure storye seyth, 1940
On a fryday, right for this entente [1] The next 2 stanzas are transp. in Ar. 20.
That, sith she faught soo strongly for oure feyth,
Men wene therfore it was conuenyent

the same day that Jesus died.

That this same day whiche oure ihesu went 1944
Oute of this world, that same day his mayde
Shuld deye for hym—thus oure Autour sayde. 1946

Bk. V. Ch. 35.

Ca[m]. 35[m].

The grete myracles whiche ben at hir graue 1947
   Arn ny vnknowe, right for grete distauns
Be-twyxe that and vs; but this knowleche we haue

Oil runs still from Katharine's tomb, which heals all sores.

That oyle it renneth euere in abundauns,
With whiche oyle of soores alle grevauns 1951
Whiche men suffre, it wil[1] be hooled[2] anoon. [1] MS. wel [2] so all MSS.
Somme men say þat if thei bere a stoon 1953

1926 sithe þat þis. a om. 1928 fulle good 1931 be 1933 sey . stand 1935 if þat 1937 pusauns 1938 scarsly . laboured ; it om. þeis 1939 þat hathe 1947 be 1948 are . onknow 1952 wilbe holyd

MS. Arundel.] *Capgrave has heard other Miracles, not proved.*

[1]Of the[2] same graue, whider þat þei it bere
It wil sweten euere þat same licoure—
Thus seyn the pilgrymes þat haue ben there,
This sey oure bookis whiche ben made in honoure
Of this sweete mayde,[1] of this vertuous floure—
It longeth to flowres swhiche lycoure for to swete.
I herde men eke of other myracles trete,   1960

Of laumpes hangynge be-forn hir sepulture   1961
ffilt with þat oyle, whiche brenne[1] a mannes lyue
And of her light neuere maken forfeture,
Though thei brenne yeeris ten & fyue.
In this mater pleynly I wil me shryue :   1965
I may weel leue that swyche meruoyles þer bee,
But for be-cause I haue noon auctorite,   1967

I dar not wryte heere her declaracyon,   1968
lest that I poyson alle myn forsayd weerk,
lest þat men eke of myn owne nacyon
Shulde ymagen þat I, whiche am a clerk,
Might of swiche thyngis take a wrong merk ;   1972
Wherfore I commytte al this thyng in-feere
On-to the[1] discrecyon of hem þat shul it heere,   1974

ffor I wil determyne noo conclusyon   1975
as in this mater ; but fully I beleue
That hoo-soo myghte see that solenne stacyon,
he shulde knowe thyng whiche we can not preue.
Of this mater thus I take my leue.   1979
God oure lord for his hye mercy
Graunte vs heuene after thys mysery ! Amen !   1981

Soli deo honor et gloria . Per Cappegraue.

1954 þat . wheder 1955 swete . same holy 1956 sey . be 1957 be 1959 licoures. for om. 1961 before 1962 brenne 1963 make 1968 hire 1969 poysene . my 1970 eke mene 1974 the om. 1978 to whiche

           Col. Per Capgraue
Iste libellus constat Willelmo Tybbe Capellano (by the same hand).

# VARIOUS READINGS TO THE RAWL. TEXT.

1. FROM MS. ARUNDEL 168, fol. 15.[1]

1 O (Initial marked by a small o). criste. croune. maydyns 3 Amonge 4 ledyste thies . rithe . þis boke. 5 alle her herte . one 6 her love here pleasaunce. one overl. sette. 7 lorde . cane not lette 8 Rith . ordire 9 modire . resone 10 rithe . here 11 schape . heme . Ioy . thate . note 12 Bute nexte . blisse 13 ffolowithe . whiche 14 we om. thynne 16 previleges whiche beth . founde 17 Are sete . hire . degree 18 thies richly . abounde 19 þies . worlde . rounde 20 leuyde 21 shalle 22 ʒavo . Iohne 23 owne . whane . shulde 24 euyne 26 wolde 27 Oute . hade 28 hire . graunte 29 Whiche . mylk . ryth om. ate 30 Rane oute . mene sein . tokynynge 31 martirdame . maydynode rithe 32 medelyde to-gedir. doutere one-to . kyngis 33 þies . thingis 34 his aungels . gode 35 Ritho . he om. dide 36 hire 37 hire . grauntede . almyghte 38 mane . womane 39 Askith . hire . righte 40 wille . ife . aske . righte 41 ellis 42 þou 43 Purchasede . lovers 44 serue þe as (so om.) . cane 45 Ande . lyfe . mor þat (þat overl.) . shalle. 46 womane . mane 47 There . fulle wane 48 ffore . labour . lyfe 49 lyue . thirtene yeres . fyfe 50 ʒit . fonde . grete 51 ffere 53 More glade . basnet brith or 54 Thane . preste . whane 55 blisside . saide 56 salace . ioy 57 made . liffe . welle 58 yite . do 59 scharpe wheelle 60 leffe . yite . do 61 made . þerto 62 Right 63 dede . haste 64 make . liffe 65 Oute 66 & wiffe 67 haste suffercde . whate . haste 68 lorde . dore vndoo 69 Suspire . wittes . preuy 70 hyme 71 preste . whome . spake 72 tellithe ate h. d. 73 þat om. 74 martire 75 hire modire . hire sere 76 yeres 77 Withe . fastynge colde . mychil 78 laste . reuelacione 79 Alle . hyde al 80 thoughte 81 honeste clothide . schoroude 82 Whiche . vpone . preste 83 what . ame 84 thinge . why . came 85 hande . helde 86 rotene . rente 87 preste . behelde seems corr. to beholde 88 ententc 89 wote . wele . haste soute . mente 90 mouthe . boke . eke inst. of ete 91 do . wille . shalle . noʒte 92 lorde seide . hyme. 93 shulde . boke 93 rotene bredes þies leues derke & dyme 95 mouthe 96 mouthe . smale 97 wille breke . cheules 98 likely . no 99 sayde . muste . booke 100 shalle elles . mouthe 101 hoke 102 Lete . go downe 103 bake 104 mouthe bytter . wilbe 105 sumtyme to þe eʒ. 106 preste . tooke . mouth anone 108 othir mane 109 preste . stounede . þouʒ 110 ioy . thoughte . hade . þane þer 111 glade 112 blissede 113 Aftere . longe . felde 114 floures . herbes . smal 115 fonde 116 rith 118 laide þer . knythe 119 Armarake . knythis 121 fonde . amonge elde tresoure 122 kynge petirs 123 fonde 124 Vrbane . as om. vnderstonde 125 felle 126 Which . herde . yit . ʒe om. 129 taughte hire . coude deuyne 131 hire 132 I-turnede vn-to criste & vne-to . faith 133 hire ledere . seith 134 liffe 135 hire . laste 136 saw hire martyrede . hyme-selfe 137 hire liffe 138 seruaunte vne-to hire 139 þis 140 hire chaunceler . secretarie 141 hire . thorow-oute . parties 142 hire faderes 143 hire . row 144 paiede 146 hire kyne 147 hire 148 hire . liffe 149 hire . customes while 150 hire 151 saw . aungels who . hire 153 veniaunce . who. 154 eke om. . hire dethe 155 saw . maxiense . slayne 156 downe . ryuere 157 Diede . sodenli . payne 158 fforth . drawe . helle-fiere 159 Aungels . hire . devels . h. bere 160 sondry . synne 161 þe othire in helle w. 162 Longe

[1] For want of type, the dashes on n m t ll d g are replaced by e, nobl̄ article by nobile articule. The variants of this MS. are for the most part merely orthographic.

406 Various Readings: MS. Arundel 168. Book I.

aftere . maxience   163 Byschope . Alisaundre . Cite   164 same mane   165 whiche . myche   166 wote . verely ʒite ife   167 which   168 Whiche . ofe-tyme synge.   169 diede euene . ane   171 liffe   172 hye   173 dede   174 oute   175 liffe   176 speke oftyme   177 Both . hire . ende   178 love hire liffe had   179 gostely   180 sikire   181 sprynge   182 ony . any   183 Twelf   184 what . myth   185 ther vsage   186 miche   188 liffe   190 founde   191 eritykis   192 both þe leffe & brede   193 soughte   194 gode . hy   195 fonde . noghte   196 noghte .   nobile   198 A hundrede   200 miche   201 passede   202 tonge both   204 in-to   205 I-sought . broughte   206 hyde alle in . amonge   207 vne-to . mans hande   208 whene . note vnderstonde   209 righte   210 liff . kepte   211 Neuer-þe-lesse . dide miche thinge   212 nobile . goode mane   213 lede . way . dore vne-doo   214 myche . better   215 þoutʒ   216 helpe . wyth₂ om.   217 Whiche . purchace.   219 diede . many a yere   220 nye fro . leste   221 Yit . diynge . grete   222 aperede   223 glade . moste godely   224 rewarde   226 speche . bi   227 seint   228 Cite . wile   231 vne-to   232 Aftere   233 sette   234 Tristynge   235 helpe .   cas . wrigh   236 parte . heuenly   237 appollo . seint   238 makith . grow .   mans   239 wite whate   241 Oute   242 Vn-to . brotherode whiche   243 gife   244 fadirs   245 Whiche . Austeyne   248 paiede   250 whene   251 heuene   252 Thoroughe.

The titles of Books and Chapters are wanting.

I.

1 Some tyme þe . grece   2 Sipire boþ lorde   3 telles . olde   4 reulede   5 gouernde . alle his e.   6 Costus þo mene . kinge. þoo here om.   7 losede   8 lione   9 liste   10 wele . boþ   11 Alle thei dide . boþ ferre   13 here be-hoffe . soughte   14 helpe . whene . nedede owt   15 Iles . vne-to . gret   16 þai om.   buxome . requeste   18 hauens . weste   19 welde . righte . liste   20 marineres   21 homageres   22 reynede   23 wase   24 wilbelouede . homagers   25 nobile   26 felde . pesibile   29 wolde him   30 what . dide   31 Whene . vengeaunce   32 Prayere . a-waile   33 assaile   34 castille bette   35 Whene thei . noʒt . bone   38 Stabulle   39 hande . douthi   41 wroughte   42 sperite   43 Peas . pute   44 cleymede   45 nobile . vne-to peas . lofe   46 made . ax vne-to   47 Amonge   48 moste . wise   49 hatyde . harlottrie . vise   50 petie vne-to . thought   51 sucho a trewe   52 rithe . wise   53 thorny   55 spronge   56 Katrine . true   57 Citees .   amonge   58 largeste   59 coste . golde . fodire   63 whiche   64 high Amaliche   65 highte . egipte   66 londe . Sipre . nothinge . wante   67 of beis   68 golde   69 londe closede   70 north-weste   71 kinge . key   72 sette   74 shippe   75 peas, were it were   76 hade   77 castille   78 vne-to   79 Be causes . fredoms   80 hethnesse . cristendome   82 meire   83 noʒt   84 To   86 shippis . Cite   87 vpone . owne   88 ofe . cuntrees   90 Whiche . Cites   92 othire   94 grete . highe   95 Egipte   96 Vne-to . thoroughe   99 egipt   100 Thithere . Marke   101 bi   102 lordis   103 twiste   104 belyue   105 made . criste   106 plate   107 boke   108 theoretica . sayne   110 hermyttis   111 such   113 alle . þies   114 martirs & f . . confessours   115 maydyns wydowes . chaste   116 Nombre   117 growith . aftere   118 mythe . nombire   119 pute . sharpe asaie   120 This vessels . martirs   121 fiere . Irune . I-brente   122 fournesse . sorow . maide   123 schapede   124 turne   125 firste excersice . devyne   126 Whiche . longith . foule   127 patenus . boke   129 score(!)   132 goode conueniente . exortacione   133 Moste . whiche   134 Alisaundre whiche . nowe   135 pepile   136 thidere drowe   137 knygh . marchaunte gone   138 though . Inow whane   140 elles   141 wones   143 Alisaundre . saide   144 a om. wurthi such   145 tounge . dome   146 lofe ner   147 doth . wele myght   149 þis kingis   150 leuyde . mychille   151 suche   152 wane . lande .   scharp   153 thingis . pleyne   154 cronnycule seyne   155 Almighti   156 mo merveils . caste   157 herithe . els   158 some . tyme om. laste   159 vne-to   160 whene   161 wille   162 Whene thinge   163 wirkith . righte . wille   165 childir . not hem   167 whiche . fallene   168 halp . whene . þat om. blynne   169 holpene . mighte   170 not om.   171 alle . entente   172 þat om.   173 Whene .

Various Readings: MS. Arundel 168. Book I. 407

not   174 helpe   176 wrought   177 vnc-lyke   178 thies olde . which leuyde .
dwire   179 haue . childe . moste . moder   180 kinge . foder   181 mighte . seker .
suche a newe   182 elsabeth   183 dide Abrame . Sara . wiffe   184 conceyuede
185 lyffe   186 Maris   187 wille (= well) . suche   188 blisside   190 maydene   191
owne   192 which speketh   193 parte . hire goode preyere   194 moste   195 wille
196 come   197 Whene . þis sesone   198 maydene . lithe   199 ordeynede ite .
suche . a om.   200 whiche   201 sprynge os   203 olde   204 a om. loughte   206
kinge . febile . qwene . olde nowe   208 now lye   210 Ladys . chambire . & om.
211 come om.   213 marie   214 Excuside   215 writene   216 faire maide   217
hire fadire . kynge.   218 hire modire . saide . sche om. highte   219 doughter .
armeny   220 beaute sha . price . presse   221 Thorought . sarcenrie   222 liste
noghte . hire praysinge   224 shewede   225 hire helpe . mischef   226 whene .
passede   228 ordeynede   229 noght   232 wesche   233 lifte·. lulle   234 wipe .
roke   235 iaboure . bi   236 kepte   238 qwene . no3t . hire yee (yee on eras.)
239 norischte . nobile   241 both meke   242 tetes   243 lastede . hire . alle life
244 pleassede   245 woudre . haue   246 provede   247 sette . boke   248 Alle .
laide   249 alle . scoleres . are   250 lofe . fere   251 Made . whene she gane .
kenne   252 þe letters & wordes   253 maisters   254 hire . retrik   255 case .
nombres . such . gysse   256 verbis whiche longed . foule   258 figurs   259 persons . modis   260 Of monge alle   261 hire chauncellere   263 survioire of . w:s
264 paide hem here hyre   266 Alle . couthe   267 moste   268 alle þe longe daie
269 sauynge mesure   270 amonge . hire playe   271 say naye   272 bade . play .
sitte   273 goodnesse . hire   274 lerned . latene   276 any philisophire bi   278
alle . bodys . planettis   279 thorough besinesse   280 vne-to . sette   281 sci .
storye   282 reynede   283 alle . victorye   285 lerne . þu 3onge   286 herisye .
blasphene   287 Thorought . grece . reeme   288 ydeottes   289 apostyls . noght
290 worlde . sowne   292 wyne . fere   293 bustonesse . I om.   294 thinkethe . þis
om. case   296 ordeynede   297 worlde   298 hire   299 hire   300 faile boste   301
mythi . strenkethe . gooste.   302 Hire fadire . þies   303 nobile . owne doughter
304 Dede make   306 knytis   307 ordeynede . hire owne   308 reeste . for om.
309 telle   310 maistres . thithire . fette   311 myth strech   312 lernyde . with-
outyne . lette   313 sette   314 wele   316 craftely . I-pythe   317 cheyers . myche
318 beste . brithe   319 bi   320 Sete . weste   321 rithe   322 heuene   323 Alle .
one rowe   324 Righ aftere   325 mithe wile y-k.   326 worthiare . hye   327
Hire   328 thies . I-take   331 faste . lernyde   332 Whene   333 chauugynge .
maisters   334 nobile . mych   335 wele witte . lofe   337 made make . for hire
338 paleis wallede rith . southe   339 sonne . hire troone   340 none suche . worlde
342 Whene . bi . selfe . soule   343 In om. gardeyne . moste   344 ferre . frome .
wighte   345 ordeynede . owne device   346 lye . wrighte   347 strange   348
& om.   349 alle   350 Solatorie llffe to stodiars his comforthe   352 Whene .
schet . faste   353 sparede . truly   354 thingis . agaste   355 moste . laste   356
wordly   357 insure   358 tours . made vp so   359 sotely I-caste   360 mith .
come . foule . doþe   361 yates . faste   362 hire-selfe . laste   364 lyued . hire
366 firste . moste   367 telleth . wey   368 wrighte   369 Rethorike is þe s.   370
doþe   371 materes . colours   372 calle . dialatike   373 litille throw   375
truethe . falssede . techith   376 rithe   378 wante   379 taught hire   380 wile
(= wel)   381 hade   382 departede   384 voice   385 arne   386 lernede   387 eu-
clides bokes . purtreytures   388 Ite . myche . longithe   389 letturs   390 of ite .
schalle . forfettures   391 Agene   392 suche   393 stye   395 planettis . reyne .
hye   396 Whiche . which   397 helpe   398 þies . lernede boþe   399 moulede .
Idilnesse   400 hire . such   401 hire fadire dide gadire . londe   403 Right .
vnderstonde   404 wit . doughter . one hande   405 aposede . meny   406 That .
gaderede   408 strauuge thinge   409 lernede . life . rith   411 not . katerine .
3ynge   412 vnderstode   413 sone hath vndo   414 goode . thies clerkis þanne
415 maide . hire life   416 supposede . þat inst. of than   417 wondre how . dryfe
418 conclucione for in yeres fyfe   419 Conne   420 this wisement   421 toke
423 maide . shalle   424 wondre   425 not . haue   426 myche   428 nobile .
rewardede . wille   429 gyftis   430 Lordis dide . clerkis . dele   432 bountyfus-

408 Various Readings: MS. Arundel 168. Book I.

nesse . suche 433 rewardede 434 lefte 435 Whane . wele 437 alle hire .
ane 438 owne 439 worlde . lede . were 440 suche . vne-to 441 kynne 442
Whiche diede wy*th*-oute faith wy*th*outene cristendam 443 such one ʒite . longe
444 lordis came (corr. fr. come) 445 wronge 446 Alle hire . wurchipe only
447 nob*i*le kinge . lythe now þ*er* 448 closede . afterwarde 449 solempnite 450
wailinge 451 cite 452 wele away . what shalle 453 lorde 454 ded 455
lefte . no heire . hede 456 yonge 457 ʒite . sche wedede 460 say 461 likly .
suggete vne-to . londes 462 bonde . suffre bondes. 463 nob*i*le qwene . what
464 petie here (to₁ om.) 465 couthe 466 teres 467 yonge . hire 469 hire
470 leide . tombe 471 wite . he om. þ*er* kinge 473 Schulde not . such 474
thinge 475 Was þane saide . whiche nede 476 happely . mith 477 such 478
stille 479 dukes . Erles . knyght*is* 480 Thirti . euene 481 ranne faste . be-
gonne . pasce 482 kinge 483 haue . thinge. 484 suche lastynge 485 rith
486 gr*a*uige 487 vanysch . waste . brente 488 alle 489 gret 491 high .
grete 492 his . coste 493 þither . carte 494 cite of famagooste 495 made .
ooste 496 have . mouth 499 moste 500 þe c. . hade 501 dide 502 þis cause,
same om. 503 while . stand . loste 504 knowlege . famagoste 506 G. C
507 nob*i*le 508 thorowoute 509 wirkith*e* many a 510 worthi 511 schalle .
such . þ*er* 512 qwene . hire owne 513 Alisaundire . whiche 514 helde . hire
housbonde 515 schulde 516 bolde 518 lordes . wiste 521 londe 522 hade .
solempnite 523 custome . holde 524 tocab*i*le 527 cite 528 in whoos 531
stores 532 Al . lordis aftere 533 a lord om. 535 byldyde 537 scholde 538
wille . aftere . daie 541 Este 542 oute of . affrike 543 ryde whedere . beste
544 grete feste 545 hire . kynne 546 Oute . & mynne (þe om.) 548 semeþ
549 lond 550 reinede 552 kinge . Alexsaundire . rith . defferens 553 kinge .
Egipte . sentence. 554 wille (= well) 555 Whiche 556 which of w. r. 557
deceyuede 559 telle forth 560 Which longe . kynrode 561 after 562 Madagdalaus . high 564 Reinede 565 hiʒte 566 which spekeþ 570 clepede 571
reinede 572 rith 573 owne 574 bylyde . fadres 575 firste lyfe . iche 577 hiʒte
579 spronge . oute 580 one-to . þe f. 581 nob*i*le 583 philip fadere . Alisaundre
584 secunde 585 ʒone s. . hafe 587 wondres . Alisaundire south 588 laboure
ʒete 589 kyng om. hith 590 owne 591 mythe 592 wane . gunne 593 cesede
594 chaungede 596 made . þe om. 597 haue his . high 598 hool 599 hote . rithe
601 deie . þis worlde in 602 selue 603 lordis gafe 605 gafe . he om. mythi
606 Alexsaundire . rith 607 firste 608 whiche . lefte . now om. 609 thinge .
clerkes 610 reinede 611 ayre 612 nob*i*le 613 amonge 614 ceptire 615
which 616 reinede þ*er* 617 calle 618 reinede 620 which . reynede 622
dide 623 temp*i*le 624 nob*i*le boke . writithe 627 whane 628 askede 629
lefte 630 hithe 631 synnede bi . doughter 632 brente . brith 633 þe inst.
of ʒe . story 634 seuene 635 euene 636 reynede 637 high 640 regnede
demetirus 641 a Crowne 643 euene . regnede 645 wanne 646 mich . grete
648 sette 649 dede 650 rithe 651 lede.. fere 652 loste . fadres wanne 656
dede þane 657 euene 658 aft*er* 660 gouernde 661 þies 663 here 665
weddede . calle 666 saide 667 By . rith 668 And om. 669 mayde 670
Rithe . high 671 Sey . suche anoþ*er* 673 sone bi 674 highe 677 Sone .
fadere . alle regnede 678 rithe . haue 680 fader 681 fader . Katrine 684
schewede 685 be-high 686 reknynge 687 acordith . wy*th* cronic*u*les . be
688 fro . thing*e*s 690 þese kinges 691 & om. ; one-to oþ*er* mens rekynnynges
692 which 693 þise . degree 694 Bute . hapely 695 meneth 697 Nombires
of yeres which 699 lordschepe 700 kynrode . scherews . worschepe 701 doth
702 Criste . schrewes 703 whi . worlde 704 correcte synners 707 Katrine .
þe 708 firste 709 lordes . which 710 araiede 711 oþ*er* 712 noʒt 713
Grete 714 bi . þat ite 715 lordes wy*th* . bachilere 716 come . þider . seruice
717 Bischoppes 718 wittes 720 Sume lordes 721 ladies . qwenes 722
crounede . þe om. 723 Whiche seruede at þat 724 pr*a*yede . hire 725 goddes .
& 726 whiche 727 lordes 729 grete 730 costome 731 & to þe pouert low
732 one-to . manne 733 dayntes . reherce canne 734 plenty . in hale & in
halle 735 seruede . nedede 736 Swich*e* rule . I- om. 737 warnede . with*e*

Various Readings: MS. Arundel 168. Book I. 409

738 righe glade   739 opene bothe   740 curyde   741 meel . oþire   742 vesselle .
foder   743 voide neiþer . ne   746 pepile   748 cite   749 gentils   750 ladys .
hire   751 bothe . othere   752 loggede . Inne   753 hire fadire kyne . hire   754
othere   756 spake . whiche   757 beste   758 Summe   759 reste   761 nobile .
whiche   762 asayede eche one   764 is om.   765 reuelle . festis gunne   766 take
767 are   768 Eche . whiche . or make   769 too courseres . whiche   770 blake .
othir white   771 & silke (of om.)   772 sey   773 Summe . mantyls white .
mylke   774 whiche   775 ryde . þei om. forthe . weye   776 note elles nowe .
farewelle   777 & praye   778 storye   779 hire . holde   780 qwene   781 hire .
not blynne   782 doth . grete   784 durste   785 Ioy . & om.   786 herte . noghte
787 aftirwarde   788 Both witte . wisedame   789 Euene . renneþe   790 Sweche .
stody dede   791 whiche   792 wite . presens   793 Durste ones touche . any
794 dide   795 euer-more   796 her seruaunte   799 neuyr   800 gouernaunȝ
801 Both prevy . a-saie   802 Stedfaste . stabile   803 seynte   805 preyer   807
one-to   808 articules   809 before   810 criste . rith   811 good om. werkis   812
werkis causede . sei þis   814 hauntede . werkes . sperithe   815 Which . haue
816 vertue both   nyth .   817 nedeth . myche . eye lithe   818 wele . fole   819
hire nobile presens   821 whene . coude . ony mysorawte (!)   823 loue   824 fulle
wisely   825 honeste   826 reulede . is om. beste   827 whanne   828 noghte .
truly   829 lokith   830 menbires . body   832 deyneth   833 what   835 rulere
836 worlde . falle (be- om.)   838 schul . I-wis   839 goode lordschipe   840 whane .
þat om.   841 nobile   842 hire   843 homely   844 comforth   845 glade . disporth
846 Sade . whane   847 Goodely . hire   848 whane . no hede   849 kepte . disolate   850 hertis hangynge . þe lede   851 commons gruchynge . at debate   852
no rule   853 pepile . surre   854 kinge . lythe . ny   856 oþire   857 helpe crye
858 come . too   859 alwey thoughte   860 who . stande   861 loste . lande   862
commyth amonge   863 elles . bokes   864 Lete . londe . & renne   867 ȝete
myth alle   868 blynde . who turnyste . wheele   869 low   870 Lith   871
supposede . conqure . his   872 not have   873 hole   874 vnsekirnesse . variabile
875 worldely . arte . vnstabile   877 ȝete . sarsenrye   878 lefte . one-to . womans
879 muste . mayde   880 summe kynge . not þus   881 if om. wurchip   882
weldeth . are made   883 schul . þis   884 per golde   885 lyve . tende   886
haue . myrth . any   887 euene . now om.   888 haue   890 nobile kynge   892
pepile saide   893 Iustice   894 sette . schire . cessiones   895 Righe . liste . nowe
896 no-thinge to   898 schalle   899 abile   900 pepile   902 capteyne ony ; oþer
om.   903 rankyre   904 laye . lande   906 alle . hande   907 sche one-weddede .
ȝonge   908 lykynge   909 abile . housebande   910 nedes . safe   913 certene
915 þanne   917 moste goodely   918 on-to om. qwene   919 hire modire whiche
921 ladys   922 suffre   923 olde   924 serteyne . writene   925 ladys   926
know   929 oþire . whiche . honde   930 to-gedire   933 leue   934 hertes .
pitouse   935 lette   937 pepile   938 oute   939 welle   940 vndire . nowe   942
riche . whych (corr. fr. whech)   944 leue . reste . pees   945 crie . I-sees   947
gouernde . werke   948 Thinkithe   949 summe-what   950 sume . oute   951
Suffre . pepile . sume   953 perfore   954 appolyne   957 one-doo   958 seene   961
desireþ alle oure grete counselle   962-3 transp. and 961 & 962 are marked b a.
962 of alle þe londe be-dene   963 weddede   964 Lete hire . choise   965 Choise .
hire   966 soule   967 nowe   968 ane   970 suche   971 to-morowe . oute . bede
972 ere   974 answerde . rithe . agene   975 algatis mote   976 leue   977 any
978 hire . heretoo   979 hire doughter   980 weddede hastely . sume   981 hire .
sente   983 qwene . surre   986 passede . dede . hire pepile   987 aloweth   988
done   989 hire doughter . sume   991 hire . to om.   992 were   993 fayne   994
fynyschede   995 hire   998 neithere   999 leke . say . naye   1001 doughter
1002 ȝet   1003 wighte   1005 hire . plithe   1006 rithe   1007 caste   1008 hire
1010 certeyne   1011 noȝte   1012 muste   1013 elles   1014 fertheste   1015 weel
1018 schulde . elles   1022 come . his beste   1026 lettede   1028 pepile . apaiede
1029 voise   1030 endiþ þe b.   1031 which hire . kynrede   1033 sende   1035
which . worchip   1037 be-twixe . hire   1038 which . rially holde   1039 stoute
1043 reste rithe.

II.

(Title om.) 1 brithe 2 fiere . faste 3 rithe 4 tellith it so 5 neither . ne 8 Thies . wordis . þis . dedis 9 Which . leuande 10 tokens . hire 11 hire gostely . fonde 12 honde 13 hath tokyns 14 alle . ȝet 15 criste 17 Brennethe . hire 18 hire . sittithe 19 dew . þe om. whiche 20 made . neste 21 wille . reste 22 speche . commende 23 whiche . with inst. of we 24 Amonge vs 25 duly 26 which 27 desireth 28 weddede 31 chidis 32 qwenchede 35 sercule . rounde 36 othir 37 calleth . felawe 38 to-gedire . sistire . as om. brother 39 Eche . drawe 40 suche . hire 41 haste . laste 42 hire serclede . caste 43 hire . þies 44 ferre 45 whel . caste hire 46 hire . tiede 47 so swetely take 49 bounde to-gidire 50 welle . thinkith . hire 51 liffe . hire . hafe 52 Thise latene bokes . þe same 53 hire . sey 54 destroie 58 Soundith . hire 60 destroiede . hire 61 Thies . hire 62 synne 63 schete oute . sperde 65 onworthi 66 þi langure 69 which . sufferede 70 streith 71 elles 72 Messengeres 74 beste 75 Clerkis muste 76 lordis 77 tary 79 thider . grete 80 wyth . grete 81 erle 82 mene myth . beste 83 phaphone . þider 84 ane opire 86 rialle 87 wyth (overl.) fulle 88 þise reall om. 89 solempnite 90 receyuede 91 is om. 92 Laste . thidire . approche 93 owe 94 calle . anteoche 97 both . rith noȝt 98 wille . hire 99 daie . which assynede 100 gaderede 101 lenghte . hundrede 102 certeyne . whiche 103 Sittynge 104 mette . hemeselue 105 Swiche . worlde 107 telle hire . þei sei 108 wote 109 wente . easly 110 rith before . fas 111-12 last half-lines transp. : ȝe schul note be dismaide 112 My s. lady, þane þus he sayde. 114 trueth . muste 118 alle . lordes . other 119 excepte rith . certeynly 120 cas . rith 122 duke . eme 125 muste . bokes 126 take . bi brokes 128 lyue 130 phelisophire . wille I sey 131 hardely 132 no pleasaunce 133 pleassith 134 peple . housbonde 135 rialle . whiche 136 goddes 138 pepile . shulle 139 Excusith . note 140 suche choise . refuside 141 myth 142 haue . myche 143 now om. 144 wey 147 desireth 148 seruauntes 149 yow om. 150 liste 152 Rith alle 153 rith . liste . 154 thise 155 alle 157 though 158 qwene 160 preuy . whiche . longe 161 muste . wronge 162 schew . longe haue 163 preuyeste poynte 164 suerly 166 veyneglorie 167 please 168 pepile . rith 169 concele . councelle 170 alle . pepile 171 deny 172 telle 173 Which . falle 174 herte . sette 175 suche . lette 176 ȝete . ageyne . owne 178 mynde . fareth . rith 179 schepe . whane . beste 180 eschapede . wawe 181 schipe 182 poynte . broughte 183 leffe . ease 184 muste 185 pepile 186 muste 188 knoweste 189 haue 190 mythe 195 thought . hire-selue 196 softely 197 myth þane h. 198 saide . goode 199 feldes 200 poynte 201 one me tille 202 alle 203 both reste . habundaunce 204 welle 210 grete haste . haue rith 211 ȝonge . welle 212 haste 214 ȝeres . paste 215 both loke . taste 216 anyse 218 not 219 suer . housbonde 222 to yow lenger 223 faste . lith 224 lith 226 it om. thinkith 227 pepile . while . iangile & carpe 228 Speke . luste . wone 229 choyse 231 summe 232 grete 233 riche 234 wordis . taugh 236 wite 237 thoughte 238 owne . aboute 239 fadire . londe 241 pounde . hande 244 hider 245 aske 246 avisede 248 I 250 sekire . birde 252 pro-fitable 253 gresse 254 hungre 257 grow 261 law 262 traitours . rowe 263 lordes 264 kende 265 blode 266 slayne . owyne om. 267 bowels cute 269 mene 272 mythe 273 make . falle 274 beste . þinke 276 Which . sinke 278 have 279 Rith . make 282 faders 284 þouȝ . lyuede 285 myth 287 such 288 while 289 selue . þouȝ 290 enmys 292 fadere . dede 293 yeres be-fore 294 dede . doth 296 obeyede 297 rowe 298 durste . þan om. 300 dide 302 loste . sumtyme 304 thefte . grete 305 hyde . crafte 306 summe . pun-chide 307 ofte . rith noȝte 308 þis same wise . wroute 309 ryde 310 Go . enmys which 312 be neke þat . honge 313 neuer 314 lete 315 goode . rith 316 a reall om. eke with-alle 317 capadoce 318 knes 321 this . hyde 322 And om. Yit may ȝe note neyther . byde 323 haue . soule 326 lykely 327 I-passede 328 lefte 329 lykith . wele 330 wonderfulle we þinke 332 in om. synke 333 youre . myth 336 satille 337 myth . alle 338 ordeynede

Various Readings: MS. Arundel 168. Book II. 411

rith 339 castelle 340 pepile . þei . schente 342 alle . I now 343 muste . kepe 344 þe om. faireste 347 ʒe om. 348 brynge forth 349 please 352 hyde . kepte . closse 353 mythe 354 capadoce 355 whiche myth 356 raunsome . gode 357 thinge consente 358 wiseste 359 thinge . wante 360 selue 362 Mythe . strenghte . wante 363 haue beaute 364 ʒit 365 Bodely strenghte wherwith . opresse 366 wikkede . whiche . now om. . ryffe 367 veniauns 368 or wiffe 369 telle . sekere . kinges 370 haue . wurchipe alle 371 Summe . pepile . ofte . muste 372 Thise thinges falle . thinkethe 373 wille 374 Ordeyne . mene . leue 375 ʒit 377 Spede . longe 379 sere 381 welle 382 worchipe 385 to be-holde 386 welle 387 streyte 388 Whiche disese . leke . dele 392 true 393 rith noʒte 394 lordschipes . wonne . handes 395 wroughte 396 faute . no om. londes 397 prisoners whiche . lede . bandes 399 borders 400 soudyours 401 rith noʒt . couet 403 noʒte . sende 405 noʒte . fynde 410 swyche . halde 411 drope 412 gunne 413 Rithe . wedede 416 pepile . wille . schalle 417 make 418 graunte 419 hange 421 swone 422 Mith graunte . þouʒ 423 dede . fadere 427 note 428 kinges . herte 429 suche fredome . rithe 430 smerte 431 myne 432 punche . scherewes 433 euelle dedes . daye 434 nedethe 435 Suche deputes sires . feele 436 suche maters . muste 437 þat om. fithe . ande 438 oficers . sekerly 440 sleithe . are . case 441 lase 442 Alle 443 faders 444 lete . lete 451 rith 452 perilous 453 fulle sone be 454 any sisme 457 pepile 458 lande 459 Renne 460 fiʒte . flite . & om. 461 Alle . araye . sette . noʒte 462 alle thinge 463 sitte 464 olde 465 luste . elles 467 bokes . wille 468 beste . dulle . mannes 470 you firste 471 hangede 472 suche 473 heme 477 goddes loue . pepiles 478 liffe . lete . boke 479 letters 480 trouthe 481 Tende vne-to . take 482 heyle . querte 483 myche . haue . herte 485 Rith . noʒte 488 any gode . rithe noʒte 492 I-wisse 493 euene . pepile 494 tachede . pouer 495 amende . a-mysse 496 muste helpe 497 litelle 498 helpe . I om. 499 true 500 hertes 503 plithe 504 þane say . rithe 505 pepile 506 amyse 508 I-wise 509 blisse 510 nabugodonysore 511 pepile 512 preste 514 breste 515 & om. pestelense 516 which . offense 517 such 518 amonges leons 519 pute . pepile 520 durste . withstande 521 muste . þouʒ 523 goddes 524 Whiche . seruede . myth 525 made om. 526 suche low pepile . kenno 527 pepiles . cryinge . kinge . oftene 528 such 530 meuede . him 531 haue 533 muste . boke 534 sers . helpe 535 worldely 536 þise . mans prowe 537 such nowe 538 alle 539 faste . growe 540 witte 541 hith . wiffe 542 whiche 543 saw . rede 545 muste 547 faders . knowe 548 conqueste 549 tolde 550 dede 551 telle 552 Swiche . thingis . hade 553 sire . muste yow lete 554 law . mannes 556 prestis are 557 þe feeste . the halidaie 558 suche 559 Eythire . Iupiter 560 carpe . summe 561 Blamethe no suche thinge 563 semethe . byde 564 to om. suche wordis 566 mayntene alle . thinge 567 Whiche . goddes . offerynge 568 sire arcules 569 grete 571 here . whiche 572 autorite 573 grete 574 wordis 576 suche 578 either yere 581 new . ware 582 commeth . late 583 is 586 ferre a-sundire fer fro 587 Whiche 588 oste 589 such 590 salte watire row 591 any 593 londe 594 mote nedis 596 goste 597 saile . londe 600 hande 602 suerly . schulde wille 603 schulde 605 myche . ofte 608 dothe bi 610 sire 612 myche 615 noʒt 616 I-bouʒte 619 tende 620 alle . wille now þerof . wante 621 sette . plante 622 maners 623 lerne . Iuste . here 624 grete . whiche . alle 625 knyth 626 haue wurchipe þouʒ . haue 627 teche . schaftis . bene 628 schalle . habunde 629 note 631 fadere . note 634 wedede 635 easede 636 wise 637 herte felle . or l. 638 mythe . alle thise 639 Whiche . rithe 640 plenteuosely alle 641 Whiche kepte 642 armles 644 ʒe myth he note . faste inst. of softe 645 rith 646 laide 648 leide rithe 649 plas 651 herisie 652 rithe 653 reste 654 kynde 655 Whiche . rith . leste 656 departede . beste 658 now inst. of lo . dwellis 660 muste 661 alle . cooste 662 reste him 664 Rith 666 duke 667 he be-gane . say 668 ʒonge . rith . dide 669 pepile muste . obey 670 dey 672 hertely bow 673 kinge 674 pepile . hye 675 Rith . amonges 682 thise thinges . seel 684 one (to om.) 685 othire 686 wille obey 687 weddede . summe 688 law 693 laste . muste

412 Various Readings: MS. Arundel 168. Book II.

bow . hardelie   694 Sire . suche   695 Rith . whiche . enforcede   697 insuer yow   698 thouth   699 it . ooste   701 kepte . whiche   703 wille (= wel) . in om. 704 resons   705 Whiche   706 liste . such þinge   707 sire   708 That inst. of As . fadere . he om.   reste   709 lykly   710 any   711 one-true   713 crowne   714 liste   715 grete . stode . bi   716 scharpe   717 thoughte   718 one-to   719 þise . alle   720 ȝit . arte   721 pringnauntly . parte   722 arne . thei be noghte   723 lesse . þouȝe   724 thoughte   726 Greteste . alle   727 preise . supposede   728 whiche   729 inhaunse   730 alle   731 poynte . not   732 herte   733 I-wisse 734 drinke to . trow   735 moste   736 Whiche . semethe . wedede   737 counselle 739 langore   740 Whiche . one-to . fikille whel   741 spousaile . olde   742 Valarye . moste   743 suche   744 suche . grete om.   745 whiche   747 saide wele 748 longe sith . rith   752 such . alle thinge   753 wede   754 wysche   757 schate . longith . rith   759 gouernenoure . goode   760 alle   761 purpose   763 Beholdithe   764 stedfastely   766 othire   768 purpose . warye   769 Lete   773 ȝonge . goode   776 wondire meche   778 þat om.   779 which   780 note   781 suche thinge   782 Such   783 Neither . othire withe   784 grete disspithe   785 efte-sone   786 alle vnthir   788 weddede   791 Both . myne faders . moders 793 Which . ordeynede   794 Which . decense   795 grete   796 such   797 wele . kinge . alle   798 Ouere   800 and 802 transp.   801 maytene rith . wronge   802 kinges myth . hardely   803 such helpe . wele   804 liste . say . parte   805 sire . truly . arte   806 pretendede   808 myne . stabely   809 suche   811 purpose   816 kinge . lorde   817 lete   818 brynge . hole bunche   819 make . vnche   820 haue . beste   822 leste   825 suche   827 choise   828 whiche   829 no.   830 to corr. to o ? muste . bow   831 entente . efte . newe alow   832 schulde . & ȝe schal   833 sire 835 thise   837 such   840 othire   841 scathe . note   842 to om.   843 no-thinge 844 maters . ouer   846 which   848 wille (= welle) . rith . seyne   849 liste   850 Whiche   851 londe . wiste   852 myth . suche . fiste   853 Draw mych . euene 854 rith welle   856 note leke . leuynge   858 lorde rith   860 eke om . amonges any   862 answerde schortly   863 Sire   864 poynte . which   865 liste   866 mayden-hede . twiste   870 too   871 wede ȝete . thinkithe   873 liste . graunte . to   874 withoutene   876 grete   877 rith   878 wisdame   879 frendes . sittene   881 grete namede loos   885 suche thinge   888 thise . witte   889 vsede   893 know . beste 895 schende   901 wote . beste   902 suche   903 know . frende   904 If ; se om. 905 liste   906 deynte   907 counte   908 suche   914 such . neither . luste   915 suche þinge   916 Drede   918 pepile   920 putte oute . whiche   921 falsede   922 which . reeme   927 lykly . note om.   929 such   931 wene . opresse   933 Sire 936 mych to   937 conceyte   938 suche . witte   939 wittes.   940 Leke . egile . alle   943 fostere . whiche   944 Dispise . noghte . þat om.   945 liche   947 Growe . witte . I-nowe   948 thowe . witte . suche   949 goode wille muste   950 mene (mens ?)   952 haunce . witte oute   953 lettithe   954 seruauntes   955 counceille . whiche   956 telle   957 bettire ende   958 broute . hedis   961 witte . whi 963 bydde . commaunde . sende   964 such   965 alle   966 his om. . londe . lyme 967 stryffe . þe debate   968 Amonges . pepile   969 staunche both enuy   970 compellede   972 kinge   973 streuen . thinge   974 whane   976 anothire   977 brothir   978 Ageyne . sone . struethe   979 rithe . entente   980 brynge . thinge 981 Sume . witte   982 ande sume   983 trew, on erasure . wittnesse   984 kinge 985 pepile   986 seene   988 pepile   991 choise   993 abouthe   994 selue . muste þei louth   995 herte   996 whate . telle . plate   997 smerte   1000 if om. stronge hyme-selue   1001 fith . alle   1002 wille   1003 Lete   1004 bringe   1005 con-naunte   1006 wele carpe   1008 lete . falle . mende   1009 I-now   1010 mornyde 1011 saw . drow   1013 sy   1014 douthire . note   1015 suche   1018 worlde 1019 suche   1020 grete   1021 haue   1022 impossibile . craue   1023 anothire daie   1024 thouthe   1025 suche araie   1026 suche thinge . noghte   1027 Cursede . brought   1028 doth   1029 That euer thei poynte þei uarie euer for soth   1030 thinge which   1033 clyuethe   1034 Wheder   1035 counselle   1038 lorne (I om.)   1039 xalle . schalle   1043 here om.   1044 duke   1047 brouth . to   1049 myche   1050 suche   1051 one-to   1052 highe . hire homagere   1053 myche   1055 kynrede   1056 mythe . alle . entente   1059 ȝonge . wise   1060

Various Readings: MS. Arundel 168. Book II. 413

thinge . law . for-byddith   1063 wille . wytte whate   1066 rith   1068 sote
1070 Brouth . lith   1071 steppes   1072 wronge elles . childerne   1073 Whiche
1078 douthere . both maide   1079 councelle . þus   1081 hew   1084 bore . myth
1087 myth   1090 distruccione   1092 worchipe   1094 haue   1100 diede . elles
1101 louyde beste   1102 myth falle . happe   1103 breste   1104 parte . reste
1106 entre while   1107 councel . suche   1108 Which   1109 I . gladnes . euer
is   1110 pleasaunce . medelith   1111 lyve . dispise   1112 sewerte   1113 haue .
londe   1114 grete   1117 hire crafte . suche . hire   1118 philosophire . deuyne
1119 Whiche . termes   1120 ȝeueth . prise   1123 selue   1125 ȝit stode   1127
haue   1128 What . haue   1129 note ȝe   1130 alle   1131 wote   1132 which . my
1133 sothly   1134 goode   1135 witte   1136 haue . wrouȝt   1138 lordschipe .
noȝte   1139 bouȝte   1140 elders   1143 wordes whiche semede   1145 rith   1146
suche . prise   1148 haue   1150 whiche . þise   1151 witte . sadnes   1152 one-
too   1153 othire . reulede   1154 Lete   1156 neyboure   1158 heme . othire . carpe
1159 he om.   1160 Whethire   1161 wele   1162 This v. wanting   1163 Alle
1165 werkes . dyrke   1170 answere   1172 to-gidire   1174 wille   1175 which
1176 þise   1177 say neither . strenghe   1179 landes . lenghe   1181 suche . banne
1182 suche   1186 worchipe   1187 sikirly   1188 wed not   1191 wise   1192
whiche longith   1193 nyse   1194 holde   1199 Athanes   1200 longe   1201 peple
1202 choise . þere &   1203 whate . whiche . heede   1204 in . stede   1208 goode
1209 & your   1210 semethe   1212 elders   1216 phelosophie . is ite   1218 take .
sote   1219 bokes   1221 all þise   1222 Eythire   1223 herte displesith   1224
oncurteisely   1226 duke   1227 grete   1228 schewe . haue   1230 Were . witte
1231 Athanes   1232 Wo . ouȝte . lete . take þidere   1233 endewede   1234
worldely   1235 soffyne   1236 motyffe   1237 voyde . weel   1239 heede . ofte-
1240 o . growinge diuers   1242 rede . white . diuers   1245 acorde   1246 diuers
1249 hardely   1251 Whiche . clouene   1252 gryffe . gryf   1253 myne   1254
schulde   1255 I schalle   1256 certenly   1258 ffare weel . ffare welle   1259
counseile . profitabile   1260 sweche . stabile   1261 saide   1262 asundire   1263
Comonde . wittes stille   1264 hopynge . after   1269 Whiche . wise . cunnynge
1271 lernynge   1272 thinge   1273 whiche . vtter   1274 all om. loste   1276
Whiche . wedede   1278 firste   1279 oure   1280 worlde whiche   1281 fulle sone
be   1283 beaute . mote   1284 leuethe   1285 leste   1286 blissid . whiche   1287
thirde   1288 Whiche   1289 falle   1290 fourte . grete   1291 Whiche . telle
1295 pepile   1297 roialle   1302 Alisaundere . worlde wanne   1303 kynge   1304
Whiche . babelle   1305 lyuynge   1306 enhaunsede hyly . grete   1307 hede .
goddes   1308 weddede   1309 kynrode   1310 othir . brithe Beaute   1312 yee
1313 Swiche . hardely   1314 flatere . sekerly   1315 preyside . booke   1316 wyth-
outyne   1317 poynte   1318 schapithe parfithlye   1319 vnder   1321 mankynde .
eyȝe   1322 schappe   1324 rithe   1325 brithe . with-al   1329 þinge . certeyne   1331 Whiche   1332 takithe hede   1334 suche a faire maye   1335 sekirly
1336 rithe   1340 wille   1342 suche thinge   1343 Suche goodly . hyde   1345
thirde poynte . whiche   1346 grete lernynge   1347 wittes . suche   1348 kynge
1349 mythe . wele troste . cunnynge   1350 selue   1352 commone . othire   1354
firste . your   1355 Whiche . sterres . hye   1356 wisdame   1357 to þis entente
1358 sente   1359 heede . parelle   1361 drawe   1362 speke nowe   1363 myche
1364 fourte poynte . þise . laste   1365 whiche   1366 worlde wondrith   1368
witte   1370 parte . wone   1371 beste like if . kinge   1372 askynge   1373 swete .
wiȝte   1375 whiche . dede endyte   1376 plate   1378 alle herte   1380 sente .
whiche . wante   1382 wyse . warante   1383 muste purpose . ane   1384 a housbonde goode . deboneayre   1385 I inst. of ȝe   1386 lyte   1388 passe   1390 wolde
knowe   1391 argumente   1392 worthieste   1393 muste . þe om. alle   1394
rith   1395 heede   1396 wise   1397 suche lenage   1398 suche   1399 haue .
wele   1400 stande   1402 my housbonde   1403 alle . muste   1405 muste . stabile
1406 purpose . sette   1407 suche   1408 haue   1409 muste . wise . know   1410
amendede   1411 rerede   1412 suche   1414 fynde such   1415 muste . suche
mythe   1416 nede . helpe   1417 selue . þe om. rithe   1418 myth   1419 me
suche one   1420 haue   1421 Herkeneth   1423 mennes   1426 herte   1427

414 *Various Readings: MS. Arundel* 168. *Book III.*

askide. ony þinge   1428 askynge   1429 muste   1430 muste passe   1432 goode.
schynynge   1433 Passe. whiche   1436 alle. noghte   1437 Alle. bute if   1438
grete. soughte   1440 alle. wile. alle. blis-e   1441 suche welthe   1442 telle.
desire   1443 strenkithe. alle þise faile   1444 leste   1445 whiche. disseuer   1448
warante   1450 I craue   1451 noute   1454 Which   1455 fader e. asundere   1457
this. o lowde   1460 wepynge. gune   1461 felle. rounde   1462 swounede
1464 lifte vþe   1465 laste. caute   1466 nye om.   1467 we₂ om. such   1468
wele hire   1470 such one. hade   1472 suche   1473 seeke. muste   1474
scorneth. iche one   1475 faste   1478 satte   1479 cursinge. maistirs   1481
lordschip   1482 sende. realme   1484 grete   1485 meche. grucchynge   1486
asunder. iche   1487 lykynge   1488 qwene wrothe. iche one   1489 lefte. dwelle
1490 write   1491 fynchede. white   1492 Iss. herte   1493 chaungynge   1494
alle   1495 loste. endynge   1496 whiche. pletynge   1497 alle. legemene.

III.

2 goode   4 ffadire. heuene. sone   5 rith   6 it om.   þe beste   7 goste   9 noble-
hede   10 grete disputynge   13 suche. beste   15 Whiche   17 telle. ordire   18
criste   19 merueylously   22 þe rederes   23 Whethir   v. 24 overl.   25 writene
26 Miche þinge. hyde. diuers   28 Kepte   29 wydder   31 liffe. hire   32 While.
lyffe   33 medecyne   34 treacle   35 deuele   36 streite. to om.   37 blissede.
coumforte   38 such   39 muste lofe   40 lerne om. troste   41 better. troste
46 it om.   47 knelynge   48 preste. sothly   49 songe   50 sleep   51 counceile
52 longe   54 bapteme   55 schorge   57 was om. ordeynede   60 wente. lady   61
hermyte   62 bodely. gostely   63 criste. mayde   64 stronge. stabile   66 worldely
68 wroute. passith   69 worldly. agaste   70 speke. passith. gnaste   73 mythe.
strenghte   75 leuyde. vitaile   76 he om.   77 lande hye   78 schippis. fasteby
80 Sixti. lede sothly   84 lede   85 alle   86 ermytes   87 dwelte. six   90 wyth-
outene   91 þis wordis   92 hermyte. falle   93 myth. bedes. wonte   95 Rith
bi. scharpes   98 werkis   99 sittithe hye   100 wele   102 sekirly   103 faste
105 goodnes   106 Deme. mythe   107 desirithe   108 blissede. allowede. sithe
109 mythe   114 sithe. þouthe   115 walkede   117 blissede sith   119 Passinge.
myche. erdly   120 Alle   121 brithe   122 wote   125 lyte   126 þinkith. selue.
lithe   128 sith. thinge   129 benedecite. merueile   130 ʒynge   131 hydyr om.
morenynge   132 noþer inst. of now here.   133 Nother. fletynge   134 mervel-
ynge   135 wente   136 thoughte   137 firste. entente   138 omnipotente   139
heuene   141 hermyte   143 myschape   144 desese   149 one-to   150 troste   151
do. werkes. rithe   152 vsethe. brithe   153 sere. messagere   154 wille. wordis
156 forsake   158 cōnaunte   159 breth   160 feche. maydens   161 Speke   163
Arte. haste saide   164 nyth   165 no^t (^t overl. by another hand), þing om. wroth
168 meyne rith   170 petous uoyse hathe criede both. nythe   171 dulnesse
172 mythe   173 massagere. gostely   174 to om.   176 buske   178 suche   179
alle. worlde   181 rialle   182 bodely. schalle   183 rith   188 straunge. astōnede
192 ordeynede   193 meche   194 wede. myth   195 ordeynede   198 alle   199
wille. telle   202 shalle   203 goodnes   204 ffirste. wite. qwene   205 rialle.
wise   206 worlde suche   209 raynes   210 sonnes   211 sothnesse   212 in alle in
215 worldly. eke om.   216 worldly   217 hyer   218 sche om.   219 muste.
meche þinge sertayne   221 pouerte   223 Or om.   225 hire. fyʒte   226 Ageyne.
herysie. phelosophie   227 all om. lite   228 sophymys   230 mytily. schal.
arte   231 draw. parte   232 telle. sekirly   233 suche   234 lyue partitly   237
as om. a gl. ende   239 þinge   240 hermyte. plate   241 aferde. swonynge
242 lifte. agayne   243 sayne   248 I om.   249 commerous   250 commynge
251 witte. verely   253 hire seruaunte. caste   254 pleynte   255 þinge. agaste
256 knowe. certayne   257 thoughte. souerayne   258 rekles   260 petous. praye
261 punche. leste   262 nyth   263 obediente rith. requeste   264 beste   265
sewerly. grete   266 dede   267 note   268 certeyne   269 rith   270 fulfille.
biddynge   272 þider. haue. mych   273 weys   274 wildernesse   275 weye.
wikkede beste   276 hastely   277 schalle. leste   278 not a-reste   283 sayne

Various Readings: MS. Arundel 168. Book III. 415

284 rialle   285 not om.   stumbille   286 suche   287 comste. in om.   288 speke
292 onworthi. mythe. dispyse   293 selue. muste   296 rialle   298 doungione.
walle   299 schalle   300 ffynde   302 alle   304 Rith. crouche   306 lette   309
walles. new   310 smal. schape   311 faste sew   312 note. rape   313 ope
lithly. swape   314 shalle entre. fynde. swete   316 wouудre. any   317 Mithe
entre. preuy   318 rith   324 postelles   325 stande   327 loller wyche   328
dismayde. gyf   329 suche   330 Rith   331 Suche wondire. stōnede   332
Criste. endew. elde rekles   336 hire   337 sothnesse   338 leuande   339 vertue
340 wedde. schorte   341 massagere   342 hire. one-to   344 tokene   345
enquere. thidire sente   349 durste   350 wurste   351 hire   352 sotil cunnynge
354 alle. stodyinge   355 faste. hider. hire   357 Take. stafe   358 rith. waye
359 Trostynge. suche. longe   360 þouȝe. aungels   361 ledynge brouthe   362
longe. euene   364 runne   365 thinge   366 þe om. worlde. liste   367 werkynge   368 cis'.e   369 stronge. beste   371 Rithe   373 chase   374 is om.   gone
forthe   375 hille. wildernesse   376 is om. as om.   377 stodyinge   378 entrede. is he   379 too   382 sodenly   383 Be-fore. rithe   384 conceyte   385
stoynede (a om.). certayne   386 fonde. lokynge   387 stody. solatorie   388
amonge. looke   389 suche beaute   391 blissede mythe   392 brithe   394
Wende. suche a. leuynge   395 herde. womans   396 brithe. beauteouus.
thinge   397 Blissede. heuene-kynge   398 hider .399 passithe wyth-outen   400
othir   401 lokede anone one. stoynede   402 mythe. þe walles   403 elles   405
selue. laste   406 faste   410 brithe were   411 amendede   412 sithe.   413 heile
414 rithe. agayne. seide   415 Goode. telle   419 firste. witte. muste   420
Wheþire. wuste.   421 mythe. maistirlye   422 walles   423 enchauntemente
424 entrede   425 witte. þinge   430 lyue   431 neþire   432 preuy. ite is   433
take suche þinge   434 falle happely   435 now om.   436 boldnesse   437 witte
439 founde   440 wende   441 rithe   442 agayne   444 sayne   447 leste   448
state   453 yeene haue   454 boldly make. commendynge   455 passithe. thinge
456 ferre   457 what-so. liste   458 dede   459 Ine. wiste   460 wroth.
schapithe. fiste   461 ȝow om.   463 worde   464 dede euer er before   465 any
466 leide. tresore   467 Rith. herte. emprentede   468 massagere   469 criste.
selue   470 Rithe os   472 a mane   473 ȝonge   476 dede   478 ferre. knowlechynge   479 smerte   480 turnythe. þinge   481 lefte. apposinge   482 seyinge
483 worthi a   485 worchiþe. witt   487 ȝette   488 lithe. fayne. it   489
hire. wheþer. lordlesse   490 þinges   491 Wheþer. lyuynge   492 soole   493
weddede sekirly   494 Meche. wille. bow   495 rowe   496 And om. leue. selue
497 ofte   498 Rithe. abouthe   500 oute a doute   503 welle   504 suche   506
lordschipe. souerayne   507 heuene. erde   508 sothly. sayne   509 comethe.
sunne   510 & of   511 Such. myth   512 lordschipe. stronge   514 truly.
wronge   516 mythe   517 leue   518 mechil   520 Modire. norse   521 to-gidere
522 ȝete efte   523 bythe   524 moder   526 Sire   527 ȝe so   531 merveile we
more   532 arayde. sympile. massagere   536 suche   537 longe. seruauunteȝ
538 cloth. worschipe   539 clothinge semyth. rithe   541 telle   542 make.
massager. dide   544 hardely   545 suche   546 alle. muste. rithe   548 gostely.
passithe   549 Bodely disgisinge   550 suche   551 clerkis   552 truth   554 sente
555 Desirithe. inwardely araye   556 clothes spredde   557 boldely   559 brithe
560 Suche   563 sende   564 wille   565 feele   566 frenschipe   567 wordly.
parte   568 noȝte   569 noȝte   570 thouȝte   571 lyuynge   574 dwelle. blisse
576 blissede. dide   578 massager   579 ȝone maydene   580 enprentede   582
sittinge   583 princis   585 kynge   586 stronge. mythy   588 endewede. goode
590 þat om.   591 leue. fiere   594 wille   597 þise   598 any   601 wordis   602
daie areste   604 note   605 mervelous   606 is modire his   609 worlde   611
mythe. & pitte   614 suche. wheþire   615 suche   616 wheþer   617 þinges   622
seithe   623 ermyt. blisse   624 thouth   625 þinge longe   626 & alle hire
goodes. noȝte   628 caste. worlde   630 bere it   632 rith   634 ony   637 sire
639 þou. not excersyse   643 ȝite. ilke   644 haue a. he om.   646 dide   647
be-gynne   649 sleep. swowe   659 goode   660 Proue. alle þinge   662 sunne.
brithe   664 rememberauns. telle. plite   665 othire   666 þise. werkes   668 telle

416 Various Readings: MS. Arundel 168. Book III.

any merkes 669 proueabile . clerkes 670 wittes muste 671 suche 672 Leke 673 aylede . myth 674 freile 675 bettere 676 lekynge 678 offendede . witte 680 Inne 682 Inne 683 leuynge . delice 685 dwelle 686 semeth 687 merchaunte 689 avaunte 690 dide 698 wikkede 699 acorde . grete 700 longe . stronge 706 Loke . herisie 707 phelosophie 709 passithe 710 failithe 712 þise 713 medille 715 thinge 716 myche better 717 poynte . gyue . warnynge 721 suche thinge 726 credulle . childere 727 thiso 729 thinge 730 one-to 731 alle . wildynge 732 blissede 739 How . blissede 742 ȝow 743 coupelynge 744 too . cryst om. 745 wille proue 747 arbitoure . tonge 749 Too . haue 750 skille 751 noȝte 752 þene . thies . wille 753 in appetite in werkynge & in thouȝt 754 bouȝte 757 wille . vne-to 758 How 760 kynde 761 mynde 762 Alle thynge . muste 763 herisie 764 Whiche too 765 heme 766 firste mouer 767 mouer 769 shalle 770 owne 771 þies 772 Assoilyde . þis 773 Vne-to . laste 775 bote . too 777 þat shalle 778 Thies wordis wente . lefte 779 astoynyde . wote . verely 780 Wheþer 781 elles 782 wordis . vnlyklye 783 ane inst. of & 785 þei inst. of men 786 liche 787 ffewe wordis 789 proude 790 counceile 792 hermyte 795 see 796 thoroughte . Cetee . gune 799 house 800 How . or ȝates . myth 801 smothe . sekenesse 802 aurisia . heme 803 sekere 804 astoynyde . shalle 805 hande . þene 806 cetee 808 lete . chide now & 809 knowithe it now whethere 810 forthe walkynge 811 Tille . house 813 wone 814 is but wildernesse 815 waylide 816 caste 818 Goode lorde . leste 819 hyȝte . geste 820 how 822 herde . sekirly 825 myȝty 826 lede 827 turnythe 828 lokethe . cooste 829 sodenly 832 wene 833 vntrew massagere 834 queene 835 verry . how 838 turmentede 839 Tel . þat om. stande . now om. 840 Counceile . lesse ne mynne 841 lefte . house 842 wente . sente 843 straunge inst. of meruelous 845 olde 846 thouthe 848 þis mane 849 feche 851 suffere . diuersyte 852 straunge 854 good om. lithe . sekernesse 855 saide 856 haue . troste . þene myne-selue 857 entrede 858 passe 859 noȝte . beste 861 saue vs 862 thoute 863 gruben . make . new agayne 865 sayne 866 dwellynge 867 gruchynge 868 counforte 871 syȝtes . swete 875 lede . kyngdome 876 hade 878 glade 879 goodly 881 loste . wille 882 truly . th'nge 883 ȝondere . nowȝte 884 wonderfulle walles shynynge . sunne 885 Swiche . thynge . wroȝte 886 suche thynge . erthe . begunne 887 bryȝte . robes . dunne 888 merely . note yondur sighte 889 yondere . bryȝthe 890 noȝte 891 Noþer 892 blissede . brouȝte 895 haue felte 897 wepte 900 seithe . bryȝtere 901 othere . olde . growene . grase 902 olde . newe 903 ȝaue 905 ȝonde . ȝonde 906 ledynge 907 presse 908 graunte 910 ye. me om. 912 Desirynge . goodly 913 folowede whene 916 whene . ȝates 917 receyuede 918 suche 919 noȝte 920 suche 921 whene . thiþer brouȝt 922 hire thouȝte 925 þies 926 suche sithes . for om. 928 rauyschede 929 Whethere . noȝt 930 nouȝte 934 truly 935 Bute ife . ȝonge 936 olde 937 what-so-euer . liste 938 myche thinge 939 receyuede . firste 940 betture 941 Whene 942 swettere . mete . þene 943 hundrethes 944 þene 945 þies 946 Welcum 949 verry 950 any 952 Thies goodly folkes . wonderfulle 954 knytis 955 mene . abites . briȝte 956 successores 957 colours 958 hire 960 ledde 962 welcummynge . suche 963 welcum 965 felle . bones 966 alle ate ones 967 abites certeyne tokens 968 a t. 969 Aftere . passions . sufferde 970-1 transp. 970 tokens 971 þer 973 erth come 974 whene . brouȝte 975 one . here 976 thouȝte 977 suche 979 suche heuenly 981 wakede 982 folowede 983 Thene . sche om. alle . makede 985 rialle 986 thynge 987 commynge 989 souȝte 990 witte 991 þis 992 is om. on om. 995 suche 997 leyede 999 Leȝte 1000 note haue 1002 lifte 1003 goode 1004 heuynesse . passede 1005 Alle . disport 1007 housholde . haue 1010 Rithe 1011 maydens 1013 tellithe note . seker 1014 ynow 1015 myche . bothe 1016 þies 1017 almithi 1018 compeny . þer 1019 stoode 1022 solempnite 1023 wordis whene 1024 Sone . thinge 1025 haue brouȝte a 1026 þer (st. þi?) sp. . louyste . hire I hire brynge 1027 shalle . rynge 1035 haue the . thinge 1036 shalle . siȝte lastynge 1038

Various Readings: MS. Arundel 168. Book III. 417

Washide 1039 whiche 1040 Clensede . merkede . marke 1042 Whene . erthe 1043 Whiche . ofte · vnkynde 1049 she hathe 1450 Brynge . me to 1051 suche . tokene 1053 preste 1054 goste 1055 Parforme 1056 note 1058 ȝite ȝowe . mythe 1060 baptise . erthe 1061 ȝite . note 1062 suche 1063 moste riȝthe 1064 wyȝte 1066 discomfortede . wey 1067 sons . sekernesse 1068 moste 1072 make 1073 myȝthe 1075, 2 do ye . deligens 1076 please 1077 ȝonde . baptistarye 1079 walkyde 1080 one-to 1081 fonde . funte 1082 watere 1083 callide . pepile 1088 suche 1091 watere 1093 clothis 1094 thinge 1095 ye 1096 Riȝthe . tokenynge 1097 know . oþer olde . ȝynge 1098 Shalle 1101 thynge . trew 1102 wilis wrouȝte 1103 suffre 1104 spoylide 1105 spoilynge 1106 feeste . teeme 1107 baptise . blissede 1108 fadre . sonne . gooste 1109 In þe . witnesse 1110 one-to criste 1111 booste 1112 Loke . dowghter 1113 one 1114 kirke 1116 dide wyrke 1119 vndefoulede . presente 1120 wittnesse 1121 answerde . þies articules 1122 sire 1124 founte 1126 wille . souerayne 1127 rithe 1129 renewede 1131 dide . clothis 1132 Alle . ilke 1133 blyndnesse . ermytis 1136 lyȝte receyuede 1137 myrthe 1138 easly 1139 sekerly . efte 1140 thankithe 1141 to om. 1145 writhe . tende 1146 bade . sekerly . dide 1148 How . he . elles . how 1151 ȝite . goynge . swetely 1153 shalle 1154 sekirly 1155 Suche wordis . walkynge soberly 1157 mayde 1159 Suche 1165 grauntede . hyr om. 1168 blissede 1169 myche 1172 erthe 1174 be doo 1175 þene felle 1176 here croune 1178 leuande 1180 heuene 1182 be þi modire 1184 bade . roos 1185 crounede 1186 myȝthe 1187 any . whene 1189 Katrynes . felle 1190 Plate one-to . stille 1191 telle 1192 thinge 1193 arte . erthe 1194 commaundynge 1195 Mercy y craue lorde þat ofe alle maner thinge 1196 elles 1197 lernyd 1198 lyfte 1199 welcum doughter 1201 Wonderly . beaute 1203 seruyce 1204 Iustyce 1206 welcumynge 1208 ffor my loue & . byddynge 1211 comons 1212 how lyke 1214 thies 1215 Plate . goode 1216 whene . wittis 1217 thene . kynge 1218 souereyne . alle . thynge 1219 aungels . mene . beste 1221 solempnite 1223 forgyfe 1227 sauncefaile 1232 yow 1235 house . rove 1236 broches . mantille 1237 for om. 1238 worldely thynges 1241 elleȝ 1242 thouȝte 1245 parte 1246 to om. 1247 in 1248 ordeynede 1254 alle . þoo om. 1256 one-to 1258 alle 1259 Next my modire ioynede to my presence 1260 schortly in sentence 1263 To be my wyfe for euer & my make 1264 ffor youre constaunce & stedfastnesse in virginite 1265 shalle 1266 Be-gynne . noȝte 1267 shalbe bouȝt 1268 riȝthe 1269 spousaile . nedes 1270 gyf 1271 seruede 1272 commaundede Iohñ . one-to 1274 rynge 1275 toke . rynge 1276 fyngire 1277 tokene 1279 wille 1281 wedede 1282 seene . rynge 1283 my nawtere 1284 grauene thynge 1286 callede . calsidony . cloude areyne 1287 swiche 1288 touchede 1289 autere 1290 bereere 1291 any maters . perilous 1293 debate 1295 bodyes . chaste 1296 songe . abouȝte 1297 most om. euery . myȝte 1298 Wordis 1300 songe . songyne . it om. 1301 þe same 1303 wil 1304 aungels 1305 songe 1306 wrechednesse 1307 The 1308 Cherche . y may 1309 wedynge 1310 liste 1312 hande . dide 1314 blissede 1319 sekenesse 1320 kepe . trew. 1321 reue 1322 shalte 1325 & om. sone . goste 1326 godede 1328 alle . truste 1329 commaundemente 1331 treuly 1332 Eche day whil sche (wylle I se crossed out) 1334 solempnite 1337 ertly 1338 aungels shalle 1341 erthe dyede 1344 passede . myrth 1345 brygthe 1347 þe Chapelle . fount . lyȝthe 1349 celle 1350 lefte . amonge 1352 how. þan om. 1353 swone 1355 watur . comethe 1357 to om. 1358 rubyde . chekes 1361 lady om. 1362 pake 1363 do we lake 1364 chere inst. of rere 1365 ffalle . sorowe 1367 nouȝte 1368 fforsake 1369 ande thouȝte 1370 wille . myche rouȝte 1371 worldely . erthly pleasaunce 1373 tho 1374 Weddyde 1375 how 1376 blisse . shulde 1377 suche . sekernesse 1378 rynge 1379 weddynge 1380 muste yow 1381 sekire . pleyne 1385 godhede . grounde . alle 1386 telle . shalle 1387 Thus 1389 besily 1390 suche 1391 sekirly . wretyne om. 1395 &₁ om. sone . goste 1397 moste 1398 coste 1402 goste . with-outyne 1403 wille haue

KATHARINE. E E

418 *Various Readings: MS. Arundel* 168. *Book IV.*

1404 my3te . ly3the   1410 fad*ur* . sone   1412 sone . blisse   1413 begotene .
gooste   1414 beleue   1415 my3the . co*n*nynge   1416 Goodnes . goste   1417
any   1418 my3te . goodnesse   1419 allmythi . sone   1422 thise   1423 the
cy3te   1424 saide . mor*e* om.   1426 þe   1427 better*e* . thoughte þene   1428
to*n*g*is* . broke   1430 ly3te   1432 bry3ter   1433 Aungels . seuene   1434 longith*e* .
her*e*   1435 emprise . heuone   1437 dede Iohñ   1439 þe om.   1440 my3t   1443
Doughtur   1444 goode blissynge   1446 telle . a maner   1447 tyraunte . lyuynge   1448 reigne   1450 stylle . owne   1451 tirauntrye   1452 in-dew   1454
muste . suffre . velony   1455 3our, om.   goodes   1456 liste   1459 no3t   1460
doughtur . þe   1462 like   1463 eke inst. of ete   1465 dede . ry3th   1470 croune
1471 thi*n*g*is*   1472 how   1473 warnyng*is*   1474 whiche, þe om.   ded   1475 y-
passede   1476 no3t discomfortede   1479 Shal . dwelle   1482 lyuyng*is*   1483
prayere . elmesdede   1484 3eue 3e . þe om.   1485 passede   1486 þene . make .
ende   1487 doughtur   1489 mynde   1491 euerlastynge   1496 Whedur . theþer
1497 note   1498 dyd . mysse   1500 ordeynede . souereyne   1504 please   1505
say . a voise.

IIII.

1 Thies . dwellers . leue   2 Are lyknede . dwel   3 els   4 farithe   5 Sume .
summe   6 diuers eke   7 laborers are lykned   8 law   9 flouers   10 to om.   13 thies
14 alle   15 be n. prophetabile   16 waste   17 but if it . the om.   18 vne-to   20 þene .
slepe . sikere   23 ffor þat þei here þou3 . noon om.   dilectacione   24 3et in   25 encresse
28 Suffisith . ful   29 semyth   30 arayde   33 þis be-nethe   33 haue om.   34 of₂
om.   35 list   41 þis wordly   42 Agayne . slulkyde   43 þies   44 wheche   45 wheche
46 the om.   47 the om.   48 wel   51 first and om.   53 vertuse   54 dwelle   55
thene he . hyme   57 wrytyne . myche   58 mynde   60 mankynde   61 blynde
62 & clothe . olde   67 chyrches   68 trost   69 laboure   70 galy   71 welle   73
ry3t   74 lyuynge stabily   76 to hire   79 Emperours   81 Maxencius   82 thyrde
parde   83 diocleciane   84 mans   86 Dwelt   87 sacrifices dide   88 any   92 þies
93 Lefte   99 þer   100 emperours   101 empire . thei om.   or   102 shorows   103
tounes om.   104 sethe   106 And to   111 wheche   112 the om.   117 or . diede
119 in salisbury   121 the om.   þe om.   122 crounede   123 myche solempnite
125 That   126 schrot   128 or   129 Sicile . diede . dyd   130 say   132 lyeth .
abyde   133 Whedire . or elles   134 dwellithe   138 laboureth . and eke   141 or
143 dome   144 reignede . the om.   146 kepe   147 slepe   149 speke   150 ne wiff
ne no   151 whene   153 husbande let   154 set   155 þene bi   156 pepile   160
had hyme in-haunsede   161 couet   162 Romayns   163 lettoures . ded om.   164
brytayne   165 preyd . a kn3te   166 fy3t   168 þer ende   169 strenthe   170 his
171 encresse . lenketh   173 pepile   176 hostis   177 trostith . one . Cete   178
disceyuede   179 housholde . meche . and om.   180 emsampile   181 troste in .
pepile . wil om.   183 of Brytayne   184 is he   185 righfully   186 lyuynge   187
victorous   188 dide . strenghis   191 þe felde wone   195 suche maistres   197
whene . thus om.   exilede   198 fadyrs   201 letters   202 serge . honge   203
distroy   204 Theis letters   205 folowede   207 thynkit   208 dwel   210 leges .
empire   211 witt . faders   213 neþer   214 Suche . þat be   215 pepile   218
hynge   221 I om. sweche   222 meche   226 in his   227 this   229 forfete . shal
230 Sweche   231 note   232 mene ony   233 þene . secte   234 officers   235 any
236 sweche   237 shal . sweche maystres   239 the₂ om.   letters   240 Wheche
242 lest   245 dame wheche   246 messageris are . ferre   247 þies   248 selue
251 wheche . eke om.   252 meny lyued . al om.   253 dide   255 are   258 þene
260 whech   261 poyntes dide   264 wolde   265 dwelte   266 dampnacione   269
sune   273 the om.   277 Vne-to . wycchis   278 thinke   279 whene . are   283
how thei   287 pepile . stately   289 londe   290 gunnys   297 be   298 shulde
300 Castels   301 none   302 thirde   305 the   308 ceremonys   309 mytour .
crosse   312 his s.   315 witene . Iupiter . hye   317 al oþer   318 forsake   321
apparicione   323 bad . pepile . & renew   324 olde ry3tes   325 faders . any
327 who   328 heilth   330 make   333 orribile ly3tenyng*is* eke   334 þis shewede
336 lesse . not om.   337 þies   338 amonge   339 shepperd*is*   340 ful wil   342

Various Readings: MS. Arundel 168. Book IV. 419

sey þies 344 be 345 þat shalle ȝeue 348 councelle 351 þe g. 354 laude 355 þat s. 356 no overl. of om. 358 is 359 is 362 is 363 pepile 364 els. song 366 did he 367 shulde 373 diede 375 bouchers labourede 376 waishyng. carcays done 385 pepile. solempnite 388 suspectione 389 sume are 391 bryȝte sune 397 whene 398 þene. veniaunce 400 arayde 402 y-purtrayde 406 dispyse 408 offeryngis 410 slee & flee. þies 412 mynstrals. shul 414 elde. sey. per 415 Suche 416 ways 420 amonge 421 solempnite 423 þise 424 are. in mychelle 432 sprede 433 worldly. are 434 þat tyme 435 ryȝte inst. of lyke 436 mayde 441 sers 444 elde 445 Riches 447 wit 448 pore 450 þei þat agayns 452 is om. 454 Suffisithe. lyue 455 commerows. any 457 we om. 458 shal 459 begynnythe 461 faders 464 þo drede 465 councelloure 466 one yow v. 467 om. 468 that om. 470 Whene þis mayde. þise 471 how 474 be 475 to$_2$ om. 476 talkynge 478 þis q. 484 conant 485 baptene whene. waishede 488 thorow 490 rudy 493 enprentede. 494 worldly 496 ffro 497 þene 498 for om. 499 þene. trewe 500 þo inst. of loo 506 my housbonde 507 sonere 508 & brede 509 Allace. any 510 boldly. drage 511 Ageyne. trueth 512 suche 513 chyrches 516 Who louethe. worlde. wille heme 518 shall 520 his palays 524 be-tuex 525 al þat 526 pepile 528 the om. porters 531 stand 533 Thies solempnites 534 no om. to no 538 offerynge 540 emperours. þies 541 whene. sey. & so 543 speke 544 seide. pepile 545 Are 546 not 548 vne-to 549 strenghe 552 to þis 553 þene. lyke. 557 y-wisse 558 thies. blisse 559 one 560 grete 566 wolde 567 sitt 568 þe om. 569 þene 573 such deuels þat be 574 sothly sere 576 for 577 his c. 581 þene 582 Thise. mene om. 584 Agayne. agayns 589 are. deuyles 591 wit 592 þise 593 of om. 596 þi hert frome 598 one-kynde 599 Agayne 602 shal. an om. 604 how 605 suche pepile 609 be myxte white 610 he om. begane 611 Astonede. beaute. pleasaunce 614 veniaunce. 615 haue take 617 þene 621 Be. sistire 622 veniaunce 629 gybet 630 the om. 631 mayd 632 Who. þis 644 þene 645 are 646 how. whene 648 pepile. deceyue 652 besyli þo. mynde 653 strenth 654 ensamples. kynde 656 seide 663 now om. 664 womb 665 a mayd 669 such 672 ben om. 674 Suche. o lyue 675 herisies. hath be take 679 Theis conceyteȝ. thei om. 680 þise. semythe 683 now to you 684 littithe. such deliaunce 685 are. trew 688 neuer 687 take. yee 690 such 691 customs 694 no rose 696 wille 698 ferre abouene. any 701 þise stokkis. goode 706 no such 707 wil preue 711 oure 715 lange. dobile 718 verrey trueth 720 þene 721 treuth. any 722 Thow myȝt. sayne 724 þene. sume. gune 725 þe Idols 728 Vne-to. thei om. pleasaunce 732 gune 735 gunne thei crie 736 and om. 737 inst. of & 741 thinkith. gunne 744 haue 749 þene 750 Mayde. gune 752 sune 754 yow 757 veniaunce 760 wille 762 me perfor. elleȝ 763 his om. Rebelleȝ 767 beems 768 ner nere 770 are 771 are 774 be. pusaunce 775 suche 779 Certene 780 Dispise 783 tho om. traytours 785 semyth 787 frome 789 Whene. besily oure helth 791 solempne 792 Loke ȝe 793 shul 795 that t. 796 thise. brestis 798 þene 802 sunne 804 Wherfore 805 punch 807 no-thinge þerby 809 encresse 816 for 819 counceile. ryȝt thus. 822 sentence 824 sonest distroie 827 messageres. letters wilde 829 þat wil. lyueloode 832 are write. ichone 833 messagers. þise. are 835 þise lettours 837 þe lettours 842 þere 843 pepile. on om. 844 kynrode 845 al his 847 are 848 witte 849 counceile 852 þise. folke. pepile. to om. 853 suasiones 854 swheche 857 Meche 859 nygromancye 869 are. lettours writene 870 þat mayde 871 palayse 873 pleasaunte 877 alle. of om. 878 þene any 883 of om. shul 887 suche 890 þise 891 ryght om. 895 vp om. 896 þene 897 lorde aboue 898 forsake 904 þi. suche 905 pronounsede 909 dispise. stand o row. 910 are 913 my 916 mynes om. 918 are 919 such. our. land 921 hande 922 trumpis. before. stande 925 forto 928 þene 932 malicolye 935 take 937 he kepe. so so she. goo om. 938 he dey 943 theme. are 945 telle yow 950 vnderstande 951 sese. begunne 952 gunne 955 massageres. þe haue 956 thies 958 & þus 960 philosophirs are. coun-

E E 2

420 *Various Readings: MS. Arundel* 168. *Book IV.*

ceile 961 witte. for heme hath 962 any 964 thise maistirs 965 phelosophie 967 were 969 & alle 970 none heme 971 groundis 973 seith. entrynge 974 Maisters 976 Reneyhithe. suche. vse 977 falle 978 þe (ye ?) 979 is into þis e. 981 truethe 982 be 983 thinkith reuthe 985 berne 987 the om. 989 are. cunnynge 991 þat t. 992 þat same 993 leuyde 996 suche. cumpanye 999 þise 1002 theme bi autorite 1003 resone 1005 þat wheel 1006 I om. 1011 her om. 1012 special. suche 1017 counceile 1018 availede note 1020 wil. mayde. proporcionis 1022 Stately 1027 Agayne 1032 aune sistere 1034 whedere. stille om. 1035 holde 1039 lesse 1044 sire. lekithe 1045 alle worldly 1046 alle worldely 1050 be. trew 1054 suche 1055 þus wille 1059 os 1061 Thinke. kynrede 1062 neuer none. theme. suche 1068 wiche 1070 suche 1072 he hire þus 1073 in om. 1075 wheithere o 1078 hat om. 1080 sikerly 1082 seide 1085 stande 1086 hangede 1090 nedis muste 1091 enmyse 1092 þene speke 1099 a om. 1101 meche 1102 of wheche. sweche 1103 nouʒt 1107 whiche 1111 enmys 1112 trew 1113 oribile 1114 tungis 1118 wrechis 1120 nede 1122 sere 1124 belyue 1128 philosophirs are. counceile 1129 sirs 1130 cunynge 1131 maisters 1133 the om. are haylede 1135 sey 1136 many mene 1138 yit. that om. 1140 Suche. rouse. þo 1145 a-taste 1146 waste 1151 she seide lorde 1152 syttis 1153 seconde 1154 Dyede 1155 fynde 1158 þise 1162 worldly 1163 graunte, to om. apostyls 1164 Whene. stande. & kynge 1167 shuldis 1169 the om. 1171 strenghe 1172 resones shrape 1173 chirches 1174 maners 1177 cunnynge 1178 troste 1179 commes 1180 noʒte. loste 1181 makiste. froste 1182 þowe 1184 pleasaunce 1185 estere. please 1186 solempne 1191 Whene. that om. 1192 fro 1193 mervelouse 1195 prisone 1197 corners 1202 sayde 1204 fro heuene om. I ame come now 1208 þise 1209 clerly 1212 theme 1213 shal om. theme. autorite 1214 lede 1217 dye 1218 prophesye 1219 determynde 1220 Thies. shal now despute 1222 grete troste 1223 þe om. 1227 Shal. meche 1229 meche. you om. 1232 shal. þise 1233 trew 1234 spirith 1238 weiʒte 1239 Whedire. be. lyʒt 1243 spouse 1244 suche 1247 confortede 1248 prisone. suche 1256 cunnynge 1261 stande 1266 she om. is best 1268 þise 1269 Maistirs. þis e. 1273 glewide 1274 shaftis. yow 1275 Thene 1276 strange chalenge. in 1277 þise. in om. 1280 ye 1284 shalle 1286 þene 1287 trew 1288 thies 1292 I-now 1293 dameselle. tow 1297 garede. to om. v. 1300 overl. and on the margin. wolde 1305 emperours 1306 mayde. write. eghtene 1309 know we 1310 thanne om. 1311 shal. puruey 1312 answere 1313 conveye 1316 þene 1319 Thene speke 1320 the om. 1321 pronounce. leeste 1324 auctours 1326 be 1330 yow 1333 erely 1339 alle om. 1340 meche trewere 1345 Beholde. Maistirs. þise mens 1348 hardely 1351 sweche 1352 wheche euer shal 1354 is gode 1356 fyere. or 1359 borne 1360 one-to. thirty 1361 þene 1362 hynge 1365 sundrie 1368 ite inst. of is 1375 reignede erthlye 1378 whene 1379 Wype ʒe þe. hillide 1380 whene 1381 shal. ful om. 1382 my om. 1383 haue ; me om. þer 1384 oute bi 1389 sauacione 1391 science make. soo om. 1392 trueth 1395 maters 1398 be 1407 speke. þene 1408 citeceynes 1410 shalle. to om. 1411 endewid 1412 wysdome 1413 suffre þise 1414 such 1417 here he seide 1418 noʒt. vnderstande 1420 þise 1422 say. be. vnkynde 1423 benefitis 1424 ʒynkith. kynde 1425 for om. 1426 colours 1427 deuels 1429 here offence 1431 Thise lewede folke. liste 1432 resones 1435 suche prechours 1436 hidere 1441 y-now 1442 conuicte 1449 lewide. note worth 1451 say. lyfe agayne 1453 harde Iewis sayne 1454 stale. rayne 1457 þise 1458 She om. 1460 my 1461 is he per. any pere 1462 or 1464 his fadire is 1465 þene 1466 ferdere procede now 1467 before 1468 eterne 1473 no om. 1474 newly 1477 dide 1480 are 1481 gruntyne whene þei eilith 1483 trueth. flede 1485 þise resones 1488 has done. sow 1489 sikire. whene 1490 wolde 1491 shal 1492 þo stode 1493 mayde. suche 1495 vnderstande 1496 make 1498 note. no 1499 be 1501 Like. þis 1504 are thise y. 1513 New chapter. mayde 1514 þise. wheche þe worthieste 1515 stande. arow 1516 perseyue. dignite 1517 þene. 1518

Various Readings: MS. Arundel 168. Book IV.

lynede 1520 þat same 1521 a om. 1524 owene childerne 1526 Banischide.
harborow 1527 sistire 1529 þise are 1530 stande 1531 Whene. bilide.
brithil bande 1532 maydons 1533 violent 1534 Wulcane. cokkolde 1535
suche 1536 are. theme are 1537 vnelene 1538 Thise. vylonyes. fro heme
shoue 1539 whechcraft 1540 suche 1541 whene. dronke 1542 þene wolde.
Iangile 1543 deuine 1544 tresorye 1546 Thies. þat om. 1549 ȝe om. 1550
commythe 1552 y-rounge 1553 be wisse 1560 þis. whene 1561 make relees
1570 self 1571 þise 1579 amonge 1585 þene 1586 suche thyngis 1587 My
nowne 1593 I wheche. suche v. 1594 om. 1598 Gladede 1601 bere hire
nowe. koyo 1604 tho om. þe 1606 figur. colour. wone 1607 ley 1608
Are 1609 se theme 1610 sune 1611 the be 1612 are. graue 1613 kene
1614 are. 1616 shadow 1619 shul euer stande 1621 be for to be 1623 be
1625 þene are 1628 are. nethere. the om. 1632 philosophirs 1634 are 1635
harde. suche 1639 a womane suche 1641 entendaunce 1642 worlde. stande
1645 lestene 1648 be 1650 stodyinge 1651 be 1656 is he. þis wyndo. rayne
1657 suche. þene inst. of thei. I sayne 1661 theme 1664 are. rediare 1671
sei 1672 one p. 1673 parfiȝtly 1674 no syche 1675 counseile 1677 one.
merveile 1678 mans 1684 he om. 1685 hym blynde 1690 ate þat lorde
1693 dyede 1696 ffor þat theme. same om. 1700 conuercione 1701 mer-
ueilithe. his 1704 yite 1706 Be 1707 be. one p. 1708 suche 1715 be bot
bare. 1716 tho om. 1720 solempne 1721 þis w. 1723 laȝer 1724 ley fourty
1726 do 1728 he 1731 vrouȝte. þise mervailes 1732 Meche 1735 truethe
1736 ful om. reuthe 1737 his 1739 mete 1740 þenne 1742 thies 1743
preue 1747 cane 1749 þise 1751 auctours 1752 meruosly 1754 leke 1755
laide 1756 shal 1757 þise autrix 1761 thies 1762 is. blessede 1763 hynge
1764 come 1770 saye 1771 waye 1772 suche 1775 wol 1776 Wyth-outene.
no om. 1777 suche. ye shulde 1778 resones 1779 constryne 1781 leue
1782 loffe 1783 houe 1784 this om. 1786 ful goode 1788 as om. 1790
matere now e. 1794 were inst. of bere 1795 are. þus om. þise 1799 whame
1801 Whene 1802 any 1803 Suche 1804 this thyng 1805 are 1806 walke
1811 cunnynge 1815 þise 1816 shal. now om. þene 1818 þat 1820 meche
thingis 1822 Iche 1829 heme 1831 freilere. stabely 1833 holde 1836
resones 1837 þat be 1838 pepile 1840 þingis. shuld 1841 be-gynne 1842
he is 1848 thus om. theme 1854 passith 1855 thenkithe. stande 1860 for
þis 1871 marrithe 1872 rekynynge 1873 any 1874 birthe. liethe 1875
borne. octouyane 1876 betheleme. lewede 1877 note fully ȝet. hundreth
1878 was of his modire 1879 suche 1880 thingis 1882 thowsandis 1883 er
þat. lyffe 1886 pepile. fyere 1890 Sweche 1892 sire 1893 oo om. 1896
countithe 1897 not om. wheche þat 1899 ago 1902 vnedo 1903 merveile
1905 begynnynge. shal 1909 of 1910 kynde 1911 kynde. his om. 1913
not om. suche disease 1914 þise. couplynge 1915 faders. please 1917 manhode 1918 manhode. not om. 1920 yit inst. of þat 1922 mayde v. 1923 on
the margin 1924 betheleme 1926 Whene 1927 stonyde. marryde. mynde
1929 kynde 1933 motyffe 1935 left. lyffe 1939 þene 1940 not om. rialle
1941 maistirde. soo om. 1942 noȝte sende (a om.) 1944 Suffire suche 1945
suffirde 1946 note 1947 selfe 1948 þene. take 1951 thorne 1952 enmys
1953 thinkith 1955 noyede 1956 lerede 1958 fyȝte 1959 suche kynde 1961
be. mankynde 1964 parfyȝt 1966 blesside. or 1968 money. dyede. a om.
1971 fyȝte 1972 þe tre. bore—1973 Ioye om. 1974 þat. blessede 1975 a
om. 1979 he om. 1980 lady om. v. 1986 om. 1987 note verely ȝit 1991
þise. no 1993 witnesse 1997 sune 1999 trew 2001 hundrethe 2002
endewede 2005 reignande 2006 suche 2007 communicacione 2008 be 2009
resones 2012 be assailede 2016 Suche sundrie 2023 thundire 2024 is he.
reignynge. aboue 2025 yite 2029 folowith 2033 lere inst. of sir 2034 & of
2036 chose 2037 a 2038 reigneth. any 2040 chosyne. commyth. bi 2042
cache 2049 are 2052 þat gode 2058 al 2059 maistire. þene 2062 maistres
2065 drunke. a. cupe 2066 secrees. þene 2069 wil 2070 enterely 2072 any
2074 knowlege 2080 comoursly 2081 consente 2084 ȝite. vttire 2087 pepile.

422   Various Readings: MS. Arundel 168.   Book V.

incressede   2088 lede   2089 are   2090 loy . bede   2091 flede   2095 whate is þene   2096 ych . preuyly . dide þei   2097 þise   2098 dispise   2100 þene þer 2101 looketh om.   2104 any . shul   2105 wisere . sawe   2106 ʒit   2109 meche thynge   2112 resones   2114 lye   2116 maters   2119 maistire . þe lande   2124 Distroye   2126 we seene   2127 wilde . þeme   2129 uictoure . þene   2130 solemply   2133 be   2134 ʒite . my þees   2135 þis m. þus   2138 it om.   2141 wunne   2142 victour þo   2145 before haue be   2146 thinkithe   2147 suche 2148 I inst. of it   2149 pursew   2152 thinkithe   2154 thies   2156 Wolde 2161 mans   2164 in his   2169 mayde   2170 Wyth-oute any   2171 mankynde 2173 myche   2174 Bute of . be   2177 sitithe þus   2178 whene þat   2179 leke . sune   2180 Like . lykene . maydens   2181 sune   2182 thorow   2184 downe came   2187 carnacione   2188 neuer   2189 be   2191 fonde . vntrew   2193 Repliynge   2194 suche   2196 Suche . douʒtes   2197 suche thingis   2199 auctours   2200 speke . pringnantly   2204 þus   2206 o   2211 sune   2214 sune 2215 be . one   2216 iche   2217 þene are   2218 one   2219 wrihith   2225 þene 2232 truethe   2233 dide . ruethe   2235 meche   2240 here   2241 sey . fadirs 2242 wheche . gouerne om.   2251 alle mankynde   2255 sonde . preuydence 2261 of om.   2262 sey   2266 alle þe hoste . philistees   2267 on om.   2268 a om.   2273 ordeynde   2278 Eentereferede   2279 longe   2281 plede . hyme   2285 chapitere . thinkis   2289 þise   2290 special   2292 as amasede   2293 speke o 2294 hoost   2295 make . mayde   2296 are   2297 spoke . saluacione   2301 any 2303 coude note . resones   2305 go   2307 trewere   2308 note   2309 blesse 2310 his sone is   2311 beleue   2312 beleue . dyede   2315 erthly . fyndes   2316 note   2318 The . alle þo . þat om.   2319 had om. lyue   2320 kepe   2321 perlyous   2325 the om.   2326 Praynge   2327 hem om.   2328 shul it þus   2329 þise   2330 Crying e   2332 forgife   2333 Deme . lorde note   2334 lorde petous 2335 we om.   2336 oure om.   2340 wil we   2343 þat heuene-b.   2344 Were . loke . þat face   2345 mene . be.

V.

5 fauourede   7 thirde & eke . ferthe   10 me   15 like . deuysede   17 Thies 18 cleue   19 rede flowers kepte   20 Or   21 þene   23 wiffe   24 sharpe   25 Wheche   31 yite   32 þies . clyue   33 are   34 stante . wyth-oute dage   35 are . wone . grow   36 Thise. wel   37 one h.   38 & date   40 lyuede   46 oppiniones . note   48 thride   52 alle   55 are   56 Reignynge   60 whelis   61 pepile toke þo 62 translate . latene   63 the om. of₂ om.   64 þise   65 alle þat . crudelite   66 emperours   67 speke   68 alle   69 disputous   71 a om.   72 a om. make   73 counceille   74 worldly   77 note . what þat þe pepile   78 sey   80 þat same   81 alle om.   83 Whene . hiper . alle   84 cunnynge . mekil   86 cunnynge   87 Thinke   88 note . þene   92 stande   93 be   94 haue   96 fare   99 þeme   106 yow . pykyde . compeny   109 þe om.   110 Theologe   111 an om.   113 or 117 velonye   118 wage   119 we om. worldis   124 hange   125 spech   131 my bowels . gane   133 alle   135 refuesse   136 renounce . the om.   137 know   138 here rowe pawe   142 mankynde   146 shal yow   152 thise   153 dye   155 and om.   157 Clerkis   158 more in   162 fyere . hastely   164 saturne   165 þise 166 ffrye heme . be om.   169 rosyne   172 dey   173 very om.   174 Iewesse thate ite be do   175 do . shal   176 theme   177 theme   180 gyf . hem om. suche . vylence   181 be   182 theme schape   184 one ashes   185 to om.   186 theme   187 more om.   189 shal   191 wrestil note   194 þis   195 þeme . at om. 198 self . coumforthe   199 tiraunde . any   201 to þat   202 are riʒte gaderede 203 a   206 merour   215 Alle   216 waishithe   217 waishide   222 refewsede 223 rewe   224 leuede . on-trew   228 for om. lye   230 are . þeme   232 his om. 233 sitte   235 he   236 seste   237 are   238 kende   240 wayshede   243 please 247 al þis   248 eche   250 dispence   252 be   254 yow   256 daie   257 waish-ynge   258 shal . aungels shal   262 alle   263 suffire   264 harde ay y. c.   265 demp   267 fyere . purgyne mans   269 are baptiʒede   270 funte   271 are   272 þat dey   273 are   275 deyene   277 þe knyʒtis   279 noʒte   280 now om.   282

Various Readings: MS. Arundel 168. *Book V.* 423

officers 284 theme . as₁ om. 285 pavide 289 fyere . are 290 gune . amonge 291 feche 292 fewelers shulde 293 throw þem 294 are 295 alle 296 suche 297 theme 298 theme . þat om. 300 go 302 ande f. . theme 306 fyere 307 þise 308 þeme before . þeme 309 sey 312 of om. 313 meruelous for to 314 myrthe 316 diede þise 318 þe laie 319 body 321 þis sey the pepile . meruelede 324 folke 326 solempne 327 þo 331 mayde 334 þene shulde þei 335 mayde 337 selfe 340 fekylnesse 342 lost . ryʒtes . elders 347 & om. wite 348 Beaute 351 shalle 354 temporal 355 myrour . parfith 359 þeme 360 ʒe om. are 363 Deceyuours . pepile v. 365 om. 366 smyte . take 367 þem 370 please theme . for inst. of soo . be 371 & om. be 375 al . shal 376 Obeynge 379 leue 381 leue 383 suche thynge whiche 386 any 387 goode 388 pleasaunce 391 Whome 393 Be-tuex 398 reame 399 shal 401 solempne . Emprise 402 like 405 Whene . shal 414 for-ʒeue 415 be 416 Suche 419 pleasaunce 430 suche 431 chaungeoures 432 so om. myche 434 Suche 438 a 442 rych 445 to om. 446 beaute . represente 447 be . pleassaunce 448 theme . worldly 449 know or 452 theme 453 wite 455 Or 456 yene 457 it shal 458 suche . cane om. 463 tunge 469 your₂ om. 471 Stande like . þat flye ab. 474 vnclene 475 ymage 476 suche a guerdone 477 shul defile 478 one-to 481 thinkithe 482 troste . fonnyde 483 feynynge & fykyl 485 shal 487 childrene 491 deuyls . stant 494 loue₁ 498 be . ease 499 such . profyʒt 500 thinketh . please 502 dilectabile . colours 503 encresse 504 sekenesse . relesse 505 it om. 507 Ne 509 suche 511 thyng om. þene 512 promesse 514 before 516 parfyʒte 520 It wil 521 Ite shal note 524 is om. alle 525 is₂ om. 527 on om. 528 The more benyngly 530 shal 531 ye 532 lyfe 539 nede 540 noʒte 542 at my promysses . at om. 544 fyere 545 sonere 547 shal 548 pepile 549 are 550 bi þer 551 passe . suche 552 punchide 553 be 554 welcum 556 smyte 558 myscheuys 560 lyuede 561 Pouerte 562 had om. 565 blasphemoures. 566 Gevynge 567 any 571 or 574 haue we 575 offerde 576 hoste 577 offire 578 & to 582 yow shal 591 encresithe 594 shal 596 menye 597 Shal 599 fynde 600 þus shal 605 gete 608 mayde . strepe here 609 hir om. 612 speke 613 galale . deuyne 617 tormentours 619 yrne . may 620 bete 621 come 622 bete 623 conforth 624 Thise 627 purgede 628 puruyaunce 632 yow sent . me om. 638 amonge 639 þe om. beters 640 mayde 641 herisye 643 shal 644 Or 647 suffre 648 wheþer 649 shameful dogide 651 thi om. 652 Be-thynke . wille 653 oute inst. of now 654 pepile . is om. 655 kepe 656 dye . worldly 657 ffolow 658 Where þat 660 oribile 661 shal 662 shal . bounde 663 shal 664 suche 665 yow . hy 666 shal 668 Lyinge . shal 669 shal . hastely 670 shal þou inst. of fulfille . malicolie 672 a om. 673 anone 674 mayde . hir lede 675 put 677 this om. 678 þise 679 slate 682 mout 683 Whene 684 þat om. 685 straitly . wyth-oute 690 rydyne . menye 695 forgotene 696 þise 697 leue . lyke 699 aungels 700 of om. 702 disease 703 suche 709 aungels . kepte 712 sarris 713 merveilede 714 note . on om. 715 courte 716 Sprenge 719 Iaylers 720 dongione 721 þis w. goth aboute þe courte s. 723 & of 724 mayde . any 728 And om. was om. 730 lande 732 shal 734 þise . he om. 736 pite 737 þise v. 740 on the margin. a stody 742 & to . preuely 743 Thise . folke . no wronge 744 bye 746 Now & now 747 of om. 748 Glotons . dronkelew 749 pleassithe 751 nouʒte 753 sey 754 mykyl 756 my . gynnyth 759 selfe 761 hade hyme 762 alle 765 folke 768 she saide porphirie . be 769 he 771 trobile . the om. 773 or 774 maner 775 lyfes 776 tho om. 779 gaylers . y-now 781 vow 784 my 787 suche . shal 790 shal 791 be 792 thinkithe . sufferith 793 horibely bete 794 no 795 oft-tyme . one þis 797 whene 801 gyfe 803 you om. 804 Comythe 807 slepe . prisone 809 þei come þer þei too 810 prisone . se 811 doun om. wyth-oute 812 to om. be om. 813 lyʒtynynge 814 sey 817 þe lyʒt 818 felt . suche 820 suche 822 borne 824 Be 825 chose 829 aungels sey 833 beaute . softly 837 a 839 Thies 840 delyʒte 842 on om. 845 thithere 849 note 852 sistere 853 Shal 854 be

424 Various Readings: MS. Arundel 168. Book V.

855 shal. a om. euerlestyng   858 theme   859 þise   860 shal. writyne. lyue
861 sers   863 Thise. þe booke   864 þer synnes. wyte.   865 theme   867 that
om.   receyue   868 elders. one-to oþer   869 presious. sitte   871 yow   872
precious   875 suche   878 Shal   880 þise folke. take   883 prisone   884 suche.
herde   886 suche   887 fulle   888 Wyth-oute. þise   891 Abacuche   893 prisone
. þus fede   894 diuers   895 brout   896 gostely or bodely. it om.   898 fadirs
899 þene   902 norchide. erthe   905 so om.   906 þe om.   909 erdly   910 but
om.   911 wille   914 be   916 thise   918 sey   920 aungels   921 suche   925
alle. dissease   927 please   928 worldly   929 Thinke. leue   931 a. shal   932
or. parte   933 pepile shal   934 a housbonde. wydow   935 ffor. maumentrie.
shal ye returne   936 theme. soiorne   939 lokithe   940 Returnethe   942 liste
944 be he   945 comende   946 Whene his. are   950 be   953 Alle   954 pepile
955 are. haue. dispyte   957 thinke   961 þat wheche   963 to om.   stirt   964
smarte   966 for hire   967 pynede   968 wyth qwyte   972 traytures. shal dye iche
one   974 fede hire   978 shal   979 forfendede   980 bynde. yrne   981 mayde.
escuse   982 suche   984 alle   986 shulde. punche   988 thise   992 messagers   993
Alle. hyme   994 sere   995 þise   996 nouʒte   997 angelles   998 No   1001 nouʒte
1002 thise   1004 suche   v. 1005 om.   1009 to þe kinge   1010 seruyne   1012
are. alle   1013 certene wicchis   1016 are traytours   1019 yife. wycherafte
1020 be. to om.   a kepte   1021 maisters lerde   1026 sewirly   1027 note-wyth-
stande   1028 mute nede   1029 pepile. stante   1031 sueche   1033 þene   1036
yrne. rente   1040 Thene   1042 the om.   1043 encresse. dye one a   1048
gruche   1052 are   1053 whene   1055 posibile   1057 þene   1062 pleasaunt.
dilectabile   1063 kyine. caluerync. alle   1065 lefully   1068 veniabile   1072
shal   1073 shal   1074 shal   1075 þi dedis. are   1079 fle   1081 be. þene.
solemply   1084 adawe   1086 alle   1087 wil   1089 þies   1090 Thise   1093 wol
1095 prophetysse   1101 fyʒte   1102 one-to   1103 pusaunce   1104 ytai'e.
ynglonde   1108 alle   1111 markede   1112 sundre   1113 Alle. trew   1114
Bot. þis wordis   1115 pepile   1117 falle   1118 Suche   1119 þis   1121 wheche
1123 goodly lyuers. shal   1127 thynkis   1130 a om.   1133 hir₂ om.   yrne
1135 bet   1139 sey   1141 lyfe. pepile   1142 lede. to   1143 pepile. gane   1147
alle   1148 aske. are   1149 dispise   1153 alle. beaute   1156 nouʒt   1157 it
om. þene. uelensly   1162 counsellede   1164 lese   1165 lese   1166 Alle   1167
thynke   1168 lede   1169 special   1170 pepile   1172 Alle   1175 alle   1176
councel   1179 be   1181 þise. no   1183 counceel   1185 thinge   1188 leue
1193 dye   1194 of ryʒt   1196 þene   1197 fykyl   1201 be   1202 Such   1204
senew. weynes   1206 alle   1208 lofe   1212 þene   1218 pepile   1221 dye   1225
prisone   1227 sey   1229 seris   1231 dye   1232 rysynge   1233 theme. herde
1237 wyth-draw   1238 priuyly   1241 mayre. pepile   1243 mekyl   1244
Venemhous. any   1245 Dispitous veniabile   1251 O   1252 standiste   1253
lystyne. councel   1257 orrybile   1259 this om. thynge þat (þat overl.)   1265
controllere   1268 bysy   1269 whelis   1270 suche   1272 shal   1275 Shal
1276 y-fastenede. alle   1279 come   1280 alle   1281 know   1282 shal   1283
whele   1284 suche. shal   1285 Iche. theme   1286 shal   1287 shal   1288 a
1289 þies   1290 be   1291 be   1292 lyuynge. sey such whels   1293 please
1294 shal   1295 ʒendur   1297 Thise whelis shul. anone   1298 gane   1299 are
calde   1300 smythes   1302 whels must   1303 it om. thride   1304 whels are
1307 whels   1308 seithe   1309 grugith   1310 shal ye   1312 meyre   1313 hath
stodyethe. alle. mende   1321 yne   1322 suche   1323 bothe om. sunne   1326
hydist   1327 crye   1330 orribile   1333 þi   1335 easy. suche   1336 pepile.
meruelous   1339 stande   1340 thynke. my   1341 tunges   1345 she om.
1346 & om.   1352 þat om.   1355 a horibile   1357 or eyʒte   1358 whels. fley
1359 sprynge   1360 Sum mane hath. or   1361 mene om.   are   1363 take om.
1365 veniaunce   1368 his   1375 theme   1376 fere   1379 fere   1380 whels.
alle om.   1385 heraudes nombire   1386 his   1389 for om.   1391 Meche folke
1393 Lyfte   1394 alle   1395 are   1396 are. gunne. frunttis   1397 folke.
hathe   1398 Summe mene. veniaunce   1399 o   1400 suche   1401 mesire
1402 and falleth om. shulde now   1405 aune   1406 repungynge   1409 thies.

Various Readings: MS. Arundel 168. Book V. 425

smythis 1410 makith 1411 is it . þe 1414 thynkis . wondire 1415 alle 1419 before 1420 whate may falle 1422 the om. 1425 wrestilliste 1428 shal 1430 fyʒtiste . þou shal 1433 þi . mans 1437 dide 1438 o 1439 selue 1440 comounnys 1441 lye 1442 hyme þane 1443 o . suche 1444 I counseyl om. 1448 gyfe (for- om.) 1452 ye spoke 1453 on om. þis 1454 or þat 1455 oribile 1456 kynrode 1457 þat hye maieste of þe 1458 þat . gracyous om. þe kynge 1459 þis fondnes 1460 an om. 1462 riʒte welle 1463 broke one 1464 wichcrafte 1466 youre . trechorie. 1467 one þe rene 1468 noʒt 1470 illucione 1472 ministirs 1473 yrne wyere 1474 shal . right om. 1475 I . þei shal do it 1476 L. sorow . and woo om. þat his . wyf om. 1479 traitours 1480 haue . haue om. deserue 1482 it om. ly . ite shalle 1483 it om. dispite 1484 his mene 1485 oribile 1486 from 1488 Alle . and₂ om. alle blody 1490 euene inst. of ryght 1491 pilere 1495 be . sufficiaunte 1501 þis holy lyfe to turne agayne to synne 1502 or 1503 þe c. of þis 1504 alle . lyʒte 1507 maydene 1507 alle 1509 þe loue perfore of oure kynge 1511 she 1513 disease 1514 leste 1515 please 1517 se 1519 þat om. before 1521 he be 1522 amende al thynge 1523 in om. 1526 be . neste 1531 bostous 1533 hire tetis now 1534 ere . & aftur 1535 a om. smyʒt 1536 O. l. g. strenghide hire to susteyne 1537 peynes 1538 is she . soule is to þat l. 1541 wensdaie 1543 vnberyed om. 1544 Lyinge per ful white & eke ful rede 1545 wynde ite 1547 And om. meche . folk om. 1550 most om. 1552 byriynge . to om. 1553 callede . one-to 1554 dyrk 1555 Katerine 1558 oyntmente 1559 this . he om. 1561 on om. 1562 after om. is per 1563 biriede 1564 falle . suche 1565 berie þis same body 1566 of . folke 1567 were . bi . officers 1568 ful boldly 1570 Sithe . shulde 1571 thus om. 1572 þyne owne wyfis 1573 hast 1574 Thise 1575 doo om. 1576 thyne i. 1577 & þi i. 1578 shul om. 1580 þat om. Biriede . me thouʒte it no tresone 1581 But . weel om. acordande one-to 1582 þe 1583 seyn suche 1584 ʒet to . robbours . are 1585 haue 1587 neybours 1589 kynde . and om. 1590 lerde 1592 write . autours 1593 ne eke 1594 man-kynde . defoule 1596 note þise 1597 Thise . are 1598 maxience hert 1604 lyue 1606 gyue 1607 take 1609 stikede . cradylle. 1610 ffor om. alle my 1612 A om. P. here 1613 good om. gentel om. þus is he lost 1614 whichcraft . gynnythe . to om. 1615 reste in here 1616 alle 1617 suche 1618 deceyuede . now om. 1620 My . ite waxite . as₁ om. as þe lede 1622 a₂ om. 1623 alle 1625 haue do 1626 but 1627 shal 1628 els 1629 þis 1631 meche 1633 shal note 1635 hyme þus sone 1636 þe olde trew 1637 fadirs kepte oute of 1639 this om. 1640 the om. his courte . & be one 1641 examede 1642 thouʒt þis m. 1644 Beholdethe. 1645 sodenly . y-falle . meserie 1646 not om. 1647 hyme now 1648 be ye. 1649 Wheche þat 1650 suche renagatis 1652 seide thei 1653 know 1656 we om. or cane 1657 hym om. We wil . serue . ande bane 1658 ande smyte . þou om. 1659 shal 1661 departe 1662 truest 1663 to fro 1664 are appliede . þene shal 1665 are . thus om. 1666 þe stone 1669 suche renagatis 1671 sunne 1672 are . to 1674 comfort 1675 presede where 1676 Suche 1678 fle . pepile . thus om. sodenly 1680 wheche þat 1682 menbris 1683 vnderstande 1684 or 1687 go 1688 Wherfore euene after 1689 bounde & forthe eke 1690 heritikis . fiere 1692 hundrede 1694 per 1695 we left . doges 1697 autores 1699 hire 1707 of inst. of and 1708 ffer . made 1710 hire modire 1712 þe knottis þat ye 1713 & om. 1714 Mayde . lyue 1715 þi 1716 counselle 1717 magik . & om. wepe sore 1718 þou were 1719 suche 1720 þyne eyne . be om. 1722 saye . the om. 1724 on om. to þe 1725 folowe 1726 on om. councell 1728 þi . alle 1729 forgyffe . þi 1730 alle þo 1731 the om. 1732 falle 1734 are 1735 shal 1736 on þis m. y wil deuyse 1737 smyte þyne heede of 1738 none faile 1739 warante. 1740 sewire . ilk 1743 þyne . councelle . to om. 1744 þene . meke 1746 hange 1747 þis daie . be 1748 worldis 1749 ffor om. To þe a q. & alle 1750 one om. 1751 wene þe falle is 1752 is 1753 Summe mene wene . dye 1754 ful s. 1755 deceyueabile 1756 lese 1758 hethe 1759 lawghynge 1760 haboundithe 1761 hate 1762 the om. 1763 theder om. 1764 dye 1766 haue 1767 dyspise . þi o. 1770

426 *Various Readings: MS. Arundel 20. Book I.*

couet 1771 aungels 1772 shulde astounede 1773 misteris 1775 þat stande 1777 spente 1779 waishide 1785 fere 1786 thise . ʒeue 1788 is . draw 1789 folow . prese 1792 sweche 1793 modirs . maydens 1794 my 1797 myschyff 1801 brynnynge fiere 1803 meche thyngis 1804 swere . be 1805 wyth-oute 1806 And om. 1808 dye 1809 smyte 1810 or 1811 sey 1815 eyne & handis 1819 þat trostyne 1822 to þi college amonge . maydens 1823 þe b. 1824 with 1825 enmy 1828 remenberaunce 1838 at eue 1843 shal 1844 mute 1845 þi 1846 bother 1849 þi 1850 aungels 1851 þi maydens 1853 þi 1855 Amonge þi . þat 1857 sodenly 1858 herde 1860 & om. mayde 1862 as beste 1869 before 1870 Maydens are 1871 Aungels are . þi s. eke to 1879 relees . alle 1882 forgyue 1887 þi 1889 stande 1890 forgyfe 1893 holly alle 1895 wode & rage 1902 þene suche 1904 Suche 1905 watirde alle 1906 aboute 1909 hathe 1913 aungels 1914 like . wyngis 1915 come . autoris 1916 toke 1920 the om. 1921 & of this v. 1923 on the margin. Poule . suche 1927 þe mounte 1928 hastly 1930 for om. 1931 be 1933 sey 1935 if þat 1936 autor 1937 pusaunce 1938 labourede . it om. þise 1939 byne . hane 1944 weche 1945 day om. 1947 be 1948 are . onknowe 1949 knowlege 1952 holede 1954 þat . wheder 1955 swete . þat same holy be lycoure 1956 sey þei p. be 1957 Thus . be 1959 suche lycours 1961 before 1962 mans 1963 hire . make forfiture 1964 or fyue 1967 autorite 1968 nouʒt 1970 eke om. 1971 ymagyne . a om. 1974 the om. shal 1977 solempe 1978 to wheche
Col.: Explicit vita sancte Katerine facta per Doct. Capgrave

2. FROM MS. ARUNDEL 20, fol. 1.

I.

Prologus (v. 1—252) om.
1us liber 1 grece 2 surry . both lorde 3 clarkis . olde storece 5 gouernde 6 calde . to inst. of þoo 7 luffyd . ful om. 8 lambe . lyone 9 nootyde . ʒow lyst 10 be-knowne 11 dyd . omage 12 bachalere 13 theyr . sought 14 þei nedyd ought 15 yles longyd . þoo om. vnto (so always) . londe 16 to hys 17 he had . honde 18 havens 19 weldyd þem . ryʒt . lyste 20 marchandis . maryners 21 omagers 22 pece . reynyd . ʒerys 23 feyr 24 belovyd . omagerys 25 nobile . seyd 26 felde . pessabulle 28 pennes 29 wolde hym 30 dyd . xulde yt 31 began vengance 32 Prayer 34 bet . ryʒt 35 lawys 37 meyd 38 Stabulle . euermore. I- om. 39 man₂ om. 40 þem 41 thyngis . þer wrouʒte 42 pytus . spryte 43 Pece 44 clynyd 45 on- om. & to 46 als mete . axe vnto 47 lordis . ther inst. of þoo 48 wysse 49 hatyd he hardely, harlotry & vysse 50 pete vnto . thouʒt 51 such . xulde hethyne 52 wysse 53 Ouʒt . hard thorne brymbulle tre 54 growys . rosse . ʒe mey 55 Iues 57 Two . othur 58 large & grete a. þe tothyr alle 59 fothur 60 & walle 61 þe tothyr . bokis 62 or 63 whych . kyngis there crownyd 64 hyʒt Amelech . stande 65 þe tothyr . Alexander . Egyp 66 same om. land 67 & eke of 68 frewte . I-wysse 70 surry . douʒt. 71 key 72 alle þe kyngdome . trone 73 surrey . must cum . wey 74 mey . shypp 75 els 76 hayvene . hooge . ful₂ om. 77 castels 78 Oppun to . wolde cum 79 theyr fredomes . feyr 80 ouʒt . heythnes . crystyndum 81 repeyr 82 Vndyr . meyr 83 xulde . ffeylle 84 wyth mete men & vyteylle 85 Alexander 86 schyp s. cyte 87 owne lordshyp 88 of . cuntresse 89 in toune felde or one see 90 whych 91 done 92 othyr 93 egyp . standis 94 & large . grete fame 95 must 96 Vnto . way & wayre 98 must 100 sent 101 By seynt p. sent 102 þem 103 so þer þei alle yt wyste 104 ffor . theyr 105 theme 107 whyche 108 xalle 110 þer 111 Munkis . suche 113 þeis 114 Alle . martyrs and fulle 115 meydyns wydous 116 numbyr 117 medow . shourys 118 Than numbyr theme I trow not he mey 119 assey

Various Readings: MS. Arundel 20. Book I. 427

120 Theys vessels . ma*r*tyrs 121 fyer . yern*e* . sleyn & brent (I - om.) 122 fournesse 123 scapyd 124 xulde . Intent 125 devyne 126 longys 129 after 132 an holy 133 callyd 135 large & ry3t fulle . pep*i*le 137 ga*n* . than om. 138 xulde 140 nou3t els 141 wones 142 callyd theyr . no nothyr 143 alexander 144 wordy suche 146 ne*þ*e*r* louys nor 147 do 3yt . my3t 149 evyn*e* . þis kyng*is* deys 150 lyvys here in . mykkell*e* 151 long*is* . lawes 152 land*is* . assays 153 thyng*is* . now om. 154 cronacc*u*les 155 As mythy, all*e* overl. mak*is* 156 mo m*a*rvyls 157 how . Ere 159 whete vnto h. whete . quaste 160 must ned*is* . when*e* 161 muste nedys 162 fardyst 163 wyrk*is* . won*d*yrs ry3t 165 þe om. chyldyrn*e* . þe*m* 166 þe*m* 167 falne 168 helpt þe*m* . wha*n*. þ*a*t om. 169 helpt þe*m* sone*r* 170 bene . þeyr 171 changyd . theyr 172 þe*m* . þ*a*t om. 173 not 175 saue3oure 177 vnlyke 178 þeis olde . lyvyd 179 haue . mother 180 fodder 181 sykker . suche new 183 dyd habraam*e* . sara 186 Marys . bryngars 188 feyr thyng, blyssyd my3t 190 vnto . meydyn*e* . hathe chosse 191 own*e* 192 whych . spek*is* 193 hyr 196 vnto 197 Whan*e* . þe om. seasone xulde 198 to lyue 199 ordynd yt . suche 202 þe w. wondryd 203 how . old*e* . xulde v. 204 follows v. 208. 205 was 206 olde 207 Shall*e* . xall*e* 208 lye now. 204 a om. lough 210 lordyes 211 cu*m* . begy*n*nys 212 Cryes a waylys . dose 214 Excusyd 215 wryttyne 216 meydyn*e* 217 Hyr father . callyd const*us* 218 Hyr mother . seyd . hy3t 219 dougher 220 beawte . presse 226 passyd & gon*e* 227 holde 228 wordy . ordynd 229 t*r*avyll*e* . þer*e* om. 230 rou3te 231 abou3t 233 lule 235 þeyr 236 xall*e* 238 hyr eye 239 nurryshyd 241 boþe om. 242 teet*is* 243 lestyd . hyr . lyue 244 ful om. 249 scolers 250 nor f. 251 ga*n* (beom.) 252 lettars . þe₂ om. sch*e* om. spellyd 253 He . mast*er*s 254 hyr (so always) 255 case . numbyr 256 modys . ve*r*bs 257 lernyd 259 þe modes om. and þe tence 262 maste*r* 263 servyoure 264 ore . peyd þe*m* theyr hyre 265 a hye clarke 268 sche om. 273 Inclynyd . all*e* hyr 276 any 278 bodys 279 bysynes 280 Whych was w*yth* hyr . thus om. on*e* þis w. 281 seys 282 Ageyns . reynyd þa*n* 284 be a rewlyd 285 3ung god 286 xalt ov*er*-cu*m* 287 grec*e* . þe reme 288 ydiotes 289 mene . appostels. 290 worlde 292 wysdome 293 bustyusnes . we xuld 294 thynk*is* . caas om. 296 ordynyd . gyffe 297 worlde . xulde not hyr 298 Nor 301 mythy . strengh of þe holy goste 302 wold þ*a*t . þeis aretys 303 dougher 304 palyce 306 knyghys 307 ordynde 308 for to . ryce 309 And eke hyr to nurtur 310 masters 315 hyer master 316 I - om. 317 chayrs . myche 318 glasyd 322 þe hoke 323 on*e* rowe 324 aftyr₂ om. 325 knowe, I- om. 326 w*er* 328 Vnto þeis clark*is*. 329 only om. now þ*us* newly 330 now inst. of þan 331 waxt 332 on*e* . gone 335 wele wyt . louys 337 made make 339 Oppu*n* 340 none . worlde 343 In om. 344 fro*m* 345 devysse 346 & stody*e* ry3t 347 treesse . off strange wysse 348 & om. rysse 350 Solatory to stodyars of lyff*e* to them*e* comforte 351 gardyn*e* & no moo 352 shyt 356 worldly . nor 357 wyse ma*n* seys 358 walls . towrs . made vp so 359 cast (I- om.) 361 shyt 364 lyvyd 366 ly3t 367 tellys 368 how . wry3t 369 hys ply3t 370 arays 371 colours . displays 373 lernys . lytyll*e* 374 be om. 375 trouthe fro*m* . falsed . techys 376 þa*n* om. folows 377 co*n*nyng*is* 378 xalt 380 in þ*a*t 381 master 383 meture 384 A. ys wyse 385 are 386 gemetry 387 ynglysh (!) 388 Yt ys . mych . long*is* 389 letturs 390 of yt. 392 I ca*n* . mak*is* 393 stythe 394 st*e*ring . standy*ng* 395 reyn*e* vppon*e* heyth 397 it om. 399 dulnesse 401 dyd gadyr . 402 clark*is* 404 wyt . dougher . on*e* hand 406 gaddyrd 407 þe*m* 408 all*e* hys c. of any 409 þ*a*t he hath l. all*e* hys . ful om. 411 no3t 413 Theyr problems . vndo 415 haue . thyng*is* 417 how . hyr a. 418 Or hyr c. for in 419 Ca*n* 421 þan om. tha*n* all*e* 422 certene 424 mey lyue 425 ned*is* 426 myche 427 wysse 428 þe*m* 429 gaue þe*m* . gyfft*is* 431 off theyr l. 432 theyr bountisnes . such 438 takyn*e* . own*e* fathyr 439 worlde 440 long*is* vnto 441 loggyd . loord*is* 442 dycd . & c. 443 3yt 444 great 445 don*e* . done wr., grete om. 446 þeir 447 lythe . now om. 448 clothyd . after (ward om.) 449 solemnyte 451 no noþ*er* noyce . cyt*e*. 452 weleawey . xall*e* 455 no ayre 456 3ung*e* 457 3yt 458 father . þus om. 459 bene . sykernes. mor*e*₂ om. 460 sykerly 461 subiect*is* to o. laud*is* 462 must . baud*is* 463

428 *Various Readings: MS. Arundel* 20. *Book I.*

nobile. what. þat om. 464 to here om. 465 gladde 466 terys 467 changyd hyr 469 hyre 470 tombe 471 mey wyt. a kyng 472 anoyntyd. balme. neþer 473 nor. suche 474 thyngis 475 Was þan. whyche nedis 476 hapely. warsse 477 suche. ryʒtis 478 lorde 479 byschops. knyghys 480 deys for evyne so v. was 481 run. begynne. passe 482 theyr 483 Must haue 484 suche lastyng whych. feylle 486 enteylle 487 vanysh. rotun 488 to þis intent 491 ameleke 492 Thys. oute om. 493 dythyr cum. seke 494 must now alle clepe þis cyte 495 coste 496 must haue. it om. 500 myche loy and myrthe 501 In þis c. eke dethe dyd hyme doune falle 502 cawsys. thys n. 503 stand. not 504 knowlege 505 ys yt callyd 507 standis 508 þis ys yt namyd 509 walkis. werkis many a. 510 worthy 511 schrewys xalle. þeir 512 hyr owne 513 Alexander 514 had. husband 515 xulde 516 cum 520 One 521 kyngis in. land 522 solemnyte 523 custome 524 trobulle. þer (-for om.) 525 Many a. parlament 526 kynred. hyre 527 foundyd 528 in whose 529 now om. 531 storys 533 Sodene 534 egyp. babbelle 537 nor 540 lesse 541 standis 542 ouʒt off 543 wheþer 545 hyer ryalle 546 babbylle 547 seyd 548 grettyst. vnto 549 land. egypp 550 wyche. reynyd 554 athanas 555 makis 556 same om. 557 deseyvyd 559 & other 560 longis 562 Madagdalaus hyʒt 564 Reynyd 565 seys 566 No. spekis 569 wordy 573 owne 574 fathers 576 must. treuly 577 gorgalus ʒunger. mardaemius 580 mardamy. þo 583 father 585 gorgalus ʒung. haue 586 whyle om. 587 wonders. souʒt. lyue 588 ʒyt. ryve 589 conquestyd 590 araby. fenyse. owne 591 gorgalus 592 wan. gunne(?) 593 sessyd 594 calde 597 haue hys 601 When. dye. in 602 alle alone. sumtyme om. 603 gaue 604 Surre 605 þat om. He gaue. a mythy 609 onys. clarkis 610 reynyd 612 so dere (!) 614 septure 615 callyd anthiocus 616 þer xv; ʒere om.. rosse 617 callyd 621 Iewys ʒyt 622 dyd 623 robbyd 624 wrytis þeis 625 þe c.. and tresun 627 when 629 the same plyʒte 630 phileplator. sey 631 wyth. dougher. vnkyndly 632 a bryʒt 636 any om. 637 þat hyʒt 642 þe kynge. þer-too 644 callyd 645 No new chapter. þis t.. romayns wan from 646 Myche 648 In mene 649 þat inst. of for. feyne 651 in₂ om. 652 landis. faders wan 653 reynyd evyne þe r. 656 dyd 659 calde hys 660 governd. lande 661 þis. seys 662 þe om. 663 t. from theyr h. 664 elyus adryames 665 dougher tylle. calde phalome 666 on- om.; to þis seyd 667 surre to þe r. 668 And om. to þem cessyd 670 þei seyd þat hyr dyd s. 671 þei saw. suche 673 sone. solabre 674 fathyr 675 archecyone & 676 glaudace 678 barus 680 custos fathyr 682 ʒow. of₂ om. 683 meydyne inst. of lady 684 holly 685 behyʒt 686 þe rekkunnyng. ame 687 accordis. cronacules. be 690 d. in many thyngis 691 othyr mens rekkynyngis 692 gyfe 693 þeis. men om. in ordyr ryʒt as þei xulde be 694 apply reply 695 menys 696 rekkun 697 Numbers & reherse. wh. wylle 698 thynkis 700 kynredd. not worschypp 701 perto. dothe 702 shrews. seys 703 how. cam 704 correk synnars 705 ware 706 genology 707 standis. þe same 708 to om. 710 ageyns 711 vyteylle. oþer 712 þer inst. of þat 713 off alle m. v. 714 so om. 716 cum 717 to-gydder 718 shew now 720 cum. omage 721 ladyes 723 mace 724 þem av. 725 gods 726 lat þer 727 how 728 hyr sewtys 729 began. enowgh 731 to þe povert lowgh 732 foysyone. vnto 734 in bowrs & in halle 735 þe. nedis 736 had (I- om.) 737 wyght 739 nyght 740 boredys. coverde 741 meele. anothyr 742 vesselle. 743 neydyr om. 744 & men 745 palyce. standis 746 pepile 747 among lordis. or X 748 þus þei kept þeyr state. eke om. 749 gentyls 750 ladeys 751 cam. othyr 753 fathyr. & sum. were om. 754 curtasy. cam inst. of game 755 spake 758 best. warre. 759 theatur 760 euery man was þer fythyng. 763 Also. wrostyllyng 764 And whan. was. & ylk dele done 765 Iustyng rewylle. þan began to 766 homward ychone for to. 767 had fully. I- om. 768 þat had. or make 769 gyffne. coursars. þe tone 770 þe tothyr whyʒt 771 of₂ om. 772 eke om. 773 war gyffne mantyls whyʒt. þe om. 775 þei ryde. forth om. 777 And preyd 778 tellys 779 kepyd. helde. þer 780 quene þat þer stylle dwels 781 for om. she can þerof 782 Hoo. þei dyd grete 783 þis 785 & hyr 787 ffor

Various Readings: MS. Arundel 20. *Book II.* 429

hy 788 grete wyt & . hert om. wels 789 rynnys frome . wels 792 þat was 793 any evle 794 And he þat dyd 799 neuer 800 court 801 perte 802 þat q. 804 was 805 ʒyt hys 811 good om. 813 meydyn . bapt. not 814 vsyd . spryth 816 bothe be 817 mech om. þe eye 818 wyt 819 þat 821 spy . mys wroʒt 823 nor inst. of or 826 he₂ om. 832 deynys 833 thys 836 falle (be- om.) 837 þat lord ys ever and xalle be in blys 843 also þow . was 850 as any 852 kepyd no r. nor none a. 855 landis 856 must 861 both oure 862 cummys 863 lovys 866 to₂ om. 868 turnys 870 lyth . beneyth 871 ys now alone 872 He ys dede & beryed & leyd fulle depe. 873 we be hole . be we₂ om. 874 o₂ om. 876 now w. k. now 878 Into 880 not þus 882 weldis 884 þeyr 887 now om. lykly 888 xalle 889 eke om. 890 ryalle k. 891 conselle 893 land . in₂ om. 895 os 896 for oure prow 897 xulde to batylle 898 ho . xuld be 899 kynd . ʒyt neuer 901 a st. . wyngis 902 chesse . a captene 905 a om. 907 þat feyr ʒyng thyng 910 must 911 Appone . matere om. 912 wythe ; oute om. 913 hath. 914 That om. xulde 916 wryʒt 917 þis matter 919 is om. . þer lady 921 Os 922 þeis l. 924 on 925 ladeys . helder . ʒyng 926 now om. knowne . lande 927 spokun 928 lyke . bannde 929 hathe . hand 930 Os 931 ladeys 932 Appon . appone 935 lat 938 alle þe 941 alle inst. of ylde 942 þat long to ʒowe now 943 Shall 945 ceasse (I- om.) 947 wyrk after 949 veylle 951 of þeyr hertis desyre 952 þe men 955 owne 956 xulde be soo 957 for þat wolde yt vndo 958 nor 960 for om. 961 desyrys 963 ʒyng . must nedis 964 let . chosse 965 on om. 966 Spede ʒe 969 myʒt 970 a om. 971 ʒyt inst. of ryʒt . or ouʒt of bedd ʒe rysse 974 ryght om. 976 al-wey inst. of alone . yt wylle not be-seeme 982 in₂ om. . skylle 983 & of 987 She lovys . hyr meydynhede 989 on om. 991 to om. 992 so om. 993 wylde . þing om. 994 bene . tyme om. 995 lyggyne in me or my w. 996 I thynk . ʒe sey 999 nor 1000 ʒow ; selue om. wysse 1001 xalle to ʒoure wylle 1002 ʒyt asseyd neuer 1003 nor me in no 1004 As om. neythyr nay nor 1005 pleyne inst. of blame 1006 dose . as om. 1007 castis 1008 oppose 1010 same om. . touchys 1011 nor to 1012 land therto 1013 þer (of om.) 1014 fallys 1015 wyt . wele om. 1016 must nedis. 1018 xalle . eke inst. of ellys 1019 muste 1020 lat. . matter . lengare 1022 now cum . hys 1024 sey theyr alle 1025 þerto I make god 1026 speke he what he wylle 1027 off þe olde quens bylle 1028 wer 1029 thus wyth one v. 1030 endis þe fyrste b. 1031 kynred 1032 Ys d. now at thys tyme 1033 she myʒte send. 1034 A new boke now begyne xalle wee 1035 on- om. 1037 be-tweyne hyre l. 1040 Vnto þe 1041 or þis 1042 prosse inst. of pause 1043 And a reste ryght here at þis same clausse.
Explicit primus liber vite beate virginis Katerine.
Incipit prosa (!) in 2ᵐ librum.

II.

2 fyer . to om. 3 mey 4 tels 5 gosse . nor 6 there be ffyer 7 In þ. s. m. I sey be þis blyssyd ladye 10 tokuns 11 no tylle 12 knew 13 Os . xalle . hasse tokyns 14 knew . roote. 15 knew . hard 17 brynns 18 sytte om. abouue 19 þat (inst. of þe qwech) one 24 Among vs 25 duly thynk one 26 ffor whyche ensampyls went 27 desyryd 28 must . nede 29 burne 30 þis ys no d. 31 frome þe thyne. 32 be₂ om. 33 vertue 35 ffor she gaffe hyr fully þerto þat stounde. 36 ryth om. 37 cum yt callys . ffelow 38 to-gydder as s. & brother. 39 yche . alle om. dose . drowe 40 To þei be cum alle suche ys þeyr l. 42 sercule & course . lo om. 44 ffar past 45 þat fro þem she casts 46 & þem are 47 she hathe so swetly takyne 48 metis and mats 49 bonde 50 accordis . me thynk om. 51 lyvyng 52 þe same 53 say . it om. 55 menys . ney 56 þus om. 57 or—ryne om. 58 Soundyth . hyre 60 neyde 62 synne 63 þer 64 ys inst. of art 65 vnwordy 68 & eke dyuersyte 70 streche . (fol. 9 & 10 are transp.) 71 rynne 74 þeir 79 þei cam 81 loppyne . ryth om. 82 ho cowde . syt or 84 many oþer 85 saracene 86 ware . there om. ryalle 87 & fulle 88 þe ryalle 92 there 93 awne . ny om. 94 callyd 95 now he xulde 96 one 97

430 *Various Readings: MS. Arundel* 20. *Book II.*

bothe om. 99 now om. assynyd 100 gaddyrd alle togydder 101 spas 102 so om.
Was in certene 103 at þeir . þe 104 it om. 105 Syche 106 chosse . among þem
107 þei seyd 111 þus om. 112 My . lady om. xalle 113 forgyue 114 sey to ȝow
trough 115 take om. 116 many a 117 chosyne 119 exceppe . ryght om.
mothyr 120 certenly inst. of ryght. 121 wylle sey þat ȝe 124 lengar 125
ȝoue 126 tak om. 127 & on 128 olde awncetre 129 xalle falle 130 Nor.
here om. 131-3 Yt ys no plesance þat ȝe xulde þus wrye, Yt plece þem better
and ȝe consent þer-too, þat ȝoure awnswere myȝt breke theyr wo 134 husbande
137 must nedys 138 ȝe xalle therby amend 139 Excuse 140 chosse 143
now om. 145 cr. & hys . rathyr wolde he 146 wysse 149 yow om. 150
Oppyne 151 case 153 Oure p. oure s. 154 theysse 155 astunnyd 156 hard
157 now om. 158 nor . wyt nor 161 me thynkis 164 thynkis suerly 166
cums 167 scruffis . plece 171 theyr 172 þem 173 thyng yff 175 mey
176 yt ys ȝyt 177 sworne 180 cums 181 fellys 185 mothyr . & inst. of if 186
must 189 alle om. 190 mey . ȝet om. 192 my stody 194 loffyd . how xulde
196 sythyng 197 þei harde hyr 198 lord 199 & alle ȝoure wones 200 at p.
205 curtasy 206 syne 209 fle me thynkis noþer but ȝe 210 but I 211 abyed
213 þeis matters now for a w. 215 The whyls 216 I inst. of & . avysse 217 nysse
219 swere 222 to yow lengar tale m. 223 loop 224 sey . lythe 225 w. one
wysement wyrk 226 it om. thynk 227 for om. bark 228 theyr lyst . wont
229 chose . must 231 as om. 233 seyd 235 eke þe more and lasse 236 þat casse
238 my awne . bouȝt (a- om.) 241 yore inst. of þoo 243 ȝe inst. of oþir men.
244 cum hydder 246 a om. avyssyd 248 but a lytylle. 249 ȝe yt
253 whyls þe gyrs growys 254 sterffe 255 now om. knowys 257 clark
one 261 xulde . arre 262 traytois 263 þeis lordis . warre 264 ffor ȝ.
gouernance and ȝour kynd þis ys f. fare 265 abyed 266 men so sleyne . owyne
om. 267 theyr w. 268 þem whyls þei are 269 men seruffyd . scruffe . lambe 270
Throw 271 þeme drawne by (cute om.) . or 272 petyus 274 as me thynk
276 se hem om. 277 & suffyr 279 lengar 280 growys 281 vnto þeis wordis
282 father 285 one 286 a 287 nedis 288 one 290 þe enmys 292 fathyr
293 ȝers . ȝede 294 do 295 chase . captyne þan 296 alle in þis 298 þan om. ney.
299 sers 300 mey ȝoue 301 nede ȝoue now to . blame. 302 was om. 303 Was
wun . als w. 304 thyng inst. of theft 305 frome 306 ware punnyshyde 307
& off þis punnyshment ȝyt he k. 308 þis ; same om. weyse 309 I wytsaue .
ryne 311 þeir cuntre . brynne 312 hem om. 313 othyr 315 lyke as 316 a
ryalle lorde & ryche wyth-alle. 317 calde . þe prince 318 knesse 320 ȝoure
feyrnes Is sprung 321 þei . knowne 322 And om. ȝyt mey ȝe not nethyr . nor
324 Os . gone 325 or ȝyt calle 326 care & om. 327 what xalle . I-pased &
om. now goo 328 for om. 329 lykis . weel om. 330 chaunce 332 wysse
334 trouthe 335 fyngers 336 settylle 338 ordenyd 339 castels 340 peple .
þei . no 341 weys went 343 must om. 344 feyryst . berys 345 so do m.
347 awne . wylle 349 xulde plece . þat om. 350 mothyr 351 Rychese . xuld .
aveylle 352 coffer . kepyd 353 myȝt . bothe plate . meylle 354 land . capa-
dosse 356 Wylde pey . raunsum 357 on- om. 358 þe om. wysyst 359 ȝet om.;
ȝe haue not one 361 wylle not nor can not 362 nor strengh . for þat þei w. 366
þe . reyne 367 þoo om. 368 in₂ om. in₃ om. 369 sykker . knythys 370 þeis
worshypps . at easse 372 me thynk 373 þat inst. of & 374 Ordyne 375 Spous-
aylle . os ȝyt ȝe neuer 376 þis ys my tale and ours fully therto. 377 in synnne
seuene 378 warde . boþe om. ; oure l. & exspense. 379 Gramerce . þan om. 381 I- om.
382 worshyp & my honour wolde 383 syre om. 384 spake 386 thynkis . awyse
388 desesse . wylde lyke 389 þus om. pretendythe 390 noþer . nor 391 all
om. 392 thynk 393 als . conquestis . seres om. 394 lordshypps . wer wone
395 þat om. 396 no om. 397 presoners . layd 398 were, seyne þat 400
sowiers. 401 ne om. we no covyt þat ȝe do 402 a-fere 403 A. ȝe 405 P.
ȝe . vnto ȝoue 406 in a. 408 peyns gyffyne 409 semys 411 My . drope
412 gane 414 must nedis 417 To om. Make fre or make to hyme presonare
419 hope to hang and drawe 421 swone 426 awȝt. 429 haue suche fredom g.
hyme w. 430 nor 431 þere ys offycers 432 þe shrews . nor. 433 ylle . i. dey

Various Readings: MS. Arundel 20. Book II. 431

þus mey ȝe 434 ned*is* . not om. 435 offycers 436 must þe*m* 437 slesse fyȝt*is* 438 xalle 439 Nor þeir dede but 440 slesse þeys me*n* þat are. 441 Serwand*is* to þe l. 443 Os . fathers 444 let . lat . or saue. 445 long*is* 446 meydyn*e* 447 be hem om.; thow þei dam*p*nyd be 448 to þe Iugg*is* b. k. & q. to se. 451 began . ryght om. to r. 452 p*er*lous 454 rysyng at any seasone war steryd 455 afferyd 457 ȝowe . how 459 me*n* om. 461 thynk 462 It f. þat off alle þis ȝe ne r. 463 sytt*is* 464 an . eke om. 465 be om. were . Iustyes 468 Nother . nor . ma*n*s mynde. 469 And peyr . yene 470 t. ȝowe 471 myȝt . be 472 hath· om. 473 þe*m* 474 boke 475 how 476 fulle s. 479 lengare . þe lettars 480 wyll*e* 482 full om. holle and in quarte 483 xalle 484 wyll*e* 486 gryme 489 xulde . a ma*n* þa*n* more þa*n* ȝe drede 490 als w. 494 ewle tacchyde . yt ys. 497 it om. 498 os . xalle 499 on- om. 500 lat 501 lande 505 here now how þe pep*i*le . þeyr 506 to₂ om. 507 I now shew 510 babilon*e* 515 dethe 516 On*e* 519 ryth om. 522 repentand 524 I wolde 526 loue 527 oft tymes 528 opynyons . fomyd 529 Make oftymes a l. 530 hyme ouȝte at herre 531 theyr wytt*is* 532 þat om. 535 warldly . ware 536 ware 538 slyd*is* . ȝe knowe 539 fulle fast ageyn*e* 542 þat om. 543 saw . wrete om. ane evyn*e* 544 þe boke 545 Reseuyd os ȝyt . thynk . must nedys. 546 yt tellys 547 how xulde we k. 548 wordy . eldyrs 549 toldo þe*m* 550 what 551 Where 553 oppynyons . ser*e* now om. ȝow lett 554 gods 555 þat 556 p*re*chars are feyne . one rowe 557 haly 560 we om. *þ*erfore inst. of þa*n* . a noþ*er* 561 stand*is* . full om. 562 master . I wylle 563 semys 564 to om. 566 meyntyne 567 long*is* . godds 568 calde 569 of₁ om. 570 theyr pesse 573 þoo om. 576 cause . must 578 byde (a- om.) . one ȝere 582 cu*m*s 583 hens om. agoo 585 land*is* 586 fare a. farre fro þe 591 wyth*o*uȝt 592 thynk 595 Whyche þat xalle wele . eke om. 599 we . lande one se & 601 studdy 602 thynk*is* surely . xulde do wele thus 603 xulde 604 lesure 606 no . wherfor 607 one . vaffe 608 do . counselle 613 os 614 and cypre 615 drede I 616 so I dere yt b. 617 þat om. 620 þ*er*-offe not wante 621 xulde set a p. 622 ȝynge 623 lere 624 ek om. 626 xulde . had 627 þe om. be so 628 presyng ȝoure t. xalle 630 now om. 632 farthermore 633 yff yt . newe om. 638 at alle 639 Whyche off ȝoue spake 640 plentuosly 641 frome 642 savyd . os . a vale 643 Os off . borne 644 ryde 646 yt 647 fun 649 On*e* 650 for om. 651 is om. c. has as 655 Whyche as . euene om. 656 hathe d. to þe*m* þus þa*n* 658, 659 dwels . at 661 owte om. 662 & inst. of Ete . rest hyme and eke at evy[n]e 663 þeyr 665 no fyculte 667 þore . þus began 668 ȝunthe 669 a kyng 671 bon*e* 672 we om. hartely 673 sworne 675 Ryȝt so & 678 yt ys 679 xall*e* now m. 685 not om. no noþ*er* 690 cu*m* affray 694 style 695 in ȝour wyt ȝe enf. 697 I inst. of ȝe . swere 698 to om. 699 yt xulde 704 rehersyd 705 awnswer 706 for om. . thyng*is* 708 þat for . he om. 710 þe*m* sesse 711 And om. But yff 713 gylte 714 þat om. 715 þ*er* stode 717 þoo om. delffe 717 deppar . to (vn- om.) 720 hert 721 perte 722 are 727 ȝow 728 in þe whyche . are indosyde 729 ȝoure ylke 730 eylys 731 beleue 732 lady om. harte ys surely sett 734 ȝe so sore drynke 735 most om. 737 concelde . tylle 738 ȝay 740 febulle wele 741 os wryt*is* þe 743 þe om. oft suche dystance 745 now lady ȝowe 748 ryght om. 750 but yff 752 as is 754 nethyr in wake nor 755 as here 756 stand*is* 757 on- om. 758 Seyne . grauntyd þe*n* 760 hathe ȝoue . we wylle craue 764 I- om. vp om. one p. 765 thynk . chaunge 766 Now and þa*n* wylle ȝe now are ȝe not of Ioynt 767 Now wyll*e* 768 know om. 772 ned*is* ffor ȝowe care 774 be 775 nor 777 þat ȝe sey . myche mervylle 780 hartyly 781 wylle 782 were no bohoue 783 nor 784 dysseyuer . spyȝt. 785 sey also þat 786 all om. 788 Os to . xalle be. 790 known*e* 791 fathers . on₂ om. mothers 793 ordynd . gods 794 eke ys 796 ware . yn*e* þat n. 798 leegys 799 it were om. buttraces 800 shew 801 meynty*n* 802 ys full*e* small*e* herdely 803 als w. 806 p*re*tendys 810 & xalle I trow 812 lere 815 Þ*er* ȝe sey fully þat 817 be but 818 all*e* þe bunche 819 of an*e* ynche 820 I put case I gafe ȝow a b. 821 folowys . þ*er*of þat om. I gaue 822 I mey . pey ȝoue 823 And gyue ȝoue an horse 824 cu*m* . þe 825 arestotels . & made . such a gyse 826 lernys þe*m* 827 chose 828

432 *Various Readings: MS. Arundel 20. Book II.*

chose 829 vp om. 831 I ȝyt eft 832 xalle . & om. 833 þis ys 834 þoo om. lamosines 835 here now 837 mervylle 840 a faryd 841 skeyth 842 had om. 843 But yt ys 844 mattyrs 846 ffor þe loue 847 Accep 848 do wele 849 ȝe lyst 855 hym alle 856 leke . vs om. 857 haue rest nor no esse 858 ware . lyke as . are 859 wele 860 many of 861 herd 863 sche sayde om. troste 864 one . þe inst. of to 865 loste 866 wost 868 eyre 869 cum 871 thynkis 873 haue om. ȝow om. 876 amerelle 877 can 879 thynkis . syttis 880 now om. myre 881 loose . now om. losse. 882 yt ende þus (!) 885 thyngis 887 wolde thynk 890 sey 891 dose lyke 892 dose a f. 893 frome 894 Be ware 895 nor 896 now om. wylle 899 man off d. d. 902 here om. 906 dente . leue 907 not om. 908 sullyne 909 hathe byddyne 912 not I . þe g. 914 nor loue 915 þe . thyngis 917 Be . telle . mo thyngs 918 among 919 ful om. 920 be . so om. 921 vsys 922 reme haply 923 Seyne 927 ful om. note om. 930 ȝe . correk . ȝoure-s. 931 wolde o. 932 þan began 933 cald 935 ful om. 936 ȝoue madame . ful om. to b. 937 Os 938 of₁ om. 939 wyt 940 lyke as . Egylle 941 in als m. 942 fallys 943 whyche þat ȝe loue 944 not theme . þat om. 948 But þow 953 lets . beleue 954 be om. 955 shal om. 956 xalle 957 end om. 958 þe om. 959 yt ys . as om. 960 ffor inst. of sore 961 wyt þe cause off ȝoue 962 meyny . shal om. þe g. 963 to send forthe . both om. 964 þat om. 965 One . hath om. off 966 off londe lorde . and lyme 967 olde . debate 968 Among . þer reynyd 971 soo inst. of thoo 972 why þat þei chasse 974 ffor qwan om. Ther was not els 975 Þer was non þan wylld 976 seyd . xulde 977 oft fallys betwene 978 Ageyns . stryvys 981 ware chosun 982 strenghe & sum 985 Excellys . þow þei be as 988 wer 991 chosse 992 drawne 993 Nor 994 heed om. must þei 995 my 998 Nor 1001 he om. 1003 as om. 1005 cunnand . ne om. 1007 be behynde 1008 fawle 1009 eke om. 1010 morenyd sore & 1011 saw 1012 þei om. 1013 gane om. 1015 pereylle 1016 dayes om. 1017 wyt 1018 ne rome 1019 not such a m. 1020 yff inst. of of 1022 or craue 1024 To þat . be ch. 1025 turnyd now 1027 hath brouȝt 1028 do om. 1029 Þat euer þey poynt þey v. euer for s. 1031 who om. my 1033 clyvys 1035 not yt 1036 I-wey 1037 wepyd 1038 ys lorne 1039 sey speke or els doo 1040 þe tyme om. 1041 though . is om. 1042 I wyt nevyr 1043 mey wyt hyr answere. 1045 cum . auȝt farther 1046 doyne 1047 me₁ om. stunnyd . to abey 1049 but om. 1055 kyndrede 1056 all om. 1057 one 1058 elys 1059 ȝyng 1060 for-byddis 1062 turne 1063 ȝoure entent 1064 frome 1066 lyke as 1067 here bef. 1068 cume ne set 1070 lyue 1071 folow ȝoue . stepps . ȝede 1072 þe chyl-dyrne 1074 decesse 1075 I hope 1077 þat om. xalle 1078 dye . meydyne 1079 þus yff ȝe conceyff 1082 getyne 1083 lerne . lessone om. at me 1084 thynk 1086 Vnkylle . ware I 1089 land 1090 eke om. vnto 1094 bothe gouerne 1096 my hart 1099 my harte 1100 ellys om. 1104 ware 1105 my hart . to do alle þing 1108 nor 1110 oft medlyth 1112 haue 1113 londe 1115 þe inst. of þoo 1116 nor 1119 dredys 1120 What so e. gyffis . prysse 1121 os 1123 seyne tyme ȝe 1126 Os yt standis . land 1127 One th. þat ȝe Ioy 1129 not om. gyffyne 1131 longis to þat 1132 regalyte . my 1133 standythe 1134 eke om. wyrkyng 1136 how we 1137 werke and laboure 1138 lord-shyps . xalle not 1139 it om. brouȝt 1140 gyffyne 1141 seruff . be ȝoue sworne 1142 lord om. 1143 semyd 1144 þoo om. 1145 þan om. in 1146 astate 1148 haue 1150 haue 1153 Os 1155 he om. wrytis . þe astr. to me (!) 1156 how . not om. naypur wyrk 1158 xulde . barke 1159 man om. 1160 wheythere₂ om. 1161 i- om. 1163 xalle 1164 xalle fele and se 1165 dyrk 1166 xalle 1168 xulde one 1171 of ȝoue she seyd 1172 myȝt 1173 at þis t. ȝoure p. 1174 wele . put m[e] in d. 1175 I put case . xulde 1176 oure l. 1177 nor 1178 rewle ȝe 1179 lengh 1181 thyngis 1182 ware 1183 hertis . full om. 1186 nor 1190 holde 1191 seyne (= syth) 1192 one th. þat longis to þe regalyte 1194 if om. holde 1195 it₂ om. 1196 for om. 1198 ȝyt knelyd doune before þe q. 1199 Þe Ryche duke off Athenys þe Cyte 1200 of scole 1201 chosyne (I- om.) also inst. of þoo 1202 theyr chose . as om. 1203 wheche om. l. to be þeyr h. 1207 descendyth 1208 bothe Ientylle 1210 semys . of þat k. 1211 ware . nor

Various Readings: MS. Arundel 20. Book III. 433

1212 eldyrs 1213 Os greyne ryally grounc . theyr 1215 ware lyke 1216 in om. þus om. 1218 soote 1219 Farther-more 1220 lyke thy*n*g hys l. 1221 semes 1223 despyt*is* . os. 1224 vncurtyslye 1226 answard þus 1228 þat om. hathe 1231 of wyt yt berys 1232 He þat 1233 indwed 1234 wardly 1236 I mey 1237 ʒoue ; resoun om. 1238 tent 1240 one t. 1242 berys . he om. suete 1244 eke inst. of & 1245 & in þat 1246 In þis we dyflyr 1247 semys . graffe 1248 I- om. olde 1249 and savour 1251 clyvyd a fore 1252 graffe 1253 farys . be₂ om. myne 1254 xalle . lyue 1255 Os do now I . I xalle 1258 ffadyr om. 1260 I wylle chose suche lyue as ys 1263 Kestyng 1264 hopyng 1265 þis seyd m. it om. 1268 chase . theyre althyrs 1272 hath formyd 1274 but yf 1275 is in ʒoue 1276 for om. 1279 none þer 1281 fulle wele asp. 1283 myʒt 1284 lyvys . se 1285 For ʒoure feyryde no man can decerne 1287 gyvne . ʒow om. 1288 yt over ʒoue ys so leyd 1289 frome 1291 nere s. 1294 vnto ʒoure 1299 xalle . inclyne 1303 þe nob*i*le 1304 þat om. þe name 1305 & many othyr of ʒoure lynageyng 1308 Seyne . ylkone 1309 do . kynred. 1310 for ʒour 1311 and byde therby 1314 ame not 1316 wyth-owtyne 1317 pay*n*t 1318 schapys 1319 is om. 1320 vyser 1321 gyue . nose 1324 gyffne 1325 fayre om. 1328 thus do . mey s. hath 1329 thy*n*g whyche 1330 do alle-wey . þat hyr dysdeyne. 1332 take 1333 lesse . helde 1336 it om. 1337 forther-more . myʒt 1338 & inst. of þow . coppyllyd . one 1342 thyng*is* 1343 thyng*is*. 1344 wolde she 1345 poynt om. 1346 lyueyng 1348 for and ʒe 1351 os . thynk 1352 ʒow commyne þeis gyfft*is* 1353 gyffne . þem 1354 man inst. of mever 1355 sytt*is* 1356 gafe 1357 haue sum xx*ti* . to 1358 xuld commun 1359 therto . peryle 1360 man . sytt*is* 1363 os 1364 poynt om. & þe last poynt 1365 to ʒoue ys 1366 wondyrs 1368 os 1371 xalle be best 1375 endyʒt 1376 sey 1378 alle my 1379 haue bene 1383 ane eyre 1384 a husband 1385 wele inst. of syre . þat om. 1386 lye 1387 set vs aboue 1389 þus I 1391 Thys argume*n*t ys ʒoure awne lare 1392-8 om. 1399 none 1402 whyche I wolde 1403 wyth-owtyne 1405 vawe 1406 sett*is* 1407 such one, h. wylle I none 1413 sykkerly 1416 he nede 1421 H. what I wylle also more sey 1423 ned*is* . mens 1424 in e. þat xulde be hym lych 1425 so Ientylle of blode 1427 onys om. ask*is* 1429 he₂ om. 1430 ameable 1431 seyne 1434 on om. seruau*n*t om. 1437 but yf 1438 seyne 1439 Os . semys . alle amysse 1441 feylle 1443 alle thys feylyth 1448 xalle . þat he 1449 wylle . newe om. 1451 Els myʒt ʒe wene þat I. 1452 Os 1454 Wh. þat 1455 eke om. mother 1459 as þan om. 1460 so sore . can 1463 sees 1465 takyne w. 1466 nye om. 1469 wot*is* 1470 wher xulde 1471 desyrys 1474 scornys . euery chone 1475 lat 1478 sat 1481 xulde þus . combird 1482 a kyng . werys 1484 a om. 1486 yche . on om. 1487 go to ryde . us þeyr 1488 are þei ylke one 1490 bothe reherse 1491 fynyshyd 1492 lyvys 1496 tretyd 1497 betwene þe . & hyr lordys legemen.

Explicit 2ᵘˢ liber hui*us* benignissime vite s. Katerine virginis

Incipit prosa in 3ᵐ librum vite sanctissime virginis Kate*r*ine.

III.

1 Sythyne . here om. present lyue 3 þe holy gost. frome 4 and off 5 frome vs 6 þat yt ys 7 þe holy gost 9 kynred 11 how she 14 no₂ om. 15 on- om. 16 now om. myne 19 mervously she ys enteryd in to hys t. 23 Whedyr 24 do om. haue bene 25 never cam 31 be hyd 32 Inclyne 33 hyre inst. of my 34 ageyne . venu*m* 35 dewle h. gyffne to 36 vnto 37 Kate*r*yne inst. of may . þou om. me now 38 was . & so gode a 42 hathe done Explicit prosa. Incipit Terci*us* liber huius vite sanctissime virginis Kate*r*ine 43 hermyt . old 44 fulle grete 45 seyd . þoo om. selle 46 þat om. 47 full om. 50 Slept . walkyd . he had 51 off holy meyd 53 spake afore . thane not 56 xalle 57 ordynyd 59 vnto egyppe 60 more om. 61 harmyt 62 bodely . wark 67 wythe f. d. 68 passys 69 men om. 70 passys . goste 75 hys lyvyng wane 76 ffor to no t. . euer 78 shypps þat saylyd . þere om. 79 had om. 81 frome þis

KATHARINE. F F

434   *Various Readings: MS. Arundel* 20.   *Book III.*

82 a partye . & a partye . hys om.   84 armyt   86 armyttis . þei om.   87 dwellyd fromc townys   89 were om.   dwellyd   90 wyth-owtyne   92 was fallne in grete a.   97 eylys now þe   98 and werkis   99 seyth . syttis   101 Os . wont   103 nor   105 alle þat   106 Demene me not   108 to be abou3t in thy s.   112 and meke   113 he had   114 þo om.   115 w. by hys selle vp   116 I- om.   117 vnto   118 saw   120 accordythe wele   121 croune   122 not best what ys to doo   124 Into   125 hathe cau3t comforth of a new l.   126 3onged he th[i]nkis & hys my3t   129 mervylle hath I   130 feyr freche &   131 here . morenyng   132 ne boote ne om. nowhere (!)   133 nor   136 to hym also 3.   137 fulle gode meke   139 þe3 om.   145 my3t   146 þat om.   148 full om.   151 dose   152 mey   153 massyngere . ware   154 for om.   155 þan seyd thys   157 & om.   158 cunnand   159 me om. my br.   160 To . a meydyns   162 the meyd   164 preyd . whan þi my3t   165 of no thyng   166 nor . wyth₂ om.   ffebylyte   167 yke . hard   170 haue . boþe om.   172 for om.   173 eke om.   175 haue . newer   179 sethe   182 boldly   184 gretys   185 commaundis   187 xalt   188 astunnyd   189 þe om.   191 Seyne   192 was made   194 wed   195 ordynde   197 xalt   198 do om.   203 cunnyng hyr godenes   205 A ry3t ryalle / a ryche / a w.   207 nor . no eyr   208 lyfe . heyr   209 reyns   210 sonnys   211 in sothe also . ryth om.   213 schewde . in w.   214 spence   215 Ryches   217 for a hyer   218 not 3yt knowys   220 whyche she now in flowys   222 Os .   þe sothe   226 off theyr ph.   227 ly3t   228 sothly   230 mythy . xalle   231 off g. p.   233 a . othere om.   235 Os   237 ane ende   238 kynde   241 & om. . ravysshyd . swonyng   243 can . þoo om.   244 And om.   247 recheles . bustous   248 late om.   249 comborous   250 to me was   251 gone . þan om.   252 my   254 allas₂ om. wryttyne   256 ho . knowne·. forgottyn   258 fulle rechles . but late   260 pyteus woyce   261 punnyche . snyb me   262 euermore redy   264 do om.   265 suerly . & large   266 spake   267 nor   268 hard   269 wylle I doo   271 werenesse   272 full om.   276 hastyly . now om.   277 in . xalle   278 Ordync   285 fade inst. of stumble   286 gyed   287 cummys . þe   291 xalt   292 here   293 And one suche thyngis þei wolde Iangylle & clatter   294 þer-ffore þi wordes kepe only.   295 xalt . þe   296 þat om. on- om. palyce   300 þere om.   gaatis   301 3epe   302 ffrom   306 Nor . eke om. þe om.   307 dwels she   308 xalt   309 walls   310 of₂ om.   311 þat₂ om.   312 nedyth om. þou nethyr (noght om.) . nor   313 oppyne   314 þou entyr wyth xalle   315 be to hyr a f.   317 in om.   318 blode   320 casse   321 nor   322 þat þou xalt   327 calle 3oue loller   328 Be   331 stunnyd   332 olde . rekeles om.   333 whech om. ry3t inst. of full   334 specyalle   336 wylle she þerto   338 haue   339 for₂ om.   341 xalt   342 c. ry3t to   343 w. any s.   344 þou xalt   345 and inst. of if . inquere   347 chosse   348 chose . full om. I- om.   349 so os   350 warst   351 xalt   355 hydder   356 well om.   358 ryght om. one   359 whych long   360 þer . nor   361 led hyme   362 þat . were   363 day om. . full om.   364 gone . ryne . full om.   365 god þat vnfullykly th.   366 Os . lyst   367 chese   368 & aye awey . cast   370 In þe Epystols . þat om.   371 wyth-ou3t any   373 chose   374 gone   375 hylle   376 wher þat . empryce   377 gardyne . þan om.   381 mervyld   382 can   383 þer ry3t   384 Os   386 leynyng   389 suche a . saw   390 Os . see   391 my3t   392 þoo om.   393 O   394 never such a creature to a fonde l.   395 as off   396 nowne . bewteus   399 passys oure mesure   402 þe   404 Cropyne . mervyld   405 ffor hyr-s. . bene   407 began   411 hundryth   413 knelyd . seyd   417 suddenly   418 & cum . any oþer   420 be t.   422 whych þat   424 ey   425 wyt   426 ho gaf 3e   427 entyr wyth-in.   430 if om.   rechesly   431 nor   432 yt ys   434 haply   435 now om.   438 man þorow whome   439 if om. mey be . mene   440 xalle 3oue . frome   445 grettyr . yf þat   446 dwellys   447 longis   449 weyne   450 os   451 tylle   452 Nor   453 ffor hyre & 3oue both . wyth eyne om. sene   455 passys   456 poure   457 þat om.   460 scapys   461 wyll om.   462 frome   464 in hyr   465 for criste   466 ermyte om.   467 hert om. prentyd . suere   468 os   470 os . from   473 freche . 3ung   474 or . on- om. meydyns   476 wyll om.   477 was cum   478 3yt far he was as to h. knolegyng   480 turnyd   481 ore   482 procedyng seyd vnto   483 wordy a   484 Os   485 hye om.   486 we wene wer we   488 lyggis . land   489 wheythere om.   492 lyffys . os I   494

Various Readings: MS. Arundel 20. Book III. 435

wele . must 495 she 499 þis wyt 501 whedyr yt be 502 ys most 504 as yt xalle 509 cums . nor dews nor eke r. 511 pover 513 þat om. 520 mothyr . nurryche 522 eft 523 leue . be 527 so preche of so hy 528 sey þus 529 passys 530 be₂ om. 532 ylle . symepylle 533 ys bene (inst. of it had be) 534 not to send 536 os 537 hyr inst. of alle 539 semys 540 wylle 541 wylle 543 þat om. had 547 wyt 548 passys 549 both in hye & lowe 550 cete 551 clarkis 552 in many 553 Elyne . gryce 555 dysyrys . m. g. þan worldly 556 in body 563 I mene 564 on- om. 566 ladys . now om. 567 must . parte a twynne 568 welthys om. settis 569 xalle 570 must 573 wher 579 ʒone 580 I toke þan so emprentyd 583 erls 584 þis₂ om. 585 wyld . nor 586 pere 588 war 592 drownyd nor 593 euyr om. 597 þis . plentyus 598 any 599 vertue 600 Cum ʒoue 603 xalle 607 & om. she ys meydyne 609 syns of þis . clensyd 611 in₁ om. in₃ om. 614 stand 615 suche a 616 þe sothe . wottis 618 & wh. 619 leue om. 621 tylle . mannys 622 se 624 hath 625 haue om. 626 hyr₁ om. gode & hyr godds settis 627 Infyryd 628 castis . maryed 629 per to 630 enformacyone 631 þat of om. one th. 634 wythouʒt 635 at om. & om 638 þe inst. of of 639 wey . not excercysse 641 Nor . but þat hye 642 can devysse 643 knowys 644 haue a . he om. . sowys. 648 on- om. 649 same om. slept 650 þan ouʒt 652 Sythyne 653 poure 656 chosyne hath . ʒour om. & ʒyt 657 of þis 660 proue be gode r. 661 Seke . of om. leffe 664 & telle 665 ware . ethyr 666 Than om. Seyne þat 667 yt ys 668 xulde haue merkis 671 as we 672 lat 673 eyls 677 ever wyth mankynd 679 can now . vs om. 682 Inne 684 boþe om. 686 semys . a w. ; fulle om. 687 marchande 688 crose dyd sp. 689 þis same 690 weshyd 691 gretiste 693 perfore om. 694 how . comple . ʒe 695 erthe inst. of eyre 698 suffyrd . hande 700 grete pascyone 701 how . lyue . eye 702 is om. complete 703 of om. god and man 704 haue takyne . seyd 705 is om. 706 loke now ʒoure speche þat per be now no heresye 707 offendys 708 questyone 711 standis 712 of om. 713 in no 715 & inst. of if 716 ʒour om. 717 one . gyffe 718 of oure 719 Nor . sole . xalle ʒoue 720 old 722 know . þat om. 723 on- om. 724 þat w is bounden sumwhat wyth a bande 726 credulle as chylderne 728 haue inst. of hem 730 commaundis . on- om. 731 hasse 733 byddis . xulde 734 Suffythe 736 arguue 738 þat om. 740 þinge inst. of most . precius 743 coppyllyng 746 awne 747 arbytor . oune tong 749 wyth-ouʒt 751 þe tone desyrys þe todyr . not 752 Contrary be þeys ij þan in wylle 753 & þouʒt 754 in þis 755 Be . wyls 756 ryght om. 760 know . tretis 761 determe . mynde 763 þe 764 be-gynnyng puttis 765 chosun 766 man 767 man cums o. c. 769 xalle 770 In . owyne om. thys mey ʒe ssee 771 þe ermyte om. hard 772 And soylyd . many one 773 at last 774 seyd 776 and wyth þis lady speke 777 þat xalle 779 no v. 781 frome 784 awysyde 785 whane þey 788 semys . and chere 789 Os . haue provyd 793 folowyd 794 in þe halle 795 nor saw off 796 Thus passyd they bothe þorow þe place 798 went . ryʒt thus s. þe b. 799—805 om. 806 c. blynyd thane 807 I w. 808 lat . or b. 809 knows 811 cam at the ground 813 wont . ys go 815 ʒede 819 as om. to c. 822 full om. suerly þe weys 825 hym 826 a. þat lede 827 morenys . turnys 828 lokys 829 he fallys 831 xuld 833 & vntr. 837 ʒe 840 haue . nor myne 841 my 843 contrary 844 Alle is gone drenchyd or brent 845 old 846 my 847 must 848 Than 849 the inst. of ʒow . seche 851 in suche dyuersyte 854 good om. lyggis . tyme om. 855 be ʒoue 857 þe om. a om. ; but lete 858 cythyr 859 Be . nor 861 beleue . soo om. 862 now ys now 865 ys gone 867 lady om. 868 myʒt 871 sythys & of so swete 874 from þe shypp 875 take kept 879 and trosty 880 on- om. aswage 882 telle ʒoue 883 se ʒoue 884 as þe sone 887 þe rowffe yt not dyme 888 ʒendyr 889 ʒendyr . shynys 890 sawe 891 wals ne ʒatis, gret s. 892 ware . borne 894 haue done 895 lyvyand 897 Ther 899 in a noþer 900 sees 901 olde . growne . grace 902 olde . was large 904 now om. 905 ʒoure towre 906 Trust . off no l. 907 preys 910 ʒe me om. 912 for inst. of sore 916 to 917 resevyd off 918 of₂ om. 921 saw 922 hyr . nor hyre 927 evyne one 929 not . was . þe 930 but þe bodye 933 creme

F F 2

436 Various Readings: MS. Arundel 20. Book III.

938 do . þat   942 & myche.   met hyr   943 A C. . can we   944 vddyr . sene   945
on om.   946 Welcum   947 haue   951 þei om. .   ledes   952 wedis   954 Emprowrs
955 abyttis fulle b.   956 creatours   957 þe freche and gay   958 saw . hyr   959
lyffe   960 þoo om.   forthe þus .   f. grete   961 gate   962 þoo om.   963 Welcum
now   964 Os .   but fulle   965 fell om.   966 Os   968 man₂ om.   969 pascyons
971 Þer tokyns .   þeyr ryȝt   972 What   973 þe erthe cam   975 l. one h. leders
how þei l.   976 þeyr m.   978 in to a tr. . nor   980 it om.   982 in to þe holy p.
983 saw   984 Wh. þat callyd . vnto . nobulle   985 ryally   988 wost . he was
989 hym   991 þis   992 euyr om.   on- om.   þe om.   995 thyng   1001 nyer
1002 Thane . lyft   1009 now om.   for me must ȝ. l.   1011 meydyns   1013 tels .
we   1014 enoughe assynyd   1015 had lothe   1017 walkyng   1018 þei om.
walkyng þer a.   1022 ordynyd a p.   1025 a   1027 desyrys . xuld   1029 haue
bene   1032 seyd . ȝow know   1034 to lok of . do   1035 no noþer   1036 xalle .
blys l.   1038 Weshyd from . be om.   dyrk   1039 whych   1043 to me fulle ;
ofte om.   1045 hafe om.   1048 lat   1049 mark   1053 & om.   1055 perfurme
1056 My aungels   1057 w. any d.   1058 ȝet om.   1066 Be . discomforth   1069
a om.   1070 on- om.   or to   1071 a baptyȝyng   1073 run   1075 do ȝe   1080
Vnto . vnto   1082 wyed   1083 from . assyed   1086 now om.   1087 cr. men
1089 the now here   1090 baptyȝyd . lordis   1091 crystynned   1092 commaundyd
1093 of om.   1094 als n. . redy om.   1095 Þis n. . xalt . cleppe   1096 for₂ om.
1097 eythyr old   1098 an om.   1101 þat we   1102 are om.   nor   1104 Þer
1106 solemp . þe tyme   1107 here om.   1111 vn- om.   1113 one   1116 B. in þe
1119 vndefylde   1123 ame   1125 for ch.   1127 yt ys   1129 renewde   1130
there   1133 ey   1134 þeis werkis . sey   1138 essely . now om.   1139 hathe
sene   1140 thankis   1141 vnto   1142 dane   1143 þis om.   þat inst. of wheche .
saw   1145 tent to   1147 o. here   1148 els cum   1149 þis lady   1150 enteryd
1153 xalle   1154 Or   1157 medyne   1159 tale om.   1160 myȝt   1161 þe here
1162 humbynes   1163 That om.   1165 hyr om.   1169 ys . meche om.   to þe
bothe beh.   1170 ful om.   1175 vnto   1176 of om.   1182 be thy mothyr   1184
rysse . rosse   1185 crownyd . or she was   1186 Þore . was   1187 came   1188
þoo om.   1190 to om. . os   1192 of om.   1196 nouȝt els   1197 þe wels ; is om.
1202 hem om.   on- om. . deyte   1203 þat m.   1204 Than   1205 xalle   1208
my l. &   1209 ȝow om.   1210 þe same   1211 communs assent   1212 Chosse .
lyke ȝoue   1217 þan ageyne to   1218 athyng   1219 O maker off aungels of man
best &   1221 coppylde   1223 forgyue   1224 seruande   1229 on- om.   1232
þoo om. . ȝowe   1234 castylle   1235 roue   1236 Broche & ryng   1238 delec-
tacyuns   1240 þis wote   1241 & of none els   1244 os   1247 in   1248 ordynyd
1254 þe meydyns   1260 shortly to sey   1262 receue . a om.   1263 Aboue alle
creaturs here I ȝoue make   1264 My wyff for ever here constant in virginite
1267 offendis   1268 Than   1269 Sythen . spouseylle must   1271 gyffis   1273
alle blody one þe tre   1275 þe r.   1276 & put   1277 off þat sannde   1279 vnto
1280 berys   1282 hath sene   1283 os my   1284 sey . grene   1287 ellys om.
1289 auctor seys   1290 To bere of . þat om.   1293 þe bate . & strete   1295
þem inst. of here body   1296 Ther . abowyn   1297 most om.   þat any man
1298 s. þer . fulle ewyne   1299 þo s.   1300 sunge . it om.   1302 þe awnswer
1303 semys   1309 endis   1310 Now lyst   1312 þe s.   1314 hyr inst. of þis
swete   1315 seyd   1316 lat . nor   1318 þat yt ys   1321 I make   1322 Os .
xalt   1325 & om.   1328 now om.   1330 wylt . sone om.   1333 Informe   1336
gyffe   1337 lyffe   1338 xalle   1340 sene   1341 dyed   1342 þus . my dere
1345 þe   1346 Alle om. I- om.   1347 þe . þe . & lyȝt   1348 now om.   1350
Was . tresse   1351 for om.   1352 swete meyd   1353 swone . os . þer   1355
cummys   1356 gane to hyr sey   1357 came . to om.   1358 þe cheekis   1360
Tylle she woke   1363 do we   1365 sorowe   1366 Thynk now ȝ. l.   1367 Haue
1368 os   1369 ȝowe be . in₂ om.   1370 mys wrouȝt   1371 nor erthly   1372
no thyng ȝow   1373 Os   1376 Þe s. b. ageyne sum tyme xalle t.   1377 suernes
as xalle   1378 be   1379 of ȝour   1386 ȝoue, my aune   1383 ȝoue   1384 soke
1387 ȝoue   1388 ware   1391 as om. off hyme wryttyn I fynde   1392 is
om.   1395 &₁ om.   1397 nor   1398 evyne of   1399 plurelyte   1400 in any

Various Readings: MS. Arundel 20. Book IV. 437

wyce 1402 Nor. þe holy gost 1403 One. in alle thyng 1406 madame om. 1411 & haue 1412 begetis 1413 begottne. from them two 1416 þus om. 1420 hath. haue 1421 wyt 1424 þan I rehers cane 1425 But at þis tyme suffythe 1426 þe 1427 þei may om. 1430 cam. from 1431 ys þan 1432 semys 1433 þore 1434 longis. theyr. dew om. 1435 emprice 1436 cam þer 1439 eke there 1441 vnto þat 1444 gretis. godly 1445 behest. cum 1447 a_2 om. 1448 reme 1449 ȝoue, nor þat ȝe flee. 1450 Abyde. ryght om. 1451 tyrauncy 1453 none; woman om. 1454 must. suffyr. velanye 1455 ȝour, om. 1460 so ffeyr 1461 was 1465 bothe inst. of she 1468 dyuersnes. or rode 1472 done 1473 warnyng 1474 þe₂ om. 1475 I- om. and layd 1476 But om. Be. dyscomforthe 1481 ȝe om. 1482 Kepe 1484 gyff 1485 I- om. 1486 ane ende 1489 mynde 1490 now om. 1492 I- om. 1493 Os 1494 my 1495 þat om. rede how 1496 on dey or weke 1497 now þer 1500 ordynd 1501 we hath 1503 off crossed out; vnyte wyth-ouȝt discorde 1505 a v.—
Explicit 3us liber istius vite beatissime virginis Katerine
Incipit prosa in 4^m librum.

IIII.

1 dwellars 2 lykkynyd. dwelle in a h. 3 els. draynes, off ȝe 4 farys. theyr 6 þere bee om. dyuers eke 7 laborars are lykkynnyd 8 gode l. 10 lerne and soke bothe teche and drawe 12 conseyt, wele savourd sauoures 13 bene v. 14 om.: MS. Othyr þer be þat prophytabull no thynge 17 but yf. tabylle 18 vnto þat wark. fulle grete. 19: Theyr bodyes to stuffe and make þem more abylle, To vyeyus lyvyng to be Inclynabylle 20 slepe 21 dranys 22 þe draynes 23 ffor þat þei here þouȝ they haue d. 24 ȝyt in 25 nor 27 no om. 28 Suffythe þem here to haue theyr reste 29 semys 31 And holy kyrk The hyue I-wys 32 Wyth many stormys of tyms affrayd 33 vertuese. haue om. 34 hyr. to hony & waxe 35 menys. lyst 36 lere 37 owlde 38 þis ys to hyme. succure 39 stabulle 42 flukyng 45 Of euery wyȝt was feyr to sene 46 ouȝt of hony grete holynes 47 can 51 first and om. 52 one syde 53 one a cl. n. 55 Ware. he. on om. hym 57 eke she gaddyrd 58 truly to kepe euer 61 eke om. 62 of clothe. olde 63 laborying and hyr 64 sukkyd. bettyr 65 flours 67 in to h. chyrche 68 os 69 labur 70 any galye 74 lyuyng stabully 75 heynly 76 hyr p.—Explicit pro huius 4^{ti} libri. Incipit 4us liber vite sancte Katerine 78 os 79 Emprowrs 81 galarius 82 hight om. thyrd 84 mans 85 galarye 86 kept stylle þe 87 sacryfyce. þer 88 any 89 presse 90 and to. 93 left þeir. resynyd 94 excusse 96 avaylde. nor inst. of now 99 Resynyd. vnto 100 Emprours 101 empyre. or cane 102 hatels. shours 104 seys. Ieste 105 assynyd 106 And þe. tho om. 107 to kepe L. 109 cuntreesse 110 ware 111 brytan. land 112 lyke as I ȝoue telle 113 Thys 115 a om. batelle 117 or. dyed. lyue 118 os. caryne 119 lat. in salysbery 120 Thane. took om. romans 121 on om. tho om. 123 & wyth g. 124 oute om. vnto m. 125 þat inst. of and 126 þat 127 cum 128 or. doune cast 129 cycille. dyd he lere 130 As c. tels whych l saw l. 132 lythe. abyed 133 wepe or els 134 dwelt 136 þis om. 137 bothe om. 138 be ryght 139 for sothe to seyne 140 reyne whe[n]. was 141 or. to 142 soiours 143 dome 144 regneth om. 145 Now os alone 146 kepe 147 slepys. ellis om. 148 reynyd. al om. 149 speke. what so euer 150 no wyffe meyd nor m. 151 must nedis cum 153 What man þat let. it om. 154 Appone. xulde set 156 pepile 157 oppun. þore 160 poure. had 161 covyd. wylde 162 Thane. romayns. cummyne assent 163 ded om. wryȝt 164 brytane 165 preyd. os. knyȝt 166 cum. ageyns. fyȝt 169 greyt strenghe 170 lande 171 encresse. lenghe 172 by whyche 173 Ytaly. up om. pepile 177 trustyd. one 178 lefte 179 howsholde. myche 180 weel om. 181 in 182 and streyt frome 183 ouȝt off bretane 184 þis same 185 deseuyd 186 lyvyng 187 os a man 188 strenghtes 189 os 190 cald 191 þe felde wun 192 ȝyt put. wars 193 þe ende 195 suche mastres 197 exaltyde 198 and om. fathers 199 waxde 200 more om. In-

3 I *

438 *Various Readings: MS. Arundel* 20. *Book IV.*

clynyd   201 lettyrs to   203 he seyd truly . wolde . þe   204 came   205 hem om.
207 Wryȝt . thynk   208 dwelle   210 greetis . legis . empyre   211 ȝoue wyt .
fathyrs . before   213 batelle . neyther om.   nor lore   214 Suche . gods þat be
wyce   215 os   217 we . frome suche v. laws   218 specyally from . honȝ one a t.
220 man inst. of god   221 I- om.   suche   222 myche   223 now dwellyng . lande
224 nothyr . nor   226 os   228 sermones   229 xalle   230 Suche . deseruff   231
lordshyps nor ryches   232 men any   234 offycers   235 any   236 We xalle
ordene . Iett   237 xalle . suche mastres   240 vnto   241 knyghys and lordys
242 cum . b. þe more & þo l.   243 vnto   245 þat inst. of whiche   246 massyngers
are . fare   248 abyede   249 Into . as om.   vnderstande   250 mythy hande   251
cetye   252 meny . levyd euer in preyr   253 cam om.   255 are . os   257 specyal
om.   258 þer inst. of the cytee   259 storyd ther wythe m.   260 cum   261 þer
dyd   262 w. were   263 stode in sentence   264 wolde   269 gods   270 now om.
271 ful om.   274 Ther . cum   276 what we gyff   277 Vnto suche wyches . far
278 thynk   279 are   281 þat he   282 þat þei   283 Who   285 brytayne   287
pepile . stouȝt pouere   288 tretor   289 Os . entyryd   290 gunnys and engyne
291 nor . þer   294 seys   295 conquerre   296 on₂ om . þat c.   297 prayd . were
298 xulde . bowys   299 gyftis   300 and landis . castels   301 nede þei none
302 thyrde   304 wylle   305 þe seruyce . þe newe   306 godds wer ordynd by þe
commyns   307 seys xalle . þe more mercyfulle to vs   308 þat om. sermonys
309 þer . crosse   310 Suche . þan   311 cryed þan . closse   312 moughe . hys
saw   313 a lytylle wyth-drawe   315 wyt . hye   316 haue . conseruatyue   318
forsakyne . falne   319 we inst. of me   321 apparycyone   323 bad . teche þe
pepylle   324 sermones . ryghes   325 fathers . knew, vsyd overl. any   326
knythys   327 Who gyffis . fyȝthys   328 holdis . vpp hyme   330 make . mastryc
331 quakis   332 makis   333 lyȝtnyng . makis   334 Alle þis shewys he to vs .
forsakis   335 ful om.   336 or ȝe be shent.   337 Leue   338 gods   339 schep-
pardis . plowmen   340 wyt fulle wele . standis . mans   341 Vnto   342 Os seyth
þis c. of criste os s. þe b.   343 alle þe syns from þe worlde he toke   344 be . shal
om.   345 xalle gyfe   346 longis   347 euerlastyng   348 Repelle from   349 I
gyne ȝoue   350 sowlys . bodys . shame   351 off þe . grete om.   sermones   354
wolde   356 of om.   358 was   359 ys . replenyshed   360 & wyth   363 pepile .
grete and also so st.   364 nouȝt els   365 cum   366 borne . þei dyd   367 there
om.   xulde   368 Serche . mynstralcye   372 trumpettis   373 Myche . dyed
375 bochers laborycle os . bene   376 weshyng . carkas doune   377 moredyr . the
om.   379 the₂ om.   380 byschops . areyd . theyr seruyce   381 mattyns . seyd
om. nor   382 gane   385 þe s.   387 eye   388 had . suspeccyone   389 are   391
sune . owres   392 graffene (I- om.) . sotelle   393 The next   394 welys . hyr
meydyns   396 Wyth hys sykkylle in hys h.   397 no nothyr   398 vengance
399—405 om.   406 awe . I not avance   407 Myche   408 was . offeryng   409
nethyr oxe hors nor   410 sle and fle, þus was theyr crying   411 þe prestis &
byschops . thyng   412 mynstrals   413 makis   414 The olde pepile seyd . sawe .
deys   415 os   416 haue . weys   417 goulds   419 ȝunge . Iolely   420 rewylle
among   421 at þe solennyte abouȝt   422 harde   423 þeis syers so stouuȝt   424 are .
wyth fulle mykylle pryed   425 lokyd   426 dose . gods   428 holy inst. of noble
429 longis   430 hir om.   431 stylle inst. of tho   432 frome   433 worldly welthys
are . frome   434 þat t.   435 ryȝt os.   436 meyd . hard þis grete c.   437 now
om.   438 menys   439 knythys   441 scrys qwat   442 þan . annolde seruaund
443 he om.   444 He hathe c. euery man to haunte   445 ryches and seruyce
447 and inst. of if . wyt.   448 off lyue . pore . state   450 þei þat ageyne   451
clossyt   452 poure   453 Lat þem   454 Suffythe . and . lyue   455 cummorouse .
any lece   457 we om.   458 cytyners off þe cyte . xalle   459 os . begynnys   460
tauȝt anon vppon theyr gods   461 þeyr fathyrs   462 hard   463 cum . ower
464 þo drede   465 receyffe . concellouro   466 vppone   468 þe . that om.   ware
470 þis meyd . hard   471 remembyr how   473 She spake þus to me & seyd my
meyd   474 be   475 to₂ om.   476 & suche   477 vnto   478 oure   479 behestyd
me yt ys . I- om.   482 reysys   484 þer . remembyrd þe cunnand þat   485 baptyme . weshyd   486 sadd   487 nor . lesse   488 war throwne . cawdurun   489

Various Readings: MS. Arundel 20. Book IV. 439

chosse 490 þan waxyd she feyr & ruddy of colour lyke þe rosse 493 enprentyd 494 worldly. fykkylle 495 nethyr. nor 496 ffro. hart. yt xalle 497 þan softly 498 fful om. astunnyd. for om. 500 she þoo 502 eke om. gyffne 503 þis inst. of tho 504 & towne 505 trough 506 Vnto my 507 soner cum 508 nought om. but sorow & quede 509 euere om. any 510 boldly 511 trewthe 512 suffyrs. now om. 513 chyrchys. seruandis 514 One. I wele 515 xalle 516 Ho louys. world. þat om. hyme wele to spylle 517 ordynd 518 xalle. frome. No new chapter. 519 walkis 520 place 521 folowyd. þe place 524 purpose 525 Scater. þat 526 pepile 527 replete. entyr 528 on om. poretars 529 lat. errande 530 Vnto 531 stand 534 vanytes nor to no 536 at om. 537 þer. strong 538 hyre offeryng. 1- om. 539 þeyr 540 emprours 541 saw þis bry3t meyd and sh. 542 ful om. 543 speke 544 seyd. pepile 545 Ar cum frome farve 546 a done 548 ry3t to 549 strengh 551 manes 552 entyrde 553 ry3t as 555 kynde. curtasye 557 3yt. myche 560 done ageyne. grete 562 Þus take. frome 563 gyff 564 not help. nor. eke om. 566 woldest om. 567 knowe om. syttis 570 vnto. & do 571 vnto. os 572 agenst. causyst. to rysse 573 suche duels os be 574 sothly 577 & fro. wykyd 578 gane 579 Vnto 580 xalt 581 yet om. trost þis 582 I- om. 583 ydols magre off theyr 584 Ageyne. resones 585 & eke 586 pyk & burnstone off 587 for þem. no nothyr 588 ware. do 589 gods are duels 590 dyscevers. covytyse 591 als wele 592 nor 593 ete nor drynk. of om. 594 wythowtyne. fote þei mey 595 thei om. no thyng 596 þi. illneyone 597 þat þe and alle thyng made (made on the margin) 598 vnkynde 600 þe amend. mayst 602 xalle. an om. 609 coloure waxyd why3t 610 & he begane 611 Astunnyd. a party 612 aremys to hyme gan he 613 seyd ageyne 614 vengance 615 hathe take 617 þeir 619 hath ordynd to þem 621 syster 626 ware 628 ware 629 Iebytt 630 That 3e. godds 631 Thane. meyd 632 Who. gods 634 xalt 635 ware 637 so s. 638 land 639 father 640 ytale 641 þan reynyd 642 calde hyme w. þe dobile 643 lokyd. & to 645 þan are þei 646 ware 647 longis 648 3e þe pepile dysceyff and clade 649 nor 652 tho om. mynde 653 strenghe 654 ensample. kynde 655 trow. stabyle 656 seyd 658 lat 659 oppynly 660 whyche þat 662 þe om. Impossybyls 663 sadly om. hepe 665 meyd 667 imp. ys vnto 668 Remeue. hart 669 soo om. 670 That om. þou3 þat 672 be 675 os. herrysye 676 seyd 677 frome. man chyld & wyffe 678 And fro euery meyd. ychone 679 Þeis fonde 680 Vnto. semyd 681 awnswerd 683 now inst. of on-to 3ow 684 lettis 685 are 686 nethyr. nor. the om. 687 take. eye 689 fruet 690 ys 3oure rage 692 freute 694 sekis rosees. rooses 697 yt. among 698 far. any pere 701 stokkis 703 Leue yt 705 gyffis 706 no suche. gyffe 707 ensampylle. 3oue inst. of than. preffe 708 rottyne. thyng 709 by3t 711 oure 714 haue 715 also long 716 rudenes & crokyd o. 717 xalle. sykkerly 720 habile 721 the om. what so euere any 722 Thene my3t men a sene 723 men. I- om. cherde 724 ere om. & theyr browys gan þe b. 725 þe ydols 726 & deth. afferyde 728 vnto 730 vnto 731 hyre 732 haue. begyne 734 nor into suche 735 gane þei crye 736 saw 737 begane. þe colour in 738 ylle 739 Vnto 741 My oune. thynkis. thei om. gane 744 haue. mervously 745 now om. 748 bewte 749 vnto 750 Meyd. seyd. begune 751 vnto 752 3o om. sune 754 3e spend. 3oue slake 758 I- om. 759 dampe 761 stoppe 762 þer-for. ware. els 763 rebels 764 any 768 walkis. nor 769 master 770 are bune 771 traytours are 772 spendythe. great 773 ensampile 774 be. ful om. pusance 778 cace 779 menye 780 deffye 783 þe traytours. lyne 785 semys by. creatore 787 frome. honore 788 xulde hathe. þat he 789 When. byselye oure helthe 790 gyue. dewls 791 solemly off 793 Traytours. os. xalle 794 wylle þe 3oue not 795 Vnto þat 796 lat. frome 798 xalle 799 stunnyd 800 alle þeyr wyttis. for om. are 801 vexyd. harte 802 to2 om. nor 803 low3t. the om. 804 Wherfore. thynkis. right om. harte 805 punnyshe. peyns 806 strangylle hyr sle. brynne 807 3yt. þerby nothyng 808 thynk. rynne 811 resones

440 *Various Readings: MS. Arundel* 20. *Book IV.*

814 councelle 815 þer can 816 frome 817 whedyr 819 ry3t þus 820 clarkis 824 sonyst dystroye 826 I- om. 827 massyngers. wylde 828 laude 829 þe clarkis þat. lyuelode 830 cum 831 Vnto 832 þe lettars are wryttyn & now selde ychone 833 massyngers. are 834 as for 835 Sclyd þeys lettars 836 gravyne (I- om.) 838 off inst. of if 839 Bee om. ffor þe leste 3yt 841 haue 842 off councelle. cete 843 ffathyr vnto. on om. kynrod 845 Sendis. clargye 847 lordshyppe. are 848 wytt 849 Vnto. prudence 850 nethyr taxe nor deme 851 oure feythe & sekte 852 makis. to om. 853 seyence 854 musse 855 moost om. now haue we cau3t 857 myche 858 frome 860 pervertys. lande. wysse 861 byd 3owe þat. wysse 862 now om. 866 xalle. cristynyd. and eke 867 avaunsyd xalle 868 rychece 869 are. lettyrs wryttyne. I- om. 871 Vnto. palyce 873 vnto 874 many om. behestys to hyr he hyght 877 of₂ om. 878 any 879 on om. 882 in₂ om. 883 of om. gyffe 884 Vnto. as to. goddece 885 that om. lyffe 886 xalle. lece 887 wordynes 890 þeis promysees 892 euer inst. of tho 894 hem om. 895 wylle he 896 w. grete sadnes 897 þeis wordis. lorde aboue 898 forsake hym wylle I neuer more 899 man. nor 900 my. frome 901 ful om. there om. lyke 902 dye 903 Vnto 904 seyne. þi. my3t 905 Os. promysyd 906 lat 907 rasse 908 nor 909 os. stand 910 are 912 wolde. xulde. inclyne 913 my 914 vnknowne 915 dyscens. tastament 916 os. myn om. 918 Seyne. are 919 suche mastres in vddyr mens landis 920 tennans 921 offryng. handis 922 trumpyttis. tabors. before. stande 923 or my lysence 924 to god & to me grete o. 926 vnry3tffulle 927 þair byddyng 928 ageyns 929 went 932 Thane 935 xulde take 937 soo om. þat she 938 þat om. horryblye. 940 Os. spouce. chambur 941 nor nothyng 943 are 946 ys þus in þ. so closydde 947 ryddyne. lande 948 as I supposyd 949 bande 950 cetees. vnderstand 951 cessyone. begune 952 Yche. off othyr. gune 953 But whan þat he hys lurney had spedd 954 cum. hom om. 955 messangers 956 þeis clarkis 957 Are cum wythe bookis chargyd many a weyne 958 þus are met 959 are 960 are entyrd. concelle 961 wyt. for them hathe 962 any ffeylle 964 masters chosse 966 if om. 967 My awter 968 in₂ om. 969 & alle 970 none theme 971 studdyd. grounde 972 now om. cummyng 973 seythe 974 Masters 976 renythe. suche. vse 977 fallyd. þe 979 ys Into 980 dewls 981 supposse. trouthe 982 be 983 suche a 3unge. thynkis yt reuthe 987 To cast. the om. how inst. of now 988 cum 989 aunswers are 990 sykker 991 Vnto 992 Vnto. hyer father 993 hyer mother 994 whiche om. 3e doo 998 studyous 999 þeis masters 1000 nede. cunnyng 1001 on om. 1003 resone 1004 goddes 1007 cum 1008 hard. wher a w. 1009 And after. semonyng. on om. 1010 commandis 1011 her om. 1012 specyalle 1013 longis vnto 1015 destresse. No new chapter 1016 odyr. cum 1017 assey. a prevye councelle 1018 vaylythe 1019 hys resone wylle not veylle 1020 meyd. proposycyon 1021 tho om. 1022 Stale. experyence 1023 armony. þer 1024 hyer 1026 macedony 1027 Ageyne. not hyr 1028 provest 1030 resones 1031 mayd 1032 syster. hedir om. 1033 Before 1034 whedyr 1035 holde 1036 renye 1038 persone 1039 streue 1040 meydyns. roosse 1041 longis. gloosse 1043 Vnto 1044 I haue. lykis 1045 alle worldly. yt ys 1048 know 3e. for a fulle certeyne 1050 be 1051 Thane 1052 laborde 1054 now must 3ow 1055 Os longys. traytorus. þus wylle raffe 1057 or els 1058 ermony 1059 on om. 1060 leue 1061 Thynk. 1062 neuer none 1063 3ow 1064 vnto 1065 þer 1067 knowne 1068 wyche 1069 in wycheralfte he had þe name 1070 wysdome 1072 and hyr þus r. 1075 wher ys 1076 wordy. to om. 1077 wold 1078 the om. wysdome & þe treuthe wyth-owtyn mysse 1079 erle. macedony. caspanas 1080 Vnto þat. thus om. 1082 borne 1085 stand. casse 1086 hangyd 1088 Vnto. wysse 1090 frome. nedys must 1094 Vnto 1095 seruandis 1096 peyne om. 1101 myche. on om. 3ow echone 1102 off whyche 1103 are gone 1104 vnto payns 1105 frome 1106 bounde sore 1108 Nor 1110 þe. was 1112 ware 1115 þe 1117 barkyng. on om. 1118 any wreches 1119

Various Readings: MS. Arundel 20. Book IV. 441

and off so hye d. 1120 must 1121 proveste 1122 þeis clarkis. lat 1123 kene 1124 must. dye 1125 no nothyr 1126 clatteryng 1128 are entret into. concelle 1129 seyrs. owre 1130 wylle se 1131 masters do 1132 from 1133-4 But yf ȝe spede oure feyth wylle sone slyede, ffor þe pepile wylle turne one euery syde 1136 many man 1138 any 1139 Ageyns. nor 1140 rosse. þer 1141 lat. cum 1142 ware 1143 gone to presone to hyr 1144 Ientylle 1146 nedys. for om 1147 thydyng 1149 Thane. al om. 1150 hyr and hyer cause euer to g. a. 1152 seruffe. whyche þat syttis 1154 Dyed 1155 vnto. fyndis vnkynd 1157 canne 1159 þi d. 1160 wondis blowe. wanne 1161 gyffe 1162 gan. worldly 1164 stande 1166 nor 1171 mey haue str[e]nghe. for om. 1172 reasons 1173 chyrches. can 1174 frome. maners 1176 Os 1177 my h. 1178 truste 1179 cums. but only 1180 lat 1181 makis 1182 þerfore. þowe 1183 ȝyt. ȝet₂ om. 1185 ester. plece hyr answere 1186 solempe 1189 causse 1190 clausse 1194 Os. os 1195 woutis 1197 dyrke cornars 1200 cummyng 1204 And as hys messanger he sendis me now 1205 greetis 1206 þis matter 1207 commaundys 1208 not om. 1209 clerely 1210 ȝet om. xalle 1211 now om. 1214 lede. vnto petrus 1215 fygures. seys 1516 xalle 1217 xalle dye 1218 whyche þat 1219 determyd 1220 þeis clarkis xalle now 1222 xalle now from þem 1223 þe om. 1225 sauȝoure 1227 xalle suffyr. myche 1228 lesure 1229 þis myche. gyffe. ful om. 1230 for om. þe kynge 1231 dye evyne In 1232 xalle 1233 gyue. messyngere 1234 spryte. dobulnesse 1236 of heuene om. haue 1238 pays. weyght 1239 be 1240 beleue 1241 ordynyd 1243 spons 1246 be 1247 comfortyd 1248 suche inst. of swete 1250 þat om. 1252 herte om. 1253 nor frome 1257 cum. owre 1259 paretye. elles om. 1261 stande 1262 þey 1263 þe l. sat 1264 and be 1265 meyd. eke also 1266 was best 1267 one hye 1268 exortyd he 1269 Masters. þis concyanatryx 1270 off whome 1271 devyour 1273 gluede. from 1274 cunnyng 1275 vnto 1276 strange chalaunce sayng 1277 Vnto. in om. 1278 os 1279 guerdome grete off price 1280 that om. 1281 thynkis. hath ȝe 1282 ȝowe. guerdome 1284 xalle leyff 1285 as om. take & know 1287 Iuste Iuge and man trewe 1289 on- om. 1290 has 1292 thynk. enowe 1293 lat. damselle. towghe 1294 Entermyte 1295 ful om. 1296 Than. meydyne to 1297 Seyne 1298 Appone 1299 myȝt 1300 mynd frome 1301 frome 1302 lat. any. to me now 1303 Than 1304 a 1305 cum. seyd. emprours 1306 meyd 1308 cum. know we 1309 lyggis 1310 Seyne. araye 1311 xalle purvey 1312 hens away 1313 sykkerly. convey 1314 þe 1315 councelle 1316 aunswer xalle we 1321 pronounse. þat om. þe leste 1322 vnworthy 1323 sethe þe tyme. þat om. 1324 loste. auctorytees 1325 fynde. fructe 1326 be gone, gyffne. els 1328 fathyr 1330 ȝe dyd 1331 Off alle þem haue I take now 1332 þeyr. In ternys & in proce 1333 erely 1334 gloce 1335 chosyne 1336 eke om. 1338 takyne. Escalape 1339 alle om. heyr. serchyng 1340 myche trwer. susteyne 1341 euery creature 1342 eke om. 1343 done 1345 Beholde. masters. þeys mens 1346 studdyd & laburde 1347 sottelle 1348 lyffis 1350 laste 1351 lerenyng 1352 treetis. þat xalle 1354 alle creature 1355 whyȝte 1356 fyer. or. ys 1359 borne 1360 vnto 1361 prophyt 1362 hyng 1363 here inst. of tho 1365 knowne. was om. sundre 1367 abeyd 1368 eselye. is om. 1369 saw 1375 reynyd erthlye 1376 suffreyne 1377 tumbile. wawe 1378 Troste not in þem, ffor nowght ys theyr myght 1379 whych blyndis 1381 þei xalle. ful om. 1382 my om. 1383 xalle. haue, me om. 1388 of ȝe b. 1390 not. ne om. 1391 seyence makis ȝe 1392 more om. 1393 ys þat þat makis 1395 matters 1397 bettyr 1398 be 1400 and om. makis 1402 ane. tho om. 1403 os þowe 1404 Master. calde þei 1405 angure 1406 he styrt vpp in þe p. 1407 Thane 1408 cytynars 1410 xalle. ȝe for to calle 1412 wysdome 1413 suffyr 1414 in suche vengabile 1416 lande 1417 here om. 1418 vnderstande 1419 Many of þem be brent wyth a brande 1422 sey. that om. be vnkynde 1423 benyffyttis 1424 ȝungyst. womans kynde 1425 so for to 1426 al om. coloure 1427 dewles 1428 &

442 *Various Readings: MS. Arundel 20. Book IV.*

thys ys warste 1431 folke . lyste 1432 resones . I- om. 1433 frome 1434 cum 1435 prechars . ageyns 1436 novylte 1437 be-gynnys 1438 calde . prophyte . galalee 1439 cals 1440 Off sande off se off water and off erthe 1441 Inowthe 1442 convicte 1444 greate dobbylnesse 1445 sey 1448 whyche know alle men ys 1451 frome 1452 was 1453 hard Iwys 1454 stale . prevely 1455 master . I- om. 1456 and so 1457 Vnto 1458 She om. 1460 take . my 1461 wythow3t any 1462 One . or 1464 hys fader ys 1465 seyne 1466 procede farther-more 1467 before 1468 eterne in hevyne reynynge 1470 noted om. 1474 newly 1477 dyde . ware 1480 And 3oure . are 1481 ffor þei . grunt . þei aylle 1482 Os ffaue In þis matter os 3yt I haue sowght 1483 frome 1484 now ame 1485 than . reasons 1486 trubbylde 1488 sowne 1489 cum 1490 wolde 1491 maners xalle overl. 1492 clarke . þer 1493 Vnto . meyd 1495 vnderstand 1496 make . diffence 1498 nor . no 1499 be 1501 lyke 1502 betokyns 1504 are . tokyns 1505 gyue . harte 1506 Not ffor theme but ffor theyr s. 1509 now sum-what 1512 To do theyr d. men þat go þem bye 1513 meyd 1515 stand one . rowe 1516 perseue 1517 þan in ane oþer 1518 lyvyd 1521 Veniabulle dispeteus . a om. 1522 condycyons vnstabile 1523 a whyle wyth hyr abyede 1524 chylderne kylde 1525 gyltee . father 1526 He banyshyd hyme and made hym hys harborow to seke 1527 syster 1528 ffather . he om. þe lande 1529 þeis are 1530 feythe þus eternally stande 1531 byggyd . bryttylle lande 1532 I'lato wyth (!) r. of þeis meydyns vyolent 1534 Walcane . cukkolde 1535 such a persone . any 1537 encressys . vnclene 1538 þis . vyolence . from þem shoue 1539 god om. 1540 so-erye 1543 suttel'e reasons . þan 1545 sothe seyd 1548 habomynabile 1550 cums 1551 haue 1552 wer þus ; openly om. I- om. 1553 be 1554 ffle 3e . drede 3e 1555 Thane 1556 one worde to hyr 1557 so hys harte dyd b. ; tho om. 1558 Vnto . latt 1559 os 1560 xalle . thei om. 1561 wysdome . make sone r. 1562 clark 1563 so inst. of tho 1569 commune . Intent 1572 mocyons 1576 despreue 1579 Os . now amongis 1580 os 1581 Hym take we . & eke Iuno 1582 takyne . ayer . gyffys 1584 Resembled . that om. sempyterne 1586 over suche thyngis . be eterne 1587 My awne 1593 founde 1594 Off theyr godds but for a conclusyone 1595 þis man haue 1596 preue 1598 Gladdyd 1599 waxyd 1600 frome 1601 bere hyr now . koye 1603 lat . here 1604 tho om. vnto þe master 1605 hyed 1606 fygure . coloure 1607 ley 1608 Are 1609 se 1611 þey be 1612 are . graffne 1613 easye 1614 are not nor 1615 arre 1618 planyttis 1619 xulde stande 1621 bene 1623 alle planettis be 1624 farther 1625 þan be they 1626 hei om. 1627 wyth inst. of alle 1628 are . nor 1629 Vnto 1630 off 3oure errour 1631 haffe 1632 mervelyd 1634 are 1635 hard 1636 can declare . be 1637 master . tho om. 1638 the om. 1639 a woman . attayme corr. to attame 1640 Lat . felows 1641 gyue 1642 world . standis 1645 laste 1647 Whyche þat . thus om. 1650 devyne . farre . euer-more studyinge 1651 I haue hene . semys 1652 demys 1653 alle thys 1654 lerne off h. þe platt and þe pleyne 1656 ys he 1657 I- om. 1658 ys he 1659 now to lerne 1662 þeis same men . she dyd 1663 Seyne . now þe forme . a scolere 1664 are . redyare . mysteres 1665 as for 1667 one 1669 ful om. 1670 in god 1671 auctor seys 1672 one 1673 commun 1674 none suche 1675 ordynyd . councelle 1677 one . fulle myche mervelle 1678 consydered . mans myche 1679 þeyr substance 1681 theys iii 1684 falne 1685 can hyme 1686 Among . off grete delice 1688 in erthe abulle 1690 þis lorde dyed 1691 in to . into 1693 dyed 1695 master 1696 same om. 1697 Ioye (ful om.) 1699 puregyd 1700 And made . correccyone 1701 mervelythe . Infyrmacione 1702 wyth 1703 One 1704 conceue as 3yt very clere 1705 coppyllyng 1706 Be 1707 be . in one 1708 none suche 1709 and inst. of if . he must 1715 be 1716 tho om. þis 1717 conceue 1719 coppylyd 1722 enowght 1723 raysyd lasare frome 1724 leyne 1726 He . os . dyd . þe greue 1727 þati om. 1728 tyed 1729 on om. dydd glyde 1730 and sowle 1731 þeis myracles 1732 myche 1733 gyffyng . 3ow 1735 Indewe 1736 ful om. 1737 hys 1738 shews . & man 1739 right om. 1744 that om. . slepyd 1746 wele inst. of pleynly 1747

Various Readings: MS. Arundel 20. *Book IV.* 443

can 1750 werkyng. whyls 1753 blysse 1756 wolde. what om. I xulde vnto 1758 a. amyttyd 1759 ʒoure 1760 Berys 1763 hange 1764 cum ʒowre a. 1767 meyd 1769 overtanne 1770 preyd 1771 his om. 1773 falle 1774 makis 1775 Ageyns. qualle 1777 xuld 1779 mans 1781 ho þat. thyng 1783 Vn om. 1784 desyrys 1786 fulle gode 1787 wylle scruffe h. as þis t. 1789 Vnto 1790 matter 1791 them 1792 þat þei xulde n. m. t. one þeyr old l. 1794 abouuʒte 1795 are Ioynyd to-gydder þeys ii. 1799 frome 1800 els. owre 1801 qwykk 1802 any 1803 for om. serche 1804 Beleue ʒe þis thyng 1805 are. now om. 1806 In euery. walke 1807 for to 1808 it om. I- om. 1809 warkyng 1812 cum 1813 haue. from. þe 1814 seyne 1815 knolege 1816 than off ʒowe now 1817 ʒowe inst. of ful 1818 ʒowe. þat l. . haue 1819 ʒoue 1820 þat om. 1821 gyffne 1822 Yche. there a. 1823 mervelous to ch. 1824 ware 1829 where om. prechyd þem so t. 1830 forsoke þem 1831 freyler 1832 worthye 1835 The thodyr seyd 1836 saw 1837 stunnyd. þat be theyr 1839 and om. experyence 1841 begane 1842 he om. ys 1844 bones aremys 1846 many 1847 astunnyd 1848 Cowardis chorls 1850 now inst. of thus 1851 moost om. 1852 Or. shul be om. 1854 passys 1855 thynk. stande 1856 Ther 1859 nor 1860 So off þis matter as he now a-fesyde was 1861 sothly 1863 sundre 1864 Contradyccions in theme fulle sone. ffune 1865 ys fulle wele knowne 1866 Os. seyd. fulle rownde 1868 that om. haue 1869 seyd 1871 Provenyng 1872 made om. rekkynnyng. wylle 1873 Among. any 1874 bookis 1875 borne ffulle trewly 1877 not ʒyt fully 1878 Seyne. was off hys mother 1882 þat inst. of thyng. thowsandis 1883 þe d. or he. than om. 1884 an om. 1886 þeis syempulle pepile 1890 haue 1891 on om. 1892 grounde 1893 takyne one parte 1894 the tother 1895 falls. rekkynnyng 1897 þe b. 1899 ago 1900 Vnto. ler gar 1902 But as for þis matter þis mystry. vndoo 1904 Os. semys 1905 begynnyng. first om. xalle 1906 god om. haue. oure lorde Ihesu 1907 lyvande 1909 off 1910 kynde 1911 kynd. his om. 1913 decesse 1914 cuppyllyng 1915 plesse 1916 & þe fals dewls þus. fesse 1917 manhode 1918 manhode 1919 haue he bene 1921 þat 1923 dyd hynge 1925 haue bene 1927 stunnyd. mynde 1929 of om. and alle þe kynde 1931 þer. wyth a grete crye 1932 Os 1934 off cryst hys feyth & 1937 þer awey, tho om. 1939 Whan. eke gane felle. 1940 his om. ryalle 1941 mastyrd 1942 not he. massynger 1944 losse. myght 1945 wer mythy 1948 take 1950 þane om. 1951 thrune 1953 me thouʒt 1955 haue. I note 1956 Os 1958 fyght 1959 ouercam. suche kynde 1960 wele 1961 be. by mankynde 1962 among 1964 parfytt and 1965 that om. so stabile 1966 or 1968 dyede 1970 a tre 1971 fyght 1972 In þe tre. was wo 1974 þat tre. a om. 1975 a om. 1978 appoysaylle 1980 Os. lady om.. one-syede 1981 Os. abyed 1984 But &. cum 1985 one 1986 prophycye 1987 not ʒyt veryly 1988 spekis 1990 whome. singler 1991 noo 1992 moo 1993 prophytis. berys wytnes 1996 to om. in h. 1997 haue 2000 calde 2001 prophyttis vn-to 2002 induede. ful om. 2004 How forbare ʒow 2005 raynyng 2008 syne. be 2009 reasons. lady om. vaylle. raakis 2012 haue. be 2013 calde 2018 you om. 2019 meryte 2020 yff ʒe 2021 nor nevyr none were 2024 reynyng 2027 Thow callyʒ 2029 folows. the om. 2030 þer where ʒe. can 2031 ther be godds thre fowlous 2032 syttis 2033 here inst. of sir. among 2035 as om. , 2036 chose 2037 a. stylle 2038 reynys. any 2039 but yff 2040 cums 2041 My. breke 2042 perfore thys conceyt ir ʒowre hartis now founge 2043 raynys 2044 pyte haue calde. to om. 2045 right om. 2047 euere om. 2048 Reynyng 2049 are. chylderne 2051 eft ʒyt legge 2052 balaam 2054 rehersys. dede om. 2055 þe. prophyttis. hy s. 2056 dyvynars 2058 alle þat ther ere 2062 masterys 2063 avaylys 2064 gyue 2065 haue. a 2067 passys 2068 spekis 2069 seys 2070 harte enterly 2072 what so any 2073 xalle. my 2074 one. knolege 2075 I haue 2076 Lat 2078 breke 2080 anone inst. of concoursly. one 2081 þe consent 2082 One. þei alle wyth one voyce 2083 commandis 2084 þei wylle 2085 vthyr 2087 increasyd 2088 haue we ladd 2089 are knowne 2090 ware.

444   *Various Readings: MS. Arundel* 20. *Book IV.*

leyne   2092 holdyn . a vanyte   2095 but on*e* þei wot ys saturne   2096 Ych to thodyr . prevyly . thus om.   2099 falsed   2100 þat was inst. of there thanne   2101 lokyd   2102 thus om. renythys   2104 any maydyn*e*   2105 wyser in hyer sawe   2106 grevys   2109 myche . vntrew   2110 On*e*   2111 was cu*m* off newe   2112 reasons þ*er* othyr   2113 my   2114 lye þer full*e* s.   2115 þat inst. of lete   2118 dey inst. of lady   2119 master . þe   2121 now wyll*e* we   2122 chosyn*e* . commy*n*   2123 þat om.   2124 dystroy   2126 we see   2130 vp om. solemly   2134 my pece   2135 þis matter þus . dowʒtlece   2138 it om. greate   2140 fro . fykkull*e*   2141 haue om. that om.   2142 victor þa*n*   2144 off cryste   2145 beffore haue   2146 thynk yt ys   2147 farther   2152 thynk*is*   2153 A-fore   2154 from*e* . þis   2156 wolde   2157 ʒyt   2160 Seyn*e*   2161 gyffne . manes . as a   2164 call*e*   2166 balle   2168 proue þe*m* wele   2169 meyd   2170 any   2171 mankynde   2173 myche . ageyns   2176 or off velanye   2177 sytt*is*   2178 harborage   2179 cu*m*myng . lyke . sun*e*   2180 lyke . lykkinid . meydyns   2181 shynys thorow   2183 peresyd   2184 farde þe   2185 hyer   2186 co*n*ceyvyd   2188 neu*er*   2189 be   2190 xall*e*   2191 ʒe xall*e* not fynde me vntrewe   2192 movyd   2193 sore om.   2194 full*e* sore & hard   2195 vttur   2196 strong   2197 my . thyng*is*   2198 yet om. v*n*nethys   2200 spek*is* . more om. preng*n*antly   2202 þat syre   2203 ʒoue . myre   2204 vnto   2205 bothe inst. of hough   2206 coupylde   2208 not he   2209 done . as I gesse   2213 on*e*   2215 Seyne . be . on*e*   2216 yche   2217 are   2218 eke om. on*e* . accord*is*   2219 a om. thynk*is* . wrythys   2220 seyd   2221 Oon om.   2222 Wherto   2223 thus.   2224 Seyr*e* . worde   2225 off inst. of on-to   2226 folowys   2227 p*er*reyeyd   2228 vnto   2229 long*is*   2232 trow   2234 myche   2235 not farther   2236 wysdome . nouʒt   2237 os   2238 But ʒyt   2239 Vnto   2240 here   2241 sey . vnto . faders   2242 longys . whyche . gouerne om.   2243 longys   2244 wysdome . a om.   2246 Wher . be h. long*is*   2248 folowys . seyn*e*   2249 in om.   2251 mankynde   2252 Intent   2256 Os . tho om.   2258 on*e* god   2259 emsampil*e* . we om.   2260 putt*is*   2261 wryghys þeroff in . of om.   2262 sey   2266 phylystens   2267 parylle   2268 þat thyng   2273 ordynd   2274 burdyne   2275 and secunde   2278 Entyrferryd whyche   2279 Os . thynk*is* . long*is*   2280 occupythe   2281 m hyre . hym*e*   2284 shortly inst. of as of this book   2285 Off þis dysputacio*ne* . thynk*is* . it om.   2286 Seyn*e*   2287 vnto . mynde   2288 Know   2289 haue . þeis masters all*e* b.   2290 inspecyally   2291 yt vaylys   2292 stand*is* now m.   2294 gode oste   2295 maken om. meyd   2296 are   2297 after om.   2298 whedyr   2299 & off hys progressyon*e*   2300 At all*e* tyemes þis l.   2301 any   2303 ffrom*e* hyr reasons he cowde   2304 Vnto . ffelows . thus om.   2305 vnto   2309 off on*e*   2310 leue . hys sone ys   2311 holy goste . knytter   2312 dyed   2313 clensyd be them*e*   2314 Vnto   2315 hartely . from   2317 sey now ʒe   2318 aunswerd . new   2320 kepe   2321 p*er*lous   2323 leyue   2324 and plato . sudiorne   2327 purchesse . hem om. vntrewe   2328 haue inst. of shulde   2330 fulle grete   2331 gloryous p.   2332 forgyff   2333 lorde not   2334 Os . pyteus . þou om.   2337 mayntyn*e* & s. yt.
  2339—2345 follow after V, 329.   Vv. 1—63 of the V. book are wanting. Book V. begins v. 421.
  2339 martyryʒed . I om.   2344 loke . þat f.   2345 gladds all*e* me*n* . be.

[V.]

  64 *complent*   65 all*e* om. credylyte   66 emprours hart . to ffaynte   67 speke   68 coviete   69 dyspytyous   71 truste   73 exp*er*yence   74 reyvyd . al om. worldly   76 ioye om. long*is* vnto   77 pepull*e*   78 sey . haue   81 þe om. (twice)   82 bene   83 heder om.   84 mykkell*e*   85 Lat . you om.   86 losse   87 Thynk   88 Be not . losse   89 lyfte . hart*is*   92 stand . hartlesse   93 be astunnyd   95 myʒt haue bene   96 fare . though om. boundyn*e* . w. a lyne   97 gyue   98 vaylythe   99 maister om.   100 þat I spake off   101 he om. begane   102 Vnto . came   103 Thys   106 ʒe   107 & in þe a.   109 Indewyd . þat s. þat þei   111 To inst. of Tyl   þat   113 or   114 reason*e* . beʒ om.   115 neu*er*   116 w*er*   117 velanye   118

Various Readings: MS. Arundel 20. Book V. 445

wage 119 than . worldys 120 it om. 121 wot not 122 mak*is* . in a traunce . 123 semys now, it om. 124 spek*is* . whyche hang & was rent 125 to þe p. 126 no p*ur*chace 127 as om. solemnyte 128 mak*is* 129 curyalyte 130 mystely harde h. speke 131 mye bowels began*e* to ; sore om. 134 p*ro*ferde 135 refusse 136 renouns 137 ʒowe . knowe 138 þeyr row bowe 139 ʒe . p*re*ue 141 hys blyssyd p. 142 ma*n*kynd . hym*e* inst. of now. 143 Vnto 145 burn*e* & put to destresse 146 xall*e* ʒe 147 to om. hart*is* 148 baptyme 149 off vs he 150 felows . Intent 151 sytt*is* 153 wyll*e* forsake 155 and om. 156 wolde haue falne 157 chorlys 158 more in 160 tho om. 161 seyd 162 now om. hastely 164 saturn*e* 165 þat þeis renegatt*is* þat 166 grece 167 nor 169 rosyn*e* 171 Vnto . any 172 dye 173 very om. 174 & se myselue þ*a*t yt be d. 175 done . xall*e* 176 ʒow . in om. handes 177 vnto 178 mythy . bandes 179 boodes . nor . her om. 180 gyue . hem om. vylence 181 be 182 escape . no 184 vnto ask*is* 185 fast now on*e* thys 186 haue 187 no mo w. more om. 189 cu*m* and aske ʒoure mede 190 drawn*e* . velanye 191 Vnto . wrastelde not þ*er*-ageyn*e* 192 eye 193 dare now 194 þeys men*e* 196 nor 198 felows . now comfort 199 any 201 ledys vs 202 are gaddyrd 203 In hevyn*e* a Ioyffull*e* 204 haue . from*e* 206 myrroure 209 dye 211 a . wark*e* 212 causys . and f. ek*e* . it om. induth*e* 213 mark*e* 214 cryestes stepps sewys 217 wasshyn*e* 219 this om. 220 now om. 221 off-tyme 223 & euer-more xall*e* rewe 225 ys now 226 seyn*e* . must vs dye 228 for om. lye 230 are purched 233 for godd*is* loue . sytt*is* 234 crosse 235 to hym*e* for vs þ*a*t ys 237 lyvy*n*g . are 240 weshyd 241 baptyme . þe better 243 prayr 244 þ*a*t thyng 245 wyll*e* 247 ffor all*e* þis mey he do ffor he 248 lovys . eu*er*y 250 ʒe 251 may om. 252 be 253 on om. 254 ʒo 256 dye . luff 257 þe h. 258 xall*e* 260 scruffys 263 þ*a*t þei suffyr ffor god to theyr g. m. 264 leff*e* þis d. troste eu*er* on*e* ʒoure c. 265 þ*a*t om. 267 fyer purge manys 269 are 270 water eke . fonte 271 are puregyd . full*e* clene inst. of I wene 272 þ*a*t dye os 273 are . beleue 275 dye 276 callys 277 There (fore om.) . knyghys 278 clayme now 279 Be 281 ware 282 ca*m* 283 bound . euene om. 284 as₁ om. myʒt 285 On*e* a. pavyde 286 he 287 hy*m*-selue inst. of tho 288 on*e* 289 fyer . are . heppe 290 gan*e* . amo*n*g 291 renn*e* feche and leppe 292 not om. 293 bende . feyte . threw . fyer 294 and full*e*. eke om. 298 now to hym*e* þat he wolde 299 lengar*e* 300 go 301 gr*a*unte 303 nor c. . of berd 304 bowys feyr and bent 305 fayre om. 306 mak*is* . þe om. 307 þis fyer 308 before styll*e* þ*a*n myʒt 309 men*e* seyde om. cryed all*e*-wey thus 310 knew neu*er* err*e* 312 now om. no-man*er* 313 forto 314 thei om. 315 Vnto . gan*e* 316 dyed 317 sememy*n*g 319 body . ek*e* om. 320 colours 321 þis saw þe pepull*e* 324 Myche folk*e* 326 solemp*e* 329 end*is* . martyrdom*e* . evy*n* inst. of right.

Then follow IV, 2339—2345, and the Colophon : Explicit 4us liber huj*us* beatissime vite virginis devotissime Kat*er*ine m*a*rtiris. Incipit prosa in 5um librum in folio sequenti (but this prologue, v. 1—63, is wanting ; v. 64—322 form the end of the 4th book ; 330—420 are wanting).

421 lewhe . hard 423 vnto 424 What þ*a*t . þ*u*s me 425 make 429 If om. 431 chaunchors xall*e* . no reste 432 myche . weste 436 Suffythe 438 a 439 full*e* ʒern*e* 440 dye 441 langage 444 þou inst. of that 445 synge . right om. Intent 446 represent 447 be . ful om. 449 know or I 453 My . wolde wyll*e* 455 Or . thyng om. 456 xuld 457 þei xall*e* 459 full*e* wele wordy . ful om. 460 beleu*e* 462 no ma*n* . yt can*e* 463 to om. 464 Vnto . & eke to 466 þis . werk*is* . mastrye 467 so om. 469 & gret*e* e. 471 Stand lyke . þ*a*t fly*e* abouʒt 472 Os 474 vnclen*e* . xall*e* 475 ymage 476 querdome 478 shakyd 480 worlde 481 a om. 482 feynyd 483 but veyn*e* and feynyng fflatorye 484 it om. als f. 485 xall*e* 486 honord w*yth* 487 chylder . cu*m* 488 xall*e* . þ*er* make 490 from*e* 491 dewls . stand*e* om. 492 repte 493 nor 494 leyff . leue 496 sir om. 497 neuer*e* om. ffor to 498 be bettyr at esse 499 statute 500 thynk 502 colours 503 Vnto . wyll*e* gyue 506 hele . comforth*e* 507 Nor nouʒt aveyll*e* . nor 508 long*is* 510 þ*a*t yt . leue 511 as a thy*n*g p*ro*phytab*i*le . receue 512 vnto a 513 a om. 514 b*e*ffore 515 groundyd . mysse 518 Leue 520 wyll*e* not 521

446 *Various Readings: MS. Arundel* 20. *Book* V.

. xalle . nor arte 526 Thane 528 benyngly 529 Os . semys 530 xalle 531 Ioy or dethe . what ȝe 532 ȝow 533 xalle . grete d. 534 þe hye m. 536 Os 537 Redressys 538 Spredis . ther-too 539 chosse yt must 540 avaylys . not om. 542 at my p. at om. prysse 543 xalle . shortly 546 encreasse 547 xalle 548 peple . be 549 hartis are 551 passe 553 xalle be 556 he sle flyght curse or b. 557 skyls 558 myscheyfis 559 suffyrd . myche 560 Whyls . lyvyd 561 ful om. 562 haue om. 564 But and . cum 566 gyffyng ensampile . of very p. 567 any 568 purposyd. 569 and his J. 571 and r. 574 xalle we haue 575 offerd . vnto 576 vndefylde 577 And om. 580-81 transp. 583 vsys 584 pover . settis . grete om. 585 sore 586 in ffyer 587 xallt þou 589 threttis 592 frome 593 menye 594 þi . xalle 597 xalle . leyue 599 fynde 600 frome . xalle 602 the om. 603 nere 605 geyt ȝardis 606 eke om. ful om. 607 right om. 608 meyd . modir om. 609 ȝe xalle 611 feese 612 speke . bedleeme 613 Nor . galale 614 rather hyr 615 þat mey be besye p. 617 takyne 619 yrne . mey 620 bet 622 bett . spous 623 trustis . cums from 626 rune 627 purchyd 628 vnto 630 I that I 631 I thank 632 þat om. senttis 634 as om. 635 euer & more 638 among þe 639 þe betyrs very 640 meyd 641 holde erysye whyche ȝe be in f. 642 now calle 643 xalle . or els 644 Or 645 þus ageyne 646 strengare 647 suffyr 648 wheþer 649 vnshamfulle 650 wylle 651 thi om. 652 Bethynk 653 mast sle & bryng ouȝt adaw 655 kepe 656 dye & passe þis worlde fulle wele I know 657 folow 658 nor done 659 and In alle 662 bound 665 hy 666 whane þat we are in 667 wythowtyne any 668 xalle 669 in happ . hastely 670 shew inst. of fulfille 671 suffyr 672 a om. 674 þat þei take . hyr lede 675 And put hyr 676 hyre 677 seyd þæt she fowle fylthe in dede 679 for to 680 gyue . ne om. 682 myȝt 684 þat om. 685 wythouȝt 686 any maner 687 any 688 commaundment 690 ryddyne . menee 691 land 697 leue . lyke 698 from 700 of om. 701 lord om. commandis 702 decesse . sobur 703 xalle 704 now om. 705 rynnys 707 comforthet 709 kepte 711 dyd crepte 712 cornars 713 are þei mervelyd 715 men . cuntre 716 Sprong . þer inst. of soore 717 from 718 frome 719 Iaylers 720 sertyne . dungyone 721 goth abouȝt 722 thydyngis . cum vnto . eyre 724 meyd . any 728 And she þerfor in presone lyggyng to be shent 730 land rydyng 732 nor 733 hungure 734 Þeis wer þe last wordyes that he seythe 735 gyue . deythe 736 pyte 740 studdye 742 And to . þus prevyly ; ful om. 743 folke 744 by . peye 746 sey 747 of om. wey 748 gloterous nor drunkyn 749 plesys 750 I had bene 752 sene . drewe 753 wolde sey 754 mykkylle dolle 756 my hart . there om. begynnys to 761 cum evyne as god had hyme 762 nobulle 763 councelle 764 and leedyr 765 ȝung folk 766 porphyr in story 768 she seyd porphyre . be 769 be . myche . aveylle 770 concelle 771 trubbylde now newly . the om. 772 cane inst. of may . nor 773 or . begynnys 776 tho om. 777 nedis now see þis meyd 778 Ordyne 779 gyf . ynowgh 780 ȝow myne owne mane 781 þis lady vnto, for to g. 782 nor so rowgh 783 wyth hyr or els I must 784 my hart 785 Porphyr 786 purvey 787 dorsse xalle . vndoo 789 and I 790 xalle. 791 ffor wyth . I haue bene 792 thynkis . suffyrs 793 orybile bet . frome 794 no . do 795 oftyme . ouer 796 Seyn . hard 799 that om. lesure 801 gyftis . gyue 803 chambur . you om. 804 Cum 805 whane ȝe here me c. 806 are c. . porphyre 808 right om. seys oure storye lyer 809 came 810 sawe 811 ffelle . doun om. wythouȝt 812 to om. a bene 813 þe 814 saw per so wonderly bryght 815 wyttis are gone 816 falne 818 felt . seys 819 þe s. 820 Thane . vnto 822 borne 823 he om. 824 Be 825 haue calde . to hys 826 ffor many cawses now to thys place 827 tyed 829 saw . syed 833 myche 834 whyls . þat om. 837 and inst. of than . ane nowre 838 comforth 839 thei om. 840 lyghte inst. of delight 841 eke om. 842 gyffyng . vnto 844 numbur 849 cane om. 850 frome 852 syster . þeis 853 xalle 854 Os . be 855 xalle . a om. 856 Vnto . man þan 857 Whyls . in hyr hand per syttyng 860 xalle . wryttyne 861 serys 862 wryȝt 863 þe b. 864 wyȝte 865 Þat from . þe xalle no more desevyr 867 þe t. . that om. receyue þis 868 olde men vnto hyr ageyne 869 syttis 870 O quene 871 askis 875

Various Readings: MS. Arundel 20. Book V. 447

haue om. 876 þowro. councelle 877 þat þorow þeir f. b. 878 xalle 880 hathe þeis folke. take 881 hart. ful om. 884 haue hard 886 dare vysyt hyr. now om. þe fere 887 thus om. 888 wyth-ouȝt 891 soo om. 892 veytalle 893 soo om. 894 storys. dyuerse 895 frome 896 Whedyr bodely. for om. 897 seynt Awstyne seys 898 fathers 900 seys 901 it is om. þat suche 902 nurryshyd. erthe 904 þe erthe 905 þe s. 906 wher he trettis off mervylle 907 donne 908 mayde om. gan hyr 910 but om. 914 wythouȝte. rowthe 915 þis p.. levyd she þis ys trewthe 917 in presone 918 sawe a. 919 cum 920 aungels 921 meydens 922 falne 924 Dowgher loke vp he seyd. se ȝowe 929 Thynk. leue. hart 931 a hart. xalle 932 oure. or. parte from 933 numbur. peple. xalle 934 a 935 ffrom. mawmentry 936 sudiorne 939 to she se 940 þan returnyd. preyare. tho om. 941 tresure 942 lyst 943 hartly 944 be hee 946 hys causys was. to an ende. 947 þe emproure I mene 948 cum. he om. begane 949 be hys knyghys 950 be. wylle 951 xalle. it om. 952 mey be provyd. gaue 954 pepulle 955 are. hath 956 Vnto 957 thynk 960 concyanatryx 961 wyche. harte 962 ys she so sore infyxt 963 from. to om. 966 for hyr 967 bene pynyd 968 lokyd. quyk. ruddy 969 angure. hart. nere sleythe 972 Traytours. xalle. euerychone 974 commendment 978 xalle 979 that we forbyddyd 980 bynde In yerne 981 meyd 983 þou art an emprour a grete so mene. 984 ordynd. 985 þi law 986 xuldis 987 doste. dost ageynst 989 me om. nor 990 in a nother 992 massyngers. be hand 994 canst 997 aungels þis mete my lorde 999 he nolde suffyre 1001 nor. desevyr 1002 dubl ylnes 1003 þat stode 1005 hart 1006 hyd in. nevyme 1009 a kyngis dougher to 1010 seruffe 1011 borne 1012 are. al om. 1013 wychys 1014 kepe ȝe 1015 petyr mary 1016 are traytours prevyd 1019 gyffe 1021 maysters 1024 soo om. 1025 worde. vngodely 1026 cawsys 1027 no wyghtstandyng so haue I 1028 but I must 1029 peple. stand 1031 deme 1032 denye 1033 eke om. 1036 els wyth yerne xalle 1037 meydyne 1040 any 1042 to þe 1043 ffor hys loue I ame redy to dye one k. 1045 þow þat. cum. owre 1047 nor 1048 gruche. and my 1049 honowrment 1050 a om. changoure 1051 ledys 1052 are 1053 commys. bryngis. þe preue 1054 seys. bybylle 1056 Vnto. þe 1057 seene 1060 Bryne 1063 kyne calvys and shepe 1064 offyr 1066 Os 1068 vengabylle 1069 Thane xalle I go to that hye felycyte 1070 To hyme þat was offyrd In caluery one a hylle 1071 after þis inst. of yet efte 1072 heer-after om. dede 1073 Not 1074 Intent 1075 þi dedys. are 1077 landis 1078 And take 1079 sley 1080 gare inst. of make. smyȝt 1081 be. thanne om. solennlye 1082 Vnto 1083 that om. wryȝt 1084 a dawe 1086 grete om. 1089 standis 1093 semys. meydyne 1095 That om. hyr here. prophytesse 1096 cummannde 1098 ys seyd 1099 stoorys 1101 fyȝt 1102 vnto 1103 pusaunce 1104 ytale. yngland. spayne om. 1105 þat inst. of tho 1107 dyscomfyt hym 1109 Os 1110 þat. borne 1112 yt knewe 1113 þat euer 1114 þeis 1116 he þan. now om. 1117 falne 1119 suffur þus a woman here to 1121 wyche 1123 lyvers. xalle 1126 cryed he 1127 me thynkis as men. ware 1129 barkyt. þe 1130 done one þe crosse 1131 gane he. to om. 1133 Irne. plumbys 1135 bet now þan beffore 1136 dispetuously 1137 þer 1139 say 1141 pepulle 1142 bune. in to 1143 can 1144 not ȝe 1145 Vnto 1147 It om. toore 1148 aske. are 1154 farther 1155 Seyne. holdyne 1156 vnto 1157 þat vylensly 1158 we trowe 1159 ȝe mey 1160 longis. vnto þe h. 1161 Seyne. why om. 1162 wylde. councelld 1164 ȝow lese þe god in ȝow plentyously sett 1165 erytage. lese 1167 solemly. that om. hart 1168 ȝe lede nor rewle 1169 to ȝoure aweylle 1171 Remembyr 1173 feyne ȝet. syne 1175 mercye askyng 1177 shynes 1179 be. done 1180 wh. þat now 1181 Hyer in þeyr deys r. none canne 1186 þe bewte 1187 þat om. 1190 not ȝe 1193 in erthe wyth w. 1194 ffor þat longis to vs off equyte and ryght 1195 pr. of god allmyȝt 1196 Ihesu owr lord. xulde. soo om. 1197 wylle so sone 1198 as om. 1200 hye deyte 1201 bees (?) 1203 þat þei 1204 nor synnews. nor 1207 vnclene 1208 lechyry 1209 or w. 1212 it om. 1213 fleche. shal om. 1215 e om. hoot (be- om.) 1216 soo om.

448 *Various Readings: MS. Arundel* 20. *Book V.*

for to 1219 ffolow . go 1221 bodely 1222 baptyme . þe 1223 traweylle 1225 Vnto 1226 scape . after 1227 sawe 1228 I b. þis thyng and troste 1229 sers as for 1230 dyrknes 1231 dye 1232 rysyng . ageyne om. 1233 hard 1237 Wythdrew . frome 1238 any 1241 mayr . ledare . pepulle 1242 Vnto 1243 mykkylle 1244 Crewlle in hys a. . any 1245 dyspyteous vengabulle wythowtyne 1246 Cursate . oute om. 1247 saw 1248 in fere 1249 O lorde emprour . wysdome 1252 standis stunnyd os þouȝ. wart 1253 lystyne to 1254 sawe 1256 Intent 1257 horrybile 1259 lat . ons 1260 thanne om. 1261 vnto 1262 master 1264 marke 1265 countroller . clarke 1269 whelys . xalle 1272 xalle 1273 xalle 1275 xalle . neylys 1276 ffestynyd 1277 berys 1278 hart . nor 1279 cummys neuer 1280 in peecys 1281 knowe 1282 xalle 1283 vnto . whele 1284 xalle 1285 yche 1286 xalle cum . cowrsys 1287 xalle 1288 & þus make 1289 made and þat now 1290 betwene þem ryght . þat om. 1291 be 1292 þat hathe 1294 cursate . xalle 1295 ȝendyr 1297 whels 1298 þis cursate 1299 are calde 1300 Carpentars . smythys als f. 1301 leue now we 1302 muste 1303 it om. cum . thyrde 1304 whels are . xulde 1305 Kataryne om. 1308 reende om. seythe 1309 grutythe 1310 ascape 1312 meyr . ymagenyng 1313 stodyd . hart . mynde 1314 ffor to 1315 from 1316 the om. 1318 hyer l. . dressyd 1320 chaunge 1321 Hyer yne 1323 bothe om. 1324 ys alle-mythy 1326 hydyst nevyr 1327 þe folk . crye to 1328 preyar . mast 1329 Intent 1331 leyvyne 1333 vppone now 1334 power now 1335 easye 1337 ys 1338 I lord . not om. for no 1339 stand 1340 thynkis . my hart 1341 wordys & tungis 1344 þis prey I shortly in a clawse 1346 And om. 1347 from 1348 clepe 1349 hart 1353 frome 1354 þer 1355 orrybylle 1356 owre the om. 1357 or viii . ffyre 1358 flew 1359 sprong 1360 Sum man had 1361 men om. are 1362 fyer flew . wonderfully 1363 myche . takyne . feesse 1364 hart 1365 from . veniance . styrte 1367 Makeyng . preyare 1368 hys electe 1370 colde 1371 What . ffett 1372 fyer by 1375 lady is om. 1376 fyer flewe 1377 oftyme 1378 Nor . nor 1380 alle om. 1383 and leyd . alle om. row 1384 caytyffis . shrow be shrowe (rith om.) 1385 heroddys numbyr 1386 holy om. reste 1387 sobere preyare 1388 & þe fyer . bothe om. 1389 To þe p. for om. 1390 cummyng 1391 Myche folke 1393 vp ageyne frome þat grete frey 1394 al om. 1395 are . þe hethyne 1396 Who are . who can . forheddis 1397 folk . hathe . fyer 1398 Sum men . nor 1399 þe too . þe tother 1402 feylys and falsys . now om. 1403 abytt 1406 repugnys vnto (is om.) 1409 cyclops smythys 1410 makis 1411 it om. thy 1414 thynk 1416 one 1417 What vnto . borne 1419 before 1420 what so 1421 cum 1423 wrechyd man . hathe . I- om. 1424 turmentis . wrongly om. 1425 wraystyls 1426 makis . & wyth 1427 pyne 1429 Whedyr 1430 fyȝtis . & þat 1433 bestyalyte vnto mans kynd 1435 wyrkis . wonderfully 1439 Smote 1440 þe om. communars 1441 lye ȝendyr 1442 hym þen 1444 I counseyl om. 1445 rede þe 1447 whyls 1448 forgyue 1449 xalt 1450 hard 1452 ȝe spake 1453 on om. thys 1454 ȝe 1455 orrybulle . þat om. 1456 nor 1458 gracyous om. þe kyng 1459 frome þis fondnesse 1461 Os 1463 haue brookyne a whele 1464 nygramansye 1465 ordyne 1466 ȝoure 1467 art þou one þat oure goddis now dysdene 1468 I count not at shyttyne bene 1469 forsaakis 1470 takis 1472 byddys hys sarvantis 1473 sotelle . yrene and wyre 1474 xalle . right om. 1475 þei xalle do yt 1476 L. sorow . and woo om. wolde he þat hys w. xulde 1477 lat . now om. 1478 done loke ȝe hyr take 1479 þer wher traytours 1480 haue om. deseruffe and teye 1481 smyȝt 1482 lye . hungre 1484 Os . þeis men 1485 pullyd off 1486 frome 1487 vaynys . doth rysse 1488 alle raggyd alle blodye 1489 ȝyt vnto 1490 preying . ryght om. 1491 pyller . moost om. 1492 vnto 1495 be 1496 cum 1500 orrybulle 1501 þis holy lyue to turne ageyne to synne 1502 or 1503 xalle 1505 Prow ȝow 1506 vnto 1507 hathe forsakyne 1509 þe loue þerfore off oure k. 1511 Os . make ȝow 1512 whosse . ȝe suffyr 1513 hartely . desess⁊ 1514 last 1515 per-wyth 1516 haue 1517 se 1518 mery 1519 When ; þat om. cum before 1520 land 1521 husband . he be 1522 amend alle þing 1523 dwellys 1524 haue . non om. dyversyte

Various Readings: MS. Arundel 20. *Book V.* 449

1525 vnto 1526 be . frome . neste 1528 stabelyd myȝtly 1529 knyghys 1531 boustyous . & strokis eke 1532 and bad þem make annende 1533 and off hyr teetis wyȝtly rende 1534 Os . and after wyth g. p. 1535 smyȝt 1536 god om. strenthys hyr to susteyne 1537 þeis grete peynys þat she suffyrd for hys ryȝt 1538 ys she . ys to þe lyȝt 1540 at om. 1541 on þe wedynsdey 1543 vnberyed om. 1544 lyggyng ther fulle whyȝt & eke fulle rede 1545 to om. wynd yt 1547 And om. myche . thouȝt. 1548 come and om. vnto 1549 gone . byedyng 1550 porphyr . ryght h. 1553 callyd . vnto 1554 ful om. dyrk. 1555 Kateryne 1557 in hyr lynnyne evyne as 1558 oyntment 1559 bawmyd 1560 preyr . and wyth 1561 layd . in to 1562 after om. ys þer made 1564 falle . suche 1565 berye þis same bodye 1566 off suspeccyone . folke 1567 Wer be-restyd 1568 porphyr 1570 Sythe . a lorde . xulde 1572 wyffys . dyd þou off 1573 hast . euer inst. of sore 1574 Intent 1575 þus inst. of now. doo om. 1576 thyne Ire 1577 leue þi b. leue þis deuoracyone 1578 shul om. 1580 þat om. me thouȝt yt no treasone 1581 But . vnto 1582 vnto 1584 ȝyt to. Robbers . are 1585 haue 1587 neyburs 1589 kynde . reasone 1590 byrdys 1592 wryghys . auctors 1593 nor eke 1594 Vnto mankynd . deffowle 1597 porphyr . are 1598 maxence hart 1601 Soundyd 1604 O I . lyue 1606 vnto . gyue 1609 stykkyd . credylle yt had bene þe beste 1610 ffor om. reyvyd . alle my 1611 porphyr now off 1612 A om. Porphyr here þe b. 1613 good om. gentel om. and þus ys he loste 1614 deceyvd be . begynnys 1615 rest wyth-in 1616 standis . comforthe 1618 deceyvyd . now she ys 1619 & þat grevys 1620 My hart waxys hevy as any 1621 comburde . thouȝt 1622 porphyr 1623 kyngdome 1624 xulde no man þe make 1625 haue . grete om. 1626 desceyvyd my w. ȝyt deceyff not 1629 þeys 1631 myche lentylle 1632 now þis cursyd 1635 hyme þus sone . renye 1636 þe olde trewe 1637 fathers kept ouȝt off 1640 & be 1641 examenyd 1642 þouȝt þis 1643 dulfully 1644 seyd . how om. my gode 1645 soddenly . falne vnto . meserye 1646 hoppe . fulle inst. of not but 1647 faver hyme now . þis 1649 Whyche þat 1650 renegattis 1652 seyd þei þus . stode now there 1653 knowne 1654 þat inst. of and . whyche þat þis s. meyd 1655 honourd 1656 god we om. or cane 1657 hym om. we wylle . scruffe 1658 smyȝt . þou om. turment 1660 so swete 1661 departe . hartely 1662 ffrome 1663 frome 1664 are peyd xalle þou þan 1665 hartis are . thus om. 1666 asį om. stabulle os þe 1672 are . vnto 1673 porphyr . now om. had 1674 he dyd comforthe . mythy 1675 Vnto . preysyd where 1676 wordyes 1677 nereand 1678 þeis pepylle . thus om. 1679 lat 1680 perylle . councelle . befalle 1681 Vnto . lande 1682 menbyrs 1683 vnderstande 1684 comforthe . or 1688 Wherfore evyne after 1689 now om. 1690 erytykis . ffyer 1691 martyrdome 1692 ware þei . one not 1694 endyght 1696 crystys 1697 auctorus . in this legent doth t. 1698 sothfastnes . wryȝtis 1702 clepyd 1704 sottelle . vnto 1705 sottelle entent 1706 gylte . seyth 1707 porphyr off. & off 1708 from . madis 1709 socery 1710 resort off þeir mother 1711 father 1712 persewe þe knottis þat ȝe knytt 1713 & om. 1714 lyue 1715 Not-wythstandyng þi 1716 councelle . vnto . fondnes 1717 magyke . & om. wepe sore 1718 þou was 1719 gyue . porphyr . ewle concelle 1720 Lat thyne eyne wyth water now þi cheekis reylle 1722 sey . cause þat blode ys spylte 1724 an om. on- om. to þe, holy 1725 folow 1726 on- om. 1729 forgyue 1730 xalt . alle þe b. a. 1731 the om. 1732 lengare 1734 are 1736 one þis maner I wylle devysse 1737 þi . to be smyte 1739 warand 1740 sure . yche 1741 fleche . or els 1742 caruffe 1743 thyne . ye repent 1744 meke 1745 dye 1746 was om. hangyd one þe croce 1747 þis dey . be 1748 vnto weredys aye 1749 ffor om. se . and alle 1750 on om. to dethe now 1751 wene þe falle ys m. 1752 men om. ys 1753 Sum men wene . dye 1754 fulle s. 1755 deceyvabile 1756-7 transp. 1756 I sey om. We lesse þat thyng whyche ys fulle of stryff 1757 land 1759 þer xalle we haue grete loy 1760 aboundys 1761 ys sykker yt had 1765 lengar 1767 thyne lawe 1769 haue 1770 So wylle I desyre for to se hys face 1771 & here þe aungels whych are 1772 þem . woltis astunnyd 1775 castels þat standis by

KATHARINE. G G

3 2

450 *Various Readings: MS. Arundel* 20. *Book V.*

ʒone roche 1776 aproche 1777 spent 1778 alle þis . shape om. 1779 þe whyche w*yth* h. b. 1780 O. wrechyd s. weshyd 1781 bothe inst. of ful 1782 folows 1783 Cu*m* 1784 abyed 1785 nor 1786 þe sentance . gyffne 1787 as I was avysyde 1789 folow . preys 1791 so wrechydly 1792 velanye 1793 mothers & maydyns 1794 my 1796 inclyne 1799 hathe . & whyche 1802 þat om. 1803 ʒowr godd*is* . myche 1804 swere . be 1805 w*yth*ouʒt 1806 if om. yow om. ryght so 1807 was s. she came . þe 1808 xulde dye, and þe*r* ys þe ma*n* to 1809 smyʒt . preyd of 1810 or . frome 1811 sey 1812 In om. medytacyons vnto 1813 hir₂ om. 1815 eyne and hand*is* 1816 W*yth* meke harte she seyd w*yth* sharpe sounc 1817 whosse . vnto nevyn*e* 1819 þat trust*is* 1821 num-byrd 1822 þe collage amo*ng* 1824 me now w*yth* 1826 lorde for thy 1828 haue . reme*m*brance 1829 ellis om. in hys 1831 hartely 1832 any relesse 1833 þe*m* theyr 1834 Os 1836 pestelence nor . myʒt 1837 and₁ om. nor o. meserye 1838 alle om. ewle 1839 but lord off þi me*r*cy þe*m* gyue 1840 off h. 1841 land*is* abyed 1842 Lord graunt 1845 vnto 1846 tyrant . nor 1848 To þe I. cr. 1849 Vnto 1850 þi aungels 1851 Cu*m* . frome . þi 1852 vnto 1853 now inst. of lord . thy 1854 feleshyppe 1855 Amo*ng* þi . þ*a*t . so bryght 1856 scarsly 1857 preyr. 1858 frome . harde þer . swoune 1859 noysse . ca*n* 1860 My . spoosse 1861 cu*m* . vnto 1862 þou arte fulle stedfastly ffeste 1863 yt ys 1864 now redy 1866 xallt 1867 abyede 1868 thy eternyte 1869 before 1870 are 1871 are ordynyd þi sowle eke . for om. 1873 xalt 1874 dowgher inst. of in haste 1876 wyll*e* one þe 1877 harte thy 1882 forgyue 1883 Confermy*ng* . hem eke om. 1885 vnto . smyther 1886 calde to a f. . now om. 1887 thou om. 1889 & stand 1890 forgyue 1891 þis c. 1893 holly 1895 & rage 1896 þe bodye 1897 þe*r* lere 1900 clennes at þat t. 1901 no noþ*er* . rune 1902 os 1904 thyng om. w*yth*-in . þing om. came 1905 plentyously . wattyrd 1906 as a most me*r*velusse 1907 Here 1909 meydynhed . berys 1910 wytnes 1912 was sene eke 1914 lyke . wynggi*s* 1915 þus auctorus 1916 toke . bare 1919 gaue 1920 Vnto . Iuwys . ledys 1921 cryest*is* 1923 poull*e* . mak*is* 1924 long*is* 1926 gyed 1927 Vnto þe . stand*is* 1928 for vs . hastely 1929 wysshe 1931 be 1933 seye standys 1934 from*e* Arabye . of lond om. a full*e* 1935 In om. Iurneys 1936 My . seys 1937 gyedys . pusance 1938 þei labure . it om. 1939 are but f. here . hathe made þ*a*t seys. The next 2 stanzas are transp. 1947 are 1948 Are . vnknowne 1949 knowlege 1950 þat yt runnythe oyle 1952-3 Whyche me*n* suffyr on*e* bodye or on*e* bone, þis holy oyle wylle hole þe*m* anone 1940 The passyon*e* of þis holy meyd as þe story s. 1941 Was one . right om. 1942 seyn*e* 1945 þe same 1946 auctours 1954—1981 These last stanzas are wanting ; Ar. has instead the following 2 stanzas :

>Hyr dey ffals newlye eue*r*y ʒere
>Þe xxv*v*ᵗⁱ dey of þe monythe off nouembyr,
>Suche tyme as she was ma*r*tyryʒed here,
>Os wytnesse berys eue*r*y kalender.
>He þ*a*t thys lyue wryʒt*is*, red*is* or els evthe here,
>Cryste, kyng off glorye, graunt þe*m* þat grace
>Off all*e* þeir synnes me*r*cy to purchace.

>Þorow þe Inte*r*cessyone of oure lady sey*n*t mary
>& þe medys off þe passyon*e* of þis gloryos meyd,
>bry*n*g vs, lorde, to þi hevynly concistory
>ffor whom most specyally þis holy meydy*n* preyd.
>Now, gloryous Kate*r*yne, be to vs an*e* eyde ·
>And specyall*e* succur yn*e* þis pe*r*lous pylgrymmage,
>Þ*a*t afte*r* þis lyue we mey cu*m* to thy cage.
>Amen.

INDEX OF NAMES.

By THOMAS AUSTIN.

ADRIAN, Roman Emperor, A.D. 117—138, 57/664.

Adrian, a hermit monk, 173/43; lived sixty years on a rock, 175/80; Virgin Mary appears to him, 177/118; is sent by her to St. Katharine, 179/148; swoons, 185/240; tells the Virgin Mary that he will obey her, 187/272; is told how to find St. Katharine, 189; reaches Alexandria, and finds Katharine, 193; tells her of the Virgin, 199, etc.; tells her of Christ, 213, etc.; asks Katharine to go with him, 217; quits Alexandria with her, 219; finds his cell has disappeared, 219; enters the Holy City with Katharine, 227; baptizes her in Heaven, 239; teaches Katharine, 250.

Alexandria, in Egypt, one of the chief cities of King Costus, 21; its Divinity School, 25; built by Babel, and called the Lesser Babylon, 49; Athanasius writes of its foundation, 51; its former kings, 51, etc.; Parliament held there, 59; Katharine's coronation there, 61; a Parliament meets there to consider on her marriage, 83, etc.; the city gathers to hear Katharine's discussion with the Philosophers, 302.

Alfragan confuted by Katharine, 325.

Amalek, a city in Cyprus, and the port of Syria, 21/64; is one of King Costus's chief cities, 21; ruled by a Mayor, 23; its name is changed to Famagost, 47.

Amphos of Athens, 303.

Ananias, Earl of Joppa, comes to Alexandria, 83/81; urges Katharine to marry, 107.

Antioch, in Syria, is built by Seleucus, 51/574. It was the capital of the Greek kings.

Antiochus I., or Soter, King of Syria, B.C. 280—261, 51/566, 53/612; he was the son of Seleucus I.—Antiochus II., or Theos, B.C. 261—246, 51/570, 53/615; son of preceding.—Antiochus III., or Great, B.C. 223—187, 55; son of Seleucus Callinicus.—Antiochus IV., or Epiphanes, B.C. 175—164, 55/637; he was the son of Antiochus the Great, and had also the name of Epimanes.—Antiochus V., or Eupator, B.C. 164—152, 55/638; son of preceding.—Antiochus VII., or Sidetes, B.C. 137—126, 55/642; he was the son of Demetrius Soter. — Antiochus VIII., or Grypus, B.C. 125—96, 57/659; he was the son of Demetrius Nicator.—Antiochus, son of Archibelon, 57/676.

Antigonus, King of Asia, B.C. 316—301, 57/676. He was one of Alexander's Generals.

Apollonius of Tyre, 55/633. He was a Stoic Philosopher, and lived in the time of Ptolemy Auletes.

Appollymas is silenced and converted by Katharine, 321.

Arabia, subdued by Alexander the Great, 53/590.

Archenon, King of Alexandria, 57/675.

Archibelon, King of Alexandria, 57/675.

Armenia, King of, Katharine's uncle, argues with her, 295.

Arrek finds St. Katharine's Life, 5; englished it, 7/57; has a vision, 9; Capgrave adapts Arrek's version, 17; turned into Latin St.

452   *Index of Names.*

Athanasius's *Life of St. Katharine*, 13/173, 15/199; died at Lynn, 15/219; was Rector of St. Pancras, London, 15/227.
Aryot disputes with Katharine, 330; converted by her, 336; openly professes Christianity, 342.
Astenes argues with Katharine, 306, etc.; is silenced, 309.
Athanasius, St., teaches St. Katharine, and is converted by her, 11/128; wrote her Life, 11; was afterwards Bishop of Alexandria, 13/162; is Katharine's Chancellor, 33/261.
Athens, Duke of, argues with Katharine, 153.

Babel, Sultan of Assyria and Egypt, built Alexandria, or Babylon the Less, 49.
Baldake, Prince of Palestine, urges Katharine to marry, 147.
Borus, King of Alexandria, 57/678.

Candia, 73, 75.
Capgrave takes St. Katharine's Life from Arrek's version, 17; born at Lynn, 17.
Cappadocia, Prince of, comes to Alexandria, 83/80, 99.
Clamadour, Duke of Antioch, addresses Katharine, 135.
Clarus, Prince of Cappadocia, comes to Alexandria, 83/80; urges Katharine to marry, 99.
Claudas I., King of Alexandria, 57/676; Claudas II., 57/679.
Clement of Alexandria, A.D. 200, 25.
Constantine, Lord of Britain, 265/112; is appealed to by the Romans, and drives out Maxentius, 267.
Costus, King of Greece, father of St. Katharine, 17; a good man, 19; his chief cities, 21; is old at time of St. Katharine's birth, 29; builds her a palace, 35; dies, 43; is buried, 45.
Cursates, Mayor of Alexandria, constructs wheels to tear Katharine to pieces, 379.
Cyprus, part of King Costus's dominions, 17.

Damascus, the Duke of, comes to the Parliament at Alexandria, 85, 119.
Daniel, 111/518.
Darius III., or Codomannus, King of Persia, conquered by Alexander, 53/589.
Demetrius, King of Alexandria, 55/640; Demetrius I., or Soter, son of Seleucus IV., or Philopator, B.C. 162—150, 55/644.
Diocletian, 264/83.

Euclid, 41/387.
Eugenius, Lord of Nicopolis, urges Katharine to marry, 149.

Famagoost. See *Amalek*.

Garaencen, the Duke of, comes to the Parliament at Alexandria, 85/85.
Gorgalus, son of Antiochus I., 51/568.
Greece, 17/1.

Hercules, Prince of Paphon, 85/83; urges Katharine to marry, 113.

Iaf. See *Joppa*.
Janus, 282/642.
Joppa, the Earl of, comes to Alexandria, 83/81, 107.

Katharine, St., her Life written by St. Athanasius, 15; her father Costus, 19; born in her parents' old age, 29; her mother Meliades, 31; her teachers, 33; her father builds her a palace for study, 35; she learns the Seven Liberal Arts, 39; her pedigree, 57; is crowned at Alexandria, 61; her great goodness, 65; her people wish her to marry, 69; a Petition is sent to her, 73; a Parliament is called in reference to her marriage, 79; meaning of her name, 83; the Parliament individually addresses her on the necessity of marriage, 89, etc.; she craves delay, 93; is urged by her mother, 141; her beauty, 159; has an ideal husband, 165; her refusal

Index of Names. 453

angers her Lords, 169; the Monk Adrian seeks her by command of the Virgin Mary, 193, greets her, 195, tells of the Virgin, 199; she is told of Christ, 207, 215; Adrian asks Katharine to leave Alexandria with him, 217; she leaves the city, 219; sees the Heavenly City, 225, and is welcomed there, 227; is taken to Christ by the Virgin, 233; Christ orders her to be baptized, 235; is baptized in Heaven by Adrian, 239; is taken to Christ, 241; consents to wed Christ, 244; weds Christ, 246; Christ comforts her, 248; goes to Adrian's cell, and is taught by him, 251; the Virgin Mary visits her, 256; her death foretold, 258; is at Alexandria, 269; reproaches Maxentius for his idolatry, 279, etc.; refuses the Emperor's hand, 290; is imprisoned by him, 291; they try to convert her, 292, etc.; she is threatened with death, 295; prays for help, 299; gives up her heathen books, 304; argues with Astenes and silences him, 308; denounces the heathen gods, 310; expounds the Trinity, 315; effect of her arguments, 320; Appolymas questions her, 321; she converts him and Alfragan, 323, 328; the Emperor is wrath at her victory, 329; she disputes with Aryot, 330; converts him, 336; comforts the martyrs, 345; refuses to turn heathen, 352; declines a statue, 353; is flogged, 358; Angels visit her in prison, 361; the Queen's visit to her, 365; Christ visits her, 368; her death ordered, 375; torture wheels shattered at her prayer, 383; she comforts the Queen, 388; is sentenced to death, 397; is beheaded, 401; her tomb, 402; miracles there, 403.

Lymason, Earl of, comes to Alexandria, 85/87.
Lynn, in Norfolk, 15/219; Arrek died there, 15/219; Capgrave born there, 17/240.

Madagdalus, son of Babel, succeeds him as King of Alexandria, 51/562.
Mardemius, second son of Gorgalus, 51/577.
Maxentius, Emperor of Rome, A.D. 306—312, his death, 11/155; made Emperor of Rome, 265; is a tyrant, 266; flees from Constantine, 267; flees to Persia, and becomes king, 267; orders Christians to be persecuted, 268; comes to Alexandria, 269; his edict against Christians, 270; festival on his birthday, 273; warns Katharine, 281; sends for Clerks to convict Katharine, 288; offers to wed Katharine if she recants, 289; threatens her with death, 295; reproaches his philosophers, 340; orders the converts to be burnt, 343; tries to win Katharine over, 349; orders her to be flogged, 358; imprisons her, 360; orders her death, 375; orders his wife to be tortured, 386, and beheaded, 389; threatens Porphyry with death, 392; has 200 knights beheaded, 394.
Maximian, 264/82.
Maximinus II. or Galerius, A.D. 305—314, 264/81; made ruler of the East, 265; dies in Sicily, 265/129.
Meliades, daughter of King of Armenia, marries King Costus, and is mother of Katharine, 31; summons a Parliament, 47; agrees with those who want her daughter to wed, 75; the Monk Adrian seeks her, 193.
Meliore, wife of Mardemius, 51/581.

Nicopolis, ? in Africa, 149/1142.
Northfolk, or Norfolk, 17/240.

Origen, 25/130.

Pancras, St., London, Arrek Rector there, 15.
Pantænus, 25/127.
Paphon, or Paphos, in Cyprus, 85/83.
Phalon, King of Alexandria, marries Solaber, the daughter of Hadrian, 57/665.

Index of Names.

Philip of Macedon, father of Alexander the Great, 51/583.
Philo, *De Vita Theoretica*, 23/107.
Philosophers summoned to argue with Katharine, 292.
Porphyry visits Katharine in prison, 364; rebukes the Emperor, 390.

Salence, the Duke of, comes to Alexandria, 85/85.
Seleucus I., or Nicator, King of Alexandria, B.C. 306—281, 51/572; cousin of Alexander, 53/606; Seleucus II., or Callinicus, B.C. 246—226, 53/617; Seleucus III., or Ceraunus, son of Antiochus II., B.C. 226—223, 53/618; Seleucus IV., or Philopator, B.C. 187—175, 55/630.
Severus, ruler of Lombardy, 265/106; raises an army against Maxentius, but is slain by his own men, 266.
Solaber, daughter of Hadrian, marries Phalon, 57.
Surry, or Assyria, 17/2, 51/569, 57/667.

Tholome, or Ptolemy, the astronomer, 149/1155.
Tyre, 77/1016.

Valerius, a writer against marriage, 123/735.
Virgin Mary appears to the Monk Adrian, 177, etc.; takes Katharine up to Christ, 233; gives directions for her baptism, 237.

Zozymus, King of Alexandria, 57/674.

GLOSSARY.

By THOMAS AUSTIN.

ACRISIA, *sb.* 218/802. See *Aurisia*.
Afrayed, *pp.* ? assaulted, 262/32.
Almyght, *adj.* almighty, 5/37.
And, *conj.* if, 43/424, 144/1079.
Apeyr, *vb. t.* impair, 106/469.
Apposayle, *sb.* apposal, examination, 189/321.
Appose, *vb. t.* examine, 40/405, 76/1008, 297/1127.
Apryse, *sb.* price, value, 302/1279.
A-rere, Arrere, *vb. t.* gain, win, 34/284.
Armonye, *sb.* harmony in music, formed of symphony and euphony, 40/384.
Arn, *vb.* first pers. pl. of present of *be*, 45/461.
Arsmetryk, *sb.* arithmetic, 38/377.
Arts, Seven Liberal, 39/365. They are Grammar, Rhetoric, Dialectic, Arithmetic, Music, Geometry, Astronomy.
Asay, *sb.* trial, affliction, 24/119, 27/152.
Asayle, *sb.* assail, assault, 19/33, 35/299.
Astoyned, astounded, stupefied, 277/498, 281/611.
Astronomy, 41/393.
A-taast, A-taste, *vb. t.* test, try, 298/1145. O. Fr. *ataster*.
Attame, *vb. t.* attack, meddle with, 314/1639. Fr. *entamer*.
Auctrix, *sb.* authoress, authority, 318/1757.
Aurisia, *sb.* a disease of the eyes, 219/802. Gr. ἀορασία, blindness.
Avysyon, *sb.* vision, 6/80. O. Fr. *Advision*, *avision*, vision, dream.

Banne, *vb.* curse, 54/621, 97/301.
Barm, *sb.* bosom, 383/1376.
Bate, *sb.* strife, contention, 248/1293.
Beck, *sb.* brook, 401/1901.

Be-dene, *adv.* together, 74/961, 169/1478, 246/1256.
Behest, *vb. t.* promise, 256/1445, 277/479.
Behest, *sb.* promise, vow, 277/486.
Beye, *sb.* bracelet, 63/774.
Beyn, *adj.* bain, ready, 210/670.
Beuerych, *sb.* beverage (of melted lead poured down throat), 280/586.
Biled, *pp.* built, 310/1531.
Bille, *sb.* letter, proclamation, 78/1027 ; article, item, 213/691.
Blaspheme, *sb.* blasphemy, 34/286.
Ble, Blee, *sb.* complexion, 166/1432.
Blowe, *vb.* blow, publish, divulge, 320/1811.
Blynne, *vb.* blin, cease, 27/168.
Boteras, *sb.* buttress, 127/799 ; "botraces" on page 126.
Boystysnesse, *sb.* boisterousness, outburst, 34/293.
Bredes, Bredys, *sb.* boards of a book, 7/86, 9/94.
Bregge, *vb. t.* abridge, 327/2041.
Brethel, *adj.* brittle, 310/1531.
Brymbyl-tree, *sb.* bramble-tree, 20/53.
Busk, *vb.* hasten, 219/792.
But if, *conj.* unless, 73/936, 939, 250/1330.
Buxum, *adj.* obedient, 18/16.
Byrd, *sb.* a byrd in your fest (fist), 93/250.

Calle, *sb.* caul, net for head, cap, 168/1482.
Carnacion, *sb.* incarnation, 332/2187.
Carpe, *vb.* speak, converse, 113/560 ; prate too much, 121/703.
Carpynge, *sb.* talk, conversation, 63/755.
Cast, *vb. t.* purpose, devise, 77/1007.

Glossary.

Cessyons, *sb.* sessions, 71/894.
Chalcedony, its virtues, 249.
Chaueles, Chaules, *sb.* jowls, jaw-bones, 8/97, 9/97.
Chauncelere, *sb.* chancellor, secretary, 10/140.
Chepe, *sb.* cheap : "Grete chepe," good bargains, 59/713.
Ches, Chees, *vb.* chose, 222/860.
Cheuentayn, Cheuetayn, *sb.* chieftain, 130/850.
Circumlocucyon, *sb.* evasive way of speaking, 312/1591, 322/1887.
Circumuent, *pp.* circumvented, 300/1208.
Clappe, *vb. t.* strike, smite, 281/621.
Claryfy, *vb. t.* purify, make pure, 231/993.
Clatere, Clatyr, *vb.* chatter, talk noisily, 140/1006.
Cloggis, *sb.* blocks, logs, 347/290.
Clospe, *sb.* clasp of a book, 8/101.
Clynk, *vb. t.* jangle, 364/796.
Collusyon, *sb.* deceit, trickery, 236/1102.
Colour, *sb.* disguise, pretext, 307/1426, 313/1606.
Comered, *pp.* cumbered, encumbered, 168/1481, 392/1621.
Comerous, Comorous, *adj.* cumbrous, stupefied, stupid, 185/249, 276/455.
Communycacyon, *sb.* converse, conversation, 335/2276.
Comoun, *vb. t.* common, make common, communicate, 161/1352, 1358, 315/1673.
Compendiously, *adv.* briefly, 350/378.
Concionatrix, *sb. f.* oratress, public speaker, 302/1269, 370/960.
Conclude, *vb. t.* redargue, confute, 293/1002, 300/1211.
Concludyng, *sb.* conclusion, summing up, 322/1894.
Conclusyon, *sb.* end, close, 258/1456.
Concoursly, *adv.* in concord, together, 328/2080.
Confeder, *vb. t.* confederate, 315/1678.
Conferme, *vb. t.* confirm, strengthen, 400/1883.
Consent, *pp.* consented, agreed, 46/488.

Conservacye, *sb.* protection, 271/316.
Conuersacioun, *sb.* way of life, habits, 10/148.
Convict, *vb. t.* convirce, confute, 289/867, 300/1213, 303/1283, 307/1417, 308/1442.
Corown, *sb.* crown, 240/1176; *vb.* 242/1185.
Cote, *sb.* cot, covering, *fig.* of the body, 4/31. Compare *Kage,* 332/2180.
Coude, *vb.* could, understood, 32/266.
Counterollere, *sb.* controller, 380/1265.
Crede, *sb.* creed of St. Athanasius, 12/167.
Creke, *vb.* make a disturbance, 140/1006, 276/453.
Creyn, *vb.* cry, 227/945.
Cristen, *sb.* Christianity, 293/1978.
Crope, *vb.*; crept, *pp.* 195/404.
Cruelnesse, *sb.* cruelty, 54/625.
Crysme, *sb.* holy oil for baptism, 235/1082.
Crystendom, *sb.* Christianity, baptism, 43/442.
Cure, *sb.* care, 32/267.
Cyse, *sb.* assize, 71/894.

Dalf, *vb.* delved, dug, 8/115. See *Delue.*
Dame, *sb.* dam, 308/1445.
Dawe, *sb.* brynge . . . of dawe *or* a dawe, put out of life, kill, 374/1084.
Dawe, *vb. int.* dawn, 363/773.
Debate, *sb.* strife, contention, 18/43.
Debater, *sb.* quarreler, bully, 310/1519.
Declaracyon, *sb.* explanation, tale, 50/558.
Declynacion, *sb.* declension of nouns, 33/259.
Delectacyon, *sb.* delight, pleasure, 245/1238, 262/23.
Delice, Delys, *vb.* delight, 213/683, 316/1686. Fr. *délice.*
Delirament, *sb.* raving, insanity, 307/1421.
Deliuer, *vb. t.* bring to end, decide 74/966.
Delue, *vb.* dig, 150/1166.

Glossary. 457

Deme, *vb.* deem, give sentence, 105/444.
Demene, *vb. t.* manage, conduct, 165/1418. O. Fr. *Demener.*
Dempt, *vb.* deemed, judged, 258/1464.
Depute, *sb.* deputy, 105/431.
Dere, *vb. t.* harm, injure, 115/613, 248/1316.
Despouse, *vb. t.* bestow, betroth, wed, 233/1028.
Dever, *sb.* devoir, duty, 235/1075.
Deyn, *vb.* die, 229/980, 347/275.
Deyte, *sb.* deity, godship, 286/764.
Dialetike, *sb.* dialectic, one of the Seven Liberal Arts, 39/372.
Dilatacyon, *sb.* extension, prolongations, 335/2278.
Diuerse, *vb.* differ, discord, 59/688.
Do, *vb. t.* do off, take off, 239/1131.
Dome, *sb.* opinion, judgment, 35/314.
Domynacyon, *sb.* rule, dominions, 270/265.
Doole, *sb.* sorrow, trouble, 33/257, 69/866, 314/1643.
Doubilnesse, *sb.* duplicity, 301/1234, 308/1444.
Drane, *sb.* drone bee, 261/3, 262/21.
Dreedful, *adj.* timid, fearful, 67/844.
Dresse, *vb.* address, apply, 83/70.
Dreynt, *pp.* drowned, 206/592.
Dun, *sb.* dun is in the myre, *Prov.* 143/1046: *i. e.* "I am at a loss," or "in a fix," *Dun* being a horse's name.
Dwere, *sb.* doubt, fear, 27/178, 89/172, 105/418, 271/304, 284/698, 299/1165, 308/1461.
Dyme, *sb.* dime, *lit.* tithe, 289/850. L. *Decima,* Fr. *Dîme.*
Dysdayn, *adj.* disdainful, 161/1330.

Eem, *sb.* uncle, 87/122; "hem," on page 186.
Egal, *adj.* equal, 334/2269. Fr. *Égal.*
Egaly, *adv.* equally, 346/249.
Eke, *adj.* ilk, same, 57/662.
Elenk, *sb.* proof, main point of argument, 128/825. Gr. Ἔλεγχος.
Elmesse, *sb.* almesse, alms, 175/82.
Em, *sb.* uncle, 124/753. See *Eem.*
Emprende, *vb. t.* imprint, 205/580, 260/1488, 277/493.

Enbraas, Enbrace, *vb. t.* embrace, engage, 71/897.
Endoos, *vb. t.* ? endorse, magnify; ? endow, 132/882.
Enforce, *vb. t.* strengthen, 299/1183.
Enprende. See *Emprende.*
Entayle, *sb.* intaglio, 45/486.
Enterfered, *pp.* mingled, mixed, 335/2278.
Entermete, *vb.* interpose, meddle, 303/1294. Fr. *S'entremettre.*
Erde, *sb.* earth, 242/1193, 250/1341.
Erdely, *adj.* earthly, 252/1371.
Erdely, *adv.* on earth, 250/1337.
Ereeth, *vb. t.* eareth, plougheth, 27/157; herþ on p. 26.
Erthely, *adv.* on earth, 305/1375. See *Erdely.*
Euphonye, *sb.* euphony, in music, 40/385. See LANE, *Continuation of Chaucer,* p. 20. "Melodie proceeds out of musickes euphonie."
Ex, *sb.* axe, 18/46.

Faculte, *sb.* college, body of professors, 37/319.
Fane, *sb.* vane, weathercock, 277/494.
Faste-by, hard by, 275/439.
Faunt, *sb.* child, 275/444.
Febilte, *sb.* feebleness, 181/166.
Feer, *adv.* far, 284/698.
Feere, *vb. t.* fear, frighten, 249/1316.
Feet, *adj.* feat, nice, pretty, 21/77.
Fele, *adj.* many, 256/1438.
Felle, *sb.* skin, 181/159, 245/1243.
Fere, in-fere, in company, 59/717.
Fese, *vb. t.* attack, annoy, 115/590, 321/1860, 323/1916, 358/611.
Filiacion, *sb.* affiliation, 335/2297.
Fix, *adj.* fixed, inveterate, 370/962.
Fle, *vb. t.* flea, flay, 357/581.
Fleete, Flete, *vb. t.* float (as a witch), 95/276.
Flyght, *vb.* strive, contend, 107/460.
Fonge, *vb. t.* grasp, 327/2042.
Fonned, *pp.* fond, foolish, 110/528, 283/679, 349/341.
Fonnednesse, *sb.* fondness, folly, 395/1716.
Font, *sb.* source, spring, 251/1347.
For, *prep.* on account of, to prevent, 37/330.

Glossary.

For-barre, *vb. t.* forbear, decline, reject, 326/2004.
Forby, *adv.* by, along, 219/798, 241/1155.
Forfete, *vb.* incur a charge, be guilty, 269/229.
Forfeture, *sb.* crime, error, 41/390.
Forlore, *pp.* forgotten, 14/201.
Forth-brynger, *sb.* parent, 28/186.
Fother, *sb.* weight of about a ton, 20/59, 27/180, 61/742.
Foulhed, *sb.* foulhead, foulness, 67/831.
Foyson, *sb.* plenty, 61/732. Fr. *Foison.*
Fulfilled, Fulfyllyd, *pp.* filled full, 22/110.
Fundament, *sb.* grounds of belief, 330/2124.
Fy, sey fy, say fie, 342/152. Comp. Fr. *Faire fi de.*
Fyn, *sb.* fine, end, 76/1019. Fr. *Fin:* Lat. *Finis.*

Gaule, *vb.* bawl, yell, 98/325.
Geometry, one of the Seven Liberal Arts, 41/386.
Gette, *sb.* ? get, prize, 269/236. This may be *Jette*, fashion, but the subst. *Get* is used thus.
Glose, *sb.* lie, 295/1041, 327/2028; gloss, 304/1334.
Glose, *vb. t.* deceive with fair words, 349/335.
Gnast, Knast, *sb.* spark, snuff of candle, used in derogatory sense, 26/159, 174/70. Compare *Snast*, in E. Anglia.
Gonne, *sb.* ? any warlike weapon, 292/952. See *Gune*.
Goost, Gost, *sb.* flesch & gost (spirit of life), 114/596; Holy Ghost, 35/301, 170/3, 334/2246.
Gramer, *sb.* one of the Seven Liberal Arts, 39/366.
Gret-namyd, *adj.* great-named, renowned, 132/881.
Grew, *sb.* Greek—the language, 82/56.
Gripe, Gryppe, *vb. t.* get hold of, 145/1085; catch, get the better of, 147/1116.
Grope, *vb. t.* seek into, 175/73; explore, 231/995.

Grotch. See *Grutch*.
Grubbe, *vb.* grub up, 222/863.
Grugge, *vb.* he gruggeth with his teeth, grinds his teeth, 381/1309: compare next.
Grutch, *vb.* murmur, take in dudgeon, 67/851, 97/301. O. Fr. *Gruchier*.
Gryf, *sb.* graft, 155/1247.
Gune, *sb.* gun, 52/592. It is applied in *Cath. Angl.* to an engine for throwing stones, or one for attacking walls. See *Gonne*, above.
Gye, *vb. t.* guide, 264/87.

Hale, *sb.* hut, tent, 60/734. Properly a wattled hut. L. L. *Hala*.
Hame, *sb.* ? skin, film, 239/1132.
Hard, *vb. t.* harden, 297/1098.
Hardyly, *adv.* hardily, surely, 87/131, 121/693, 203/544, 305/1348; firmly, 346/264.
Hardynesse, *sb.* courage, boldness, 299/1177.
Hatte, *vb.* be named, 47/491; "hyght" on p. 46.
Haunt, *vb. t.* frequent, 301/1223.
Heende, *sb.* end, death, 12/177.
Helve, *sb.* handle of axe, *fig.* 18/46.
Her, Here, their, 2/5, 6, 18/13, 30/225, 35/298, 267/185.
Herburgage, *sb.* abode, dwelling, 331/2178. O. Fr. *Hébergage*.
Herne, Hyrne, *sb.* nook, corner, 312/1587, 313/1622, 343/182, 352/438.
Herr, Herre, *sb.* hinge, 132/891.
Hethenesse, *sb.* the heathen world, 21/80.
Heyl, *vb. imp.* hail, 298/1133. It is used transitively for *Hail upon*.
Hille, Hylle, *vb. t.* hele, wrap, cover, 30/227, 306/1379.
Homager, *sb.* one that does homage, a subject, 19/21, 24.
Hoore, *adv.* ere, before, 195/410.
Hope, *sb.* expectation, 105/419.
Horse, *sb.* grey horse, *prov.* 95/253.
Houe, *vb.* ? loiter, ponder, 134/915.
Hyght, *vb.* See *Hatte*.
Hyng, *vb.* hung, 246/1273.
Hyȝe, Yȝe, *sb.* eye, 65/817.

Iape, *sb.* jest, 127/782.
Ildes, *sb.* isles, 19/15.

Glossary. 459

Impossible, *sb.* impossibility, 282/662.
Indignacyon, *sb.* contempt, 89/170.
Induction, *sb.* counsel, instruction, 401/1923.
Inn, *sb.* abode, mansion, 278/539.
Inquietude, *sb.* molestation, annoyance, 38/355.
Insolible, *adj.* insoluble, insolvable, 316/1713.
Intrusore, *sb.* intruder, 270/289.
Iornay, *sb.* day of battle, battle, 97/296.
Iust, Iusten, *vb.* joust, 116/623. O. Fr. *Jouste*. It is properly a combat between two knights, for honour.

Kepe, *vb.* keep, intend, mean, 245/1246.
Keye, *sb.* key, *fig.*: main defence, 20/71. *Clavis* also means "endroit fermé," or fortified place.
Knettere, *sb.* knitter, bond, 336/2311.
Kynhod, *sb.* kindred, kinsfolk, 49/526; it is spelt "kynrode" on p. 48.

Lame, *adj.* unsound, crippled, dishonoured, 48/537.
Lappe, *sb.* lap of garment, 191/356.
Laught, *vb. pp.* of *Lacchen*, got, 328/2062.
Leche, *vb.* leech, heal, 212/685.
Leed, *sb.* lead, the metal, 348/306.
Leke, *sb.* leek, "not worth a leke," 54/628.
Leke, *vb. t.* like, please, 200/504, 318/1748.
Leones, *sb.* lions, 111/518.
Lette, *vb. t.* let go, abandon, 112/553.
Lette, *sb.* let, hindrance, 35/312.
Lette, *vb. t.* let, hinder, 266/153, 269/227.
Lettyng, *sb.* hindrance, 36/330.
Leue, *vb.* believe, 346/264, 273, 381/1301, 393/1659.
Leve, *vb.* live, 42/424.
Leuene, *sb.* lightning, 54/632, 369/938.
Leuynge, *adj.* living, 345/237.
Leuys, *sb.* leaves of a book, 329/2114.

Lewed, *adj.* foolish, 313/1596.
Lofte, on lofte, aloft, above, in this world, 266/146.
Lollard, used as a term of abuse, 191/327.
Lomb, *sb.* lamb, 17/8.
Loos, *sb.* honour, fame, 133/881. O. Fr. *Los.*
Lope, *sb.* leap, 92/223.
Lordles, *adj.* lordless, husbandless, 201/489.
Losyd, *adj.* honoured, 16/7. See *Loos.*
Loute, *vb.* bow in worship, kneel, 287/803, 320/1825.
Low, *vb.* laughed, 352/421.
Loy, Loyn, *pp.* lay, lain, 329/2090.
Lyme, *vb. t.* lime, with bird-lime, 341/115.
Lyn, Lyne, *vb.* cease, rest, 52/593, 76/1020.

Magre, maugre, in spite of, 280/583.
Male, *sb.* mail, trunk, 333/2219.
Marred, *pp.* amazed, thunderstruck, 192/381, 206/610, 274/386, 322/1871, 323/1927. It seems to mean *senseless* on p. 322.
Massager, *sb.* messenger, 324/1942. Fr. *Messager.*
Maument, *sb.* idol, 279/563.
Maumentrye, *sb.* idolatry, 22/104, 45/477, 271/318. L. L. *Mahomeria;* O. Fr. *Mahomerie.*
May, *sb.* maid, 297/1108, 302/1265.
Meke, *adj.* meek, domesticated, 309/1475.
Mene, Meny, *sb.* retinue, attendants, 72/936, 196/439, 269/252, 286/777. O. Fr. *Mesniée, Meyné.*
Mere, *sb.* ? measure, 332/2203.
Meuere, *sb.* mover, 319/1798.
Mocyon, *sb.* motion, proposition, 151/1169, 316/1714.
Modes, Modys, *sb.* moods of verbs, 32/259.
Modir-naked, *adj.* naked as a new-born child, 358/608.
Moone, *sb.* moan, 314/1629.
Motyf, *sb.* argument, idea, 321/1856, 322/1884, 324/1954, 333/2227.
Mowled, *vb.* rusted, 40/399.
Musyk, one of the Seven Liberal Arts, 39/379.

Glossary.

Myn, Mynne, adj. less, 49/546, 104/431, 387/1501.
Myne, sb. mine, 270/290.
Mysdraught, sb. misbehaviour, 65/821.
Mysty, adj. dim, uncertain, 312/1566.

Nase, sb. nose, 159/1321.
Ne were, were it not for, 113/555.
Noblehed, sb. nobleness, nobility, 171/9.
Not, vb. ne wot, know not, 141/1031.
Noye, sb. annoyance, trouble, 313/1600.
Noysed, pp. celebrated, 330/2120.
Nugacyon, sb. trifling, 329/2115. Lat. *Nugacio*.
Nyce, adj. foolish, effeminate, 65/822, 108/493; fastidious, 310/1522.
Nygramauncy, sb. necromancy, 289/859.

Omager, sb. See *Homager*.
Onlykly, adj. unlikely, unlike, not in keeping, 217/782.
Onreuerently, adv. irreverently, 285/752.
Onrightful, adj. unjust, 291/926.
Onsekernesse, sb. uncertainty, mutability, 69/874.
Oppresse, vb. t. keep down, keep under, overcome, 101/365, 289/863.
Ouere-leede, vb. t. draw over, win over, master, 328/2060.
Ouere-thinke, vb. t. repent; compare "remember it," 369/951.
Overt, sb. overture, 248/1302.

Palustre, sb. palæstra, arena, 288/830.
Partye, sb. side, 322/1893. Fr. *Parti*. Party ... party, partly ... partly, 289/859.
Passyble, adj. possible, 316/1712.
Passyon, sb. suffering, death, 393/1668.
Pathed, pp. paved, 347/285.
Pere, sb. pear, value of a pear, fig, 133/907.
Peroracyon, sb. peroration, close of speech. 278/536.

Peyse, vb. t. pese, weigh, 301/1238. Fr. *Peser*.
Plat, adj. flat, flatly, used as *adv*, plat and pleyn, 22/106, 139/996, 315/1654.
Plesauns, sb. plesaunce, pleasure, 2/6.
Plete, vb. plead, 164/1400, 300/1189. L. L. *Placitare, Placitum*.
Pletyng, sb. pleading, 170/1496.
Pluk vp your hertis, pluck up your courage, 103/402.
Plumb, Plumme, sb. plum, plummet, 375/1133.
Point, vb. t. cause to appear, 316/1698.
Portrature, sb. figure (in Euclid), 41/387.
Potestate, sb. potentate, 361/692.
Povert, sb. poverty, poor people, 61/731.
Pregnantly, adv. significantly, 122/721, 154/1237.
Processe, sb. matter, cause, 264/76, 306/1401. Comp. French *Procès*.
Procession of the Holy Ghost, 335/2299.
Progression, sb. a royal progress, or visit, 187/280.
Promission, sb. promise, 256/1429.
Proue, vb. int. attain, reach, 367/874.
Prouost, sb. viceroy, proconsul, 294/1028.
Prow, sb. profit, 111/536, 115/592. O. Fr. *Prou*.
Pryme, sb. prime; the first Roman Catholic service (after Lauds), 12/168.
Pryme, sb. spring, 316/1698.
Puple, sb. people, 119/669.
Purchace, sb. purchase, hold, grasp, 161/1333; compare nautical usage.
Puttyng at the stoon, putting the stone, 63/763.

Quayll, vb. int. fail, give way, cower, 294/1019, 318/1775.
Queke, vb. t. quick, quicken, make alive, 319/1801.
Quenchere, sb. q. of vice, extinguisher, 65/820.
Qwat, what, 6/67.
Qweche, which, 12/167, 80/19.

Glossary.

Qwert, qvert, *adj.* sound, hearty, 108/482.
Qwhy, why, 6/84.
Qwome, whom, 6/71.

Race, *vb. t.* tear, destroy, 290/907.
Rake-stele, *sb.* rake-handle, 326/2009.
Rap, *vb.* rynge ne rap, at a door, 189/312.
Rayle, Raylle, *vb. t.* array, 245/1230, 294/1020. Compare *Nightrail.*
Rayle, *vb. t.* range in line, 377/1168.
Real, *adj.* royal, 153/1213, 181/181. O. Fr. *Real.*
Regalte, *sb.* regality, royalty, royal power, 122/726.
Regalye, *sb.* regality, royalty, 286/778.
Remembre, *vb. t.* remind (with two accusatives), 253/1379.
Remene, *vb. t.* interpret, 335/2271.
Reney, *vb. t.* reject, disown, 293/976, 294/1036. Fr. *Renier.*
Repayr, *sb.* repair, resort, 22/81. Fr. *Repaire.*
Repleshed, replenished, 278/527.
Replicacion, *sb.* reply, 310/1508.
Resultans, *sb.* resultance, origin, 213/704.
Retoryk, one of the Seven Liberal Arts, 39/369.
Reuers, *vb. t.* upset, overcome, 306/1396.
Reve, *sb.* steward, delegate, 251/1321.
Revers, *vb. int.* ? be perverse, 355/529.
Reyle, *vb. int.* rail, flow, 395/1720.
Ront, Runte, *vb.* ? scold, 177/96.
Roos, Rowse, *sb.* rouse, stir, 298/1140.
Rought, Rowth, recked, cared, 253/1370.
Row, *adj.* rough, 72/942, 94/262, 114/590, 200/495.
Rowne, *vb.* round into ear, whisper, 329/2096.
Ryf, Ryffe, *adj.* rife, evident, 246/1280.

Sacrifye, *vb.* sacrifice, 274/389. Fr. *Sacrifier.*

Sadly, *adv.* soberly, in a settled way, 16/5, 315/1662.
Sadnesse, *sb.* soberness, steadiness, 148/1151, 290/896.
Sale, *sb.* opportunity, 208/635. See *Seel.*
Saluatour, *sb.* Salvator, Saviour, 270/270.
Sare, *adj.* sore, used as *adv.*, 242/1188.
Sarsynrye, *sb.* Saracenry, 68/877.
Sarysbury playn, "let him go walk on Salisbury plain," *prov.* 265/119.
Saunsfayle, without fail, 245/1227.
Say, *vb.* saw, 10/136; sayn, 252/1383.
Scar, *sb.* chink, 361/712. Comp. Armor. *Skarr.*
Schape, *pp.* shaped, prepared, 246/1257.
Scysme, *sb.* schism, party disturbance, 106/454, 108/486, 292/951.
Seel, *sb.* opportunity, occasion, 121/682. A.S. *Sæl.*
Selkouth, *adj.* strange, 179/128.
Sempiterne, *adj.* eternal, everlasting, immortal, 282/647, 312/1586. L. *Sempiternus.*
Sencyall, *adj.* essential, 294/1012.
Sere *sb.* sir, 275/423, 441. Fr. *Sire, sieur.*
Serge, *vb.* search, 319/1803.
Servage, *sb.* servitude, subjection, 57/654.
Sewe, *vb.* pursue, follow, 2/7, 60/728.
Shene, *adj.* radiant, beautiful, 279/541.
Shew, *vb. t.* display, 30/224; *vb. int.* 31/224.
Slides, *sb.* burning brands, firebrands, 81/31.
Shour, *sb.* shower, squall, in fig. ' sense, 165/102, 298/1132.
Shrew, *sb.* wicked person, 47/511, 59/702.
Sisme, *sb.* schism, 107/454.
Skyl, *sb.* skill, reason, 59/702.
Slughed, *adj.* slugged, slothful, 263/42.
Slyde, *vb. int.* slip, be forgotten, 72/935, 91/213.
Smytyng, *sb.* smiting, striking (of

Glossary.

musical instruments, as harp), 40/384.
Snebbe, Snybe, *vb. t.* snub, reprove, 187/261.
Soke, Sook, *sb.* suck, 2/2.
Solen, Solenne, Soleyn, *adj.* solemn, terrible, 132/908; sacred, 317/1720.
Solennyte, *sb.* solemnity, 265/123, 273/385.
Sonde, *sb.* message, dispensation, 12/194, 334/2255.
Soonde, *sb.* See *Sonde*.
Soothsaw, *vb.* speak truthfully, 311/1545.
Sophem, *sb.* sophism, sophistical argument, 185/228.
Sophie, *sb.* learning, 372/1020. Gr. σοφία.
Sowdyoures, *sb.* soldiers, paid troops, 102/400. O. Fr. *Soldaier :* comp. M. Fr. *soudoyer*.
Speker, *sb.* speaker, one who presides at a meeting, 84/107.
Sperd, Spered, Speryd, *pp.* barred, closed, shut, 38/353, 275/432.
Spousesse, *sb.* wife, 231/999.
Spyce, *sb.* species, manner, 2/20. Fr. *Espèce*.
Staker, *vb.* stagger, hover, 278/525.
Stakeryng, *sb.* staggering, 388/1510.
Sterne, *vb. int.* starve, die, 157/1285, 295/1039.
Stenene, *sb.* voice, 193/361.
Stodieres, *sb.* studyers, students, 37/350.
Stoyn, *vb. t.* astound, stupify, 9/109, 287/799, 320/1837.
Surveour, *sb.* surveyor, overlooker, 33/263.
Swap, *sb.* blow, at a blow = at once, 189/313.
Swete, *vb.* sweat, distil, 403/1959.
Swow, *sb.* swoon, deep sleep, 209/649, 242/1214, 252/1353.
Symphonye, *sb.* symphony, related to harmony, 40/385.
Syse, *sb.* size, conceit, self-esteem, 128/845.
Sysed, *pp.* app. set, 338/17. Comp. Fr. *assis*.

Tarie, *vb. t.* tarry, delay, 291/930.
Tary, *sb.* tarry, delay, long study, 12/186.

Tast, *vb.* try, 287/815. O. Fr. *Taster*, L. L. *Tastare*. See *Ataast*.
Teche, *vb. t.* teach, 291/925.
Teene, *sb.* anguish, pain, 7/77 : Tene, 6/77, 12/186.
Tetched, *pp.* taught, 108/494.
Tetys, *sb.* fro þe tetys, or teats, *i. e.* from infancy, 30/242.
Thenswart, thenceward, *i. e.* to depart thence, 231/1015.
There = where, 47/506.
Þoo, those, 246/1254.
Thurify, *vb.* burn incense, sacrifice, 349/350.
Tight, *adv.* tite, quickly, 350/385.
Touch, *vb. t.* touch on, allude to, 331/2157.
Trace, *vb. t.* track, rove through, 90/193 ; *vb. int.* (of a dance), 275/421.
Trappure, *sb.* trapping, array, order, 240/1166. Fr. *Trappure*.
Trayn, *sb.* treachery, artifice, 267/185.
Treacle, *sb.* theriac remedy, 173/34.
Turbe, Turbel, *vb. t.* disturb, trouble, 49/524.
Twyst, *vb. t.* turn aside, 22/103 ; destroy, 131/866.

Vengeable, *adj.* vindictive, 310/1521.
Veniable, *adj.* vindictive, revengeful, 307/1414. See *Vengeable*.
Vinolent, *adj.* given to wine, 311/1533.
Vlix, *sb.* Ulisses, as a crafty person, 302/1271.
Vnch, *sb.* inch, 129/819.

Wade, *vb.* dive, flounder about, 120/703, 314/1624.
Wale, *sb* within the wale = on board of, 117/642. The wales are thick planks which give the form of a vessel.
Walk, *vb.* be off, go, 210/672.
Want, *vb. int.* be lacking, fail, 80/26.
Wared, *pp.* guarded against, saved, 100/378.
Warn, *vb. t.* warn a gate, forbid it, 61/737.
Wave, *vb. int.* waver, totter, 183/199, 207/593, 306/1377, 350/390.

Glossary.

Wawe, *sb.* wave, 89/178.
Wayr, *sb.* wear, lock, 22/96; thorow wey & thorow wayr, by road and by river.
Wecch, Wetche, *sb.* watch, in wecch, *awake;* 125/754.
Weede, *sb.* weed, clothes, array, 229/952, 259/1484.
Weent, Went, *sb.* bent of mind, course, 291/929.
Weniaunce, *sb.* vengeance, 10/153.
Werre, worse, 263/55.
Weyne, *vb. t.* waive, decline, 354/510.
Whanse, Wanyse, *vb. int.* vanish, disa͑ pear, 47/487.
Wilfully, *adv.* willingly, of free will, 47/516, 305/1361.
Wisse, *vb. t.* teach, 402/1929.
Wonder, *adj.* wonderful, 289/860; *as adv.* 313/1608.
Wondyrly, *adv.* wonderfully, 242/1201.
Wone, *sb.* house, abode, in wones = at home, 18/26, 25/141; property, 163/1370. In 25/141 it seems almost equivalent to *once.*
Word, *sb.* world, 53/600.
Wordly, *adj.* worldly, 299/1162.
Woundyr, *adj.* wonderful, 42/424.

Wrake, *sb.* wreck, harm, ruin, 18/29, 69/866.
Wreche, Wreke, *sb.* wrath, vengeance, 326/2014, 339/61.
Wyte, *sb.* weight, 301/1238.

Xalle, shall, 40/390.

Ya, ʒa, yea, 123/738.
Yave, *vb.* gave, 5/22.
Yche, *adj.* ilk, same, 50/575. See *Eke.*
Ydiotes, *sb,* ignorant people, unlettered men, 35/288.
Yeede, ʒede, *vb.* yede, went, 45/466.
Yefte, *sb.* gift, 271/299.
Ylde, *sb.* isle, 72/941.
Yongthed, ʒonthyd, *pp.* youthed, made youthful, 179/126.
Youe, *pp.* given, 7/63.
Yryn, *sb.* iron, 24/121; "yern" on p. 25.

ʒaue, *vb. t.* gave, 4/22.
ʒerne, *adv.* eagerly, quickly, 352/439.
ʒonthyd, *pp.* made youthful, 178/126.
ʒoue, *pp.* given, 6/63.
ʒyng, *adj.* young, 40/411.